W9-DGK-462

METHODS AND MATERIALS FOR
SECONDARY SCHOOL PHYSICAL EDUCATION

Charles A. Bucher, A.B., M.A., Ed.D.

Professor of Education, New York University,
New York, New York

Constance R. Koenig, B.A., M.S., Ed.D.

State University of New York at Brockport,
Brockport, New York

FIFTH EDITION

with 125 illustrations

THE C. V. MOSBY COMPANY

Saint Louis   1978

FIFTH EDITION

Copyright © 1978 by The C. V. Mosby Company

All rights reserved. No part of this book may be reproduced in any manner without written permission of the publisher.

Previous editions copyrighted 1961, 1965, 1970, 1974

Printed in the United States of America

Distributed in Great Britain by Henry Kimpton, London

The C. V. Mosby Company
11830 Westline Industrial Drive, St. Louis, Missouri 63141

Library of Congress Cataloging in Publication Data

Bucher, Charles Augustus, 1912-
    Methods and materials for secondary school
physical education.

    Bibliography: p.
    Includes index.
    1. Physical education and training—Teacher
training. I. Koenig, Constance R., joint author.
II. Title.
GV363.B73 1978   613.7'07'12   77-10805
ISBN 0-8016-0873-2

GW/VH/VH 9 8 7 6 5 4 3 2 1

PREFACE

A methods and materials course must be continually updated to provide the prospective teacher with the wherewithal to teach effectively in modern society. Similarly, a methods and materials text must be revised periodically so that institutions providing preservice and in-service education for teachers and leaders of physical education will have ready access to up-to-date material and information. As a result, this text has undergone major surgery to make it the most effective tool possible for teaching physical education.

In keeping with new developments in education each chapter in this completely revised text initially sets forth the instructional objectives and competencies to be achieved by the student as a result of his or her reading this chapter. Then, at the conclusion of each chapter there are postassessment tests to assist students in determining whether the material and competencies presented in the chapter have been mastered.

In addition to the instructional objectives and competencies and postassessment tests much new material has been added. Since the secondary school student represents an entirely new breed of student, two chapters, rather than one, are now devoted to this important subject in order to provide the prospective teacher with a better understanding of the consumer of physical education services. A systems approach for developing a relevant curriculum in physical education is presented.

Twenty-six innovative ideas are discussed that have proved effective in practice by physical educators who teach in the secondary schools of the nation. Two new chapters on the teaching process and learning outcomes are presented, stressing the cognitive, affective, and psychomotor domains. The space devoted to the methods and materials of teaching various physical education activities has been increased twofold, and in addition the activities are presented in a manner that will enable the teacher to achieve cognitive, affective, and psychomotor goals. The subject of mainstreaming is considered, and the methods and materials for teaching the handicapped student are provided. New illustrations are utilized throughout the text to update the book.

These are only a few of the changes that have taken place in this text. The result is a book that is in keeping with the times and the many educational changes that are taking place in general education as well as in physical education. Students and teachers will benefit as a result.

Charles A. Bucher
Constance R. Koenig

v

CONTENTS

PART FOUR
Teaching physical education

PART FIVE
Class management

PART SIX
Evaluation

METHODS AND MATERIALS FOR
**SECONDARY SCHOOL
PHYSICAL EDUCATION**

1

SECONDARY SCHOOL PHYSICAL EDUCATION IN A CHANGING SOCIETY: AN INTRODUCTION

INSTRUCTIONAL OBJECTIVES AND COMPETENCIES TO BE ACHIEVED

After reading this chapter the student should be able to—

1. Describe some of the major changes that have taken place in American society and culture in recent years.
2. Draw implications from the changes in education and physical education that have taken place.
3. Identify some of the important changes that have taken place specifically in the secondary schools of the United States.
4. Describe what is meant by such terms as accountability, the feminist movement, competency-based teacher education, Title IX, open education, free schools, and minischool and to understand how these developments affect education and physical education today.
5. Outline the major areas needing change in education and physical education today that have particular implications for the methods and materials for teaching physical education in secondary schools.

The United States and the world are not the same as they were 10, 20, or 50 years ago. Changes are taking place that affect the way we travel, what we eat, where we go for a vacation, how we heat our homes, and the positions to which we aspire. Why have some of these changes come about?

Americans have lived for many years in a beautiful land where each generation has been richer, freer, and better educated than their parents' has been. It had been hoped that progress was being made toward the elimination of poverty and even of most work. However, today's realities show this not to be the case. Wars, urban decay, and a host of other problems have prevented this dream from coming true.

Americans consume 35 percent of the world's basic, irreplaceable resources, although we represent only about 6 percent of the world's population. This consumption of a major share of the world's resources by Americans has helped to decrease American popularity in the rest of the world and has caused many environmental problems.

The United States has become painfully aware in the last ten years that there are limits to its military and economic influence on the rest of the world and as a result has lost much prestige abroad. American technology has produced airplanes, television sets, and beautiful automobiles, but it has also produced smog, pollution, and many urban problems.

1

American scientific knowledge has prolonged the average length of life by ten to fifteen years, but it is also partially responsible for one-half of our hospital beds being occupied by patients with mental illness and the increase in the incidence of heart disease, cancer of the lung, and accidents. The American desire for material possessions and power has contributed to the destruction of the country's values with the result that many citizens have lost faith in their nation's government and leaders.

CHANGE IN SOCIETY AND CULTURE

Our modern society is dynamic, flexible, demanding, and self-centered. The space age is freeing men and women from the confines of their atmosphere and has permitted them to reach into outer space, even the moon, and to probe the depths of the seas. This era is having an increasingly profound influence on society. The skilled worker has had to become a highly trained technician, and the professional has had to become a specialist. Widespread use of computers, which are the children of the space age, has increased the pace of life. More people need more education to understand and control the machines that are the core of modern life. Each highly complicated electronic vehicle that is launched into space or dropped into the sea is the result of increased technology and of the refinement of the machines of science, industry, and education.

Our world becomes more complicated year after year. Not only are there many problems that affect us domestically, such as the need for more education, increasing specialization among vocations, problems of the inner city and of the environment, and a faster living pace, but there are also growing international problems.

Only a little over fifteen years ago our world was a relatively uncomplicated place in which to live, become educated, and earn a living. There were brief periods of world peace, and domestic and international unrest were not in the forefront of the news. Students in high schools, colleges, and universi-

ties were willing to adapt themselves to required courses and curricula in order to have a job and a steady income. Today's youth, however, realize that schools and universities must change as the world changes and are calling for improvements in curriculum, faculty, and administration. The activism and militancy of students have shown that they will no longer endure outdated pedagogy. We have "new" secondary school students, and we are gradually giving them "new" secondary schools geared to the needs of tomorrow.

Today's secondary school students live in a computer card world. They have never known international peace or domestic stability, but instead they are intimately familiar with a constantly fluctuating society, community change and upheaval, electronic marvels, and educational evolution. It is not technology per se that has brought about the changes in secondary schools but the effect technology and new developments have had on all the factors that combine to influence and control secondary education. Society at large, the changing structure of communities, the student and parents, educators, administrators, and the schools themselves are all intimate parts of educational evolution.

Today's society is, for most people, an open one. People have become highly mobile, and more money is spent on more and more consumer goods and services. Ease of ownership of private automobiles has helped to motivate many families to travel extensively.

This last decade has been marked by increased suburbanization. Many persons have chosen to leave the cities to seek out the supposedly quieter, more stable, and relatively more peaceful life of the suburbs. Many former urbanites prefer to commute many hours to work rather than live in the crowded, industrialized cities. Many cities are now largely the domain of the lower socioeconomic groups who cannot leave because the suburbs cannot house or employ them or because they find that society has effectively closed the door on upward mobility.

The cities represent one of the nation's

major problem areas. Transportation, crime, pollution, the high cost of welfare services, and inadequate housing are only a few of the critical ways in which cities are suffering.

Society is concerned with its environment. The pollution of the air and water, the destruction of our natural resources, overpopulation, and the increase of wastes have caused great concern among a large segment of the population.

Society is also becoming more internationally minded. New communications media, such as Telstar and its sister satellites, have helped to bring the world and even the moon into every home. News is relayed at the time it happens from country to country, shrinking the size of the world and making international understanding a possibility. The youth of today are especially concerned with international understanding and are actively demonstrating this feeling through involvement in secondary schools, United Nations clubs, and international relations clubs. Many older youth have turned to other

humanitarian activities. Young people are opposed to war and actively demonstrate against it.

Our wealthy, knowledgeable, mobile, and highly automated society is still fighting the ills of poverty, discrimination, and unemployment. Many of our citizens in this affluent society live in poverty, lack money for adequate medical care, attend schools that do not meet their education needs, and rarely venture outside their own neighborhoods. Additionally, lack of adequate education and training prohibits these individuals from obtaining employment. Political unrest and general dissatisfaction with government bureaucracy have been characterized by scandals and the misuse of public office.

Social problems, especially those of minority groups, have directly affected large segments of the population. Pollution of the environment is widespread throughout the country. Environmentalists are deeply concerned that outdoor recreational resources are being threatened and that potentially

Fig. 1-1. Cities represent one of nation's major problem areas. City of Seattle, Wash. with the Kingdome in the foreground.

hazardous living conditions for future generations are being created.

The energy crisis has resulted in the price of oil and gasoline skyrocketing as well as a shortage of these commodities. As a result, many activities requiring travel have had to be curtailed, and most people have had to make adjustments in the consumption of energy.

The feminist movement has resulted in women playing a much more important role in all aspects of societal endeavors. It has helped to open up new job opportunities, has provided equal pay with men in many positions, and has made it possible for girls and women to participate in new experiences, such as sports that formerly were solely the province of the male.

IMPACT OF A CHANGING SOCIETY ON EDUCATION

Changing times have resulted in many educational innovations. A sampling:

A *town in California:* A president runs a college that has no campus, no buildings, no dormitories, no cafeteria, no grades, no majors, and no required subjects.

A *city in Georgia:* A mother enters a combination school and community center with her 3-year old girl and mentally retarded boy. After picking up her welfare check, she enrolls in a course to prepare as a nurse's aide, registers her girl for day care, and has her boy tested for the center's trainable mentally retarded program. The school is the focal point for community services where educators and community agency leaders work closely together to serve the entire population.

A *village in Massachusetts:* Students design their future bodies in a class called Genetic Engineering. In a day and age when transplants and artificial limbs are commonplace it is believed that someday people may be able to choose body parts to suit their own needs and life-styles. The teacher furnishes her students with body parts in the form of pieces of colored flannel and tells them to fashion the types of bodies they would like to have in the year 2000. As a result the students better understand the po-

tentialities of biological science and the impact it may have on their own lives in the years to come.

A *city in Florida:* Students come to class to find that one-half of the desks in the room are roped off. As a result they have to double up with their classmates. They are playing a game involving the effects of overpopulation.

A *large city in California:* Five hundred adults, many of them handicapped, are taking high school classes via the telephone. Teachers sit at a special telephone console and through a special phone hookup the teacher can talk with students individually or as a group and students can converse with each other.

A *community in Indiana:* A high school has a total of 170 minicourses scheduled, and a computer keeps track of each student's progress.

Education is one of the most important facets of changing modern life. Today, there is an emphasis on providing education for everyone regardless of age or social class, and many more people are thinking in terms of continuing their education beyond the secondary school. A minimal education, they realize, is of limited practical value in the demanding job market of the computer age.

There is another group of persons in our society who question the value of education, particularly beyond the high school level. They compare salary schedules of persons in the professions with what persons earn in the trades and crafts and wonder if it might not be better to forego a college education and enter the field of work immediately upon graduating from high school.

It is at the secondary school level that the most startling educational changes are coming about. Some of the implications of the computer age for education have already been realized. The earliest teaching machines, in the form of manual Skinner boxes, have already been superseded by complex electronic devices such as talking typewriters, videotape and instant playback machines, recording and playback hardware, and the machinery specific to the language laboratory.

Individually paced learning has become feasible in many curricular areas through the use of electronic equipment. With such equipment the teacher is free to decrease mass instruction time while increasing individual instruction time. Thus the teacher can introduce new material more effectively and efficiently and can supplement group instruction with individualized machine instruction.

In many secondary schools, scheduling of classes and room and teacher assignments are programmed by computers. Register keeping, once a time-consuming task, is also adaptable to computerization, giving the teacher additional hours of teaching time. However, the most profound influence of the computer age has occurred in the curriculum itself. Static and classic curricula have been forced to undergo extensive revision and continued evaluation. Not only the sciences but the languages and social sciences as well are updating all phases of their courses to

meet the advancing tide of innovation such as programmed instruction.

Some secondary schools, however, do not have any of the hardware of the computer age, even though the computer has become increasingly important as an aid to education. Secondary schools that fail to keep up with modern educational methodology cannot hope to offer their students a competitive education by adhering to outdated educational processes. The full implications of the computer age for general education will not be known until society finds that it has exhausted the last frontiers of knowledge.

Accountability

Accountability is a general term that denotes various ways of making persons answerable for their performances. Performance or productivity may be measured by prespecified goals, the outcomes of which must meet certain standards. Accountability in education often includes students as well as teachers and administrators.

The feminist movement

The feminist movement is primarily responsible for making people aware of the inferior position of women in many areas, including civil rights, jobs, and salaries. As a result of this movement, Title IX legislation was passed, female applicants for educational positions are actively sought, discriminatory personnel policies are being eliminated, and policy changes are being made at all levels of education.

Competency-based or performance-based certification and teacher education

A most significant development in education is competency-based certification and teacher education. Competency may be defined as a *demonstrated ability* that can be required for performance in a specific occupational or professional role. The major purposes of competency-based programs are as follows:

Fig. 1-2. A mechanized ball-throwing machine used in physical education program at Wheaton High School, Wheaton, Md.

- To identify and state educational goals in terms of competencies learners should acquire
- To develop procedures whereby individ-

uals may be assessed and awarded credentials when these competencies are mastered

- To develop educational experiences that will result in the attainment of competencies

Traditionally, learning has been assessed on how persons compare with others in, for example, the comprehension of subject matter and mastery of skills. Competency-based learning, however, stresses the results of the learning. It is the competency of the individual that matters, not his or her competency compared to others.

Title IX

In 1975, the president of the United States signed Title IX of the Education Amendments Act, a law that affects virtually every educational institution in the nation. The law prohibits discrimination by sex in educational programs that receive federal money. The spirit of the law is reflected in the opening statement of the act: "No person in the United States shall on the basis of sex be excluded from participation in, be denied the benefits of, or be subjected to discrimination under any education program or activity receiving Federal financial assistance. . . ."

The law was originally introduced in 1971 as an amendment to the Civil Rights Act of 1964. Following congressional debate and changes, the law, signed on June 23, 1972, emerged as Title IX of the Education Amendments of 1972, a broad-scale bill covering a range of federal assistance programs.

Some of the highlights of Title IX as it affects physical education and athletic programs are as follows (see also Chapter 7):

- Physical education classes must be

Fig. 1-3. As result of competency-based certification and teacher education, teachers of physical education must demonstrate competency for teaching various physical skills. Physical education teacher demonstrating her competency in teaching tennis as part of Hampton Institute's training program, Hampton, Va.

grouped on a coeducational basis. However, this does not mean that all activities must be taught coeducationally. Within classes, students may be grouped by sex for certain sports, such as wrestling, boxing, and football, and also classes may be grouped on an ability basis, even if this results in a single-sex organization, as long as sex is not the yardstick for such grouping.

• Separate teams for boys and girls must be established by schools or provided for by having coeducational teams. For example, if there is only one swimming, track, or tennis team in a school, both boys and girls must be permitted to try out for these teams.

• There must be provision for equal opportunities for both boys and girls with respect to equipment and supplies, facilities, medical and training facilities, coaching opportunities, travel, per diem allowances, and housing and dining accommodations.

• Although it is not necessary to have equal aggregate expenditures for any program, institutions may not discriminate on the basis of sex in providing necessary equipment and supplies, and so on.

Open education

On the assumption that children vary widely in their learning abilities, interests, and attention spans, the classroom is decentralized around a number of "interest centers," which appeal to different abilities and interests of students. In this type of educational climate children are free to move, for example, from the science area to the reading area or to some other area of the room that they wish to study and explore. Open education is also based on the assumption that students will learn more if they discover answers for themselves as a result of being motivated by their desire to know. In this type of classroom the teacher performs such tasks as furnishing the materials for the interest centers, answering questions, and guiding the discussion.

Nongraded schools

This innovation is based on the premise that individual differences exist among stu-

dents. Therefore, grade levels are abolished and children with similar abilities study together regardless of their chronological age. For example, a science class might have students ranging in age from 5 to 8 years. A student progresses as rapidly as desired, based on individual potential.

Free schools

In this type of educational atmosphere, students meet with their teachers and plan their own education. Classes are usually planned on a daily basis and generally do not observe time limits but continue as long as student interest exists. No established curriculum or formal classes exist. Freedom is the watchword on the assumption that students work harder and retain what they learn longer if they participate in the decisions that concern their own schooling.

Bilingual education

This type of education usually is found in large city programs where a different language, such as Spanish, is spoken by a significant segment of the population. In bilingual education, instruction is given in English and the foreign language. The policy is based on the assumption that the United States is a pluralistic society and that students should not be converted into a narrow American mold.

The minischool

This type of educational innovation is usually found in high schools. It provides for a decentralization of the administration, faculty, students, and program. For example, a 1,600-student high school could be separated into four 400-student sections, each with its own student body, administration, and faculty. Each would adhere to its own educational philosophy. In this way it is felt that student needs can be better met. For example, minischools make it possible to stress such areas as a straight academic curriculum, performing arts, independent study, health care, industrial arts, computer science, and others.

MAJOR AREAS NEEDING CHANGE

Six major areas* exist in which secondary schools need to change. These areas indicate important considerations not only for education in general but also for physical education if programs are to be relevant to the times in which we live.

Humanization and involvement

Our world and schools have become so large, complex, and remote that young people feel powerless to affect the course of their own lives. Unfortunately, many schools are impersonal, cold, and unresponsive to students as individuals. Change is needed to humanize our schools so that students feel a sense of identity and belonging and are actively involved in the decision-making processes that affect them. Physical education programs need to be concerned with humanization and involvement processes.

New ways of learning and development

Many secondary school students are deeply concerned about problems in the United States, such as poverty, race relations, war, environment, and urban life. At the same time, they feel the school does not focus its energies sufficiently on these significant problems. Methods of instruction are often outmoded, suject matter areas are too traditional in approach, some school practices are restrictive, and dynamic learning materials are not always available. Change is needed to utilize stimulating innovative methods and materials and to provide a broad range of learning options. Physical educators must seek new ways to make their subject matter more exciting and useful to students and also relevant to the problems with which society is faced.

Making opportunities equal

If students are to have sufficient opportunities available to them, it is necessary for them to acquire certain levels of skill, par-

ticularly in reading and quantitative thinking. Change is needed to help all students achieve desirable levels of accomplishment. What is true of teaching reading is also true of teaching skills in physical education. Change is needed to help each student, whether normal, atypical, or somewhere in between, to achieve a level of skill appropriate to individual physical resources that will provide him with the opportunities and vitality that can be enjoyed throughout a lifetime.

The community as school

Education should not be confined to a school building. Change is needed whereby the resources of the community are included in the curriculum, thus expanding and vital-

Fig. 1-4. New ways of learning and development represent an urgent need for the future. The University of Northern Colorado, Greeley, Colo., includes rock climbing as a new activity in their physical education program. (Courtesy Barry Iverson.)

---

*The Task Force on High School Redesign of the Office of High Schools and the Chancellor's Center for Planning: Toward the 21st century, New York, 1971, New York City Board of Education.

izing learning experiences under the auspices of the school. Physical education has a wealth of community resources it can tap as part of its educational program.

Service and responsibility

Frequently, more walls than bridges arise between such groups as black and white, young and old, and student and teacher. Change is needed whereby young people establish a sense of personal identity while developing a sense of common humanity. Experiences should be provided whereby young people develop abilities that balance rights and responsibilities and where they also acquire self-discipline. The gymnasium, playground, athletic field, and other physical education settings offer laboratories where service and responsibility may be learned.

Mastering the future

The many changes taking place in modern society make it difficult for young people to establish goals, career choices, and directions. Young people need to be better prepared for dealing with an unpredictable future. This can be achieved in part by giving each student some grasp of the vast opportunities of the world of work and guidance in making wise career choices that will avoid psychological and occupational dead ends. Physical education instructors should present a realistic picture to students concerning the career opportunities in its field of endeavor.

WHY CHANGE?

Physical education has been slow to change. In the past, physical education had adhered primarily to its traditional approaches to curriculum content, scheduling, programming, methods of teaching, and grading practices. However, such recent developments as the elimination of required programs in some school systems, austerity budgets, reduction of personnel, and parental and student protests have resulted in the recognition of the need for change in physical education. Therefore, one of the major purposes of this revised text is to help physical education to be more relevant to the times.

Teachers must accept change. Those of us who are teachers must face change today. We cannot escape it. The times demand it. The following are some reasons that make such change necessary: For the first time in our history we now have a youth culture with its own music, dances, and way of life. As adults we cannot become a part of it, although it is very important that we understand it. We are living in a period of great technological accomplishment. We are living in a drug culture, a culture that has never before existed in the way it does today. We are living in an era of violence where physical attacks on public figures are prevalent. We live in a society characterized by urban problems that most of us never experienced in our earlier years—only 40 percent of us lived in the city in 1940. We live in a society where a black man looked into the future and said, "I have a dream," and his dream has yet to be realized. We live in a time when poverty, injustice, inequality, and other human ills exist. Change is needed since education can and must do something about these twentieth century conditions.

Change is essential to physical education. Many of our programs, procedures, methods, and materials are as obsolete as the old Bentley and Pierce-Arrow automobiles. We can no longer produce the responses that will enable us to survive. We have to innovate and develop programs that are up to date and relevant to today's society, education, and student. This means creative thinking, outstanding leadership, and teamwork that will help our students develop the resources and capacity to effectively express themselves. Progress will not be possible without change. One producer of change is research. Scholars in physical education and other disciplines have made discoveries that unfortunately have not been applied to our field of endeavor. The challenge is how can we close the gap between theory and practice. It must be done if we are to move ahead.

Physical education appears receptive to change today. The profession is receptive to change today because of the pressures being exerted upon it. Pressures are being exerted on the one hand from dissatisfied parents who feel their children are not getting much out of their classes and on the other hand from frustrated students who consider the schools too rigid and the program too boring. There are also pressures from the racial minorities who believe the schools should help them more than they are at present. We recognize that these pressures are many times deserved and we believe in change.

Physical education is receptive to change because of economic necessity. Austerity budgets have forced retrenchments in many schools as a result of problems with the economy. Taxpayers and administrators are asking how more can be accomplished with fewer resources.

In being receptive to change, physical education should be a aware of the goals of the current reform movement. These goals include greater flexibility and greater involvement of students in the planning of their own education. The reform movement also stresses that we need teaching based on scientific facts, new ways to enable students to learn on their own outside the classroom and gymnasium, and more productive use of the student's time and of educational facilities.

The emphasis on change in the area of methods of teaching includes a change from the traditional emphasis on the group to the present emphasis upon the individual, from a stress on memorization of facts to an emphasis upon inquiry, from a sterile classroom climate to one where there is a zest for learning, from regularly scheduled classes to greater freedom for the student involving such things as independent study, and from teaching as telling to teaching as guiding. Physical education in the future will incorporate these changes and in addition will be based more on a scientific approach, such as the teaching of skills based upon sound principles of motor learning, more emphasis upon audiovisual aids, and greater stress on the individual, whether normal or atypical.

Physical education must become more educational in nature. Physical education has not always kept its *educational* goals clearly in mind. This may be a partial answer to why

Fig. 1-5. Physical education needs to be more humane. Secondary school students receive individual attention at Regina High School in Cincinnati, Ohio.

some programs are being dropped in high schools and colleges across the country. If physical education is to grow and prosper it must be compatible with the goals of general education.

Physical education needs to be more humane. Physical education needs to stress humanization, to become more personalized, and to provide custom service to all persons in our society. This means that girls and women must be provided with budgets, equipment, facilities, and other essentials on an equitable basis with boys and men. It means that the handicapped student must receive as much attention as does the non-handicapped student. It means that the practice of cutting from athletic squads must be reexamined, because the students who are cut may be the persons who can derive the greatest educational worth from the activity. It means that we need to take a look at elimination games in our program in which poorly skilled, obese, or handicapped youngsters are usually the first persons to be eliminated. We need to stress adult fitness more; we should not be solely interested in the young. For example, only 3 out of every 100 adults engage in any formal fitness program, and 49 million adults 22 years of age and older do not engage in exercise for the sake of physical fitness. We need to help our students find success in our classes—not failure. This means not class standards but individual standards must be established. Alternate programs should be provided and self-paced instruction given.

In physical education, we need to have more teachers like the one who wanted to make sure that each member of her class was successful and at the same time be challenged by the activity of jumping over a rope. At first she thought she would place the rope horizontally at 2 feet above the ground, but she knew this would not be challenging for all students. Then, she thought about placing it at 6 feet above the ground but she knew that many students would fail at this height. She finally fastened the rope diagonally so that each student could jump at the height he or she was able to accomplish. As a result,

each child had a successful physical education experience.

Physical education needs to stress the cognitive domain. This means that facts, knowledge, understanding must be communicated to our students. We have traditionally stressed activity and exercise, and as a result, we have to a great extent physically trained rather than physically educated our students. Activity by itself is good, but it is not enough. We must get at the *why* of the activity as well as at the performance of the activity. Physical education should mean education *about* the physical as well as education of the physical. Such topics as posture, fitness, the relationship of exercise to the healthful functioning of the various organic systems, nutrition and fitness, how we grow and develop physically, first aid, and a multitude of other topics should be a part of our program. If we are serious about making our field truly *physical education* rather than physical training, we need to get across some subject matter, become a science, and graduate physically educated students rather than just physically trained students. Furthermore, this subject matter needs to be aimed at changing the behavior of our students so that physical activity becomes a meaningful part of their lives.

Physical education needs to emphasize the affective domain. In recent years there has been much stress on values and valuing. This has come about as a result of many Americans feeling this country has lost many of the basic values that helped to make it a great nation in the first place. For example, a Harris survey showed that faith in our Congress, our legal system, and our press has fallen considerably in recent years. The explanation for this drop is that needless wars have been waged, there has been corruption of men in high office, racial abuses have been commited, and a high rate of crime exists. Physical education should be concerned with helping to establish a sound system of values and with assisting our students to evaluate their own values. Since the individual has to be the architect of his or her own intellectual and moral development, we should help each individual to make personal commitments to standards and values. Our program offers many opportunities to emphasize honesty, integrity, playing according to the spirit as well as the letter or the rules, respect for one's opponent, playing a person when he or she is at his or her very best. Students should know when they participate in our program that such traits as honesty and personal honor are important.

THE CHALLENGE

If physical education programs are to be strengthened, changes are needed. A new physical education must emerge. Physical education must be identified as an important part of the education of each student. Academicians, parents, and the public in general must clearly understand and identify the values and contributions physical education can make to students and to people in general. They must understand that physical education is closely linked to the educational process and is essential in preparing a person to meet life's challenges.

Self-assessment tests

These tests are to assist students in determining if material and competencies presented in this chapter have been mastered:

1. Without consulting the text, state in your own words the major changes that have taken place in American society and culture in recent years.
2. Prepare a chart that identifies on one side of the sheet the major changes that have taken place in American society. Opposite each of these major changes list the implications each has for education and physical education.
3. You have been requested to prepare a paper on the educational changes that have taken place specifically in the junior and senior high schools of the United States. Prepare this paper and present it to the class.
4. Write a one-sentence description opposite each of the following terms, indicating clearly that you understand the meaning of the term and its implication for physical education:
   Accountability
   The feminist movement
   Competency-based teacher education
   Title IX
   Open education
   Free schools
   The minischool
5. Prepare a unit for teaching a physical education ac-

tivity. Include a statement of methods and materials that will be used. Provide in your unit for each of the following:

Humanization: developing each student's sense of identity and belonging

New ways of learning: enhancing student learning through some innovative method

Equalizing opportunities: Providing each student with ways of achieving a desirable level of accomplishment

Responsibility: encouraging each student to become involved and accept some responsibility for the welfare of the group

Points to remember

1. Why the United States is very different from what it was 5, 10, or 15 years ago.
2. Why our modern society is dynamic, flexible, demanding, and self-centered.
3. Why secondary schools have changed as society has changed.
4. How schools, society, and students have changed.
5. The impact of a changing society on education.
6. The important changes taking place in education today.
7. Provisions of Title IX.
8. Major areas needing change that have implications for methods and materials for physical education.
9. Why methods and materials of physical education must change with the times.

Problems to think through

1. How has the computer changed education and physical education?
2. What are some of the problems faced by large cities in the United States?
3. How can innovative ideas contribute to better physical education?
4. To what extent is physical education accountable to students?
5. How will Title IX change the physical education program?
6. How can methods and materials of physical education be changed to provide for the changes that have taken place in education and physical education?

Case study for analysis

Society, education, and physical education are undergoing change in today's secondary schools. You know of a school system where the physical education faculty has resisted change. The members of the faculty maintain that the physical education programs that have existed over the last 25 years still represent what is best for the students and that most of the changes taking place result in less effective physical education programs rather than better ones. The principal of the high school and the superintendent of schools of the school district insist on change. Analyze the situation and develop a plan for effective action.

Exercises for review

1. Why should physical education change from traditional types of programs that existed many years ago?
2. How have the feminist movement, the minischool, and competency-based learning affected education and physical education?
3. How can physical education provide a more humanizing experience for the students?
4. Prepare a speech on *the new physical education* that takes into account the many changes taking place in education today.

Selected readings

American College of Sports Medicine: Encyclopedia of sport sciences and medicine, New York, 1971, Macmillan Publishing Co., Inc.

Billings, T. A.: About people who never grew up. . . . by one of them, Phi Delta Kappan **57**:18, April, 1976.

Broer, M. R.: Efficiency of human movement, Philadelphia, 1973, W. B. Saunders Company.

Bucher, C. A.: Administration of health and physical education programs, St. Louis, 1975, The C. V. Mosby Co.

Bucher, C. A.: Foundations of phycial education, St. Louis, 1975, The C. V. Mosby Co.

Bucher, C. A.: Physical education for life, New York, 1969, McGraw-Hill Book Company.

Cassidy, R.: Societal determinants of human movement; the next thirty years, Quest **16**:48, 1971.

Levine, D. U., and Moore, C. C.: Magnet schools in a big-city desegregation plan, Phi Delta Kappan, **57**: 507, April, 1976.

Lewis, F. C.: Self-abuse as a teaching device, Phi Delta Kappan **57**:533, April, 1976.

Patton, C. V., and Patton, G.: A year-round open school viewed from within, Phi Delta Kappan **57**:522, April, 1976.

Schurr, E.: Movement experiences for children, Englewood Cliffs, N.J., 1975, Prentice-Hall, Inc.

PART ONE

The community, school, and student

Courtesy Strix Pix.

2

THE CHANGING COMMUNITY AND SECONDARY SCHOOL

INSTRUCTIONAL OBJECTIVES AND COMPETENCIES TO BE ACHIEVED

After reading this chapter the student should be able to—

1. Describe how the community affects the physical education program.
2. Indicate how the physical educator may work most effectively with community groups.
3. Discuss and diagram the various types of administrative structures for the community and the school.
4. Relate how physical education fits into the administrative structure of the school.
5. Identify how the makeup of communities and schools differ.
6. Indicate the titles and roles of key administrative personnel in a school district.

THE COMMUNITY

The vast changes taking place in our society and culture, which were discussed in the introduction, are leaving their imprint to a greater or lesser degree on each school and community in the United States. Some communities, because of their location, conservatism, or other factors, are changing more slowly than other more progressive localities. However, most communities are different than they were only a few years ago.

The nation's economy has resulted in austerity school budgets with cutbacks in physical education, including athletic programs. Research conducted by the National Education Association has disclosed that many of the nation's largest school districts are operating under crisis conditions because of financial problems. Students are requesting more involvement in school affairs and are questioning whether some educational requirements, including physical education, are necessary. As a result, some physical education programs are becoming voluntary rather than required.

The demand for an end to discrimination against minority groups has resulted in community discussions regarding such things as bussing, hiring of black teachers, and equal salaries and opportunities for women as well as men teachers. The population mobility has raised questions about what kind of educational program is needed for a nation on wheels. The alarming dropout rate in our schools, with large numbers of youth leaving with neither the skills nor the self-reliance needed for gainful and satisfying employment, has brought forth a recommendation to assign top priority to career education. More community and parental concern for education has led to a demand for such things as greater accountability on the part of educators. Computers have made school class scheduling and record keeping easier. In the large cities of the nation there has been a move to decentralize large cumbersome school districts and in their place make small community districts, which it is hoped will result in better administration and more lay involvement in the running of the schools.

The school and the physical education program reflect, as in many ways all education does, the community in which they exist. The community is that subdivision of people, homes, and businesses that make up a school district. It may coincide with the geographical limits of a city, town, or village, such as San Diego, California, or Denver, Colorado; or it may include two or more political subdivisions, such as the Bedford School District, which includes the towns of Bedford, New Castle, North Castle, and Pound Ridge, New York.

In any event, the local community plays an important part in the philosophy and formulation of the school physical education program. A knowledge of the community and the secondary school are important to the teacher so that he or she may better prepare for the experiences to be encountered.

What is the structural organization of the community? What factors play a part in the financing of the schools? In regard to the schools, who is responsible to the citizens of the community? What influencing factors should be considered in establishing a philosophy of education? How is the physical education program affected by the community?

In this chapter these and other problems as they relate to the community and the schools and specifically to physical education will be discussed so that teachers may be better able to understand and work with their particular situations.

Community relations policies for physical educators

The relations between physical educators and the community are affected by many divergent interactions varying widely in scope, complexity, and intensity. The implications for physical educators are of great depth and latitude, ranging from the seemingly innocuous task of answering the telephone to being able to effectively utilize public communica-

tions media. Because of the inherent dissimilarities in communities, any discussion here must be relatively broad in scope. Some community relations policies that physical educators should think about very carefully include the following:

• *Physical educators should work closely with the community in goal setting, planning, and subsequent program evaluation.* Although the "how" of the school operation is essentially the responsibility of professional physical educators, they should constructively enlist the abilities, interests, and drives of persons in the community in respect to many school activities. By utilizing citizen cooperation at its highest level better programs can be developed, community needs can more readily be met, citizen involvement in activities such as parent-teacher associations and neighborhood clubs can be enhanced, and greater public interest can be gained.

• *Physical educators must be guided by the knowledge that public reaction to school personnel and practices creates the basis for community approval or rejection of many aspects of school affairs.* They should be familiar with the community's traditions, beliefs, resources, limitations, and, most importantly, its people. In working with the community, physical educators must use integrity in all relations and must be efficient in their daily functions and services, for these have significant value.

• *Schools, actively assisted by physical educators, should offer learning opportunities that meet the needs of the community as well as its students.* Within legal limitations and within rules and regulations of the Board of Education, physical educators should assist in making the school a community center by helping to provide recreational and educational activities for adults as well as children and youth. Furthermore, physical educators should participate in community efforts and activities as resource people. Finally, physical educators should utilize appropriate community facilities and resources to enhance the program of physical education in the school.

• *Physical educators should develop the physical education program with the community in mind and flavor it with acceptable habits, customs, traditions, ideals, resources, and problems of the community.* To accomplish this task most effectively, physical educators should be familiar with such things as the community's historical background, social pursuits, economic status, political philosophy, leaders, and channels of organized communication.

• *To be most effective in community relations physical educators must develop professional skills to make their role as effective and as extensive as possible.* Physical educators should be capable of utilizing available communications media in the community, make adjustments and improvements to meet changing needs, maintain continual communication with various groups, and keep school and community leaders informed regarding school and community activities.

Community factors influencing education

There are many factors that have a bearing upon the school system and the program within the school. These factors could be termed external, in that they are related to influences outside the school and the teacher-pupil relationship. Their importance, however, cannot be overemphasized.

When developing a program for a particular community, it must be kept in mind that the community is the real focus of decision making. The program must be planned around the needs and interests of the community and the students. It further must be remembered that the school is only one community agency that contributes to the education of the children. Therefore, the physical education program must be related not only to the individual but also to the family and the community as well.

Economic conditions. One of the problems facing every community today is how to ob-

Fig. 2-1. The physical educator should play effective role in community. Physical educator at Hampton Institute, Hampton, Va., demonstrates tennis grip to student.

tain enough money to close the gap between the amount and quality of education that is needed and the financial support that is available. The following factors that determine the cost of education are listed by the National Education Association: the problem of securing an adequate number of teachers at salaries high enough to attract and hold them, the need for counseling and guidance, the need for adequate facilities, equipment, and the like, the need for enough classrooms to implement a modern program, and the need to lift poverty-stricken districts to a respectable level of support.

The community that is able and willing to meet these needs will have a sound educational system. In relation to physical education, this means well-planned physical plants —both indoors and out—and enough qualified personnel to administer a sound, safe, and varied class program, an inclusive intramural program, a full interscholastic program, and a practical adapted program.

In poorer areas many students have after-school jobs and, furthermore, because of crowded conditions cannot study at home. In this type of situation, nearly all educational experiences must take place in the school if they are to take place at all. Special dress or equipment requirements must be kept to a minimum because of the financial status of the families of most students. The physical facilities and equipment available will depend to some extent on what the community can afford to pay. In densely populated areas the schools may be crowded. Class size must be a component of program design if the maximum benefit within the limits of facilities and number of students is to be achieved. If there is not an overcrowding problem, many more options are open in choosing a curriculum. In the community that is not able to afford what it should have, there are lower salaries, larger classes, less equipment and supplies, fewer personnel, and limited intramural and interscholastic programs.

Fiscal problems have no easy solution, but the implications for physical education, as for all education, are monumental. The economy of a community may have particular impact upon the physical education program. In an economically weak situation the classes are apt to be overcrowded, with far too many students for an effective teaching-learning situation. There may be inadequate locker and shower facilities, as well as inadequate teaching stations both indoors and out. Equipment may be worn or inadequate, and new equipment may be difficult to obtain. In a situation where students may be employed after school, it may be difficult to operate an intramural program. Lack of staff may dictate that physical education personnel assume a variety of nonteaching duties, such as lunch hour supervision and study hall and bus duty. In a community where the schools enjoy strong economic support the reverse will be true.

Religious groups. Fifty to one hundred years ago, religious groups had a great and direct influence upon the administration of a community's affairs, including the program in the schools. In recent years the separation of church and state has been greater, to a point where the influence of religious groups is less than it was before.

The church school is another consideration. Many children spend part or all of their school life without going to a public school. With conditions as crowded as they are in many public schools, this helps alleviate further overcrowding. Support for public education, however, is understandably less from this group.

A few religious groups frown upon certain activities that a school endorses. This may include social dancing, Saturday or Sunday athletic contests, and family life courses. Where a particular church has considerable influence, it may mean a complete breakdown of some parts of the program, even though they may be needed and wanted by the other students.

To meet these problems, physical educators must base programs on educationally sound principles and should be certain that the school administration is supporting the program. If a question arises, they should be prepared to explain the program with supportive evidence to representatives of the community's churches and to listen carefully for valid criticisms and suggestions for improvement.

Politics. In communities where school boards are appointed, merit and qualifications for the job may be taken into consideration. However, in other instances, appointments may be made on the basis of political patronage. Where board members are elected, the entire voting community has a voice in who runs the schools. However, this system may also have drawbacks. Interested candidates who will do a good job run and often win election. However, aspiring politicians often run for the school board and then use their position as a stepping-stone in their careers. The process of education is frequently only a minor consideration to such politically motivated individuals. Further, in a community that favors one political party over another, the candidates of that party, rather than the best person for the job, may be elected.

Not only the school board but local politicians as well may have a voice in running the schools of a community. The local press and radio reflect local political views in regard to the schools through editorial comment. It is the school board, however, that hires and fires teachers, approves budgets, and decides on new construction. The teacher is ultimately responsible to the school board, which as a group is responsible to the community.

Strong support of a school board by the community will be reflected in the physical education program. Qualified staff will be hired, and they will teach in a healthful environment and, if satisfactory, be retained for further service. Budget requests and appropriations are most likely to be honored where the school board receives community support and in turn supports its teachers and their programs. Where the school board is ineffective and inefficient because it is politically maneuvered, all of education suffers.

Climate. Another consideration is the geographical location of the community. Planning must take the following aspects into consideration:

1. Amount of time it will be possible to be out-of-doors. It would be unreasonable and detrimental to outdoor facilities to spend large amounts of money in equipping and maintaining an oversized gymnasium in southern California or Florida where the amount of time spent out-of-doors will be much greater than that indoors. Conversely, in the northern states more time will be spent inside because of the weather.

2. Activities that will be of interest to local residents. The inclusion of and emphasis on skiing and ice skating in the program in northern states would certainly be understandable, whereas more emphasis on tennis would be reasonable in Arizona and Texas. This does not exclude ice skating from the program in the South or the Southwest, although facilities would have to be available. The emphasis on winter sports in the South, however, would not approximate that in the northern section of the country.

It is necessary to determine the activities and interests of the community as they relate to the climate and make efficient use of funds in the light of it.

Sociological and cultural backgrounds. The composition of the community has a bearing upon the physical education program. The races or nationalities, wealth or lack of it, educational backgrounds, and ages of the residents are just a few of the sociological and cultural factors that should be considered when planning a program.

The program in a low socioeconomic area should include many opportunities for active participation as an outlet for aggressive tendencies that may be more apparent in this type of area. In requiring proper gymnasium attire it is important to recognize that some pupils may not have the money to purchase sneakers or gym suits. It may be possible to stockpile uniforms as pupils outgrow them. It is necessary, however, to be tactful when making them available to pupils. It is also important that showers be taken because some of the pupils may not have other opportunities to take baths.

If the child resides in the inner city, play space is usually limited to the streets and neighborhood playgrounds. It is up to the school to provide a well-rounded program of motor experiences for such students. If the parents of a child work and are poverty-stricken, there will be little money for recreational activities. If different ethnic groups are represented in the student body, new sports and activities may be included in the program to enhance students' pride and respect for their own heritage. This is in keeping with making activities relevant to students' backgrounds. It makes much more sense, for example, than trying to teach deck tennis to inner-city children.

The community residents may be college graduates and fairly well-to-do. The physical education program should make use of the educational interests of these fathers and mothers to encourage support for programs, facilities, special equipment, and supplies. The program may include individual activities such as golf, tennis, and archery, since the students will probably be able to make use of these skills out of school.

The great problem of meeting the needs of children from varied backgrounds presents a challenge to the teacher in working not only with pupils but in working with parents as well. It is therefore important to know the parents of children in the community. Such knowledge could come from an analysis of the following items concerning the parents: (1) interest in the parent-teacher association, (2) participation in various organizations that are important in the community (groups such as the League of Women Voters, garden clubs, and Junior League may indicate a higher educational background and socioeconomic status), (3) participation in hobbies and leisure activities (golf and tennis clubs and riding stables may indicate a higher socioeconomic area), (4) interest in school sports activities, which may indicate interest and potential support if properly channeled by the physical educator, and (5) the desire to conform (the danger lies in the possibility of conforming to mediocrity).

Differences in taste, attitude, and race or nationality are minimized in the gymnasium and on the athletic field. Breaking down false beliefs, recognizing ability, and giving a feeling of belonging can be accomplished in the field of sports. Physical educators can help combat the harmful social and cultural variances within the community by means of a good program.

Attitudes toward education. Is the community willing and able to support the schools? How have they voted in recent referendums relating to school expansion or expenditures? Do they regularly cut the school's operating budget? If they have, it is possible that the community is either unable or unwilling to meet desirable educational expenses.

A beginning physical education teacher should be conscious of the handicap of working where the equipment and supplies are old or in short supply, classes are overcrowded, or facilities are inadequate. The amount of relief that can be expected is largely dependent upon the attitude of the members of the community.

Another aspect worth noting is the degree of acceptance of educational trends approved and used in other communities or sections of the country. For instance, are antiquated strength tests, an excessive amount of formal work such as calisthenics, or heavy apparatus being used? Is the term "physical training" still used? The answers to these questions indicate attitudes of the community and schools that may have a part in the eventual success of the physical education program.

Consideration must be given to parents' ideas for their children's education in the design of any school program. All social groups have goals for their children, and these determine what programs the community will support and sanction. There is a need for clear lines of communication between curriculum planners and the community.

Pressure groups. A pressure group can be defined as an organization or group of people working to achieve a common goal. There are groups or organizations in every community that attempt to bring pressure to bear to elect a certain candidate, repair a street, reduce a tax, or perhaps change the physical education program. Examples of pressure groups are a dads' club desiring to sponsor a football league, a church group wanting to eliminate social dancing in the school, and a citizens' group trying to rally support for a school referendum.

Not all pressure groups try to tear down the program. In fact, quite the opposite is true. It is possible that one of the strongest allies in combating the goals of one pressure group will be another group. It is also true that many organizations believe they are helping the physical education program by their actions when in reality they are doing a great disservice to the students. For example, a fraternal organization that gives expensive prizes or awards or sponsors a football league at the elementary school level usually does so out of a desire to be of service to the community and the school. It is only by fostering an understanding of the possible harm that can be caused that the physical educator can effectively combat these influences.

When physical education teachers are members of the community, there are often opportunities to discuss ideas on an informal basis. Such discussions provide excellent opportunities to encourage, dissuade, or rechannel a group of interested community members. Speaking at meetings, interpreting a good program, and sending home happy, understanding students are probably the best ways to combat undesirable group pressures.

Community structure

Through a knowledge of the composition and governing bodies of the community, teachers will be better able to understand the problems facing the community. It is also true that any suggestions for improvement of the curriculum, school plant, facilities, number of personnel, or school philosophy will be more meaningful when they are based upon local community conditions. It is necessary, therefore, to investigate and obtain information about the community, evaluate these facts in the light of professional knowledge, and plan a course of action.

Size. Is the community a compact indus-

trial area, such as Scranton, Pennsylvania, or does it sprawl over the countryside, as does Berkeley, California? The answer to this question has much significance for the school and the physical education program. In a compact area, for instance, there is little or no transportation problem. Afterschool activities such as intramurals and varsity team practice are not greatly affected, because public transportation is available to take students home. In the sprawling community, lack of public transportation can be a deterrent to the conduct of many activities. Solutions to these transportation problems may include convincing school authorities to provide extra transportation, enlisting the aid of the local parent-teacher association, and coordinating efforts with other departments, such as music or dramatics, thereby involving enough students to warrant extra transportation.

Another problem of community size involves future growth, particularly with regard to the current exodus to suburbia. Has the community reached its peak growth, or is it still expanding? Do facilities amply provide for the number of students they are now handling? What are the plans for the future regarding new facilities? Do these plans properly provide for physical education space, facilities, and teaching stations?

Type. Are you going to teach in a predominantly residential community such as Darien, Connecticut, or Berkley, Michigan? If so, you may assume that the parents will take time to inquire about and be in on the planning for education. Active and interested parents are a great help to the school when they put their energies to work in helping the administrators and teachers. Interested parents can help the physical education program by supporting its activities, helping to obtain new facilities, equipment, and supplies, and gaining an understanding of the program. In an industrial community or in a culturally disadvantaged one, residents may be less inclined or may have less time to concern themselves with education. In Flint, Michigan, however, a public interest in education has brought more people into the schools at night than during the day.

Flint has developed the school-community idea to the point where each school has an evening center and most have gymnasiums that are at least 100 by 100 feet in area, as well as other community rooms. In addition to the evening recreation centers, there are a child health program, in-service training for teachers, an outdoor camp, Big Sister organization, adult education programs, tots and teens groups, a stepping-stone program, and other programs.

This program was begun in 1935 by the Mott Foundation in cooperation with the Flint Board of Education. Its purposes are threefold: (1) to make possible the maximum utilization of school buildings and school facilities as well as other community resources—personnel, material, and organizations; (2) to act as a pilot project in testing and demonstrating to the local board of education and other communities the possibilities of what may be accomplished; and (3) to stimulate, by demonstrating what can be done, constructive influences not only in this community but eventually in other parts of the state, the nation, and the world.

The values of the Flint program are obvious. Important also are the attitudes of the taxpayers when they are able to see and use

the buildings for which they pay. Flint was blessed with the Mott Foundation, but most communities can achieve community-centered schools for very little extra cost.

You may find yourself in an industrial or business community like Flint, Michigan, but where the village, town, or city does not have a positive attitude toward education. There may be little room for playing fields and recreational areas. There may be a large populace of older residents who no longer have school-age children. The attitude of the public is of great importance because many residents may feel little sympathy for public school problems, particularly since most solutions to the problems involve an increase in taxes.

In addition to the older residents, there are those parents who send their children to private or parochial schools and who have no desire to pay twice for education. They must pay their taxes, which are used for public education, but they have a vested interest in minimizing these payments.

Although there are always many parents interested in the schools and their problems, the support of a majority of the population is necessary. This requires public interpretation. In Flint this positive attitude has been achieved through a community-centered

Fig. 2-2. Soccer at Brockport Central Schools, Brockport, N.Y.

program. In Norfolk, Virginia, an interest has been manifested in education through a program of health instruction, activity instruction, and intramurals. This program developed because of close cooperation in the fields of health and physical education, which led to an integrated core of instruction.

If community support is not present, it is the responsibility of the school and of every individual in the school to foster it through careful planning.

Governing body. There are three main types of governing bodies that determine the form of local government: the mayor-council, the commission, and the city manager.

The *mayor-council plan* places primary control of administrative matters in the hands of an elected mayor. The council, elected by the citizens, handles local legislation. There are variations in the organization of this plan. Some communities have a dominant mayor, others divide the responsibilities of the mayor and the council relatively equally, and still others have a weak mayor, with the majority of the duties being handled by or through the council. The mayor-council plan is still the most prevalent. The majority of small cities use it in one form or another, as do such large cities as New York, Boston, San Francisco, and Detroit.

The *commission plan* has had its period of growth and is now generally regarded as being in eclipse. The city of Galveston made this plan popular just after the turn of the century. There were five commissioners elected by the people. One was designated as mayor, but only for the purpose of presiding at the meetings. He had no veto power and only a proportionate share of the administration with the other commissioners. This type of plan is still used by some municipalities, but its popularity is on the wane.

The *city manager plan* is growing the most rapidly of any type of city government. In

Fig. 2-3. Students working on balance beam. (Courtesy New York University.)

Fig. 2-4. Self-defense class. Regina High School, Cincinnati, Ohio.

this plan, a career person trained in public administration is appointed by the council. He is responsible for the conduct of municipal administration. There are variations in this plan, such as that wherein the council keeps certain appointment rights. The majority of plans leave only two duties in the hands of the council: (1) the right to pass necessary ordinances and resolutions and (2) the right to select the city manager. The trend in many municipalities is toward the city manager type of government.

The growth of the city manager plan has numerous implications for education. The concentration of powers in a professional person (the manager is supposed to be nonpartisan and is generally chosen from an approved list) usually brings about wider use of modern administrative procedures, which generally are credited with unusually effective standards of modern administration.

The implications of the governmental structure, whether it is city, village, town, or other type, in your community for the school and the physical education program are numerous. Knowing it well will provide an understanding of the following:

1. The chain of responsibility—that is, who the local district leaders are and

what they have to do with appropriated moneys
2. The use of modern governmental structure—that is, the degree to which the community is operating under an archaic form of patronage or an efficient modern structure that attempts to cut unnecessary costs and meet today's challenges
3. The pressure points in the community structure—that is, how public sentiment for needed school expenditures can best be made known and brought to bear on local officials

It is your responsibility as a teacher as well as a member of the community to know as much as possible about your local government.

Board of education. The board of education, or school board or committee, as it is known in some areas, is the administrative unit whose responsibility it is to develop policies for the educational program in the local schools. Some communities have a single commissioner of education, but most cities and districts retain the board plan. This is true in spite of the widespread movement to single-headed departmental control in such areas as police, fire, and health. This

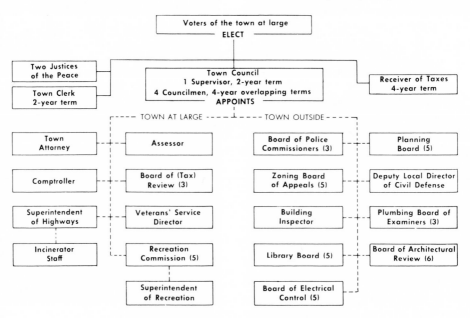

Fig. 2-5. Structure of a town government.

may be because of the reasonable success of the board plan and the caliber of board members, who are able to remain aloof from local politics. Whatever the reasons, the board plan appears to be here to stay, especially since most educators seem to prefer this type of administration.

A board of education may be financially independent, allowing it to fix its own tax rate within limits set by the state and to spend the money as it sees fit. In many cities of more than 25,000 people, as well as in some smaller communities, the boards are financially independent. When a board is fiscally dependent, it recommends the amount it needs to cover the cost of its budget, but the municipal administration decides upon the amount the board will receive. If the full amount is not given, the board must reduce, eliminate, or adjust budget items to fit the amount allotted.

It is important for the physical educator to keep the board aware of problems facing the teacher and to recommend some realistic solutions. It is necessary to channel this information through the principal, director or supervisor, or superintendent.

Composition. Boards of education for school districts evolve from acts of state legislatures. In most cities, boards are elected by the voters. There are places, however, where they mayor appoints members. Regardless of how they obtain their positions, their terms vary from one year to about four years. The usual term is three to four years. Terms are frequently overlapped to ensure continuity in membership.

Size. Boards of education are gradually diminishing in size, from the thirty- and forty-member boards of yesteryear to the five- and nine-member boards seen most commonly today. The number of board members ranges from three, who represent a small local district, to fifteen, who constitute the board in some large cities. The smaller boards of today seem to produce better results by working more efficiently and with greater harmony. As a rule, most members serve without compensation, although very nominal salaries are given in certain areas.

The National School Boards Association has indicated the following characteristics of school boards in forty-two cities throughout the nation having more than 300,000 population.

Most of these school boards have seven, five, or nine members, in that order. Three cities have boards with fifteen members. The composition of school board members (3% of whom are women and 13% of whom are blacks) is broken down as follows: businessmen, 103; lawyers, 66; housewives, 51; physicians, 22; ministers, 11; and college professors, 8.

Most of the 137,000 members of the nation's approximately 25,000 school boards are elected. Among the large cities, only Philadelphia, Pittsburgh, and Washington, D.C., choose boards through a committee of court judges. In Boston, Detroit, Los Angeles, and St. Louis, school boards are elected.

Duties. The board of education's responsibilities may be summed up as follows:
1. Establishes policies and legislates
   a. Curriculum—including physical education curriculum (in accordance with certain state regulations)
   b. School calendar—including time and days when interscholastic contests may or may not be played
   c. School entrance age—set by the state in some areas
2. Provides means for carrying out policies
   a. Prepares budget—including salary scale, arrangements for time off or extra pay for coaching, and policy regarding coaching duties
   b. Hires superintendent and other personnel (upon recommendation of the superintendent)
   c. Votes tax levies, if fiscally independent, or recommends adequate levies to those who have the fiscal responsibility
   d. Plans and executes building and maintenance program (within limits mentioned above)—including new physical education plants and facilities

3. Sees that policies are efficiently carried out
   a. Visits schools
   b. Receives oral and written reports on progress

The board also represents the public in the preparation of its policies and budgets, interpreting to the public the needs of the school in terms of plant, facilities, and working conditions. Although there are some specific duties and responsibilities of boards of education and of superintendents, there is no exact line where the duties of the board end and those of the superintendent begin. This must be worked out together toward a common goal. The superintendent of schools, however, is the professional education leader, and members of the board of education are lay personnel. This, of course, has implications for the responsibilities of each.

There is a growing awareness among professional and lay leaders alike of the need for reform in respect to school board operations. Reforms have been advocated by such an important group as the New York Committee on Educational Leadership and are receiving support in some of the more progressive sections of the country. These reforms include (1) the transfer of all administrative functions that encumber school board operations to the superintendent of schools, (2) better procedures for screening school board members so that the "office seeks the man rather than the man seeking the office," (3) elimination of annual public votes on school budgets where required and substitution of budget hearings, and (4) improved procedures for selecting superintendents of schools.

State and national influence

Education is a state function. The state legislature is responsible for education. Although most states follow similar administrative structures, they differ in details. In every state there is usually a commissioner or superintendent of education as well as a board of education.

State departments of education emphasize cooperative planning. They do not serve merely as law enforcement agencies. Although most states have the power to change school districts, they prefer to leave as much choice as possible to the local districts; however, they will bring pressure to bear where necessary. They are always ready to provide consultant services to help in the solution of local problems.

Recently, at the request of an eastern city, the state department of education conducted a school survey in that city. The recommendations included in the survey covered many aspects of education. The imminent threat of the withdrawal of state aid was one of the factors that hastened the city's compliance with many of the basic recommendations made in the survey. In the field of physical education the survey resulted in the addition of teachers, an increase in allocation for supplies, and the expediting of plans for reconditioning and enlarging existing physical plants.

A knowledge of the minimum state standards will enable the beginning teacher to determine whether the school has provided the educational essentials. If the recommended standards have not been met, an attempt to make improvements should be made. Since one responsibility of state departments of education is to improve physical education programs, consultants are usually available to local schools and districts for (1) evaluation of program content, (2) assistance in curriculum revision, (3) guidance in problem situations, and (4) assistance in public relations. State department representatives will usually work to find ways of improving the profession, curriculum, standards, and facilities.

Since the Constitution of the United States does not carry any provision for federal education, the state has assumed the responsibility. The state has limited its own action primarily to guidance and the specification of minimum requirements, leaving a major part of the obligation of education in the hands of the local district and thus placing more responsibility on the physical educator to constantly interpret his program.

THE SECONDARY SCHOOL

The school, as the hub of the educational program, should reflect societal changes that are meaningful and important to the students who attend these institutions. Furthermore, the school should work directly with the community, parents, and students in a manner consistent with the changes taking place. For teachers and school administrators to do this intelligently, the structure and role of the secondary school must be clearly understood.

The beginning teacher, particularly, in order to perform his or her role in the most effective way possible, should know and understand the way the school system is structured in the community, how the secondary school fits into this structure, the personnel who play key roles in the educational process, the facilities utilized, and the programs being offered. The lack of such knowledge and understanding can result in personnel problems, disregard for proper channels of communication, and failure to utilize important program resources or get innovative ideas accepted.

The school has the responsibility of educating tomorrow's citizens. Although the goals of education are similar, the means to the end will differ from one school system to another. In this section a picture will be presented of the organization and structure of schools so that beginning teachers of physical education can be better prepared to take their places in the educational system.

Structure

School district. A school district is that subdivision that is responsible to the state for the administration of public education. Districts vary greatly in size and function. They may be formed on township and city lines, according to elementary or secondary levels, or using other divisions. The trend is away from having many, overlapping, ineffectual districts and toward the use of larger, more effective districts. The National Education Association reports that from 1948 to 1958 the number of school districts in the United States dropped from nearly 102,000 to 48,043. In recent years the number of school districts has been reduced; at the present time there are approximately 30,000.

Since public education is not mentioned in the federal Constitution, the state has assumed this obligation. Local school districts operate under authority granted by the state. The school district, which is administered by a board of education, is therefore legally responsible to all the people of the state, not to those of the school district only. The fact that a great amount of local freedom is allowed does not alter the legal responsibility. The school board's duties are explained earlier in this chapter. The agents of the board, such as superintendents and principals, are the administrators who concern themselves directly with school problems.

The implications of district reorganization bode well for physical education. As districts become larger, their ability to support and maintain proper physical education plants, personnel, equipment, and supplies should increase—hence, the probability of a more comprehensive program.

School system. The size of the system dictates the number and type of duties its school administrators have. In a small system the superintendent performs many separate functions. In a larger system he or she is concerned primarily with coordination and public relations, while the many details are handled by assistant or deputy superintendents, department heads, subject supervisors, and principals.

The pattern of school organization at the elementary and secondary levels is in a period of transition. Some of the present patterns of school organization are as follows:

1. In the traditional high school, or 8-4, system, the four-year high school is preceded by the eight-year elementary school.

2. In the combined junior and senior high school, or 6-6 or 7-5, plan, the junior and senior high schools are combined under one principal.

3. In the three-year junior high school, or 6-3-3, system, the junior high school is grouped separately under one principal. Although the junior high school usually includes grades seven to nine, there are exceptions to this organization.

4. In the four-year high school, or 6-2-4, system, the four-year high school is similar to

the traditional high school in organization, and the junior high school consists of two grades.

5. The middle school plan, for example, the 4-4-4 plan, retains the old high school idea but groups the upper elementary grades, such as grades five to eight, in one unit.

There are many arguments that can be set forth for each plan of school organization. The physical, psychological, and sociological aspects of the school setting and of child growth and development, the need for effective communication between schools, the range of subjects, the facilities provided, and the preparation of teachers are all pertinent to the type of administrative organization selected. One survey of 366 unified school systems with pupil enrollment of 12,000 or more, conducted by the Educational Research Service, showed that 71 percent of

these school systems were organized on the 6-3-3 plan, 10 percent on the 8-4 organization, and 6 percent on a 6-2-4 pattern. Other patterns included 7-5, 6-6, 5-3-4, and 7-2-3.

Elementary school. In most elementary schools the pupil is with one teacher most of each school day. The only change comes when a specialist handles the class for a period one or more times each week. These specialists may include the physical educator, music teacher, science teacher, art instructor, and an occassional resource person. In very small rural schools one teacher may instruct grades one through six—in the same classroom.

In some elementary schools all physical education is handled by the classroom teacher. In other situations a physical education teacher may meet with the elementary class weekly or biweekly and prepare a program for the classroom teacher to use during

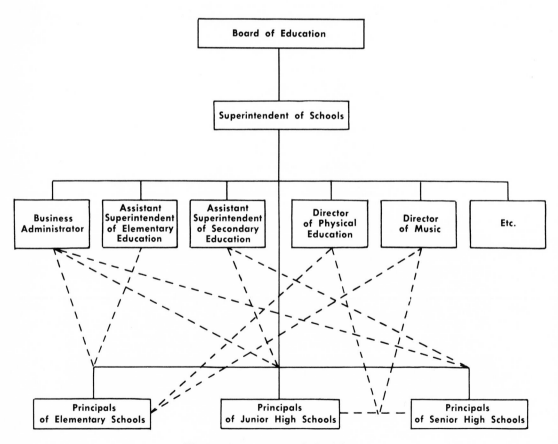

Fig. 2-6. Basic structure of school district.

the intervening days. In other elementary schools the physical education specialist sees the children two or three times weekly.

Middle school. One pattern of organization being considered by many school systems is the middle school concept. Most simply stated, a middle school is for boys and girls between the elementary and high school years—grades six, seven, and eight, and sometimes five. Communities that have embarked on the middle school pattern are Bridgewater, Massachusetts; Bedford Public Schools in Mount Kisco, New York; Sarasota County, Florida; Saginaw, Michigan; Easton, Connecticut; and Independence, Ohio.

Some of the advantages of the middle school include the opportunity for more departmentalization, better stimulation of students, special teachers and special programs, and better student grouping.

Some of the disadvantages of the middle school include the lack of evidence to support its value, the social adjustment problems occurring when ninth graders are placed with twelfth graders, the possibility that youngsters in the middle school will be pushed too hard academically and socially, and the ne-cessity of altering administrative techniques and procedures.

Secondary school. The junior high school is usually composed of grades seven, eight, and nine, and the senior high school is composed of grades ten, eleven, and twelve.

It is difficult to present a picture of a typical secondary school because of the variety in the size of the schools. They range from small rural schools with fewer than 100 pupils to large city schools that house student bodies numbering in the thousands. There are, however, certain basic factors that are true regardless of size or location:

1. Secondary education is usually coeducational.
2. Guidance is offered in most schools by specially trained personnel.
3. Extracurricular activities are an important part of the program.
4. Secondary schools are prepared to offer terminal education as well as college preparation.
5. Individual courses of study are prepared for the students.
6. Teachers are specialists in subject areas.

Fig. 2-7. Demonstration and instruction in horseback riding at Bel Air, Md., Middle School.

There are many limiting factors to the small high school that have brought about the present tendency toward centralization and consolidation. Some of them are listed below:

1. Meager curriculum offerings—inability to hire teachers for small groups of gifted children
2. Inadequate equipment—such as library, gymnasium, shops, laboratories, and so on—because of lack of funds for these expensive items
3. Inferior opportunities for social development—small number of children of comparable age and interests
4. Inferior staff—lower pay scale and living conditions as a result of lack of available funds

The larger high schools are generally able to offer a much more varied curriculum. Many educators have pointed to the necessity of challenging our gifted pupils and bringing along the slower ones. In the large high school the opportunity to meet these and other objectives is more readily available. Among recommendations for improving American secondary schools are the following:

1. More student involvement
2. Minischools
3. Use of paraprofessionals
4. Use of community resources
5. Teacher accountability
6. Flexible scheduling
7. Differentiated staffing
8. Individualization of programs
9. Self-paced instruction
10. Grouping according to ability

The opportunity to meet children's needs is greater in a larger school—one with a graduating class of at least 100 pupils. In a large school there are usually a sufficient number of gifted pupils to fill a special class. The more experienced and better teachers are attracted to the larger school by better salaries and working conditions. The curriculum is more varied because full-time teachers are hired to teach the slow readers and the languages, sciences, and other needed courses. Guidance personnel are also more readily available.

Fig. 2-8. Physical education class at Mount Pleasant Senior High School, Wilmington, Del.

Specialists almost always handle the physical education program on the secondary level. In some junior high schools the arrangements are similar to the elementary school procedure, but more and more schools are using physical educators to handle the entire program, as they do in senior high schools.

Personnel

Responsibility for the operation of the local schools rests with the board of education. The board hires a professional educator to administer the school system. This practice is about 140 years old. It started when education grew to be more than could be handled by the existing town officials. Now, as then, administrators attempt to solve the ever-present problems of public education.

Superintendent. The chief school official hired to supervise a school system is the superintendent. In a small community he or she may double as the principal of a high school and may be referred to as the district supervising principal. In larger communities he or she has an office staff and possibly an assistant to handle myriad responsibilities. In large cities or towns numerous assistants, deputies, or associates assist in various duties. Included in the superintendent's charge are these responsibilities:

1. School organization—establishes the school structure for the system
2. Curriculum development—establishes groups to conduct curriculum revisions in all areas
3. Personnel recommendations—recommends to the board those individuals needed to fill vacancies
4. Administration of all the school plants and facilities—supervises maintenance, construction, and repair of all plants and facilities
5. Budgetary recommendations—submits budget recommendations to the board of education
6. School-community relations—fosters good public realtions through public appearances, meetings, and so forth
7. Advice—advises the board regarding policy changes, procedures, and practices, presenting educationally sound, workable suggestions
8. Publicity—keeps the board informed,

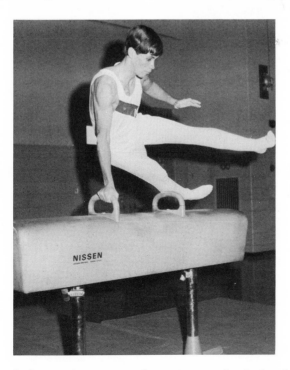

Fig. 2-9. Physical education class at Mount Pleasant Senior High School, Wilmington, Del.

giving reports on educational trends and notice of special school activities

To assist in these responsibilities and make recommendations to the superintendent there may be any or all of the following individuals as part of the administrative organization in the school system: assistants for secondary education and/or elementary education; business administrators; school health assistants; personnel assistants; public relations assistants; curriculum assistants; and directors of special areas such as art, music, library, industrial arts, physical education, and buildings and maintenance.

Principal. In each school within any system, the principal is the chief administrator. His or her duties vary, depending upon the size of the school. In a small building the principal may teach some classes in addition to supervisory and administrative responsibilities. In larger schools he or she not only is relieved of teaching duties but also has some administrative assistants. They may include an assistant principal, guidance personnel, department heads, deans of girls and boys, and a custodial head.

The principal's responsibilities are similar to the superintendent's. They consist of executing the educational policy as outlined by the superintendent, directing the instructional program, promoting harmony and a democratic feeling within the faculty, encouraging and directing good school-community relationships, and supervising the maintenance of the physical plant.

It is usually difficult for a principal to know all the pupils in a large high school, but as a rule the pupil-administrator relationship will be much better when the principal is able to know pupils personally. Many administrators drop in at a rehearsal, team practice, or sports event not only to observe the teacher but also to let the students know that they are interested in their activities.

The principal also works closely with parents. He or she plays an important role in the local parent-teacher association and in community affairs. The principal meets with parents to discuss student problems regarding college, grades, or discipline or acts as the intermediary to bring parents and teachers together to discuss these problems. The work is time consuming and tedious.

One of the responsibilities of a principal is to establish a democratic administration. This means that faculty members participate in the formulation of policies. Of course, it is the principal's decision to use or to discard any suggestions, but it is the successful and wise administrator who listens to faculty suggestions—whether in open meetings, through committees, or in personal conferences. Faculty committees are usually appointed by the principal to work with specific problems such as grading, graduation, discipline, and the honor society. The committees present their recommendations to the faculty and the principal, to be used in the formulation of school policies. A knowledge of the formation and the functioning of these committees can be invaluable to the new teacher. It is also important to know the function and frequency of staff meetings and the channels through which problems, questions, and innovating ideas may be presented. Knowing how to approach the supervisor can play an important part in the satisfactory adjustment of the beginning teacher.

Department heads. Depending upon the size of a school system, there may be heads of special subject matter areas. These heads assist the superintendent by coordinating the work of the teachers and programs in their special fields.

Similarly, in larger high schools there are department heads to assist the principal. These people usually teach a number of classes, but their assignment also includes supervision, organization, and guidance. In smaller schools a department representative is often appointed by the principal to act as a liaison between the administration and the department when it is inconvenient to meet with the faculty as a whole.

In the field of physical education it is the usual practice in the larger school systems to have a director or supervisor who coordinates the work and supervises all the physical education teachers. In the smaller systems the superintendent or an assistant in charge of secondary or elementary education may supervise the physical education teachers.

Teachers. Teachers are hired by the board of education upon recommendation from the superintendent. A recommendation generally comes from a principal or department head.

In small schools a teacher may teach two different subjects and possibly on two educational levels. This situation is not usually prevalent in larger schools. Physical education teachers on the secondary level usually teach physical education full time.

It is becoming more common to use specialists in health to handle all health instruction; however, in many systems the physical education teacher still doubles as the health teacher and possibly as the driver education teacher as well. Specific problems and details that the new physical education teacher must face are discussed in Chapter 13.

Custodians. Responsibility for the maintenance of the building rests with the principal. It is customary for a principal to delegate this responsibility to a head custodian. The importance of this aid to good teaching be-

comes evident when the temperature is too high or seats are in disrepair and conditions are not satisfactory for effective learning. A means of communication from the teacher to the custodians is usually established so that these environmental factors can be quickly controlled and kept at optimum standards.

The school's custodians are often the physical educator's best friends and allies. Where they are treated with respect, the gymnasium and locker and shower rooms will be kept in spotless condition. Frequently, the custodians are also responsible for maintaining the playing fields and for marking lines. If the physical educator takes cognizance of these individuals, his or her work can be made much easier. Where good relationships exist, the custodians will go out of their way to help repair a piece of equipment, to build a special item, or to mow the field an extra time. Poor teacher-custodian relations can have disastrous effects on the entire physical education program.

Specialists. The size of a system usually determines how many specialists will be part of the professional staff and just what their duties will be.

Fig. 2-10. Administrative structure of school district with director of health and physical education.

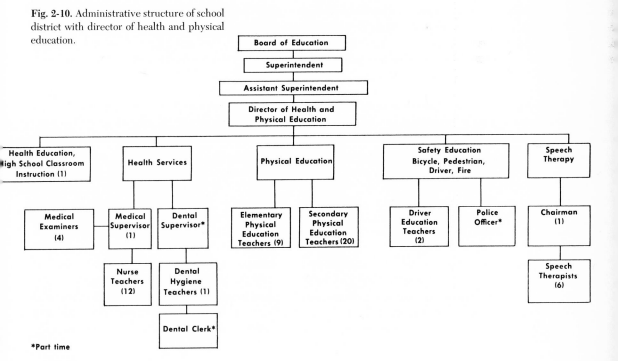

Medical staff. A large system may have a full-time physician in charge of the nurses and part-time physicians who assist in the yearly examinations, follow-up of remediable defects, examination of athletic team participants, and the like. The medical staff in a smaller system may consist of a nurse who is assisted for a few hours weekly by a local physician.

Some schools authorize the nurse as the only person who can excuse a student from a physical education class for the day. She can assist the physical education department by observing and referring students who need advanced medical or dental treatment. She also has knowledge of those students in need of a modified program and can act as a liaison between the physical education department and the family physician. The school nurse is an invaluable resource person as a member of the physical education team.

Supervisory personnel. The range in this area will be from numerous assistants in the large system to a superintendent or supervising principal who is the primary supervisor in a small school.

Curriculum specialists. Responsibility for the curriculum may be placed in the hands of committees of classroom teachers, or it may be delegated to curriculum specialists.

Guidance specialists. Professional workers in guidance may include psychologists as well as other guidance personnel. Some students manifest various behavioral and emotional problems. The school guidance counselors have dossiers on each student and can guide the physical educator in the most effective way of handling a particular problem. The guidance people are usually backed up by school psychologists and social case workers, who may have or who can obtain further helpful information. The physical educator should seek the assistance of these people. A mishandled problem can create further problems, especially where a chronically disruptive pupil is concerned.

Because of their unique position in the school, the guidance counselors are often in a good position to observe and evaluate the physical education programs. They fre-quently hear the student's point of view in counseling interviews and can relate non-confidential comments to the physical educator.

Business administrator. The details of business administration may be assigned to an individual or to a staff responsible for the maintenance and repair of all plants, as well as the preparation of distribution of all supplies, texts, or equipment.

Cafeteria personnel. Supervision may be handled on an individual basis in each school, or it may be handled through a head dietitian responsible directly to the superintendent.

Facilities

An excellent educational program does not necessarily require an ideal plant, nor does an ideal plant guarantee a good program; however, they complement each other. School construction is a major problem in the United States. Since the physical education department is one of the most expensive items in the school, this problem is of particular interest to the physical educator. Multiple use of the physical education areas, such as the gymnasium, playing fields, and pool, undoubtedly engenders more support from the voting public for school construction. This implies the use of the facilities during evenings, weekends, holidays, and summers, in addition to school hours. Some communities that make extensive use of their school plants are Oakland, California; Spokane, Washington; and Norwich, Connecticut. Public reaction to educational expenditures is generally more favorable in such communities. This is undoubtedly true because many of the residents themselves are involved in the use of the school building, have a better understanding of where their money goes, and are therefore more inclined to support educational referendums.

Multiple use of facilities is not a panacea for education but has implications for the physical education teacher. Extensive use of facilities and proper interpretation to the public may help alleviate some of the problems relating to plant and facilities.

Curricula

Today's secondary schools vary greatly in the type of courses offered and in size and organization. If the trend toward centralization and consolidation of districts continues, it will help most schools to offer comprehensive programs and greatly raise the level of education.

There are three basic curricula offered on the secondary level. Some schools offer all three, which is a sound, comprehensive program. Others offer only one or two of these types.

General. The general curriculum is usually a terminal education program. It meets state requirements for graduation and covers the basic courses in English, history, science, mathematics, physical education, art, and music.

College preparatory. This program includes the same courses as above at an advanced level plus added units in any or all of the following subjects required for college entrance or used for advanced standing: foreign languages, sciences, mathematics, music, and art.

Vocational or career education. The vocational curriculum includes basic courses in English, history, practical mathematics, and physical education, as well as specialized courses in such vocational areas as bookkeeping, typing, welding, auto mechanics, food trades, and designing.

In most schools grades seven and eight follow the required courses; grade nine allows for some exploration; and the tenth, eleventh, and twelfth grades allow students to follow their chosen course of study. This pattern is usually selected through the joint effort of the pupil, parents, and guidance personnel.

In some small schools the choice may be limited; therefore, students may be forced into patterns they would not select if given a choice. In some larger cities special schools meet the needs for special courses. In many cities there are schools that concentrate in a particular area, such as science, music and art, machine and metal trades, aviation, and food trades.

The type of course a student follows in high school has no bearing upon the amount of physical education required. It is generally accepted that this instruction is necessary for all students.

Physical education in the school

For beginning teachers to better meet their responsibilities, it is necessary to understand the place of the physical education department in the school and the responsibilities of the personnel in the department.

Structure. The positions of physical educators sometimes are more complicated than those of other teachers. As teachers, they will be under the direct supervision of the principal of the school. In many systems, however, there is a director or supervisor of physical education who represents the superintendent of school in his special area. One would expect this supervisor to have direct control over the members of his department. This is not usually the case. Although the director is responsible for the coordination of all physical education in the system, his or her role is primarily that of an advisor to the principal and superintendent. The relationship of physical education instructors, their director, and the principal is a delicate one and should be understood by new teachers so that they may avoid obvious pitfalls. Beginning teachers should find out the chain of responsibilities in the system.

Personnel. In the field of physical education, the responsibilities of personnel will depend upon the size of the system. In a small school one person may handle all the physical education duties from kindergarten through the twelfth grade. In other communities the responsibilities may be divided by director, chairman, and teachers.

Director or supervisor. There is a trend that recognizes the necessity for one person to oversee and coordinate all physical education in a school system. In at least one state a physical educator may become certified as a Director of Health, Physical Education, and Recreation. This person's responsibilities are to help establish policy, see that it is carried out, organize and administer girls' and boys' physical education programs at all levels, check facilities, coordinate programs, supervise teachers, help prepare the budget, organize all athletic programs, including scheduling, arranging for officials, transportation, equipment, and insurance, and assume responsibility for all equipment and supplies. In some communities these responsibilities are divided between the coach at the high school and an assistant or deputy superintendent.

When the director has been charged with administering the fields of physical education, health, and recreation, responsibilities include the following duties:

General duties of the director

1. Implement standards established by the state department of education and the local board of education.

2. Interview possible candidates for positions in the special areas and make recommendations for these positions.

3. Work closely with the assistant superintendent in charge of business affairs, the assistant superintendent in charge of instruction, and subject matter and classroom teachers.

4. Coordinate areas of health, physical education, and recreation.

5. Supervise all inside and outside facilities and equipment and supplies concerned with special areas (this responsibility includes maintenance, safety, and replacement operations).

6. Maintain liaison with community groups; for example, hold educational meetings with doctors and dentists to interpret and improve the school health program, schedule school facilities for community groups, and serve on various community committees for youth needs.

7. Prepare periodic reports regarding areas of activity.

8. Coordinate school civil defense activities in some school systems.

9. Serve on the school health council.

Physical education duties of the director

1. Supervise total physical education program (class, adapted, intramurals, extramurals, and varsity interscholastic athletics).

2. Administer schedules, practice and game facilities, insurance, and equipment.

3. Maintain liaison with county, district, and state professional groups.

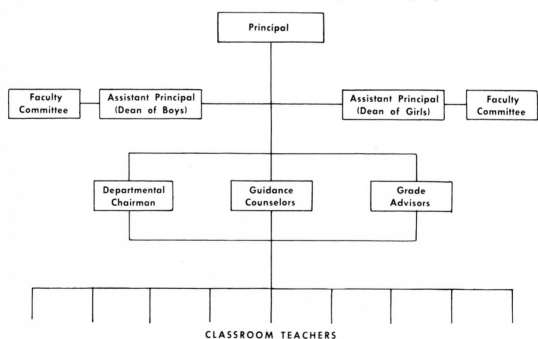

Fig. 2-11. Administrative structure of one secondary school.

4. Upgrade program in general.

Health duties of the director

1. Supervise health services, including supervision of school nurse-teachers and dental hygiene teachers, coordination of the work of school physicians, preparation of guides and policies for the program of health services, organization of health projects, and obtaining of proper equipment and supplies.

2. Supervise health science instruction, including supervision of health education programs throughout the school system, preparation of curriculum guides and research studies, and upgrading of the program in general.

3. Promote healthful school living through general supervision of the school plant, attention to psychological aspects of the school program, and making of recommendations for improvement.

Recreation duties of the director

1. Supervise various aspects of recreation program, including, in addition to the school program, summer and vacation playgrounds, teen centers, and the like.

2. Obtain, where necessary, facilities, equipment, personnel, and supplies.

3. Plan and administer the recreation program.

Chairperson. The chairperson of a depart-

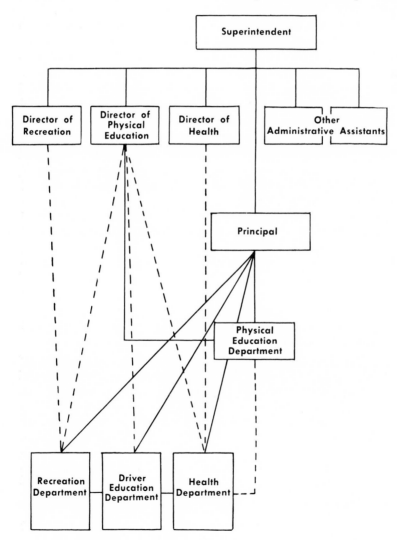

Fig. 2-12. Administrative structure of physical education in a school system.

ment is usually appointed by the principal or superintendent of schools. In some schools there is no formal department head; an individual is appointed by the principal to act as representative of the department. In most instances this person is the immediate supervisor of the physical education teachers. Part of his or her responsibilities may be to assist in the evaluation of a new teacher's performance. The person involved with this administration may teach a full program and receive extra compensation for duties rendered, may be relieved of some or all teaching responsibilities to allow time for administrative duties, or may merely be the department representative and have no supervisory responsibilities. He or she may be the athletic director, which means planning all interscholastic athletics. However, this may or may not be in addition to the responsibilities assigned as the department head.

Teachers. Teachers of physical education handle physical education classes, assist in curriculum evaluation, make suggestions for the improvement of the program, handle intramural and interscholastic programs, and assume other obligations to the school that fall to the lot of every teacher.

In a small secondary school the physical education program may be conducted by only one teacher for the girls and one for the boys. In such a situation, each teacher must assume total responsibility for all areas of the program, including teaching, care of equipment, budget making, and directing intramural and extramural programs, as well as assuming any other responsibilities that may accrue from being all things to all phases of the job.

In a large secondary school there are frequently several male and several female physical educators. One of these teachers may serve as department chairperson and in turn be responsible to a supervisor of physical education who serves the entire school system. In this kind of hierarchy, each teacher is usually asked to assume the responsibility for a particular area, such as equipment maintenance or the ordering of library materials and audiovisual aids. This arrange-

ment fragments the operation of the overall program but frees each teacher to devote more time to teaching. Similarly, department chairpersons and city supervisors can devote more time to serving as resource people and to general supervision of the program.

Two of the main responsibilities confronting a new physical education teacher are to be accepted as part of the total school and as an important part of the physical education department.

1. Part of the total school picture. One way in which a physical educator may gain the respect of colleagues is to share the so-called boring, routine jobs that are so much a part of the school day. These may involve distribution of supplies, detention assignments, lunchroom duty, or graduation practice. It is well worth the effort to shoulder one's share of the day's responsibilities.

As a member of a school faculty, the physical educator should show an interest in school activities and projects of all kinds. There is always something to be done, such as helping with the annual concert, the dramatic presentation, or the magazine drive, as well as participating in parent-teacher association meetings, staff meetings, and even faculty social functions. The physical educator should know the teachers in the school so that they will have the opportunity to gain a new respect for and understanding of the physical education department. This could very well lead to a more honest evaluation of the physical education program and to new supporters for its rightful place in the school curriculum.

2. Member of the physical education department. As is true for any new faculty member, the physical educator must demonstrate capability, flexibility, and sincerity to his or her peers. To do this he or she must do the job as efficiently as possible and respect the experience and seniority of colleagues.

Interscholastic athletics. The interscholastic athletic part of the physical education program may involve controversy. It is unfortunately true that there are some coaches who go to extremes in the handling of their teams. These coaches drive their teams unmercifully, attempt to pressure teachers to keep players eligible, believe they have to win at any cost, and devote too much of their time and energy to their teams—to the detriment of their physical education classes.

It is important to have interscholastic sports program in its proper place in the total program. It has great value in that it challenges the athletically gifted child, kindles and keeps aflame the spirit of a student body, and unites the members of a school and gives them a proud feeling of belonging, in addition to having many other worthwhile aspects. It is, however, only one part of a physical education program.

Interpreting physical education.* Too often the physical educator or coach is considered apart from the education staff: the faculty educate students; physical educators exercise them.

The challenge of this attitude must be met by physical educators. They must have a sound philosophy of education and an understanding of the place of physical education in the development and growth of the child. They must also be exemplary in the performance of duties. Finally, the interpretation of physical education must be directed not only to faculty members but to the community as a whole.

Physical educators have many means of interpreting the program. Speaking at meetings of the Parent-Teacher Association, Rotary, Elks, Masons, Kiwanis, and other clubs is an accepted and effective method of presentation. Physical education demonstrations, sports nights, and athletic contests can also afford good publicity.

The best selling point, however, is the student in the physical education class. If

*See Chapter 11.

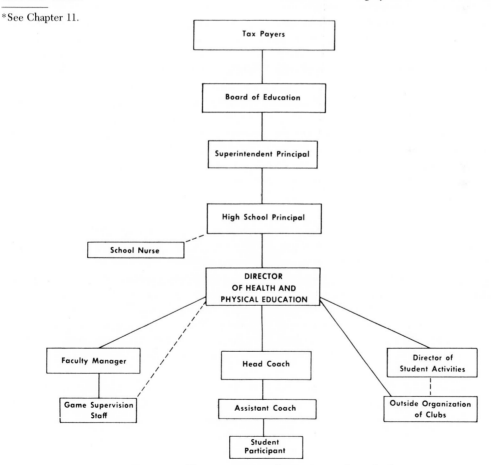

Fig. 2-13. Athletic organization chart in a secondary school.

pupils understand why they spend hours on the playground or in the gymnasium, their reactions and comments at home are the best means of interpreting the program to parents. To accomplish this, however, students must receive more than a chance to play ball. There must be an understanding of the accumulated values of a well-rounded program. Students, then, can be the physical educator's best salespersons. If they are educated well, the opportunity to do an even better job will generally be forthcoming because of increased school and community support.

Keys to success in physical education

Indicated below are some characteristics of a secondary school that are essential for a sound education and physical education program.

Administrative philosophy and policies. The administrator of a secondary school may or may not view the physical education program with favor. Where the administration values physical education, it will be easier to have homogeneous classes, and physical education will not be the last class to be scheduled. Where the administration is cooperative, the physical education program will be put on a par with academic courses. The administration often sets the policies in regard to uniforms, excuses, and the grading system. The teacher must abide by these policies. The administration also assigns extra duties to teachers. Where physical education is given its rightful place in the curriculum, the physical education teacher has a minimum of extra duties during the school day. Lack of homeroom duties means time to ready the equipment for the day. Lack of study halls and lunch duty frees the physical education teacher for teaching, and lack of afternoon bus duty allows time for the conduct of a good intramural program. In any case the physical education program must be conducted within the existing administrative framework.

Faculty relationships. Teachers should work together not only to coordinate subject matter but also to support and coordinate those special events that are so much a part of school life. The efforts of all teachers should be harmonized to culminate successfully in a music festival, school dance, general organization membership drive, athletic event, or other school-sponsored project.

The physical educator must strive to maintain cooperative relationships with the rest of the faculty. Social conversation with other faculty members allows for an interchange of ideas. Understandings are developed and concepts formed about other areas of the curriculum. It is also here that the physical educator can articulate the relationship of the program to the rest of the school. The physical educator should always maintain professional ethics and refuse to discuss confidential information about students or to participate in a discussion that is concerned with gossip about students, other teachers, or the administration.

Teacher-parent relationships. When teacher-parent relationships are good, parents believe that they can approach their child's teacher to discuss any problem, and the teacher believes that he or she can call on parents for assistance when necessary. The relationship is one of mutual respect, providing the basis for a frank discussion between parent and teacher of problems and possible solutions.

To know the parents helps the teacher to understand the child. By joining the parent-teacher association and attending its meetings and socials, the teacher is able to meet the parents in a relaxed and informal atmosphere. It is here that the teacher can explain his or her program and answer any questions the parents may have. The physical education program in a secondary school thrives on good public relations, and this starts with the parents of the community.

Teacher-student relationships. When teacher-student relationships are good, mutual respect exists between pupils and teachers. The teacher is aware of the need and the methods for earning this respect from his or her pupils and, therefore, is the one to foster this feeling. He or she is able to establish rapport with pupils, which greatly contributes to the success of his or her program.

Besides teaching students, the physical educator must know and guide them and try to inspire them. In some schools, student respect for teachers is totally lacking, and good discipline is difficult at best to maintain. Safety alone requires that physical education classes be well disciplined. A new teacher must be especially cognizant of the fact that students will test him or her. They want to know how the teacher will react to disrespect, horseplay in class, and bad conduct in general. Where the school administration has set strong behavior policies, the teacher will receive backing in maintaining these standards. Where behavior policies are weak, the teacher must set high standards and be consistent in applying them.

A martinet never develops close rapport with students. The good disciplinarian who respects and knows students as individuals will be able to develop good rapport. Discipline must be tempered with understanding and respect for the student.

Good teacher-student relationships also develop in, and are carried over to, areas outside the classroom. The teacher who attends football games and concerts and helps to chaperone dances and social affairs has the opportunity to develop a working and companionable relationship with students. Students will respond in kind to respect, understanding, and interest.

Allied fields

The fields of recreation and leisure services and health education are closely allied to physical education. The positions that are established to handle these responsibilities may or may not be within the department of physical education. It is obvious that cooperation is necessary regardless of the local structure. The city of Norfolk, Virginia, has shown how the objectives of education can better be reached through close cooperation in the fields of health and physical education. Flint, Michigan, has proved extensively the values of cooperation in the fields of recreation and physical education. The accomplishments made through mutual effort can be limitless when a community sets its mind to the task.

Recreation and leisure services. Before discussing recreation and leisure services, it is first necessary to define it. Recreation is a leisure activity—that is, an activity performed during nonworking hours. It is enjoyable and wholesome—something that contributes to one's satisfaction and happiness. It is voluntary—something in which the individual participates because he desires to do so.

There are many types of recreational and leisure activities. There are those that challenge the mind and those that challenge the body. There are those that call for cooperative effort and those that involve only the individual. Integrated physical education and recreation programs can be of great value to each other in at least the following ways: (1) programming, in which recreation programs are used as a testing ground for skills learned in physical education class; (2) extension of the intramural program; (3) facility construction, in which duplication is avoided by constructing one unit to serve both the school and after-school programs; and (4) economies, in which common use is made of personnel, supplies, and equipment.

There are different means of coordinating physical education and recreation and leisure services. In one Minnesota city, the administration of community recreation is vested in a board composed of one appointed representative from each city ward, one member-at-large, and three ex-officio members representing the school board, park board, and common council. In one California city the superintendent of recreation and leisure services coordinates and administers the program, and the costs are borne by the board of recreation, the board of education, and the city. In other areas similar plans are in effect, varying in many details except the important one, which is coordination, or cooperation.

Communities that have minimized the duplication of personnel and established a person or board responsible for recreation and leisure services and physical education

---

Checklist of selected items for evaluating the secondary school's physical education program's relevancy to the community

		Yes	No
1.	The physical education program utilizes such community resources as parks, swimming pools, bowling alleys, and so on as well as people with expertise in various physical education activities and such methodology as visual aids, curriculum development, and other areas in providing a rich experience for the students.	☐	☐
2.	Physical education takes into account the economic background of the community in planning activities (for example, weekend skiing trips may be too expensive).	☐	☐
3.	Physical education takes into account the physical needs of the residents of the community (physical fitness, nutritional needs, and skill levels).	☐	☐
4.	The physical education program takes into account the climate and other natural features of the community, making greatest use of the out-of-doors, providing seasonal activities, and the like.	☐	☐
5.	Physical education works cooperatively with closely allied community agencies such as Boys' Clubs, PAL, YMCA, YWCA, CYO, YMHA, and YWHA.	☐	☐
6.	The physical education program provides for the interests and needs of people in the community with different ethnic backgrounds, in respect to its offering of games, dances, and sports.	☐	☐
7.	Physical education interprets articulately the value of its offering to the children and other residents of the community.	☐	☐
8.	Physical education works closely with the community's communication media to properly interpret the program, including the role of educational athletics in the school.	☐	☐
9.	Physical education interprets the athletic program to the townspeople and encourages proper behavior of spectators at sports contests so that their behavior reflects favorably on the school.	☐	☐
10.	Physical education interprets the need for community utilization of its facilities to school authorities in order to further its objectives for the adult population.	☐	☐
11.	Physical education takes into consideration the attitude of the residents toward education and the level of aspiration for their children.	☐	☐
12.	Physical education takes into consideration such community problems as drugs, violence, and school dropouts in its curriculum planning.	☐	☐
13.	The physical education program takes into consideration the religious beliefs of the community in planning and carrying out its offering.	☐	☐
14.	Physical education provides a viable program, where feasible, during school vacation periods.	☐	☐
15.	Physical education provides advice and counsel for community physical fitness and athletic programs.	☐	☐
16.	Physical education does not yield to community pressures to utilize questionable professional procedures to develop outstanding athletic teams.	☐	☐

---

list the following values: (1) dollar savings, resulting from lack of duplication of facilities and use of the same personnel; (2) stronger programs, with continuity of school and out-of-school activities; and (3) greater participation, resulting in better understanding of programs and better public relations.

In some communities the recreation and leisure services board and the school board have no administrative tie, and although they work together on particular activities or problems, they also have their differences, with no ready means of working them out. The importance of cooperation between physical education and recreation and leisure services programs cannot be overemphasized.

Health. The fields of health and physical education share much in common, although they are two separate entities. It is only in recent years that the differences have become more commonly recognized. There were times when the job of health was everyone's job—from members of the mathematics department to the custodial staff—and so it was really no one's job. Today, some states have moved so far as to certify people in the field

Fig. 2-14. Health education. (San Diego County Schools, San Diego, Calif.)

of health education, while other communities have put the responsibility in the hands of the director or supervisor of health and physical education. The degree to which this person is able to coordinate and guide is an important factor in establishing a good program. This is especially true when one realizes that a school health council may include any or all of the following: school principal, physician, dentist, nurse, health educator, teacher of physical education, teachers of biology and home economics, psychologist, members of guidance staff, teacher for the physically handicapped, nutritionist, dental hygienist, custodian, student representatives, parent representatives, and representatives from community health organizations.

In some communities cooperative health services may be organized by a school health coordinating council. In other communities a joint cooperative plan involves the park board, board of education, board of health, and volunteer agencies. School health policies are formulated by the board of education

and rendered by the town health department.

Coordination in the fields of health and physical education results in the following: (1) better total education—using coordinated means to reach the goals; (2) better program planning—avoiding duplication and providing more available hands to operate a complete program; (3) minimizing of clerical work in handling special problems, which is more economical and provides readily available records; and (4) more prompt and complete follow-up of remediable defects through sound and convenient use of physical education and health personnel. Coordination and cooperation are obviously the key to better health and physical education programs.

Self-assessment tests

These tests are to assist in determining if material and competencies presented in this chapter have been mastered:

1. Describe the community in which you live and give specific illustrations as to how it has affected the school's physical education program.
2. Prepare a plan that you would follow as a physical educator to ensure an effective working relationship

between the community and your school's physical education program.

3. Draw a governmental organizational chart of your community. In this chart show the various offices and positions that exist.

4. Prepare an administrative organizational chart of your school district. Include in this chart a detailed breakdown of the various administrative units in the high school and how physical education fits into this administrative structure.

5. You are presented with the proposal that the administrative structure of your school be changed. Discuss how schools differ and what administrative plan you feel would be most helpful to implement a viable physical education program.

6. List the key administrative positions in a school district. Opposite each position list the duties performed by the person holding that position.

Points to remember

1. There are different types of communities in which teachers work; the nature of each type of community has many implications for physical education.

2. Many community factors, including economic conditions, religious groups, climate, sociological and cultural backgrounds, attitude toward education, and pressure groups, affect education and physical education.

3. There is an urgent need for cooperation between physical education, health and recreation.

4. The structure of a school district has implications for physical education.

5. The many types and characteristics of secondary schools.

6. The place of the physical education department in the total school picture is important to the program's adequate functioning.

Problems to think through

1. What are the advantages to the physical education department in a community where the board of education is fiscally independent? Fiscally dependent?

2. What would you, as the physical educator, do in a community where there is a movement to organize a highly competitive sports league for junior high school students?

3. What are the implications for physical education in the drive to consolidate or centralize small school districts?

4. What are some of the considerations that face a new teacher?

5. How may a coach avoid alienating members of the school faculty?

6. What are the advantages of a secondary school that has a graduating class of 100 pupils?

7. What value would a director, chairperson, or supervisor of physical education be to a school system?

Case study for analysis

All teachers are responsible to their principal. Many physical education teachers are also supervised by a de-partment chairperson and/or a director or supervisor of physical education who represents the superintendent of schools. Analyze the chain of responsibility of all physical education teachers in a school system containing one senior high school, one junior high school, and four elementary schools. Consider possible friction points between the supervisory personnel. How can physical education teachers avoid difficulty in their relationship with their supervisors?

Exercises for review

1. Describe the composition of the board of education in your community and the powers and qualifications of the members.

2. Who are the pressure groups in your community that may affect the physical education program?

3. List five facets of a program of physical education that are successfully performed in communities near your own.

4. What are the responsibilities of the superintendent of schools regarding physical education?

5. To whom may the new physical education teacher turn for help and guidance? Indicate the specific areas needing assistance and the individuals who may be of greatest value.

6. Prepare a speech that you could use to interpret physical education to a parent-teacher association, men's club, or sports night dinner.

Selected readings

Bannon, J. J.: Leisure resources—its comprehensive planning, Englewood Cliffs, N.J., 1976, Prentice-Hall, Inc.

Bucher, C. A.: Administrative dimensions of health and physical education programs, including athletics, St. Louis, 1971, The C. V. Mosby Co.

Bucher, C. A.: Administration of health and physical education programs, including athletics, ed. 6, St. Louis, 1975, The C. V. Mosby Co.

Calam, J., and Patenaude, J.: The schools ain't what they used to be—and probably never were, Saturday Review, April 29, 1972, p. 52.

Colo, R. L., et al.: The beginning teacher, Today's Education **60**:54, 1971.

Hahn, R. O., and Bidna, D. B.: Secondary education: origins and directions, ed. 2, New York, 1970, Macmillan Publishing Co., Inc.

Hecht, G. J.: What must be done to meet the needs of all American children? Parents **47**:10, 1972.

Kalakian, L., and Goldman, M.: Introduction to physical education—a humanistic perspective, Boston, 1976, Allyn & Bacon, Inc.

Penman, K. A.: Planning physical education and athletic facilities in schools, New York, 1977, John Wiley & Sons, Inc.

Resnik, H. S.: The open classroom, Today's Education **60**:16, 1971.

Singer, R. N., et al.: Physical education foundations, New York, 1976, Holt, Rinehart & Winston.

Van Til, W.: Curriculum, quest for relevance, Boston, 1971, Houghton Mifflin Company.

3

THE SECONDARY SCHOOL
STUDENT—I

INSTRUCTIONAL OBJECTIVES AND COMPETENCIES TO BE ACHIEVED

After reading this chapter the student should be able to—

1. Identify the characteristics and needs of secondary school students.
2. Understand why teenagers act as they do in searching for identity.
3. Appreciate the developmental tasks that boys and girls face in their teens.
4. Trace the growth and development of young people through their early teens, middle teens, and late adolescence and the problems they cope with during these years.
5. Identify the characteristics that determine when a young person reaches maturity.

The many changes taking place in American culture in recent years have left an imprint upon our young people—our students. As a result, unless teachers of physical education know and understand their students—their characteristics and needs, their goals and aspirations, their developmental tasks, the factors that affect the development of their personalities, and a multitude of other forces and facts that play upon them—they can never have a successful physical education program. Therefore, in light of the fact that we have a new breed of students in our

secondary schools and that boys and girls are our chief concern, considerable space is devoted to this most important consideration.

Part I will be concerned with a discussion of secondary school boys and girls as they pass through the adolescent period, that is, the things that are important to them during their teen years, how we as teachers can help them in their search for identity, the factors that will contribute to their development into mature adults, and many other important considerations vital to the needs of every boy and girl.

Part II, using as a background the general discussion of the student covered in Part I, identifies specific physical, emotional, social and intellectual characteristics of students and draws implications from these facts for the teaching of physical education in the secondary school.

As a result of this study, the reader should have a much better understanding of the consumer of his or her teaching and services and thereby be much better qualified to make a worthwhile contribution to the pupil's education and welfare.

THE TEEN YEARS

During childhood, students live in the environment created for them by others. Adolescence, on the other hand, is really the halfway point in their life cycle—a bridge between childhood and adulthood. It is a period of "growing up" when they prepare to go out on their own. It is, in the words of one authority, "the period during which a young person learns who he or she is and what he or she really feels." It is the time during which a student becomes a person in his or her own right. Another important fact for physical educators is that it is the time when the foundations of a physically active life are being formed and when the student develops positive or negative attitudes toward physical education.

Adolescence is therefore the span of years when the student can take care of "unfinished business" left over from earlier developmental stages. This does not mean the student fights old battles or nurses old hurts. But, if he or she has not built a strong and satisfying self-image, the teens offer the opportunity to try out new ideas and work out more satisfying behavior patterns.

The teens can be divided into three phases that differ from one another and that come to young people at different times. *Puberty* (controlled by endocrine changes) is marked by rapid development of the reproductive system accompanied by the "gang spirit." It is followed by the *transition period* during which interest shifts from same-sex to opposite-sex friendships. *Late adolescence* is characterized by idealism and by romantic

Fig. 3-1. Adolescence—a bridge between childhood and adulthood. An adolescent student in the Brockport Central Schools, Brockport, N.Y.

attachments to members of the opposite sex. In addition to the overall developmental tasks of adolescence, each of these phases has something special to contribute to the growth of personality.

Who am I? The question of identity

How does a human being with new properties and new functions fit in with the self-image developed in childhood? A teenager often asks the question, "Who am I?" This is because the self of teens is not the self of childhood or later adulthood. Young people may be drawn in two directions and may not always be sure whether in a given situation to act like a child or an adult. They cannot leave childhood permanently behind until their identity (incorporating the physical, mental, emotional, and social changes that have taken place) has been securely established.

During the teens young people try on a number of personalities in the same way they try on hair styles and clothes to find those that best suit them. In establishing a true identity a host of mannerisms and attitudes may follow one another. This accounts for the rapid changes in many teenagers' friendships, interests, and plans. The midteens especially may be a period of moods that swing like a pendulum from high to low.

During the teens students may have feelings of dissatisfaction and may need a boost to their self-image. For this reason they are most sensitive to criticism. They may feel out of step as they replace one personality with another. They want to know who they really are because their self is in a state of flux.

Search for self

The search for self that takes place in the teens may assume such outward forms as the choice of a new name or spelling the old one differently. This device reflects a wish to announce the "new me" independent of the infant named by parents. Parents may find it hard to remember that the Patsy of yesterday is the Patricia of today, or that "Sonny" or "Junior" are now to be called by their proper names. Teenagers often experiment with handwriting and try to project their new personalities by adding flourishes or adopting a different slant in their penmanship. On the more serious side they may also join in rallies and movements to attack social injustices—often to the consternation of adults. All of these attitudes and mannerisms (and there are likely to be many more) contribute to the formation of a life style typical of themselves and no one else.

The ideal self

By the time students reach the teens they have a pretty good idea of the kind of person they want to be. In terms of personality, this is their *ideal self*. It is based on many models and various experiences. The ideal self allows them to match their actions against a standard. Their ideal self helps direct the resources of their personality toward unifying the various selves established in earlier stages of development. Thus their self-image in the teens has two sides—a "real" (natural) self and an "ideal" (moral) self.

They are constantly working to balance their self-image—their real self—with their ideal self. Unless they do this they may be in a state of conflict or tension. When their real self harmonizes with their ideal self, they feel comfortable and at ease. They are happy with themselves. When there is a gap between what they are and what they would like or expect themselves to be, feelings of guilt and inferiority crop up.

To the degree that they accept or reject their self, their life will be pleasant and satisfying or disquieting and tense. Physical education offers many opportunities to help students accept themselves and bring into more harmonious balance their self-image with their real self.

Fig. 3-2. Teenagers often ask the question, "Who am I?" Girls in physical education in the Brockport Central Schools, Brockport, N.Y.

Developmental tasks

Young people abound in energy during their teens. They are ready and eager to test themselves in new situations and will work to overcome obstacles and difficulties. Developmental tasks are usually undertaken in a spirit of adventure. Most teenagers like a challenge and welcome responsibility. Those who felt insecure as children, however, or whose wills were given too little chance to develop at the appropriate time, may shrink from new challenges.

Because the teens pose many special problems the developmental tasks of this period deserve separate consideration. Some tasks persist throughout the teens, and some predominate during one or another developmental phase. A mature personality brings the physical, mental, emotional, and social achievements and failures of all developmental stages together into an individual identity. When this has been done, all the resources of the personality can be directed toward self-actualizing activities.

Reality principle. Children and adults characteristically act to secure their needs in different ways. Children usually act according to the pleasure principle. That is, they follow the path of least resistance to meet their needs. The pleasure principle spurs them to act on impulse. To act on the pleasure principle is sure to cause problems because it ignores the fact that actions have results.

Mature people can put off gratifying their needs until the appropriate time. This basis of action is called the reality principle. To act according to the reality principle requires a person to consider the effect of what he or she is going to do before doing it. Children lack the experience to link cause and effect. It is a developmental task of the teens to change the base of action from the pleasure principle to the reality principle.

Reality checking. Teenagers can draw upon a wealth of past experience to meet the challenges of daily life. All present impressions must be checked for accuracy against past experience. This process, called reality testing, measures current observations,

ideas, attitudes, and reactions against other things one feels, knows, or has experienced.

Reality testing is one of the important mental functions to be developed in the teens. A person cannot respond to the environment appropriately unless he or she first tests reality. Reality testing must be employed to gauge strengths and limitations accurately. A realistic personal assessment leaves one free to use, shape, and develop abilities. Reality testing helps to base what one thinks and does in every area of life on a dependable foundation. It helps to distinguish fact from fantasy, reason from emotion, and evidence from wishful thinking. Thus it is the basis of sound decision-making.

Toleration of stress. Change, conflict, and tension are to be expected in life. After the period of protected childhood, teenagers may suffer considerable tension when first exposed to the "hard facts of life." Mature people can endure physical hardship and discomfort. They can also withstand repeated and intense disappointment, failure, and other real stresses. They can tolerate failure or the possibility of failure as well as success. To tolerate stress does not mean to give in or avoid it. It means to continue in spite of it—to overcome, rather than to be overcome. Each experience in the teens should contribute to tolerance of stress and thus prepare for the more complex problems to be encountered in adult life. Physical education offers many opportunities to tolerate physical, social, mental and emotional stress. It can provide a laboratory for meeting problems head on whether it involves losing hard fought athletic contests, failure to achieve a high rating in a physical fitness test, or one of the many other situations that constantly occur in this program.

Conflict between generations. Because they are adventurous and willing to take responsibility, teenagers want to make choices on their own. They resent interference in choice of clothes, hairstyle, friends, books, and recreation. Each generation has a different point of view concerning appropriate behavior. Teenagers who insist on having their own way may be considered rebellious and disobedient. The teenager's conflicts with adults are most likely to center around friends, a car, money, use of time, and telephone privileges.

Sometimes the gap between the generations makes communication difficult. A teenager may feel for a time that adults just "don't understand." Parents, too, may shake their heads over the fact that they just do not seem to "get across" to their children. They will express concern as to "what the new generation is coming to."

Relations to authority. One's personality needs guidelines throughout life. During the teens parental discipline, firm but reasonable, is still helpful. This form of guidance, which respects a young person's individuality, reinforces feelings of trust and security.

Parents who have shared in their children's early efforts to adapt and socialize will not need to worry about control and discipline in the teens. All their training in discipline will have taken place long before. By midteens, self-discipline should be well established. Teenagers who do not get along well with parents, however, will usually resist authority from other sources. They may protest the supervision of teachers, the regulations of the police, as well as the advice of parents.

It is sometimes hard for parents, teachers, and children to give young people enough discipline to assure trust and enough freedom to support individuality. Sometimes teenagers are more vocal concerning their rights than concerning their responsibilities. It is a developmental task of the teens to demonstrate self-discipline before asking for greater freedom.

Early teens

To grow up one must break certain ties with the past, a past that includes family and friends. These ties may be based on affection, authority, respect, responsibility, closeness, or possessiveness. Breaking these childhood ties and forming new ones is a developmental task of adolescence.

Teenagers come to see that those who were loved in childhood are neither all-powerful nor all-perfect. At first this recognition may cause shock, pain, and disillusion. When they realize that "nobody is perfect,"

Fig. 3-3. Physical education offers many opportunities to tolerate stress. Student engaged in rock climbing exercise. (Courtesy University of Northern Colorado, Greeley, Colo., and Barry Iverson.)

they can accept other people's flaws and imperfections without loss of respect and affection. They should also be able to face their own.

In addition to making new friends, adolescents have the developmental task of forgoing adult ties of interest, acceptance, and concern for the family. To see parents as human beings with their weaknesses and strengths and their favorable and unfavorable personality traits and to feel strongly about them in spite of these is a big step in the process of growing up.

In the early teens teenagers live in their own society with many of its own standards and values. This state lasts for about as long as they look back across the teen bridge to childhood. It becomes less important in the midteens as they look forward to taking their place in adult society.

One of the crowd. At every stage of the life cycle teenagers want to feel that they belong. A child's feeling of belonging centers in the family. In the early teens group membership, characterized by the "gang spirit," takes the place of family dependence.

During the early teens the opinion of peers is more highly valued than that of adults. Teenagers may ignore family or teacher approval and turn instead to the crowd for support and reassurance. Their approval reinforces individual self-confidence. Teenagers often excuse their actions by saying "everybody's doing it."

In the early teens boys and girls are still largely separate from one another in interest and activities. Friendships are formed among members of the same sex. Being one of the crowd gives boys and girls the feeling that there is safety in numbers. Boys seem more attracted to moving in a gang than do girls, perhaps because in the teens their aggressiveness (an emotional by-product of increased endocrine activity) takes more active forms. Boys, moreover, are intensely loyal to the group, whereas girls tend to be more personal when loyalty is involved. When girls do move in gangs they often affiliate with a group of boys.

In the early teens groups of boys and groups of girls are likely to socialize with one another. One reason that a hangout—drugstore, pizza parlor, street corner, record shop, youth center, or other—may be popular is that it provides neutral ground for groups of boys and groups of girls to enter separately and without prearrangement. The fact that girls mature sooner than boys changes this relationship. As time goes by, boys and girls no longer look at each other with the indifference of childhood. For a while new feelings may make them uncertain of how to behave. By the end of the teens, however, they should be at ease in one another's company.

Clubs and gangs. Many clubs are organized to promote common interests among teenagers. Shared enthusiasm for drama, folk music, stamps, cars, chess, or science holds some groups together. Club membership strengthens personality by making the individual less self-centered.

Gangs often form because of a mutual gripe or grievance. Even though a gang may not always seek socially approved goals, membership in it can increase a person's ability to share with others and to lose self-centeredness. So far as the individual member's personality development is concerned, this is helpful. Sometimes individual gang members feel powerless as individuals and consequently use group force to gain their ends. This not only injures society but damages the individual's personal development. Just when young people should be building a secure self-image they become overly dependent on others.

Group membership serves a positive purpose if it contributes to independence. If conformity to group standards replaces dependence on the family, however, one form of dependence has been replaced by another. When instead of depending on the family a person depends on the group, there is no net gain in independence.

The person who depends on the group for approval may have a weak self-image and be overly dependent on others for clues as to his or her true worth. It may be that the individual's personality is too weak to stand without group support. If it lasts beyond adolescence, group membership without other independent interests may be a sign of immaturity.

Difference and conformity. To break with the past a person must be different from the way he or she was in childhood. Although teenagers want to be different from children, they do not want to be too different from their peers. Teenagers feel a strong urge to adopt group standards as a mark of being "in." If a young person has not developed a strong sense of self-worth, being different in any way can be a source of misery and humiliation.

But group approval usually requires conformity in dress, behavior, speech, mannerisms, possessions, and attitudes. Fads in attire (dress, hair styles) and behavior (posture, speech) become badges of membership in the "in" group. As people develop strong individual personalities, they gradually discard such conformity in favor of making their own choices.

Following the leader. The group—be it a club or a gang—usually takes its identity from one person who initiates action and inspires loyalty. But who is the leader? He or she is a person who has a secure (not necessarily mature) self-image.

The leader's "power" is usually based on qualities that group members would like to possess. They identify with the leader's weaknesses and strengths and may imitate oddities of dress, speech, and behavior. Such loyalty provides followers with a chance to develop weak areas of their personalities. But the leader may have the problem of being too sure of being "grown up." He or she may feel there is too much to risk in giving up any personal traits and so may fail to mature further. As a result, there is failure to understand that the loyalty and admiration on which he or she depends is bound to pass.

Search for popularity. In the teens, group acceptance is usually measured in popularity. Being popular can be an important goal to a teenager. To be accepted by a club, a sorority, an athletic team, or a fraternity may be the last word in popularity. Some teenagers will sacrifice anything in the quest for popularity and approval. This is especially true if they felt rejected in childhood. Popularity should not serve as a crutch for a faltering self-image. It can never substitute for the inner security that comes with a strong self-image.

The middle teens

Group activity leaves one need unmet—the need for a person who can share secrets and discuss problems. As the gang stage passes, boys and girls enter the transition period of the middle teens. At this time they often have a "best friend." The need to expose their feelings to someone else is very strong in this period. Personal feelings may be expressed privately to a friend or in a diary or publicly in messages on tree trunks, subway posters, fences, and walls. This is a time when best friends keep each others' secrets, whisper and exchange notes, and engage in marathon private telephone conversations. All these activities are part of the attempt to find out who they "really are."

Boys and girls together. More and more the social standards in the United States and in other countries accept women as equal partners in life with men. Since Title IX was passed and since business, the professions, and politics have opened their doors to women, the two sexes must learn to appreciate each other as co-workers and companions. For this reason, one of the tasks of teenager development is for boys and girls to learn to think of each other as human beings.

Boys and girls who know each other as friends, who talk openly on a variety of subjects, and who participate together in physical education activities are learning to accept one another as persons. They have a chance to see the ways in which they are alike. They can also observe the social, psychological, and emotional ways in which they complement one another. Not every relationship that boys and girls or men and women share is romatically inclined. When romance develops out of friendship, however, it is much more likely to strengthen self-concepts than does romance based only on physical attraction. Solid friendships with boys and girls

Fig. 3-4. High school physical education coeducational activity. (Courtesy Bill Henderson, Toms River, N.J.)

bolster self-esteem and self-confidence and improve the individual's self-image. The midteens are the time when boys and girls have the widest opportunity to develop friendships with the opposite sex.

Friendship encourages the spirit of sharing. It is a developmental task of the teens to learn to share not only material possessions but thoughts, feelings, and ideals. By the end of the transition period a boy and a girl may share with each other secrets and problems in the same way that they once shared them with a best friend of the same sex.

In the period of shared interests personal qualities such as politeness and consideration are strengthened. Interest in personal grooming gains importance. It is a time when many things are shared in preparation for the sharing required in marriage. Friendships with members of the opposite sex enable

teenagers to test personal relationships in anticipation of making a permanent choice in marriage.

Emotional transition. At about the age of 13 or 14 in girls and about 15 in boys, a phase of self-absorption sets in. This is a period in which the teenager appears to be given over to self-examination and often to long periods of wanting to be left alone. A new point of self-discovery is often preceded by a period of depression. This may reflect a fear of not meeting adult expectations. Parents and teachers are likely to be surprised by this sudden change because it is in marked contrast to earlier gang activity and "bosom buddy" loyalties. This period usually precedes a person's first real interest in a member of the opposite sex.

During this time young people feel a strong need to be close to the parent of the

Fig. 3-5. A high school student in physical education. (Brockport Central Schools, Brockport, N.Y.)

opposite sex. Boys at this age will be more gallant and protective toward their mothers. Girls become especially affectionate and considerate toward their fathers. When, through force of circumstance, parents are neither physically nor emotionally close to a child, these feelings may spill over to teachers, relatives, or older friends. This form of intimacy helps young people to understand the needs, interests, and personalities of people unlike themselves. Much of the sensitivity and understanding young people later bring to marriage is learned in this phase of life. A successful relationship with parents in this stage increases self-confidence and strengthens personality.

It is possible at this time to become overly attached to a parent. This usually reveals insecurity held over from earlier developmental stages. It suggests that the individual was not prepared by his parents or parent substitutes for true psychological independence.

If the parent has also felt emotionally deprived, he or she may place too much emotional reliance on youngsters in this stage

and may have difficulty letting go when the time comes. A too intense attachment between children and their parents may hinder rather than promote personality development.

What do they believe? The question "Who am I?" can hardly be separated from the question, "What do I believe?" For this reason, it is important as the teen years pass for young people to formulate a philosophy of life. Their philosophy of life is an overall system of ideas that determines what they believe and how they will behave. To maintain their psychological balance they must follow a consistent code of conduct. This does not mean merely establishing predictable behavior, because even conditioned behavior is predictable. Human beings who function like clockwork have lost an important element in the enjoyment of life.

People's values differ according to their education, environment, and personal needs. Some people act on "common sense" in daily life. Others embrace a religious teaching. Some people operate in line with material considerations; others formulate a philosophy based on intellectual or spiritual values. No set of rules imposed by others can cover every detail of one's life. As one gains in experience, a pattern gradually emerges that shows the kind of behavior that balances different areas of one's personality and brings peace of mind. These ground rules form part of the young person's way of life.

A sound philosophy is one that is consistent in terms of inner personality and appropriate in terms of outer reality. It promotes good adjustment and brings personality into harmony with the environment. A weak philosophy upsets the steady state. Without a philosophy of life or at least a personal guide for action it is difficult to make day-by-day choices in terms of long-range goals.

The mature conscience. In a classic example of cinema art, Walt Disney told the story of Pinocchio. Every time the puppet did something wrong, his conscience in the form of an insect, Jiminy Cricket, was there to "bug" him. In a dramatic way, this characterized the role of conscience in personality.

A mature person recognizes conscience not as an outside force directing action like a policeman directs traffic but as a necessary and functional part of his or her inner life. Conscience plays the part of an outside critic, but it is still a real part of each person.

Conscience monitors the relations between the real self and the ideal self. A person's real self is the self of needs and drives. The ideal self develops with experience and education. Children handle their instinctual demands in such a way as not to break rules set by their parents or other people who may punish them. However, although fear is a natural and necessary emotion, one cannot seek the "right" thing to do out of fear without damaging one's personality. A pattern of behavior based solely on fear makes demands incompatible with psychological well-being and mental health. Acting on fear, a person may appear well behaved, but his or her adjustment will only be on the surface.

The gratification of instinct is always primarily pleasurable, but emotions, depending on their nature, may be pleasurable or painful. A mature personality has established some form of harmony among its impulses. This cannot be accomplished without the expenditure of considerable energy. A mature conscience helps a young person to behave so that he or she not only does the right thing but feels the value of such socially constructive emotions as honesty, kindness, generosity, loyalty, and perseverance.

Establishing goals. Young people have earned the right to make their own decisions when they assume responsibility for them in terms of the reality principle. Each decision that is made and attitude adopted influences future growth. Thus it is always important to select positive aims and goals.

Goals established in the light of the reality principle are usually positive. Positive goals are unifying. Negative goals upset the steady state. In a general way we can call positive goals "right" and negative goals "wrong" to the degree that they promote personality harmony. Each person must select goals that harmonize his or her personality. To do so, one must assess abilities and admit shortcomings.

Late adolescence

Several important developmental tasks remain in the final stage of the teens. At the end of adolescence, students will be young adults and must apply personal energies to the achievement of economic independence. To do so they must select an occupation or career and decide whether they can realistically expect to do such work. Young people must also be prepared for effective citizenship and for constructive use of leisure time. Finally, young people must be ready to make a most important personal choice—the selection of a mate. To live and share one's life with another person and to accept family responsibility requires sound preparation in the teens.

Fig. 3-6. At end of adolescence, student will be a young adult. Student in physical education class, Regina High School, Cincinnati, Ohio.

Teenage idealism. The search for the perfect object in love, politics, sport, and art is part of the general high-mindedness characteristic of late adolescence. In the late teens, young adults are often disturbed by the difference between the way things are and how they would like them to be. In late adolescence, teenagers feel about things (for a time at least) in "all or nothing" terms. They admire honesty and sincerity but are quick to detect phoniness or hypocrisy.

If they have learned to share interests and ideas with other individuals, a feeling of identity with *all* human beings may develop. People who have never established a feeling of closeness with *one* person can never develop a sense of sharing with *all* people. By the end of the teens, many people have learned to feel sympathy for the misery and suffering of others and to be horrified by deceit or injustice. Unless they can apply reality testing to their actions they may do impulsive things spurred by idealism.

First love. Strong interest in members of the opposite sex is characteristic of late adolescence. Writer Atra Baer described it as the time when "Johnny Jones now writes in chalk, his love for Mary on the walk." Before the individual becomes seriously interested in one person, he or she has usually been interested in the opposite sex as a group. The attraction is a general one. A boy has usually been "in love" with a number of girls at the same time. A girl has sought and enjoyed the attention of more than one boy.

It is in late adolescence that most people have their first real experience of love. In first love, adoration and blindness to the other's faults and shortcomings is typical. Romantic love implies feeling without action and worship from afar. It focuses only on perfection and ignores flaws.

The experience of young love can ripen into mature love and some "childhood sweethearts" have made successful marriages. Those who have strong self-images and who have completed their developmental tasks are most likely to make lasting marriages early in life. A happy marriage brings together all the feelings of friendship, companionship, romance, and family life that the individual has previously known. This kind of love is a part of emotional maturity where all earlier experiences are brought together. It is not achieved when a person is trying to "make up" for a lack of love in childhood.

"Real" love. Love (unlike fear, anger, or sex) is not an instinct but a group of emotional tendencies. It includes tenderness, friendship, admiration, devotion, pride, respect, agressiveness, submission, protection, loyalty, and adoration. Each of these has previously been felt separately in the course of personality development. In the mature personality they attach to both persons and ideas. Thus love is not a feeling only but a relationship involving the whole personality. The part each emotion plays in a relationship varies with circumstances and the individual. Friendship, for example, looms large in a marriage between childhood sweethearts, who are more likely to be aware of each other's faults and shortcomings and so marry with a realistic view of one another.

Physical attraction plays an important part in real love, too. Physical fitness and a strong physical image are assets for young people. There is a biological basis for beauty; it fills a biological function in the creation of new individuals. When strong and fit individuals marry and raise families, their children will usually inherit strength and fitness, too. Natural beauty has survival value for the human race. To a large extent beauty goes with health, and healthy parents can better care for and protect their offspring. Survival of offspring after birth also requires tenderness, protectiveness, and patience. These are qualities of emotional maturity. Establishing a stable home for the development of new personalities involves the cooperation of mature people. Without it, children are exposed to insecure family relations. In such a setting warped personalities are likely to develop.

Developing sound skills. Each person has different talents or abilities. When these are accepted realistically, one can turn their energy to developing and refining those that will be most stimulating and most useful to society. Because their muscular systems are now fully developed, teenagers can learn a whole range of new physical and other activities. It is an important developmental task of the teens to identify, cultivate, and perfect skills necessary for social and economic independence and for enjoying leisure hours.

Achieving self-direction. When all parts of the personality are in harmony, the young person has achieved *self-direction*, that is, is able to use personal resources to reach self-made goals. Establishing self-governing behavior is an important developmental task of the teens and is made possible by the successful completion of earlier tasks.

To maintain a steady state for the total personality the appropriate rules, regulations, and values of society must be made a part of each young person. When this has been done, one's life is guided from within and is not subject to the "whims of fate." It has become *inner directed*. This capacity develops throughout the teens as the conscience, aims, goals, and values are built into the personality.

When developmental tasks are completed, the young person's personality has become aware of itself (self-conscious) and critical of itself (self-critical). To be self-conscious or self-aware means that one part of a person's personality recognizes the other. Most important, it is in command of itself under the direction of the will (self-controlled).

Maturity

When all the elements of an individual's personality—body, public personality, inner self—combine, we say that personality is integrated or mature. Personality has become a reliable unit that one can take for granted and depend upon. It maintains a steady state in which physical and psychological needs are faced and met. One can feel that this stage has been reached when he or she can say, I am the kind of person who (1) has come to accept myself, physically and mentally, (2) has accepted the selves of others, (3) is accepted by others, (4) has learned to master and adjust to my environ-

ment, and (5) acts on the basis of my own values and experience.

Maturity, however, is not the end stage of growth. It is rather, the secure foundation on which continuing growth and self-realization take place.

A final developmental task of adolescence is the foundation of a sense of commitment. That is, the entire personality, unified toward satisfying goals, is directed toward self-completing activities. It is concerned not only with what is best for itself, but what is best for others and for society as a whole.

EPILOGUE

The developmental tasks of secondary school students have been discussed. The task of physical education is to better understand these students and their developmental tasks and to play a key role in helping them to achieve these goals. If physical education can play such a role and accomplish such a task there will not be any question about its worth in education today. Part Two spells out in some detail how many of these needs may be met through physical education.

Self-assessment tests

These tests are to assist students in determining if material and competencies presented in this chapter have been mastered:

1. Prepare a table and list the principal characteristics and needs of a boy and a girl in each of the grades 7 to 12.
2. Think of some teenaged boy or girl that you know. List some of the mannerisms, interests, plans, and attitudes that he or she expresses that show how he or she is searching for identity.
3. Prepare a list of developmental tasks that boys and girls face in the secondary school.
4. Draw up a list of problems that young people face today. After each problem indicate at which developmental stage (early teens, middle teens, late adolescence) each problem is most pronounced.
5. Define the term maturity. Describe in specific terms how you would know when a boy or girl reaches maturity.

Points to remember

1. The characteristics of secondary school students.
2. The needs of secondary school students in light of these characteristics.
3. The question of identity for teenagers.
4. Developmental tasks of secondary school students.
5. Important considerations of secondary school stu-

dents during their early teens, middle teens, and late adolescence.

6. Maturity and what it involves.

Problems to think through

1. Why do some teenagers belong to "gangs"?
2. How can physical education help teenagers to achieve a sense of identity?
3. Why is there a generation gap between some students and adults?
4. What is meant by teenage idealism and what should the teacher do about it?

Case study for analysis

You are assigned to a high school in your community. It is your responsibility to develop a physical education program that meets the needs and characteristics of one of the grades in this high school. Analyze the student body and develop a physical education program from this analysis.

Exercises for review

1. List several reasons why it is very important for teachers of physical education to know and understand their students.
2. Why is adolescence called a bridge between childhood and adulthood?
3. What should represent a wholesome relationship between the student and authority?
4. What are some signs of peer group influence and how can this affect physical education?
5. To what extent should teenagers make their own decisions?

Selected readings

Arnheim, D. P. E., Auxter, D., and Crowe, W. C.: Principles and methods of adapted physical education and recreation, St. Louis, 1977, The C. V. Mosby Co.

Arnheim, D. P. E., and Pestolesi, R. A.: Developing motor behavior in children—a balanced approach to elementary physical education, St. Louis, 1973, The C. V. Mosby Co.

Caldwell, S.: Toward a humanistic physical education, Journal of Health, Physical Education, and Recreation **43**:31, 1972.

Clarke, H. H., editor: Individual differences, their nature, extent and significance, Physical Fitness Research Digest, October, 1973.

Riley, M., Games and humanism, Journal of Physical Education and Recreation **46**:46, 1975.

Snyder, E. E., and Spreitzer, E. A.: Family influence and involvement in sports, Research Quarterly **44**: 249, 1973.

Stallings, L. M.: Motor skills: development and learning, Dubuque, Iowa, 1973, Wm. C. Brown Company, Publishers.

Taggart, R. J.: Accountability and the American dream, The Educational Forum **39**:33, 1974.

Toffler, A.: Future shock, New York, 1970, Bantam Books.

Vodola, T. M.: Individualized physical education program for the handicapped child, Englewood Cliffs, N.J., 1973, Prentice-Hall, Inc.

Williams, W. G.: Does the educational past have a future? Kappa Delta Pi Record **11**:103, 1975.

Yee, A. H.: Becoming a teacher in America, Quest **18**: 67, 1972.

4

THE SECONDARY SCHOOL STUDENT— II

INSTRUCTIONAL OBJECTIVES AND COMPETENCIES TO BE ACHIEVED

After reading this chapter the student should be able to—

1. Show how physical characteristics of students affect their personalities and self-image.
2. Describe the physical, emotional, social, and intellectual changes that take place in the adolescent person and the implications for teaching physical education that these changes produce.
3. Identify the differences between boys and girls in regard to height, weight, skeletal changes, and primary and secondary sex changes, and the implications these changes have for teaching motor skills in the physical education program.
4. Indicate the characteristics of boys and girls in relation to their social development and how an understanding of these characteristics may help the physical educator in better meeting the needs of secondary school students.
5. Determine how the variations in intellectual abilities of secondary school students should condition the teaching methods used in physical education.

Teachers in today's secondary schools face student populations quite different from those found many years ago. Teenagers and their environments have undergone extensive changes that need to be understood because of their implications for teaching.

THE NEW BREED OF STUDENT

National attention is being focused on the struggle of adolescents for existence, and it is this increased interest in teenagers that has brought about further changes in their environment. Students in several communities, for example, have evaluated their own secondary school curricula and suggested changes.

Today's students are being studied while they study and are being influenced while trying to exert influence. The student has achieved a unique importance in the structure of education, and it is this individual that the teacher must try to understand. The forces and pressures being exerted upon adolescents while they undergo an important phase of personal growth and development combine to make adolescence a difficult period of adjustment. The teacher must try to assist them in every way possible.

Teacher expectations in a secondary school population

In a school of 500 students a teacher should be prepared to find 500 different individuals, each one advancing through various stages of the adolescent process, and each one at a

60

different level of development. While many of the students may be college-bound, others require education to fit them immediately for life.

Secondary school students will have a variety of cultural backgrounds and bring with them a vast assortment of needs, fears, hopes, abilities, and problems. Those individuals who require special attention—the mentally retarded, the culturally disadvantaged, and the physically handicapped—must be identified so that programs may be tailored to meet their needs. At the present time the federal government is spending increased sums of money on special education programs for these individuals. Yet less than one half of the eight million handicapped persons are receiving the special programs they require. Many of these students are still enrolled in public secondary schools. Physical educators have a responsibility for providing these students with an opportunity to

develop their physical capacities equal to the opportunity provided for regular students. This may be done through the adapted program of physical education or through assignments within the regular class program. The individualization of teaching can best accomplish the goals.*

What is the role of the school?

The school must identify and recognize the nature of each student. It must strive to help all secondary school students to find themselves, for this is the central problem of adolescence. The development of self-esteem and the identification of the self are vital concerns of every teenager. Too often schools provide threats (through class distinctions and values and unrealistic standards of behav-

---

*Chapter 19 discusses the different types of atypical students and the contribution that physical education can make to each.

Fig. 4-1. Secondary school students will have a variety of cultural backgrounds and bring with them a vast assortment of needs, fears, abilities, hopes, and problems. Secondary school students in the training program at Hampton Institute, Hampton, Va.

ior) rather than reassurances to students. Too often schools demand conformity rather than independence of thought and action. If the purpose of the school is to develop worthy citizens, it must start by helping them to feel worthy and competent within themselves.

The physical education program provides excellent opportunities for the development of these needed competencies. The feeling of importance derived from team, group, or squad membership, the feeling of freedom of expression in movement, and the pride in accomplishment when points are scored for a team are all competencies that are natural outcomes of physical education activities. More important, however, is the recognition of the self as defined by a body concept developed through participation in a well-balanced program. Research indicates a close relationship between a body concept and a self-concept in terms of the confidence needed to face life. The individual who feels satisfied with the ability of his or her body to move, express, attract, feel, and react is more apt to feel satisfied with his or her total adjustment to life. On the other hand the unhappy student is frequently one who is dissatisfied with his or her own body image. Physical educators have a vital responsibility for the development of healthy attitudes toward the body and should therefore provide the necessary experiences through well-planned and well-executed programs.

Understanding the complex changes of adolescence is a large task, for students and for teachers. The implications for teaching are many because of the relationship between student development and achievement in education. It will be the purpose of the remainder of this chapter to describe the physical, social emotional, and intellectual changes that take place in the adolescent and also to indicate the specific implications for teaching physical education that these changes produce.

PHYSICAL GROWTH AND SELF-IMAGE

Physical changes in the teens have a dramatic effect on personality development, but there are also many carry-overs from childhood. Illness or injury, the level of nutrition, and the amount of sunshine and exercise received during childhood will have physical after effects in the teens. Irregularities in hormone secretions can cause startling physical and personality changes. Endocrine imbalance affects height, weight, growth, and development. In the teens, normal changes in the endocrine system herald the onset of puberty.

The teens, as a time of rapid growth, are sometimes an awkward age. Just as second teeth looked so large to students when they were in the first grade, their arms and legs seem to grow at different rates while they are in high school. In the teens their noses and chins may also seem out of proportion for a while.

It is sometimes hard for young people to accept the fact that wide differences in rate of growth, muscular development, and coordination can be expected at their age. Teenagers differ from children and also from adults. They differ physically, biologically, and intellectually among themselves. Some differences are controlled by genes, and others are the product of environment. Still, human beings put the "finishing touches" on their own personalities. Many of the things that make them different from other people are the results of their own ideas and efforts.

Personality and appearance

Physical appearance influences personality because, after all, it is the first thing people notice about individuals. Physical differences may or may not be "handicaps," depending on their effect on self-image. Extreme good looks or startling beauty can be liabilities if they interfere with personality development. Many people develop fine, strong personalities in spite of disabling physical handicaps. Helen Keller triumphed over the triple handicap of blindness, deafness, and mutism to make meaningful contributions to the world. Some people, because of a weak self-image, magnify a small defect so that it cripples development.

Physical characteristics affect the self-image of boys and girls differently. Tallness, for example, has a favorable effect on a boy's self-image, whereas a girl may be unhappy if she seems taller than the boys and girls around her. A person whose skin is marred by acne feels differently about himself or herself than does one whose complexion is clear.

Basic feelings of acceptance or rejection toward onself are often expressed in personal hygiene and grooming. Neglect or excessive care may reflect feelings of inferiority. A desire to falsify appearance may reveal an individual's negative self-image. Extreme tastes, either in dress or grooming, may cover up feelings of rejection. A girl with a poor opinion of her looks may use too much makeup. A boy who does not feel he is accepted as a young man may grow a beard or moustache. On the other hand, indifference to detail in dress and grooming sometimes reflects a self-image which is so secure that no outward "show" is needed to support it. As a person's physical appearance alters and he or she gains experience, the self-image changes and personality grows.

PHYSICAL DEVELOPMENT

The secondary school student passes through four stages of development, which are generally labeled preadolescence, early adolescence, middle adolescence, and late adolescence. It should be understood that each individual develops according to his or her own growth pattern, but in general the stages may be identified at certain age levels.

The classification of adolescent development offered in Table 4-1 is a guide to the use of these terms throughout the discussions in this chapter of physical, emotional, social, and intellectual development.

Because of the complexity of adolescent physical development and the differentiation between boys and girls, it is necessary to con-

Table 4-1. Stages of development*

	Girls	Boys
Preadolescence or childhood	11-13	13-15
Early adolescence	13-15	15-17
Middle adolescence	15-18	17-19
Late adolescence	18-21	19-21

*From Cole, L.: Psychology of adolescence, New York, 1954, Rinehart & Co., Inc., p. 4.

sider each phase of their growth separately. Height and weight, skeletal changes, and primary and secondary sex changes will be discussed, with the differences in boys and girls explained at each level of development. The implications for physical education will also be included in the discussion.

Height and weight

Probably the most obvious physical changes during adolescence occur in height and weight. These changes can be accounted for by increased hormone production, which in turn causes the sudden growth spurt of the preadolescent and early adolescent period.

Girls 11 to 13 years old become taller than boys of the same ages but then show slower increases in height until late adolescence. A rapid increase in weight also takes place at this time or following the growth in height. Girls are frequently heavier than boys at ages 12 to 14 years, but with the onset of menstruation a leveling off period occurs.

The sudden growth spurt in boys does not come until approximately two years after that of the girls, and it continues to a greater extent until around 20 years of age. Boys shown an even greater increase in weight and also continue this gain for a longer period than do girls.

These changes have definite implications for the physical education program. First, boys and girls have a real concern for their physical development. Participation and total involvement in physical education activities provides an opportunity for them to forget their own self-concerns and to lose themselves in the enjoyment of the game.

Second, in regard to regular class activities in which height is an important factor, as in volleyball or basketball, it may be advisable to distribute the tallest boys and girls among the squads for the best playing results. Also, the coeducational program at the junior high level, where differences in sizes are most obvious, must be carefully organized to minimize any undue embarrassment experienced by both boys and girls. Dancing activities may be difficult to conduct because the boys are shorter than the girls, whereas relays, games of low organization, badminton, volleyball, and similar activities may have great success. However, it should be noted that in communities where social dancing is established and promoted for this age level, this activity will probably meet with success.

One of the most important factors that the physical education teacher should consider is the personal self-consciousness and embarrassment suffered by teenagers in regard to their physical development. This is particularly true in physical education classes, where emphasis is placed on physical skills and bodily coordination. Students who are concerned with overweight or underweight conditions frequently seek excuses from class participation, showers, or exercise because of their discomfort, fatigue, and ineptitude. The teacher of physical education has a real opportunity for guidance in such cases by offering suggestions on healthful nutrition and proper exercise. A sincere interest and understanding of individual problems can direct the student's self-interest toward a solution of problems and motivate him or her to put forth increased effort.

Skeletal changes

Some of the adolescent increases in height and weight may be attributed to inner changes in the skeletal structures, which cause differences in body proportions at this time.

The bones of the growing youth change in length and breadth as well as in density (mass). Studies of x-ray films show that a definite relationship may be found between skeletal age and age of puberty. In other words, a child's bony growth continues at approximately the same rate and time as other facets of development and is complete when the sexual function is mature.

These skeletal changes cause differences in body proportions common in adolescence. The long bones of the arms and legs are extended, with accompanying growth of the superimposed muscles. Facial contours change, and as the nose lengthens, the hairline changes, and the second molars appear.

Several implications for physical education are involved here. With these constant changes occurring in their skeletal framework, adolescents need considerable exercise for their large muscles to maintain competent physical skills. The teacher must use caution, however, during strenuous activities and guard against fatigue and strain in this age group. Adolescents also need a broad understanding of the changes taking place to offset disappointment and discontent when skills suddenly seem less effective.

In relation to the competitive aspects of the intramural and interscholastic programs, especially among early adolescents, skeletal growth, muscle strain, and fatigue should be considered. Physical educators must, of course, follow state regulations in regard to competition.

Primary and secondary sex changes

Besides the sudden spurt in height and weight, the next most obvious adolescent change is in sex characteristics. There are two levels of changes to be considered here: the primary sex changes, which involve the reproductive organs, and the secondary sex characteristics, which include those traits generally attributed to masculine and feminine appearances. Growth of facial hair on boys and breast development in girls are examples of secondary sex characteristics.

The primary sex change in girls is the development of the organs of reproduction (ovaries and fallopian tubes), which signal their maturation with the onset of the menstrual cycle. This signpost of adult function is of major importance to growing girls and usually occurs between the ages of 12 and 14 years, although it may be earlier or later in a few cases.

The implications of this cycle in teaching physical education are many. In the first place it is essential that a healthy attitude toward menstruation be fostered by requiring all students to dress for classes and to participate in some, if not all, the activities. Girls should not be allowed to pamper themselves on these occasions but should learn to lead a regular, normally active life. There are, of course, exceptional cases—girls who are under a doctor's care and who may need rest at this time.

Instruction in proper hygiene and cleanliness, as well as in helpful exercise to relieve tensions, is another area in which the physical education teacher can do great service to adolescent girls. Special provisions for showering may have to be made, however, to spare them real embarrassment. In schools where individual stall showers and dressing areas are provided there is no problem, but in other instances girls having their menstrual period may need to shower earlier or to substitute a sponge type of bath for a shower at the end of class.

The reproductive organs of boys (penis and testes) do not mature until approximately two years later than girls' reproductive organs, or around the ages of 14 to 16 years. Because growth of the male organs is external in nature, overdevelopment or underdevelopment is often a cause for much self-concern. Teachers should show care and understanding and should foster on the part of all students an attitude of acceptance of individual variations. Locker room antics and teasing about this personal characteristic can develop an unhealthy dislike for physical education and should not be permitted.

The main female secondary sex characteristic that develops in adolescence is the mammary gland. Other minor changes include growth of pubic and axillary hair, settling of the voice, and broadening of the hips. These changes begin the slow process of development at around 10 years of age and continue long after the menarche.

In boys the changes termed secondary sex characteristics are similar to those of the girls: pubic and axillary hair, plus facial hair, as well as a deepening of the voice, broadening of the shoulders, and development of a waistline. These changes generally appear around the age of 12 years and continue into late adolescence.

The teacher of physical education should recognize the great importance these changes have in the minds of the students and the deep concern they feel about their growth and development. The teacher

should help the students to understand the process of growth itself and should guide their thinking toward an appreciation of individual differences.

The teacher should also assist students in overcoming some of the problems that usually accompany sex changes. Acne, caused by the increase in glandular activity, and body odors, for example, may both be discussed by the physical education teacher, and hints may be given for improving these conditions. Group instruction on personal cleanliness and hygiene and individual, personal consultations in extreme cases are services that the teacher can perform for adolescents.

Other systemic changes

Other physiologic systems undergo further development along with the previously mentioned areas of growth. The circulatory system, which includes the heart and blood vessels, continues to grow steadily during adolescence. This growth may be identified by a normal increase in blood pressures. However, the pulse rate seems to decrease in adolescence, although girls maintain a higher rate of speed than boys.

Respiratory system changes are also evident in adolescence, as seen by measurements of vital capacity. Large increases are registered in both boys and girls from ages 10 to 14 years, with a subsequent slowing down in girls' capacities, while boys' capacities continue to increase.

The digestive organs continue to grow during this time, necessitating more and more daily nourishment and thereby making greater demands on the adolescent body.

The nervous system is more fully developed before adolescence than are the other systems, but there is thought to be an increase in the complexity of brain connections, with a subsequent increase in the types of thought processes. These developments continue until late adolescence.

Systemic changes should be considered as part of the total adolescent developmental picture, each having some bearing on the teaching program. In regard to the respiratory and circulatory changes, adolescent students should be watched carefully for signs of fatigue and exhaustion. Their appetites are usually large because of changes in digestion, but improper food habits are generally prevalent, and students need guidance in this respect. The further development of the nervous system, with increases in the types of thought processes, has implications for the knowledge and appreciation that adolescent students can now achieve. The teaching program may therefore be geared to more advanced aspects of strategy, rules, and philosophical ideas.

Basic motor skills

Consideration of the basic motor skills and their development during adolescence is a very important concern of the physical education teacher. The following observations seem to hold true in many cases:

1. Accuracy. Girls are usually better than boys in this skill throughout adolescent development.
2. Agility. Girls are more agile than boys until around 13 years of age, at which time boys surpass the girls in this respect.
3. Control. Girls perform with more control than boys in early adolescence. The boys become superior after the age of 14.
4. Strength. Boys are generally superior to girls in strength, but a greater degree of differentiation is seen with their maturity.

Basic motor skills are an essential part of the program in physical education. Therefore, changes in adolescent performance of these skills have definite implications for teaching. For girls, emphasis should be placed on continuing improvement in balance, agility, control, and strength. Boys need to work, particularly in the early years, on accuracy, agility, and control, whereas in later years stress should be placed on their ability to achieve accuracy.

The differences in basic motor skill performances should be kept in mind when different aspects of the program are planned. With coeducational groups, for instance,

activities requiring strength would not be chosen because of boys' superiority. When expected athletic performances of students are estimated, these same skill differences and changes should be considered. The teacher should realize that a change in students' interest and satisfactions takes place as their motor skills change and develop. In motivating students, therefore, different techniques will be necessary at each age level.

Health aspects*

Although adolescence is sometimes described as one of the healthiest periods of life, a study of illnesses and problems of secondary school students is quite revealing to teachers.

Figures gathered from nineteen clinics across the United States indicate that the most frequent diagnoses of adolescent patients show these health problems to be most prevalent: obesity, acne, allergy, seizures, and orthopedic problems.

The physical education program should consider what contributions it might make through its curriculum to alleviate the number one problem, obesity. At the same time, physical education teachers should realize that injuries, along with upper respiratory infections, are frequent problems for their students and consider what steps need to be taken to ensure student safety and freedom from exposure to disease.

It is also interesting to note that although the death rate among adolescents is low, accidents cause about 50 percent of their deaths, and two-thirds of these are motor vehicle accidents. These statistics are particularly significant for teachers of driver training courses.

A comparatively new problem in high schools in the larger urban areas across the country involves pregnancy in high school girls. In many instances it is the girl's physical education teacher who first recognizes the symptoms, and therefore she should be aware of the type of help currently available in the schools for such students.

---

*See also discussion on health goals, Chapter 6.

Although the health and vitality of adolescents are usually good, every teacher should be aware of other aspects of student life that may cause difficulties.

The physical education teacher should take advantage of every opportunity to offer guidance in health matters. The need for proper diet, rest, and exercise is easily related to athletic performance, and discussions of these factors can be very valuable. Guidance in proper body mechanics and posture, which is also a responsibility of the physical education teacher, is very important to adolescent health. Every program of physical education should contain a unit or series of classes devoted to postural studies for the identification of defects and improvement of postural conditions.

Fitness aspects

It is of utmost importance that physical fitness be an objective of the physical education program in junior and senior high schools. Students undergoing the constant process of change need to pay particular attention to achieving and maintaining a high level of fitness. It is at this stage in their de-

velopment when a true appreciation of activity and fitness for its own sake is formulated. Fitness will be discussed further in Chapter 20. However, it should be emphasized here that the physical education teacher has a very great responsibility in this regard, for it is in this field alone where physical fitness may be promoted in the school.

The physical development of the adolescent is a very complex process. Its close association with the physical education program makes it essential that teachers understand thoroughly the various aspects of growth and development in order to meet the needs of adolescents and help them understand better the process that is taking place.

EMOTIONAL DEVELOPMENT

The emotional development of adolescents is just as complex as their physical development, but it is not as easily defined or measured because there is no exact pattern of development to follow. To discuss this phase of adolescence it will be necessary to picture briefly the basic human emotions and the adolescent adjustments and responses that

Fig. 4-2. Students engaging in self-defense exercise as part of the physical education program at Regina High School in Cincinnati, Ohio.

are distinguishable from those of chilhood and adulthood.

Basic human emotions

It must first be realized that the adolescent, like human beings of any age, experiences the three basic emotions—fear, anger, and joy—and their variations. It is in the stimulus exciting an emotion and in the response to a particular situation that the growing adolescent differs from other age groups.

Adolescent responses

Adolescent responses tend to be extreme in nature. Members of this age group are either highly excited or greatly depressed, and rapid changes of mood are typical. For this reason adolescence is sometimes described as a period of heightened emotionality.

Adolescents develop emotionally at the same time that physical, social, and intellectual maturation is taking place. Signs of extreme emotional responsiveness may be seen as early as the preadolescent stage, and the developmental process continues slowly, with completion in late adolescence. Boys mature approximately two years later than girls in this respect as well as in other phases of development.

The heightened emotional responses of adolescents can best be understood in terms of the changing needs that cause them and that in themselves form a pattern of emotional development. A study of these adolescent needs, therefore, is necessary to interpret their relationship to physical education.

Adolescent needs

The emotions of adolescents are aroused in response to the adjustment needs peculiar to their stage of development. They must adjust to a changing physical state, to a heterosexual interest, and to an environment free from parental control. Other adolescent needs that must be satisfied are shared by all human beings. They include security, achievement, affection, adventure, and well-being. Adolescents, however, in satisfying these needs, find methods that are limited to their particular age group and that undergo changes as different stages of development are reached. It is this transition in satisfaction-producing factors that provides a clue to adolescent emotional development and that should be studied individually in respect to each student's needs.

Affection. The early adolescent seeks many friendships with individuals of the same sex, whereas in middle adolescence friendships with the opposite sex begin. These friendships become even stronger in late adolescence, while friends of the same sex continue to hold interest. Also in late adolescence relationships with adults are more friendly as authority relaxes, and eventually friendships with the same sex dwindle in number as they deepen in intensity.

Problems in regard to affection usually arise either from fears centered around the making or losing of friends or from conflicts with them. Still others may stem from a desire for continued affection from parents, which is in conflict with a simultaneous need for independence from them.

All teachers need to understand the basic problems faced by teenagers in reference to their need for affection. Physical education teachers should provide many socializing situations in which friendships may be fostered and should further the process of adjustment to the opposite sex through coeducational activities.

Achievement. In early adolescence achievement is realized through success in many and varied interests and hobbies. In middle and late adolescence, as interests center upon fewer, more important areas, achievement is sensed through accomplishments in these areas. These later interests usually stem from the adult role that the adolescent determines is most suitable, and success is felt as this ideal approaches reality.

Problems of adolescents generally stem from lack of achievement in the areas of interest at each age level. For example, receiving good grades in school becomes a problem when an interest in a college education is aroused.

Teachers of physical education should

realize that many students find satisfaction in superior performance and achievement in their field. For those students who have difficulty performing in physical education, the teacher should try to provide a program varied enough so that in some particular activity or sport a sense of accomplishment may be derived.

Adventure. In early adolescence the variety of interests in many different areas provides much satisfaction of the need for adventure. Striking out on one's own with the new freedom that this age permits provides much excitement in middle adolescence, and this same satisfaction is present in late adolescence. The major problem occurs when satisfaction of this need for adventure is gained from improper experiences, as seen in the juvenile crimes of today.

In physical education this need for excitement and adventure may easily be satisfied through the challenge and thrills of sports and competition. The program should therefore be set up on a broad scale to provide satisfaction through afterschool activities for as many students as possible.

Security. The early adolescent seeks security in his or her social world through the gang or crowd. The middle adolescent finds similar satisfaction in smaller groups or cliques, and the late adolescent begins to be satisfied with more adult relationships, having found security with himself or herself.

The main problem that creates insecurity in adolescents lies within. Because of the uncertainties life holds and the doubts of success, adolescents do not dare to rely upon themselves. Instead, they seek security in whatever else they can find: the gang, the club, the world of books or music, or some other facet of life.

The physical education teacher has a very real responsibility toward the security of students in all activities. All students should feel at ease in the gymnasium, and this goal may be accomplished by giving concrete instructions and establishing definite procedures and regulations so that students will know exactly what is expected of them. This, together with consistency in handling routine procedures, discipline problems, and other everyday occurrences, ensures feelings of security in physical education.

Sense of well-being. A sense of well-being is brought about by adjusting the picture of the self through various mechanisms. Adolescents employ the same methods as all human personalities: rationalization, blame, compensation, and use of excuses, to name a few.

Superiority in physical pursuits provides one outlet for adjusting the self-picture of individuals who have difficulty in academic work. Students who can achieve in some area of physical education naturally augment their sense of well-being or sense of worth. Elementary classroom teachers have said that

Fig. 4-3. Developing skill in soccer and other physical education activities helps the adolescent develop a better self-image. (Walt Whitman High School, South Huntington Schools, New York.)

the key to all learning is making children feel good about themselves in regard to whatever they are trying to do. Surely this same principle applies to students of all ages.

Physical education teachers should be aware of the abnormal extremes to which human personalities may go when overrationalizing or overcompensating. When teachers recognize these extreme cases, they should make the proper referrals to the school psychologist for study. In this way the teacher does a service to students who need help in regaining their sense of well-being.

Adjustment to physical change. The adjustment to the changing physical self has been discussed previously in this chapter. From the emotional standpoint it should be emphasized again that this is a source of great concern to all adolescents.

Adjustment to heterosexual interest. This discussion will be expanded in the section on social development, but the close relationship of heterosexual interest to emotional responses should be pointed out here. Many adolescent fears and worries center around this particular phase of development, necessitating a real contribution on the part of the physical education program through coeducational activities to relieve tensions.

Freedom from parental control. In adolescence there is a particular need to gain freedom from parental control, yet the conflicts in treatment given adolescents by adults cause many problems.

At home adolescents begin to assume adultlike responsibilities in relation to doing household chores, baby-sitting, holding part-time jobs, and having an increased allowance. At the same time, however, they still are restricted in many things, such as using the family car, dating, and observing curfews. These discrepancies in treatment frequently seem senseless to the adolescent and are difficult to reconcile.

At school this dichotomy—treating adolescents partially as adults and partially as children—continues. Rules and regulations are established about smoking, dances, and conduct, while at the same time the students are allowed to run the school government, athletic organizations, and other school activities.

To help adolescents feel secure without depending on parental or other adult controls the physical education teacher should try to offer many opportunities for the development of self-responsibility, self-discipline, and self-reliance. This may be done through assignment of leadership positions and through class planning of rules and regulations of conduct. Students who are allowed to mutually formulate their standards of behavior better understand the necessity for having them and follow them more willingly.

An understanding of the many adolescent worries and needs helps the physical education teacher make provisions in the program to overcome these emotional difficulties. It is also important that additional problems be avoided in the school situation, and the teacher who understands possible areas of concern, such as security, is better able to provide a healthy teaching situation. Students who are emotionally upset learn little, and they need help in controlling emotional responses. It is the responsibility of teachers to assist them in achieving this goal.

Manhood and womanhood

Boys and girls are transformed into men and women in the teens. The activity of hormones on the reproductive system at the onset of the teens establishes the two sexes. The fact that men and women possess different reproductive structures and functions shapes their psychological and emotional development. Until the adolescent period personality development is largely the same for boys and girls. From the teens on they follow different paths to achieve a mature identity.

Physical and psychological functions are generally established before they can be fully used. This is also true of the reproductive function. During the teens the reproductive urge joins hunger, thirst, and safety as among the most powerful human drives. Reproduction, however, involves not only the individual but a partner and society as well. The sex drive requires special understanding so that it can be controlled and directed not only in terms of personal needs but in line with social goals.

Physical differences. At one time women were believed to be "the weaker sex." Research has shown, however, that more boy than girl babies die at birth. In general, life expectancy is longer for women than for men. Furthermore, girls mature (from about the age of 6 through the teens) a year or two ahead of boys. This is the reason girls are often taller than their male peers. Earlier emotional maturation also explains their readiness for social events sooner than most boys.

Emotional differences. The nature, strength, and timing of sexual feelings are different for boys and girls. The difference in their emotional and psychological involvement in the matter of sex is partly explained by their differing biological roles. A woman's reproductive system prepares her for child-bearing and nurture. Because of this her total personality may become involved in feelings of love. Traditionally, society considered marriage to be the fulfillment, biologically and otherwise, of a girl's personality. In the United States today, however, many question this traditional attitude. A girl's feelings (possibly because girls mature earlier than boys) may center on marriage long before

boys of her age are emotionally or economically ready for it.

Also traditionally boys accepted the fact that economic independence was required to care for a wife and family and a great deal of his energy was directed away from the home and to his work. There is an increasing tendency, however, for the man and woman to share economic responsibilities and for both to find satisfaction in their careers. Although some portions of society hold to the traditional views, many alternatives are now available to those who do not.

SOCIAL DEVELOPMENT

Social development can be thought of in terms of the adolescent's relationships with friends of his own sex, with friends of the opposite sex, and with adults. In each of these areas different stages of growth are found, appearing later in boys than in girls, and to a different degree. The developmental process itself is based on the adolescent's desire to break away from his parents and to assume selfhood in his social world.

Relationships with same sex

In early adolescence the individual finds a place in the social world by becoming part of a large group, which usually consists of

Fig. 4-4. At one time women were believed to be the weaker sex. Girl at Paul J. Gelinas Junior High School in Setauket, N.Y. disproves that statement.

age-mates of the same sex. This occurs with girls in junior high school, and somewhat later, perhaps in the ninth or tenth grade, with boys. Groupings usually evolve from similar school classes, neighborhoods, and social backgrounds. They provide standards of behavior, such as manner of dress and talk, as well as opportunities to learn how to act with people in different situations.

In middle adolescence the dictates of the peer groups continue to be strong. However, the crowds break down into smaller, more cohesive cliques that promote snobbishness and prejudices not usually found in the larger groupings. With girls these close friendships maintain an extreme importance that continues into the college years, while boys seldom rely as completely on friendships.

There are two important implications for physical education stemming from this phase of adolescent social development. One concerns leadership and the other, clique formations.

Because the development of *leadership* qualities is a fundamental phase of physical education, the program should provide many opportunities for promoting and guiding good leaders. The formation of leaders' clubs in junior and senior high school provides a structured situation wherein leadership qualities may be developed and practiced by many interested members. Learning to select good leaders may also be considered an outcome of physical education, and this factor should have carry-over value into out-of-school group activities.

Another phase of the physical education program that should have carry-over value in adolescent circles relates to the injurious aspects of clique formations. The socializing phase of physical education activities, such as the teamwork, should point out the equalities of all individuals and promote consideration for and cooperation with people of all races and religions. The harmful effects of ostracizing a few people—so frequently found in small clique formations—should be discussed during class organization, with the hope that desirable extracurricular practices will be followed.

Relationships with opposite sex

In early adolescence, between the ages of 10 and 12 years, boys and girls generally exhibit an antagonistic attitude toward one another.

In middle adolescence, girls of 13 and 14, who are now developing physically, begin to take an active interest in boys, parties, and mixed social functions. Boys, however, seem less interested in girls. Between 14 and 16 years of age boys return this interest in the opposite sex, and social activities consume a great deal of an adolescent's time and energies. It is usually at this point that pairs begin to develop. By the age of 16 or 17, adolescent adjustments to members of the opposite sex are nearly complete.

The development of an interest in the opposite sex as well as such legal requirements as Title IX have two important implications in the physical education program: the planning of coeducational activities and the individual class program.

Coeducational activities for the early adolescent in junior high school should provide an opportunity for relaxed socialization in which no undue embarrassment is felt. At this level boys and girls are at various stages of development, ranging from no interest to too much interest in the opposite sex. Activities should therefore be those already familiar to the students, such as badminton, volleyball, tennis, or recreational games. Knowing the activity helps the adolescent overcome the fear of socializing. Simple mass dancing activities may be successful when well organized and taught, particularly in communities that promote social activities in junior high school.

The senior high school coeducational program should include learning experiences that will have carry-over value when students complete their education. Bowling, golf, and other individual sports may be introduced at this level if facilities permit.

The individual program of physical education must change somewhat along with this changing heterosexual drive. Younger girls love to play all kinds of games, but with physical development comes an increased desire for attractiveness, grace, poise, and balance. This aspect of their interests can and should be served in the teaching program, with dance and fitness activities stressing these goals.

The difference in sexual roles, although changing in today's culture, has always been reflected in an unfortunate split in social values and a "double standard." That is, society sometimes approves one form of behavior for boys and men and another for girls and women. Boys have more freedom and are less subject to social criticism than are girls. The "boys will be boys" attitude is an example of this. When social conventions are disregarded girls suffer the burden of social disapproval more than boys do, although to a far lesser extent than they once did.

Relationships with adults

Preadolescents usually accept adult authority, whereas early adolescents begin to be resentful. The latter try to assert themselves above such authority, except in cases of hero worship. In middle and late adolescence the students become more receptive to adult helpfulness and seek advice from those who represent fields in which they are strongly interested. Then at the end of adolescence adults are met on a more friendly basis, and the socially mature individual finds that he can enjoy casual friendship with everyone.

This change in the adolescent-adult relationship has two important implications for physical education. One concerns class management and the other, the problem of hero worship.

Because the younger adolescent tends to be resentful of adult authority, the physical educator should try to have members of a class manage themselves as much as possible. Through guided group planning the adolescent can set proper standards of behavior, and therefore has no reason to rebel. Students are then motivating themselves and providing self-direction—thus fulfilling educational goals as well as developmental goals.

In regard to the second factor, hero worship, it should be pointed out that in physical education, in which an informal teacher-pupil relationship is likely to be maintained, hero worship and infatuations easily develop. This can become a serious problem for the student involved, for such strong feelings often become very time and thought consuming, to the detriment of the individual. If such an attachment develops, the wise teacher remains objective and tries to be friendly and helpful and at the same time remote in other relationships with the student. Fortunately these infatuations are usually shortlived, and when they are properly handled no personal misunderstandings or ill feelings result.

The social development of the adolescent is of great importance both to him or her and to the school. The physical educator should assist in as many ways as possible in this development in all three aspects: relationships with friends of the same sex, with those of the opposite sex, and with adults.

Boys and girls are less concerned about material security and more concerned with basic human values. They resent the differences between what adults say and what they do. They want to participate more in deciding their own future. They are articulate and inclined to express themselves regarding how they feel about the major issues of the day.

Specifically, here are some characteristics of today's students that have deep implications for the teacher of physical education:

• *Today's secondary school students want to be involved.* Boys and girls want a say in respect to the decisions that affect them. They want to participate in the curriculum they will follow, the rules and regulations that control their actions, and the matters that will affect their future. They want to have a voice in policy decisions, be on school committees, and evaluate courses and teachers.

• *Today's secondary school students are not inhibited.* They voice what they believe, which often is different from what adults believe. They want to know why they have to do certain things and why certain procedures and practices are followed.

• *Today's secondary school students have a new image of themselves.* Students recognize that they are human beings who have rights in this society and a say in what happens to them, what happens to their families, and what happens to their country. They are no longer content to let adults and others make decisions for them. They utilize their economic, political, and social power. They stress the individual and his value in society and the need for each person to have equal opportunities.

• *Today's secondary school students are antiestablishment.* They are skeptical of adults, of the school administration, of government, and of older people in general. They have seen the materialism, discrimination, pollution of the environment, war mongering, and other evils associated with past generations and want to bring about a change.

Fig. 4-5. The new breed of student. (Ellensburg Public Schools, Ellensburg, Wash.)

• *Today's secondary school students have different goals than do adults.* Students have different goals from adults, particularly in respect to such things as money, security, challenge, and position. According to a recent survey young people indicated that their three greatest sources of satisfaction listed in priority order are family, leisure, and occupation.

• *Today's secondary school students are educationally oriented in different ways.* Instead of memorization of dates, they want to know the reasons for the movements and events behind the dates instead of merely knowing about historical events to understand the underlying forces that resulted in these significant events.

• *Today's secondary school students are not part of the crowd.* Each student wants to be considered for his or her own self and talents. Girls, for example, want to have the same rights as boys. Students do not want to be treated in an impersonal manner and exposed to an impersonal curriculum. They do not want to be required to perform the same school tasks that other students, whose abilities, needs, and interests may be different than their own, are required to perform. Students feel they must be dealt with as they are and not as they are expected to be.

To illustrate what the secondary school student wants is shown by the demands of students as listed in a study conducted by a student task force in North Carolina. The survey covered students from representative high schools in the state. Their major demands included the following:

• Administrators should maintain a constant dialogue with students.
• Legitimate requests of students should be dealth with promptly and fairly.
• Student dissent should be sanctioned if it is legitimate and does not disrupt the educational process.
• Seminar sessions should be held regularly with students for discussion of current school problems.
• Students should be permitted to form committees with powers to investigate

and propose solutions to problems of unrest.

- Students should be urged to respect the school as their institution of learning.
- The local high school should be given responsibility for all rules and regulations.
- Clear communication lines should be established between administration, faculty, and students.
- Student government should be given as much responsibility as possible.
- The principal should write a column in school newspaper as an avenue of communication.

As a result of these demands new and innovative methods and educational programs in North Carolina were established, students were given a voice in planning their own course of study, and they were appointed to committees and given a chance to revamp the grading system.

INTELLECTUAL DEVELOPMENT

The teens are a period of mental growth. A teenager's interests extend in many directions and are stimulated by new experience. The fact that students are no longer confined to the narrow limits of their immediate environment opens new horizons in the teens. Heightened learning and planning ability and improvement in the capacity for self-expression help teenagers to develop minds of their own.

The ability to conceptualize and to grasp abstract ideas increases rapidly in the teens. During this time young people can approach the upper limits of their intellectual potential. With these new powers the teenager undertakes the most complex tasks of the life cycle—establishing a system of values, forming lasting personal relationships, choosing a career, and developing a philosophy of life.

The adolescent does not go through a great intellectual growth spurt or change as in other phases of development. At this time there seems to be an expansion of powers, however, as well as an increase in capacities. The continuing growth toward intellectual maturity is extremely varied in individuals,

with a high degree of this development being reached at any time between the ages of 16 and 25 years. Boys and girls are alike in this respect, and the wide range of ages points out the individualized nature of intellectual growth.

Adolescent intellectual advancement may be discussed in reference to four general areas: memory, concentration, imagination, and reasoning power. The power of memory, which is so strong in childhood, seems to decrease in adolescence. Actually, however, it is the adolescent's lack of interest in making use of this capacity to memorize that causes this decline.

The powers of adolescents to concentrate increase, particularly in areas of work in which they are greatly interested. The adolescent's ability to use imagination also increases at this time. Of greatest importance in relation to schoolwork is the distinct increase in adolescent powers of reasoning and judging. It is this phase of intellectual development that distinguishes growth away from childish ideas and permits the student to generalize from past experiences to formulate moral values and knowledge, together with a philosophy of life.

The importance of this intellectual development of adolescents to the physical education program lies in its relationship to teaching methods and the influences exerted by the teacher.

In regard to the first point, teaching methods, the teacher must be sure to consider the variation of intellectual abilities when presenting instructions and explanations. As students progress through high school, the material presented in physical education class should require more and more reasoning power and judgment. Thought questions should be included in tests rather than simple true-false or multiple-choice types. Strategy and game concepts should become a part of the teaching program, for adolescents are now able to understand more fully this phase of physical education activities.

The teacher should also make use of teaching methods that promote creative thinking on the part of adolescent students. Units on modern dance obviously foster creative thinking in girls, but sports units for both boys and girls may be constructed to take advantage of improved adolescent powers of imagination and thinking. Students should have an opportunity to work out team plays in basketball, for example, or to develop their own exercise patterns, drill formations, or football plays. The teacher can use the problem-solving technique to accomplish this, asking the students to think out some specific solution to a given game situation.

Checklist of selected items for evaluating the physical education program's relevancy to the student in the secondary school

	Yes	No
1. Activities are provided that will enable each student to be successful and feel that he has worth.	☐	☐
2. Students are helped to relate to one another, to members of the opposite sex, and to adults.	☐	☐
3. Students are provided an opportunity to have a say in the development of the physical education curriculum and consequently will be more highly motivated to participate in the program that is meaningful and interesting to them.	☐	☐
4. Students are helped to understand the why of the activity in which they are participating.	☐	☐
5. Students are grouped in classes according to their abilities.	☐	☐
6. Teachers know all students and help in solving their problems.	☐	☐
7. The community is involved in the physical education program, for example, father-son and mother-daughter activities.	☐	☐
8. Instruction is provided in new sports, such as scuba diving, in which students have an interest.	☐	☐
9. Students have a voice in policy-making decisions, are represented on important committees, and participate in the evaluation of courses and teachers.	☐	☐
10. Physical education program is kept abreast of the changing times in society and the changing nature of students, with student needs being met in a realistic, meaningful manner. (Today, some students find their programs repetitious, time consuming, giving little emphasis to the unskilled, and so on.)	☐	☐
11. The program gives equal opportunities to girls and boys.	☐	☐
12. Opportunities are provided students for leadership roles.	☐	☐
13. Students are represented at faculty meetings.	☐	☐
14. The physical education program meets the needs of minority groups.	☐	☐
15. Communication channels are available whereby students can submit their grievances to the administration.	☐	☐
16. Intellectual as well as physical capacities of students are challenged.	☐	☐
17. The curriculum provides for a sequential advancement from basic skills to more advanced skills.	☐	☐
18. Individualistic hair styles and dress codes are permitted where they do not affect the health, safety, and performance of students.	☐	☐
19. Physically handicapped, mentally retarded, emotionally distrubed, and culturally disadvantaged students are provided for in the physical education program.	☐	☐
20. Sufficient variety and progression exist in activities to satisfy individual differences.	☐	☐
21. The intramural, varsity athletic, and other extracurricular activities meet the needs of students.	☐	☐
22. The program is designed to develop the optimum potential of each student.	☐	☐
23. The objectives of the physical education program are clearly understood by students.	☐	☐
24. Students have the opportunity to participate in activities where identification and acceptance are manifested.	☐	☐
25. Students have the opportunity to participate in activities that will be of value to them not only now but also in the future.	☐	☐

The other important aspect of adolescent intellectual development that affects the physical education teacher lies in the student-teacher relationship. Because adolescence is the period in which adult attitudes, moral values, and a philosophy of life become formalized, the teacher of physical education should exemplify those ideals that are most suitable to mature living. For example, the physical education teacher should try to promote positive attitudes toward health and physical fitness: a desire to maintain good health, a desire to continue physical pursuits for enjoyment, and an appreciation for the outcomes of physical exercise. As an influence on adolescent moral values, on their concepts of right and wrong, and on their prejudices, which are now taking final shape, the physical education teacher should have clearly defined values that are consistently applied and worthy of imitation by the students. The ideals of respect for all individuals, no matter how different they may be, should be promoted in physical education, together with the real meaning of sportsmanship.

The philosophy of life that shapes an individual's outlook and actions is also formulated during adolescence. Religious doubts and philosophical questioning are increasing concerns of the adolescent. Physical education teachers never know when their actions, thoughts, or beliefs may be idealized or when guidance and advice may be sought. They must therefore be ready to serve and to answer students to the best of their abilities and must recognize that many values are best learned from example.

Self-assessment tests

These tests are to assist students in determining if material and competencies presented in this chapter have been mastered:

1. Describe the physical appearance and characteristics of someone you know. Discuss how this person's physical characteristics and appearance affect his or her personality and self-image.
2. Complete the following chart regarding changes that take place during adolescent growth and the implications these changes have for teaching physical education:

Changes that take place during adolescence	Implications for teaching physical education
Physical changes	
a. _____	_____
b. _____	_____
c. _____	_____
Emotional changes	
a. _____	_____
b. _____	_____
c. _____	_____
Social changes	
a. _____	_____
b. _____	_____
c. _____	_____
Intellectual changes	
a. _____	_____
b. _____	_____
c. _____	_____

3. You are in charge of a ninth-grade coeducational physical education class in volleyball. How would you provide for differences in height and weight and other physical differences in boys and girls in the class?
4. Title IX requires coeducational physical education classes. Indicate the social characteristics of high school boys and girls and how you would provide for these social characteristics in the high school physical education program.
5. Describe how you as a physical education teacher would provide for variations in intellectual abilities among your students.

Points to remember

1. The process of adolescent physical development and the stages undergone are different in boys and girls, and each individual follows his or her own particular growth pattern.
2. The emotional responses of adolescents are different from those of adults because of their varying needs.
3. Social development in adolescence is recognizable by the changes in relationships with friends and adults.
4. Intellectual growth is experienced during adolescence and plays an important part in mature living.
5. The process of growth and development in adolescents has many implications for the physical education program.

Problems to think through

1. How can we capitalize on the varying interests exhibited in junior high school students?
2. How can we promote and further good social relationships in junior high school students when heterosexual interests develop?

3. How can we develop in students an understanding of the physical growth that takes place during adolescence?
4. How can we develop good habits of cleanliness and proper hygiene techniques during early adolescence?
5. How can we prevent cliques from controlling or damaging class and afterschool activities?
6. How can we capitalize on the heightened interests and abilities of the older high school pupils?
7. How can we further the development of leadership techniques in students not usually given opportunities to demonstrate them?
8. How can we relieve extreme emotional tensions that develop during adolescence?
9. How can we promote attitudes of honesty, fair play, and consideration of others?

Case study for analysis

Tina was the rather unfortunate nickname given to a very large eighth grade girl, recently moved into a small community. Physical education classes met twice a week for all eighth grade girls and once a week with boys and girls together. Embarrassment over her size and her lack of abilities in physical activities forced her to try every conceivable technique to be excused from class, especially the coeducational class, where she was completely ill at ease. How should Tina be motivated to enter into activities to derive the benefits she so badly needs?

Exercises for review

1. What points of good grooming should be emphasized with junior high school girls? Boys?
2. What steps should be followed in helping a student whose emotional adjustment is questionable in a school where a nurse is not in daily attendance?
3. How would procedures regarding monthly periods be outlined to a class of seventh grade girls?
4. In what way could proper class and locker room management benefit the ostracized high school boy?
5. What adolescent individuals in the modern world of sports should be singled out as examples of athletic achievement?
6. What advice should be given the adolescent youth, ordinarily proficient in physical activities, who finds himself falling below par?

Selected readings

Berg, K.: Maintaining enthusiasm in teaching, Journal of Physical Education and Recreation **46:**22, 1975.

Berlin, P.: Prologomena to the study of personality by physical educators, Quest **13:**54, 1970.

Bronson, D. B.: Thinking and teaching, The Educational Forum **39:**347, 1975.

Bucher, C. A.: What's happening in education today? Journal of Health, Physical Education, and Recreation **45:**30, 1974.

Caldwell, S.: Toward a humanistic physical education, Journal of Health, Physical Education, and Recreation **43:**31, 1972.

Clarke, H. H., editor: Individual differences, their nature, extent, and significance, Physical Fitness Research Digest, October, 1973.

Friedenberg, E. Z.: Coming of age in America, New York, 1965, Random House, Inc.

Friedenberg, E. Z.: The vanishing adolescent, Boston, 1959, Beacon Press.

Gregory, S.: Hey, white girl! New York, 1970, W. W. Norton & Co.

High school kids "turned off" by education, White Plains Reporter Dispatch, October 20, 1971, p. 10.

Morsbach, M.: The Negro in American Life, New York, 1967, Harcourt, Brace and World.

Murphy, G.: What can youth tell us about their potentialities? Bulletin of the National Association of Secondary-School Principals **50:**10-24, 1966.

Oliva, P. F.: The secondary school today, New York, 1967, World Publishing Co.

Rand, L.: Teen-agers and money, National Education Association Journal **56:**34, 1967.

Snyder, E. E., and Spreitzer, E.: Family influence and involvement in sports, Research Quarterly **44:**249, 1973.

Some popular myths on youth (editorial), Wall Street Journal, June 28, 1971.

United States Department of Health, Education and Welfare: Dialogue on adolescence, Washington, D.C., 1967, U.S. Government Printing Office.

Youth's faith . . . (editorial), New York Times, May 8, 1970, p. 20.

PART TWO

The goals and program

5

DEVELOPING GOALS—WHAT SHOULD PHYSICAL EDUCATION BE DOING FOR THE STUDENT?

INSTRUCTIONAL OBJECTIVES AND COMPETENCIES TO BE ACHIEVED

After reading this chapter the student should be able to—

1. Describe the nature and importance of having goals in physical education.
2. Identify the bases and procedure for determining the specific goals that physical education should strive to achieve.
3. Outline and discuss the objectives of general education.
4. Name and present a rationale for the major objectives of physical education.
5. Present data to support a priority of objectives of physical education.
6. Show how methods and materials for teaching physical education are important to the realization of the objectives of physical education.

What are the objectives toward which physical education should strive in the secondary school? Will the selected goals, when achieved, contribute to the physical, mental, emotional, and social well-being of the student? What are the main contributions that physical education can make to the new breed of student who is attending junior and senior high schools of this country?

Thus far in this text we have considered the secondary school in a changing society, community, and school. We then looked at the student. A logical next step is to identify the goals and objectives that physical education hopes to achieve. In so doing, it is well to keep in mind four basic guidelines.

• *Goals must be clearly identified and should be understood by the student.* The goals toward which physical education is working should be clearly set forth and be understood and identified by the student. Surveys indicate that the purposes for which physical education programs exist are not always clear in the minds of students or are thought to have little value. This should not be the case. When students take physical education they should clearly understand at the outset the purpose of the program and the benefits and values to expect as participants. In addition, the goals should have been so carefully thought through and selected that the student will identify with them as important now and in the future.

• *Goals should have scientific worth.* The physical educator should select goals that are backed by scientific investigation and that can be achieved. Unfortunately, some teachers make wild claims for physical education that they cannot prove scientifically or achieve.

DEVELOPMENTAL OBJECTIVES OF PHYSICAL EDUCATION

ORGANIC

Proper functioning of the body systems so that the individual may adequately meet the demands placed upon him by his environment. A foundation for skill development.

Muscle Strength

The maximum amount of force exerted by a muscle or muscle group.

Muscle Endurance

The ability of a muscle or muscle group to sustain effort for a prolonged period of time.

Cardiovascular Endurance

The capacity of an individual to persist in strenuous activity for periods of some duration. This is dependent upon the combined efficiency of the blood vessels, heart, and lungs.

Flexibility

The range of motion in joints needed to produce efficient movement and minimize injury.

NEUROMUSCULAR

A harmonious functioning of the nervous and muscular systems to produce desired movements.

Locomotor Skills

Walking   Skipping   Sliding   Leaping   Pushing
Running   Galloping   Hopping   Rolling   Pulling

Nonlocomotor Skills

Swaying   Twisting   Shaking   Stretching
Bending   Handing   Stooping

Game Type Fundamental Skills

Striking   Catching   Kicking   Stopping
Throwing   Batting   Starting   Changing direction

Motor Factors

Accuracy   Rhythm   Kinesthetic awareness
Power   Balance   Reaction time   Agility

Sport Skills

Soccer   Softball   Volleyball   Wrestling
Track & Field   Football   Baseball
Basketball   Archery   Speedball   Hockey
Fencing   Golf   Bowling   Tennis

Recreational Skills

Shuffleboard   Croquet   Deck tennis   Hiking
Table tennis   Swimming   Horseshoes   Boating

INTERPRETIVE

The ability to explore, to discover, to understand, to acquire knowledge, and to make value judgments.

A knowledge of game rules, safety measures, and etiquette.

The use of strategies and techniques involved in organized activities.

A knowledge of how the body functions and its relationship to physical activity.

A development of appreciation for personal performance. The use of judgment related to distance, time, space, force, speed, and direction in the use of activity implements, balls, and self.

An understanding of growth and developmental factors affected by movement.

The ability to solve developmental problems through movement.

SOCIAL

An adjustment to both self and others by an integration of the individual to society and his environment.

The ability to make judgments in a group situation.

Learning to communicate with others.

The ability to exchange and evaluate ideas within a group.

The development of the social phases of personality, attitudes, and values in order to become a functioning member of society.

The development of a sense of belonging and acceptance by society.

The development of positive personality traits.

Learnings for constructive use of leisure time.

A development of attitude that reflects good moral character.

EMOTIONAL

A healthy response to physical activity through a fulfillment of basic needs.

The development of positive reactions in spectatorship and participation through either success or failure.

The release of tension through suitable physical activities.

An outlet for self-expression and creativity.

An appreciation of the aesthetic experiences derived from correlated activities.

The ability to have fun.

Fig. 5-1. Developmental goals of physical education. (From Annarino, A. A.: Journal of Health, Physical Education, and Recreation 41:25, 1970.)

- *Goals should be relevant to society, education, and the student.* The aims of physical education should reflect the changing society, education, and student discussed in the earlier pages of this text. Physical educators will be remiss if they fail to evaluate and select their goals with these changes in mind.

- *Goals should relate to the cognitive, affective, and motor domains.* Objectives of physical education should reflect directly or indirectly three domains, namely, the *cognitive*, with its emphasis upon knowledge and the development of intellectual abilities and skills; the *affective*, which relates to attitudes, values, interests, and appreciations; and the *psychomotor*, which refers to motor and manipulative skills. Furthermore, the interdependence of the three domains in relation to learning and the student should be recognized. For example, students do not think or behave without feeling. Instead, they respond as total organisms.

STUDENT-PARENT CONFUSION

Many students and parents are confused about the real worth of games and sports as part of the school program. Over the years we have had the opportunity to discuss physical education with many people. Some of their comments reflect this confusion: "It's exercise done to command." "A matter of arms and legs and good intentions." "Something that entertains the students—a necessary evil." "A good device to keep the kids off the street." "Just an extracurricular activity—a frill, a fad." "It certainly isn't part of the educational program—merely an appendage." "Too much time should not be devoted to it—above all, don't take time away from learning science and mathematics."

If physical education and play do not mean more than these comments indicate, they should be abolished from the school program. After all, there are more than 100,000 leaders getting paid several million dollars annually in this specialized field today. Approximately sixty million school children are being exposed to their programs. Gymnasiums, swimming pools, playgrounds, and recreational facilities are being constructed at a cost of billions of dollars to taxpayers. An up-to-date gymnasium costs at least $400,000 and a 75-foot swimming pool $100,000. Even the basketball that the kids bounce up and down the floor costs $30. The average gymnasium is one of the most costly parts of the school building and takes up space equivalent to ten to fourteen classrooms. Why pay all these teachers, construct these expensive facilities, and take up valuable space unless they are going to produce results—unless they are an important phase of education?

Students and parents are demanding the answers to such questions. They have become vitally interested in education. For parents, this interest has mushroomed until today there are over fifteen million members of parent-teacher associations throughout the country. They want to make sure their children have the benefits of worthwhile educational experiences. They vote money only for things they consider sound.

As these parents scan the educational programs of their communities, they should become increasingly aware that boys and girls do not learn, grow, and develop only during those hours spent at their desks in reading, writing, and working with paper and pencil. There are other times that may be even more important—time spent in taking a trip to the zoo, going to camp, making a doghouse, attending a dance, and YES, playing on the field, in the gymnasium, or in the swimming pool.

KNOWLEDGE OF OBJECTIVES— AN IMPORTANT CONSIDERATION

Upon the shoulders of the teacher of physical education rests the responsibility for interpreting to students, their parents, and the public in general the objectives of their specialized field. This responsibility cannot be met unless the teacher understands clearly the goals of education, students, and physical education. Furthermore, all these goals must be compatible with the educational development of each boy and girl in the secondary school and must contribute to it.

Each student of physical education and each teacher in the schools should know the objectives they are trying to reach. These aims represent the worth of this specialized field, they show the contribution that can be made to young and old alike, and they provide a guide for action in our day-to-day programs.

It is impossible for teachers of physical education to do a worthy educational job unless they know the objectives of the field and how they fit into the total education picture. Trying to work without such vital information would be analogous to a carpenter's trying to build a house without blueprints to guide him.

DEVELOPMENT OF GOALS FOR THE PHYSICAL EDUCATION PROGRAM

Physical educators in the secondary school should use a logical, step-by-step approach for arriving at the goals they wish to accomplish in their programs. The following steps are suggested as a specific way in which goals may be determined. Each step is presented in a form of a question, and the questions proceed from general to specific considerations.

What is the purpose of education?

Physical educators should be aware of the purposes for which formal institutions of learning exist. This changing nation has basic objectives for educational programs that are well grounded in democratic ideals. Some of these objectives, discussed later in this chapter, were formulated by the Educational Policies Commission.

Physical educators should next determine how physical education can best help to accomplish the basic goals of education. Furthermore, they should recognize the place of physical education in the total sphere of general education. As will be discussed later, physical education makes a contribution to the physical, mental, emotional, and social development of the student.

What is the school's philosophy of education?

Physical education goals should be in keeping with the philosophy of education within the school where the physical educator works. Therefore, the physical educator should be familiar with the goals of education of the secondary school and relate them to the physical education program. A careful study of the school's goals should be made, and where there is doubt in regard to the school's philosophy, it should be clarified through discussions with the administration. Most schools have specific goals of accomplishment that have been put in writing. If not, there should be some research to identify existing goals. One school, for example, points out that it has as its goals the following: "To promote healthful living by developing physical fitness, emotional stability, and appreciation of the ideals of good sportsmanship. . . . In our entire program we consciously support good physical and mental health habits, which are specifically taught in physical education, family living. . . . Through sports and other extracurricular activities we encourage participation in and enjoyment of rewarding recreational activities."

What are the needs and interests of the students?

The physical education program is for the students, and thus their needs and interests are a vital consideration. These needs and interests may be determined in a number of ways and by using a variety of resources, including school records, observation of students, talks with parents, making inventory of students' interests and suggestions, examining the literature that specifically relates to this subject, studying the professional research, and talking with specialists in the school program, such as the school physician, the nurse, and the guidance counselor. Any program that is developed should be compatible with the needs and interests of the students in a specific school. The procedure of studying students carefully should be a continuous one so that the goals are flexible and meet the changing needs of the students.

What are the influencing factors relating to such items as facilities, state regulations, and staff?

A basic premise for the development of physical education goals is that they must be established within the framework of factors that are essential for their accomplishment. For example, it would not be a worthwhile goal to indicate that each student should know how to swim, if there is no swimming pool or water available for such instruction, or, if a state regulation does not permit the use of a trampoline, it would be foolish to list such an activity as a goal. Individualized instruction in many activities is not possible without adequate staff. In addition, there are other influencing factors, such as climate, local school regulations, equipment available, and administrative philosophy, that must receive the attention of the physical educator in the development of goals.

What does the nature of the community indicate is the type of program that is needed?

The community itself—its social, economic, political, and physical makeup—

A

B

Fig. 5-2. A, The needs and interests of students are a vital consideration in the physical education program. **B,** Students in the physical education program, Brockport Central Schools, Brockport, N.Y.

should play an important role in the development of goals. For example, Americans are becoming aware that a different type of education is needed in the inner city and in poverty areas of this country than in suburbia. The program must be geared to the boys and girls who dwell in these neighborhoods. The fact that they are physically, emotionally, socially, and educationally disadvantaged has implications for education. The fact that many of the students are antiintellectual must be taken into consideration. Ethnic considerations are pertinent.

The physical education program has particular value and can make a valuable contribution to many boys and girls if it is related particularly to the conditions that exist in their communities and to the type of educational program needed to meet their needs and interests.

A consideration of the community is also important from the standpoint that its support and cooperation are needed if an excellent program of physical education is to be developed.

What is the physical educator's personal philosophy of education and physical education?

After all the previous steps have been taken into careful consideration, physical educators should give thought to their own personal philosophy of education and physical education. Their training, experience, and thought have resulted in a realization of what is valuable, what is educational, and the type of program that will make the greatest contribution to young people. When the first five steps, plus the development of a personal philosophy, are synthesized, they should provide a valid formula that, when implemented, will result in an excellent physical education program.

OBJECTIVES OF GENERAL EDUCATION

Teachers of physical education must be concerned with general educational goals before thinking of the goals of their special field. Since physical education is a part of general education, it is important to understand the purposes of education—why schools, teachers, and curricula exist. Physical education is one part of the educational program, as is geography, science, mathematics, foreign languages, or art. Each field of specialization needs to keep its sights on the purposes of general education if it is to justify its rightful place in the schools. If each area of specialization in secondary education established its own objectives irrespective of the overall goals of education, chaos would result, and programs of education would probably conflict and become distorted, depriving the students of a well-balanced educational experience. Therefore, each area of learning must realize that it is a part of the whole, and that the whole is greater than the sum of its parts.

For purposes of this discussion the goals of general education set forth several years ago by the Educational Policies Commission may be used. This influential policy-forming group pointed out that there are four major categories of educational objectives: (1) self-realization, (2) human relationship, (3) economic efficiency, and (4) civic responsibility. As one studies these objectives it can be seen that they relate to the cognitive, affective, and psychomotor domains discussed on pp. 89-90.

The objectives of self-realization are concerned with helping the individual to become all that he is capable of becoming. For example, education should help each boy and girl to speak, read, and write effectively, to acquire fundamental knowledge and habits concerned with healthful living, and to develop ability to use leisure time in a wholesome manner.

The objectives of human relations are concerned with assisting the individual to fully understand and relate to human beings working cooperatively with other human beings. Thus education should help to develop such things as an appreciation of the home, friendships, courtesy, the value of human welfare, and the ability to work harmoniously with one's fellowmen.

The objectives of economic efficiency relate to the individual as a producer and a worker and also as a buyer and a consumer. Therefore, these objectives stress, on the one hand, such things as the importance of good workmanship, selecting one's vocation carefully, occupational adjustment, appreciation, and efficiency and, on the other hand, such things as consumer judgment, buying, and protection.

The objectives of civic responsibility pertain to the function of the individual in a law-abiding society. These goals apply to such things as the citizen's responsibility to one's fellowmen, to country, and to the world; one's responsibility for being tolerant, scientific, critical, sympathetic, and cooperative as a member of a free society; and one's responsibility for developing an unswerving loyalty to the democratic way of life.

The four categories of objectives outlined by the Educational Policies Commission point to the overall purposes of education. The goals of physical education, therefore, must be compatible with and reinforce these objectives. The education that takes place at the gymnasium, playground, dance studio, swimming pool, and other play facilities can contribute much to the accomplishment of these worthy objectives.

GOALS FOR SECONDARY SCHOOL STUDENTS

Teachers of physical education, in addition to understanding and appreciating the goals of general education, must also be familiar with the goals that are peculiar to boys and girls who are pursuing their secondary school education. General educational goals and physical education objectives must be interpreted and delineated in terms of what students need at each stage of development and at each educational level through which they pass. At the secondary level teachers should be aware of the developmental goals and tasks that boys and girls are accomplishing and continually try to utilize the physical education program as a means of helping them to accomplish these worthy goals. Some of the developmental goals of secondary school students include the following:

1. Understanding of self. Students understand themselves physically, mentally, emotionally, and socially—how each aspect of self is reflected in personality and how to strive for integration of the various aspects of self so as to function harmoniously as a whole.

2. Feeling of security. Young people have security because of skills that have been developed for such tasks as protecting against danger, earning a living, and meeting physical needs. They have security within, and this sense of security embraces such conditions as being loved, possessing self-confidence, and having a feeling of belonging.

3. Realistic attitude. Young people have discovered their abilities and interests, have grown in understanding of self, and know their needs and capabilities. They are realistic in self-appraisal, accept themselves, and deal with situations and problems honestly and objectively.

4. Self-sufficiency. Young people become increasingly self-sufficient. They develop skills and interests that provide freedom from dependency on family and group. They are increasingly able to make decisions, do original thinking, and work out personal plans.

5. Flexibility. Young people profit from the thinking and experiences of others and are tolerant and understanding of the feelings of other people.

6. Social-mindedness. Young people establish satisfying relationships with boys and girls and with parents and adults, serve as participating citizens in school and community, learn about the social environment, gain experience in group living, learn to respect the rights of others and conform to the standard of acceptable behavior.

7. Balance. Young people have a variety of interests and are not interested in only one activity, such as basketball or reading, but develop a variety of interests that may include sports, drama, music, and history.

8. Sense of personal worth. Young people have self-respect and self-esteem and a sense of pride, achievement, mastery, usefulness, and success.

9. Emotional stability. Young people exercise self-control and adjust to changes in a mature manner.

10. Intellectual improvement. Young people develop basic mental skills, acquire knowledge, learn about the natural and physical environment, acquire better understanding of the scientific approach to learning, grow in ability to listen, read, think, speak, and write, and are motivated by learning.

11. Value consciousness. Young people appreciate what is right and wrong and the importance of striving for excellence, scholarly behavior, and proper ethical conduct.

If the boy or girl in secondary school can achieve these developmental tasks before completing this phase of education, he or she will have gone a long way toward becoming an educated and well-adjusted person and thus will have laid the foundations for productive, happy, and healthful living. Physical education can play an important role in helping each young person to be successful in accomplishing these goals.

WHAT THE PROGRAM SHOULD DO FOR EACH STUDENT

The physical education program should accomplish the following:

1. *Develop physical powers*

Body awareness	Coordination	Balance
Strength	Flexibility	Accuracy
Endurance	Speed	Posture
Muscular power	Agility	

2. *Develop skill in many activities*
   Movement fundamentals
   Fundamental activities (running, jumping, skipping)
   Individual sports (tennis, golf)
   Team sports (basketball, baseball, track and field)
   Gymnastics (tumbling and apparatus)
   Aquatics (swimming and diving)
   Rhythmic activities (dance)

3. *Facilitate understanding of physical activity*
   Movement principles (role of gravity, force)
   Contribution of physical activity to physical health (weight control, muscle tonus, relief of nervous tension, relaxation, absence of fatigue)
   Contributions of physical activity to mental health, for example, a desirable body image (research indicates the attitudes and feelings of a person toward one's body affect personality development); outlet for aggressions; release from tensions
   Contributions of physical activity to academic achievement (research indicates there is a correlation between motor development and academic achievement because of physical fitness, development of motor skills, better self-concept, and so on)

4. *Provide a meaningful social experience*
   Success in play activities
   Recognition and a feeling of belonging
   Learning to play by the rules
   Developing such social traits as honesty, sportsmanship, and reliability, which contribute to the development of a socially desirable personality
   Development of respect for other members of the class
   Development of respect for leadership
   Contribution to proper group adjustments

MAJOR OBJECTIVES OF PHYSICAL EDUCATION

The general objectives of physical education are usually stated in broad terms, with no distinction made for boys or girls. The physical education profession has selected, through its leading authorities, the general objectives of physical development, cognitive development, motor development, affective and social adjustment.

Physical development

Physical development refers to the building of organic power through development of the various systems of the body. It is concerned with a state of vigorous health and physical fitness. Physical power is built into the individual partially through participation in a program of physical activities. Such participation, if engaged in wisely and adapted to the needs of the individual, results in the ability to sustain adaptive effort, to recover, and to resist fatigue. The value of this objective is that an individual will be more active, have better performance, and be healthier if the organic systems of the body are functioning properly. Physical activity helps these organs to function properly. Through vigorous muscular activity the heart provides better nourishment for the body and the person is able to perform work for a longer period of time with less expenditure of energy. Such a condition is necessary for a vigorous and abundant life. Throughout the entire day a person is continually in need of vitality, strength, endurance, and stamina—both to perform routine tasks and to meet emergencies. A well-planned physical education program can help equip the student with these essential items.

Motor development

Neuromuscular skills are concerned with proficiency in the performance of physical activities. They include the coordination, rhythm, accuracy, and poise that lead to excellence in executing various games, sports, and physical skills. Motor development is concerned with cutting down waste motion, with performing physical acts in a proficient, graceful, and esthetic manner, and with utilizing as little energy as possible in the process. This has implications for one's work, play, and any other activity requiring physical movement. This objective is sometimes referred to as "motor" development, a name that is derived from the relationship between a nerve or nerve fiber that connects the central nervous system, or a ganglion, and a muscle. As a consequence of the impulse thus transmitted, movement results. The impulse the nerve delivers is known as the motor impulse.

Motor, or neuromuscular, development is essential to physical education. With increased cortical control of the body there is less waste motion; consequently, coordination and skill are increased. Greater skill and

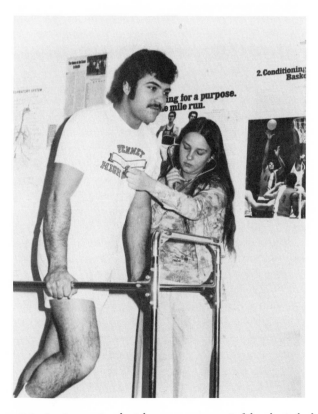

Fig. 5-3. Students participating in exercise physiology program as part of the physical education program at Penny High School, East Hartford, Conn. Girl is listening to boy's heart rate.

proficiency and fewer errors mean more enjoyment of the activity and a greater desire to engage in it. It is human nature to like to do those things in which one excels. It is very important to the physical education profession, to the individual, and to society in general to develop many and varied skills in the individual. In this way, the desire and motivation will be present to spend time regularly in activities that will result in a more totally fit population.

Cognitive development

Cognitive development involves knowledge and judgment, attendant on performing physical activities. It is concerned with an accumulation of knowledge essential to enriched living and the ability to think and to interpret situations continually encountered in day-to-day living. The accumulation of knowledge takes place when the person gains information concerning the body, the importance of exercise, the need for a well-balanced diet, and the values of good health attitudes and habits.

Cognitive development also includes knowledge of the importance of sanitation, factors in regard to disease prevention, community and school agencies that provide health services, rules and regulations in regard to various games and allied activities, techniques and strategies involved in organized play, human relations, and many other items useful in living a full life. The ability to think and to interpret situations is developed through many experiences in games and sports. These experiences foster alertness, the ability to diagnose a situation under tense conditions, the ability to make a decision quickly and wisely under highly emotional conditions, and the ability to interpret human actions. A body of knowledge is stored away so that it can be called upon at some future time to help in making discriminatory judgments, discerning right from wrong, and distinguishing the logical from the illogical.

Affective development

Affective development is concerned with helping the student adopt or establish ac-

ceptable interests, appreciations, attitudes, and values relating to physical education and physical activity. For example, this objective relates to the worth or value a student attaches to physical activity in his or her or other person's lifestyle, as well as to such things as personal behavior in game and sport situations. This can range in degree from a desire to improve group skills to assuming responsibilities for the effective functioning of a group such as a squad or team. Through participation in an excellent physical education program each student can learn desirable ways of associating with others, the need for cooperation, and the importance of being dependable, courteous and honest.

Affective development is also concerned with the development of an attitude that fosters good health habits and where a person seeks to develop a personal regimen that will contribute to physical fitness. The student appreciates the contribution that physical activity can make to his or her physical, mental, social, and emotional welfare.

Social development

Social development entails adjustment to self and to others and development of desirable standards of conduct essential to good citizenship. It represents one of the main contributions of physical education to modern society. Through physical activities the individual, under qualified leadership, can be aided in making adjustments. Physical education carries its own drive. Most children and youth do not have to be motivated to engage in many of the activities that are offered. They want to participate as a result of their own free choice and as a result of an inner drive that propels them into action. Under such conditions rules can be established and a framework of conduct set forth, and the individual will conform in order to participate. Good human relations are developed when there is respect for ability, one's desires are subordinated to the will of the group, aid is given to the less skilled and weaker players, and the realization exists that cooperation is essential to the success of society. Physical education further aids in developing a feeling of belonging, regard for the rules of sportsmanship and fair play, courtesy, sympathy, truthfulness, fairness, honesty, and respect for authority. All are essential to good human relations—one of the most important keys to a peaceful and democratic world.

BEHAVIORAL AND PERFORMANCE OBJECTIVES

Behavioral or performance objectives are terms frequently used in recent years and represent a method of specifically stating educational goals by observing and measuring student behavior.

It is generally agreed that students exhibit behavior in the three domains previously discussed: the cognitive, affective, and psychomotor. Behavioral and performance objectives may be developed for each of these domains, and they should contain two essential parts: the observable behavior and the criteria of acceptable performance. It is extremely important that behavioral and performance objectives be specific. For example, a behavioral objective might be as follows: the student will return the tennis ball in a forehand position over the net. This objective in the psychomotor domain specifically states that the observable behavior is returning the ball in a forehand position, and the criteria of acceptability is that the ball be returned over the net. The important point to remember is that physical educators must be specific in the behavior they want to elicit from the student.

PRIORITY OF OBJECTIVES IN PHYSICAL EDUCATION

Leaders of physical education are beginning to ask such questions as: Is one objective of physical education more important than the others? Where should the emphasis in physical education programs be placed? Physical educators cannot do everything— what comes first? Does physical education have a master purpose? Is there a hierarchy of objectives?

Historically, we have seen that physical education in its early days was primarily concerned with organic development. However, at the turn of the century with the introduction of the "new physical education," other objectives more closely identified with general education, such as social development, were included. Today, there are varying viewpoints in regard to the question of priority of objectives.

A survey of selected leaders in the field of physical education, asking for their views as to a priority of objectives, produced some interesting information. Most professionals contacted felt that organic development and motor development are the objectives that should get highest priority. They listed such reasons as they are most uniquely tied in with physical education, they are essential for fitness throughout life, they provide the impetus for the program, and they represent the objectives that can more readily be achieved. After organic and neuromuscular development, the leaders surveyed indicated that the objective most widely accepted as important is cognitive, mental, or interpretive development. The reasons listed for the importance of this objective included the fact that it is important to develop a favorable attitude toward physical education if any objective is to be achieved at all. Also included was the fact that education is primarily involved with developing a thinking, rational human being in respect to all matters, whether it be concerned with his physical development or other aspects of living. Social development ranked lowest in the survey. Reasons given to support this place on the priority listing were that all areas of education are interested in the social objective and that it was not the unique responsibility of one field, such as physical education. Therefore, the other objectives should receive a higher priority rating.

The survey of national leaders in physical education brought out another important consideration. Many professional leaders stressed the point that with the national curriculum reform movement taking place today and with increased emphasis on educational priorities, physical educators should rethink their positions in regard to their place in the educational system. They should reexamine how they can contribute their greatest effort

92 *The goals and program*

Table 5-1. Comparison ranking of objectives of physical education*

Objective	Ranking
Organic vigor	1
Neuromuscular skills	2
Leisure-time activities	3
Self-realization	4
Emotional stability	5
Democratic values	6
Mental development	7
Social competency	8
Spiritual and moral strength	9
Cultural appreciation	10

*From Rosentswieg, J.: A ranking of the objectives of physical education, Research Quarterly **40**:783, 1969.

Table 5-2. Ranking of objectives by sex*

Objective	Ranking	
	Males	Females
Organic vigor	1	2
Neuromuscular skills	2	1
Leisure-time activities	3	3
Self-realization	4	4
Emotional stability	5	5
Social competency	6	8
Democratic values	7	7
Mental development	8	6
Spiritual and moral strength	9	9
Cultural appreciation	10	10

*From Rosentswieg, J.: A ranking of the objectives of physical education, Research Quarterly **40**:783, 1969.

and make their greatest contribution in today's changing world.

Rosentswieg* conducted a study in which he had 100 college physical educators in Texas rank ten objectives of physical education. Rosentswieg's findings showed that these 100 physical educators ranked the organic and neuromuscular objectives higher than all the rest. When the men physical educators were compared with the women physical educators, there was disagreement upon the primary objective of physical education. The statistical results of the study are illustrated in Tables 5-1 to 5-2.

LEADERSHIP—THE KEY TO ACCOMPLISHMENT OF PROFESSIONAL OBJECTIVES

Leadership is essential in the field of physical education if the goals that have been set for this profession are to be realized. The most elaborate facilities can be provided and the necessary materials can be at hand, but unless there are qualified leaders available, programs will fail. These leaders must have certain general and specific qualifications if they are to do an acceptable piece of work. Leaders will be better able to accomplish physical education objectives if they possess the following qualities:

---

*Rosentswieg, J.: A ranking of the objectives of physical education, Research Quarterly **40**:783, 1969.

1. Sound judgment, logical thinking, common sense, and the ability to discriminate right from wrong.

2. Functional use of written and oral English. Since the use of English is so essential in effectively presenting programs to the public, this qualification is required. In addition, because physical education leaders are emulated by the thousands of youths who engage in their programs, they must set a good example by using correct English.

3. Acceptable health. Leaders should be free from any physical or mental defects that would prevent successful leadership. Because of the important part leaders play in shaping the lives of those they lead, persons with any health handicap that would adversely affect the consumer of the product should not be a part of this profession. Leaders should be in a state of buoyant, robust health so that they may carry out their duties regularly and effectively. They should be able to teach by doing and to participate in the activities they recommend to others. Good health is essential if this function is to be performed effectively. Most important, however, the physical education leader should be an example for the profession that stresses the importance of a healthy body.

4. Pleasant personality. Such traits as enthusiasm, friendliness, cheerfulness, industry, cooperation, dependability, self-control, integrity, and likableness are essential to working with people in a manner that will

ensure the success of the programs concerned.

5. Interest in and understanding of human beings. Leaders should be familiar with the needs of the atypical as well as the normal individual. They should be conscious of the interests and capacities of those with whom they will work. Leaders should enjoy working with people. They should get along well with others, be interested in people, be able to obtain their respect, and be able to adapt to various social settings. Such qualities as patience, loyalty, tactfulness, sympathetic attitude, sincerity, friendliness, tolerance, reliability, and a good temperament are some of the essential attributes to develop if this qualification is to be met.

6. A sincere interest in the profession. Leaders should be willing to contribute generously of time and effort to the advancement of the profession. Individuals must believe in what they are doing and conscientiously strive to promote their work so that more people may share its benefits.

7. Skill in many of the activities that constitute the program. Skill is essential in appreciating and demonstrating good performance, instilling confidence, knowing the work that constitutes the profession, and adequately interpreting the program to the public.

8. Technical training. Specialized training is essential for the field of physical education. An understanding of the fundamental sciences and of scientific principles in the areas of philosophy, administration, and methods and materials, in addition to many other areas of knowledge, is necessary to the development of physical educators.

The qualifications that have been listed are essential to one who desires to become a leader. Physical education work has appeal to many, but not all are qualified to become leaders in this endeavor. Only those who meet the essential qualifications should be considered. In the hands of good leadership, methods and materials may be used effectively and wisely.

Physical education leaders often remark that inadequate facilities are preventing them from doing a job, that it is impossible to have a good program without essential indoor and outdoor equipment, and that the program is not recognized because of these deficiencies.

Acres of beautiful green grass, spacious gymnasiums, and special equipment for sports and other physical education activities are very helpful. Other things being equal, they result in programs that better meet the needs and interests of the public than do programs that have poor resources. However, one must strive to do an effective job with what is available. Programs must be built on the status quo while effort is expended to obtain more and better facilities. Many needs can be satisfied by improvising and by obtaining auxiliary playing fields and space to tide over an emergency period. Doing an effective job with what is available is one of the best ways to stimulate good public relations to the point where additional facilities will be provided. The public must recognize the need for the program and how it is helping to build a better community. When the community is able to see how it can be further aided by additional facilities, the response will be greater. This will not be the situation if the leader exhibits apathy, indifference, and lassitude because ample resources are not provided.

There is an increasing need for better qualified leaders in physical education. There must be a stringent selective policy for all preprofessional students, and standards must be established that allow only qualified individuals to become members of the profession. Only in this way will it be possible to adequately meet the needs and interests of the public, obtain their respect and enthusiasm for this work, and realize the potentialities of this great profession.

The fact that many undergraduate students and leaders in physical education do not have sufficient knowledge of the many activities that comprise their programs presents a problem. Better professional preparation in our colleges and in-service education in the schools will help in solving the problem.

Another problem encountered by many professional leaders is that of large instructional groups. Under these conditions the ratio of leaders to participants is usually very low—a few leaders are responsible for many students. To do a sound instructional job under such conditions, many important factors cannot be overlooked. There must be advance planning that takes into consideration all the equipment, visual aids, and other materials that will be needed. There must be good organization of the class, of materials, and of other essential items. Good teaching methods and proper techniques must be utilized. Safety precautions must be stressed. These items deserve attention even in smaller classes but must have special attention in large groups.

IMPORTANCE OF METHODS AND MATERIALS IN REALIZING PHYSICAL EDUCATION OBJECTIVES

Where do methods and materials fit into the total picture of leadership and teaching of physical education? The goals of physical education are worthy ones and should be accomplished in the most economical, thorough, and beneficial way possible. Since the activities that comprise physical education are the media through which the objectives are to be achieved, they should be taught by utilizing the best methods of organization and presentation that can be compiled. The methods and materials that are used should represent the experience and training of those who have worked with these activities for many years and who, through their training and experience, know the method that is most effective under various situations. The use of such methods and materials will result in the best teaching and learning situations, with consequent interest, acquisition of knowledge and skill, and proper attitudes on the part of the learner-participant.

This book shows how activities may be presented with a minimum of equipment. Improvisations, sport and game variations, and teaching aids and materials that provide the best results under existing circumstances

are set forth. The material allows for the presentation of activities in situations where limiting factors such as inadequate facilities are present. Also included are various techniques of presenting activities, teaching, and evaluating, as well as other aids that are useful in program development.

Self-assessment tests

These tests are to assist students in determining if material and competencies presented in this chapter have been mastered:

1. Given: two departments of physical education in two different secondary schools. One department has clearly outlined goals it wishes to achieve. The other department has not given any thought to such goals. What do you project as to what will be the nature and scope of each department's program of physical education?
2. Develop a modus operandi for determining the goals that you feel a physical education program should achieve.
3. Without consulting the text, state in your own words the objectives of general education.
4. You have been asked by the Parent-Teacher Association to give a speech on the major objectives for the physical education program in a secondary school. Prepare an outline of this speech indicating each objective and your rationale for selecting it as a goal.
5. List what you consider to be the order of importance of each of the objectives of physical education. Present documentation to support your thinking.
6. For each of the objectives of physical education indicate how methods and materials are important to the accomplishment of that objective.

Points to remember

1. An understanding of the goals of physical education.
2. Importance of knowing the objectives of physical education.
3. Scientific principles upon which physical education programs need to be based.
4. The role of the leader in accomplishing the objectives of physical education.
5. Importance of methods and materials in achieving the objectives of physical education.

Problems to think through

1. Why is a teacher who does not know the objectives of his or her profession somewhat like a ship without a rudder?
2. Why should the goals of physical education give support to and help accomplish general education goals?

Case study for analysis

Select a secondary school and study the program of physical education to determine how well this educational system is accomplishing the four major goals of our profession.

Exercises for review

1. Read four professional books in the field of physical education and list and discuss the goals of physical education as described by the authors.
2. Categorize the specific values of physical education under each of the four major objectives.
3. What knowledge should a student possess in regard to physical education?
4. Describe a physically educated boy and a physically educated girl.
5. Why is leadership so important in the achievement of educational objectives?

Selected readings

American Alliance for Health, Physical Education and Recreation: Knowledge and understanding in physical education, Washington, D.C., 1969, AAHPER.

Annarino, A. A.: The five traditional objectives of physical education, Journal of Health, Physical Education and Recreation 41:24, 1970.

Ariel, G.: Physical education: 2001, Quest 21:49, 1974.

Bloom, B. S., editor: Taxonomy of educational objectives. Handbook I. Cognitive domain, New York, 1956, David McKay Co., Inc.

Bloom, B. J., Hastings, J., et al: Handbook on formative and summative evaluation of student learning, New York, 1971, McGraw-Hill Book Company.

Cratty, B. J.: Teaching motor skills, Englewood Cliffs, 1973, Prentice-Hall, Inc.

Dillon, S. V., and Franks, D. D.: Open learning environment: self identity and coping ability, The Educational Forum 39:155, 1975.

Gronlund, N. E.: Stating behavioral objectives for classroom instruction, New York, 1970, Macmillan Publishing Co., Inc.

Harrow, A. J.: A taxonomy of the psychomotor domain, New York, 1972, David McKay Co.

Jewett, A. L., et al.: Educational change through a taxonomy for writing physical education objectives, Quest 15:32, 1971.

Martens, R.: Social psychology and physical activity, New York, 1975, Harper & Row.

Maslow, A. Psychological data and values theory. In Abraham Maslow, editor: New knowledge in human values, Chicago, 1971, Henry Tegnery Co.

Park, R. J.: Alternatives and other ways: how might physical activity be more relevant to human needs in the future? Quest 21:30, 1974.

Robb, M. D.: The dynamics of motor skill acquisition, Englewood Cliffs, N.J., 1972, Prentice-Hall, Inc.

Rosentswieg, J.: A ranking of the objectives of physical education, Research Quarterly 40:783, 1969.

Tanner, D.: Using behavioral objectives in the classroom, New York, 1972, Macmillan Publishing Co., Inc.

6

ACHIEVING HEALTH GOALS THROUGH PHYSICAL EDUCATION

INSTRUCTIONAL OBJECTIVES AND COMPETENCIES TO BE ACHIEVED

After reading this chapter the student should be able to—

1. Show the relationship of physical education to the health of the student in the secondary school.
2. List the objectives of the health program in the secondary school.
3. Demonstrate how the physical education program can contribute to the students' health knowledge, health attitudes, and desirable health practices.
4. Describe effective methods and materials for teaching health knowledge, attitudes, and practices in the secondary school.
5. Outline the guiding principles that will help physical education in achieving relevant health goals.

A recent study for the National Institute of Alcohol Abuse and Alcoholism found that 28 percent of the nation's teenagers are problem drinkers. More than one out of every four were drunk at least four times in the last year or their drinking got them into trouble with peers or superiors at least twice in the last year. The research further pointed out that beer was the teenagers' most popular beverage, boys drank more often and more heavily than girls, and children of drinking parents tended to drink more frequently than offspring of parents who were abstain-ers. Only 18 percent of the nation's 17-year-olds had never taken a drink, although the legal drinking age in all states is at least 18.

This study illustrates only one of the myriad of health problems that affect the secondary school student population. In addition, the incidence of smoking, venereal disease, poor physical fitness, inadequate nutrition, and many other problems are prevalent among our students. In many instances, physical education can help to contribute to the health of our younger people. Therefore, this chapter is included to show some of the ways by which physical educators can help to promote better health habits among their students.

State departments of education and health, voluntary and official health agencies, and other interested groups, individuals, and organizations are mobilizing their resources in an all out effort to acquaint boys and girls with the need for good health and the practices necessary to achieve this goal. Physical education must also contribute to this important objective.

Physical education has a direct relationship to the health of secondary school boys and girls. The ultimate objective of any health education program is to maintain and improve the health of the youngsters in the schools. This refers to all aspects of health, including physical, mental, emotional, and social. The school has the responsibility to see that all students achieve and maintain optimum health, not only from a legal point of view but also from the standpoint that the educational experience will be much more meaningful if optimum health exists. A child learns more easily when in a state of good health.

Physical educators will find many teachable moments when it is possible to contribute to the achievement of health goals. The opportunity is provided to impart scientifically accurate information that will contribute to better health habits on the part of students when they ask: "Why will it be necessary to take showers?" "Must we bring clean towels?" "Why must uniforms be clean?" Physical educators are trained in the biological sciences. This foundational science information provides accurate factual information on various health subjects that have a direct bearing on the health of students.

Physical educators can see that the health services of the school and community are understood and utilized by the students in the physical education program whether they involve emergency care, health appraisal, communicable disease control, or other health measures.

Physical educators should provide an environment that promotes health, growth, and learning. For example, they should cooperate with the custodian in providing safe and sanitary facilities that meet acceptable health standards; in providing proper ventilation, heating, and lighting in the settings for physical education activities; in seeing that all equipment is in a safe and clean condition; and in providing a proper social and emotional atmosphere for the conduct of the program. They should conduct regular inspections of facilities and equipment, institute rules that will promote safety in various activities, establish procedures to be followed in the event of illness or injury to participants, and provide proper insurance protection.

Fig. 6-1. Instructor in physical education at Hampton Institute in Hampton, Va., helps students to achieve health goals.

Physical educators should be cognizant of the health of students in the conduct of the program, being continually alert to their health practices and encouraging them to improve. They should take an interest in each student's total physical, emotional, social, and mental health.

Physical educators can help in the attainment of several specific objectives that the health program is attempting to accomplish in the schools. They are (1) to provide boys and girls with *health knowledge* that is reliable and based on scientific facts, (2) to help young people develop desirable *health attitudes*, and (3) to stimulate students to develop desirable *health practices*. This chapter outlines some specific ways in which the physical educator may help in the achievement of these worthy objectives.

HEALTH KNOWLEDGE

Physical educators have many opportunities to present and interpret scientific health data for purposes of personal guidance. Such information will help students recognize health problems and solve them by utilizing information that is valid and helpful.

It also will serve as a basis for the formation of desirable health attitudes. In today's complex society there are many choices confronting students in regard to factors that affect their health. A reliable store of knowledge is essential to making sound decisions.

Young people should know such things as how their bodies function, causes of infections, methods of preventing disease, factors that contribute to and maintain health, and the role of the community in the health program. Such knowledge will help boys and girls to live correctly, help them to protect their bodies against harm and infection, and impress upon them the responsibility for their own health and the health of others.

Presentation of facts about health varies with different age groups and educational levels. For young children in the early grades there should be an attempt to provide experiences that will show the importance of living healthfully. Such settings as the cafeteria, lavatory, and medical examination room offer excellent opportunities for such learning. When a boy or girl becomes a secondary school student, the underlying reasons for following certain health practices

Fig. 6-2. Education should try to develop sound attitudes toward safety—a goal in the New York City schools.

and ways of living can be presented. Some of the areas of health knowledge that should be understood by students and that can be presented by physical educators include nutrition, the need for rest, sleep, exercise, and protection of the body against changing temperature conditions, contagious disease control, the dangers of self-medication, and community resources for health.

The following are a few areas of health knowledge that can be imparted by physical educators at the secondary school level:

1. Safety education as applied to physical education activities
2. Accident prevention as applied to physical education activities
3. Dangers of self-medication
4. How to dress for warmth, comfort, and protection
5. Sanitary practices involved in physical education participation
6. Available community health services
7. Organic systems of the human body
8. Good body mechanics
9. Physical limitation and fatigue
10. Effect of depressants upon the human body
11. Effect of stimulants upon the human body
12. Structures of the human body
13. How to safeguard eyes and vision
14. Physical defects and how to correct or live with them
15. Communicable and noncommunicable diseases and minor health disorders— how to prevent and control
16. Nutrition and weight control
17. Good grooming
18. Importance of an adequate and a balanced use of free time for relaxation and recreation
19. Relationship between exercise and good health
20. Need for physical activity to develop and strengthen the body
21. First aid procedures
22. Amount of sleep and rest a student needs
23. Necessity and importance of the medical examination
24. Physical fitness and health
25. First aid
26. Drugs and physical health and athletic performance

HEALTH ATTITUDES

Health attitudes refer to the health interests of persons or the motives behind health practices. All the health knowledge that can be accumulated will have little worth unless the student is interested and motivated to apply this knowledge to everyday living. Proper health attitudes, motives, drives, or impulses will cause a boy or girl to seek out scientific knowledge and utilize it as a guide to living. This interest, drive, or motivation must be dynamic to the point where it results in behavior changes.

The physical education program should be directed toward developing those attitudes that will result in optimum health. Students should be motivated to be in a state of buoyant health, feeling fit and strong, well rested and well fed, to have wholesome thoughts free from anger, jealousy, hate, and worry, and possess adequate physical power to perform life's routine tasks. If they have the right attitudes toward health knowledge, healthful living, and such health services as medical examinations, proper health practices will be followed. Health should not be an end in itself except in cases of severe illness. Health is a means to an end—it aids in achieving noble purposes and living an enriched life.

Another factor that motivates boys and girls to good health is the desire to avoid the pain and disturbances that accompany ill health. They do not like toothaches, headaches, or indigestion because of the pain or distraction involved. However, developing health attitudes in a negative manner, through fear of pain or other disagreeable conditions, is not as desirable as the positive approach to achieving proper health attitudes.

A strong argument for developing proper attitudes or interests centers around the goals the students are trying to achieve in life and the manner in which optimum health is an aid in achieving such goals. This is the strong-

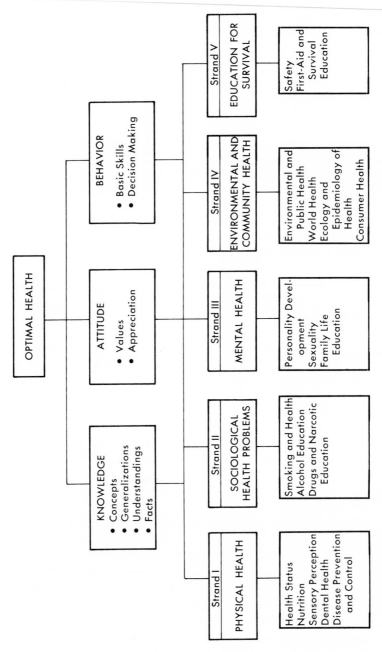

Fig. 6-3. New York state optimal health chart. (University of the State of New York, State Education Department, Albany, N.Y.)

est incentive or interest that can be developed in the individual. A great artist, an outstanding businessman, or a famed dancer is greatly benefited by good health. It is important that the study, training, hard work, trials, and obstacles encountered be met successfully. Optimum health will aid in the accomplishment of such goals. As Jennings the biologist pointed out, the mind can attend to only one thing at a time. If attention is focused on a headache or an ulcer, it cannot be satisfactorily focused on essential work that has to be done.

Some of the health attitudes that the physical educator can help to develop include an interest in the following:

1. Attaining and maintaining good health
2. Obtaining accurate scientific information concerning health
3. Forming proper nutrition and eating habits
4. Preventing accidents
5. Recognizing the roles of physical activity, sleep, rest, and relaxation in physical fitness
6. Separating health fact from fancy
7. Understanding one's physical limitations
8. Correcting any remediable body defects
9. Developing good health habits
10. Evaluating one's health habits and making needed changes
11. Understanding how one's body can function to utmost capacity
12. Using the body in an efficient, graceful manner in sports activities and daily life
13. Mastering and enjoying a wide range of physical activities
14. Providing for play and large-muscle activities, as well as daily relaxation, in order to realize optimum achievement in physical and mental well-being
15. Knowing how various organic systems of the body work together
16. Acknowledging health responsibility as a member of a school, community, and family
17. Accepting reasonable responsibility in keeping the school, home, and community environment neat and clean
18. Participating in social and play activities with others
19. Being a good sportsman and taking failures and successes in stride
20. Learning to accept physical handicaps of self and others
21. Recognizing the effects of drugs, alcohol, narcotics, and tobacco on performance in physical activities

HEALTH PRACTICES

Desirable health practices represent the application to one's routine of living of those habits that are best, according to the most qualified thinking in the field. An individual's health practices will to a large extent determine his or her state of health. Harmful practices or habits, such as failure to obtain proper rest or exercise, overeating, overdrinking, and oversmoking, as well as the failure to observe certain precautions against contracting disease, will often result in poor health.

Knowledge does not necessarily ensure good health practices. An individual may have at his or her command all the statistics concerning the dangers of speeding on the highway; yet this information is useless unless it is applied. The health of an individual can be affected only as applied to that which is known. At the same time, knowledge will not usually be applied unless an incentive, interest, or attitude exists that impels its application. It is important, therefore, to see the close relationship that exists among health knowledge, health attitudes, and health practices. One contributes to the other.

Listed below are a few health practices with which every physical educator teaching at the secondary school level should be especially concerned:

1. To prevent the spread of infection, insist that each member of an athletic team or physical education class have an individual towel and drinking cup and personal articles of clothing.

2. To prevent the spread of infection (such as colds, influenza, mumps, and measles), do not allow students to exercise or engage in a strenuous workout while an infection is still resident.

3. Give proper first-aid treatment promptly to floor or mat burns or other abrasions and wounds suffered in physical activity.

4. Have a physician present at all interscholastic contests in which the injury hazard is great.

5. Do not allow a player to reenter a game following a severe injury, particularly when unconsciousness or injury to the head or spine has occurred.

6. Work closely with the medical adviser and health department in all matters that are medical in nature, such as treating infected wounds. Honor all excuses from physicians.

7. Maintain a sanitary environment in the locker and shower rooms, gymnasium, swimming pools, and other facilities of the physical education department.

8. Insist on clean clothing, towels, and so on for all types of physical education activities.

9. Discuss with physicians, the medical society, nurses, and other qualified persons the school policy that should govern excuses from physical education for health reasons.

10. Encourage students with colds and other illnesses to remain home.

11. Make the health and welfare of students the primary considerations in planning all physical education and athletic programs.

12. See that students have adequate medical examinations if they participate in any of the various phases of the physical education program.

13. Conduct an athletic program in which contests are adapted to the physical capacities and other needs of the student.

14. Plan the playing seasons for athletics so that they will be of a reasonable duration, with no postseason contests. Make sure players are well conditioned before competition is conducted.

15. Encourage all boys and girls to receive proper sleep, rest, and nutrition and to develop other desirable health practices essential to physical performance and sound health.

16. Do not include boxing as part of the physical education program.

17. Be qualified in first aid.

18. In planning classes, allow time to permit change of clothing and showering.

19. Provide an opportunity for each student to participate in physical education class and the intramural sports program.

20. Give appropriate guidance to community groups sponsoring organized competitive athletics.

21. Offer a wide variety of activities based upon students' interests and needs.

22. Group students for participation on the basis of their abilities and needs.

SELECTED METHODS OF TEACHING HEALTH KNOWLEDGE, ATTITUDES, AND PRACTICES

Some methods of teaching health information to students are as follows.

Discussions. The classroom, gymnasium athletic field, and other places where students gather offer many desirable moments for presenting and discussing important health information.

Example. A teacher's example is a very powerful method.

Films and other visual aids. Many excellent health films are available from state departments of health, voluntary health agencies, universities, and professional associations.

Reading assignments. There is a considerable amount of health material available, in a pamphlet form as well as in book form. Bucher's high school physical education text, entitled *Physical Education for Life,** contains several chapters on health matters relating to the physical education program.

---

*See Selected Readings.

By being selective, teachers of physical education can assign readings that will give meaning to the health principles they are trying to impart.

Speakers. The school doctor, team physician, outstanding community personality, professional sportsman, or other person can be brought in from time to time to accent the importance of health.

Special projects. Health Day, Physical Fitness Week, Clean-up Week, Work Day, and other projects can be utilized to focus attention on various aspects of health.

Awards. An award in the form of a letter, certificate, or other form of recognition can be given to the healthiest student or to the boy or girl who ranks highest on the physical fitness tests, on a health knowledge examination, or the like.

Experiments. An actual experiment such as feeding two rats different diets will work wonders in putting across health information to students.

PRINCIPLES TO KEEP IN MIND IN FURTHERING HEALTH OBJECTIVES

1. Physical activities should be included in the program only as the pupils' health status warrants. This means that such factors as students' strength, organic or functional disorders, muscular development, physical disabilities, and coordination, as ascertained through medical examinations, are taken into consideration.

2. All students should participate in the physical education program.

3. Class size should be sufficiently small to permit effective instruction and activity. A general guide would be to enroll not more than forty pupils in a class.

4. Every precautionary measure possible should be taken to provide for safety and to prevent accidents.

5. The intramural, extramural, and interscholastic athletic programs should be laboratory periods for the class instructional program and should be conducted in the light of the welfare and health interests of those who participate.

6. Every school should have a well-defined plan that provides for the proper medical and health considerations of each pupil. This means that there should be well-thought-through policies governing procedures for prevention of disease, emergency care in event of accidents, environmental sanitation, medical examinations, and so on.

7. The physical education program should establish and enforce sound hygienic standards.

8. The physical education teacher should be sure that each student understands the impact of food, drugs, smoking, and the use of alcoholic beverages on physical performance.

9. Teachers of physical education should have an understanding and an appreciation of the school health program and a desire to further the health of their pupils.

Self-assessment tests

These tests are to assist students in determining if material and competencies presented in this chapter have been mastered:

1. You have heard a classmate say that the physical education program has little to contribute to the health of the secondary school student with the exception of teaching him or her physical skills. Present a rebuttal to your classmate's statement, showing the relationship of the physical education program to the health of secondary school students.
2. A parent wants to know the major objectives of the health program in the secondary school. What will be your answer?
3. Prepare a chart in which you show the following headings or goals: (a) health knowledge, (b) health attitudes, and (c) desirable health practices. Opposite each of these headings indicate the various ways in which physical education can help to achieve each of the goals.
4. Prepare a unit for the teaching of a physical education activity, such as basketball. Indicate the methods and materials you will use to impart and develop health knowledge, attitudes, and practices in the students as part of the unit.
5. Prepare a plan to submit to physical educators in a department of physical education that proposes a set of guiding principles to follow in achieving health goals in the physical education program.

Points to remember

1. An understanding of the relationship of physical education to the health of the student.
2. An appreciation of ways in which the physical educator can contribute to the health of the student.
3. Health facts that physical education can teach to students.

4. Health attitudes that physical educators can help to develop in students.
5. Health practices that physical educators can help to develop in students.
6. Effective techniques and means of presenting health information.

Case study for analysis

Through a program of testing and observation, determine the amount of scientific health knowledge possessed by a high school boy and girl, their attitudes toward health, and the health practices that are a part of their daily routine. Analyze this health information in light of the contribution a physical educator can make.

Exercises for review

1. What are some of the outstanding objectives of any school health program?
2. What should each secondary school student know about his or her body?
3. What is the relationship of attitudes to health practices?
4. What are some methods of motivating high school boys and girls to develop good health practices?
5. Why is it better to use the "positive" approach in the teaching of health?

6. Discuss and illustrate five methods of presenting health information to students.
7. Prepare a list of basic principles essential to making physical education a dynamic force in furthering the health of secondary school students.

Selected readings

Bucher, C. A.: Physical education for life, New York, 1969, McGraw-Hill Book Company.

Bucher, C. A.: Administration of health and physical education programs, including athletics, ed. 6, St. Louis, 1975, The C. V. Mosby Co.

Bucher, C. A., Olsen, E. A., and Willgoose, C. E.: The foundations of health, New York, 1976, Prentice-Hall, Inc.

Diehl, H. S., et al.: Health and safety for you, New York, 1975, McGraw-Hill Book Company.

Haag, J. H.: Health education for young adults, Austin, Texas, 1973, Steck-Vaughn Co.

Miller, B. F., and Burt, J. J.: Good health, personal and community, Philadelphia, 1972, W. B. Saunders Co.

Schriver, A., et al.: Your health and safety, New York, 1977, Harcourt, Brace, Jovanovich.

Willgoose, C.: Health teaching in secondary schools, Philadelphia, 1977, W. B. Saunders Company.

7

A RELEVANT PHYSICAL EDUCATION PROGRAM: IMPLICATIONS OF TITLE IX

INSTRUCTIONAL OBJECTIVES AND COMPETENCIES TO BE ACHIEVED

After reading this chapter the student should be able to—

1. Describe the component parts of the total school physical education program.
2. Indicate the role of the basic instructional physical education program as it relates to the other component parts of the total program.
3. Define what is meant by the adapted program and mainstreaming and the contributions they make to the secondary school student.
4. Compare the intramural and extramural with the interscholastic athletic program.
5. Enumerate the changes that should take place in the physical education program as a result of Title IX.
6. Evaluate a physical education program.

Physical education is an integral part of the total education process and has as its aim the development of physically, mentally, emotionally, and socially fit citizens through the medium of physical activities that have been selected with a view to realizing these outcomes. This is the definition of physical education that is recommended for this important field of endeavor.

• *Physical education should be an integral part of the total system of education.* Its value is determined by its contributions to the objectives of education in general. It is one part of the total educational process and therefore must contribute to the achievement of the objectives of general education.

• *Physical education should promote the optimum physical, mental, emotional, moral, and social development of each student as a contributing member of a free and democratic society.* It is concerned not only with training the physical self but with the mental, social, and emotional aspects of human development. Its worth is associated with such things as health, organic efficiency, character, and personality. It helps each pupil in the process of normal growth and natural development.

• *A study of needs and interests of students is essential in determining the type of program content and methods for a physical education program.* The program does not exist apart from the student. The program must be made to fit the needs and interests of students, not the students made to fit the program.

Components of the secondary school physical education program have been listed by many authors and under a variety of terms.

The four components of the school physical education program used here are (1) the basic instructional class program, (2) the adapted program, (3) the intramural and extramural programs, and (4) the interschool program.

THE BASIC INSTRUCTIONAL CLASS PROGRAM

Where sound basic instructional class programs of physical education exist, they have been developed on the basis of the physical, social, mental, and emotional needs of the students. A broad and varied program of activities, both outdoor and indoor, progressively arranged and adapted to the capacities and abilities of each student, is offered.

Following are some important considerations for the basic instructional class program of physical education at the secondary level for boys and girls.

Instructional nature

• *The physical education class is a place to teach the skills, strategy, appreciation, understanding, knowledge, rules, regulations, and other material and information that are part of the program.* It is not a place for free play, intramurals, and varsity competition. It is a place for instruction. Every minute of the class period should be devoted to teaching boys and girls the skills and subject matter of physical education.

• *Instruction should be basic and interesting.* Skills should be broken down into simple components and taught so that each individual may understand clearly what he or she is expected to accomplish and at the same time how it should be done. Utilization of demonstrations, loop films, models, slide films, posters, and other visual aids and materials can help to make the instruction more meaningful and interesting.

• *Instruction should be progressive.* There should be a definite progression from simple to complex skills. Just as a student progresses in mathematics from simple arithmetic to algebra, geometry, and calculus, so in physical education the pupil should progress from basic skills and materials to more complex and involved skills and strategies.

• *Instruction should involve definite standards.* Students should be expected to reach individualized standards of achievement in the class program. A reasonable amount of

Fig. 7-1. Students engaging in judo exercise as part of physical education program. Courtesy New York University.

skill—whether it is in swimming, tennis, or another activity—should be mastered, depending upon individual differences. Laxity and indifference to achievement should not be tolerated any more in physical education than in any other subject area in the curriculum. When boys and girls graduate from high school they should have met definite standards that indicate that they are *physically educated.*

• *Instruction should involve more than physical activity.* All physical education classes do not have to be held in the gymnasium where physical activity predominates. A reasonable proportion of class time, perhaps as much as 10 percent to 20 percent, can be devoted to discussions, lectures, independent study, working on learning packages, and meaningful classroom activity. Outstanding coaches often have chalk talks for their players, in which they study rules and regulations, strategies, execution of skills, and other materials that are essential to playing the game effectively. This same principle can be applied to the physical education class period. There is a subject matter content that the student needs to know and understand. Physical activity should not be conducted in a vacuum; if it is, it has no meaning and will not be applied when the youngster leaves the class and school. As the student understands more fully the importance of sports and activities in life, what happens to the body during exercise, the history of the various activities in which he or she engages, and the role of physical activity in the culture of the world, the class takes on new meaning and physical education takes on new respect and prestige.

• *A textbook should be used.* Just as other subjects in the secondary school program utilize textbooks in their courses, so can physical education profitably use a textbook. Assignments can be made, discussions held, and tests given—all of which will provide the student with a much more meaningful learning experience. Physical education should not be a "snap" course. It has content, and knowledge and appreciation are to be gained from this subject just as they are, for example, in American history. Bucher has written a high school physical education textbook for student use—*Physical Education for Life.**

• *There should be records.* Adequate records should be kept by the instructor to provide tangible evidence of the degree to which objectives are being met by the students. This means that data on physical fitness, skill achievement, knowledge of rules and other information, and social conduct—such as sportsmanship—should be a part of the record.

• *There should be homework.* It is just as reasonable to assign homework in physical education as in general science. There is much subject matter to be learned and many skills to be mastered. If teachers would require their students to work on various activity skills and knowledge outside of class, there would be more time in class for meaningful teaching.

• *Each student should have a health examination before participating in the physical education program.* An annual health examination should be regarded as a minimum essential to determining the amount and nature of physical activity that best meets each student's needs.

• *The teaching load of physical educators should be determined not only by the number of instructional class periods assigned but also by the total number of activities handled by the teacher both in class and outside of class.* To do efficient work a teacher should have a normal work load—not an overload. Some professional standards have established that class instruction should not exceed five hours, or the equivalent of five class periods per day.

Student requirements

Physical education represents a need of every child, just as do English, social studies, and other school experiences. Physical education became part of the school offering as a required subject to satisfy such a need and

---

*See Selected Readings.

therefore should be continued on the same basis.

All students should take physical education. No one should be excused. If a boy or girl can come to school, he or she should be required to attend physical education class. At the same time, this presupposes that a program adapted to the needs of *all* pupils is provided.

The student is compelled to take so many required courses that elective courses are limited, if not entirely eliminated. If physical education is not required, many students will not have the opportunity to partake of this program because of the pressures placed on them by the required courses. In addition the student looks upon those subjects that are required as being the most important and the most necessary for success. If physical education is not on the required list, it becomes a subject of second-rate importance in the eyes of students.

Various subjects in the curriculum would not be provided for unless they were required. This is probably true of physical education. Until state legislatures passed laws requiring physical education, this subject was ignored by many school administrators. If physical education were on an elective basis, it could be crowded out of the school curriculum in many communities. Either the subject would not be offered at all or it would have to be eliminated because of low enrollment.

Even under a required program, physical education is not fulfilling its potentialities for meeting the physical, social, and mental needs of students in most schools. If an elective program were instituted, deficiencies and shortages would increase, thus further handicapping the attempt to meet the welfare and needs of the student.

Physical educators should try very hard to convince administrators, school boards, and the public in general of the place of their special subject in the curriculum of the secondary school. Only as this is done will the subject occupy an important place in the school and become a required offering that is respected.

Daily period

On the secondary level there should be a daily period for physical education or, through flexible scheduling, a system that provides adequate time for a meaningful physical education program. Although this does not exist in many schools at the present time, it should be a goal toward which all leaders should work. The great amount of subject matter, skills, and activities to be covered and the need for regular participation in physical activities are two good reasons that a daily period is so essential.

Credit

Physical education should be given credit like the other major subject matter offerings. It is included in the curriculum because it contributes to educational outcomes. The credit is justified by the contribution physical education makes to the achievement of goals toward which all of education is working.

Variety of activities

Some physical education activities that should be covered in the secondary school are as follows:

- *Team games:* baseball, softball, basketball, touch football, volleyball, soccer, and field hockey
- *Dual and individual sports:* track, badminton, table tennis, deck tennis, handball, horseshoes, tennis, archery, golf, and shuffleboard
- *Rhythms and dancing:* movement fundamentals, social dancing, folk dancing, rhythms, square dancing, and modern dancing
- *Aquatic activities:* swimming, diving, lifesaving, scuba diving, water games
- *Outdoor winter sports:* skating, snow games, ice hockey, skiing, and tobogganing
- *Gymnastics:* tumbling, pyramid building, apparatus, rope climbing, and acrobatics
- *Other activities:* self-testing activities, relays, corrective exercises, camping, and outdoor education

To best meet the needs of the secondary

school student, the types of activities should be wide and varied. The junior high and early senior high school programs should be mainly exploratory in nature, offering a wide variety of activities, with the team games modified in nature and presented in the form of lead-up activities. Toward the end of the senior high school years there should be an opportunity to select and specialize in certain activities that will have a carry-over value after formal education ceases. Furthermore, many of the team games and other activities should be offered in a more intensive manner and in larger blocks of time as the student approaches the terminal point of the secondary school. This allows for greater acquisition of skill in selected activities.

As a general rule, boys and girls at the secondary level, including both junior and senior high, can profit greatly from rhythmic activities such as folk and social dancing; team sports such as soccer, field hockey, softball, baseball, touch football, volleyball, and speedball; individual activities such as track and field, tennis, paddle tennis, badminton,

hiking, handball, bowling, archery, and fly casting; many forms of gymnastics, such as tumbling, stunts, and apparatus activities; and various forms of games and relays. These activities will comprise the major portion of the program at the secondary level. Of course, the activities should be adapted to boys and to girls as they are played separately or on a coeducational basis.

THE ADAPTED PROGRAM AND MAINSTREAMING

The adapted program and mainstreaming refer to that phase of physical education that meets the needs of the individual who, because of some physical, mental, or cultural inadequacy, functional defect capable of being improved through exercise, or other deficiency, temporarily or permanently may have difficulty participating in certain physical education activities. The adapted program can correct faulty body mechanics, develop physical fitness, and provide a meaningful program of physical education for students who may otherwise not be able to benefit

Fig. 7-2. Girls archery, Hughes Junior High School, Los Angeles Unified School District, Los Angeles, Calif.

from such an experience. The word "adapted" is used here, although in many books and schools this special program is known by other terms, such as "corrective," "handicapped," "individual," "modified," "remedial," "atypical," and "restricted."

Mainstreaming is the educational strategy that integrates the handicapped student with nonhandicapped student. Many educators are now suggesting that mildly mentally and physically handicapped students achieve more and are happier in regular classes. Mainstreaming may also be defined as the placement of students from emotionally disturbed, mentally deficient, culturally deprived, and partially handicapped classes into regular class or a physical education class to provide them with experiences offered in a regular class program.

The discussion of the relevant program of physical education in this chapter is concerned with outlining the main aspects of an adapted-mainstreamed program. Chapter 19 will cover the subject of mainstreaming in more detail.

Health examinations such as medical or physical fitness tests often indicate that some of the pupils are not able to participate in regular physical activity programs. The principle of individual differences that applies to education as a whole should also apply to physical education. Physical education leaders believe that as long as a student can come to school, he or she should be required to participate in physical education classes. Adherence to this tenet means that programs must be adapted to individual needs. Many boys and girls who are recuperating from long illnesses or operations or are suffering from other abnormal conditions require special consideration in their program of activities.

It cannot be assumed that all individuals in physical education classes are normal. Unfortunately, many programs are administered on this basis. One estimate indicates that one out of every eight students in our schools is handicapped to the extent that special provision should be made in the educational program.

Special provisions under an adapted type of program also need to be made for such students as the mentally retarded, the physically handicapped, the poorly coordinated, and the culturally disadvantaged in the secondary school population. Culturally disadvantaged students, for example, often have had only a limited physical education experience, either because their families have moved frequently or because they may have attended inner-city schools that did not have adequate facilities and staff for a sound physical education program.

Culturally disadvantaged students benefit from an adapted type of program because they have so often not had prior training in physical education activities, nor have they developed the fitness needed to cope with a regular physical education program.

In summary, students having such atypical physical conditions as the following may profit from an adapted program: (1) faulty body mechanics; (2) nutritional disturbances (overweight or underweight); (3) heart and lung disturbances; (4) postoperative or convalescent problems; (5) hernias, weak and flat feet, menstrual disorders, and the like; (6) nervous instability; (7) poor physical fitness; (8) crippling conditions (such as infantile paralysis); (9) cultural disadvantages; (10) mental retardation; (11) disruptive tendencies; (12) poor coordination; and (13) gifted or creative minds.

An adapted physical education program can help these students develop the skills, fitness, and ability they need to find enjoyment and success in sports, games, and recreational activities.

Scheduling and mainstreaming

There is a strong feeling among physical education leaders that scheduling handicapped children and youth in separate groups is not always satisfactory. Instead, they should be mainstreamed. Many educators who have studied this problem believe that the atypical child should receive his or her physical education along with the nonhandicapped children and, in order to accommodate his or her handicap, that the program be modified and special methods of teaching used. In such cases, the administrator should be certain that the modification of the program is physically and psychologically sound for the pupil. Sometimes mental and emotional defects can be minimized if the teacher acquaints other pupils with the general problems of the handicapped child and encourages their cooperation in helping the child to make the right adjustment and maintain self-esteem and social acceptance. There also seems to be a trend in secondary schools to follow an adapted sports program rather than to have a corrective type of program.

In some schools it sometimes has been possible to schedule special classes for children with certain types of abnormalities. This procedure has not always proved satisfactory, however, because of the financial cost and the feeling that boys and girls should be scheduled with nonhandicapped children for social and psychological reasons. Therefore, including the handicapped in the same classes with other students is becoming a common practice.

In other schools students needing an adapted program have been scheduled as a separate section within the regular physical education class. In some cases group exercises have been devised, and pupils have been encouraged to assist one another in the alleviation of their difficulties. These methods are not always satisfactory, but according to the schools concerned, they are much better than not doing anything about the problem. In still other schools atypical pupils have been scheduled during special periods in which individual attention can be given to them.

The procedure followed by any particular school in scheduling students for the adapted program will depend upon its educational philosophy, finances, facilities, and staff available and should be guided throughout by the needs of the students.

Principles underlying a sound adapted-mainstreamed physical education program

1. A thorough medical examination is a prerequisite to assignment to the adapted program.

2. Through conferences the teacher can gain from the student much information concerning his or her interests, needs, limitations, and abilities.

3. The program of activities should be adapted to the individual and his or her atypical condition. Special developmental exercises, aquatics, and recreational sports can play an important part in most adapted programs.

4. There should be a periodic evaluation of student progress.

5. Complete records of each student should be kept. Such information as the nature of the handicapping condition, the recommendation of physician, special activities, interviews, progress, and other pertinent data should be recorded.

6. Excellent teacher-student-nurse-physician-administrator rapport is essential to an effective program.

7. The teacher of adapted physical education should work very closely with medical and guidance personnel.

8. Teachers of adapted physical education should have a sincere interest in handicapped students and should recognize the real challenge in helping them.

INTRAMURAL AND EXTRAMURAL ATHLETIC PROGRAMS

Intramural and extramural activities comprise that phase of the school physical education program greared to the abilities and skills of the entire student body. It consists of voluntary participation in games, sports, and other activities. It offers intramural activities within a single school and such extramural activities as "play" and "sports" days that bring together participants from several schools. It is a laboratory period for sports and other activities whose fundamentals have been taught in the physical education class. It affords competition for all types of individuals—the strong and the weak, the skilled and the unskilled, the big and the small. It also includes both sexes. It is not characterized by the highly organized features of varsity sports, including their commercialization, many spectators, considerable publicity, and stress on winning. It is a phase of the total physical education program that should receive considerable attention.

Relation to interschool athletics

Both intramural and extramural and varsity interschool athletics are integral phases of the total physical education program, which is made up of the required physical education class program, the adapted program, the intramural and extramural programs, and the varsity interschool athletics program. Each has an important contribution to make to the achievement of physical education objectives. The important thing is to maintain a proper balance so that each phase enhances rather than restricts the other phases of the total program.

Whereas intramural and extramural activities are for the entire student body, varsity interschool athletics are usually for students who have a greater degree of skill. Intramurals are conducted primarily on a school basis, whereas extramural and varsity interschool athletics are conducted on an interschool basis.

There is no conflict between these phases of the program if the facilities, time, personnel, money, and other factors are apportioned according to the degree to which each phase achieves the educational outcomes desired, rather than according to the degree of public appeal and interest stimulated. One should not be designed as a training ground or feeding system for the other. It should be possible for a student to move from one to the other, but this should be incidental in nature, rather than a planned procedure.

If conducted properly, each phase of the program can contribute to the other, and through an overall, well-balanced program, the entire student body will come to respect sports and the great potentials they have for improving physical, mental, social, and emotional growth. When a physical education program is initially developed, it would seem logical to first provide an intramural program for the majority of the students, with the interschool athletics program coming as an outgrowth of the former. The first concern should be for the majority of the students. This is characteristic of the democratic way of life. Although the intramural and extramural athletics program is designed for every stu-

Fig. 7-3. Intramural basketball at Regina High School, Cincinnati, Ohio.

dent, in practice it generally attracts the poorly skilled and moderately skilled individuals. The skilled person finds his or her niche in the varsity interschool athletic program. This has its benefits in that it is an equalizer for competition.

Junior high school level

In the junior high school the main concentration in athletics should be on intramural and extramural activities. It is at this particular level that students are taking a special interest in sports, but at the same time their immaturity makes it unwise to allow them to engage in an interscholastic program. The program at this level should provide for all boys and girls, appeal to the entire student body, be well supervised by a trained physi-

Fig. 7-4. Wrestling at Brockport Central Schools, Brockport, N.Y.

cal educator, and be adapted to the needs and interests of the pupils.

The American Alliance for Health, Physical Education, and Recreation, the Society of State Directors, and many other professional groups have gone on record in favor of a broad intramural and extramural junior high athletics program. They believe that it is in the best interests of youth at this age level.

The junior high school provides a setting for developing students' fundamental skills in many sports and activities. It is a time of great energy—and a time when physiologic changes and rapid growth are taking place. Youth in junior high schools should have proper outlets to develop in a healthful manner.

Senior high school level

At the senior high school level the intramural and extramural athletics program should develop its full potential. At this time the interests and needs of boys and girls require such a program. These students want and need to experience the joy and satisfaction that are a part of playing on a team, excelling in an activity with their own peers, and developing skill. Every high school should see to it that a broad and varied program is part of the total physical education plan.

The program of intramural and extramural athletics for boys and girls should receive more emphasis than it now has at the senior high school level. It is basic to sound education. It is a setting in which the skills learned and developed in the instructional program can be put to use in a practical situation, with all the fun that comes from such competition. It should form a basis for the utilization of skills that will be used during leisure time, both in the present and in the future. Since this is the time when so many young people lose interest in physical activity, the intramural and extramural program can help to maintain such an interest.

Corecreational activities should play a prominent part in the program. Girls and boys need to participate in activities. Many of the activities in the high school program adapt themselves well to both sexes. Play and sports days also offer a setting in which both sexes can participate and enjoy worthwhile competition together.

Principles underlying sound intramural and extramural programs

1. The goals of the intramural and extramural programs must be consistent with

Fig. 7-5. Intramural volleyball at Regina High School, Cincinnati, Ohio.

those of general education and physical education.

2. The supervision of the intramural and extramural programs should be the responsibility of qualified physical education personnel.

3. The planning and conduct of the intramural and extramural programs should be based upon democratic principles and allow for participation by students as well as faculty.

4. The facilities of the entire physical education department should be available for the intramural and extramural programs to permit a wide variety of activities and the maximum participation possible.

5. The units of competition in intramural and extramural programs should depend upon such factors as the size of the school, needs and interests of students, natural formation of groups within the school, and other considerations that will lend flavor to the competition.

6. Tournaments should be so conducted as to permit maximum participation of students.

7. Eligibility requirements should be designed to enable maximum participation of the student body and to protect the health and welfare of the participants.

8. Achievement can be recognized by some token of recognition, but awards should not become a primary motive for participation.

9. Officials should be well qualified so as to promote better play and maintain safety.

THE INTERSCHOLASTIC PROGRAM

Varsity interschool athletics have a definite and important place in senior high school. Whether they should exist at the junior high school level is controversial. Varsity interscholastic competition at the senior high school level can help players achieve a higher standard of mental, moral, social, and physical fitness, provided the overall objectives of physical education are kept in mind.

Varsity interschool athletics represent an integral part of the total physical education program. They should grow out of the intramural and extramural athletics program. Athletics, with the appeal they have for youth, should be the heart of physical education.

Junior high school level

There has been considerable discussion as to the advisability of varsity athletic competition at the junior high school level. The resolutions passed by some professional organizations and the stands taken by leaders in the field point to the fact that highly organized interschool athletics programs are questionable as a part of junior high school programs.

There are two sides to the question of junior high school varsity athletics, and at times they both sound convincing. Opponents have offered facts to indicate that it is risky business to permit boys and girls to play varsity interschool athletics at this level of growth and development. Those who favor these activities have shown that programs have been conducted in a safe and sound manner.

Both sides would agree, it seems, that more research is needed to determine the right policy to follow. Probably educators would be on the safe side if they waited until more research has been conducted before encouraging this kind of participation. Above all, the following principles are basic:

1. The main object of athletics should be healthful participation and fun.

2. Every student should have opportunities to participate in a varied program of many physical activities and sports both in a physical education class and in intramural and extramural programs. These phases of the total physical education program should receive priority for the junior high schools.

3. Occasional competitive experiences in selected activities on an informal basis such as sports days and play days can be conducted with profit.

4. A complete medical examination is a prerequisite.

5. Proper leadership consists of persons who know and appreciate the physical and emotional limitations of students, the fundamentals of first aid, the sport itself, and how to condition and train players for the activity. A certified physical educator should handle such activities.

Senior high school level

The high school level is the logical place to start interschool athletics on a more highly organized basis. This is the place where students may find an opportunity to experience exhilarating competition and test their skill against that of teams in neighboring communities.

The following principles should guide the program:

1. High school varsity interscholastic athletics should be voluntary in nature. All students who desire to be on a team should be allowed to play on the squad. In theory no one should ever be cut from the squad. Every attempt should be made to have sufficient junior varsity, or grade "B," "C," and other teams, so that any interested student will have the opportunity to participate at his level of ability.

2. Athletics should be conducted in out-of-school hours. The class period should never be utilized for practice.

3. Players should not be excused from physical education class. Programs may be adapted, but every player can receive some benefit from participating in the class program.

4. The interschool athletic program should be organized and administered with the needs of the participant in mind. What will benefit the spectator should never influence the program.

5. A wide variety of activities based on the needs and interests of students should be offered. The number of students that can be accommodated in a wide variety of sports and other physical education activities should be the basis on which an interschool athletic program is founded and developed.

6. The coach should be selected on the basis of his or her knowledge of the game, ability to teach, understanding of the partici-

pant, and character and personality. Some physical education preparation is an essential.

7. Through interschool competition the player should become physically, mentally, emotionally, and socially more fit.

8. One of the first requisites for every participant in an athletics program should be a medical examination to determine physical fitness and capacity to engage in such a program.

9. Everything possible should be done to provide for the safety of the participant.

10. Every school should have a written policy in regard to financial and other responsibilities associated with injuries. The administrator, parents, and players should be thoroughly familiar with the responsibilities of each in regard to injuries.

11. Some form of insurance plan to cover injuries should be in force in all schools.

12. Title IX regulations, which prohibit sex discrimination in physical education and athletic programs, should be strictly adhered to.

13. Officials should be well qualified. They should know the rules and be able to interpret them accurately, recognize their responsibility to the players, be good sportsmen and be courteous, honest, friendly, cooperative, and impartial, and be able to control the game at all times.

WAYS OF IMPROVING PHYSICAL EDUCATION PROGRAMS

An analysis of present-day physical education programs shows that they can be improved in the following ways:

1. Outlining clearly defined goals to be achieved by students at each grade level.

2. Developing meaningful programs that are developmental in nature and that are characterized by progression from kindergarten through grade twelve. Programs should also utilize performance and behavioral standards to assess accomplishment.

3. Individualizing programs for each student (normal student, physically handicapped, mentally retarded, poorly coordinated, culturally disadvantaged).

4. Utilizing effective teaching techniques

such as team teaching, independent study, student involvement, alternate programs, and applying the techniques that promote motor learning.

5. Having sound instructional materials for each activity in the program. Materials on activities graded according to skill ability, audiovisual materials, such as records and films, materials on the human body, such as charts on organic systems, posture, safety and first aid, physical education textbooks that can be placed in the hands of students, should be included.

6. Evaluating each student's progress toward established goals, for example, utilization of valid and scientific tests of physical fitness or skill and sound grading system.

7. Having a meaningful record system of each student's skill achievement, physical fitness, posture, physical defects, medical examinations, and so on, which follows the student from kindergarten to grade twelve in the same way that scholastic records follow the student.

8. Providing for a consulting service and in-service education of faculty. Teachers and administrators should have ready access to experts in all phases of physical education including curriculum development, testing, teaching techniques, and instructional materials. Also, there should be provision for periodic in-service workshops for teachers of physical education and coaches.

TITLE IX

Today's relevant physical education program must take into account the passage of a very important law by our national government, namely, Title IX. On May 27, 1975, the President of the United States signed into law Title IX of the Education Amendments Act of 1972, which prohibits sex discrimination in educational programs that are federally assisted. The effective date of the regulation was July 21, 1975.

Title IX affects nearly all public elementary, secondary, and postsecondary educational institutions. This includes the nation's 16,000 public school systems and nearly 2,700 postsecondary institutions. As

Fig. 7-6. Coeducational physical education activity. Courtesy Bill Henderson.

a first step the regulations provide that educators should perform a searching self-examination of policies and practices in their institutions and take whatever remedial action is needed to bring their institutions into compliance with the federal law.

Reason for Title IX

The main reason for the enactment of Title IX was such testimony before Congressional and other committees as the following:

• Girls were frequently denied the opportunity to enroll in traditionally male courses and activities.

• Girls and women were frequently denied equal opportunity, such as the case cited where a program for girls was inferior to that provided for boys and another case in which rules in one state prevented the best tennis player (a girl) in a high school from competing on the school's tennis team.

• A national survey conducted by the National Education Association showed that although women constituted a majority of all public school teachers they accounted for only 3.5 percent of the junior high school principals and 3 percent of the senior high school principals.

• A study by the National Center for Educational Statistics revealed that women college faculty members received average salaries considerably lower than those of their male counterparts.

Implications for physical education and athletic programs

• *Physical education classes must be set up on a coeducational basis.* This regulation does not mean that activities must be taught coeducationally. Within classes, students may be grouped by sex for such contact sports as wrestling, basketball, and football. Also, within physical education classes, students may be grouped on an ability basis even though such grouping results in a single-sex grouping. However, sex must *not* be the criterion for grouping. It must be something other than sex. Furthermore, if an evaluation standard has an adverse impact on one sex, such as a standard of accomplishment in a physical fitness test, different evaluation requirements may be used.

• *Schools and colleges must establish separate teams for boys and girls and men and women or provide a coeducational team.*

Questions and answers on Title IX*

The Office of Civil Rights of the Department of Health, Education and Welfare has provided answers to some commonly asked questions concerning Title IX. They are listed here for the reader's information.

Question: What is Title IX?

Answer: Title IX is that portion of the Education Amendments Act of 1972 that forbids discrimination on the basis of sex in educational programs or activities that receive federal funds.

Question: Who is covered by Title IX?

Answer: Virtually every college, university, elementary and secondary school, and preschool is covered by some portion of the law. Many clubs and other organizations receive federal funds for educational programs and activities and likewise are covered by Title IX in some manner.

Question: Who is exempt from Title IX's provisions?

Answer: Congress has specifically exempted all military schools and has exempted religious schools to the extent that the provisions of Title IX would be inconsistent with the basic religious tenets of the school.

Not included with regard to admission requirements ONLY are private undergraduate colleges, nonvocational elementary and secondary schools, and those public undergraduate schools that have been traditionally and continuously single-sex since their establishment.

Even institutions whose admissions are exempt from coverage must treat all students without discrimination once they have admitted members of both sexes.

Question: In athletics, what is equal opportunity?

Answer: In determining whether equal opportunities are available, such factors as these will be considered:
- Sports selected and the interests and abilities of both sexes
- Provision of supplies and equipment
- Game and practice schedules
- Travel and per diem allowances
- Coaching and academic tutoring opportunities and the assignment and pay of coaches and tutors
- Locker rooms, practice and competitive facilities
- Medical and training services
- Housing and dining facilities and services
- Publicity

Question: Must an institution provide equal opportunities in each of the above categories?

Answer: Yes. However, equal expenditures in each category are not required.

Question: What sports does the term "athletics" encompass?

Answer: The term "athletics" encompasses sports that are a part of interscholastic or intercollegiate club or intramural programs.

---

*Office of Civil Rights, U.S. Department of Health, Education and Welfare, *Final Title IX Regulation Implementing Education Amendments of 1972 Prohibiting Sex Discrimination in Education.* Effective date: July 21, 1975.

Question: When are separate teams for men and women allowed?

Answer: When selection is based on competitive skill or the activity involved is a contact sport, separate teams may be provided for males and females, or a single team may be provided that is open to both sexes. If separate teams are offered, a recipient institution may not discriminate on the basis of sex in providing equipment or supplies or in any other manner.

Question: If there are sufficient numbers of women interested in basketball to form a viable women's basketball team, is an institution that fields a men's basketball team required to provide such a team for women?

Answer: One of the factors to be considered by the director in determining whether equal opportunities are provided is whether the selection of sports and levels of competition effectively accommodate the interests and abilities of members of both sexes. Therefore, if a school offers basketball for men and the only way in which the institution can accommodate the interests and abilities of women is by offering a separate basketball team for women, such a team must be provided.

Question: If there is an insufficient number of women interested in participating on a women's track team, must the institution allow an interested woman to compete for a position on the men's track team?

Answer: If athletic opportunities have previously been limited for women at that school, it must allow women to compete for the men's team if the sport is a noncontact sport such as track. The school may preclude women from participating on a men's team in a contact sport. A school may preclude men or women from participating on teams for the other sex if athletic opportunities have not been limited in the past for them, regardless of whether the sport is contact or noncontact.

Question: Can a school be exempt from Title IX if its athletic conference forbids men and women on the same noncontact team?

Answer: No. Title IX preempts all state or local laws or other requirements that conflict with Title IX.

Question: How can a school athletics department be covered by Title IX if the department itself receives no direct federal aid?

Answer: Section 844 of the Education Amendments Act of 1974 specifically states that: "The Secretary shall prepare and publish . . . proposed regulations implementing the provisions of Title IX of the Education Amendments of 1972 relating to the prohibition of sex discrimination in Federally assisted education programs which shall include with respect to intercollegiate athletic activities reasonable provisions considering the nature of particular sports."

In addition, athletics constitutes an integral part of the educational processes of schools and colleges and thus is fully subject to the requirements of Title IX, even in absence of federal funds going directly to the athletic programs.

The courts have consistently considered athletics sponsored by an educational institution to be an integral part of the institution's education program and therefore have required institutions to provide equal opportunity.

Question: Does a school have to provide athletic scholarships for women?

Answer: Specifically, the regulation provides "to the extent that a recipient awards athletic scholarships or grants-in-aid, it must provide reasonable opportunities for such awards for members of each sex in proportion to the number of students of each sex participating in interscholastic or intercollegiate athletics."

If there is only one swimming team in a particular school, for example, then both boys and girls are permitted to try out for this team. In other words, if a school fields a team in a noncontact sport for one sex and not for the other, members of both sexes must be allowed to try out for the team.

The regulation does not enumerate what activities and teams a school should provide. However, under the regulation, equality of opportunity means that schools and colleges must select sports and levels of competition that provide for the interests and abilities of both sexes. This means that where the interests and abilities of members of both sexes are not provided for on one team, the institution is required to provide separate teams for males and females.

• *Schools and colleges must provide equal opportunities for both sexes.* This is true in respect to such items as facilities, equipment and supplies, practice and games, medical and training services, coaching and academic tutoring opportunities, travel and per diem allowances, and housing and dining facilities.

Equal opportunity means that the sports and activities offered must reflect the interests and abilities of students of both sexes.

Adequate facilities and equipment must be available for both sexes in every sport. Furthermore, one sex cannot dominate the facilities or the new equipment.

Also, adequate time for practice and games must be provided for both sexes in every sport. Again, one sex cannot dominate.

• *Schools and colleges must spend funds in an equitable manner.* Although equal aggregate expenditures are not required, an educational institution cannot discriminate on the basis of sex in providing proper equipment and supplies.

• *Title IX takes precedence over all state and local laws, and conference regulations that might be in conflict with this federal regulation.*

• *If an institution receives federal aid it must be in compliance with Title IX even though its athletic or physical education program does not directly receive any of this aid.*

• *There can be no discrimination in respect to personnel standards.* No discrimination can exist in respect to personnel standards by sex for employment, promotion, salary, recruitment, job classification,

Fig. 7-7. Coeducation activity at Brockport Central Schools, Brockport, N.Y.

marital or parental status, or fringe benefits.

• *Scholarships must be awarded on an equitable basis.* The regulations require an institution to select students to be awarded financial aid on the basis of criteria other than a student's sex.

Compliance with Title IX

Title IX will be enforced by the Office for Civil Rights of the Department of Health, Education and Welfare of the federal government. The first step will be to seek voluntary compliance. If violations are found, federal financial support may be cut off and other legal measures taken, such as referring the violation to the Department of Justice for appropriate court action.

The Office of Civil Rights is trying to approach Title IX in an constructive manner.

They wish to achieve the goals of Title IX in the shortest time possible, that is, to end discrimination against women. However, opportunity for women is the law of the land and must be enforced. The aim will be to utilize HEW's enforcement machinery by giving priority to systemic forms of discrimination rather than following an approach whereby individual complaints assume priority. This means that the total picture of noncompliance will be assessed, taking into consideration information received from individuals and groups, as a means of determining enforcement priorities and compliance reviews.

Title IX regulations have been evolving for a long time. They should result in increased physical education and athletic opportunities for all students.

Checklist of selected items for evaluating the physical education program's relevancy to a modern secondary school

Educational philosophy

	Yes	No
1. Educational philosophy of the school encourages innovation.	☐	☐
2. Close school-community relationships are encouraged.	☐	☐
3. Educational program is relevant to the times.	☐	☐
4. Faculty and students are actively involved in the total educational program.	☐	☐
5. Education is individualized for each student, including culturally disadvantaged, physically handicapped, mentally retarded, and so on.	☐	☐
6. Worth of physical education program is recognized.	☐	☐
7. Clear written statement of educational philosophy exists, with educational objectives enumerated.	☐	☐

Administration

	Yes	No
1. Administration represents a means to an end (an excellent educational program) rather than an end in itself.	☐	☐
2. Administrative structure enhances and facilitates the implementation of the educational program.	☐	☐
3. The school, including physical education, has a meaningful and accurate system of record keeping.	☐	☐
4. School records are accurate and up to date.	☐	☐
5. School is open to the community.	☐	☐
6. Faculty and students play an important part in decision making and policy formation.	☐	☐
7. School utilizes community resources.	☐	☐
8. Adequate facilities, supplies, and equipment exist.	☐	☐
9. Sufficient teaching stations exist to carry on a meaningful physical education program.	☐	☐
10. Scheduling is done in an effective manner, including the utilization of flexible scheduling.	☐	☐
11. Meetings are held regularly with the faculty to share new ideas and methods and discuss common problems.	☐	☐
12. Students have representation at important administrative and faculty meetings.	☐	☐
13. School facilities are utilized on a twelve-month basis.	☐	☐
14. Facilities are designed to meet program needs, permit effective instruction, and ensure pupil safety.	☐	☐

Continued.

Checklist of selected items for evaluating the physical education program's relevancy to a modern secondary school—cont'd

Administration—cont'd

15. Community is kept informed concerning educational objectives. ☐ ☐
16. Equipment and supplies are checked periodically to ensure that adequate amounts are available and in good condition. ☐ ☐
17. Administration is democratic. ☐ ☐
18. School building is utilized to its maximum potential. ☐ ☐
19. Administration is receptive to innovative teaching techniques. ☐ ☐
20. Office practice is efficient and represents a valuable service in carrying out educational objectives. ☐ ☐
21. Administration understands the needs of physical education and its contribution to the achievement of educational goals. ☐ ☐
22. Channels of communication are readily available to faculty and students. ☐ ☐
23. School conforms to Title IX regulations. ☐ ☐

Students

1. Students participate in curriculum planning. ☐ ☐
2. Students have the opportunity to evaluate the physical education program. ☐ ☐
3. Students are assigned to physical education classes on the basis of their physical development, needs, and achievement. ☐ ☐
4. Students find school and physical education a pleasurable and worthwhile experience. ☐ ☐
5. Students participate in a program that meets their individual needs. ☐ ☐
6. Students are properly grouped for activities according to ability and other relevant factors. ☐ ☐
7. Students have good rapport with teachers. ☐ ☐
8. Students have opportunity to develop leadership potential. ☐ ☐
9. Students are permitted to pursue individual dress and hair styles providing they do not interfere with the rights of other students or their own health, safety, and performance in school activities. ☐ ☐

Teachers

1. Teaching assignments are made with regard to teacher's interests, strengths, and experience. ☐ ☐
2. Opportunities are available to experiment with new teaching methods and materials. ☐ ☐
3. Beginning teacher is provided with proper orientation to school and role to be played. ☐ ☐
4. Evaluations of teachers are objective, with a view to improving teaching ability and service to students. ☐ ☐
5. Accountability is required for outstanding teaching and service to students. ☐ ☐
6. Salaries are given according to the role teachers play in the educational process. ☐ ☐
7. Faculty meetings are attended regularly. ☐ ☐
8. Leadership is provided for the community in teacher's specialty. ☐ ☐
9. Excellent relationships exist with students. ☐ ☐
10. Student leaders and paraprofessionals are utilized to develop leadership qualities of boys and girls and to devote more time to teaching. ☐ ☐
11. Creativity is regarded as an important quality. ☐ ☐
12. New developments in special field are well known, understood, and applied. ☐ ☐
13. Harmonious working relationships exist with other members of the faculty. ☐ ☐
14. Professional activity is recognized as being important. ☐ ☐

Physical education program

1. Innovative ideas are utilized. ☐ ☐
2. Students participate in the development and evaluation of the program. ☐ ☐
3. Classes are of sufficient length to permit meaningful participation in scheduled activities. ☐ ☐
4. Intramural program provides for maximum participation of all students. ☐ ☐

Checklist of selected items for evaluating the physical education program's relevancy to a modern secondary school—cont'd

Physical education program—cont'd

5. Transportation is provided for athletic events. ☐ ☐
6. Close working relationship exists between the physical education and health programs including school physician and health services. ☐ ☐
7. Provision is made for individual differences. ☐ ☐
8. Progression is a characteristic of the program, with a smooth transition from elementary to junior high school and from junior high school to senior high school. ☐ ☐
9. Physical education is an integral part of the total educational offering. ☐ ☐
10. Program evaluation is done periodically with necessary changes being made. ☐ ☐
11. Program is relevant to the times, the student, and the role of education in modern society. ☐ ☐
12. Title IX regulation is adhered to. ☐ ☐

Self-assessment tests

These tests are to assist students in determining if material and competencies presented in this chapter have been mastered:

1. Draw a diagram of a school physical education program showing its component parts.
2. A colleague has suggested that intramural physical education activities be conducted during the basic instructional physical education class period. Prepare your answer to your colleague outlining the purposes for which the basic instructional class period exists.
3. Develop a physical education unit of study for the teaching of swimming for a secondary school class where mentally retarded boys and girls are mainstreamed into the regular program. Include in the unit the methods and materials that will be used and how the class will be conducted.
4. Utilizing the activity of tennis, demonstrate how it can be conducted most effectively on an (a) intramural, (b) extramural, and (c) interscholastic level.
5. Prepare a plan for implementing the various provisions of Title IX into a secondary school physical education program.
6. Develop what you consider to be an effective checklist for determining whether a secondary school physical education program is excellent, good, fair, or poor.

Points to remember

1. A workable definition of physical education.
2. The four components of the physical education program.
3. Basic considerations in the required class physical education program.
4. Nature and scope of adapted physical education program.
5. Characteristics of intramural and extramural physical education program.
6. Considerations for an interscholastic athletic program.
7. Provisions of Title IX.

Problems to think through

1. Why is it essential to consider all four components of a program of physical education in order to best meet the needs and interests of all boys and girls?
2. Why is it that many schools do not have an adapted physical education program?
3. Why is it that many schools do not follow resolutions of professional associations in regard to interscholastic athletic programs?
4. Why was Title IX passed by the federal government?

Case study for analysis

Select a secondary school and make a careful study of its class, adapted, intramural and extramural, and interschool athletic programs. Make a list of commendable aspects of the school's physical education program and a list of points that are weaknesses and require attention.

Exercises for review

1. Define physical education.
2. Why must the class physical education program be instructional in nature?
3. What are some important considerations in developing an effective instructional class program?
4. Make a study of what four physical education leaders say are important characteristics of the class physical education program.
5. Debate the issue—Resolved: Interschool athletics should be banned from all junior high schools.

Selected readings

Bannon, J. J.: Leisure resources—its comprehensive planning, Englewood Cliffs, N.J., 1976, Prentice-Hall, Inc.

Barron, A. A.: Report of the first DGWS national conference on girl sports programs for secondary schools, Journal of Health, Physical Education, and Recreation, **42**:14, 1971.

Bell, M. M.: Are we exploiting high school girl athletes? Journal of Health, Physical Education, and Recreation, **41**:53, 1970.

Bucher, C. A.: Physical education for life, New York, 1969, McGraw-Hill Book Company.

Bucher, C. A.: Female sports barriers are crumbling (syndicated newspaper column), Washington, D.C., July 29-30, 1972, President's Council on Physical Fitness and Sports.

Bucher, C. A.: Girls and women in sports: pros and cons (syndicated newspaper column), Washington, D.C., August 5-6, 1972, President's Council on Physical Fitness and Sports.

Geyer, C.: Physical education for the electronic age, Journal of Health, Physical Education, and Recreation, **43**:32, 1972.

Kidd, F. M., et al.: Guidelines for secondary school physical education, Journal of Health, Physical Education, and Recreation **42**:47, 1971.

Larson, L. A.: Foundations of physical activity, New York, 1976, Macmillan Publishing Co., Inc.

National Advisory Council on Education Professions Development, Mainstreaming: helping teachers meet the challenge, Washington, D.C., 1976, National Advisory Council.

Nelson, W. E.: Need we fear voluntary physical education? Journal of Health, Physical Education, and Recreation **43**:63, 1972.

Penman, K. A.: Planning physical education and athletic facilities in schools, New York, 1976, John Wiley & Sons, Inc.

Report of an AAHPER Conference: Perceptual-motor development: action with interaction, Journal of Health, Physical Education, and Recreation **42**:36, 1971.

Schochet, M.: We can't remain just a high priced repetitive recreation program, Journal of Health, Physical Education, and Recreation **41**:24, 1970.

Singer, R. N.: Motor Learning and human performance, New York, 1975, The Macmillan Publishing Co., Inc.

Singer, R. N., et al.: Physical education: foundations, New York, 1976, Holt, Rinehart and Winston.

Stanhope, C. L., et al.: The new physical education, Journal of Health, Physical Education, and Recreation **42**:24, 1971.

Studer, H. R., et al.: Instructional technology, Today's Education **59**:33, 1970.

University of the State of New York, The State Education Department, Mainstreaming: idea and actuality, Albany, N.Y., 1975, The University of the State of New York.

U.S. Department of Health, Education, and Welfare, Office for Civil Rights, Final Title IX regulations implementing education amendments of 1972—prohibiting sex discrimination in education, Washington, D.C., 1975, U.S. Department of Health, Education and Welfare.

8

A SYSTEMS APPROACH TO DEVELOPING THE CURRICULUM IN PHYSICAL EDUCATION

INSTRUCTIONAL OBJECTIVES AND COMPETENCIES TO BE ACHIEVED

After reading this chapter the student should be able to—

1. Discuss why curriculum reform is essential to the future of physical education as a profession.
2. Apply the procedure for developing a curriculum in physical education to a specific situation.
3. Demonstrate how physical education activities should be selected for any given group of secondary school students.
4. Plan a yearly, unit, and daily program in physical education for the tenth grade.
5. Utilize a systems approach to the development of a physical education curriculum.
6. Propose a plan for bringing about desirable changes in a school's physical education program and outline the procedure to be followed if changes were necessary.

Traditionally, physical education curricula have been developed in a haphazard manner. Activities have often been scheduled during the fall, winter, spring, and summer seasons of the year without any logic, scientific basis, or systematic method being used. Sometimes teachers of physical education have scheduled those activities in which they are most interested and proficient without any regard to what is best for the student. Sometimes there has been insufficient consideration of the objectives that are sought and how the curriculum relates to the achievement of these objectives.

In recent years many physical educators have tried to develop a more logical means of determining the activities and other considerations that should be included in a curriculum. In some cases formulas have been created that help to determine the activities that should be scheduled. In other cases, step-by-step procedures have been developed that provide a rationale for matching goals that are sought with the activities that are provided. Such methods of curriculum development are very encouraging since they represent an attempt to make curriculum development in physical education a much more scientific procedure.

This chapter discusses the many changes taking place in the physical education curricula of secondary schools, the information needed and steps to be taken to develop a curriculum, the principles that should guide the selection of activities, and some of the factors to be considered in planning the yearly, unit, and daily programs.

This chapter also includes a *systems approach* to developing a physical education curriculum. This approach should be very helpful to the secondary school physical educator. It provides a scientific, logical, and systematic method for preparing a program of physical education that will meet the needs of boys and girls in secondary schools.

The physical education program in secondary schools will experience many changes in the years to come. Students will play an increasingly active role in determining the type of program that will best meet their needs and interests. This will be reflected in such innovations as more electives, from which students can select those activities in which they wish to specialize. In addition, there will be independent study, in which a student may spend an entire semester working on some sport or other project. Furthermore, students will be permitted to take tests that, if passed, will provide exemption from part or all the physical education requirement. In addition, performance and behavioral objectives will see wide use.

The physical education program will become more instructional in nature. Physical education will emphasize involvement in community programs and greater utilization of community resources in the organization and implementation of the curriculum.

The years ahead will see the extensive utilization of computers and measuring instruments to accurately group students in physical education classes according to abilities, traits, skills, physical fitness, and previous experience in physical education. Textbooks will be used in physical education classes as in other subject matter fields. The movement emphasis will permeate the program throughout the school life of the student. The adapted program will receive much more emphasis. The program of physical education will be aimed at developing physically educated students, with a trend away from teacher-induced learnings toward student-motivated learnings. The conceptualized approach will be utilized with the identification of the most important concepts to be transmitted to the student. These concepts will define the domain of physical education and the most important contributions the field makes to human beings.

A well-developed curriculum is a prerequisite for teaching and learning and the key to successful daily programming. It requires much time and thought to construct an extensive course of study that encompasses the present and future needs of an ever-changing student body and community. However, it must be done if students are to pursue a relevant curriculum in physical education.

REDESIGNING THE CURRICULUM— WHAT ONE STATE IS DOING*

Physical educators were invited from various sections of New York State to a workshop on the concept of "Redesign of Physical Education." As part of the preliminary features of this workshop participants were asked two questions, the answers to which are particularly relevant to this chapter concerned with developing a curriculum in physical education. One question asked each participant was: "If I had the power to change my physical education program, the first problem that I would work on would be —." Some of the selected answers given to this question by physical educators indicate new directions for physical education:

- Individualize learner goals.
- Relate physical education to the rest of the curriculum.
- Step up electives.
- Improve staff and student communications.
- Reevaluate the relevancy of objectives.
- Reinforce basic classroom learning through physical education.
- Eliminate repetitious content.
- Provide relevant course choices for each student.
- Meet needs of students.

*The University of the State of New York, The State Education Department: Final report on the workshop on the concept of "redesign" for New York State physical educators held at Stamford, New York, October 11-13, 1970, Albany, November 20, 1980.

- Reinforce the curriculum in behavioral objectives.
- Provide a more relevant curriculum.
- Develop a program that is interesting to all students as well as enjoyable.
- Revitalize staff.
- Recognize individual abilities and offer challenges to each.
- Provide flexibility in program.
- Redesign entire curriculum.

The second question that was asked of physical educators who attended this conference is especially pertinent to the development of a relevant curriculum: "What will be the characteristics of physical education in the 1980s?" Some selected answers to this question were:

- Recreation oriented
- Elective in nature
- Less structured physical education classes

- Greater use of resources in community
- Stress on individuality
- Growth of girls' interscholastics
- Pupil planning
- More coeducational activities
- Individualized curriculum
- Increased voluntary participation
- New concepts in facilities
- Interdisciplinary curriculum
- Use of audiovisual television aids
- Teacher-student/teacher-teacher/student-student planning
- Involvement of community and student in planning curriculum
- Emphasis on behavioral change in students
- More guidance on an individual basis

Previous to the physical education workshop, experts in education had developed what they called "Redesign—the twenty-four characteristics of the New System of

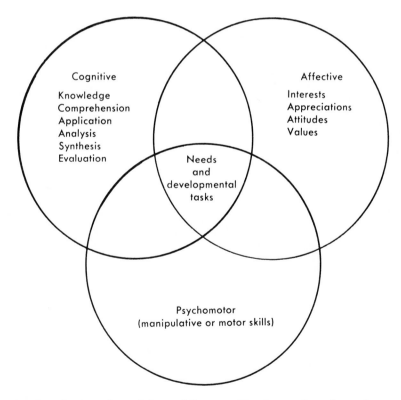

Fig. 8-1. Reinforce the curriculum in behavioral objectives. Note the interdependence of cognitive, affective, and psychomotor domains and their relationship to the learner's system of needs and developmental tasks. (From Tanner, D.: Using behavioral objectives in the classroom, New York, 1972, Macmillan Publishing Co., Inc.)

Education." These twenty-four characteristics were developed from the best thinking of experts in many educational disciplines, including educational psychology and philosophy, and specialists in innovative programs and learning resources. Many consultants assisted the New York State Department of Education in the process. One task of the workshop was to relate physical education to each of the characteristics of the "New System of Education." Since these characteristics have many implications for physical education programs of the future and for the development of a relevant curriculum, they are briefly stated here for the information of the reader:

1. The New System of Education (NSE) ensures that everyone in the community has the opportunity to be a student or staff member at any time during his or her life.

2. NSE manages learning resources under its aegis and coordinates all learning experiences using community resources. Resources are continually added and subtracted.

3. The general community is encouraged to use educational facilities and resources. Facilities are open, convertible, and flexible; resources are easily available and responsive.

4. NSE is self-renewing.

5. NSE ensures that the organization is flexible and responds quickly to program needs.

6. NSE is based on the best we know and is constantly searching for and implementing new ideas.

7. NSE is continually evaluated at all levels by its own operations, as well as by outside resources.

8. Staff development is a continual, integral part of the program.

9. Staff members have a wide range of functions; different staff members perform different combinations of functions, which are constantly changing and evolving.

10. NSE guarantees that decision-making power is in the hands of those who are affected by the decision.

11. NSE sees that each student has an individual personal plan that is continually updated and changed as necessary to maximize his potential.

12. NSE provides many alternate ways of attaining the goals of the students.

13. NSE is continuous and open; students may be in any program at any level in which they are capable of performing.

14. NSE emphasizes processes rather than information.

15. NSE emphasizes human values. Establishing a positive self-concept and a feeling of control over one's environment through active participation in decision making are major goals.

16. NSE provides a range of learning experiences that emphasize direct, real, and relevant experiences.

17. NSE emphasizes human interactions; equipment and facilities are means.

18. NSE exists to serve the needs of people in the community. It is responsive to their needs and is held accountable; failure represents system failure only, not that of students.

19. NSE is a zero-reject system (never excludes people).

20. NSE functions full time, all day and all year, is available everywhere, and provides personal educational programs throughout the student's entire life.

21. NSE has evolved by a process through which the community has gone.

22. NSE has a stated set of goals translated into performance objectives and learning activities based on predictions about the future, extrapolation of the past, and designs based upon what people would like their future to be as well as consideration of today's needs.

23. NSE has a student population with widely diverse backgrounds.

24. NSE has a carefully written plan, which describes it in detail.*

---

*The University of the State of New York, The State Education Department: Final report on the workshop on the concept of "redesign" for New York State physical educators held at Stamford, New York, October 11-13, 1970, Albany, November 20, 1970.

DEVELOPING THE CURRICULUM

A well-developed physical education curriculum is more than just a course of study or a program of activities. It is a statement of the philosophy behind the physical education program. It is a set of principles guiding the staff in all phases of classroom and extraclass instruction. It is a series of objectives and goals to be achieved by those who learn. It is the program, progressive in nature from year to year and season to season, providing the best opportunity for education to the majority of students as often as possible. It is the measuring rod beside which the achievements and accomplishments of students and staff alike may be evaluated. The curriculum is all these things—a culmination of the united efforts of the many people who serve to develop it.

Purpose

The purpose of a curriculum is to provide the best type of physical education program possible for students in a particular school situation. One task of a curriculum committee is to determine the type of program to be presented as well as construct an appropriate progression of activities.

Curriculum committee

The curriculum committee is usually established by the administrator of a school or superintendent of schools and is directed to develop or to revise the course of study. The head of the physical education department may serve as chairperson of the group to develop or revise the physical education program, or the committee may select its own leader. Other members may include the physical education staff, a representative from the administration, such as a school principal, individuals from the health and recreation departments of the school or community, and selected classroom teachers from the elementary grades.

The size of the committee can vary and depends largely upon the size of the school and community to be served. The group may be further enlarged by visiting specialists or consultants in curriculum design who are called in to advise and guide the workshop meetings. In some school systems, developing a new curriculum may be labeled in-service education, and members serving on committees may receive credits toward salary increases for their participation. When university personnel are used as consultants for curriculum workshops, committee members may be able to receive graduate credits. Serving on the curriculum committee should be a very rewarding and enriching experience for new and experienced teachers. Although completion of the study may require a full school year and after-school meetings, if a worthwhile program of physical education is the result, the entire school system and the community benefit.

Steps in curriculum development

Collection of data. Many facts and details should first be gathered by the committee to serve as a background or foundation upon which to build the new curriculum. Several factors influence a course of study, and they should first be identified, analyzed, and understood. To prepare for constructing a curriculum, therefore, subcommittees should be established to investigate the following areas:

• *The current program of physical education.* The present program of physical education should be evaluated in terms of student achievements and progress. Specific weaknesses and strengths of the program should be identified and areas for expansion studied. Are the proper activities being scheduled for students? Are students meeting or exceeding minimum physical fitness standards? Are more teachers or teaching stations needed at any level? These and similar questions need answering.

• *The needs of the students.* A curriculum is successful only to the extent that the students benefit from it. They learn, they achieve, they develop, and they are better prepared to face the future as a result of experiences in physical education. Therefore, it is essential that the basic needs of the stu-

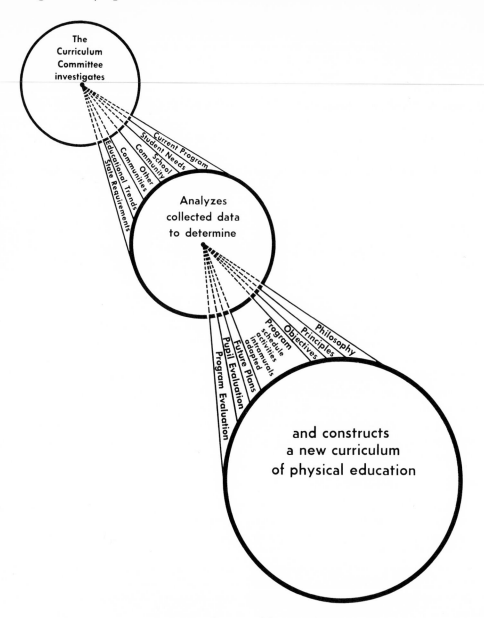

The
Curriculum
Committee
investigates

Current Program
Student Needs
School
Community
Other
Communities
Educational Trends
State Requirements

Analyzes
collected data
to determine

Philosophy
Principles
Objectives
Program
schedule
activities
intramurals
adapted
Future Plans
Pupil Evaluation
Program Evaluation

and constructs
a new curriculum
of physical education

Fig. 8-2. Development of the curriculum.

dents be identified. Two areas require investigation in this respect. Current research findings related to adolescent growth and development should be studied, and a survey of student interests and attitudes should be taken. The results of these two studies of the needs of students should yield helpful information and background material.

The school's community. A curriculum should fulfill the specific needs of the school's particular community. It is essential to survey the community in terms of its prospective growth and change, school population expansion, and recreational needs. Similarly, it is important to survey community feelings in regard to the physical education program itself. Would the community approve construction of athletic facilities for increased interscholastic programs, for example? Is there a desire for adult recreation programs using school facilities? Is there an increasing need for other recreational activities? All these areas should be fully investigated before beginning the actual development of a curriculum.

The surrounding communities. The physical education curricula of schools in neighboring communities should be surveyed, as well as those of distant schools similar in size, geographic location, and climate. Much can be learned from the successes of others, and valuable ideas may be gained in this way. For example, if a course in scuba diving has been successful in other schools, the curriculum committee may want to consider such an activity in its own school program.

The current trends in society and education. A study should be made of recent trends in society and in the field of education in general, as well as in physical education. The latest techniques and methods of teachings, such as team teaching, learning packages, self-paced instruction, and programmed learning, should be considered. Research findings in relation to the learning process, grouping, and group dynamics should be studied. The identification of learning theories and concepts regarding motor learning that are compatible with today's physical education programs should be given careful consideration. Information on improved equipment, new resource materials, new films, and new books and games should be collected. It is in this area in particular in which real stimulation and impetus may be found for changing a program. At the same time provisions may be made for program experimentation and research.

The state requirements. An investigation of state regulations and requirements should also be made to ensure acceptance of a new or revised curriculum. At the same time it should be determined whether any changes in state standards are anticipated or are in progress, in order to fulfill any future specifications that may be enacted.

When the subcommittees have completed studies in each of these six areas and have gathered as many facts and materials as possible, the committee as a whole should then

be ready for the next step in curriculum construction.

Analysis of materials. The materials thus collected should be considered by the entire committee and serve as a basis for rebuilding the new curriculum. Recommendations of the subcommittees should be heard, and the committee as a whole should then determine the direction for the program and outline the present and future changes needed.

Development of the curriculum. When the data have been thoroughly analyzed and the committee has agreed upon the fundamental directions of the new curriculum, smaller working groups may again be appointed for the purpose of constructing the curriculum. Using the committee findings as a basis upon which to work, these new committees might prepare the following:

1. A statement of philosophy of the physical education department compatible with the school's philosophy of general education

2. A set of principles for teaching incorporating new methods, materials, and techniques at specific grade and ability levels

3. A set of goals and objectives for students at each grade level with provision for individual differences

4. An outline of class activities identifying levels at which new materials should be introduced to ensure progression within the program

5. A schedule of classes, including suggested size of classes, time allotment, class sessions per week, and teacher assignments

6. An intramural and extramural program outlining activities to be included and standards for participation

7. An adapted program including methods of appraisal and referral and suggested time and types of activities for class sessions for each type of atypical condition

8. A prospectus for the years ahead suggesting additions needed in facilities and equipment and increases needed in the teaching staff and budget to accommodate innovations and expansion in the activities program and the school population

9. A synthesis of evaluation techniques covering individual record cards for students

at different levels and methods of reporting and assessing achievement of objectives

10. A technique for the yearly evaluation of the total curriculum and staff, with suggested methods for curriculum revision if necessary.

It should be noted here that a curriculum does not dictate to a teacher exactly what must be taught during a particular class hour. Rather, it serves as an overall guide for the establishment of the program within a school. It provides consistency, progression, and structure for the total physical education program, without binding or stifling the individual and collective creativity of the staff.

Adoption of the curriculum. After it has been developed, the committee as a whole should reconvene to amend and to adopt the curriculum, which should then be sent to the administration for approval and action. A curriculum of physical education should be revised as frequently as the need dictates.

SELECTION OF ACTIVITIES

The program of physical education consisting of activities such as team sports, individual and dual sports, rhythms, calisthenics, self-testing, and leisure-time and movement education activities should receive special attention. To provide students with a program consisting merely of popular team sports is neither adequate nor bene-

ficial. Therefore, the following principles are offered as a partial guide for determining the activities to be included in a balanced program of physical education.

Selected physiologic principles for determining activities

1. The physical education program should provide ample opportunities for a wide range of movements involving the large muscles.

2. The facts related to human growth and development are important considerations in curriculum construction.

3. The differences in physical capacities and abilities found among students should be provided for in the program.

4. The physical fitness needs of students must be met by the physical education program.

Physiologic characteristics are a major consideration in the selection of activities. It is necessary to understand the physical characteristics of boys and girls at all levels of growth and to meet them in selecting activities. The program must be rewarding for all levels of ability.

Selected psychological principles for determining activities

1. The physical education program should consist mostly of natural play activities.

Fig. 8-3. The curriculum should be rich in activities adaptable to use in leisure time. A canoeing class at Litchfield High School, Litchfield, Ill.

2. Activities should be selected in the light of the psychological age characteristics of the student. For instance, the program should provide more coeducational activities for adolescents, because this type of program meets the needs and interests of this age group.

3. Activities that are valuable in providing an emotional outlet for the student are needed.

4. The selection of activities should provide for progression. In the junior high school the fundamentals of tumbling and apparatus work, along with simple stunts, may be taught. In the senior high school the student should progress to more advanced work and more challenging combinations.

5. The selection and placement of activities should allow for sufficient time for the basic fundamentals of the skills to be learned.

6. Activities should be taught so that each student develops a more desirable self-concept and experiences a feeling of success.

7. Activities should be selected that best meet the seasonal drives and other interests and abilities of the students.

8. Psychologically speaking, the activities should provide a healthy outlet for boys and girls; they should be challenging, yet within the students' physical and mental capabilities. There must be an opportunity to continually improve and develop knowledge and skills—that is, there must be a progression that will keep interest high and develop abilities to a point where an activity can be enjoyed for the pleasure of doing it correctly.

Selected sociological principles for determining activities

1. The curriculum should be rich in activities adaptable to use in leisure time. For example, such activities as golf, tennis, and swimming should be in the program, if possible.

2. The activities should be selected for their possible contribution to the youth's training for citizenship in a democracy. The opportunity to participate in a team sport, select a captain, and be a member of a cohesive unit should be available with proper teacher guidance.

3. The curriculum should be suited to the

Fig. 8-4. The physical fitness needs of students must be met by the physical education program. Students at Wheaton High School, Wheaton, Md., developing physical fitness.

ideals of the community as well as to its needs. It may be of value, for example, to include square dancing, swimming, or bowling in the curriculum to meet the interests and needs of a community.

4. The activities that are particularly rich in opportunities for individual pursuit, such as gymnastics, are especially desirable.

5. Activities that reflect nationwide interests should be provided in the program. It is important to understand and have a working knowledge of popular American pastimes such as, baseball and basketball, because of the values inherent in these team sports and because of their national recognition and acceptance.

6. The curriculum should provide opportunities for students to develop leadership qualities.

PLANNING THE TOTAL PROGRAM

The goals of physical education can be achieved only through the execution of a well-made plan. The teacher in the physical education program has the responsibility to set up the daily learning situation in direct relation to overall objectives. This can be done only through careful and thoughtful planning of every physical education experience, so that it may be a purposeful one for each student and a step toward the attainment of the goals.

Planning the yearly program

The program of study for a single year is based on the overall curriculum, with specific objectives and activities selected according to the age and grade level of students. The program for the year should be exact and yet flexible enough to accommodate the changing needs and abilities of the students. Steps in planning for the year include both selection of objectives and activities and evaluation.

Objectives. In planning the yearly program, teachers should select specific objectives from those outlined in the overall curriculum. Selection is based on the particular age group and developmental status of the class. A secondary objective of the goal of

physical fitness, for example, may be the development of accuracy. A subordinate objective based on this factor may be the improvement of accuracy in the lay-up shot for basketball. Similarly, the methods of teaching activities should be selected specifically for the purposes of meeting these objectives. Plans must be flexible, however, since some students may already be proficient in the skills.

Activities. The activities to be included in a particular year of study are usually outlined in the overall curriculum. However, the teacher should determine the amount of time to be devoted to each activity, according to the needs and desires of the group. In schools that promote student planning, the teacher may base some decisions on the outcomes of discussions with students. For example, one class of ninth-grade girls may wish to study field hockey exclusively in the fall, while another group may want to combine field hockey with tennis. However, the teacher must ultimately decide the program for the year, after considering such things as the seasons of the locality, the facilities and equipment available, and the size and needs of the group.

Evaluation. Methods of evaluating the year's work should be planned in advance. Student achievement and program content should be surveyed in terms of the established objectives. Procedures for evaluation are outlined in a separate chapter, but the teacher should realize that planning is an essential part of the yearly plan.

Planning the unit of teaching

A unit of teaching refers to the period of time during which a particular sport or activity is studied. The program for the year has several units of teaching, some scheduled for six weeks, eight weeks, and other amounts of time. The use of units in teaching physical education is of great importance to the quality of the learning experience. Unit teaching provides direction and structure to each class meeting, and the students recognize each session as being a distinct part of a whole. The physical educator, guided by the unit goals, offers progressive instruction for their attainment, and the students should be aware of the purposes of activities within the unit. In planning the unit of teaching the teacher must consider the specific objectives and activities to be included in the unit. Because this phase of planning is the basis for daily instruction and the learning experience itself, its importance must not be underestimated.

Objectives. Specific objectives established for the year form the basis of the subobjectives in the unit plan. There should be subobjectives relating to all four goals of physical education (see Chapter 5), for it is these subobjectives obtained in the unit course of study that are the steppingstones to achieve-

ment of overall goals. Following is an example of the way in which objectives may be broken down for a unit: (1) *goal*—physical skill; (2) *objective*—to develop throwing power; (3) *specific objective (yearly plan)*—to improve pitching accuracy; and (4) *subobjective (unit plan)*—to pitch fast balls over the plate. Subobjectives would be established for each of the four goals in this manner, with the age level and developmental needs of the students the determining factor in estimating accomplishment.

Activities. The choice of activities to be included in each unit of study should be made on the basis of the subobjectives established. Certain principles should be kept in mind while planning the activities, in order

Fig. 8-5. Volleyball action at Brockport Central Schools, Brockport, N.Y.

to make the unit a complete series of learning experiences.

1. Provide a variety of learning experiences (relays, games of low organization), techniques (drills, skull sessions), and materials (audiovisual aids, outside reading).

2. Provide activities that are appropriate to the needs, age level, and developmental achievements of the group.

3. Provide activities that are progressive in nature.

4. Provide flexibility in planning so that unforeseen interruptions and delays during the course of the unit do not hinder achievement of unit objectives.

5. Provide a definite form for the unit by introducing new skills and activities on a weekly basis or with each class session (depending upon the frequency of classes), so

that students recognize progress within the unit.

6. Provide activities that promote the greatest amount of participation for the greatest number of students by utilizing all facilities and equipment available.

7. Provide for appropriate ending activities in the unit: methods of evaluation based on predetermined, specific objectives, as well as some type of special, climactic activity such as a tournament, demonstration, performance, or similar presentation toward which the work has been building throughout the unit.

Table 8-1 is a sample unit taken from the yearly plan with its activities and subobjectives.

An alternative to the unit plan, called the day's order, is sometimes used. In this ap-

Table 8-1. Sample basketball unit (six weeks)

	Physical fitness	Physical skills	Knowledge and appreciation	Social development

Week 1	Endurance
	Speed
		Passes
		Dribbling
			History
			Safety
			Rules: ball and
			  line violations
			Assign notebook
				New squads
				Discussion:
				  leadership
				Elect captains

Week 2	Endurance
	Speed
	Agility
		Review passes
		  and dribbling
		New: reverse
		  turn and pivot
			Rules: footwork
			  and fouls
				Group responsibility in drill
				  practice

Week 3	Endurance
	Speed
	Accuracy
	Agility
		Review pivot
		New shots: lay-
		  up, chest, and
		  one hand
			Offensive techniques	Safety-shooting
				  practice

Week 4	Endurance Speed Agility Accuracy Balance	Review shooting New: foul-shooting	Defensive techniques Planned plays	Teamwork Group planning

Week 5	Endurance
	Speed
	Agility
	Accuracy
	Balance
		Review shooting
		Tournament
			Etiquette in
			  tournament
			Strategy
			Review rules
				Continue group
				  planning and
				  teamwork

Week 6		Evaluation of
		  skills
			Written test
			Notebook due
				Evaluation of social cooperation
				Needs and plans
				  for next unit

proach the program of activities varies from day to day. However, within a semester of teaching, the same amount of time would be devoted to each activity as in the unit plan. When scheduling problems prevail, this plan facilitates use of gymnasium space by more than one class, for one group could be working on basketball while the other class concentrates on trampoline or apparatus work on the sidelines.

Planning the daily lesson

The final step necessary in the planning phase of teaching is the actual lesson plan itself. This has as its basis the unit plan of objectives and activities but is a complete analysis of the step-by-step procedures to be followed during each class session. This plan is probably the most important one, because it represents the real contact with the students and what they should be learning. It therefore needs to be very carefully thought out from beginning to end, with many principles followed in selecting procedures and definite objectives established for attainment.

Objectives. Each lesson must have its own set of definite objectives. Unless the teacher knows exactly what should be accomplished during the class period, the students also will not know the daily objectives.

Procedures. An outline of procedures should be written down for each class meeting. The various methods of teaching and the progression from one type of activity to another need to be carefully worked out. The following principles for the daily lesson plan should be helpful in planning procedures for a single class period:

1. Provide maximum participation for all class members. When choosing a method of teaching, the physical educator should consider the size of the class, the facilities and equipment, and the time allotment and select those procedures that allow the greatest amount of practice for the most students.

2. Provide maximum instruction and supervision. The physical educator should select formations and drills that allow instruction for small groups and supervision for the entire class.

3. Provide for safety of students. Group formations and game situations should be set up in such a way that students are protected from danger. This includes hazards from stationary equipment and from adjacent practicing groups.

4. Provide for the health of the students. Methods of instruction should be selected in accordance with capacities of students in respect to overexposure, fatigue, and extreme heat or cold.

5. Promote student interest and enthusiasm. The physical educator should strive, by varying the teaching patterns (games, drills, relays) and increasing the complexity of the work, to heighten student responses.

6. Provide for the growth and development of the students. The choice of methods should be dependent on the skill levels and accomplishments of the participants, and performances far above or below the estimated limits of their abilities should not be required.

7. Promote learning by proceeding from what is already known by the group to what is unknown. The students will thus be able to understand the relationship of new learnings to that which they have already learned.

8. Provide for self-evaluation by students of their abilities and for evaluation by the group and the physical educator of their daily accomplishments. In this way improvements and progress are recognized and advancement toward specific goals is kept in mind.

9. Promote carryover values and transfer of learning into daily life situations. Students who learn cooperation and good sportsmanship on the field or in the gymnasium, for example, need help in applying such learning to other experiences. The physical educator should make references to everday situations to pave the way for application of these traits to daily life situations.

10. Promote creativity on the part of each student. Contributions of new ideas and theories from all the students should be sought by the physical educator. An atmosphere should be established in which all students feel free to express themselves.

One final note in regard to the daily lesson

SAMPLE DAILY LESSON PLAN
(Based on unit plan, week 2)

Date: January 10
Class: Ninth grade boys and girls (approximately 30)
Teacher: Mr. EJM
Activity: Basketball (pivoting)

Equipment: AV loop film; six basketballs
Time: 48 minutes
Area: Gymnasium
Group organization: four assigned groups

Behavioral objectives

1. Each student will practice/drill with partner for eight minutes or until he has successfully completed 25 of each of the three types of passes (overhead, underhand, and chest) as previously taught. Passing station is in southwest corner of gym.
2. Each student will improve by one second his/her score for performing the zig-zag dribbling course set up in the northeast corner of the gym. Improvement should be shown within eight-minute practice/drill at this station.
3. Each student will view loop film on pivots in northwest corner of gym, actively following directions provided for practice of pivots. Practice and viewing should take place in approximately eight minutes.
4. In the southeast corner of the gym each student will follow given directions on pivoting drill, actively working with a partner to complete passes with pivots. Practice will continue for eight minutes or until successful completion of 25 passes to partner, using pivots off of left side and right side.
5. Each student will record his own progress at the end of class.
6. Each group leader will be responsible for the conduct of his or her group and will record progress of each member of his or her group on progress charts at end of class.

Time	Learning activity	Organization	Teaching behaviors
0-5 min.	Preparation for class. Individualized shooting practice at baskets	Free organization for shooting at six baskets.	Assist practice Check roll as class enters gym
5-37 min. (approx. 8 min. ea.)	At learning stations: 1. Review passes 2. Review dribble 3. Observe pivot loop film 4. Practice/drill pivoting then	Four groups, one at each station. Rotate at 8-min. interval, or individuals rotate upon completion of tasks	Assist groups (emphasize safety: keep balls under control, in assigned areas; throw only to a *ready* receiver)
	At baskets for shooting	Individual shooting practice if completed four stations	Work with pivoting.
37-39 min.	Evaluation reporting	Report to leader	Collect balls and progress charts
	Question period	Informal around teacher	Question group
39-48 min.	Showering and dressing		Supervision

Questions for evaluation

1. How many of you were able to complete all your passes? To improve this skill?
2. How many of you were able to take one second off of your zig-zag score?
3. What is the purpose of a pivot? Why should we be able to perform to both sides? Describe balanced position. What violations pertain to pivoting?
4. Did you all record your scores with leaders?

Notes for next time:

Fig. 8-6. Football at Paul J. Gelinas Junior High School in Setauket, N.Y.

plan is concerned with flexibility. Although it is essential that this plan cover the full time allotted to the class and should be adhered to as closely as possible, the physical educator must be sensitive to the group's response to the procedures. If it is seen that the class tires quickly in a particular drill formation or that one of the procedures is not successful, the physical educator should go on to a different phase of the lesson. It is always wise to plan more than the time allows, so that in such instances valuable time will not be lost for lack of organization or preparation. During the outdoor season, alternate daily lesson plans should be prepared for use indoors on rainy days. In this way no time is lost because of inclement weather.

A daily lesson plan drawn from the ninth-grade unit on basketball is included as an example.

A SYSTEMS APPROACH TO CURRICULUM DEVELOPMENT IN PHYSICAL EDUCATION

The systems approach to curriculum development in physical education includes seven steps:

1. *Identify the overall basic or developmental objectives of physical education* (ex-

ample: organic development, skill development, cognitive development, social-affective development). These represent the objectives physical educators are attempting to achieve for each boy and girl. For a fuller description of each of these objectives see Chapter 5.

2. *Delineate each of the basic or development objectives listed in the first step into meaningful subobjectives desirable for each boy and girl to accomplish.* Identifying the subobjectives brings into sharper focus what needs to be accomplished and makes much more manageable the achievement of the overall basic or developmental objective. Here are some examples of subobjectives of each of the overall developmental objectives:

Organic development objective
Subobjectives:

Cardiorespiratory endurance	Posture
Muscular strength and	Flexibility
endurance	Speed
Coordination	Agility
Balance	Accuracy

Skill development objective
Subobjectives:
Locomotor and nonlocomotor activities
Movement fundamentals
General motor ability

Specific motor ability in game and sport skills

Cognitive development objective

Subobjectives:

Understanding of principles of movement (role of gravity, force)

Knowledge of rules and strategies of games and sports

Contribution of physical activity to health

Contribution of physical activity to academic achievement

Problem solving

Social-affective development objectives

Subobjectives:

Sportsmanship

Valuing

Participation

Group orientation

Attitude toward physical education

Respect for other students and leadership

3. *Identify the characteristics of the students in terms of each subobjective identified in step 2.* A characteristic, for example, of seventh-to ninth-grade students in respect to the subobjective of cardiorespiratory endurance under the basic development objective or organic development would be that boys and girls at this level tire easily due to the rapid, uneven growth that takes place during this growth period, whereas at the tenth- to twelfth-grade level students have or nearly have reached physiologic maturity and therefore are much better equipped to engage in vigorous activity for an extended period of time.

The characteristics of students at each educational level would be determined in respect to each of the subobjectives identified in step 2. Where pertinent, characteristics of boys and girls would be differentiated. As a result of accomplishing this step in curriculum development it is now possible to see the relationship between the goals that are desired to be accomplished and the specific characteristics of the students for whom the goals are desired to be accomplished.

4. *After identifying the characteristics of students it is now important to determine the needs in relation to the characteristics as outlined in step 3.* This means that for each sub-objective the needs of the students concerned would be identified. For example, in light of the fact that a characteristic of the seventh- to ninth-grade students in respect to the subobjective of cardiorespiratory endurance as a subdivision of the developmental objective of organic development indicates that boys and girls tire easily due to the rapid, uneven growth that takes place, a need that could be identified for these students would be that physical education experiences should be provided that overcome fatiguing factors associated with time, distance, and game pressures. On the other hand, since a characteristic of tenth- to twelfth-grade students indicates they have matured physiologically to a much greater extent indicates a need for activities that are more vigorous in nature. In addition, students need guidance in respect to such items as amounts of activity, food habits, rest, and sleep.

5. After identifying the developmental objectives, subobjectives, characteristics, and needs of students and seeing how all of these relate to boys and girls, *the next step is to identify the activities that are appropriate in light of these considerations.* For example, in light of these factors that we have identified for students in grades seven to nine, we can point out that the activities scheduled should include such sports as soccer or field hockey and other physical activities (named in accordance with specific school's facilities), utilizing modified rules (could be spelled out), which include such factors as shortened periods of play, smaller playing areas, frequent time outs, unlimited substitutions.

6. In conformance with a recent trend in curriculum development, this systems approach in curriculum development in physical education suggests the *listing of specific performance objectives for students in relation to their objectives, characteristics and needs and the activities appropriate to their age, physical condition, and abilities.*

For each of the subobjectives specific performance objectives will be listed. For example, in respect to the seventh- to ninth-grade group of students a performance objective for the cardiorespiratory endurance subobjective could be "Given an exercise that measures cardiorespiratory endurance, for example, running a quarter of a mile, the student is able to perform without undue fatigue and with a quick heart rate recovery." A performance objective for the tenth-to twelfth-grade group of students might be "The student runs one-half mile and is able to perform without undue fatigue and with a quick recovery of pulse and heart rate." Of course, it is understood that all performance objectives would take into consideration the characteristics and needs of the specific students. Performance objectives provide specific levels of accomplishment that indicate whether the desired objective and goals have been accomplished.

7. The final step is to identify the best methods and procedures for instruction that will be most effective in achieving the desired goals. These methods would provide variety for the students and would include the application of sound motor learning theories (for example, mass versus distributed practice) and the understanding and appreciation of certain basic concepts relative to the accomplishment of the objectives (for example, follow through helps to guarantee accuracy), a concept in skill development.

An example of a method that could be utilized in respect to the development of the subobjective of cardiorespiratory endurance for seventh-to ninth-graders might include a laboratory experiment with conditioned and nonconditioned animals, an explanation of the role and worth of cardiorespiratory endurance in organic development and physical fitness, an explanation in student language of some research that indicates the physical fitness status of their age group, actual participation in activities that develop this quality, and an explanation of performance objectives and practice for their accomplishment.

The seven-step systems approach to curriculum development in physical education provides a logical step-by-step method that results in scientific method for determining what activities will be offered in light of the objectives sought and the characteristics and needs of students and then establishes performance objectives to assess whether students have met each objective. By utilizing such a systems approach a much more meaningful physical education program may be provided. It represents a program that is aimed at helping students to become physically educated in the true sense of the word and in making well-planned physical education that achieves specific outcomes a viable offering in our schools.

Fig. 8-7. Running activities at Paul J. Gelinas Junior High School in Setauket, N.Y.

To recapitulate, the systems approach to curriculum development in physical education consists of the following steps:

1. Identify major developmental objectives of physical education.

2. Delineate each major developmental objective into meaningful subobjectives.

3. Identify characteristics of students in respect to each subobjective listed in step 2.

4. Identify the needs of students in light of their characteristics as listed in step 3.

5. Identify the physical education activities that meet the conditions outlined in steps 1 through 4.

6. List performance objectives for each physical education activity in light of conditions in steps 1 through 4.

7. Identify the best methods and procedures for instruction.

ROLE OF STUDENTS IN CLASS PLANNING

The teacher of physical education should devote some thought to the role of students in program planning. How much opportunity should they have in planning their own course of study?

The answer to this question lies in the philosophy of the department concerning student creativity and free expression. It may be believed that students should share in many phases of the planning or that they should contribute only to planning within a single unit or part of a unit. Some measure of student contribution should be sought, however, because of the inherent values of increased motivation, understanding, and creativity it affords.

Motivation. When students assist in making plans for class work, they are motivated and stimulated to participate to a greater extent. They believe that they have a share in the goals and have a genuine desire for their accomplishment.

Understanding. The discussions necessary to bringing out student suggestions require leadership and guidance from the physical educator. Some of the purposes of physical education might be pointed out to the students at this time to widen their understanding of the program as a whole. In this way their suggestions become consistent with their needs and with the goals of the program.

Creativity. Developing individual creativity is a goal of all education and one that should be included among the physical education objectives. Allowing students to contribute their own ideas and express their feelings is one way in which a creative atmosphere can be produced. While it may be

Fig. 8-8. Field hockey in Lexington Public Schools in Lexington, Mass.

more difficult to promote this type of rapport, it is indeed worthy of the attempt.

Problems. There are certain problems connected with student-teacher planning and the incorporation of the students' ideas into the program. In a large school where use of facilities is tightly scheduled and a prescribed regimen of activities must be followed, students would need to take these factors into consideration.

Another problem that arises in regard to student planning stems from the type of leadership offered by the teacher. There is a real art to promoting good class discussion to bring out the contributions of all students and the physical educator must devote much time to planning key questions and ideas and to developing skill in this area.

INDIVIDUALIZING INSTRUCTION

After incorporating student suggestions into the program, the instructional phases of physical education may be further individualized with the inclusion of variable goals for individual achievement. Inasmuch as each student within a class has attained a certain level of ability in a particular sport, the goal for that student should be improvement of his or her own skill level. Therefore, the student needs freedom to work at his or her own level of interest and rate of speed. The student should strive to improve according to developmental tasks based on previous record and performance. For example, in a skill such as pitching a softball or a baseball, proficiency levels for some students might indicate further practice to improve accuracy and speed, whereas other advanced students may need to advance to practicing various styles of pitching (fast ball, slow ball, inside and outside curves).

In a prescribed curriculum, this may mean that some students are working on advanced skills earlier than suggested in the written guide. It must be remembered, however, that individual development rarely follows a defined pattern. Therefore, freedom to explore and expand must be provided for.

When the teacher has completed all phases of planning—for the curriculum, the year,

the unit, and the daily lesson—and has incorporated student ideas wherever possible, the time has come to carry out the plan.

CONCEPTUALIZED APPROACH

The process of education is undergoing a revolution in many areas of the curriculum. The sciences, mathematics, and languages especially are utilizing new teaching methodology and new technological devices and are drastically revising their curricula. Today's secondary school students are familiar with concepts and areas of knowledge that formerly were reserved for college-level courses.

Physical educators are well aware that they also must adapt physical education to the demands of this era. Physical educators have found that today's students require and react well to a conceptualized approach to physical education and that this approach to teaching helps to stimulate curriculum reform in these areas.

Today's physical educators realize that the first task is to educate students about their bodies and the scientific principles that control the use of the body and to educate them to use their bodies effectively and efficiently. The conceptualized approach to the teaching of physical education helps students to better understand how their bodies move and why physical activity is so important in maintaining health and fitness. This approach to teaching physical education integrates the mental aspects with the physical.

In using the conceptualized approach, the teacher serves as a guide rather than as a storehouse of information. Students learn, for example, the principles of body leverage, hip rotation, and foot and leg placement in throwing a softball by experimenting. The physical principles involved are best understood when they are ideated by the students themselves. This approach to teaching physical education depends upon the background of the physical educator and his or her willingness to place much of the burden for learning on the students themselves. This approach, however, also demands that the physical educator utilize a textbook geared to secondary school students and that each student be assigned readings and outside work based on the text and related experiences in the physical education classroom.

The conceptualized approach to physical education helps students to understand why certain activities are selected for inclusion in the program and why such activities as physical fitness and the lifetime sports receive such great emphasis. This approach to physical education draws the student closer to the program and helps to make physical education activities a respected and pleasurable aspect of the school day.

PROJECTING PHYSICAL EDUCATION INTO THE FUTURE

What will physical education be like for the secondary school student of the future? Based on a knowledge of current advances in education and technology, some tentative projections can be made, but even these will be subject to change in the light of new events and discoveries.

The cost of education is constantly rising and physical education facilities will have to be financed and built to accommodate students and teaching staffs. New materials, especially plastics, will probably be used extensively for gymnasium floors to reduce the constant need for refinishing and to save on maintenance costs. Synthetics will be utilized on outdoor surfaces to make them more usable for longer portions of the year. Geodesic domes will house multiple-use gymnasiums and auxiliary physical education rooms, and air-supported structures will provide additional teaching stations.

An increasing emphasis on research in physical education will lead to more scientifically formulated curricula. Much of the benefit from this research will result in better programs for the atypical student. Mainstreaming will be utilized more and more. Students in regular physical education classes will have textbooks and will utilize special audiovisual aids. They will be able to analyze their performances through instant playback devices housed in physical education projection rooms.

Curricula in the secondary school will be broadened and increased, and students will be given a wider choice in the selection of activities. Alternate programs will be introduced. A wide variety of lifetime sports will be offered, along with physical fitness work, dance, and the usual variety of team and dual sports and activities. Portable pools will help to make swimming instruction a possibility for every student. There will be an emphasis on student-centered learning through the conceptualized approach, and the students will take on an increased responsibility for the program.

As physical education continues to assert itself in the secondary school curriculum, it will gain greater respect. This will help to decrease class size, to give classes a more homogeneous balance, to provide an individual program of physical education for every student, and to release the physical educator from the burden of nonteaching duties. Physical educators will become more expert in their own field, will attend more in-service and graduate courses, and will be more knowledgeable about education in general. This will help physical education to gain full community respect and support.

Athletics will become more educational for both boys and girls. The current trend toward varsity-level competition for both boys and girls as provided for under Title IX will continue and intensify, but these programs will be balanced by expanded intramural programs serving the needs and interests of all the students in the school. Interschool competition will place a stronger emphasis on the individual and the effect of competition on him or her.

As sophisticated communications and transportation media continue to make the world seem smaller, the international aspects of physical education will emerge. More and more students and physical educators will cooperate in international exchange programs, and Olympic and international sports and events will become vital parts of the secondary school program.

We cannot know or predict all the changes the future will bring. We may find that the philosophy and objectives of physical education will have to be drastically revised from year to year. Continued space exploration may result in significant advances in the understanding of man's physiology and psychology that will affect our programs. Government-sponsored research and pilot physical education programs, changes in professional preparation, and revisions in general education will also have a profound effect on physical education, as will our need to serve handicapped students more meaningfully and our efforts to stabilize domestic and world conditions.

BRINGING ABOUT CHANGE IN THE PHYSICAL EDUCATION CURRICULUM

If physical education is to grow and gain educational respect the traditional type of physical education must be evaluated carefully and alterations made in light of the changes taking place in society and general education. To bring about change, a discussion is provided that (1) looks at the catalysts that bring about curriculum change and (2) examines the ingredients essential to change.

Catalysts that bring about curriculum change

Changes occur in physical education curricula as they do in other areas of the school offering. There is usually a continuous list of myriad proposals for change. Each proposal should be considered on its own merits and put to the test of whether or not it has value.

What are the influencing factors in regard to change? A few associations, agencies, and individuals who produce change in physical education are discussed in the following paragraphs.

National associations and agencies. The President's Council on Physical Fitness and Sports is an outstanding example of one national governmental agency that brought about much change in programs of health, physical education, and recreation throughout the United States and the world. Through their speakers, publications, and communications media pronouncements, many

changes have taken place in the schools and colleges of this nation. Physical fitness in some communities has become the overriding purpose of programs of health education and physical education, sometimes at the expense of the other objectives of these fields and a wellbalanced program of activities.

Examples of other national associations and agencies that play a part in curriculum change are the National Education Association, the American Alliance for Health, Physical Education, and Recreation, the United States Office of Education (example, Title IX regulations), the Association for Supervision and Curriculum Development, and the American Medical Association.

State associations and agencies. As national organizations influence the curricula of our schools and colleges, so do state organizations. State boards of education or departments of public instruction, state bureaus, departments, or divisions of health and physical education, state education associations, citizens' committees, teachers' associations, and associations for health, physical education, and recreation are a few examples of organizations that influence curricula. Through the publication of syllabi, sponsorship of legislation, enactment of rules and regulations, exercise of supervisory powers, allocation of funds, and initiation of projects, organizations promote certain ideas and programs that initiate changes in schools and colleges.

Research. Research brings about change. As new knowledge is uncovered, more information is known about the learning process, new techniques are developed, and other research is conducted. Change eventually ensues if the research is significant, but the change may be slow in coming. It usually takes a long time for the creation of knowledge to penetrate to the grass roots, where it becomes part of an action program.

In the field of physical education, research on motor learning, the relationship of health and physical fitness to academic achievement, movement education, cognitive learning, physiologic changes that occur in the body through exercise, smoking, ecology, and the relationship of mental health and physical activity represent a few examples of research that have or will have a bearing upon programs of physical education throughout the country.

College and university faculties. The leaders in education from the campuses of the nation who serve as consultants, write textbooks, make speeches, and are active in professional associations help to bring about changes in education in general and in the special field of physical education.

Social forces. Such social forces in the American culture as the civil rights movement, automation, mass communication, student activism, black studies, sports promotion, and collective bargaining through unions are a few of the movements sweeping the nation that have implications for curricula in schools and colleges. In addition the social trends of the times involving attitudes toward sex, driving, alcohol, tobacco, drugs, and narcotics bring about curricula change. Times change, customs change, the habits of people change, and with such changes the role of educational institutions and their responsibilities to their society frequently change.

Ingredients essential to change

Change is a process that takes time. The steps through which change usually occurs are as follows: (1) Physical educators become aware of a needed innovation, for example, movement education in the elementary school. (2) As more and more people become interested in the innovation, an interest stage develops. Interest in movement education has been generated through experimental programs, workshops, writings and other means of communicating the idea to educators. (3) There is the evaluation stage, in which physical educators determine the values that the change has for their programs —values that relate directly to the student and the goals of physical education. (4) More extensive experimenting with the idea takes place. (5) The change is adopted. Movement education has gone through these steps in

many schools systems with the change being adopted. However, many of the schools in the United States have not changed their program to incorporate movement education into their schools. Therefore, more change needs to take place not only in respect to movement education but also in many other areas.

Miller,[*] in her article entitled "A Man to Fill the Gap: The Change Agent," points out that each profession needs to bring about change to lessen the gap between what they know and what they practice. Since there is a big gap between what we know and what we practice in physical education, change is needed and change agents are necessary to bring about the needed change. Miller defines the change agent as "a professional who has as his major function the advocacy and introduction of innovations into practice" or a professional person who tries to influence decisions that will bring about the adoption of new ideas. In bringing about change, the change agent, according to Miller, should be aware of seven principles. They are presented here in adapted form and are related to physical education.

• *The change agent must be well informed as to the needs and characteristics of the client system.* The students and others, such as the physical education staff in a school where it is desired to effect the change, are the client system. It is important for the change agent to base his plans on their needs.

• *The change agent must develop a close relationship between himself or herself and the client system.* There must be a confidence in the change agent. A mutual trust and respect must exist between the client system and the change agent, for unless the client system has confidence, change cannot effectively be brought about.

• *The change agent must realize that change is not a unilateral undertaking but, instead, is a mutually cooperative affair.* The autocratic director of physical education who orders the innovation will never succeed.

---

[*]Miller, P. L.: A man to fill the gap: the change agent, Journal of Health, Physical Education, and Recreation **40:**34, 1969.

Change is a cooperative procedure between the change agent and the staff of his school system. As a result, there may be compromise and modifications, but the changes that are made will be more permanent and better accepted by the staff.

• *The change agent should enlist the support of key leaders in the client system.* Key leaders among the students in the school system as well as other persons, can help to ensure that the change is accepted by the client system and is adopted. Their involvement is essential in getting the entire student body and staff to accept the new development.

• *The change agent needs a well-developed plan and strategy for introducing change.* The plan for bringing about change in an organization cannot be a hit-or-miss affair. Foresight and planning must decide the timetable for moving from one step to the next in innovating change, for identifying the key leaders who in turn will influence others, and for formally approving the change. Also, the techniques to be used, the communications media to be solicited, the persons to be seen, the meetings to be held, and the information to be imparted must all be carefully planned out so that nothing is left to chance.

• *The change agent must be willing to change himself or herself and to keep up with the times.* To be effective in bringing about change in others, the change agent must be a model of change. He or she must reflect an image of self-renewal and self-improvement. Such a person is needed to empathize with others and to be sensitive to the change process.

• *The change agent needs to help others to become change agents.* The change agent's success will be determined in large measure in how well he or she gets other members of a staff or organization to become change agents themselves. In so doing they will be abreast of the latest research findings in their field, have a recognition of the need for innovation, possess the ability to make wise choices as to what innovations will best help the client system, and be willing to try new ideas and practices.

Self-assessment tests

These tests are to assist students in determining if material and competencies presented in this chapter have been mastered:

1. A teacher has been in a school system for twenty-five years. She indicates that the physical education curriculum she developed a quarter of a century ago is the best physical education program for her school. The program includes field hockey and soccer in the fall, volleyball and basketball in the winter, and softball and tennis in the spring. What is your answer to this teacher?
2. Get permission from a junior or senior high school to observe their physical education program. After your observation apply what you consider to be a sound procedure for curriculum development and construct a physical education program for that school.
3. Given a group of seventh-, eighth-, ninth-, tenth-, eleventh-, or twelfth-grade students, indicate what activities you would select to be included in their physical education program. Justify your selection.
4. Prepare a yearly plan for the teaching of physical education for a tenth-grade class. Then, follow through and develop a unit plan for the teaching of swimming. Finally, develop one day's session plan that would be included in the swimming unit.
5. Utilizing the systems approach in the text, prepare a physical education program for a given group of seventh-grade students.
6. Imagine that you are a faculty member in a secondary school that urgently needs to have the physical education curriculum updated and revised. The faculty is composed of elderly teachers who wish to preserve the status quo. What procedure would you advocate to bring about desirable change in this program?

Points to remember

1. Curriculum planning is a group process.
2. The physical educator has a major responsibility in the formulation of a physical education program.
3. A curriculum guide for a school system is a set of minimum standards.
4. There must be understanding of the student and learning theories to produce a valid curriculum.
5. A curriculum study must fit the school system and the society in which it will operate.
6. Activities must be properly selected.
7. A systems approach may be used in curriculum development.
8. Evaluation is a never-ending process for a curriculum.
9. The daily plan, the unit plan, and the yearly plan are all outgrowths of the overall curriculum.

Problems to think through

1. How detailed should a curriculum guide be in regard to length of time spent on an activity and items to be covered in a listed activity? Why?

2. Should there be room for initiative by the physical educator working from a curriculum guide? Why?
3. Compare two schools where the same activity may be handled differently. What may make it necessary to handle this activity differently?
4. Why is it important to understand the nature of the student in curriculum planning?
5. What administrative details would limit a curriculum?
6. How can a systems approach be used to develop a physical education curriculum?

Case study for analysis

Select a secondary grade level (boys or girls) and prepare, in outline form, a curriculum for one twenty-week semester. The school has separate gymnasiums for boys and girls, an outdoor turf area, two teachers for each class of sixty to eighty pupils, sufficient equipment and supplies for the largest class, and three periods of physical education weekly for each student. Analyze specific objectives, time allotment, activities, and fundamentals. Simulate a school situation by working in a committee groups.

Exercises for review

1. What steps should be followed in the preparation of a curriculum?
2. How may a physical education teacher make a contribution to a curriculum study?
3. What principles should be considered in the selection of activities for a program?
4. Who may be a part of a curriculum study group?
5. Plan a six-week unit on badminton for seventh graders.
6. Plan a daily lesson within that unit.

Selected readings

Bannon, J. J.: Leisure resources—its comprehensive planning, Englewood Cliffs, N.J., 1976, Prentice-Hall, Inc.

Bucher, C. A.: Physical education for life, New York, 1969, McGraw-Hill Book Company.

Bucher, C. A.: Administrative dimensions of health and physical education programs, including athletics, St. Louis, 1971, The C. V. Mosby Co.

Bucher, C. A.: Dimensions of physical education, St. Louis, 1974, The C. V. Mosby Co.

Bucher, C. A.: Administration of health and physical education programs, including athletics, ed. 6, St. Louis, 1975, The C. V. Mosby Co.

Bucher, C. A.: Foundations of physical education, ed. 7, St. Louis, 1975, The C. V. Mosby Co.

Brameld, T.: A cross-cutting approach to the curriculum: the moving wheel, Phi Delta Kappan, March, 1970, p. 346.

Crosby, M.: Who changes the curriculum and how? Phi Delta Kappan, March, 1970, p. 385.

Curriculum for people, Today's Education **60:**42, 1971.

Kidd, F. M., et al.: Guidelines for secondary school physical education, Journal of Health, Physical Education, and Recreation **42:**47, 1971.

Metcalf, L. E., and Hunt, M. P.: Relevance and the curriculum, Phi Delta Kappan, March, 1970, p. 358.

National Advisory Council on Education Professions Development: Mainstreaming: helping teachers meet the challenge, Washington, D.C., 1976, The Council.

Shane, J. G., and Shane, H. G.: Cultural change and the curriculum: 1970-2000 A.D., Educational Technology, April, 1970, p. 13.

Silberman, C. E.: Crisis in the classroom—the remaking of American education, New York, 1971, Random House, Inc.

Singer, R. N., et al.: Physical education: foundations, New York, 1976, Holt, Rinehart and Winston.

Toffler, A.: Future shock, New York, 1970, Random House, Inc.

University of the State of New York, The State Education Department: Final report on the workshop on the concept of "redesign" for New York State physical educators held at Stamford, New York, October 11-13, 1970, Albany, November 20, 1970.

U.S. Department of Health, Education, and Welfare, Office for Civil Rights, Final title IX regulation implementing education amendments of 1972—prohibiting sex discrimination in education, Washington, D.C., 1975, HEW.

Van Til, W.: Curriculum: quest for relevance, New York, 1971, Houghton Mifflin Co.

Willgoose, C. E.: The curriculum in physical education, Englewood Cliffs, N.J., 1969, Prentice-Hall, Inc.

9

TWENTY-SIX INNOVATIVE IDEAS FOR SECONDARY SCHOOL PHYSICAL EDUCATION

INSTRUCTIONAL OBJECTIVES AND COMPETENCIES TO BE ACHIEVED

After reading this chapter the student should be able to—

1. Identify twenty-six innovative ideas relating to secondary school physical education programs.
2. List innovative ideas for physical education programs that stress:
   a. Personalized and individualized learning
   b. Performance objectives, competency packages, and goal setting
   c. Career and leadership opportunities
   d. Electives
   e. Flexibility in scheduling
   f. Specialized types of experiences

Webster's Dictionary defines the word "innovation" as the "act of introducing something new or novel . . . or a change effected by innovating. . . . " In other words, innovation represents a change in the way things are done. In the field of education it may represent an effort to bring about something new in respect to the substance, methods, materials, or some other aspect of education so as to provide experiences for students that are more relevant to the world in which they live.

The current educational setting is one in which much innovation is taking place. Physical education is also concerned with innovation as it tries to develop programs more in tune with the times and the student of today. This chapter presents several innovative programs in physical education that are in operation throughout the country. Many of these programs are still in the early stages of development and thus their merit and worth have not been established, therefore, we are presenting these programs as new ideas but are not necessarily endorsing them. We also recognize that many innovative practices that exist in many schools are not discussed in this chapter.

It is important for the physical educator, and particularly the new teacher, to know about innovative programs. This will broaden their knowledge, stimulate their thinking, and hopefully enrich their teaching and thus make their physical education programs more dynamic and meaningful to the students they teach.

Each of the innovative programs discussed in this chapter is presented only briefly. The purpose is to make the reader aware of some of the changes taking place in physical education throughout the country. The interested reader who desires more detailed information regarding these programs should contact the schools directly.

PROGRAMS STRESSING PERSONALIZED AND INDIVIDUALIZED LEARNING IN PHYSICAL EDUCATION

INDIVIDUALLY GUIDED EDUCATION*
Parkview Junior High School
Roseville, New Mexico

Grades and students concerned. Junior high school grades

Selected objectives
- To provide an effective medium of teaching individual sports.
- To know students better as individuals.
- To enable students to move at their own rate of learning and not to repeat skills learned previously.
- To free the teacher to work with those students needing the most help.
- To provide students with an opportunity to work on their own in the development of sport skills under teacher guidance.
- To provide an opportunity for students to progress to their own level of accomplishment.

Selected features of the program. Individualized units have been developed in such activities as apparatus, archery, tumbling, track and field, table tennis, badminton, bowling, basketball, and volleyball.

Each unit includes performance objective, explanation of unit, activities, and a test. To achieve an objective the student does such things as the following: determines what the objective is and what is to be accomplished in the way of skills to be learned, reads the directions and determines the activities that will result in the accomplishment of the objective, works on the needed skills utilizing such helps as teacher-student assistance, loop films, and books. After doing assigned work the student is tested by the teacher. The student then goes on to the next objective, and the entire procedure is repeated.

STUDENT-DIRECTED CURRICULUM*
Triway Schools
Waynesville, Ohio

Grades and students concerned. It is recommended that student age and maturity should be assessed and, in addition, such items as available facilities and the school's educational philosophy should be reviewed before utilizing this innovative idea.

Selected objectives
- To provide students with the opportunity to develop their own course of study.
- To help students to develop responsibility, creativity, initiative and communicative skills.
- To improve students' understanding of values of health and physical education.

Selected features of the program. Students and teachers work as a group in developing the physical education curriculum for the semester. Plans formulated by students become a semester's contract between student and teacher. The official course of study represents a combination of students' as well as teachers' selection of units. Field trips, visiting speakers, and some utilization of community facilities are part of the program. Evaluations have shown student feedback to be enthusiastic and positive.

SELF-EVALUATION OF OUTSIDE ACTIVITY AND PARTICIPATION*
Rutland High School
Rutland, Vermont

Grades and students concerned. High school students.
Selected objectives
- To encourage the development of positive attitudes toward physical activity as a lifetime, twelve-month-a-year endeavor.
- To develop a pattern of lifetime activities that will have a beneficial impact upon students, parents, and citizens in the community.
- To encourage students to develop skills in new and different types of activities they have not tried before.

Selected features of the program. Students earn points toward a grade when they become involved in designated activities during after-school and summertime hours.

The program provides for four groups of activities: vigorous, carryover-mild, coeducational, and new activities. Examples of vigorous activities are jogging, soccer, hiking-hunting, and bicycling. Examples of carryover-mild activities are bowling, tennis, golf, horseback riding, and badminton. Coeducational activities can be any activity in a mixed group. New activities can be any activity that the student has not tried before.

Points are awarded on the basis of 1 point for each hour of participation. A student can earn only 3 points per week from each of the four categories of activities.

Students keep a record of their points on a daily basis for an eight-week period, which constitutes a quarter. Students who engage in summertime activities during a ten-week program may earn a grade for the first quarter of the school year.

CONTRACTING†
Ft. Pierce Central High School
Ft. Pierce, Florida

Grades and students concerned. Eleventh and twelfth grades.

---

*Adapted from Barry, P. E., editor: *Ideas for Secondary School Physical Education*, Washington, D.C., 1976, AAHPER.
†Adapted from letter and material sent by Barbara L. Fast and also from article by Fast, B. L.: Contracting, Journal of Health, Physical Education, and Recreation **42**:31, 1971.

---

*Adapted from Barry, P. E., editor: *Ideas for Secondary School Physical Education*, Washington, D.C., 1976, AAHPER.

Selected objectives

- To facilitate the teaching of large physical education classes.
- To enable students to pursue activities of their own choosing.
- To assign grades to students in accordance with their achievement.
- To inject new vitality into the physical education experience.
- To utilize an objective procedure in evaluating physical education progress.

Selected features of the program. Students follow units of activity of their own choosing and report to class solely for the purpose of checking attendance.

Contracts are prepared on each activity that is offered in the physical education program. Each contract lists the requirements to be met by the student and the point value of each. For example, Contract 1 in a unit on bowling requires the student to bowl six games, keep score, list the reasons for keeping score, and identify the symbols used in scoring. Each contract is valued at 5 points. This is multiplied by the difficulty rating, which ranges from 1 to 5. The bowling contract thus has a 20-point value. Materials are provided so that students can research assignments as needed.

When one contract is completed another one is made. Students establish their own pace and set the schedule at which they wish to fulfill the contract. Penalty and bonus points may be awarded.

Worksheets are kept on each student and provide a record of such things as contracts for each student, completion dates, point value, penalty and bonus points, and final score.

Grading system is as follows: 100 points, A; 90 points, B; 75 points, C; 70 points, D. No contract results in failure. If the contract is not completed, it is returned to the student, who begins again.

INDIVIDUALIZED APPROACH TO LEARNING*
Omaha Public Schools
Omaha, Nebraska

Grades and students concerned. Fourth to twelfth grades.

Selected objectives

- To provide a student-centered learning experience in physical education.
- To provide a learning continuum in physical education.
- To provide an individualized physical education curriculum for students.

*Adapted from material sent by and article written by Shrader, R. D.: Individualized approach to learning, Journal of Health, Physical Education, and Recreation 42:33, 1971.

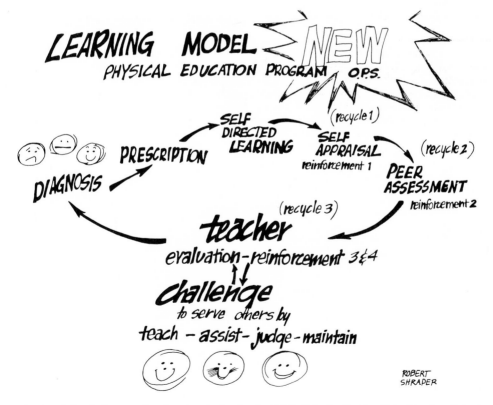

Fig. 9-1. Individual approach to learning, in the Omaha Public Schools, Omaha, Neb. (Courtesy Robert Shrader.)

- To make it possible for each student to regulate his or her own learning.
- To convert the gymnasium into a learning laboratory.
- To encourage students to assist other students in the learning process.
- To have the teacher serve as a facilitator rather than as a presenter of learning.

Selected features of the program. Students are pretested to determine present status in respect to such items as skills, knowledge and understanding, and value domains (psychomotor, cognitive, and affective).

Each student is provided with an individual prescription (called a *phy-pak*) based on test results and his needs and works toward fulfilling his or her prescription as indicated. Self-testing and peer assistance are encouraged.

Each student meets with teacher for final evaluation of prescribed task. The teacher determines whether task has been successfully accomplished based on learning objective. Records are kept on student progress and the new learning task (phy-pak) prescribed. If task has not been successfully completed, teacher offers suggestions regarding alternate ways in which learning objective can be achieved.

The phy-pak contract consists of nine parts: clarification of contract, what the prescription can do for the student, learning objectives, diagnostic test or pretest, learning tasks categorized into three parts (psychomotor, cognitive, and affective domains), learning activities, self-test, final test, and challenge activities.

PROGRAMS STRESSING PERFORMANCE OBJECTIVES, COMPETENCY PACKAGES, AND GOAL SETTING IN PHYSICAL EDUCATION

PHYSICAL EDUCATION PERFORMANCE OBJECTIVES BANK*
Montgomery County Public Schools
Rockville, Maryland

Grades and students concerned. Junior and senior high school students.

Selected objectives
- To help in the selection of objectives and units of instruction related to students, facilities, and time alloted.
- To have a teacher resource of objectives based on student and program needs.
- To identify more accurately student level of learning for the benefit of student and teacher.
- To enable the teacher to be better able to construct curricula, develop tests, select teaching aids, develop units, and identify activities for the program.

Selected features of the program. The performance objectives bank includes five parts: (1) introductory description of how cards (objectives) are utilized in the bank, (2) rationale as to the impact of the learning concepts on such things as methods and techniques of teaching, (3) classification of units with such information as the description of performance objectives for each unit, (4) measurement techniques, and (5) listing of skills and a bibliography for various activities.

The bank is divided into five sections with color-coded cards as follows: (1) *white*, introductory and descriptive information; (2) *yellow*, objectives for the psychomotor domain; (3) *blue*, objectives for the cognitive domain; (4) *pink*, objectives for the affective domain; and (5) *green*, techniques for measurement.

Each card contains either explanatory information, statement of performance, or measurement technique. For example, the yellow cards (psychomotor domain) contain specific physical performance objectives relating to motor skills. In addition to the motor skills, suggestions are included as to what should be emphasized concerning evaluation of the performance objective at beginning, intermediate, and advanced levels of learning.

COMPETENCY PACKAGES (COMPACS)*
Florida Department of Education, Bureau of Curriculum and Personnel Development
Tallahassee, Florida

Grades and students concerned. Middle, junior, and senior high schools.

Selected objectives
- To better meet instructional, assessment and organizational needs of teachers of physical education.
- To provide viable tools for teachers in providing proper sequence and progression in physical education activities throughout the various school grades.
- To assist in program development in physical education.
- To provide a more systematic method for meeting the goals and objectives of physical education.

Selected features of the program. The development of this program is called Project COPE (Curriculum Objectives for Physical Education). The documents provided in this program were developed by curriculum and physical education experts throughout the State of Florida for the Florida State Department of Education.

A series of ten clusters containing forty-four COMPACS (competency packages) are provided. The ten clusters relate to the following: (1) the body, (2) physical development and conditioning, (3) lifetime sports, (4) team games, (5) gymnastics, (6) track and field, (7) movement and dance concepts, (8) aquatics, (9) recreational games, and (10) combatives.

Each COMPAC contains the following: (1) overview

*Adapted from Barry, P. E., editor: *Ideas for Secondary School Physical Education*, Washington, D.C., 1976, AAHPER.

*Adapted from Barry, P. E., editor: *Ideas for Secondary School Physical Education*, Washington, D.C., 1976, AAHPER.

of the activity, (2) scope and sequence chart of objectives classified according to beginner, intermediate or advanced status, and motor, cognitive, and affective learning domain for each objective, (3) performance criteria for each objective with teaching tips, (4) comprehensive tests with keys for all tests, (5) enabling activities to assist in meeting goals, (6) references, and (7) suggestions for recording pertinent information in order to keep meaningful records on each student.

Clusters can be purchased from Panhandle Area Educational Cooperative, P.O. Drawer 190, Chipley, Florida 32428.

LEARNING PROCESS BASED ON GOAL SETTING*
Framingham North High School
Framingham, Massachusetts

Grades and students concerned. Ninth to twelfth grades.
Selected objectives
• To enable students to play an active role in determining what and how they are going to learn in the physical education class.
• To involve students in the decision-making process.
• To provide opportunities for students to become aware of their own human abilities and potential and to learn skills in accordance with these elements.
• To help students understand the worth of physical activity throughout life.
• To help the student function as a self-directed individual in assuming responsibility for meeting goals.

Selected features of the program. Students are first helped to understand the decision-making process as it affects their leraning and their goals.

In respect to goal setting, students are oriented to various activities and also to the steps relating to goal setting. (For example, they should know themselves, understand and be aware of what facilities and equipment are available, and be cognizant of other resources that can be utilized for learning.)

Students are given materials and guidelines and instructor assistance to help them in establishing their goals for the various activities; that is, they are encouraged to take a hard look at themselves, determine what they want to learn, delineate their goals, design a plan for meeting the goals, and develop a procedure for evaluating the degree to which their goals are achieved. The goals, plans, and the like that have been selected are written out and made a matter or record.

Class procedure includes such possibilities as solving problems relating to the activity (for example, in gymnastics—can you do a cartwheel?); working independently on goals they had set for themselves; attending a teaching lesson arranged by the teacher; reviewing posted unit charts; analyzing in written form the degree to which the students felt they had achieved their goals; then setting new goals.

PERFORMANCE OBJECTIVES*
Glenbrook North High School
Glenview, Illinois

Grades and students concerned. Ninth to twelfth grades.
Selected objectives
• To provide achievement standards for students in each activity offered in the physical education curriculum.
• To help students to better achieve the objective of education and physical education.
• To provide a guide for students in respect to what is to be achieved in each activity in which they participate.

Selected features of the program. Performance objectives were established for each grade level after the faculty evaluated the program in terms of its philosophy, the cardinal principles of education, health goals, and the objectives of physical education: organic, neuromuscular, emotional, social, and mental development.

Working committee prepared performance objectives for each activity in the four-year curriculum.

Examples of performance objectives for freshmen and seniors in one activity—basketball—include:
• *Freshmen:* (1) Dribble ten times with left hand and ten with right hand without losing control of ball while dribbling in the center jump circle; (2) During a thirty-second interval from any spot on the court make five baskets; (3) Demonstrate chest, bounce, and overhead passes across the free throw lane.
• *Seniors:* (1) Execute a three-on-two drill; (2) Make four out of ten free throws; (3) Make eight shots in thirty seconds; (4) Demonstrate and show difference between player on player and defense zones; (5) Demonstrate and explain a scissors to the basket.

PROGRAMS STRESSING CAREER AND LEADERSHIP OPPORTUNITIES IN PHYSICAL EDUCATION

RECREATIONAL LEADERSHIP†
Wheaton High School
Wheaton, Maryland

Grades and students concerned. High school students on an elective basis.

---

*Adapted from material sent by and the article by Mathieson, D., and Driscoll, S.: Goal-centered individualized learning, Journal of Health, Physical Education, and Recreation **42**:26, 1971.

*Adapted from letter and material sent by Walter D. Sherman and from article by Sherman, W. D.: Performance objectives, Journal of Health, Physical Education, and Recreation **42**:37, 1971.
†Adapted from Barry, P. E., editor: *Ideas for Secondary School Physical Education*, Washington, D.C., 1976, AAHPER.

Fig. 9-2. Outdoor education workshop in casting and angling conducted in Baton Rouge, La., for high school physical education teachers. (Courtesy Kermit Davis, Consultant, Physical Education and Recreation, State of Mississippi.)

Selected objectives

- To give students an understanding of the field of recreation and the career opportunities that it offers.
- To provide students with many varied experiences in the field of recreation through such means as field trips and guest speakers.
- To provide high school students with opportunities to participate in a variety of recreational programs.

Selected features of the program. The program is elective in nature and covers such topics as (1) agencies involved in recreation work, (2) educational preparation needed to become a recreator, (3) activities involved in recreation programs, (4) outdoor education, (5) field trips to such places as community centers, (6) student-directed activities such as arts and crafts, (7) guest speakers on such subjects as orienteering, and (8) miscellaneous presentations involving such topics as local job opportunities in recreation.

Program is planned so that no more than three days a week are scheduled for either lecture or activity sessions.

The semester is eighteen weeks in length with the program for the first six weeks planned by the instructor, the next six weeks by students and instructor, and the last six weeks by the students. This procedure provides for student involvement under instructor guidance.

Evaluation takes place in class and also from the student counselors' principals in outdoor education program.

INTRODUCTION TO CAREERS IN PHYSICAL EDUCATION*
Woodward High School
Rockville, Maryland

Grades and students concerned. High school students.
Selected objectives
- To provide students with an understanding of career opportunities in physical education.
- To provide students with practice and experience in career or avocational possibilities in physical education such as coaching, officiating, and teaching elementary school physical education.

Selected features of the program. The course covers such items as an overview of the professional field of physical education, officiating, coaching, elementary school physical education, and areas such as athletic training.

The course is conducted on a seminar basis as a no-credit, no-grade course. Students meet every other day with faculty sponsor, and on alternate days they work on their own. The program includes an overview of skills needed and goal setting by students and teacher.

Skills are practiced where possible in places out of high school, such as officiating in junior high schools and coaching community athletic teams. Students also serve as teacher aides in neighboring elementary schools.

Outside consultants are brought in, and trips are also arranged for students to visit other programs.

---

*Adapted from Barry, P. E., editor: *Ideas for Secondary School Physical Education*, Washington, D.C., 1976, AAHPER.

JUNIOR TEACHING AND RESOURCE CENTERS*
El Camino Real High School
Woodland Hills, California

Grades and students concerned. Tenth to twelfth grades.

Selected objectives
- To provide an opportunity for selected high school students to experience being junior teachers in physical education classes grades one to nine.
- To help students with leadership potential become more familiar with the nature and scope of elementary and junior high school physical education programs.
- To help students with leadership potential to understand the physical, social, and emotional needs and characteristics of children and adolescents.
- To provide a teaching experience for students that may lead to full-time employment later on.

Selected features of the program. Students electing to serve as junior teachers receive five or ten credits. The Statement of Intent is completed by a student who negotiates a contract with the teacher of physical education. Contracts are signed by students, parents, supervising teacher, and department chairman.

The junior teacher is involved in such duties as the interpretation of rules, assisting in testing for physical fitness, supervising activities, introducing various physical education activities, and helping students who are deficient in movement skills.

A staff member is assigned to each student teacher. The staff member's duties include holding seminars, conducting conferences, observing junior teacher, coordinating student's program, and evaluating results.

A resource center that contains such items as audiovisual aids and reference materials of various types is provided for junior teachers. There are also study and seminar accommodations.

PARAPROFESSIONAL PROGRAM FOR PHYSICAL EDUCATION†
Old Orchard Junior High School
Skokie, Illinois

Grades and students concerned. Sixth to eighth grades.

Selected objectives
- To enable teacher to provide more individual help to students.
- To free teacher from clerical and nonprofessional details.
- To enable teacher to utilize time for which he is trained.

- To provide a better organized and meaningful physical education experience for students.

Selected features of the program. Each physical education class (usually seventy to eighty students) is assigned two teachers and one paraprofessional (assists teacher).

Teacher is responsible for all planning, teaching, and professional responsibilities such as handling discipline problems, teaching the various activities, and beginning and dismissing classes.

Teacher supervises work of paraprofessional who handles such responsibilities as refereeing games, keeping records, leading calisthenic exercises, administering make-up tests, supervising locker room, and getting equipment ready for classes.

Paraprofessionals are recruited through area universities and advertisements. Many graduate students in professional preparation for higher education programs are used as paraprofessionals.

Qualifications to become a paraprofessional include a demonstrated interest in students, willingness to go through an orientation and training period, noteworthy physical development, and possession of knowledge of various physical education activities.

Parents are kept informed regarding paraprofessionals. Parents, in turn, approve of their use in light of the more meaningful physical education program that is provided.

PROGRAMS STRESSING ELECTIVES IN PHYSICAL EDUCATION

COEDUCATION ELECTIVE PHYSICAL EDUCATION PROGRAM*
Gar-Field High School
Woodbridge, Virginia

Grades and students concerned. The elective phase of this program is for students who have successfully completed required freshman and sophomore health and physical education with a C average.

Selected objectives
- To enable students to learn basic skills in a variety of activities.
- To enable students to choose activities in which they are interested.
- To provide individualized instruction for students utilizing pre- and posttests in skill and cognitive areas.
- To enable selected students to assume some responsibility for teaching other members of the class and assisting the teacher.

Selective features of the program. The coeducation program consists of four phases: (1) required freshman health and physical education, (2) required sophomore health and physical education, (3) elective physical

*Adapted from material written by Carol Ghens for Secondary School Conference, Washington, D.C., 1972.
†Adapted from the article by Wright, L.: Paraprofessional program for physical education, organizational patterns for instruction in physical education, Washington, D.C., 1971, American Alliance for Health, Physical Education, and Recreation, p. 63.

*Adapted from Barry, P. E., editor: *Ideas for Secondary School Physical Education*, Washington, D.C., 1976, AAHPER.

education for those students who complete phases 1 and 2 successfully, and (4) physical education aide program.

All four phases of the program provide for student choice of activities. Activities are taught in blocks of three weeks. Each of the four phases provides for team sports, individual and dual sports, rhythms and recreational activities, and students are required to select a certain number of activities in each of these areas.

The emphasis in phase 3 is on sports of carryover value and leisure pursuits.

The emphasis in phase 4 (physical education aide) is on students who wish to learn more about health and physical education by assisting the teacher in the conduct of the program.

Community resources are utilized to provide more activities for students. Independent study is also common to all phases of the program.

THE LEXINGTON SECONDARY ELECTIVE PROGRAM*
Lexington High School
Lexington, Maine

Grades and students concerned. Tenth to twelfth grades.

Selected objectives
- To provide students with an understanding of and basic skills in a variety of sport activities so that participation will be more successful and enjoyable.
- To provide students with a thorough appreciation of activities from a spectator point of view.
- To provide for better utilization of facility plant.
- To provide for more flexibility in programming.

Selected features of program. Forty-three different physical education activities are provided in this program at a variety of educational levels.

Students are required to participate in two fifty-five-minute periods each week. Extra hours for student participation can be scheduled if space is available.

The faculty consists of eight full-time physical education teachers (four men and four women). The school year is divided into four quarters, and students elect two different activities each quarter, one activity for each day they participate each week. Activities usually cannot be repeated in a single school year.

Evaluation records are kept on each student.

The program of activities is mostly held outdoors during the fall and spring sessions and inside during second and third quarters (gymnasium and large field house).

The student-teacher ratio is based on one physical education teacher for each 250 students. One dollar and fifty cents is allocated each year for each student to be spent on supplies and equipment.

---

*Adapted from Barry, P. E., editor: *Ideas for Secondary School Physical Education*, Washington, D.C., 1976, AAHPER

ELECTIVE PROGRAM*
Silverton High School
Silverton, Colorado

Grades and students concerned. Eleventh and twelfth grades.

Selected objectives
- To make physical education more meaningful for students.
- To give students a voice in curriculum development.
- To provide for student choice in the selection of activities.
- To provide activities for students outside the regular school day.
- To capitalize on local environmental resources.
- To provide activities that students may enjoy for a lifetime.

Selected features of the program. Physical education classes may consist of such activities as fly fishing in a river, weekend backpacking trip through an Indian reservation, cross-country skiing, or mountaineering.

Activities also include traditional team and individual sports, such as badminton, basketball, soccer, circuit training, volleyball, baseball, softball, and dance.

Program is coeducational and physical education activities are integrated into other areas of the general education program. For example, students on a backpacking trip study federal aid to Indians and the way Indians live when they make a trip to an Indian reservation. Home economics is involved in arranging menus for trips, and shop classes help in making bows and arrows.

INNOVATIVE PHYSICAL EDUCATION THROUGH ELECTIVES†
Regina High School
Minneapolis, Minnesota

Grades and students concerned. Ninth to twelfth grades.

Selected objectives
- To provide students with a choice of activities, both on and off campus, in which to participate as part of the physical education program.
- To develop skills that will provide for the worthy use of leisure during adult years.
- To develop physical fitness.
- To utilize the resources of the community in providing a more challenging physical education program for students.

---

*Adapted from material prepared and sent by George J. Pastor, Director of Physical Education, Silverton High School, Silverton, Colorado.
†Adapted from material sent and article written by Luck, K. Cash: Innovative physical education through electives, organizational patterns for instruction in physical education, Washington, D.C., 1971, American Alliance for Health, Physical Education, and Recreation, p. 80.

Fig. 9-3. Rock climbing taught to some future teachers at University of Northern Colorado, Greeley, Colo. (Courtesy Barry Iverson.)

- To utilize modular scheduling as a means of arranging many different types of activities and a more meaningful program for students.

Selected features of the program. The physical education program includes traditional physical education activities such as volleyball, archery, gymnastics, basketball, tennis, softball, and track and field and also includes several off-campus activities, including horseback riding, golf, bowling, skiing, roller skating, and swimming.

Off-campus activities are conducted in different settings throughout the community. For example, golf is conducted at one of the several clubs in the area, bowling at one of the local bowling lanes, and swimming at the YMCA pool. Transportation is provided for students, although there is a small fee in some cases to cover costs.

Basic skills in off-campus activities are taught. For example, horseback riding classes are aimed at developing such things as an understanding of horses, knowledge of horsemanship, and so on. In so doing students take care of their horses, including grooming, bridling, and saddling.

Additional aids used in the instructional process include audiovisual aids and computer center. (In golf, for example, the student can plan indoors and electronically measure yardage, select clubs, and sink putts on a screen.)

Computer scheduling has been carefully studied so that students can be scheduled into activities that meet their interests, needs, and abilities, plus meeting the school requirements in respect to the rest of the educational offering.

PROGRAMS STRESSING FLEXIBILITY IN SCHEDULING IN PHYSICAL EDUCATION

SKILL ACHIEVEMENT AND MODULAR SCHEDULING*
Poway High School
Poway, California

Grades and students concerned. Ninth to twelfth grades.

Selected objectives
- To assist students in achieving proficiency in physical education skills.
- To utilize modular scheduling in grouping students in accordance with their skill proficiency.
- To help students enjoy physical education through competition with students possessing equal skill development to their own.
- To further the physical fitness development of each student.
- To provide individual instruction in skills for students who need and desire such help.

Selected features of the program. First, students are assigned to classes in skill area of their choice. Classes meet twice a week, with emphasis on instruction.

Second, students are assigned to physical fitness

*Adapted from article by Welch, Ronald E.: Poway High School physical education program, organizational patterns for instruction in physical education, Washington, D.C., 1971, American Alliance for Health, Physical Education, and Recreation, p. 69.

laboratory. Testing is done periodically and records are kept on each student's progress.

Third, regularly scheduled competitive experiences or laboratories are conducted each Friday when each student competes with other students of similar skill level. Activities include badminton, volleyball, handball, touch football, basketball, and tennis.

Fourth, there is an open laboratory period where students may receive individual instruction in the various skills. Performance standards have been developed for each activity to guide student achievement and permit better evaluation. Evaluation is done on the basis of three ratings: outstanding, satisfactory, and unsatisfactory.

Computer scheduling makes it possible to schedule students for various phases of the physical education program according to their individual needs and interests.

Videotape recordings of students executing skills are utilized in aiding skill development.

Team teaching is limited to gymnastics.

Program is interpreted to parents via a student-parent handbook, articles, and an open house.

TRUMP MODEL SCHOOLS PROGRAM*
Edgewood Junior High School
Saint Paul, Minnesota

Grades and students concerned. Seventh to ninth grades.

Selected objectives
- To adapt the Trump Model Schools Program to physical education including small and large group, instruction, learning packages, and so on.

---

*Adapted and based on letter and materials sent by Jim Danner, Edgewood Junior High School, November 8, 1972.

- To motivate students to participate in physical activities on their own.
- To develop a degree of self-understanding in each student in respect to activities in the program plus a recognition of the need for physical activity throughout life.
- To provide for close teacher-student relationships.
- To measure skill progress in terms of behavioral objectives.
- To provide individual student assistance where necessary.

Selected features of the program. Large and small group instruction, learning packages, teacher-counselor relationship with students, and paraprofessionals constitute parts of the physical education program.

Students attend large group sessions once a week that are designed to orient, interest, and motivate them to participate in coming units of study involving various physical education activities.

Students attend a small group discussion once each week that is designed to build self-understanding, stimulate group dyanmics, and broaden their understanding of health, physical education, and recreation.

Students attend three two-period sessions of physical education laboratory each week where they learn skills presented in learning packages, each of which contains specific skills to be learned, behavioral objectives, the means of achieving objectives, and procedures for evaluating behavioral objectives.

All teachers engage in teacher-counselor role, with each teacher assigned to about twenty-five students or counselees. Both group and individual meetings are held where such items are covered as schedules, personal problems, school problems, and so on.

Five instructional aides (paraprofessionals) are assigned, one to each activity unit that is in operation. Aides have three major areas of responsibility: student control, skills testing, and individual student assistance.

SAMPLE LEARNING PACKAGE

Title: Wrestling—Head Lever   Learning package no.: J-6
Level: I   Department: Health, Fitness, Recreation
Written by: J. Danner   Date: November 1, 1971

1. Behavioral objective: On the mat you will put the head lever ride on another wrestler holding tight to the wrist and driving your head into the armpit while driving from your toes.
2. Pretest: Satisfy the behavioral objective.
3. Do at least two of the things listed:
   a. In the resource center view the loop film "Head Lever."
   b. Practice the skill on the mat with another wrestler.
   c. Ask another student for a demonstration.
4. Tell the aide of work done.
5. Posttest:
   a. See a teacher's aide.
   b. Satisfy the behavioral objective.
   c. If you satisfy this behavioral objective, go on to another.
   d. If you cannot satisfy this behavioral objective, repeat the things listed.

EDGEWOOD JUNIOR HIGH SCHOOL PROGRESS REPORT
HEALTH, FITNESS, RECREATION DEPARTMENT

STUDENT'S NAME _____

TEACHER-COUNSELOR _____ M F 7 8 9

Small Group Discussion Leader _____

This progress report lists the 3 year curriculum in the Health, Fitness, Recreation Department and is to be used by students, parents, and teacher-counselors as a basis for goal setting and pacing. The Curriculum Level Goal* is based on results from standardized achievement, ability, and departmental tests, past performances and teachers' observations.

Entry Date _____ Exit Date _____

COMPARISON OF GOALS AND PROGRESS							
MARKING PERIOD	1	2	3	4	5	6	Final
Curriculum Level Goal*							
Present Curriculum Level							
Work Completed							
School Within A School							

Each marking period the work completed grade is based on: A—100 points or more, B—70 to 99 points, C—40 to 69 points, D—39 or less points.

SKILLS LEVEL (5 pts. ea.)
_____ A5 Swim 25 yards
_____ A6 Agility
_____ A7 Cardiovascular
_____ A8 Power
_____ A9 Strength
_____ Participation Points

LEVEL I

BOWLING (4 pts. ea.) _____
_____ X1 Getting Started
_____ X2 Stance & Pushaway
_____ X3 Approach
_____ X4 Pendulum Swing
_____ X5 Delivery
_____ X6 Scoring
_____ Participation Points
_____ Level II
_____ Level III

CONDITIONING (5 pts. ea.) _____
_____ G1 Jogging
_____ G2 Circuit Training
_____ G3 Isometrics
_____ G4 Arm Curl
_____ G5 Half Squats
_____ G6 Military Press
_____ G7 Dead Lift
_____ G8 Bench Press
_____ Participation Points
_____ Level II
_____ Level III

GOLF (5 pts. ea.)
_____ S1 Equipment
_____ S2 Safety
_____ S3 Grip and Stance
_____ S4 Full Swing
_____ S5 Half Swing
_____ S6 Putting
_____ S7 Scoring

GOLF (continued)
_____ S8 Etiquette
_____ S9 Game
_____ Participation Points
_____ Level II
_____ Level III

INDOOR HOCKEY (4 pts. ea.) _____
_____ I1 Rules
_____ I2 Dribbling
_____ I3 Forehand Passing
_____ I4 Backhand Passing
_____ I5 Shooting
_____ I6 Goal Tending
_____ Participation Points
_____ Level II
_____ Level III

RHYTHMS (4 pts. ea.) _____
BALLROOM

CONTEMPORARY

FOLK DANCE

SQUARE DANCE

_____ Participation Points
_____ Level II
_____ Level III

SOFTBALL (4 pts. ea.) _____
_____ U1 Rules
_____ U2 Throwing
_____ U3 Catching
_____ U4 Fielding - Fly Balls
_____ U5 Fielding - Ground Balls
_____ U6 Batting
_____ U7 Pitching
_____ Participation Points
_____ Level II
_____ Level III

TENNIS (3 pts. ea.)
_____ D1 Safety & Equipment
_____ D2 Court
_____ D3 Forehand Grip
_____ D4 Forehand Drive
_____ D5 Backhand Drive
_____ D6 Serve
_____ D7 Rules
_____ Participation Points
_____ Level II
_____ Level III

TRACK (4 pts. ea.) _____
_____ V1 Running
_____ V2 Starts
_____ V3 Baton Passing
_____ V4 Hurdling
_____ V5 Long Jump
_____ V6 High Jump
_____ V7 Triple Jump
_____ V8 Shot Put
_____ V9 Discus
_____ Participation Points
_____ Level II
_____ Level III

SWIMMING (3 pts. ea.) _____
BASIC SKILLS
_____ Y1 Bobbing
_____ Y2 Rhythmic Breathing
_____ Y3 Jellyfish Float
_____ Y4 Front Float
_____ Y5 Back Float
_____ Y6 Flutter Kick
_____ Y7 Back Glide
_____ Y8 Front Glide
_____ Y9 Front Glide & Flutter Kick
_____ Y10 Back Glide & Flutter Kick
_____ Y11 Overarm Pull
_____ Y12 Back Stroke Pull
BEGINNERS
_____ Y13 Front Crawl (8 yds.)
_____ Y14 Front Crawl (16 yds.)
_____ Y15 Front Crawl (25 yds.)
_____ Y16 Basic Back Stroke

BEGINNERS (continued)
_____ Y17 Changing Directions
_____ Y18 Turning Over
_____ Y19 Front Dive
_____ Y20 Deep Water Skills
_____ Y21 Elementary Rescues

ADVANCED BEGINNERS
_____ Y22 Front Crawl (50 yds.)
_____ Y23 Whip Kick
_____ Y24 Elementary Back Stroke
_____ Y25 Survival Float
_____ Y26 Tread Water
_____ Y27 Dive & Underwater Swim

SYNCHRONIZED SWIMMING
_____ Y86 Front Crawl
_____ Y87 Back Stroke
_____ Y88 Sculling
_____ Y89 Marlin Turn
_____ Y90 Log Roll
_____ Y91 Corkscrew
_____ Y92 Tub
_____ Y93 Oyster
_____ Y94 Back Tuck Somersault
_____ Y95 Front Tuck Somersault

SKIN DIVING
_____ Y110 Fitting & Defogging Mask
_____ Y111 Flooding Mask
_____ Y112 Relieving Air Pressure
_____ Y113 Fins
_____ Y114 Snorkel
_____ Y115 Breathing
_____ Y116 Surface Swimming
_____ Y117 Surface Diving
_____ Y118 Swimming Underwater
_____ Y119 Entering Water
_____ Y120 Safety Written Test
_____ Y121 Extra Credit Activities
_____ Participation Points
_____ Level II
_____ Level III

Level I Sign-Out
This student has completed Level I. With permission of the teacher-counselor, parent, and small group teacher, this student has signed out of HFR resource center.
Date Excused _____ Teacher _____
Date Reentered _____ Teacher _____
Date Excused _____ Teacher _____
Date Reentered _____ Teacher _____
Date Excused _____ Teacher _____

LEVEL I			LEVEL II			LEVEL III		
Fitness			Aide			Health		
Health			GAA			Interscholastic		
			Health			Athletics		
			Intramurals			Large Group		
			Large Group					

COMMENTS:

HFR REQUIREMENTS: Each student shall finish Level I in the following areas over a three (3) year period of time. Students not attending Edgewood for the three year (7-8-9) period of time shall meet the requirements set by their HFR Small Group Discussion Teacher.

☐ Archery
☐ Badminton
☐ Bowling
☐ Broomball or
☐ Skating or
☐ Skiing
☐ Health

☐ Competitive Swimming or
☐ Track
☐ Golf
☐ Gymnastics
☐ Modern Dance (Girls)
☐ Rhythms
☐ Tennis
☐ Wrestling (Boys)

Choose Two
☐ Basketball
☐ Broomball
☐ Floor Hockey
☐ Volleyball
☐ Water Polo

Choose Two
☐ Flag Football
☐ Soccer
☐ Speedaway
Swimming
☐ Basic Skills
☐ Beginner
☐ Advanced Beginner
☐ Any other pool unit

Fig. 9-4. Edgewood Junior High School progress report. (Health, Fitness, and Recreation Department, Edgewood Junior High School, St. Paul, Minn.)

QUINMESTER PROGRAM*
Dade County Public Schools
Miami, Florida

Grades and students concerned. Seventh to twelfth grades.

Selected objectives
- To provide a flexible physical education program for students.
- To provide students with a choice of activities in which they wish to participate.
- To provide self-contained nonsequential nine-week units of study.

Selected features of the program. School year is

---

*Adapted from material sent by Robert F. Adams, Dade County Public Schools, and also from article by Rothstein, H., and Adams, R. F.: Quinmester extended school year plan, Journal of Health, Physical Education, and Recreation **42:**30, 1971.

broken into five nine-week terms and students are required to be in attendance during any four of the five "quins" offered each year. Students who so desire may attend all five "quins" and thereby accelerate their graduation date.

Courses are written up in detail by instructors.

Students select courses in physical education in which they have special interest and/or need.

Physical education quinmester course offerings involve team sports, lifetime sports, rhythmic activities, and physical conditioning. Most courses are coeducational.

Although no specific course in the area of physical conditioning is required, it is recommended that physical fitness tests be given twice a year.

Quinmester curriculum may be viewed as a series of minicourses, each nine weeks in length and carrying one-quarter credit.

Thirty-seven schools are participating in the program.

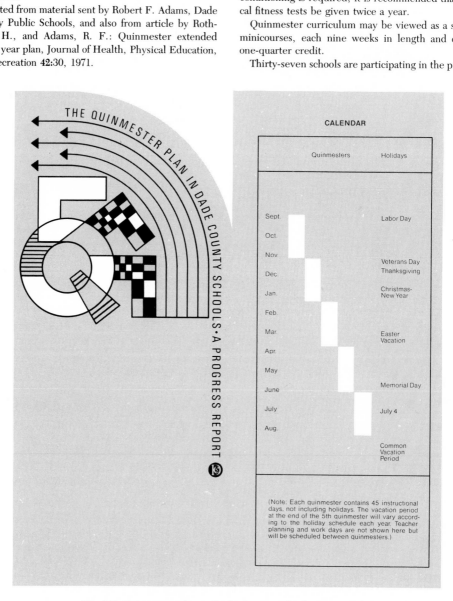

Fig. 9-5. Quinmester plan in Dade County Schools, Miami, Fla.

NONGRADED CURRICULUM*
Athens High School
Athens, Ohio

Grades and students concerned. Ninth to twelfth grades.

Selected objectives
- To provide a nongraded program in physical education for high school students.
- To make it possible for students of similar abilities to meet physical education requirements in homogeneous groups.
- To provide for the individual differences and interests of students.

Selected features of the program. Students are placed in classes according to level of skill achievement and physical maturity rather than according to their chronological age or grade level.

The AAHPER physical fitness test scores are used in determining in what phase students will be placed in the program. There are four phases: phase 1, up to the twenty-fifth percentile; phase 2, twenty-sixth to fortieth percentile; phase 3, forty-first to seventieth percentile, and phase 4, seventy-first to one hundredth percentile. If performance justifies, students can phase up or down at the end of each grading period.

Two years of physical education is required of all students. Elective activities are offered in junior and senior years. A student may start the two-year requirement cycle as a freshman, sophomore, or junior.

There are required and elective courses in the program.

Modular scheduling is utilized and this together with nongraded classes has provided for small classes, homogeneous groupings of students, additional class periods for additional work, clubs, and open laboratories.

PROGRAMS STRESSING SPECIALIZED TYPES OF EXPERIENCES IN PHYSICAL EDUCATION

CYCLING†
Dulaney Senior High School
Timonium, Maryland

Grades and students concerned. Twelfth-grade students.

Selected objectives
- To offer an instructional unit in cycling.
- To provide cycling on an elective basis for interested students.
- To provide instruction in safety procedures to be

followed in cycling and thus reduce the incidence of accidents.

Selected features of the program. The cycling program is conducted five days a week for a four-week period on the running track or on an adjacent school parking lot. Instructors have special training in such areas as safety procedures, proper cycling techniques and maintenance and care of equipment. Each student supplies his or her own bicycle and necessary tools.

Cycling skills such as the following are taught: mounting, stopping, dismounting, changing gears, hand positions, cadence and ankle technique. The cognitive areas include facts about such things as medical aspects, safety, purchasing a bicycle, cadence, types of bicycles, equipment for bicycles, care and maintenance of cycles, and cycling organizations.

Activities provided in the course include putting gears in highest ratio, cadence practice, accuracy practice, obstacle course, and riding between concentric circles.

EXERCISE PHYSIOLOGY IN SECONDARY SCHOOLS*
Penney High School
East Hartford, Connecticut

Grades and students concerned. Large group instruction for all high school students and an elective in-depth exercise physiology course for eleventh- and twelfth-grade students who have at least a C grade in biology.

Selected objectives
- To enable students to have a better understanding of the physiologic effects of exercise and athletic training on the human body.
- To equip students with specific techniques to measure physical fitness.
- To show students the worth of physical education and physical activity in their lives.
- To physically train as well as physically educate students.

Selected features of the program. The program consists of three levels and was initiated in September, 1973.

Level 1 consists of a course offered for one semester in exercise physiology for eleventh- and twelfth-grade students with emphasis on the impact of physical activity on the body systems. It specifically provides for an understanding of concepts relating to such phenomena as cardiovascular endurance, muscle strength and endurance, and athletic conditioning. This course consists of two lectures and one laboratory class each week. The laboratory work provides an opportunity for students to do such things as test muscle strength, administer physical fitness tests, and study body composition. This course carries one-half credit.

Level 2 consists of a large group instruction for all students in the school. The course is of the lecture-

---

*Adapted from article by Burson, R.: Nongraded curriculum and modular scheduling, organizational patterns for instruction in physical education, Washington, D.C., 1971, American Association for Health, Physical Education, and Recreation, p. 88.
†Adapted from Barry, P. E., editor: *Ideas for Secondary School Physical Education*, Washington, D.C., 1976, AAHPER

---

*Adapted from Barry, P. E., editor: *Ideas for Secondary School Physical Education*, Washington, D.C., 1976, AAHPER.

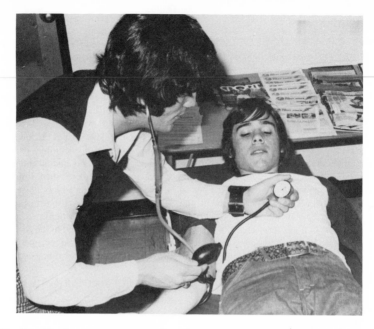

Fig. 9-6. Checking blood pressure. Exercise physiology at Penney High School in East Hartford, Conn.

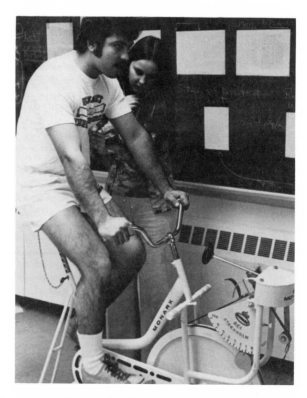

Fig. 9-7. Bicycle ergometry. Exercise physiology at Penney High School in East Hartford, Conn.

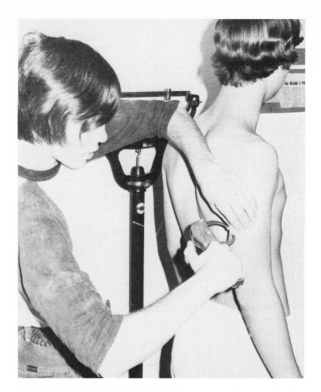

Fig. 9-8. Exercise physiology at Penney High School in East Hartford, Conn. Skinfold test to test for body fat.

demonstration type with students attending by grade level.

Level 3 consists of the regular physical education activities course. At this level the concepts discussed and demonstrated in level 2 are applied to the physical activity that takes place at this level. The physical education facility complex for the course consists of a classroom for lectures and demonstrations, laboratory, gymnasiums, and so on.

A great amount of laboratory equipment is provided by the school for this course including dynamometers, weights, tensiometers, stethoscopes, skinfold calipers, stop watches, step-up benches, and metronomes. Projectors are also provided and occasionally closed-circuit television.

A field trip to Springfield College is also one highlight of the course where advanced physiologic tests are conducted.

COURSE FOR PREGNANT GIRLS*
Cardozo Senior High School
Washington, D.C.

Grades and students concerned. Pregnant girls in senior high school.

---

*Adapted from Barry, P. E., editor: *Ideas for Secondary School Physical Education*, Washington, D.C., 1976, AAHPER.

Selected objectives

- To increase the understanding and emotional stability of pregnant girls.

- To provide an opportunity for pregnant girls to develop proper skills and attitudes and self-confidence as a means of regaining their self-image.

- To help remove fear, emotional shock, stigma in those girls who become pregnant and are rejected by parents and boyfriends.

Selected features of the program. The class is offered on an elective basis with the requirement that girls must be registered with the school nurse and must be under a physician's or clinic's care during the prenatal period.

The course outline covers such topics as proper grooming and nutrition for pregnant women, caring for the baby including such items as nutrition, clothing, and other aspects of everyday care, moral implications of pregnancy, and legal implications of pregnancy.

Many consultants are utilized in the course. An evaluation of the course showed that many girls lost their fears, had their self-esteem restored, improved their scholastic average, and graduated from high school. There were no dropouts in the course.

SPORTSMAN'S BIOLOGY*
Mayo High School
Rochester, Minnesota

Grades and students concerned. Junior and senior high school students (on a selective basis).

Selected objectives
- To have students develop outdoor skills.
- To explore the environment.
- To determine the effect of hunting and fishing skills upon the environment.
- To have students assess their values.

Selected features of the program. The course in Sportsman's Biology is taught by the physical education and biology departments; students taking the course receive one-half credit in each area. The program is conducted on campus as well as at the city's nature center, state refuges, and local waterways.

The course is team-taught by a science and a physical education instructor. The class meets daily for two hours for one semester.

The course outline includes such topics as the following: sportsman's responsibilities, stream biome, lake biome, hunter safety and shooting sports, birds and game, fur-bearing animals and trapping, game processing and mounting, sportsman's navigation, and winter limnology.

Students pay a $15 fee to cover essential supplies and equipment they will need in the course (example, fly tying equipment). A culminating fishing field trip is taken over a four-day period. The instructor is skilled and qualified in many outdoor activities (a necessary requisite).

OUTDOOR ENVIRONMENTAL UNIT*
Prairie and Buchanan School
Olathe, Kansas

Grades and students concerned. High school students.
Selected objectives
- To teach camping and backpacking skills to students.
- To teach specific skills such as first aid, survival techniques, map reading, outdoor ecology, and equipment care.

Selected features of the program. The course is taught in the classroom as well as in various community resources such as parks and open fields. Field trips are an important part of the course. The course outline includes eight topics that are covered during the nine weeks the course is taught. These eight topics are (1) first aid skills, (2) survival techniques, (3) tracks and traces, (4) setting up camp, (5) outdoor skills and crafts, (6) map reading and compass orientation, (7) purchase, selection, and care of equipment, and (8) ecology of the outdoors and basic climbing.

Local sporting goods and other establishments dem-

**Adapted from Barry, P. E., editor: *Ideas for Secondary School Physical Education*, Washington, D.C., 1976, AAHPER.*

onstrate and share their equipment with the school. The cost of equipment is about $100 per student.

The school recommends that the course be scheduled for the first or last hour of the school day so that added time will be available if necessary.

Thirty-five behavioral objectives have been established for the course. An example of some of these are (1) the student will be able to identify and name thirty selected major bones of the body; (2) the student will make a small first aid kit suitable for backpacking; (3) the student will bring to class five edible plants or nuts and describe the food value of each; (4) the student will be able to identify five common animal tracks; and (5) the student will be able to describe the first types of compasses and at least two styles presently in use.

Self-assessment tests

These tests are to assist students in determining if material and competencies presented in this chapter have been mastered:

1. Without consulting the text, list as many of the innovative ideas as possible that are discussed in this chapter.
2. Develop your own set of criteria for evaluating innovative ideas in physical education and use them to evaluate those that are discussed in this chapter. Rank each of the innovative ideas discussed in order of the results of your evaluation.
3. Discuss in detail the advantages and disadvantages of utilizing what you consider to be the best innovative ideas presented in this chapter in secondary school physical education.

Points to remember

1. Society is changing, and education, if it is to contribute to the society of which it is a part, must also change.
2. Physical education as a part of education must change to meet the needs of today's society and students.
3. Many innovative practices exist in schools throughout the United States. Physical educators should study the nature of such innovative practices and determine their value for their own physical education programs.
4. Student involvement is important.
5. Educational and physical education programs must be geared to the needs of the student.

Problems to think through

1. What are the advantages and disadvantages of each of the innovative programs discussed in this chapter?
2. What constitutes a list of innovative practices that have greatest value for modern-day physical education programs?
3. How can change be brought about in a school system where a traditional physical education program exists?
4. What are the implications for physical education of innovations that are taking place in other subject matter fields in the educational program?

Case study for analysis

Select a school system where the faculty is steeped in tradition, where the age range of faculty is 50 to 65 years, where a formalized program of physical education is in operation that has been totally prescribed by the faculty, where the students do not play a part in the decision-making process, and where citizens of the community are very much concerned about rising educational costs and wonder whether the physical education program should be retained or whether it should be dropped as an economy measure. As an interested physical educator, describe what procedure you would follow to restore physical education as a valuable and important part of the school program so that the community would not question the worth of this activity.

Exercises for review

1. Discuss five major changes taking place in education today.
2. Compare education in 1900 with education today.
3. Review the professional literature and identify school programs where you feel they are meeting the needs of students today.
4. What is the best way to bring about educational change?

Selected readings

American Association for Health, Physical Education and Recreation: Ideas for secondary school physical education, Washington, D.C., 1976, AAHPER.

Bucher, C. A.: Administrative dimensions of health and physical education programs, including athletics, Saint Louis, 1971, The C. V. Mosby Co.

Bucher, C. A.: Administration of health and physical education programs, including athletics, ed. 6, St. Louis, 1975, The C. V. Mosby Co.

Bucher, C. A.: What's happening in education today?, Journal of Health, Physical Education and Recreation **45:**30, 1974.

Journal of Health, Physical Education, and Recreation, September, 1971 (entire issue).

MacKenzie, M. M.: Toward a new curriculum in physical education, New York, 1969, McGraw-Hill Book Company.

Riley, M.: Games and humanism, Journal of Physical Education and Recreation **46:**46, 1975.

Willgoose, C. E.: The curriculum in physical education, Englewood Cliffs, N.J., 1969, Prentice-Hall, Inc.

Williams, W. G.: Does the educational past have a future? Kappa Delta Pi Record **11:**103, 1975.

10

AN INNOVATIVE PROGRAM OF MOVEMENT EDUCATION FOR THE SECONDARY SCHOOL

INSTRUCTIONAL OBJECTIVES AND COMPETENCIES TO BE ACHIEVED

After reading this chapter the student should be able to—

1. Define movement education and understand its historical beginnings.
2. Compare movement education with traditional physical education.
3. Discuss the place of movement education in the physical education curriculum.
4. Identify the role of the teacher in movement education.
5. Demonstrate movement education activities for the secondary school physical education program.

The traditional curricula of our secondary schools are currently being challenged by the students they serve. These traditional curricula are gradually being replaced by innovative and flexible educational experiences that attempt to meet the needs of the students. The new focus in secondary education is on individual creativity and individualized learning. Some subject areas of the secondary school curriculum utilize teaching machines and other technological hardware in an attempt to individualize the learning experience. These technological advances have helped to create many changes in the methodology of teaching.

Secondary school physical education programs are emphasizing the individual through comprehensive instruction in the lifetime sports and through a renewed concentration on all phases of the creative-expressive activities, such as dance and gymnastics. This increased awareness of the individual and of the individual's creativity has made education for movement a vital part of the newly developing curricula in physical education.

ORIGINS OF MOVEMENT EDUCATION

Movement education has been misunderstood, misinterpreted, and at times misused within physical education programs in the United States. Movement education is not a recent development, nor it is synonymous with dance. Movement education has been a part of physical education curricula in English schools for many years and is closely aligned with the *movement exploration concepts* integral to dance. Movement education as a foundational phase of the physical education curriculum can be traced historically to the theories of the dancer Rudolf Laban. After fleeing Germany for England during World War II, Laban established an

Art of Movement Center bearing his name. Like the kinesiologists, Laban was a student of human movement. He believed that each individual possesses inherent natural movements and felt that through rigid and formal exercises man loses his ability to move freely and easily. Conversely, Laban said, experiences in spontaneous and exploratory movement would help individuals to reach their potential for efficient and effective movement through increased kinesthetic awareness.

Prior to World War II, physical education in English schools stressed formal gymnastics. During World War II England revised its educational philosophy and its educational structure. Courses and teaching methodology were updated, and education for movement was made the central focus of physical education programs. English children are educated in movement from the earliest school years. When the concepts of the movement education approach to physical education reached the United States in the late 1950s, they were first included in basic instructional programs for women on the college level. However, courses entitled "Movement Education" bore little resemblance to Laban's principles or to the movement education methodology developed in England. Rather, these first attempts to educate for movement were closely correlated with the objectives, techniques, and methodologies associated with existing courses called "Body Mechanics," "Movement Fundamentals," or similar titles. These early courses in programs for college women used movement as a tool primarily to reeducate the body. The system of movement education as developed in England uses the body as a vehicle for enhanced motor skill development, beginning with the natural movements of childhood as the foundation for all bodily movement.

Since 1960, many articles and books have been written and published in the United States that focus directly on movement education. Research is being conducted and several pilot programs in elementary schools are well under way. Through these media,

professionals are developing an understanding of movement education and its proper application within physical education curricula in the schools of the United States. Further, a corps of experts in the specialized area of movement education is being developed, and these individuals are giving freely of their knowledge and experience to other physical educators. At the present time, these advances are helping to make movement education one of the most significant new trends in the field of physical education.

WHAT IS MOVEMENT EDUCATION?

Everything an individual does involves bodily movement of some sort. Movement education attempts to help the individual to become mentally as well as physically aware of these movements. Thus movement education is based on a conceptual approach to human movement. That is, the better the individual mentally understands a movement pattern, the easier it will be for him or her to develop physical skills. For example, softball is a popular team sport that is frequently taught on the secondary school level. Many girls and some boys never develop the ability to throw well because of physical errors in the position of the throwing arm or errors in foot position. Through movement education, the position of each body segment in relation to the whole body is perceived by the student intellectually before the physical skill is attempted. When the student is intellectually aware of the position of his or her body as an entity, rather than considering the body to be made up of independent segments, physical skill learning is enhanced.

The experts do not agree on a single definition for movement education. They do agree, however, that movement education is dependent on physical factors in the environment and on the individual's ability to intellectually and physically react to these factors. Through movement education, the individual develops his or her own techniques for dealing with the environmental factors of force, time, space, and flow as they relate to various movement problems. The mental and phys-

Fig. 10-1. Track-and-field events require adherence to basic movement principles in order to achieve best physical performance. (Walt Whitman High School, South Huntington Schools, N.Y.)

ical skill development of the individual is of prime concern to the movement educator, rather than the common skill development of an entire class or group.

The nature and scope of movement education has been defined by several authors, two of whom are listed here. Felshin* lists five components in her classification, namely, human movement as (1) basic to human functioning and performance, (2) related to culture and society, (3) an esthetic experience, (4) a source of human meaning and significance, and (5) persistent and dynamic forms.

Mackenzie† identifies seven major classifications covering the nature and scope of human movement. These classifications include (1) movement forms (descriptions of sports), (2) mechanical principles of movement (body positioning), (3) structure and function of the moving human organism (body composition), (4) movement and the person (esthetic expression), (5) learning how to move (motor learning theories), (6) movement and health (therpeutic uses), and (7) movement and meaning (philosophical and sociological interpretations).

These classifications of the nature and scope of movement indicate clearly that physical education at all educational levels should be concerned with movement and involved with the study and development of an effective moving human organism.

UNIQUENESS OF MOVEMENT EDUCATION

How does the methodology of movement education differ from the traditional methodology of physical education? As much as physical education has traditionally been taught through structured classes, classes in movement education are also structured. It may seem that movement education is nothing more than a haphazard approach to traditional physical education in relation to skill teaching and learning, but this is far from the case. In many instances, movement education classes involve a more highly structured approach and demand more of the teacher in regard to concrete philosophy, sound objectives, logical progressions, and understand-

---

*Singer, R. N., et al.: Physical education, an interdisciplinary approach, New York, 1972, The Macmillan Publishing Co., Inc., p. 12.
†Mackenzie, M. M.: Toward a new curriculum in physical education, New York, 1969, McGraw-Hill Book Company.

Table 10-1. A comparison of movement education and traditional physical education concepts*

Movement education	Traditional physical education
The program	
1. The program is activity-centered.	1. The program is verbal-centered.
2. The program is student-centered.	2. The program is teacher-centered.
3. The program attempts to develop an intellectual awareness of the body.	3. The program attempts to develop skills often lacking in intellectual comprehension.
4. The program places an emphasis on the problem-solving method, which includes exploration and discovery based on the individual needs of the student.	4. The teacher serves as a model to be imitated by the students, and the method includes lecture and demonstration based on the needs of the group.
5. Repetition of problems leads to a greater variety of solutions.	5. Repetition of drills leads to an improved performance in motor skills.
6. Syllabus develops as each class period uncovers the needs of the individual that must be explored.	6. Syllabus often unrelated to previous learning experiences is presented to the students.
Role of the teacher	
1. In the learning process the teacher educates students.	1. In the learning process the teacher trains students.
2. The teacher is imaginative and creative in the methods used.	2. The teacher utilizes the traditional methods of teaching.
3. The teacher guides students in the activities in which they are participating.	3. The teacher leads students in the activities in which they are participating.
Role of the student	
1. Motivation for learning comes from inner self.	1. Motivation for learning comes from the teacher.
2. The student experiences the joy of natural movement and unique style.	2. Individual body types are not considered.
3. The student demonstrates ability to reason logically and intelligently.	3. The student demonstrates ability to take orders and follow directions.
4. The student demonstrates independence.	4. The student often lacks independence.
5. The student faces each new situation in an enthusiastic and intelligent manner.	5. The student often exhibits difficulty when confronted with new situations.
6. The student evaluates his or her own progress.	6. The teacher evaluates the student's progress.
7. The student develops at his or her own rate of progress.	7. Rate of progress is dependent upon the norm of the student development within the class.
8. Success is based on the student's goals.	8. Success is based on the teacher's goals.
9. The student competes with himself or herself.	9. The student competes with fellow classmates.
Class atmosphere	
1. There is an informal class atmosphere.	1. There is a formal class atmosphere.
2. Varied formations are used.	2. Set formations are used.
3. The teacher exhibits permissive behavior.	3. The teacher exhibits strict behavior.
4. Individual needs of the students are the determining factor in the allotment of time to be spent in any activity.	4. The completion of the subject matter is the determining factor in the allotment of time to be spent in any activity.
Facilities and equipment	
1. The facilities are considered secondary to the need for a resourceful and creative teacher.	1. Facilities are of prime importance, although the need for a resourceful and creative teacher is recognized.
2. The equipment is created to meet the needs of the individual.	2. The individual must adjust to the equipment used.
3. The equipment is used in many different situations.	3. The equipment is limited in its use.

*From Bucher, C. A.: Foundations of physical education, ed. 7, St. Louis, 1975, The C. V. Mosby Co.

ing of proper techniques and methodology, as well as creative ability.

Movement education employs the problem-solving approach. Each skill that is to be explored presents a challenge to the student. Learning results as the student accepts and solves increasingly more difficult problems. For this reason, the natural movements of childhood are considered to be the first challenges that should be presented to the student. Movement educators feel that adult problems in physical skill performance are the result of poor habits developed in early childhood. While most children spend their preschool years in uninhibited running, jumping, leaping, climbing, twisting, and other such vigorous activities, it is pointed out that these movements eventually become stereotyped. Students do not, on their own, explore a variety of movement patterns. Through movement education, boys and girls are encouraged to walk or run or otherwise move at different speeds, in different directions, and on different levels. They are encouraged to exploit physical obstacles, such as an inclined plane or even another person, and to incorporate them into unique movement patterns. The student gains confidence and enjoyment in the use of his or her entire body for movement and begins to develop an intellectual understanding of the capabilities of the body and how they differ from the capabilities of the bodies of others. These understandings, developed as physical skill develops, help to form a basis for more efficient and effective physical movement in later years.

Traditional physical education emphasizes the learning of specific skills through demonstration, drill, and practice. Movement education emphasizes the learning of skill patterns through individual exploration of the body's movement potential. These two approaches to skill learning are not in opposition to each other. Movement education does not supplant learning that takes place in traditional physical education programs. Movement education does help the student to develop a better foundation for the learning of the more sophisticated skills. Education

in movement is the first step in becoming a physically educated person.

PLACE OF MOVEMENT EDUCATION IN THE PHYSICAL EDUCATION CURRICULUM

In the English schools, movement education begins in the first grade and is the sole vehicle through which physical education is taught in the elementary schools. In English secondary schools, girls continue to be educated in movement, but this is interwoven with the learning of specific sport skills. Secondary school boys concentrate on learning specific sports skills taught by traditional methods. However, both the boys and the girls have acquired a sound understanding of movement, and this knowledge facilitates their motor skill learning and performance.

Movement education teaches proper use of the body as a tool for movement. It is not concerned with the rules of specific sports and games, with the strategy involved in playing a game, or with teaching the mechanics of playing, for example, first base in softball or center in basketball. These areas of knowledge are the province of traditional methodology. Through movement education the student discovers the leverage, balance, force, and speed required to kick a soccer ball, dribble a basketball, execute a forward roll, or throw a softball. Through traditional physical education, the student learns the applications of these and other skills.

Particularly on the secondary school level, we find boys and girls who do not perform physical skills well. They may lack confidence, or they may not be motivated to perform well simply because they have never experienced the satisfaction of a well-performed skill. These uncoordinated boys and girls may be physically capable of a good performance but may not intellectually understand the physical criteria of a good performance. These students need to be educated or reeducated in movement.

Movement education should be an on-going part of physical education curricula. It should not be used as a short-term phase of the program included to bridge the change-over from indoor to outdoor seasons or to fill a gap of several lessons between different units of study. Movement education need not, on the secondary school level, fill an entire class period. It can be used during each class period to replace formal warm-ups or calisthenics. With careful and thoughtful planning on the part of the teacher, the principles of movement education can be used to introduce new sports skills or scientific concepts of skill performance, replacing demonstration and drill. In this way, teacher-directed learning can move toward student-conceptualized learning, thus enhancing not only the physical but also the intellectual objectives of physical education programs. Through the movement education method, students perform as individuals, and their

Fig. 10-2. Traditional physical education emphasizes learning skills through demonstration, drill, and practice. **A,** Paul J. Gelinas Junior High School in Setauket, N.Y. **B,** Brockport Central Schools, Brockport, N.Y.

performance depends in a large degree on their creativity and problem-solving ability.

ROLE OF THE TEACHER IN MOVEMENT EDUCATION

In traditional physical education programs, the physical educator explains a skill demonstrates it, and directs student drill and practice. The teacher corrects errors in performance as the students strive to perfect the skill in relation to what they have seen and been told. The movement educator does none of these things.

A movement educator sets the problems and challenges for his other students, guides the students through a thinking process, observes their attempts at solving the problem, and asks questions and stimulates their thinking through discussions of the problem. The movement educator improvises unique equipment where needed and avoids demonstrating or using formal patterns of class organization, such as circles, lines, or rows.

Whereas the physical educator sets the standards for the performance of a particular skill, the movement educator helps each student to become motivated to perform at his or her own peak of ability. Whereas the physical educator evaluates a student on the performance of a skill, the movement educator asks each student to evaluate his or her own performance and suggest ideas on how to improve performance. Whereas the physical educator tells a student that a headstand is unsteady because head and hands are too closely aligned and shows the student the proper alignment, the movement educator asks the student to suggest how the alignment of the body parts might be changed to stabilize the headstand. In this way, the student may attempt several unsatisfactory alignments before discovering the most stable one, but will intellectually understand the physical adjustments he or she has made. This understanding will transfer to other skill learnings. The movement educator guides students toward success by helping them to evaluate their own performance and by providing encouragement to each student as he or she seeks to solve a problem in movement.

Traditional physical education methodology is speech-centered; movement education is activity-centered. The movement educator employs a problem-solving approach and allows the individual student to use creativity to solve the problem. The movement educator neither dictates a solution to a problem in movement nor demonstrates the performance of a skill. Because there can be no stereotyping of a performance or imitation of the teacher's performance, the student is free to establish his or her own most comfortable movement patterns. The student is guided into using the body as the prime tool for movement rather than conceiving of the body as a force to be overcome before movement can take place.

MOVEMENT EDUCATION IN THE SECONDARY SCHOOL

Secondary school students can reap the benefits of movement education experiences whether or not they have been exposed to this method in the elementary school. Movement education leads itself to all phases of the physical education curriculum on all levels and can be adapted to use with all activities. The modification and adaptation of method will seem far stranger to the physical educator than to the student.

It would be difficult, if not impossible, to revert to the use of the natural activities of childhood in a secondary school situation. However, movement education can be employed on this level to introduce new skills and can be tailored to help in correcting performance errors in familiar skills. Further, most secondary schools offer units in dance. Dance and movement education depend on the creativity of the individual and on use of his or her body in relation to the time, space, force, and flow of a movement or series of movements. Dance and movement education are often described as systems of nonverbal communication.

The techniques and methods peculiar to movement education are suited to use with secondary school boys and girls alike. If a unit in soccer is being introduced and the dribble or pass is to be learned, the teacher may ask students to discover on their own how many different ways they can use their feet, with the exception of the toe, to propel the ball. The students are then given ample time to explore this problem. The teacher circulates from student to student, observing their progress. If the teacher discovers that a student persistently contacts the ball with the same foot, he or she will ask a question that will help the student to discover not only that both feet may be used but that there are advantages to be gained from doing so. At the end of the exploratory period, the teacher will call the students together and ask several of them to demonstrate the techniques they have discovered. Student evaluations and suggestions will be elicited, with the teacher guiding the discussion through questions. After this brief period, the teacher may ask the students to attempt to find out how they can keep the ball in motion while maintaining control of it. A third problem for the same class period may involve a problem in passing the ball back and forth with a partner over an increasing distance, whereas a final problem may be concerned with asking the students to discover how they can stop a rolling ball using their feet and legs only. Student demonstrations and discussions would follow each problem-solving period of the class

time, and the class would be concluded by using these newly discovered skills in a teacher-created lead-up game. The use of relays would not be suitable since they emphasize competition between groups rather than focusing on the achievement of the individual.

The movement education approach also lends itself to apparatus activities. Freedom of use and movement on equipment, with appropriate regard to safety, can precede problems in mounting, using the piece of apparatus, and dismounting. This approach gives each student an opportunity to suceed, since no specific movement patterns are required or demanded. In teaching the use of the trampoline, for example, an initial problem might be to move across the trampoline in any way the students desire. Some may roll across, some may choose to bounce across, and others will go on all fours, while still others will create their own unique method. All these methods deserve teacher praise for a problem correctly solved. From this beginning, students may be asked to find out in how many different ways they can bounce on the bed of the trampoline. Through exploration and student demonstrations and discussions, use of the arms and legs for control and height will be better understood and perfected, leading to learn-

Fig. 10-3. Movement education is activity with a purpose. (Marion Moore High School in Fern Creek, Ky.)

ing the proper use of the trampoline and skills unique to it. Skill learning will thus have been guided by the teacher, but the skills will have been discovered by the students themselves.

These two examples show how movement education can be used on the secondary school level to introduce new skills. Movement education can also be used effectively to perfect and improve performance in skills that have been learned previously. The physical educator begins with the observation stage and has the student suggest how performance may be improved through the exploration of a variety of new stances, positions, or techniques.

Movement education on the secondary school level is an invaluable tool for use with the student who does nothing well in physical education. By being encouraged to explore skills rather than having to mimic stylized patterns, this student can attain a measure of success and become motivated to proceed and progress at his or her own pace.

Those secondary school students who have been educated in movement in their secondary school years will benefit from a continuation of this training. Further, they can be of inestimable aid to the secondary school physical educator who wishes to teach skills through the principles of movement education in situations where a majority of students have had no prior movement education experiences.

Movement education is not a panacea that will make a highly skilled performer out of a student who is poorly skilled. It does offer a means through which the physical educator can assist the student in forming an intellectual concept of the skill to be performed or perfected. When corrections or adjustments are verbalized or demonstrated by the physical educator, the student need only attempt to mimic the physical movements, often totally disregarding any intellectual understandings that underlie the physical act.

Individual analysis of problem-solving situations is the basis for movement education. Rather than telling or showing students how to perform, the teacher guides the students through a series of possible responses as they seek solutions that are individually appropriate. In traditional physical education the teacher is a director, commander, and evaluator, while in movement education the teacher is a questioner, a guide, and an observer.

The high school boy and girl will find Bucher's textbook, *Physical Education for Life*, an informative resource on movement education. The basis of physical movement and its application to physical activities are discussed in detail in this book. (See Selected Readings at the end of the chapter.)

INNOVATIVE MOVEMENT EDUCATION CURRICULA FOR GRADES SEVEN TO NINE AND TEN TO TWELVE

Many curricula have been developed for movement education for the elementary school level; however, very few have been developed for the secondary school level. In exploring the possibility of including an innovative movement education program for the secondary school level in this text, we contacted Carol S. Rynbrandt, who has pioneered in developing a movement education curricula for grades seven to nine and grades ten to twelve for boys and girls who (1) have had an organized movement education experience at the elementary school level and (2) for those who have not. This curriculum represents an outstanding contribution to the teacher of physical education in the secondary school who desires to utilize fundamental concepts that have proved so valuable and educational in the elementary school grades. The following introduction and movement education curricula for grades seven to nine and ten to twelve have been developed and written by Carol S. Rynbrandt* and used in this text with her permission.

Inherent to the successful implementation of this curriculum are an understanding and knowledge of the

---

*Formerly, Assistant to Director of Education, Dance Notation Bureau, Center for Movement Research and Analysis, New York, N.Y.

concepts of effort/shape—a qualitative, notational approach to observing, recording, and analyzing movement based on original concepts formulated by Rudolf Laban. Throughout the curriculum references are made to the elements of the effort/shape system, that is, weight, time, flow, and so on. (*A Primer for Movement Description** is a valuable text on the effort/shape approach to movement.) Also needed is the belief that movement education is a creative and individualistic approach to learning about movement.

The following curriculum has been developed for both boys and girls, for boys as well as girls benefit from movement education. The values and aims are equally applicable to both sexes, for if within the curriculum a balanced choice of themes is offered to which both sexes can relate, then all students have the freedom of variety in response.

The curriculum is divided into four parts: (A) a program for students in grades seven, eight, and nine who have had no previous exposure to movement education; (B) a program for students in grades seven, eight, and nine who have had previous exposure to movement education; (C) a program for students in grades ten, eleven, and twelve who have had no previous exposure to movement education; and (D) a program for students in grades ten, eleven, and twelve who have had previous exposure to movement education. Previous exposure shall be defined as at least one year (two semesters) of classes.

Program A: mandatory—seventh, eighth, ninth grades

Class composition
Girls and boys. Present movement situations that are especially appropriate.

Class organization
Unstructured, informal spacing of students.
Teacher should freely move about students during the class session.
Possible class organization plans:

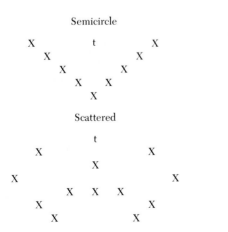

Semicircle

Scattered

*Dell, C.: A primer for movement description, New York, 1970, Dance Notation Bureau, Inc.

Equipment and facilities
1. Balls, jump ropes, medicine balls, hoops, wands, bean bags, inner tubes. THERE SHOULD BE ENOUGH EQUIPMENT SO THAT NO STUDENT WILL EVER HAVE TO WAIT TO USE SOMETHING.
2. Also benches, balance beam, mats, nets, and parachutes.
3. Record player, drug, gong, wood blocks, cymbals.
4. Spacious, well-lighted, well-ventilated room.

Content-materials*
First semester
1. Explore body movement possibilities—moving joints, fingers, limbs, different body parts. Especially be aware of movement elements of space, weight, time, and flow. Pose question—With what do we move?
2. Explore all aspects of space, and movement in space. Explore movement that is narrow, wide, high, low, on the diagonal. Again consider the four movement elements involved. Pose question—Where do we move?
3. Move with body parts other than legs. Explore twisting, stretching, bending, spiraling, contracting.
4. Work with the basic locomotor movements—walk, run, skip, jump, slide, hop, gallop.
   a. Vary speed of each of the above movements.
      (1) Slow it down.
      (2) Speed it up.
      (3) Vary speed between slow and fast.
   b. Vary size, range of each movement.
      (1) Make it small.
      (2) Make it large.
      (3) Make it narrow.
      (4) Make it wide.
   c. Vary amount of weight exerted in each movement.
      (1) Make it strong.
      (2) Make it light.
      (3) Make it neither strong nor light.
   d. Vary control of flow of each movement.
      (1) Be very tense, rigid.
      (2) Be very loose, floppy.
      (3) Be neither tense nor floppy.
5. Adapt movement to a partner.
   a. Follow the leader, changing quality, size, weight, flow.
   b. Contrast movement, move in opposition.
   c. Mirror movement.
   d. Mirror movement, but make a change a quality or element of the movement, for example, speed, size.
6. Move the arms and legs in unconventional manner.
7. Work to become aware of isolated actions, gestures.

---

*All suggestions listed under "content-materials" contain a breadth of material. Each suggestion should be subdivided and dealt with for a number of class sessions.

8. Explore movement with objects—throwing, catching balls, hoops, wands, nets, inner tubes. How do objects affect one's movement?
9. Work with occupational rhythms: sawing, cutting, chopping, stirring, sweeping, washing. Explore movements, considering elements and qualities involved. Juxtapose qualities and abstract the movement.

Second semester

1. Work with particular shapes of movements—angles, curves, numbers, letters, the feeling between different shapes. Begin by shaping single body parts and sequentially add parts to involve total body.
2. Work with qualities of movement—swinging, percussive, sustained. Utilize lightness, flow, gravity, sharp and quick movement.
3. Explore movement in the three body planes—horizontal, vertical, sagittal. Use images of door, table, and wheel, respectively, to clarify planar concepts.
4. Work with interrelating to other people.
   a. Begin to sense group rhythm and pulse of movement.
      (1) How does one's individual movement pulse differ from the group's movement pulse?
      (2) How must one alter one's movement to conform to the group rhythm and pulse?
   b. Begin to sense group quality of movement.
      (1) How does the quality differ from an individual's quality?
      (2) What must one do to conform to the group quality?
      (3) How does one feel about conforming to the group?
   c. Sense the group's use of space.
      (1) How does the group's use of space differ from the individual's use of space?
      (2) Does one feel differently when moving in group space as opposed to individual space?
5. Work with ballistic, vibratory, and collapse qualities of movement. Develop movement phrases that include two or more qualities.

Once the above material has been covered, the class should review the concepts that they had difficulty grasping. Throughout the entire semester, the teacher should at all times consider the elements of space, weight, time, and flow of movement. The understanding of these concepts is the basis for all movement.

Throughout the semester the students, in some form, should, always be asking: How do I move? What do I move? Where do I move? Both teacher and student must know that in movement education there is never a wrong movement.

Program A: exemplary class session—moving with a partner

Specific objectives

1. Develop an awareness of another person's movement.

2. Develop a deeper awareness of one's own movement through observing others and imitating their movements.
3. Strengthen student's sense for laterality of movement.
4. Develop kinesthetic sense of placement of body parts.

Concepts involved

1. Movement is a visual art, and kinesthetic perception is enhanced by observing movement.
2. Each person is unique and has particular movement nuances.

Equipment and facilities

A spacious, well-lighted, well-ventilated room; phonograph.

Content-materials

1. Have students select partner with whom they wish to work. Require that they choose someone they do not know very well.
2. One student is the leader and the other the follower. Leader starts moving simply, so that follower can replicate his movements. When "leading" is going well more complex movement may be tried, if desired. After three to four minutes students should be told to exchange roles. There should be no verbal conversation between the students.
3. The leader initiates movement and the follower mirrors that movement. Start with simple movement.
4. Change partners and repeat mirroring.
5. Incorporate big movements—jumps, hops, slides into mirroring.
6. Discuss what mirroring is and also what symmetry is.
7. With soft, slow background music ask students to move body parts symmetrically.
8. Ask the students to compose a short movement phrase using symmetry while lying supine on the floor.
9. Each half of the class performs their movement phrase for the other half.

Teacher evaluation

1. How well did the students grasp the concepts of mirroring and symmetry?
2. What didn't work?
3. How might you work with these concepts again?
4. What new ideas were realized for future sessions?

Program B: elective semesters—seventh, eighth, ninth grades

Specific objectives

1. Promote creativity, sensory perception of movement, quick reaction, dexterity, and rhythmic sense.
2. Develop a consciousness of movement exploration.

3. Develop feeling for interrelationship of all body parts.
4. Discover where a movement starts and where it naturally progresses.
5. Capitalize on spontaneous, impulsive, emotional movement.
6. Experience success in movement.

Equipment and facilities

1. Balls, jump ropes, medicine balls, hoops, wands, bean bags, inner tubes. THERE SHOULD BE ENOUGH EQUIPMENT SO THAT NO STUDENT WILL EVER HAVE TO WAIT TO USE SOMETHING.
2. Benches, balance beam, mats, nets, and parachutes.
3. Record player, drum, gong, wood blocks, cymbals.
4. Spacious, well-lighted, well-ventilated room.

Summary of approach

1. Discovery of body's movement possibilities.
2. Movement utilizing inexpensive equipment.
3. Movement with partner and group.
4. Movement utilized in games and sports.

Content-materials (one semester)

1. Work with movement in group formation. Students discover elements requisite to group movement, themes that work well, and where the individual fits in the success of group movement.
2. Experiment with movement that is basic to sports activity—throwing, catching, striking. Abstract by changing flow, quality, time, weight, and use of space to see what happens to the movement and how its efficiency is affected.
3. Work with Laban's full-effort actions—press, dab, flick, glide, float, punch, slash, wring. (See *A Primer for Movement Description* for explanation.*) Each full-effort action combines the elements of movement in a different way. Have students explore various sport movement and everyday movements to discover where full-effort actions are used.
4. Work with objects and obstacles; use medicine balls, bean bags, hoops, wands, lightweight balls.
   a. Develop movement phrase using medicine ball or bean bags.
   b. Develop movement phrase using wands, hoops, or lightweight balls.
   Begin to concentrate on body rhythm and the effect of object on rhythm.
5. Using a variety of musical instruments and recorded music, combine movement with sounds and music.
   a. How does sound/rhythm affect and alter movement?
   b. Have students accompany movement with sound—that is, the movement dictates the sound.

   c. Have students move to sounds, rhythm, and music.
   d. Work with movement and music, so that both complement the other.
6. Work with the body rhythm inherent to sport skills; the rhythm of a run, a leap, a swing, a tennis serve, and so on. Emphasize that one really feel the movement's rhythm.
7. Contrast movement elements, light versus strong, quick versus slow, and incorporate them into the three body planes.
8. Explore one's kinesphere for near, medium, and far reach. Explain the kinesphere to students and discover what basic movement patterns take place in what part of the kinesphere. Analyze sports movements in the same way.
9. The culminating activity for the semester—a lecture-demonstration for the entire school or one class, depending which is most feasible and desirable. Demonstration would be comprised of the basic elements of movement; how, what, and why a human being moves; how movement can be abstracted; the "taking apart" of a sport skill; presentation of students' own creative solo and group movement phrases. Additional considerations might be the rhythm, potential, and freedom of movement.

Program B: exemplary class session—working with balls

Specific objectives

1. To explore movement possibilities in working with a ball.
2. To discover to what extent the student can manipulate the ball and to what extent the ball forces the student to move in a certain way.

Concepts involved

1. The body imparts energy, propels and stops objects.
2. Objects affect body movement.

Equipment and facilities

Soft rubber balls, assorted sizes, enough for each student to have one; a spacious, well-ventilated area.

Content-materials

1. Each student selects a ball.
2. The student investigates the ball very carefully and explores to discover how it affects movement.
3. The student explores to see how the ball can be used. How can it be propelled with different body parts? How can its movement be stopped using different body parts?
4. How can one best maintain a controlled movement with the ball?
5. Can the ball be moved on the ground?
6. Can the ball be moved in the air?
7. The students exchange balls, working with one of a different size or weight.
8. The students are asked to simulate movement without a ball.

---

*Dell, C.: A primer for movement description, New York, 1970, Dance Notation Bureau, Inc.

9. Culminating problem: Compose a movement phrase depicting how you most enjoy moving or manipulating a ball. Once the teacher has viewed the class as a whole, combine four or five students who have similar or contrasting movement phrases. These groups would then repeat their individual movement phrases as a group phrase for the other students.

Teacher evaluation

1. How creative were the students in working with balls?
2. What size and weight balls seemed to work best?
3. What would you change if you were to present this session again?
4. Did the student's enjoy moving?

Program C: mandatory—tenth, eleventh, twelfth grades

Class composition
Coeducational, equal number of boys and girls
Class organization
Unstructured, informal, spacing of students (See Program A).
Equipment and facilities

1. Balls, jump ropes, medicine balls, hoops, wands, bean bags, inner tubes. THERE SHOULD BE ENOUGH EQUIPMENT SO THAT NO STUDENT WILL EVER HAVE TO WAIT TO USE SOMETHING.
2. Also benches, balance beam, mats, nets, and parachutes.
3. Record player, drum, gong, wood blocks, cymbals.
4. Spacious, well-lighted, well-ventilated room.

Content-materials
First semester

1. Explore breathing and body relaxation. Present three-dimensional breathing, allowing breath to flow through entire body.

The following material is taken from Program A, for whatever age the class, all students must first experience the basic concepts of movement. The important point to remember is that method of approach does vary with different age groups. The content from Program A will be restated but in a shortened form.

2. Explore body movement possibilities—joints, fingers, limbs.
3. Explore all aspects of space and movement in space.
4. Move with body parts other than legs—stretching, bending, twisting.
5. Work with the basic locomotor movements—walk, run, skip, jump, slide, hop, gallop. Vary speed, range, weight, and flow in each movement.
6. Adapt movement to a partner, follow, mirror, contrast.
7. Use the arms and legs in unconventional manner.
8. Work to become aware of isolated actions, gestures.
9. Explore movement with objects—throwing, catching balls, hoops, wands, nets, inner tubes, to see how movement is affected and altered by the objects.
10. Work with occupational rhythms: sawing, cutting, painting, chopping; washing, stirring, sweeping, typing.

Second semester

1. Work with particular shapes of movements—angles, curves, numbers, letters.
2. Work with qualities of movement.
3. Explore movement in the three body planes—horizontal, vertical, sagittal.
4. Work with interrelating to other people.
   a. Sense group rhythm and pulse.
   b. Sense group quality of movement.
   c. Sense group's use of space.
5. Continue to work with qualities of movement—ballistic, vibratory, and collapse qualities.

Methods
Present situations that relate in some way to the students' other courses. Discuss gravity when working

Fig. 10-4. Movement education in New Zealand. (Department of Education, Wellington, New Zealand.)

with weight, inertia when understanding movement flow, sociology when exploring group interaction. It is not the teacher's intention to get involved in the other course materials and so to view movement as secondary. But it is important that students realize that movement relates to all aspects of life. The class will be more meaningful if the teacher and students grasp basic movement concepts through an integrated approach.

Program C: exemplary class session—body relaxation, perception, and joint movement

Specific objectives
1. To release tension in the entire body.
2. To clearly perceive body parts and joints and gain a better understanding of body make-up and movement potential.
3. To explore movement in each joint of the body.

Concepts involved
1. The body is marvelously constructed.
2. Movement is the integrated working of the joints.

Equipment and facilities
A spacious, well-ventilated, well-lighted space.

Content-materials
This session would transpire in the second half of the semester.*
1. Students are paired.
2. Student A lays on floor, in supine position, relaxed with eyes closed.
3. The partner, student B, slowly starts feeling student A's fingers, the joints of the hand, and wrist. Student B senses how the bones are connected and how the bones can move. As student B does this, he or she also is "shaking" out any tension that exists in the specific body parts of student A.
4. Following the hand and arm, student B continues to sequentially "shake-out" student A's other hand, arm, shoulders, head, back, chest, feet, ankles, legs, knees, hips, pelvis, until all body parts have been "shaken-out."
5. Student A should be completely relaxed, so that the body can be moved in any way—body parts will be very heavy.
6. Partners reverse roles. Throughout the "shake-out" the teacher should be directing the students and aware of their progress. This process should not be rushed and can take from fifteen to twenty minutes with each person.
7. Students are standing and are asked to begin moving only fingers in as many ways as possible.
8. After movement is flowing in the metacarpals, wrist movement is added, then the elbow. It is an additive movement process incorporating all the joints of the body.

9. Once all joints are moving consecutively, the process is reversed until the fingers, which were the first to move, are the last body joints to stop moving.
10. In this session the students have experienced a state of total relaxation and also a total moving of body parts.

Teacher evaluation
1. How successful was the session?
2. How did the students respond?

Program D: elective semesters—tenth, eleventh, twelfth grades

Specific objectives
1. Promote creativity, sensory perception of movement, quick reaction, dexterity, and rhythmic sense.
2. Develop a consciousness of movement exploration.
3. Develop feeling for interrelationship of all body parts.
4. Discover where a movement starts and where it naturally proceeds.
5. Capitalize on spontaneous, impulsive, emotional movement.
6. Experience success in movement.
7. Continue to expand one's knowledge of movement.
8. Investigate the origin of movement education and the various approaches that exist.
9. Integrate movement experiences with other subjects in the school curriculum.

Equipment and facilities
1. Balls, jump ropes, medicine balls, hoops, wands, bean bags, inner tubes. THERE SHOULD BE ENOUGH EQUIPMENT SO THAT NO STUDENT WILL EVER HAVE TO WAIT TO USE SOMETHING.
2. Also benches, balance beam, mats, nets, and parachutes.
3. Record player, drum, gong, wood blocks, cymbals.
4. Spacious, well-lighted, well-ventilated room.

Summary of approach
1. Continual and fuller discovery of body movement.
2. Integration of movement education with other courses in the curriculum—history, biology, literature, sociology.
3. Discovery of "movement education" movement in sports.
4. Movement with partner and group.

Content-materials (one semester)
For those students who have had a maximum of two semesters of movement education, the content in Program B should first be presented and dealt with. Once that material has been covered, areas in which the students are weak should be reviewed, being presented from a different slant. There are endless possibilities of movement combinations that can be worked

---

*Session based on material provided by James Tyler, Instructor, New York University, Spring, 1972.

with if one considers the elements of movement, the qualities, full-effort actions, and so on. Also:

1. Work with more complex rhythmic patterns and motor coordinations. Beat a rhythmic pattern and ask students to devise movement phrase that complements the rhythmic pattern, and vice versa. Interchange gallops, skips, hops.
2. Build movement phrases from session to session.
3. Refine and alter old movement phrases.
4. Break down motor activities in sports. Discuss concepts, principles involved.
5. Allow students to suggest and initiate their own movement situations/problems.
6. Continue to utilize objects, obstacles, and music in different ways. Work to develop new effects.
7. Explore Laban's concepts of movement—effort/shape.
8. Investigate English and German systems of movement education.
9. Suggest research projects and books for reading dealing with any aspect of movement in which the students are interested.

Methods

Encourage advanced students to pursue a particular movement interest or interest related to movement education. With some students, a contract curriculum might be worked out where the student would devise his or her particular course of study, pursue it, and at the end of the semester present a "product" representing the semester's work.

Program D: exemplary class session—group rhythm (ten to fifteen students)

Specific objectives

1. To sense group rhythm.
2. To move as a group, as an integrated whole.

Concepts involved

1. Individuals must adjust personal body rhythm in order to move as a group.
2. Group harmony requires some type of conformity for each individual involved.
3. Group movement affects individuals psychologically as well as physically, for example, movement pace, speed.

Equipment and facilities

Spacious, well-ventilated, well-lighted space.

Content-materials*

1. Before the class begins any movement, they shall be instructed that they are to begin to walk, each at his or her own pace; they are then asked to begin to sense and adopt a group pace or walk, requiring that each person be very aware of everyone else in the group.
2. Once a group walk has been established, the group is instructed to gradually speed up the

---

*Session based on material provided by James Tyler, Instructor, New York University, Spring, 1972.

pace to a run and at the same time use more space.

3. Once the group has established a group run, they are to decelerate to a walk, then to a very slow walk, and finally to a standstill. As this happens the group's use of space becomes smaller, so that when the pace is very slow, the group is also very close together. This may vary in time, taking from five to fifteen minutes.
4. Begin a new group experience with all students standing still. One student initiates a walk or run. A second student begins to move at a different pace. The first student must adjust to the second student's pace. A third student begins to move and the first two students must adjust their pace to the pace of the third student. This process continues fairly rapidly until all students are moving. A group tempo is established that decelerates to a standstill.
5. Bring the students together and ask them what they thought of the experience. Talk about what group unity requires. Ask students to express any and all feelings concerning the experience or related group experiences.

Teacher evaluation

1. How did the students respond?
2. Was a sense of group rhythm/tempo established?
3. If not, why!

Evaluation of movement education

Class attendance—one fourth of grade.
Objective evaluation—one fourth of grade.
Student self-evaluation—one fourth of grade.
Subjective evaluation—one fourth of grade.

Objective evaluation (a written examination)

1. State elements of movement.
2. State qualities of movement.
3. What type of movement do you naturally find yourself doing?
4. List the three body planes and give an example of a movement in each one.
5. What type of movement is most difficult for you to do? Why?
6. Explain what the kinesphere is (advanced).
7. Execute eight full-action efforts (advanced).

Student self-evaluation (written or oral)

1. To what degree did you grasp the concepts of movement education as presented this semester?
2. Has your kinesthetic awareness of movement increased?
3. How would you rate your ability to execute the qualities and elements of movement?
4. What did and didn't you like about how the course was taught? How might it be improved?

Subjective evaluation (by the teacher)

1. Has the student's self-respect, self-worth, and self-control been improved, strengthened?
2. Is there a greater sense of kinesthetic awareness evident in the student's execution of movement?

3. Does the student think for himself or herself?
4. Does the student recognize qualities and elements of movement in other students? To what degree can the student analyze movement?
5. Can the student improve his or her movement pattern by using another student's idea?

STUDENT EVALUATIONS IN MOVEMENT EDUCATION

In traditional teaching methodology in physical education, the teacher sets the standards for the performance and evaluates student performance in relation to these standards. In the movement education approach to teaching physical education, standards may be applied to a skill performance, but the ways in which these standards are attained are quite different.

Every student in a movement education program sets his or her own goals, but because the students are reacting as individuals, they are not only directing their own learning but disciplining their learning as well. A skilled performance is thus judged not by a single standard for an entire class but by a series of standards that reflects the individual standards and differences of each of the members of the class. The physical education class becomes a laboratory experience in which the student is not only en-couraged but given the freedom to test a variety of solutions to a performance problem before arriving at the answer to that problem. When a student is given such experiences, the satisfactions gained from a successful performance help to motivate him or her to accept increasingly more difficult performance challenges. Each student can experience success because each solution attempted is a step toward the personal goals set by the student. The movement education approach helps to eliminate the fear of failure and of ostracism or criticism for failure to meet a common standard. Students achieve on their own level and derive fun and satisfaction from their physical education experience.

Evaluations in movement education can be achieved objectively and realistically. Program objectives will be student-centered and student-achieved. For each activity within the physical education class program, including the team, dual, and individual sports and activities and physical fitness and dance units, there can be a movement education approach. Within this framework, student progress can be measured on an individual basis in a cooperative student-teacher effort. Written tests concerned with intellectual

Table 10-2. A progressive program

Area	Elementary school	Junior high school	Senior high school
I. For developing skills	To develop movements necessary for basic sports skills (run, throw, catch)	To extend areas of basic skills in a wide variety of activities	To perfect techniques and capacities in basic skills
II. For physical skills	To understand basic components of physical fitness	To increase physical fitness levels through continued movement experiences	To improve and maintain physical fitness levels through movement experiences
III. For creative expression	To provide opportunity to respond freely to a variety of stimuli	To provide opportunity to experiment with many complex movements	To innovate and create new movements and new experiences
IV. For communicative experiences	To provide imaginative and dramatic opportunities	To provide more complex ideas for communication in terms of time, space, force	To innovate and create new relationships with environment
V. For understanding scientific principles	To understand basic function of balance and gravity	To develop greater understanding of forces of gravity in relation to static and dynamic movement	To understand physical laws governing motion, force, and balance as they apply to movement

understanding of the scientific principles of skill performance can be employed. Physical skill tests designed to measure individual achievement, as well as physical fitness tests, can also be applied to the evaluative process. Students on the secondary school level are capable of self-evaluation through student-teacher conferences. By combining these and other methods, a truer and more meaningful evaluation of each student's progress toward becoming a physically educated person can be derived. Total involvement of the student in all phases of the program will serve to enhance not only student achievement but the accomplishment of the program objectives as well.

MOVEMENT EDUCATION AND THE EXTRACLASS PROGRAM

Movement educators avoid group competition on the elementary school level. On that level, the student competes with himself or herself to improve performance and gain an understanding of it. Games are used, but the competitive aspects are eliminated as much as possible. Games are a means through which newly learned skills can be practiced and correct performance reinforced.

On the secondary school level, competition is a necessary part of many traditional programs. Students enjoy competition, and it serves as a stimulus to them. Within the regular class program, where movement education is employed, sports and games can be played competitively as soon as the students are satisfied that they have achieved sufficient skill ability to enjoy competition.

Intramural programs should be open to all students in a school. Participation in an intramural program should precede a student's membership on an interscholastic or varsity team. The movement education approach used in the class program will help each student to become more aware of the value of participating in sports and games of his or her own choosing outside the class program requirements. Students will also better understand the qualities needed for membership on the more highly competitive teams.

Movement education programs help to complement and supplement the extraclass offerings of secondary school physical education programs.

Self-assessment tests

These tests are to assist students in determining if material and competencies presented in this chapter have been mastered:

1. Summarize for the class what movement education is, how it started, and its growth in the United States.
2. Using your classmates as examples of secondary school students demonstrate what a traditional physical education class and what a movement education class are like.
3. Some traditional physical educators state that they do not see why movement education should be a part of today's physical education program. Write a rebuttal to these traditionalists that justifies the importance of including movement education in today's physical education curriculum.
4. Prepare a chart that compares the teacher's role in a traditional physical education class with that in a movement education class.
5. Develop what you consider to be a movement education unit for seventh-grade students who have not had any previous experience in this area.

Points to remember

1. Movement education is a significant new approach to teaching secondary school physical education.
2. Movement education frees the individual student to work and progress at his own pace.
3. Movement education helps the student to better understand the physical laws that govern human movement.
4. Opportunities for creative expression and exploration are an invaluable aspect of movement education.
5. Physical skills are developed through an individualized problem-solving technique.

Problems to think through

1. On what basis should a student be graded when the movement approach to teaching physical education is utilized?
2. Is the movement approach applicable for all the goals and objectives of physical education programs on the secondary school level?
3. Are movement education experiences as vital for secondary school boys as for girls?
4. Does the movement education approach offer a new means of motivating those secondary school students who are resistive to physical education?

Case study for analysis

A class of high school freshmen has scored low on initial physical fitness tests. The teacher has also observed that the students do not exhibit adequate levels of motor ability on a variety of skill tests. Intellectually, the class as a group expresses disinterest in and distaste for physical education. The first unit of instruction for these students will be track-and-field activities. How can the teacher interest and motivate these students as well as help them to improve their fitness scores and skill abilities?

Exercises for review

1. How does the problem-solving method of teaching help movement education to succeed?
2. In what ways can the area of dance contribute to movement education?
3. How does movement education correlate with traditional programs of physical education in secondary schools in the United States?
4. Compare the role of the teacher in traditional physical education with the teacher's role in movement education.
5. How can movement education help students to develop confidence in their skill performances?

Selected readings

Allenbaugh, N.: Learning about movement, NEA Journal **56**:48, 1967.

Barrett, K. R.: Exploration—a method for teaching movement, Madison, Wisc., 1964, College Printing and Typing Co., Inc.

Brown, M. C., and Sommer, B. K.: Movement education: its evolution and modern approach, Reading, Mass., 1969, Addison-Wesley Publishing Co., Inc.

Buchanan, E. A., and Hanson, D. S.: Free expression through movement, The National Elementary School Principal **52**:46, 1972.

Bucher, C. A.: Foundations of physical education, ed. 7, St. Louis, 1975, The C. V. Mosby Co.

Bucher, C. A.: Physical education for life, New York, 1969, McGraw-Hill Book Company.

Cratty, B. J.: On the threshold, Quest, vol. 8, Spring, 1967.

De Maria, C. R.: Movement education: an overview, The Physical Educator **29**:73, 1972.

Estes, N.: Encouragement for innovation, NEA Journal **55**:30, 1966.

Hackett, L. C., and Jenson, R. G.: A guide to movement exploration, Palo Alto, Calif., 1966, Peek Publications.

Howard, S.: The movement education approach to teaching in English elementary schools, Journal of Health, Physical Education, and Recreation **38**:31, 1967.

Lemen, M.: Implications of the problem-solving method for physical educators, Journal of Health, Physical Education, and Recreation **37**:28, 1966.

Porter, L. R.: The movement movement, Today's Education **62**:42, 1972.

Rizzitiello, T.: Movement education challenges an inner-city school, Journal of Health, Physical Education and Recreation **43**:35, 1972.

Schurr, E. L.: Movement experiences for children, New York, 1975, Prentice-Hall, Inc.

Smith, H. M.: Introduction to human movement, Reading, Mass., 1968, Addison-Wesley Publishing Co., Inc.

Sweeney, R. T.: Selected readings in movement education, Reading, Mass., 1970, Addison-Wesley Publishing Co., Inc.

Wessel, J. A.: Movement fundamentals, Englewood Cliffs, N. J., 1970, Prentice-Hall, Inc.

11

INTERPRETING THE PHYSICAL EDUCATION PROGRAM

INSTRUCTIONAL OBJECTIVES AND COMPETENCIES TO BE ACHIEVED

After reading this chapter the student should be able to—

1. Recognize and understand the need for interpreting the educational value of physical education.
2. Discuss the role of the Physical Education Public Information (PEPI) project in interpreting physical education to the public.
3. Apply sound principles and policies of public relations to physical education.
4. Identify various groups of people who need to be reached in interpreting the value of physical education and the basic considerations that need to be utilized in planning a public relations program for these groups.
5. Utilize various communication media to interpret the value of physical education.
6. Evaluate his or her own role in interpreting the worth of physical education.

Physical education has been the victim of the economy, taxpayers' rebellion, and fiscal pressures. Some budget officials and boards of education view physical education as a nonacademic subject and therefore low on the priority list when it comes to allocating money for new staff and equipment. Other educators have noted that with an austerity budget it is one of those extras they will have to do without.

A few years ago the city of Philadelphia decided to cut all extracurricular activities and reduce the physical education program requirement to the minimum mandated by state law. Fortunately, pressures exerted by responsible individuals and groups and a concerted effort to interpret the physical education program and its worth to students resulted in the programs being partially restored. As Edyth A. Fleming of the Philadelphia High School for Girls stated prior to an important meeting: "When Board of Education members meet with budget officials I hope they will be able to convince them that physical and mental conditioning go hand in hand and are equally necessary."

NEED FOR INTERPRETING PHYSICAL EDUCATION

There is an urgent need to interpret physical education to students, academic teachers and other educators, and the public in general. Accurate and significant facts need to be presented to these people so that they will understand the purposes and worth of our profession in the educational process as well as in their personal lives.

Physical education is a misunderstood profession. Surveys conducted among lay persons show that physical education is thought of as "calisthenics done to command," "athletics," "arms and legs and good intentions," or in terms of other misconceptions. Only as physical educators interpret their profession effectively will it be possible to obtain public support and to achieve its goals.

It is vital for teachers, students, parents, and the community-at-large to have a clear understanding of the important place of physical education in general education. This can be accomplished only when there is cooperation within the department, within the school, and within the school, and within the community. A public that is not informed is not likely to lend its support to furthering physical education.

Teachers, to be effective participants in public relations, must be guided by well thought through, sound educational policies. This chapter concerns itself with policies and suggestions that will assist each physical educator to be an effective public relations worker, recognizing that it is important not only to teach but also to interpret the program and its worth to various groups.

PEPI PROJECT

The Physical Education Public Information (PEPI) project is one of the major efforts by the profession to interpret physical education to the public. The project has identified some 600 coordinators for each of the nation's largest metropolitan areas who organize and interpret physical education in their own geographic area through such means as radio, television, newspapers, and other media.

The PEPI project was initiated on the premise that the tendency to curtail physical education programs can be reversed if people become aware of such basic values of physical education as:

- Physical education is health insurance.
- Physical education contributes to academic achievement.
- Physical education provides experiences and skills that last a lifetime.
- Physical education helps in developing a positive self-image and the ability to compete and cooperate with others.

PEPI has mobilized its efforts to get these messages across to the public, particularly taxpayers, students, teachers, administrators, school boards, parents, and funding agencies.

Coordinators have been carefully selected on the basis of their interest in the profession and in public relations, their reputation for working with people, and their ability to get the job done. All coordinators were required to attend several workshops in order to become oriented in the materials to be used, the procedure for obtaining time on television and radio, and other matters pertaining to the effective carrying out of their responsibilities.

Currently, PEPI is stressing that a "new" physical education exists, that physical education has changed, and that physical education is more relevant to the times through which the nation is passing.

For further information on PEPI and to help in this project, contact the American Alliance for Health, Physical Education, and Recreation offices in Washington, D.C.

AN EXAMPLE OF AN ATTEMPT TO INTERPRET PHYSICAL EDUCATION TO THE PUBLIC

Bucher has written many syndicated newspaper columns for the President's Council on Physical Fitness and Sports. The purpose of this effort is to interpret physical education so

Fig. 11-1. Cheerleaders at Paul J. Gelinas Junior High School in Setauket, N.Y.

PLAY AND YOUR CHILD'S REPORT CARD

By Charles A. Bucher
Consultant to the President's Council
on Physical Fitness and Sports

As a parent you want to help your child be a success in school. You spend long hours searching for material to be used in his reports, hire a tutor if he is lagging in arithmetic, sweat out the exams, and carefully scrutinize the report cards. You may even send a note to the principal and ask that he be excused from physical education so that he will have an extra period in the library.

Success in school, you sincerely feel, is filling the mind with historical facts, learning how to work with fractions, and developing a knack for writing compositions in English. Mastering these tasks, you have been led to believe, represents the formula for getting your child on the honor roll and into a prestigious college. As a neighbor of mine pointed out after seeing her son's report card: "I'm furious. My boy has three As, two Bs, and a D. The D is in gym and wrecks his average. He's not an athlete. It's not fair. It has only to do with his body—not his mind."

When well-intentioned parents ignore the physical aspect they are overlooking a vital part of their child's education, and ironically, may not be helping him to make that honor roll or get that much sought after diploma from a first-rate college. They are oblivious to a proven fact—that their child's mind and body are dependent on each other for maximum achievement in school, as well as in life. In other words, the chances are that their children will get better grades in school if they develop some skill and are physically fit than if they are uncoordinated and on the soft side.

More than a quarter of a century ago Lewis M. Terman, the famous psychologist from Stanford University, studied gifted children and found that physical weakness was rare among his bright subjects. Instead, most were fairly good physical specimens.

More recently, research conducted in Oregon among 9- to 17-year-olds found positive correlations between achievement in school and such physical measures as weight, height, strength, and certain physical skills. A study in England revealed that most students above average in scholarship were also above average in physique. An examination of more than 33,000 children in St. Louis found that mental mediocrity was associated with physical mediocrity. Motor characteristics of 43 underachieving boys, ages 10 to 14, enrolled in the Psychology Clinic of the University of California at Los Angeles, were studied and one-half of the boys from 10 to 12 years old exhibited poor motor performance.

Other research studies have shown that children who repeated a grade in a certain school system were inferior in weight and height to those who were not held back. Physical performance and emotional development factors among nonintellectual considerations in another educational program were most significant in achieving academically in reading and arithmetic.

There are many factors that relate to scholastic achievement in school. Intelligence, the amount of time your child spends on the books, and how motivated he is to do well in his studies will most certainly play a very important part in determining how successful he is. However, these conditions in themselves will not entirely determine what grades he gets in English and social studies, his promotion from grade to grade, and other measures of scholastic achievement.

Physical factors also play a part in your child's scholastic achievement. Parents who encourage their child to be physically fit and to develop motor ability will be giving their boy or girls the best chance to succeed. Although physical fitness and skill cannot improve your child's intelligence, they will help his learning potential.

that it will receive greater public support in communities from coast to coast. An example of one of these columns is included in this discussion.

GENERAL PUBLIC RELATIONS POLICIES FOR PHYSICAL EDUCATION

1. Each school within an educational system should develop its own public relations program, which should be an integral part of the larger school organization.

2. Before attempting to foster good public relations between the school and the community, good internal public relations should be developed, involving students, teaching personnel, nonteaching personnel, and administrators.

3. The public relations program should recognize that there are many kinds of peo-

Fig. 11-2. The aims and objectives of the total physical education program should be conveyed to the public. Basketball at Paul J. Gelinas Junior High School, Setauket, N.Y.

ple to be reached, such as pupils, parents, alumni, physicians, and administrators, and that each group requires its own unique procedures and approach for effective results.

4. The public relations program should present an articulate philosophy of physical education that clears away the misconceptions and stresses the objectives and worth of the field through the presentation of scientific evidence.

5. The physical educator should recognize that how he or she relates to other individuals within and without the department has implications for the public relations program. Consequently, such factors as a pleasing personality and appearance, provision for a healthy physical environment, and harmonious relations with students and parents are very important.

6. Before using communications media, such as radio or television, advanced planning is essential.

7. Evaluation of the effectiveness of the public relations program and the attitudes of the various sectors of the public should be determined through a carefully planned research program.

PUBLIC RELATIONS IN PRACTICE

Fifteen school systems in New York State were questioned about their public relations programs for physical education. They cited these operational factors in the conduct of their program:

1. Each physical education department has an active public relations program in operation.

2. Definite policies are established to guide the public relations program.

3. Responsibility for public relations is shared by all members of the department, with the central authority residing with the director.

4. Many media are used to interpret the program to the numerous groups to be reached.

5. Preparation and planning are essential in the use of all public relations media.

6. The total physical education program in action is recognized as the most effective medium of public relations.

7. Effort is made to interpret to the public the correct facts concerning physical education.

The fifteen school systems surveyed were asked the question, "What message are you trying to convey to the public?" A compiled list of the answers given by the directors of the physical education programs follows:

1. The aims and objectives of the total physical education program
2. The value of the total physical education program
3. The importance of the program to the student
4. Recognition and achievement of all students in physical education classes and in intramural and extramural activities, and not just in athletics
5. The importance of the physical education program for each child
6. The efforts and energies that are directed toward giving each child a sound program of physical education
7. The contributions of the physical education program to all children, not just athletes
8. The fact that even though interschool athletics receive most of the publicity, these activities do not receive priority in the program of physical education
9. The ability of the physical education program to enhance the health and welfare of the student

GROUPS NEEDING INFORMATION

Interpretation, or public relations, is basically concerned with communication. One person has defined it as getting the right facts to the right people at the right time and in the right way. Another has said it is doing good and receiving credit for it. One important consideration, regardless of definition, is to recognize that there are different kinds of people to be reached, and therefore different procedures and techniques are necessary in reaching these various groups. Six important groups that should be contacted are identified here.

Youth

Students in our schools who are exposed to physical education programs should be our best supporters. They should graduate from our schools and depart from our programs feeling that they have had worthwhile, enjoyable, and educational experiences. They should believe that the subject of physical education needs support and should be recommended to other people. Students grow up to be presidents of boards of education, directors of banks, industrial chairmen, and other important citizens in our communities from coast to coast. The experience they have in physical education will help to determine how much they will support these programs as adults.

Colleagues

Faculty members in other subject matter areas are an important group to reach. The absence of coaches and other physical education personnel at faculty meetings and other academic gatherings frequently results in a lack of adequate communication and interpretation of the program to teachers of history, science, English, and other subjects. Physical education cannot expect to be considered an important part of the school educational program if the department is not represented at important meetings. Physical educators need the support of their colleagues. They should exploit every opportunity to reach these important educators, whether in faculty meetings or in informal discussions in the teachers' room.

Administrators

School administrators make decisions affecting physical education programs, determine budget allocations, approve facility allocations, and in many other ways help or hinder our professional progress. It is important to reach this powerful group and impress them with the contributions of physical education to the total education of the student.

Parents

Mothers and fathers should understand that physical educators contribute to their children's health and welfare. If they believe that their children are receiving a worthwhile educational experience in physical education, they will be strong supporters, but if they believe that it is a waste of time because of poorly planned programs, they may fail to provide their needed support.

Alumni

The alumni of a school can be a valuable asset to any physical education program, provided they are kept informed.

General public

Of course, the general public, consisting of business and professional people, taxpayers, and other citizens, are interested in their schools. Outstanding educational systems are marks of good communities. Therefore, it is important to interpret to the general public how physical education contributes to a strong educational program.

BASIC CONSIDERATIONS

Following are some basic considerations for reaching the groups of persons noted previously.

Studies and research

The results of investigations of various aspects of the physical education program, such as improvement in the students' physical fitness or skills, are excellent publicity material. These studies should help to place physical education on defensible ground as to its worth in the educational program.

Written material

Newsletters, reports, memoranda, brochures, and other forms of written material that have been accurately and neatly prepared are excellent media for reaching the various groups.

Sound departmental policies

If the department of physical education has given time and study to policies concerning excuses, uniforms, athletic participation, class participation, grades, and other important matters, the wide dissemination of such material will reflect efficiency and a well-functioning program.

Conferences

Student, parent, administrator, or teacher conferences are important avenues for explaining purposes of programs, indicating interests, eliminating problems, and planning projects.

Integrated programs

Planning interdepartmental programs is an effective educational and interpretive device. A folk dance festival, for example, that integrates the resources of the physical education, art, music, home economics, history, geography, and other departments is an excellent medium.

Fig. 11-3. The program of physical education is the most important public relations medium. Girls engaged in cross-country race as part of physical education program in Lexington Public Schools, Lexington, Mass.

Involvement

"As you share you care" is a saying that has much merit. Administrators, townspeople, colleagues, students, and others can be involved in many aspects of the physical education program, ranging from athletics to a "careers day" project.

Internal considerations

Public relations should be considered internally before being developed externally. The support of everyone within the organization, from the top administrator down to the last worker, should be sought. Furthermore, such items as defining the purpose of the program, designating the person or persons responsible, considering the funds available, deciding on the media to be utilized, and procuring the wherewithal to carry on the program should be a first consideration.

Public relations plan

The public relations program should be outlined in writing, and every member of the organization should become familiar with it. The better it is known and understood, the better chance it has of succeeding.

Funds

There should be adequate funds to do the job. Furthermore, the person or persons in charge of the public relations program should be given freedom to spend this money in whatever ways they believe will be most helpful and productive for the organization.

Persons responsible

Individuals assigned to public relations responsibilities should modestly stay in the background, keep abreast of the factors that affect the program, develop a wide acquaintance, and make contacts that will be helpful.

Wide coverage

A good interpretative program will utilize all available resources and machinery to disseminate information in order to ensure adequate coverage.

Outstanding program

The program of physical education is the most important public relations medium. Good news travels fast but bad news spreads even faster. If the program is good, people will hear about it and, in turn, will give their support and help.

INTERPRETIVE MEDIA

Fifteen school systems were surveyed to determine what specific media were utilized by the departments of physical education in interpreting their programs to the various groups of people they were attempting to reach. The following media were listed:

Newsletter	Personal contact
School publications	Demonstrations and
Radio	exhibits
Television	Films
Newspaper	Pictures
Posters	Magazines
Letters to parents	Window displays
Public speaking	Brochures
Physical education	Sport days
program	Bulletin boards
Slogans	Professional associations

Some of the media that can be utilized effectively in physical education, along with general principles regarding their use, will be discussed briefly.

Slogans

The strength of a slogan lies in its emotional appeal—it is a distinctive phrase used to signify a purpose.

Slogans should be informational, factual, colorful, appealing, and easily understood and remembered, and they should impel to action. In addition, slogans should be timely, practical, personal, challenging, simple, based on truth, short, imaginative, and concrete. They can be used in radio, television, speeches, songs, posters, letterheads, billboards, displays, rallies, exhibits, advertisements, and handbills.

Our nation's political history has been affected by slogans. A few examples: "Walk softly and carry a big stick." "Keep cool with Coolidge." "Make the world safe for democracy." "A chicken in every pot." "54-

40 or fight." "Over the top." "Remember the Maine." "Taxation without representation is tyranny."

Slogans have noticeably affected our economic development. A few examples: "It's smart to be thrifty." "We will not be undersold." "What helps business helps you."

Products have used slogans effectively. A few examples: "All the news that's fit to print." "Progress is our most important product." "The pause that refreshes."

Ways of life are reflected in slogans. A few examples: "A stitch in time saves nine." "Time and tide wait for no man." "He who hesitates is lost." "Spare the rod and spoil the child."

Slogans have been used successfully in health, physical education, and recreation. A few examples: "It pays to play." "Give your child's mind his body's support." "Cross at the green, not in between." "Brush today to check decay." "A sound mind in a sound body." "Health, energy, and power are yours." "Fitness—a basic goal of education." "You can't sit and be fit."

Posters

Posters should catch and hold the attention of the viewer. They require an eye-catching design and should have a message that, as a rule, is short, punchy, and well-worded.

Color is one of the most important agents that help to convey a poster's messages if effectively used.

Posters should be simple, interesting, attractive, and convincing and should leave a specific message with the viewer. They should guide an observer's view from one part of the display to the other. This can be done through color, line, and various layout techniques. Posters should be placed at eye level if possible and should have good balance, with essential features in the most prominent places.

Radio

A radio program should hold the listener's attention from start to finish. Many radio stations today broadcast little other than music and news. Programs must fit into such a pattern to hold listeners rather than lose them.

Short programs are good. Very few persons turn on the radio today to listen to a dramatic play or a long discourse on some topic of the day. The program should be informative and entertaining.

Language must be simple and direct—human interest and anecdotal material are always effective. It is better to put depth into one idea rather than to cover many ideas and only scratch the surface of each. Talk *with* rather than *to* the listener. Speak in the listener's terms. Know your audience.

Consult with the broadcasters—producers, program directors, and so on. Find out the most effective methods for radio broadcasting.

Have a definite message in mind to put across to the public. Be thoroughly familiar with the method to be used to relay the information: spot announcements, editorials, news broadcasts, reporting of school activities, pannels, interviews, plays, quiz programs.

Determine the time of day at which the most receptive audience would be listening and publicize the radio program in advance. This can be done via advertisements, announcements on other broadcasts, school publications, and press releases.

Television

Explore the possibility of obtaining free time. The idea of performing a public service will influence some television station managers. Consult television stations that are reserved for educational purposes.

Be prepared with written plans that can be put into operation immediately. Sometimes one must take advantage of opportunities for television time on short notice. Being ready may make the difference between acceptance or rejection for such an assignment.

Do not overlook the fact that television programming requires rehearsals, preparation of scenery, and other work.

Have boys and girls participate in the program. When youngsters are in the act, the attention of mothers, fathers, aunts, uncles,

Fig. 11-4. High school volleyball. (Courtesy Bill Henderson, Toms River, N.J.)

grandmas, friends, and so on is immediately attracted.

Motion pictures

One of the most powerful means of informing and enlightening the public in regard to physical education is the use of motion pictures. Good pictures of daily class activity are tangible evidence of the worth of the program to parents and others. They are excellent for PTA groups, civic clubs, and the like.

Motion pictures usually receive better audience attention. The situation is not like that in television, where there is opportunity to change to another program.

Before making a film, analyze the potential audience, the message to be conveyed, and other important items. Survey the entire program of physical education in order to select the most significant and typical activities to be photographed.

Homemade film depicting daily operation of the school can be useful in interpreting the program to the public. In a do-it-yourself operation, try to obtain some professional advice—perhaps from a photography club or a camera shop. Use good equipment and material. Nothing is more annoying than

watching a poorly planned movie that consists of shots that are blurred or not in proper focus, or going through an unpleasant experience with a projector that does not work properly.

Many films on physical education are available through professional organizations, college and university film libraries, commercial organizations, and state departments of education.

Exhibitions and demonstrations

In physical education an exhibition or a demonstration can be a culminating school activity to show what has been accomplished in the program and what students have learned. Exhibitions and demonstrations can focus public attention on a program and stimulate action in support of the program.

Exhibitions can take the form of bulletin board displays, showcases, scrapbooks, drawings, or posters to point up such subjects as physical fitness or some sport or skill. They can also be used to show how expert performers have acquired outstanding skill in a particular sport.

An exhibition, for best results, should be limited to one type of activity or purpose and should be original, present facts, stimulate participation, provide new ideas, and create action.

Demonstrations can utilize all the students regardless of skill and also present a picture of what actually goes on in day-to-day classes.

Newspaper and magazine articles

Articles can be published in local papers or periodicals or in national publications. They should be factual, arouse and secure attention, contain human interest material, and be written in the language of the reader.

Magazines have many advantages since they have excellent color and layout, are read many times by different persons, reach a wide range of people varying in income and intelligence, and are found in many offices and homes.

Know the subject, the ideas to be put across, and the type of persons to be reached; then place the article in a suitable publication.

Newspaper material is often read hurriedly. Therefore, the style of writing must take this point into consideration.

Prepare all copy in typewritten form— neat, double spaced, and on one side of the paper only.

Ideas may be suggested to magazines and newspapers to be staff written.

Letters

Next to personal contact, correspondence is the best interpretive medium. Letters can be direct, are economical, and may be adapted to any situation.

Letters should be individually typed. It is important to use correct grammar and spelling.

The message contained in the letter should be friendly, cordial, warm, courteous, sincere, enthusiastic, and natural. Write your letters as though you were speaking to the individual in person.

Letters can be used to announce special programs, to indicate the necessary skills and understandings expected of students, to interpret the objectives desired to be reached, and so on.

Letters should be written in terms of the reader's wishes and needs.

Public speaking

Public speaking can be a very effective medium of interpreting. Through public addresses to civic and social groups in the community, public gatherings, professional meetings, and any organizations or groups that desire to know more about the work being performed, a good opportunity is afforded for interpreting the physical education profession to the public.

A public speech must be effective, or it may result in poor public relations. Know the subject to be discussed, have a sincere interest in the topic, and be enthusiastic. Be direct, straightforward, and well-prepared. Give a brief presentation, and use clear and distinct enunciation.

Prepare an outline of the talk in advance. The talk should be well organized. Use correct English and have an interesting beginning and conclusion, as well as a theme or central point.

Professional associations

Professional associations on local, state, and national levels can do much to interpret physical education to the public at large. Professional groups hold meetings to upgrade programs; prepare films, publications, and other materials, establish professional standards, sponsor radio, television, and other programs, publish articles in periodicals, and in many ways inform the community, state, and nation about the physical education profession. They deserve your constant support.

Professional organizations are valuable in reaching boards of education, the general public, colleagues in the profession, other teachers, pupils, and other groups.

SOME THINGS EACH PHYSICAL EDUCATOR CAN DO TO INTERPRET THE FIELD OF PHYSICAL EDUCATION

Following is a brief list of ways in which the physical educator will personally be able to interpret to others the profession of which he or she is a part:

1. Join professional associations and help them to achieve their goals.

2. Attend faculty meetings after becoming a member of a school staff. Enter into discussions.

3. Become well informed about physical education as a professional field and about education in general.

4. Seek out school administrators, other members of the faculty, and the consumers of physical education's products and services. Help them to better understand the profession of physical education.

5. Understand the scientific foundations underlying physical education: the latest research and new trends and developments. Find out what the latest thinking is and translate it into action at the grassroots level.

6. Develop the best possible program of physical education. Have satisfied children and youth go out from the program.

7. Utilize every opportunity available to sell someone else on the worth of the professional field of endeavor. If the physical educator himself is sold, it will not be difficult to sell someone else.

8. Exploit every medium of communication to put the message across.

9. Think in positive terms. Think success, and the profession's chances of achieving great things will be better assured!

Self-assessment tests

These tests are to assist students in determining if material and competencies presented in this chapter have been mastered:

1. Conduct a survey of twenty-five lay people on a public street in your town. Ask each person what he or she understands is meant by the term physical education and to what extent it has value in an educational program. Summarize the results of your survey and relate your findings to the need for interpreting the educational value of physical education to the public.

2. What do the letters PEPI stand for? What is the purpose of PEPI? How is it organized and what does it accomplish?

3. Given a secondary school program of physical education, prepare a set of guiding principles that you feel will help in educating the public as to the worth of a physical education program.

4. As a faculty member in a secondary school where the physical education program has little public respect, what groups of people would you try to reach and what specific types of information would you try to communicate to these groups to gain more respect for your field?

5. Identify the various communication media that exist in your home community. Construct a plan indicating how you would use four of these media in interpreting physical education to the public.

6. Perform a self-assessment by listing on a piece of paper in *column 1*, what you are actively doing to interpret the worth of physical education to the public and, in *column 2*, what additional things you could do in this regard that you are not now doing.

Points to remember

1. Some of the basic principles underlying a sound program of interpretation and public relations.

2. The various groups of people to whom the profession should be interpreted.

3. A knowledge and understanding of the following interpretative media: slogans, posters, radio, television, motion pictures, exhibitions, demonstrations, newspapers, magazines, letters, public speaking, and professional associations.

4. Some things that can be done to interpret the professional field of physical education.

Problems to think through

1. What are some of the common misconceptions about physical education? How did these misconceptions originate, and how can they be corrected?

2. What constitutes an adequate public relations program for a secondary school?

Case study for analysis

Choose some product that has gained national recognition, such as an automobile, cigarette, soap, and so on. Do an in-depth study to discover what techniques were used to promote it and to persuade the public to accept this product.

Exercises for review

1. Define the term "public relations."

2. What are the groups of people with which physical education is most directly concerned?

3. What are five principles to recognize in interpreting your profession to the public?

4. What do we mean by the statement, "As you share you care"?

5. Develop a slogan that can be used to promote physical education.

6. Prepare a poster to stress the importance of physical fitness.

7. Write a series of ten one-minute spot announcements for a radio station.

8. Write a letter that could be used to inform parents about the physical condition of their son or daughter.

9. What is the difference between an exhibition and a demonstration?
10. Write a 500-word magazine article on the topic, "It pays to play."

Selected readings

American Association for Health, Physical Education, and Recreation: PEPI-GRAMS, a series of communications on the Physical Education Public Information Project, 1972.

Bucher, C. A.: Administration of health and physical education programs, including athletics, ed. 5, St. Louis, 1975, The C. V. Mosby Co.

Bucher, C. A.: Back to school—what kind of education is relevant? (syndicated newspaper column), Washington, D.C., September, 1972, President's Council on Physical Fitness and Sports.

Bucher, C. A.: Foundations of physical education, ed. 7, St. Louis, 1975, The C. V. Mosby Co.

Bucher, C. A.: Play and your child's report card (syndicated newspaper column), Washington, D.C., May, 1972, President's Council on Physical Fitness and Sports.

Caldwell, S. F.: Toward a humanistic physical education, Journal of Health, Physical Education, and Recreation **43:**31, 1972.

Dapper, G.: Public relations for educators, New York, 1964, The Macmillan Co.

Geyer, C.: Physical education for the electronic age, Journal of Health, Physical Education, and Recreation **43:**32, 1972.

Heryberg, F.: Work and the nature of man, New York, 1972, World Publishing Company.

Taylor, J. C., and Bowers, D. C.: Survey of organizations, Ann Arbor, Mich., 1972, Institute for Social Research.

Torpey, J.: Interpreting physical education for the public, Physical Educator **24:**131, 1967.

Ziatz, D. H.: Practical-realistic public relations, Journal of Physical Education and Recreation **46:**69, 1975.

PART THREE
The teacher

12

BECOMING A TEACHER

INSTRUCTIONAL OBJECTIVES AND COMPETENCIES TO BE ACHIEVED

After reading this chapter the student should be able to—

1. Better assess the current employment situation in physical education.
2. Explain the new developments taking place in teacher education and the role and responsibilities of teachers in the secondary school.
3. Evaluate his or her own qualifications for teaching and becoming certified and knowing the procedure for obtaining a position.
4. Outline a teacher's responsibility to the department, school faculty, profession, and community after obtaining a position.

Aristotle once said that those who educate children well are more to be honored than those who produce them; for those who produce them only give them life, but those who educate them give them the art of living well. These wise words of Aristotle indicate the challenge that the teaching profession presents to every person who desires to enter the ranks. A teacher has the responsibility to inspire students with the desire to learn, to have them recognize the need to develop physical skills and be physically active, to see that each one develops to his or her capacity, and, to ensure that each one has a successful educational experience.

The prospective teacher of physical education today can look ahead to a field of endeavor that is much more selective in its choice of those persons who will become the practitioners. This selectivity will be based on competencies developed rather than courses taken and on behavioral changes taking place in students rather than merely the accumulation of knowledge and the development of skills.

THE CHANGING JOB MARKET

Today, many physical educators are looking to places other than schools for positions after they graduate from college. Although schools and colleges still remain a fertile source for employment, the fact that the market for positions is not as plentiful and the number of teachers trained is in excess of the number of job openings means that in many cases there is a need to look elsewhere to secure employment. Two of the areas that are proving to be excellent places of employment are industrial fitness programs and health spas.

Industrial fitness programs

Anyone who doubts the value of looking into industry for possible employment should consider the fact that some 50,000 United States firms spend an estimated $2 billion on fitness and recreational programs for their employees each year. The payoff from such fitness programs can be credited to such things as increased productivity among employees, less absenteeism, more and better work, and better relations with co-workers. Such companies and industries as Pepsico, Inc., General Foods, Rockwell International, Life Insurance Company of Georgia, Xerox, Tyler Corporation, and many others have found that these programs are worthwhile and therefore hire personnel, among them physical educators, to help in conducting activities for their employees.

Health spas

The health spa industry in the United States is an estimated multi-billion-dollar industry, which is growing rapidly because of the current national emphasis on physical fitness and exercise. Many reputable health spas provide their customers with worthwhile programs of activity and fitness advice. At the same time, there are some health spas that are "ripping off" the public through high rates, poorly trained staff, inadequate facilities, getting customers to sign contracts before they know what they are getting into, and misleading advertising. Examples of other complaints include high-pressure selling, the closing of spas shortly after opening, difficulty with refund policies, and fitness promises that cannot be fulfilled.

The National Association of Physical Fitness Centers, which was recently established, is trying to bring creditability to the health spa industry, but due to the lucrative nature of this type of business the progress is slow. Professional physical educators are needed in the health spa industry to help in making them reputable and to better meet the needs of men and women looking for such a service.

To show how health spas have grown, the European health spas can be used as an example. In the United States they have 144 locations in 80 cities and 28 states. They employ some 2,700 people, and in one year their gross sales were approximately $65 million. They have about one-half million members who attend their spas three times a week. They have men instructors for men and women instructors for the women. A typical facility costs between $250,000 to $750,000

and consists of an exercise room, apparatus, treadmills, bicycles, swimming pools, saunas, and oil baths. The activities include yoga classes, ballet classes, jogging, and many other activities.

NEW DEVELOPMENTS IN TEACHING

Five of the significant new developments in teaching that the new teacher should be acquainted with are licensing teachers with competencies, differentiated staffing, teacher aides, student leaders, and teacher accountability.

Licensing teachers

To show the degree to which licensing of teachers is changing a task force in one of the largest states recently recommended the following:

- A statewide licensing examination for all persons seeking to become teachers; included in this examination would be the requirement to demonstrate the mastery of a defined body of knowledge unique to teaching
- A successful one-year internship period before licensing new teachers
- A master's degree as the minimum requirement for new teachers
- A professional practices board, like those in medicine and law, to oversee the teaching profession

Competency-based teacher education

Probably one of the major innovations in the licensing of teachers that has swept the country is the competency-based approach whereby teachers must show that they have mastered certain competencies before receiving their teacher's license. The purposes of competency-based learning are to identify the competencies that learners are expected to acquire, to have procedures and techniques by which learners can accurately be awarded credentials for mastery of these competencies, and to provide educational experiences by which students may attain needed competencies.

The persons involved in developing lists of

competencies that they feel teachers should have may be people representing different constituencies, including learners, faculty members, administrators, professional agencies, practicing professionals, employers, and public agencies. The main requirement would be that all parties have a legitimate interest in the prospective teacher and what the competencies should be. Those involved would form groups internal and external to the educational institution and would view a competency as a specific, demonstrable ability, skill, attitude, or knowledge required for performance in a given professional role.

In addition to identifying the needed competencies to teach there is also the need to determine how they will be assessed. The assessment of whether the person has mastered the identified competencies emphasizes the results of learning. In other words, they are not assessed in terms of credits, degrees, and courses taken. On the other hand, what is important is that the learner is

able to reach a given standard of performance.

In competency-based learning the main indicator of student achievement is his or her ability to do effectively the job for which he or she has prepared. Learning can be accomplished in and out of the school. The criterion for a good teacher is the degree to which he or she can help students acquire the competencies they are seeking. The teacher is held accountable for the student's acquiring the identified competencies within the limits of his or her abilities.

Differentiated staffing

Differentiated staffing means the assignment of personnel to different roles in terms of their training, abilities, career goals, aptitudes, and interests. The primary reason is to provide a more individualized program and better service to students, to make greater use of teacher abilities, and to enable teachers to assume greater responsibili-

Fig. 12-1. Teacher at Hampton Institute, Hampton, Va., in physical education class for students.

ties and receive increases in compensation. Teachers have differentiated levels of responsibility and are paid accordingly.

Differentiated staffing recognizes the individual differences of teachers and how they can best be used to enhance student learning. In physical education there are many roles that teachers can fulfill.

Teacher aides

There has been greater and greater utilization of teacher aides. These assistants are sometimes known by different names such as "auxiliary personnel" and "paraprofessionals." Some of the tasks performed by teacher aides include clerical duties, such as recording grades, typing, and filing; nonclassroom duties, such as helping in lunchroom and playground supervision; assisting with large group instruction, such as music and art; grading papers; assisting with small group instruction; helping in the preparation and use of instructional materials, such as operating a projector; and performing work connected with the classroom environment, such as caring for bulletin boards.

Student leaders

Another development is the increased use of student leaders in schools. One reason for greater stress on such a practice today is the recognized need for more student involvement. Other reasons include the need to train leadership for the profession and the desire to render a greater service to students by providing them more individualized instruction from their better skilled classmates.

Student leaders may be utilized in several ways, such as class leaders, officials, committee members, supply and equipment managers, program planners, record keepers, office managers, and special events coordinators.

Teacher accountability

Most educational systems are giving increased attention to teacher accountability. The high cost of education and the rise in taxes to support this cost are causing the public, who pays the bill, to demand accountability in terms of what a teacher produces. The aim of such a movement is to develop objective standards as a means of improving school effectiveness. Among other things, it is designed to show which teaching and school methods have proved most effective in achieving specific educational goals. It will protect successful teachers against unfair criticisms by providing proof of their effectiveness; for those teachers who are not effective, it will indicate the additional training and help they need to become effective teachers.

It may help the prospective teacher to know the educational goals that the public thinks are important for them to accomplish. According to the Fourth Annual Gallup Poll of Public Attitudes Toward Education, the public wants children to achieve the following goals as a result of their education:
- To help children get better jobs
- To help children develop better human relations
- To help children be financially successful
- To help children be satisfied with themselves
- To help children be mentally stimulated

It will also be interesting to the reader to note that this Gallup poll indicated that approximately three out of every four persons surveyed stated that they would be very happy to have their offspring take up teaching as a career. In other words, teaching is a very popular vocation today among all classes of people.

New teachers in today's modern secondary schools face tasks and responsibilities far different from those faced several years ago. Whereas previously a teacher worked alone to teach, today's teacher may work with a team of several teachers and with many different groups. Whereas at one time a teacher had only one set of textbooks at his or her disposal, today there are films, television, cassettes, transparencies, computers, and programmed materials to assist in teaching. Once the teacher had to rely on subjective judgments to recognize pupils' attitudes, aptitudes, and interests, but today's extensive testing programs offer comprehensive guidance information instead. Yet these technological advances have not made the teacher's tasks in education any easier, for they have brought with them additional responsibilities. The teacher must learn how to operate specialized equipment. He or she must keep up with new materials being released and know when and how to utilize them appropriately.

Teachers presently graduating from professional institutions are being trained to meet these innovations in modern education. First of all, courses of study within their fields of interest are greatly specialized. For example, a prospective teacher may specialize in such areas as health, the dance, elementary school teaching, athletic training, or coaching. Moreover, some institutions offer teacher-internship programs in which a student lives and teaches in a community while gaining firsthand teaching experience. Increased knowledge of child development and the learning process has made another substantial contribution to the training of today's teachers.

Yet these improvements in teacher training have not made the teacher's task any easier either, for administrators of modern secondary schools are expecting more productivity from their staff members. Administrators expect the teacher to keep abreast of the advances in knowledge, application of the latest teaching methods, and utilization of modern equipment. Furthermore, administrators want increased professionalism through in-service workshops and advance study, plus increased commitments to their field through faculty associations and organizations.

Although the task of teaching has not become any easier, progress in education has brought benefits not only to students but also to the teachers themselves. Today's teachers now enjoy greatly improved standards and practices. Starting teachers' salaries, for example, have vastly improved from meager wages to an average of over $8,000 per year. In some sections of the country, of course,

the average starting salary is much higher. Furthermore, many schools now offer valuable fringe benefits in terms of retirement plans, medical and life insurance coverage, and tenure. Teacher organizations such as the National Education Association are developing increased powers to demand improved health standards for children and improved working conditions for teachers, such as lighter class loads, fewer nonteaching duties, and smaller classes.

Teaching is a demanding profession and an ever-changing one. A close look should be taken at the changing aspects of the teaching profession—the teacher's responsibilities within the department, to the school, and to the profession, keeping in mind specific relationships to physical education. However, the problems of personal qualifications, job application, and certification generally come first chronologically for those persons entering the profession. Therefore, these topics will be discussed first.

SOME RESPONSIBILITIES OF TODAY'S TEACHER

The role of the person who is teaching in the secondary school today is partially told in some of the highlights taken from a survey by the National Education Association:

- Approximately one out of twelve secondary school teachers is assigned to health and physical education.
- Approximately one out of seven teachers devotes more than one-half of their time to duties outside their major field.
- Approximately three out of every four have five or more unassigned periods per week.
- The weekly workload of teachers averages about thirty-seven hours.
- Most teachers teach about 180 days a year.
- Approximately four out of ten schools have team teaching.
- Approximately one out of every six teachers has aides for themselves or share with other teachers.
- Approximately 98 out of every 100 principals are males.

PERSONAL QUALIFICATIONS

The personal qualifications of the physical educator are an extremely important consideration. Administrators regard such characteristics as professionalism, promptness, and the ability to maintain control as attributes of primary importance, while students hold patience, understanding, and fairness as desirable qualities in a teacher.

There is no formula for a successful teacher to follow. The "coach" who is like a father or mother to his boys or girls may be as highly respected as the one who is a strict disciplinarian and dictator. The physical educator who is highly organized and efficient may be as well liked as the young graduate who can participate with the students.

Is being "highly respected" and "well liked" the key to successful teaching? Perhaps these characteristics are a part of the overall picture. Certainly maintaining dis-

cipline and imparting information are equally important qualities for the teaching process. The personality traits exhibited by the teacher and the relationship established with the students are the vital links between the subject and its recipients. All four aspects of the teacher's character—physical, social, emotional, and intellectual—should be worthy of emulation by the developing adolescent.

Physical qualifications

The physical educator usually has many more students in classes than do other teachers. Close relationships with students develop through the intramural and interscholastic programs. Because of the number and type of these relationships between student and teacher, it is important that the appearance of the physical educator be worthy of respect and admiration from ado-

Fig. 12-2. All four aspects of the teacher's character—physical, social, emotional, and intellectual—should be worthy of emulation by the students. Physical education class at Brockport Central Schools, Brockport, N.Y.

lescents. Uniforms should be spotless and all clothing should be neat, clean, appropriate, and in good taste. The association of health, good hygiene, and cleanliness with physical education is so close that the instructor must represent these ideals to the students.

The physical skills and abilities of the physical educator should be exemplary. To conduct satisfactory demonstrations and teaching lessons, teachers should be able to perform well in as many areas as possible. This does not mean that they must "star" in all events, but their background of basic coordinations should be well above average.

Social qualifications

Because of the many social objectives of physical education, it is important that the teacher be representative of mature social development. The teacher should meet people easily, mix well, and treat all individuals with respect and consideration. It is these qualities that the teacher emphasizes in the classroom, and the students should therefore be able to recognize them in the teacher.

As a leader the physical educator should strive to control but not dominate the group and to plan with but not for students. In so doing the qualities of leadership that should be promoted are presented to the students, and they in turn may learn to lead well.

Emotional qualifications

It is important that every teacher be a stable, mature individual, well adjusted to life in his or her chosen occupation. This is particularly true of the physical educator. The nature and tenor of the work require an emotional control and a responsiveness that are not easily defined.

To establish effective teaching rapport, the teacher must have patience and understanding mixed with firmness and composure. To meet all the individual problems that arise daily with students—their maladies, their excuses, their upsets—the teacher must offer a sympathetic, understanding ear, indicating to the students a sincere interest in their personal difficulties. In handling the everyday occurrences in the classroom, the teacher should display firmness and quiet confidence, so that the students realize that the situation is well under control.

The many frustrations that beset the physical educator striving for winning teams and competitive excellence must be met with calm self-assurance. Administrative and community pressures should not become so strong that other teaching responsibilities are neglected or that self-concern replaces consideration for the students.

Intellectual and other professional qualifications

Intellectually, the physical educator needs many qualities that are equally important both as a teacher and as an influence on young people.

As a teacher the physical educator should be efficiently organized and able to maintain order in handling the myriad administrative details. An ability to express ideas clearly and distinctly orally and on paper is also important, for students learn from what is imparted to them, and therefore materials must be intelligently presented. A professional manner and outlook enhance the profession itself in the eyes of the students, and this, too, becomes an important aspect of the teacher's personality. The image that a physical educator is a person of all brawn and no brains is slowly being overcome, and new teachers entering the field should further enhance this newer picture of the teacher as an intelligent educator.

As an influence on young people, the teacher should have many interests in and out of the field. This is important because it affords more opportunities for sharing the various interests of the students who are contacted daily. As a broader interpretation of physical education in its relationship to life is presented to the students, the physical educator is respected for more than just coaching abilities or professional skills. In this role of a counselor influencing students in their approach to life, the physical educator should have an outlook worthy of respect and imitation.

Ideally, the physical educator should have

a wholesome personality, sharing a deep knowledge and interest in the subject with students who are respected as people and led with sympathetic understanding. The personality that the teacher presents to the students may be as important as the material to be learned. Ideally, also, the physical educator should meet other qualifications and standards in addition to those of a personal nature.

PROBLEMS OF CERTIFICATION

Among the many problems encountered by any prospective teacher are those concerning the initial step of becoming properly certified. Often the confusion and red tape involved in finding appropriate information and determining personal status are so disheartening that the new teacher is bewildered before starting. The prospective physical educator is not different from other teachers in this respect, and knowing in advance about state requirements and qualifications can save a great deal of worry and frustration. Certification problems are complicated further by the continuous study and change of specifications.

Some of the newer approaches to teacher certification include a competency-based approach, a freer movement of qualified teachers across state lines, a simplication of the types of certificates issued, an approved-program approach where the preparing college or university has its teacher-preparing program approved and then accepts the responsibility for training and certifying the teachers who pursue and graduate from said program, and basing certification upon a teacher's demonstrated abilities rather than upon courses he has taken in a collegiate program.

Certification requirements

All states have established minimum requirements that must be met by prospective teachers before they become legally certified to teach. These certification requirements in teaching correspond to similar requirements in other professions, such as the licensing of doctors and dentists after state or national examinations.

The certification of teachers serves several purposes. The regulations protect schoolchildren by ensuring a high quality of teaching, the employment of only superior and qualified personnel, and unifying teaching standards. The students therefore benefit from these requirements. For teachers, however, the task of meeting the varying state requirements complicates professional preparation and certification procedures.

There are nine general areas in which most states have governing regulations for teacher certification. While many states may agree on certain factors, they may disagree on others. The prospective teacher should therefore inquire directly of the state education department, division of teacher certification, for exact requirements. To summarize these nine general areas and the requirements presently established in the fifty states, the following information is presented.

Citizenship. More than one half the states have citizenship requirements or a declaration of intention clause. The teacher must be a citizen of the United States to qualify.

Oath of allegiance or loyalty. Approximately one-half of the states do not require a loyalty oath for teacher certification. The others usually have a written statement that must be signed.

Age. The age requirement varies among states. The lowest minimum age is 17 years. In general 18 or 19 years of age is acceptable in states specifying a particular age. Some states have no stipulation in this regard.

Professional preparation. It is in this area that the greatest differences in state requirements may be found. Many states are moving toward a competency-based approach. Several states have particular courses that must be taken by candidates for certification. For example, in one state teachers must have studied American government and/or history; in another, state and federal government; and in still another, school health education. Some of these special state requirements must be complete before the first year of teaching, while others may be fulfilled within a certain period of time.

Recommendation. Most of the states require a teaching candidate to have a recommendation from college or from the last place of employment.

Fee. A fee for certification, ranging from $1 to $25, is required in a majority of the states.

Health certificate. A certificate of general health is necessary in many states. Some states require a chest x-ray report instead of or along with this certificate.

Employment. Candidates from *other* states may need to have secured employment to become certified within some states.

Course of study. Besides the general areas of state requirements, there are basic and minimum regulations regarding the course of study that must be followed to qualify for specific certification in physical education. Again, the states disagree in their requirements of hours of study and competencies necessary within the subject of physical education.

Because of these curriculum differences and the variation between states in regard to the nine basic factors outlined, a certificate to teach in one state does not necessarily permit a teacher to teach in a different state. However, reciprocity among states in the same region of the country is a growing reality, particularly for graduates of an accredited teacher preparation program.

A further problem in certification presents itself where localities within a state have specific regulations governing selection of teachers. These are often more rigid than the standards established within the state itself. Detroit and New York City, for example, have their own sets of qualifications that must be met by their teachers, and many southern cities and states require high scores on the National Teacher Examinations. Local regulations usually involve such factors as teacher preparation and experience. An applicant may also be required to pass written and oral examinations for local licensing. Information regarding local teaching requirements may be secured by writing to the board of education in the city in question.

Prospective teachers should try to determine state and local regulations far in advance, if possible. In so doing they may guide their course of study in college to meet the requirements. They should then send in their records far enough ahead of time to become certified before accepting a position.

Types of certificates

The type and value of certificates issued by the states vary nearly as much as do their regulations. In some states, for example, there are merely two categories of certification, permanent and probationary, while another state may have twenty-two variations of certificates to issue. The certificate to teach physical education is generally limited to this special field of work, but its validity may be for one year (probationary) or for life. Some states grant temporary, provisional, or emergency certificates to teachers who do not fully meet all requirements, with the understanding that within a certain period of time the candidate will become fully qualified.

The value of the certificate again depends on state regulations. It enables the teacher to teach in any public school system within that state, except those where local standards require further qualifications. It may qualify the teacher to teach in neighboring states, depending on reciprocity agreements. It may also permit him or her to teach in private schools within the state, or at least in private schools seeking state accreditation.

The prospective teacher or the experienced teacher seeking employment in a different state should not let these differences in state requirements and qualifications become a hindrance. An inquiry to the state or local department of education should bring the necessary information in time to facilitate certification.

PROBLEMS IN JOB APPLICATION

Recent surveys and statistics indicate that teaching jobs will be much more difficult to obtain in the future than they have been in the past. In the next few years, for example, according to the U.S. Department of Labor, the nation may train more than four million elementary and secondary school teachers but there will be only approximately two million jobs. Declining birth rates, oversupply of teachers being trained, and a new array of educational hardware are some of the reasons for this projection. However, positions will still be open to those who are highly qualified and prepare themselves well for their responsibilities. Furthermore, there are many bright job opportunities in the inner city and poor rural districts, in teaching the handicapped, in early childhood education, in educational research, in industry, in health spas, and in the federal Teacher Corps.

The next series of problems faced by the prospective teacher revolves around finding a job—writing a proper letter of application, having an interview, and attending to the similar details important in obtaining a teaching position. The superintendent who is forced to choose between two or more candidates for a physical education opening may allow his decision to rest on appearance, on spelling, or on the smallest of details. The applicant should therefore take great care in all phases of the process of finding and obtaining a position.

Letter of application

The prospective teacher usually hears of job openings through friends, the college bureau of appointments, an employment agency, or direct application by letter to a specific locale. The letter of application serves as an introduction to the prospective employer and should be carefully constructed to contain appropriate information.

In appearance the letter should be neat, typewritten, and grammatically correct. Pertinent details should be included concisely and yet in such a manner that the personality of the individual is conveyed to the reader. The employer wants to know about the applicant's educational background, experiences related to the field of education, and interests. Personal information such as age and health should also be included, together with names and addresses of references. If possible, the applicant should also state his or her availability for an interview.

In response to this letter of application the candidate should receive a letter stating either that there are no vacancies or that the position is open and an interview is desired.

A printed application form is often included with this reply, and it should also be filled out neatly and carefully.

Interview

Interviews of teacher-applicants generally take place at the school itself, providing candidates an opportunity to see the school in action, or at the college of the graduating candidate. In the latter case a field representative of the school system usually interviews several candidates from the college, and a request from the superintendent for a school-visitation interview follows.

In either type of interview the prospective teacher should expect to ask and to answer questions of all types, for it is the purpose of the interview to allow the new teacher to learn about the school system, as well as to give the employer an opportunity to screen the applicant.

While the employer is questioning the applicant, he or she will be observing the teacher's bearing, outlook, speech, personal mannerisms, and general effectiveness as a person. Needless to say, the applicant should be prompt, well groomed, and neatly dressed for this occasion. The prospective teacher should be ready to answer in a concise and intelligent manner questions about any phase of teaching physical education. What is the most important attribute of a good teacher? What is the philosophy behind the inclusion of physical education in the school curriculum? What are some specific objectives of the program? How are the needs of the children determined? The range of possible questions is very broad, and the candidate can make little actual preparation for them other than to know and sincerely believe in the field of physical education.

The answers given by the applicant at the interview are not the only determining factor in obtaining employment. The employer may judge to some extent on the basis of intelligent questioning by the candidate about the type of education being offered in the school and the community's interest in school affairs. Inquiries about scheduling, class groupings, extramural duties, community activities, and school organizations indicate to the superintendent or person doing the interviewing that the prospective teacher knows what is involved in a teaching position. At the same time the applicant is, of course, determining whether this particular school administration is genuinely interested in physical education and if this type of position is the most desirable and suitable in comparison to other available jobs.

There are several types of teaching jobs that the physical educator needs to consider. Is a large or small school system preferable? In a small school the teacher often has classes from grades one through twelve, while in the larger, multiple-building systems, a position may be limited to elementary, middle school, junior high, or senior high teaching. Is teaching in a large, departmentalized situation with several other persons a better position in which to start than one in which the teacher is entirely alone? These are questions that the teacher must settle in his or her own mind, in terms of personal preferences, after several school visitations and interviews have pointed out the differences.

Unfortunately, the prospective teacher does not always receive the position of first choice. A poor impression during the interview or a poor letter of application may make the difference. Other factors also enter into a failure of final appointment. Lateness of application or stiff competition for a position may be a determining factor. The teacher seldom knows the real cause of failure.

Appointments are not generally made at the interviews themselves, for the board of education must give final approval, and the applicant should have additional time to think about such an important decision. Later the applicant may receive a letter from the superintendent or other school official saying that the position has been filled or with congratulations on his or her appointment and perhaps some type of contractual agreement.

Contractual agreements

Contractual agreements between employer and teacher vary in style, form, and content, but essentially they signify a promise of payment for services rendered. In some areas a single word or handshake is the only type of agreement used, while in other areas a formalized contract carefully specifying duties and assignments is required. Each board of education has its own particular method. However, the prospective teacher should inquire about certain aspects of the agreement in order to know exactly what responsibilities and fringe benefits are contained in it.

Term of employment. The initial contract is usually a provisional one, covering one year of teaching. In many schools there is a three-year or five-year provisional period for new teachers, and at the end of that time a more permanent type of contract may be issued. Some boards of education provide "tenure" for teachers, which means that following the provisional period teachers may be assured of a permanent position in their schools, if so desired.

Persons going into teaching should be aware that teacher tenure is under nationwide attack. For example, a Gallup poll indicated that the public in general does not like the idea of tenure—namely, 61 percent of them disapprove. For those who are parents and have children in school, 64 percent disapprove of tenure. Among professional educators 53 percent approve of tenure, 42 percent disapprove, and 5 percent have no opinion.

Responsibilities. In some instances contracts contain detailed outlines of teaching responsibilities, including, for example, the number of hours of intramural activities or the number of coaching assignments required of the teacher. These duties must be performed by the teacher if he or she enters into such an agreement, unless unusual circumstances permit exemption.

Release from a contract. Unusual circumstances, such as forced leave of absence or call to military service, may release the teacher from the total contract. This is possible in most cases by application to the board of education. The prospective teacher should realize, however, that except in these unusual situations it is not wise to break an agreement with the board of education. As professionals in the field of education, teachers are expected to be reliable and dependable people, with high ethical standards, and therefore able to live up to agreements.

Salary. Written agreements between teachers and employers usually indicate exact salary arrangements. In most schools a salary scale has been established, with definite regulations governing the placement of teachers on that scale. Years of service or

---

AN ACTUAL DAY IN THE LIFE OF ONE PHYSICAL EDUCATOR

Pre-first period activities

8:20   Sign in
8:20   Confer with other teachers
8:35   Set up and check equipment to be used that day

First and second periods—8:50-10:20 (double period for ninth graders)

Locker room supervision
Student leaders check attendance
Fifteen-minute exercise period in preparation for physical fitness test
Presentation of the skills and techniques involved in the sprint start
Individual practice—instructor and the student leaders check student progress
One-hundred-yard sprint—students demonstrate the skill that they have just learned
Shower and change clothes—locker room supervision

Third and fourth periods—10:22-11:48 (double period for tenth graders)

Locker room supervision
Student leaders check attendance
Fifteen-minute exercise period in preparation for physical fitness test
Review of the basic skills and techniques involved in the sprint start with student demonstration
Presentation of the basic skills and techniques involved in the long jump: the run, the gather, the take-off (float style in the air, hang style in the air, and the hitch-kick style in the air), and the landing
Student leader demonstration
Question-answer period on basic skills and techniques
Student individual practice with suggestions offered by instructor to improve individual performance
Shower and change clothes—locker room supervision

Fifth and sixth periods—11:50-1:10

Preparation of new skills for future presentation, review of new library materials, films, and so on, setting up skill scales for evaluation purposes, and preparation of written test questions on the activity being covered
Lunch

Seventh period—1:11-1:53 (single period for twelfth graders)

Locker room supervision
Student leaders check attendance
Fifteen-minute exercise period in preparation for physical fitness test
Review of previous class instruction (beginning skill, the relay race, or intermediate skill, long jump)—student demonstration and explanation
Presentation of the basic skills and techniques involved in the shot put—8- and 12-pound shot puts are available
Individual student practice with suggestions offered by instructor to improve student performance
Question-answer period on the basic skills and techniques of this activity
Shower and change—locker room supervision

Eighth period—1:55-2:40

Preparation period—continuation of activities begun in the fifth and sixth periods

merit usually determine increments in salary, although differentiated staffing is changing this practice in some places. Where years of service are used as a basis for raises in pay, teachers usually receive regular increments in salary. In schools where a merit plan is in effect, the better teachers usually receive higher pay on the basis of certain standards of teaching that have been established for evaluation of services. A third type of salary schedule has emerged from schools using the team-teaching program. In this case the person or persons shouldering major responsibility for a course of study receive higher salaries.

Benefits. Some school systems also establish subsidiary teacher benefits that make them more desirable and attractive places in which to work. Sick leave policies and visitation days are examples of administrative consideration for teacher welfare. Provisions for sabbatical leave, health insurance, and retirement are also benefits that vary among schools and states. The new teacher should try to find out as much as possible about these fringe benefits for teachers in the particular school system offering employment.

When the prospective teacher accepts the appointment offered and signs the contractual agreement, if one is necessary, the benefits and terms are settled and the problems of job application cease. The teacher has now assumed new responsibilities and obligations that must be met. These responsibilities encompass the physical education department itself, the school faculty, the community, and the profession, and are equally important to a successful career.

RESPONSIBILITIES TO THE DEPARTMENT

Whether the school system is large or small, the physical educator has many responsibilities to the department, each of which is essential in administering a successful teaching program. These responsibilities demand the teacher's time and thoughtful consideration, but because they relate directly to the students, the results of the teacher's efforts are apparent.

In a large school

As one member of a team of physical educators, the individual instructor has definite responsibilities in relation to teaching regular classes, conducting the after-school program, and working with other members of the department. In all three areas these duties require constant cooperation and mutual understanding for a smoothly functioning program.

Teaching classes. Each teacher is officially in charge of the instructional program in assigned classes. This responsibility entails far more than just teaching or conducting classes, however. Some of the other duties entailed in class management are the following:

1. Program planning and evaluation
2. Grading and pupil evaluation
3. Testing
4. Motivating (through charts, diagrams, and the like)
5. Checking health problems
6. Counseling on student problems
7. Conferring with students and parents
8. Caring for shared equipment and facilities
9. Maintaining departmental standards in locker room, showers, and gymnasium
10. Keeping records

These duties are performed in cooperation with other members of the department, and the same or similar methods that have been approved for all are used. For example, one teacher would not keep one form of record on a student while another teacher in the same department followed a different system.

Conducting the after-school program. In addition to regular teaching responsibilities, the members of the department share in carrying out the many extra duties that are a natural component of the physical education program. Conducting an after-school program of intramural and extramural activities, as well as interscholastic athletics, involves many details, such as the following:

1. Coaching assignments
2. Scheduling games

3. Handling publicity
4. Scheduling facilities
5. Caring for uniforms and equipment
6. Arranging transportation
7. Handling finances
8. Checking custodial maintenance
9. Ordering awards
10. Keeping records

In a large school a single instructor would not be able to manage all these details alone. With the entire staff working together, however, a well-organized after-school program serving all the students may be effectively conducted.

Working with the staff. Conducting the after-school program is only one of the ways in which the members of the department cooperate. The director of the department usually considers the staff as a policy-making body that proposes and carries out progressive ideas. They plan together the direction the program will take and share with the administrator of the department the many details of budgeting, scheduling, making inventory, and so forth. In some schools the team teaching approach to physical education has been implemented. In this case the staff cooperates and coordinates all its efforts in order to capitalize on the special abilities of each of its teachers.

Cooperation promotes harmonious relationships among members of the department, and when disagreements or problems arise, they should be handled within the department itself. Ethical standards of conduct indicate that mutual support of colleagues be presented to outsiders and that individual problems of a member be taken to the department chairperson first, rather than to the principal or superintendent.

The new teacher should realize at the outset the nature of the role he or she must play as a member of a large school staff. Schools may differ in the actual delegation of responsibilities, but the teacher's obligation to share and cooperate remains the same.

In a small school

In a small secondary school it is customary to find one man and one woman on the physical education faculty. While such a situation simplifies the problems of group planning and departmental organization, the same administrative responsibilities outlined for a large school remain, and they must be carried out by these two individuals. Because the number of students served by the program is small, it may be possible for one teacher to handle the many details involved in the teaching program.

A new teacher will find that the job of teaching in a small-school situation requires much coordination between the boys' and girls' activities. The program of physical education is more effective if the instructional procedures and requirements of the two teachers are similar and methods of pupil evaluation agree. Also, their policies on intramural and interscholastic activities should be consistent, with schedules for the use of facilities for these programs mutually and equitably arranged as provided for in Title IX.

When problems or difficulties develop concerning the sharing of facilities, for example, the two teachers should try to work out the solutions together. If the answers cannot be found, the teachers should both seek advice from the next higher authority. If there is no officially designated chairperson of the department, the school principal would be the person to ask for guidance.

Working together effectively is of primary importance to a smoothly functioning program of physical education in a small-school situation. When the two teachers mutually assist and support each other in all phases of their work, this worthy objective is achieved.

RESPONSIBILITIES TO SCHOOL FACULTY

Beyond being a member of a physical education department, a teacher is also a member of a school faculty. This position carries with it many responsibilities related to administering a program of education for children. All teachers must share in this endeavor, which includes three general areas of obligation: upholding school policies, sharing mutual faculty responsibilities, and respecting the educational curriculum.

Upholding school policies

Administration of a secondary school program involves the establishment of well-defined policies concerning all phases of school life: the curriculum, school regulations, homework, activities, and sponsored functions. In most school situations teachers play an important part in regard to these policies.

In a democratically administered school system, the teachers share in the establishment of school policies. Decisions are formulated on the basis of group discussion and majority opinion. The physical educator should share with the other teachers in formulating policies at teachers' meetings.

School policies must be upheld by all members of the staff once they are determined. This includes the physical education teacher, who should not expect special privileges for members of varsity teams in respect to academic standards, for example, or request athletic considerations contrary to school regulations.

Sharing mutual responsibilities

In large and small school systems alike, the faculty shares many administrative duties. These are essential to a sound educational program, although they have no relationship to the school curriculum, and are a necessary component of school administration.

For example, there are many instances in which a teacher is called upon to act as a supervisor or sponsor of student activities. Teachers may be required to take bus duty or cafeteria supervision or to be responsible for noon-hour activities. Homerooms, study halls, club activities, and student council are all additional responsibilities, and the physical educator should expect to serve with the other teachers in any of these areas.

In many schools, faculty committees are established to study current educational problems, such as education for the gifted or elementary foreign language teaching. Committees to handle administrative details such as class scheduling, grouping, or safety may also be set up. Membership in these communities is usually voluntary, but all teachers are expected to serve in some capacity. While the conduct of the after-school program may make it difficult for the physical educator to attend committee meetings, every effort should be made to share in this phase of school organization.

Respecting the curriculum

Just as physical educators should support the methods and procedures of their colleagues within the department, so should they respect those of the other teachers in all areas of education. The teacher should exhibit a genuine and sincere interest in all phases of the curriculum and respect the work and accomplishments of the other teachers.

In return, the physical educator can expect from other teachers similar respect and appreciation of the work being accomplished by the department. This regard should be deserved, however. Teachers in other subject areas do not necessarily evaluate the physical education program in the same manner that physical educators would. Instead of rating program content with which they are unfamiliar, other teachers tend to value the teacher's seriousness of approach to teaching, the manner in which the instructor fulfills educational responsibilities, the concern shown for student welfare, and general attitudes toward the profession.

The physical educator who meets all these responsibilities as a member of the teaching staff actually promotes appreciation for physical education as a profession.

There is one further obligation of physical educators that is directly connected with their particular field and deserves special mention at this time. Good working relations with members of the school custodial staff are of vital importance to the program and are clearly as important as relations with other teachers. The service of the custodians in gymnasium maintenance and in care of equipment adds significantly to the quality of physical education and should not be forgotten.

RESPONSIBILITIES TO THE PROFESSION

Membership in a profession such as physical education carries with it certain responsibilities that the new teacher should expect and accept. They are concerned mainly with professional advancement for the teacher and the growth of the profession itself.

Professional organizations

Professional associations are the media through which members mutually assist each other in achieving benefits for the group and promoting advancement.

As educators, physical education teachers should join the educational organizations available in their district or local area. This includes the faculty association, the local education association, and the country or district group, whichever organization has been formed. It is also considered the mark of a professional to join the state education association and the National Education Association. Membership in these associations is usually made available to the teacher through the school office at the beginning of each school year.

Physical educators should also join their own special local and state organizations and the American Alliance for Health, Physical Education, and Recreation. It is through these channels that the teacher is able to keep up with the latest advancements within the profession. There are also specialized organizations on the local level for coaches, women, or teachers of a particular activity. It is in these local, small groups that the greatest benefits are derived, for the members have the opportunity to know each other well and to share mutually in the problems and issues at stake.

Membership in these associations and alliances is made possible through literature sent to the school in each locale, in most cases. If not, teachers in neighboring districts are ready to provide the necessary information to newcomers.

Professional advancement

Membership in various associations is not the only professional responsibility of the physical educator. To reap the greatest benefits and to aid in advancing the profession itself, each member must make valuable contributions.

These associations are usually organized into committees that function in a particular area, such as planning, research, fitness, and publications. Working on these committees can be a very satisfying and rewarding experience, and one that should not be missed.

Even greater contributions to the profession as a whole can be made through research on problems in the field. Sharing results or findings on a particular method of teaching or testing is a real service to other members that should be willingly performed.

Personal advancement

Continued study for personal growth and development is another major responsibility of every member of a profession. In addition to individual study, the physical education teacher has two developmental paths open: in-service education and graduate study.

In-service education takes many forms within the school system and neighboring districts. It is found in individual and staff conferences and in workshops, clinics, and study institutes. Planning sessions, orientation programs, and interschool visitations are all phases of in-service education. Any opportunity in which teachers join together with associates to consider school problems is considered to be in-service education. Real values stemming from these sessions are seen when teachers change and grow together for the improvement of the school program and the profession.

Graduate study is the other method of personal, professional advancement. Some of the purposes of graduate study include the development of a higher degree of competence and the development of the ability to evaluate, interpret, and draw conclusions from the scholarly work of others.

There are several types of graduate degrees available to the physical education teacher.

1. Master's degree. A master's degree in physical education usually requires one year of study beyond a bachelor's degree. In some

Fig. 12-3. Physical education class at Paul J. Gelinas Junior High School in Setauket, N.Y.

universities a thesis is part of the required program for a degree, while in other schools several related extra credits or a comprehensive examination is required in its place.

2. Doctor of philosophy, doctor of education, or doctor of physical education. The doctoral degrees usually require three or four more years of study. In the curriculum for a doctorate a formal dissertation or document is a requisite.

Some institutions offer a professional or specialist's certificate for thirty hours of graduate work above the completion of the master's program.

The prospective teacher of physical education should realize that a professional attitude is another important responsibility that must be developed through associations and study programs with other professionals. In this way the teacher makes a valuable contribution to himself or herself and to the profession as a whole.

RESPONSIBILITIES TO THE COMMUNITY

Another responsibility of importance to the physical educator is the relationship established with the community. This is a two-way association, for the support a physical education teacher gains for the program depends largely upon the program itself and the way the citizens interpret it. The responsi-

bilities of the physical education department in promoting this community relationship are three: presenting a sound program, joining community-sponsored activities, and supporting community standards.

Presenting a sound program

The physical educator is employed by a community's board of education to teach physical education in the finest manner possible. The program of physical education can be a comprehensive source of good public relations between a school and its community because of the many contacts that are a natural by-product of this program. It is in this field that an entire student body is excited by interscholastic competitive activities, and parents, too, share in these enjoyable events. Through the intramural programs, the demonstrations, and the testing program the parents become very much aware of and interested in the total program of physical education. The entire school administration benefits from a sound physical education program because of community interest; therefore, it is essential that the program be thoughtfully planned, presented, and evaluated.

Joining community activities

The physical educator has definite obligations to become a part of the community by joining selected community organizations, including the parent-teacher association. Furthermore, because of the close association between recreational activities and physical education, the teachers often are called to conduct evening programs and assist in sponsoring special events. While sharing in these activities the teacher has an opportunity to know the people of the community and what it is that they want from their schools. This is an advantage to the school, for it must serve its own particular community. At the same time the physical educator helps the school administration by serving as an interpreter of its philosophy to the community and helping the people understand what the schools are trying to do.

Serving the community in which they teach is a responsibility that must be met by all teachers. Good school-community relations are of primary importance to a school that is meeting the needs of its students. Physical educators must do their share by contributing in as many ways as possible, and the results will bring greater support to the program.

Supporting community standards

Throughout the many associations established with community citizens, the physical educator should support and honor the standards expected of teachers in that particular community where they are in accordance with high professional standards. It is important to remember for example, that relating school gossip or information of a personal nature about a particular student does not earn respect for a teacher in the schools and that by wiser acction the respect and status of teachers may be upheld in the community.

CODE OF ETHICS

The teacher is far more than just a teacher of physical education. His or her responsibilities extend to all relationships established with people, and all actions are governed in almost every area by a code of professional ethics. Many important principles in this code of ethics have been pointed out in relation to particular situations. The code of the

National Education Association has been endorsed by the American Alliance for Health, Physical Education, and Recreation. This code represents the combined thinking of experienced leaders in the field and therefore should be respected. Furthermore, it provides a framework of guidelines for all professional physical educators, thereby guaranteeing the professional freedom it is designed to preserve.

The code consists of four principles. *Principle 1* outlines the commitment to the *student* and indicates the cooperative, helpful, and professional relationship that exists between the student and teacher. *Principle 2* outlines the commitment to the *public* and spells out the important role of educators in the development of educational programs and policies and their interpretation to the public. *Principle 3* outlines the commitment to the *profession* and indicates the need to raise educational standards, improve the service to people, and develop a worthwhile and respected profession. *Principle 4* outlines the commitment to *professional employment practices* and explains the importance of acting in accordance with high ideals of professional service that embody personal integrity, dignity, and mutual respect.

The code is designed to show the magnitude of the education profession and to judge teachers in accordance with the provisions of this code.

Self-assessment tests

These tests are to assist students in determining if material and competencies presented in this chapter have been mastered:

1. Compare a health spa and an industrial concern with a secondary school as places to be employed in physical education.
2. Without consulting your text define each of the following terms in a way that clearly indicates you understand their relationship to teaching;
   Competency-based teacher education
   Differentiated staffing
   Teacher accountability
3. Conduct a self-evaluation of your qualifications for teaching by writing down what you consider to be your present status in respect to each of the following: physical qualifications, social qualifications, emotional qualifications, and intellectual and professional qualifications. Opposite your qualifications in each of

these four groups list what are desirable qualifications for a teacher. Compare your qualifications to this list.

4. Imagine that you are a member of the physical education faculty in a junior or senior high school. Indicate what responsibilities you would assume to ensure that you would be a respected member of the faculty.

Points to remember

1. Physical educators must fulfill personal and educational requirements to become certified to teach. These requirements vary throughout the states, as do the types of certificates issued.
2. Certain personality and character traits help make a teacher more effective in teaching and associating with students and colleagues.
3. A physical educator's relationship to the students is very important for effective teaching and guidance.
4. A physical education teacher's relationships with other teachers, the administration, the profession, and the community have an important bearing on the respect he earns for himself as a professional person and for his program.
5. A physical educator is governed by a code of ethics that protects him and other members of the profession by suggested standards of behavior.

Problems to think through

1. When is a teacher not a teacher?
2. What personal qualities are most important for a teacher of physical education—qualities that may not be as essential in teaching other areas?
3. With whom would a new physical education teacher discuss a disagreement relating to procedures in marking students (a) in a small school? (b) in a large school? With whom would he not discuss it?
4. In August a new teacher receives another job offer at a higher salary in a preferred locale. What course of action should be taken, if any?
5. What community clubs or agencies have a direct interest in the school physical education program? How would the teacher who lives outside the school's community indicate an interest in the activities of such groups?
6. An after-school intramural game conflicts with a special faculty committee meeting. The physical education teacher, as a member of this committee, must choose where his time will be spent. What factors enter into his decision?

Case study for analysis

The new physical education teacher has been asked by his experienced co-worker to help referee an important eighth grade intramural soccer championship game. The game ends in a tie, and rather than reschedule another playoff or play another quarter, his colleague rules that the team winning two out of three penalty kicks will win. The new teacher senses the keen disappointment felt by the team members with this ruling

and does not agree with his superior's decision in this case. What, if anything, should he do?

Exercises for review

1. What specific information should be included in an application to a superintendent of schools? Write a sample letter.
2. Investigate the requirements for teaching in another state and determine in what ways these requirements are being met, if they are, and in what ways professional preparation may be lacking.
3. What questions may a candidate for a physical education position in a large school system expect to be asked during an interview with the administrator?
4. What school policies should this candidate inquire about during this interview?
5. A school system is planning to build a second junior high school and the administrator asks the physical education department to share in the formulation of plans for the physical education facilities. What steps would a new teacher take in order to offer real assistance in this project?
6. A new physical education teacher discovers that the community fathers run a highly competitive Little League program. If this teacher disagrees with the type of management the program is receiving, what procedures would he follow to combat this community enterprise?
7. List some outside interest and hobbies that would add to the professional growth of a physical educator.
8. In what areas of teaching physical education would further scientific research be particularly valuable?
9. In what ways does a professional code of ethics protect the teacher of physical education?
10. What responsibilities to the profession of physical education would be most difficult for a teacher to meet?

Selected readings

Annand, V.: PELT—Physical education leadership training, Journal of Health, Physical Education and Recreation 44:50, 1973.

Berg, K.: Maintaining enthusiasm in teaching, Journal of Physical Education and Recreation 46:22, 1975.

Bronson, D. B.: Thinking and teaching, The Educational Formum 39:347, 1975.

Bucher, C. A.: Administration of health and physical education programs, including athletics, St. Louis, 1975, The C. V. Mosby Co.

Bucher, C. A.: Foundations of physical education, St. Louis, 1975, The C. V. Mosby Co.

Bucher, C. A.: Physical education for life, New York, 1969, McGraw-Hill Book Company.

Caldwell, S.: Toward a humanistic physical education, Journal of Health, Physical Education and Recreation 43:31, 1972.

Dillon, S. V., and Franks, D. D.: Open learning environment: self-identity and coping ability, The Educational Forum 39:155, 1975.

Elam, S.: Performance based teacher education: what is the state of the art? Quest, June, 1972.

Field, D.: Accountability for the physical educator, Journal of Health, Physical Education and Recreation 44:37, 1973.

Fisher, M.: Assessing the competence of prospective physical education teachers, The Physical Educator 29:93, 1972.

Longo, P.: Opening the door to the open classroom, Kappa Delta Pi Record 11:98, 1975.

Menzies, I.: The touchy teacher's benefit issue, The Boston Evening Globe 207:18, 1975.

Toffler, A.: Future shock, New York, 1970, Bantam Books.

13

THE BEGINNING TEACHER

**INSTRUCTIONAL OBJECTIVES
AND COMPETENCIES TO BE
ACHIEVED**

After reading this chapter the student should be able to—

1. Identify the major problems faced by beginning teachers.
2. Evaluate the problems faced by beginning teachers and know what ones may be eliminated before accepting a position.
3. Prepare oneself for eliminating or coping with certain problems encountered in teaching.
4. Cope with problems that are administrative in nature.

According to the annual Gallup poll of public attitudes toward education, the major problems confronting the public schools listed in order of importance were: (1) lack of discipline, (2) inadequate financial support, (3) problems of integration-segregation, (4) difficulty associated with getting good teachers, (5) classes too large, (6) lack of interest on the part of parents, (7) inadequate facilities, (8) poor curriculum, and (9) drug use. Of all these problems, one of the most important is the need for good teachers. With good teachers many of the other problems will be solved.

As the day of birth is one of the most critical for the newborn baby, so is the first year of teaching one of the most critical for the newly trained teacher. The neophyte instructor has spent four or more years in college learning a great amount of theory from professors, talking about what to do when discipline problems arise with students, and discussing how to function with inadequate facilities. Now he or she find himself or herself on the job in the classroom or gymnasium faced with a live and restless group of students. These boys and girls know that an inexperienced teacher is handling the class, and many seek opportunities to disprove all the theory that has been learned in four years of training. The big test has come. Will the beginning teacher be successful in meeting the challenge? Will the class be organized for effective instruction? Will the teaching techniques that have been mastered be equal to the practical situation that now exists? The answer to these and similar questions depends upon many factors, including whether or not the beginning teacher has been alerted to some of the problems that may arise and some of the procedures that may be followed in handling them. This chapter is aimed at helping the new teacher meet problems that are encountered the first year on the job. Although the problems of the beginning teacher are infinite, it is believed that many are common and that recommendations by experienced teachers will assist him or her in successfully completing the first critical year of teaching.

There is a high turnover rate of first-year teachers. Some teachers change jobs after the first year to improve their status; others leave the profession because of dissatisfaction and discouragement and because they have found the job of adjusting to the hard realities of teaching too difficult for them to master. Several research studies have been conducted to determine the reasons teachers give for job satisfaction or dissatisfaction. They include such items as teacher-administrator factors, physical conditions, teacher-community factors, teacher-faculty factors, teacher-student and teacher-parent factors, and salary and security factors. An example of such a study is one conducted several years ago but still true today, involving ninety-five beginning teachers who graduated from Appalachian State Teachers College. The research involved the identification of 2,537 difficulties encountered by the teachers. The three areas into which these difficulties were grouped were (1) difficulties related to personal characteristics, (2) difficulties related to instructional activities, and (3) difficulties related to community environment and relationships. Most of the difficulties pertained to (1) pupil control, (2) teaching assignment, (3) adaptation to pupil needs, (4) records and reports, (5) deficiencies in equipment, (6) teacher-principal relationships, and (7) personality.

According to a more recent study conducted by the Research Division of the National Education Association, the five major problems of teachers were identified as (1) insufficient time for rest and preparation in the school day, (2) large class size, (3) insufficient clerical help, (4) inadequate salary, and (5) inadequate fringe benefits. Less stress was placed upon such problems as lack of public support for schools, ineffective faculty meetings, and poor administration.

It is readily evident from the research conducted that problems of beginning teachers are numerous and varied. It would be of great value to the new teacher to study each of these problems in as much detail as possible and to determine the meaning they have in relation to adjusting satisfactorily to the job.

Many of the problems of teachers are "across the board" types of difficulties affecting all teachers regardless of subject-matter affiliation. However, the teacher of physical education encounters some problems caused by the nature of his or her special field of endeavor. Some of the more common problems of beginning physical education teachers that have been identified through research are associated with the following:

Discipline
Facilities
Adjustment to the school
Class organization
Student hostilities toward the program
Methods of teaching
Legal liability
Numbers of students in class
Insufficient space
Equipment
Behavior problems
Introduction of new ideas and techniques
Intellectually inferior label associated with physical education
Program planning
Status
Role of physical education in education
Personal relationships
Interscholastic athletics
Budget
Scheduling
Grouping in classes
Time allotment
Insurance

Many problems of the beginning physical education teacher appear to recur over and over again and can be grouped into two classifications, personal and professional problems and administrative problems. Before discussing some of these problems it seems important to consider how selecting the right position and having a better understanding of the school, community, and job into which the new teacher is going will reduce or alleviate the problems.

ELIMINATING SOME PROBLEMS BEFORE ASSUMING THE POSITION

The teacher should carefully evaluate the position before accepting such a responsibility. Unfortunately, some teachers accept positions in schools and communities in which they do not fit or belong and, consequently, where problems are bound to arise. If one is going to be unhappy and ineffective on the job, it may be better not to accept such a position in the first place. The many complex factors related to proper adjustment on the job are usually associated with the nature of the person, the nature of the environment, and the interaction of the two. It is therefore important to the candidate for a teaching position to carefully weigh the available position and his or her abilities and personal characteristics for handling this position effectively. If this is done, many of the problems will be foreseen, and the qualities and preparation needed to handle them successfully will be evaluated realistically.

Advance considerations

Two advance considerations important to the beginning teacher before assuming the job are knowledge of the conditions of employment and pertinent factors about the school and community.

Knowledge of employment conditions. It is imperative for the new teacher to understand the numerous details, duties, and responsibilities that he or she is about to assume, including a knowledge of classes to be handled, sports to be coached, clubs to be sponsored, homeroom assignments, study halls, length of the school day, after-school obligations, compensation to be received, salary schedules in force, sick leave, tenure, sabbaticals, health insurance, and other pertinent facts. Only as the teacher has a clear understanding of the responsibilities will he or she be able to prepare sufficiently, mentally and physically, for the position. Information can be obtained from other teachers, members of the administration, and school literature that contains pertinent school policies.

Lack of advance knowledge of unfavorable working conditions has caused many teachers to be unhappy in their positions. The following are some of the conditions most often mentioned:

1. Classes are too large.
2. The work week is too long.
3. The daily schedule is too long.
4. Clerical duties are excessive.
5. Community demands for out-of-school activities are too heavy.

In some studies it has been shown that the teacher is required on the average to spend approximately an hour each day in nonteaching, schooltime duties. Many school systems are attempting to minimize the unfavorable conditions and will undoubtedly eliminate some of them. The beginning teacher should not become discouraged but should understand these problems and be prepared to meet them.

The importance of ample preparation and knowledge of conditions of employment cannot be overemphasized. Teachers who know and understand the conditions into which they are entering are less likely to be discouraged when they do not meet the optimum or theoretical standards they have been studying in college.

Pertinent factors about school and community. A beginning teacher should have a thorough knowledge of the school and community of which he or she is a part. Items such as the following should be known: history of the school and community, traditions, curricular offerings, economic status, philosophy of education, industrial development, size, political structure, and problems and projected future growth. These factors will have implications for the type of students to be taught, the parents with whom the teacher will work, the community of which the teacher is to be a part, and the social, political, and educational climate within which the teacher must work. A more detailed analysis of the school and community are discussed in Chapter 2.

PROBLEMS OF BEGINNING TEACHERS CITED BY DIRECTORS OF PHYSICAL EDUCATION

A representative number of directors of physical education in school systems across the nation were surveyed to determine what they feel are the most difficult problems faced by beginning teachers. Since these administrators had an opportunity to observe beginning teachers as they embarked on their professional careers, their experiences should be of value in helping new teachers to have a good start. The thinking of these

Fig. 13-1. Physical education classes should be of a size that will enable all students to actively participate in the scheduled activities. Physical education class in the Brockport Central Schools, Brockport, N.Y.

administrators may be summarized under the following headings: organization, teaching, teacher-student relationships, teacher-teacher relationships, and making adjustments.

Organization

Many of the problems of beginning teachers are caused by poor organization, which can easily be corrected. Some of the beginning teachers are not accustomed to moving large groups of students from one place to another and from one formation to another. They are not thoroughly familiar with the various methods of class organization for various activities. Sometimes they are poorly organized in respect to uniforms, lockers, towel fees, and many routine duties important to the efficient running of a physical education program.

Problems concerned with organization can be easily remedied if the beginning teacher will study them, become familiar with various types of organization, and ask questions and the help of experienced teachers.

Teaching

The beginning teacher is sometimes an excellent performer in various physical education activities, and it is hard for him or her to realize that some students have no idea how to throw or jump or perform other basic skills. Often too much time is spent in teaching games rather than teaching basic fundamentals and skills. Often the new teacher does not have the ability to completely involve all members of the class in the activity. Sometimes there is a tendency to teach the units the teacher is interested in and to minimize those in which he or she is weak.

The beginning teacher needs to put into practice the tools learned during undergraduate training. This includes presenting skills

Fig. 13-2. Physical education teachers should have good relationships with their students. Physical education class in a high school. (Courtesy Bill Henderson of Toms River, N.J.)

within the ability of the pupil, utilizing appropriate teaching techniques, making lesson plans, and, finally, recognizing one's own shortcomings and trying hard to correct deficiencies through in-service training.

Teacher-student relationships

Personal relationships are involved in teacher-student relationships. Students will frequently test the authority of the new teacher, and sometimes the teacher does not meet the test. Problems may arise, and the teacher may fail to face them directly and instead may refer the students to the principal's office. The teacher may expect too much from the students, the students may not be adequately motivated, or the teacher may show favoritism to certain students.

The beginning teacher needs to establish rapport with pupils, which requires the ability to be both firm and pleasant, as well as consistent; to know boys and girls as human beings rather than just so many "numbers"; and to establish friendships with pupils without becoming "one of them." The beginning teacher should recognize that sometimes problems are a result of the teacher's lack of planning and class organization. The teacher will be respected much more by boys and girls if he or she can handle the problem rather than passing it on to the principal's office.

Teacher-teacher relationships

Physical education, including sports, tends to isolate teachers of physical education from the rest of the building and often from colleagues in other subject areas. As a result, some beginning teachers fail to realize the importance of participating in general building activities with all teachers, attending faculty meetings regularly, and becoming an integral part of the faculty.

From the very beginning the new teacher should become acquainted with other members of the faculty, work cooperatively with them, share committee responsibilities, attend faculty meetings, and try to be respected by all.

Making adjustments

Beginning teachers often find staff, equipment and other conditions on the job to be far below expectations and far from ideal. They should realize that teachers do not always have ideal situations in which to teach; in fact, very few of them do. Many are faced with poor equipment, limited facilities, changing weather conditions, and other substandard conditions.

The new teacher must adjust to the position, the school, other teachers, school policies, procedures, and routines. Regardless of the situation, the conditions that prevail should be accepted as a challenge to excellent teaching in spite of limitations. The teacher should follow through on the many duties, responsibilities, and "chores" for which he or she is responsible. Adjustments should be made to existing policies and to the curriculum, with its inherent demand for skillful budgeting of time. The teacher should recognize his or her responsibility to professional physical education standards and also to the students, faculty, and school.

Planning is necessary—even the teacher of long experience needs at least a brief written plan. A teacher's responsibility involves teaching the student *how* to perform an activity or a skill; merely telling a pupil *what* to do or simply supervising activities in a gymnasium is not enough. Rules and regulations should be established and followed. Accidents may occur when rules are not followed. Exercising foresight will help to prevent problems and is preferable to trying to get out of predicaments. For example, the climbing ropes should be tied up before the class period starts so that it will be unnecessary to shout at the students who are swinging on them after class has begun. Finally, the teacher should practice self-evaluation each day and then faithfully try to eliminate weaknesses and expand on strengths.

SELECTED PROFESSIONAL PROBLEMS CITED BY BEGINNING PHYSICAL EDUCATORS

A few of the more common professional problems experienced by the beginning physical educator, with recommendations for meeting them, are the following: (1) discipline, (2) working effectively with colleagues, (3) lack of respect for physical education, (4) inequitable use of facilities, (5) problems relative to sex roles, and (6) extra school assignments.

Discipline

Lack of discipline is one of the most common problems cited by beginning physical educators in the secondary school. Poor neighborhoods, parental neglect and indifference, overcrowded classes, student transiency, poor economic conditions, and pampered children have been cited as contributing factors. Teachers have mentioned that some students are guilty of inattention, unpreparedness, smoking, drug use, cutting classes, refusing to follow instructions, talking, and many other infractions.

If a teacher is to be a success in his or her profession, classes must be conducted in an orderly manner, and the teacher must have the respect of the pupils. Part of the difficulty in regard to discipline problems may be caused by the youthful appearance of the teacher and the desire on the part of the students to test the new teacher.

Some beginning teachers are more sensitive than others about the reasons why discipline problems arise. For example, one teacher stated that poor planning on his part was quickly recognized by the pupils, causing many discipline problems. Another teacher noted that in some schools the beginning teacher must work three times as hard as an experienced instructor to establish proper student-teacher relations. A third teacher related that the previous teacher was not respected, which made it more difficult for her to work effectively. A fourth teacher made an excellent point when she said that she did not understand the boys and girls with whom she was working. She pointed out that she lacked knowledge of their stages of growth and development and therefore of what to expect at each age level. She recognized that this problem could be alleviated only by a thorough study and understanding of the physical, mental, social, and emotional characteristics of children and youth.

Experienced teachers have recommended many techniques that should be helpful to the physical educator in working with groups of students:

1. Be firm when first meeting a group. It is easy to relax after a good relationship has been established, but it is difficult to gain control over a group that has not known discipline.

2. Maintain poise with a noisy group. Call for silence and then wait for the order to be obeyed. If necessary, call to one or two individuals to be quiet. This will often have the desired effect on the class.

3. Use a whistle only when necessary. Blow it sparingly, but require attention whenever it is used.

4. Wait for silence before talking. A murmur can multiply quickly if it is not stopped.

5. Know the pupils well in order to determine the best approach to each individual.

6. Maintain self-control. No situation should be allowed to deteriorate into a personal duel with the children.

7. Give all pupils a feeling of belonging.

Show the boys and girls that they are all part of the group and will receive your interest and attention.

8. Be liberal in praise. Every child wants to be praised by the teacher, and accomplishment should be recognized.

9. Be friendly and relaxed. The atmosphere that the teacher establishes in class will be quickly copied by the pupils.

10. Be sympathetic. Show an awareness of the difficulty of the stunt or skill and encourage the child to continue.

11. Know the subject matter; have a sense of humor; have the courage of your convictions; work for challenging, exciting programs; and be consistent, fair, and democratic.

12. Know the pupils' interests, abilities, parental and family backgrounds, and achievements.

13. Make physical education activities interesting, meaningful, and vital.

14. Find out what the pupils' problems are and try to help them solve their difficulties.

Working effectively with colleagues

A problem frequently cited by beginning teachers is the problem of working effectively with other members of the department of physical education and with other faculty members. One beginning teacher commented that it was particularly difficult to gain the cooperation of older teachers because they were inflexible. Another teacher said that some colleagues do not cooperate because a new teacher is too ambitious and too much of an "eager beaver." Another teacher believed that physical education teachers are frowned upon as not being very scholarly. Finally, another teacher commented that being young and inexperienced makes it difficult to adjust—one is looked upon more as a student than as a faculty member.

Probably the comment of one beginning teacher on this problem is the best advice that can be given. She said: "Whether or not you get along with colleagues depends upon you."

Human relations can be effective when a person is considerate, tries to help others, is not overly critical, listens to the advice of others, becomes a member of the team, and tries in every way to contribute effectively to the achievement of the goals of the organization.

It is important for the new teacher to understand that the experienced instructors have amassed practical knowledge in addition to their formal training, which places them well ahead of teachers just out of college. There are many techniques that can be learned from colleagues. The beginning teacher should watch closely and select the methods that can be of value.

The new teacher should try to follow accepted procedures and systems, fitting into the existing pattern as much as possible. Being willing to work, anxious to learn, and able to get along increases the possibility of obtaining quick acceptance by colleagues.

Another aspect of this problem is the distribution of the work load. There is the question of whether the new teacher should carry a heavier or a lighter load than the older teachers and do more or less committee work at first.

The new teacher should willingly accept assignments of teaching and nonteaching duties, but he or she should feel free to ask questions when there is some phase of the program or duties that is not clear. New teachers often run into difficulty because they are afraid to ask questions. They think this would indicate ignorance, and instead of seeking the answers, they blunder ahead, making mistakes and intensifying problems.

Each teacher is primarily responsible for his or her own preparation for the job. There is also the responsibility of the administrator, however, to help prepare the new teacher for the experiences to be encountered. Some steps that administrators can take that in the opinion of their Association* would benefit a beginning teacher include those listed here:

1. To provide all the necessary pertinent information
2. To establish workshops for new teachers
3. To assign an adviser for each new teacher

*American Association of School Administrators.

4. To hold seminars for new teachers
5. To have new teachers observe excellent teaching
6. To demonstrate teaching techniques to improve skills

Lack of respect for physical education

Sometimes physical educators are referred to as "jocks," "muscular women" or "muscle men," or given other uncomplimentary names. The effect of this situation is to separate these teachers from other teachers, who are considered educators. It is important to break down this stereotyped thinking. Only when administrators, colleagues, and the public in general understand the true purpose and philosophy of physical education will this thinking change.

Physical educators should be educators first. They should exemplify well-educated people. They should be interested in the total development of students, not just their physical development. Although the work may concern itself with the physical more than the work of other teachers, it should not deter them from an appreciation of the importance of giving high priority to the mental development of youngsters, recognizing that the physical is only a means to an end. The end must be the education of the total child.

The dress of physical educators as well as their manners will help to support or disprove the stereotype. The working uniform should be restricted to the gymnasium. Teachers would not, of course, be expected to change clothes every time they leave the gymnasium for a few minutes, but they should be properly attired for every school function, whether it is an assembly, a faculty meeting, or a conference, as well as for just going home. Furthermore, in all actions physical educators should try to show that they are well-mannered, cultured, educated human beings who rank on the same level with other educators.

Another major task for teachers is to interpret the program of physical education

Fig. 13-3. Physical education class playing soccer in the Lexington Public Schools, Lexington, Mass.

wherever they go. There is much misunderstanding in regard to the goals and values of the profession. All phases of the program—classes, adapted programs, intramural and extramural activities, and interscholastic athletics—should be interpreted correctly, together with their specific worth in the educational program for students.

Physical educators must be professional in every respect. This means joining local, state, and national organizations, recruiting outstanding personnel for the profession, continually seeking opportunities for self-improvement, being effective teachers, continually keeping abreast of the latest developments and thinking in the field, and being good public relations ambassadors for physical education. If physical educators would fulfill their responsibilities in these areas, physical education would soon be respected throughout the country.

Inequitable use of facilities

The use of the available facilities, according to many beginning teachers, seems to be a common problem throughout the country. Several beginning teachers point out that too often women are asked to give up facilities in favor of the varsity interscholastic program. It may be that a separate gymnasium or field is not available for a girls' intramural sport or that because of the varsity schedule the area is free only during the late afternoon hours. The equipment shared may also be divided inequitably. Finally, the budgetary allotments may be apportioned in such a way that the men obtain the lion's share and the women a bare minimum. The underlying causes may mean there is little administrative enthusiasm for what has traditionally been considered girls' activities. Such a problem may take considerable time to correct, and the new teacher must work slowly and patiently to build up a more favorable administrative attitude. An effort should be made to build up student and community interest in activities in which girls will participate. When interest is aroused, it may be possible to convince the administrator of the importance and value of providing a strong

coeducational program as well as activities in which girls are interested. Title IX (see Chapter 7 provides that girls and women cannot be discriminated against, so it is possible to have a strong program in this area. As a result girls and women are having much more say in the administration of the program. This in itself will hurry the solution of many of these problems. The best program possible for all girls and boys is what is needed.

Problems relative to sex roles

Male physical educators experience many different types of problems when beginning to teach. They may be required to take on additional responsibilities in the community, working with recreation, church, and various youth groups. If they are married, there are extra responsibilities that require additional funds when starting salary schedules do not adequately provide for family considerations. A beginning teacher may not be assigned teaching and coaching duties in accordance with his or her wishes.

There are many problems faced by the beginning male teacher, but the most common seems to be associated with an overemphasis on interscholastic athletics. (Under Title IX this may also become true for some female physical educators.) The pressures involved in sports, when they are influenced by local newspapers, radio, television, community, and alumni, place undue importance on this phase of the physical education program. The physical educator wants to be an effective teacher in regular classes and intramural activities but finds that community pressures often force him to spend a disproportionate amount of time on the interscholastic athletic program. Under such conditions the teacher should steer a steady course, realizing that he is associated with educational, rather than professional, athletics. The coach who puts a winning team above all else, tries to pressure teachers to keep players eligible, teaches how to win at any cost, is rude to officials, is not completely honest, and closes his eyes to improper conduct will be a credit neither to his school nor to the profession of physical education. There are many valuable contributions that sports can make to the student, such as teamwork, skill, sportsmanship, respect for ability, and greater understanding of the value and place of sports in our society. These worthy goals must receive the main emphasis as the total physical education program for all students is kept in proper focus.

Women physical educators also have many problems with which to contend during their first year on the job. Some of these, including inequitable use of facilities, have been mentioned. Other problems may involve her professional as well as her personal life.

Male physical education teachers sometimes receive extra pay for extra coaching duties, but the time spent by female teachers with intramural and interscholastic programs sometimes remains unrecognized. When an unequal pay scale exists, the female physical education instructor—together with other teachers in the school who devote extra work to the band, orchestra, dramatic group, school newspaper, or other activity—should strive to impress the administration with the need for added salary benefits. Title IX provides there can be no discrimination in salaries, so this practice is no longer legal.

The beginning female teacher may find an obvious lack of interest in physical education among secondary school girls. The students may be more interested in dates and in their social obligations than in physical education.

Personal problems may also confront the beginning teacher. If she is married, there is the problem of time to devote to the home. Physical education requires long hours, and home life may be neglected. Good planning and organization in the home as well as at school may relieve this situation. For the unmarried teacher, either too much socializing in the evening or too much fretting about domestic problems may interfere with her work at school. The teacher who enjoys her work, however, finds that self-preoccupation disappears as soon as the morning bell sounds and that the problems of the students replace her own.

Not all the problems presented here will be faced by all new male and female teachers, but some of them will be present. The teacher who keeps in mind his or her responsibilities to students, school, and profession, gets along with others, and does quality work should encounter little difficulty.

Extra school assignments

One of the most pressing problems facing beginning teachers of physical education is the extra duties required during the school day. It is not uncommon for the physical educator to be assigned to supervise a lunchroom period, to keep an eye on the entrance or exit where the students congregate, to handle traffic at school functions, to manage school dances, to monitor study halls, or to supervise the parking lot. Too often the number and type of such assignments place an unfair burden upon the teacher, sometimes to such a degree that they interfere with his or her primary responsibility as a physical educator. It is important, of course, to perform all duties to the best of one's ability. It is also reasonable to point out to the administrator in charge those instances when such assignments affect teaching, infringe upon hours that could be put to better professional use, or take an unfair amount of a teacher's free time.

SELECTED ADMINISTRATIVE PROBLEMS CITED BY BEGINNING PHYSICAL EDUCATORS

The beginning physical educator will encounter many problems that may be classified as administrative in nature. These problems involve administrative responsibilities and decisions of chairpersons of departments, principals, superintendents of schools, and other persons who work in similar capacities in school systems. These responsibilities and decisions have important implications for the physical education program. Therefore, the teacher of physical education must be alert to the problems involved and continually interpret to those in administrative positions the philosophy, needs, and policies that are necessary if physical education is to make its greatest contribution to the students.

The administrative problems discussed in this section are encountered by many beginning physical education teachers, and they involve facilities, budget, scheduling, grouping of pupils, class size, time allocation, and legal liability.

Facilities

Considerable school construction is continually in progress, and therefore many physical educators will be asked for their recommendations concerning facilities needed. Furthermore, as a specialist in this area the beginning teacher should know the basic facility requirements, adaptations that can be made to improve the program, and the best way to proceed in developing an adequate physical plant.

It is important that the beginning teacher know what a good physical education plant should contain in the way of standard equipment, adequate locker areas, and offices, including size requirements. This knowledge will be of help, especially if the plant is to be remodeled or enlarged or a new school is to be built. It is the responsibility of the physical educator to be able to work with the architects to make economical and sound suggestions. It is also important for the physical educator to know what is wrong with the existing plant so that he or she may take the necessary precautions when planning a program.

Gymnasiums and auxiliary facilities. The type, size, and number of gymnasiums should reflect the number of participating individuals, the variety of activities to be conducted, the number of desired teaching stations, official court sizes, the number of spectators, and the need for enjoyable and safe activity participation. It is preferable for a gymnasium to be in a separate wing in the school building in order to minimize the possible disturbance to other classrooms, as well as to have the gymnasium readily available for after-school use without the necessity of opening the entire building.

Multipurpose room (or large, uncluttered area). The multipurpose room is usually larger than a regular classroom. It has no permanent furniture, the ceiling is usually as a regular height, and the lighting fixtures are often without protection. It can be used for tumbling and apparatus work, relays, games of low organization, mimetics, testing, and other limited activities. At a nominal expense, the light fixtures and windows can be screened and the room used for additional selected activities.

Classrooms. It is possible to make use of an empty classroom or two for indoor physical activity if there is no multipurpose room available. There would not be enough room for running games, but there would be sufficient space for tumbling and apparatus work, for recreational activities such as table tennis, bat-back, and handball, and for some basketball where a goal-hi could be used or possibly a basket and blackboard permanently installed. With some ingenuity and modification, other activities may also be conducted.

Other areas. It is also possible to practice track work in the hallways or in the basement areas.

A modified physical education program can be conducted without a gymnasium. An important consideration in the use of any area is to plan for the *safe* use of the facility, limiting activities to those that can be conducted without fear of accident. In such planning, it will always be necessary to take into account the features listed below.

1. Obstructions. Have obstructions covered, or establish a floor plan to avoid any activity near them. Be sure that the students are conscious of these obstructions.

2. Lighting. Secure larger bulbs or more fixtures, if needed, to provide sufficient light for the activity area.

3. Ventilation. Be conscious of temperature. Be sure that vents or radiators are covered or protected and that the students are made aware of them.

4. Composition of the floor. Consider those activities that would be applicable to wood, tile, or concrete floors and make selections accordingly.

Locker, shower, and drying areas. It is important that the physical education plant have adequate locker, shower, and drying rooms. Refer to the books at the end of the chapter for necessary and standard requirements.

Where locker facilities are insufficient it will be necessary to work out a plan for their most efficient use. It is possible to have students double up or to assign certain grades permanent gymnasium lockers, while the other students have lockers only during their physical education period. It may be advisable to switch at some time during the year to equalize this advantage.

Dirty, dark, unpainted, unappealing locker rooms often can be brightened, cleaned, painted, and made more attractive. Where there is no locker room, it will be necessary to find an area that can be utilized for changing into gymnasium uniforms. This may be a vacant classroom, storage area, or lavatory. It is also possible to have the pupils wear their uniforms under their school clothes if there is no area available for changing. This should be the last resort, however, because it violates a basic use of the uniform. Students should be able to change out of sweaty or dirty clothes before returning to a classroom.

The problem of shower and drying rooms is very simple. Either there are facilities or there are not. If there are showers, it is important that they be used. If not, a dry rubdown should follow each activity period. In some cases perhaps a sponge bath may be feasible.

Special activity areas. There should be teaching stations in addition to the gymnasium for use in conducting many physical education activities. These may include rooms for remedial or adapted activities, apparatus work, weight lifting, wrestling, rhythms, squash, handball, fencing, or any other activities of particular interest. A recommended size for an auxiliary gymnasium is 40 by 60 by 24 feet.

It is possible to convert regular classrooms for certain of these special activities. Some of these rooms would need special equipment —such as ladders, bars, ropes, pulley weights, or mats—in order to properly conduct the activities. Facilities needed will depend upon the interests, abilities, and desires of the students, as well as upon the comprehensiveness of the program, the availability of staff, and the accessibility of rooms.

Outdoor areas. When outdoor facilities are planned, it is highly desirable to have them located convenient to the gymnasiums and locker areas and also to have them available for year-round use by the community.

The size of outdoor areas will vary from 10 to 40 acres. On the junior high school level the facilities should be adequate for archery, volleyball, tennis, hockey, soccer, touch football, baseball, speedball, softball, golf, and track. The senior high school field should also allow for field hockey, lacrosse, football, and baseball, as well as ample space for other activities in the regular physical education class.

When a school playfield is not available, it is still possible to have outdoor activities. Some schools may be in the vicinity of a park or recreational play area that would be satisfactory. It may be necessary to have double periods of physical education, to allow time for travel to and from this area. It will be necessary to receive permission from the school administration and the park or recreation department for the use of such space. Another alternate site may be the school parking area. It is possible that lines could be painted on asphalt and cars limited to a certain section to allow room for the physical activities. It may also be possible to use the school's grassy areas. As a last resort it may be necessary to use the street adjacent to the building. In such a case it would be essential to have the street closed, at least during school hours. No physical education class should be limited to indoor classes all year long.

An adequate physical plant can help in developing an excellent physical education program. A poor plant, however, does not mean that there will necessarily be a poor program. In most cases it will be as good as the physical educator and the school administration want it to be.

Budget and PPBS

In the future the reader will hear the initials PPBS referred to more and more. These initials stand for planning, programming, and budgeting systems. In its totality the process involves comprehensive planning. It involves the instructional program and the resources needed to make the program an effective one. The program budget provides the machinery or plan for systematically relating the fiscal aspects of the operation to the accomplishment of the planned goals for which the organization exists. In other words, PPBS attempts to provide a system whereby the resources that are allocated are used in an efficient manner in the achievement of specific objectives. In this way the budget expresses in financial terms the operational plan of the organization.

In every school system, equipment and supplies are purchased each year for use in the schools. There are many things a teacher can do to secure the proper supplies and equipment needed for the program.

There are generally two sources of money for physical education items: (1) the board of education and (2) organizations within the school.

An allocation from the board of education may consist of money allotted directly to the physical education department or given to the principal to divide among all the departments in the school. The usual procedure for using this money is for the teacher to requisition the needed items, obtain the principal's approval, and send the requisition to a central purchasing agent for processing and purchase. This procedure centralizes the purchasing power and often brings increased value for each dollar spent.

There is frequently some type of athletic association or other student organization that handles the proceeds from the sale of school general organization memberships, athletic contests, dramatic or music presentations, the school store, and other fund-raising affairs or activities. This money is used to support many of the school activities, as well as for the purchase of special supplies or equipment. It is a source of funds for items the central purchasing agent may not approve for payment out of tax money, as well as for special items that must be obtained quickly. The faculty adviser can explain the procedure for his or her particular school.

If the necessary funds are not available through these channels, there are still other means of obtaining equipment and supplies. The ingenuity of physical education teachers and pupils working together, with the cooperation of other teachers and the school administration, can solve many problems.

A small list of items that can be constructed at little or no expense in the shops or the backyard includes the following: starting blocks, hurdles, vaulting standards, crossbars, backboards, batons, chinning bars, a form of parallel bars, mat trucks, sideline markers, yardline sticks, goal flags, charging sled, and football dummies. It is also possible to call upon the home economics department to sew and clean uniforms and upon the art department for publicity purposes. Special fund-raising drives can be organized, with the proceeds earmarked for specific needs. These may include a cake sale, a white elephant sale, or a dance.

Scheduling

The importance of proper scheduling cannot be overemphasized. A school that schedules physical education classes to meet the needs and interests of the students will usually have a good program.

Scheduling should be done according to a plan. The plan for scheduling should be based upon (1) the number of students taking the course, (2) the number of teachers available to teach the course, and (3) the number of rooms or teaching stations available. This plan should provide for early scheduling of physical education.

Since English, history, the sciences, mathematics, and physical education are required of all students, it seems logical to assume that these subjects should usually be scheduled first. Physical education and science laboratory periods should also be given particular consideration because there are usually fewer physical education teaching stations and science laboratories available than rooms for other subjects. If a sound progression in physical education is to be maintained, it is important that class size be approximately the same and that homogeneity by grade be a minimum prerequisite to scheduling. The physical educator should inform the administration of the sound reasons that make it important to give physical education early attention in setting up the school program.

In scheduling for physical education, every student should be included. This, of course, is based on the premise that the responsibility of the physical education department to adapt the program for the atypical child will be carried out.

Grouping

When considering how to group pupils for physical education, there are many problems that must be thought through before a decision is reached. It is widely accepted that classes should be homogeneous. In physical education the real question is "homogeneous in what respect?" Various groupings can be made, depending upon the criteria used: grade, age, health, physical fitness, ability, motor capacity, speed, strength, endurance, or interests. The American Alliance for Health, Physical Education, and Recreation stresses the need for grouping students homogeneously, but the inability to scientifically measure such important factors as ability, maturity, interest, and capacity has been a deterrent to accomplishing this goal. The Alliance points out that the most common procedure for grouping today is by grade or class. Under Title IX, sex can no longer be a basis for grouping.

The ideal grouping plan will take into consideration all the factors that affect performance—intelligence, capacity, ability, interest, knowledge, age, height, weight, and the like. It is not administratively possible, however, to utilize all these factors in many schools.

Some form of grouping is essential to provide the type of program that will promote educational objectives and protect the stu-

dent. On the secondary level the most feasible procedure appears to be to schedule classes by grade and then to organize subgroups within the regular physical education class. Classification within the physical education class can be based on such factors as age, height, intelligence, interests, motor ability, and motor capacity.

Size of classes

The size of physical education classes will vary greatly from school to school, and it may also vary from class to class within any one school. The number of pupils in each class has implications for teacher effectiveness.

Criteria. When considering the size of classes, it is essential to consider the number of teaching stations, the supplies and equipment, and the size of the area, as well as the number of available teachers.

Many of the same principles that are applicable in an English class also apply to the gymnasium. Obviously, the effectiveness of both the English teacher and the physical education teacher will be seriously hampered if there is an excessive number of pupils. Individual attention is limited, and many children must "sink or swim" on their own. Organization of a large class takes more time, discipline may be a greater problem, and the administrative structure of the class must be more formal. Furthermore, there is less opportunity to help meet the individual interests and needs of the children.

In recommending proper class size to an administrator, the American Alliance for Health, Physical Education, and Recreation suggests that the number of pupils in a class should not exceed thirty-five.

What to do with large classes. On the senior high school level, the problem of scheduling is a difficult one because students have individual programs. Each program is made to suit the individual student's needs. In the junior high school, it is sometimes a simpler process because of the block system, in which a group of students is scheduled as a unit and goes to different teachers as a unit.

One technique suitable for handling large classes is the use of student leaders. The effective use of trained pupils to assist in the management and organization of large classes can prove helpful. The students may be trained in a leaders' club that meets during a regular club period, after school, or both. With the assistance of these students it will be possible to institute an active squad work program. It will also be possible for the teacher to work with selected groups while the others are busy under the direction of their leaders. The responsibility for the class, however, always rests with the teacher. It is important for the teacher to oversee all activities, even though he or she may spend a major part of a class period with a particular group or groups.

Time

Standards for time allotment vary. In a survey of state requirements, the differences ranged from no specific time requirements for physical education, in some states, to minimum daily requirements. Many educators and administrators realize the importance of a minimum daily period of physical education.

The amount of time spent on physical education may vary from thirty to sixty minutes. When figuring the amount of physical education a student receives, the time needed for dressing and showering should be taken into consideration. For boys, this would be approximately five to seven minutes at the beginning of a period and about seven to thirteen minutes at the end of the period. It is usually necessary to add a few extra minutes for girls, particularly if hair must be dried. This means as little as fifteen to twenty minutes of actual activity on the gymnasium floor. In some situations, it may be advisable to have physical education on fewer days with longer periods. Considering a basic forty-five-minute period, the school that schedules five daily periods of physical education weekly may total as little as 125 minutes of physical activity per week. In the same school, by using two double periods each week, it is possible to have 150 minutes of physical activity while allowing the same amount of time for showering and dressing.

Of course, with flexible scheduling it is very easy to schedule classes with different lengths of time.

The time advantage that can be achieved by longer periods should be considered, even though the thinking of most educators is for a continuity that can be achieved only through a daily period of physical education.

Legal liability

A high school student who charged that he had been paralyzed as a result of negligence after an injury in a football game was awarded over $200,000. This is only one of many cases of legal liability that regularly occur in physical education programs.

With the growth in physical education programs throughout the country, there has been a resultant increase in the problems involving legal liability. The very nature of physical activity involves a certain amount of risk, and for their own welfare, teachers must be aware of their responsibility and liability for any accident.

A teacher's liability is "tort" liability; that is, it is "liability for personal or property injuries caused through the defendant's negligence. . . . Any tort action involves proof of four elements: that the defendant owed a duty to avoid unreasonable risk to others, that the defendant failed to observe that duty, that the failure to observe that duty caused the damage which occurred, and that damage in fact occurred to plaintiff . . . "*

Negligence. Negligence can be defined as something that a reasonable person would not do or the failure to do something that a reasonable person would do. There can be no legal liability unless there is negligence. Negligence must be shown. If one did not foresee a danger of accident as a reasonably prudent person should, there is negligence. Another condition demands an unfulfilled duty toward the injured person. Every teacher has such a duty because he or she is acting *in loco parentis* (in place of a parent).

---

*From Fahr, S. M.: Legal liability for athletic injuries, Journal of Health, Physical Education, and Recreation **29:**12, 1958.

Following are types of conduct* that constitute negligent acts:

1. Appropriate care is not used by the teacher. Example: An instructor permits a student to use the trampoline without stationing spotters.

2. The circumstances under which the activity is done creates risk, although it is done with due care and caution. Example: Two softball games are played on opposite ends of an area that is not large enough to permit overlapping outfielders.

3. The teacher is indulging in an act that involves an unreasonable risk of direct and immediate harm to others. Example: The physical education instructor places a boy at a certain position to mark where the shot put landed. The instructor puts a shot that hits the boy's head.

4. The teacher sets in motion a force, the continuous operation of which may be unreasonably hazardous to others. Example: A person, without justification, frightens a horse or dog that becomes uncontrollable.

5. The teacher creates a situation that is unreasonably dangerous to others because of the likelihood of the action of a third person or inanimate forces. Example: The instructor permits a student to ride a bicycle on a playground crowded with other pupils. The result is an injury to another student.

6. The teacher entrusts dangerous devices or instruments to persons who are incompetent to use or care for such instruments properly. Example: The instructor permits students to use fencing foils without supervision.

7. The teacher neglects a duty of control over a third person who, by reason of some incapacity or abnormality, may be likely to inflict intended harm upon others. Example: The instructor fails to supervise and control the conduct of a boy who is a bully in the play area.

8. The teacher fails to employ due care to give adequate warning. Example: The in-

structor, although responsible for supervision, absents himself or herself from the area. In another example, a student is struck by a car when crossing the street between the gymnasium and the athletic field. Negligence is found because no crosswalk was provided, no safety instruction was given to the students, and no warning signs for motorists were posted.

9. The teacher fails to exercise proper care in looking out for persons who may be in danger. Example: The teacher does not clear the students from the area directly behind the batter in a baseball game.

10. The teacher fails to employ appropriate skill to perform acts undertaken. Example: The teacher is unable to perform first aid when it should be administered.

11. The teacher fails to make adequate preparation to avoid harm to others before entering into an activity where such preparation is necessary. Example: The instructor permits students to use the horizontal bar without a mat underneath.

12. The teacher fails to inspect and repair equipment or mechanical devices used by others. Example: The teacher fails to inspect flying rings and other hanging equipment periodically.

Avoidance of negligence. It should be obvious that the best way to avoid negligence is to use common sense and to insist upon safety rules at all times. Some necessary rules include the following:

1. Clear a playing area of all obstacles (equipment and obstructions).
2. Inspect all equipment regularly.
3. Lock up apparatus when it is not in use.
4. Have a health examination for all competitors.
5. Never permit a boy or girl who may be injured to participate.
6. Instruct students in safety rules before permitting participation in an activity.
7. Employ spotters at all times.
8. Repair, remove, or do not use defective equipment.
9. Have ample insurance coverage at all times.

*Based on types of conduct that create unreasonable risks to others, from Harper, F. V.: A treatise on the law of torts, Indianapolis, 1938, Bobbs-Merrill Co., Inc., pp. 171-176.

10. Never leave a class alone.
11. Always use protective equipment in contact activities.
12. Be sure the activity is suitable for the age level.
13. Do not force a student to participate in any activity that involves the hazard of personal injury.
14. Administer first aid when necessary.
15. Do not treat injuries.
16. Request in writing the repair of all hazardous conditions.
17. Insist that all participants wear proper uniforms at all times.

Defenses against negligence. For damages to be awarded, it is necessary for the plaintiff to prove that the negligence involved resulted in, or was directly connected to, the injury. The legal defense against such a charge may be any of the following:

1. Act of God. A condition occurs that is beyond the control of man.

2. Assumption of risk. When participating in an activity that involves certain risks, that individual assumes responsibilities for those risks. There is still, however, the responsibility for effective leadership and safe equipment and facilities.

3. Contributory negligence. The injured person does not act as a reasonably prudent person of his age should act. In this case the negligence of the teacher is canceled. Every person is expected to maintain a reasonable amount of self-protection.

4. Proximate cause of injury. The negligent act must be the direct and immediate cause of injury. If the negligent act was only indirectly or remotely concerned with the injury, the claim will be disallowed.

Teacher liability. Teachers are liable for their own negligence. The doctrine of *respondeat superior*, however, can relieve them of liability. This doctrine holds that employers are liable for torts of their employees committed within the scope of their employment. In Iowa, the state supreme court ruled that a teacher is not liable for charges while carrying on a government function, even though he or she is guilty of negligence. Some states, such as New York, New Jersey,

and Connecticut, have "save harmless statutes," which permit the payment, out of school funds, for damages arising through the negligence of teachers or other employees of the school district.

Many teachers, particularly physical educators, purchase liability insurance from private companies. The American Alliance for Health, Physical Education, and Recreation has made available a policy that will protect its members from liability while engaging in any activity sponsored by the school or organization. The best means of avoiding any legal liability, however, is to make good use of the basic safety factors previously mentioned.

Insurance. Since schools require boys and girls to actively participate in physical education, they have a moral responsibility to protect them financially against injury. Staff members, because of the nature of their work and the need for protection against accidents and negligence, also need coverage. Some kind of insurance program should therefore be carried. Some factors to consider in such a protective insurance program are listed below.

1. All children and staff members should be covered in class and out-of-class activities.

2. Prior to the selection of an insurance policy, a study should be made of school needs and problems, the various types of policies offered by different companies, and the insurance program that best meets the local situation.

3. Insurance policies should provide sufficient funds to cover doctor's fees, hospital expenses, x-ray examinations, dental care, and so on.

4. Commercial plans should be explored, together with athletic association plans and other plans. Although commercial plans may be more expensive, they may provide better coverage.

5. In many cases the nonallocated form of policy is the more desirable, since benefits will be paid up to a specific amount regardless of the type of injury, whereas an allocated policy limits the benefits for each type of injury, such as a broken arm.

6. Staff members and other employees should also have insurance coverage.

Self-assessment tests

These tests are to assist students in determining if material and competencies presented in this chapter have been mastered:

1. Prepare an extensive list of major problems faced by beginning teachers without consulting the text.
2. Take the list prepared in number 1 and opposite each problem indicate if this problem could have been eliminated prior to the teacher assuming the position. Indicate how the problems could have been eliminated. Under what conditions should the teacher not have accepted the position?
3. Take the list in number 1 and opposite each problem that could not have been eliminated prior to accepting the position, indicate what special preparation, training, experience, or attitude would enable a beginning teacher to cope most successfully with each problem.
4. Prepare a list of problems that are administrative in nature and list how a beginning teacher may cope most successfully with each.

Points to remember

1. The possibility of avoiding many potential problems by investigating before accepting a position.
2. The probability that discipline will be your major professional problem.
3. Some problems directed toward teachers as members of the physical education department, not to them personally.
4. The necessity of coordination between the male and female physical education departments.
5. The need for the member of the physical education department to be an educator first.
6. How to conduct a program when the facilities are limited.
7. Sources of money for equipment and supplies and procedures for using the money.
8. Why physical education classes should be scheduled early in developing the school's master plan.
9. The need for homogeneity in physical education classes.
10. Proper class size and how to subgroup for good instruction.
11. Information regarding the legal liability of teachers.

Problems to think through

1. Why is the problem of acceptance of great importance to any beginning teacher?
2. How can one best prepare for the first day of teaching?
3. What do you anticipate as your greatest problem upon entering the teaching profession? Why?
4. Select any secondary school and determine how the facilities could be improved at a minimum expense. Use only the land and buildings available. What long-range major changes would you recommend?
5. How are supplies and equipment purchased in the school that you attend? Can the system be improved? How?
6. What are the advantages of having a physical education class containing students from the same grade?
7. Explain what a teacher should do when an accident occurs.
8. Compare the advantages of having five single physical education periods weekly with those of having two double periods weekly.

Case study for analysis

Unfavorable working conditions are causing many teachers to leave the profession. Some of these conditions relate to the size of classes, the length of the daily schedule and worksheet, and clerical duties and after-school obligations. Determine the degree to which adverse conditions prevail in a school system of your choice. Analyze factors that contribute to these conditions. How may the beginning teacher help to combat this problem?

Exercises for review

1. What are some techniques that are beneficial in working with large groups?
2. What school duties may be assigned to a beginning teacher?
3. Why is the orientation period important for good teaching?
4. Of what value are interscholastic activities to the student and the school?
5. How can the female physical education teacher avoid being labeled as the "girls' coach"?
6. What can the physical educator do if there is no gymnasium available in the school?
7. What areas can be used to change into uniforms in the absence of a locker room?
8. How can a physical education class have out-of-doors activities without a playing field?
9. What departments in the school can help to minimize physical education expenses?
10. What size should physical education classes be?
11. How may student leaders help the physical educator?
12. List ten negligent acts in physical education. Give an example of each.
13. What are the legal defenses against negligence?

Selected readings

Bucher, C. A.: Administration of health and physical education programs, including athletics, ed. 6, St. Louis, 1975, The C. V. Mosby Co.

Bucher, C. A.: Foundations of physical education, ed. 7, St. Louis, 1975, The C. V. Mosby Co.

Bucher, C. A., and Reade, E.: Physical education and health in the elementary school, ed. 3, New York, 1970, The Macmillan Publishing Co., Inc.

Dillon, S. V., and Franks, D. D.: Open learning environment: self-identity and coping ability, The Educational Forum **39**:155, 1975.

Field, D.: Accountability for the physical educator, Journal of Health, Physical Education and Recreation **44**:37, 1973.

Fisher, M.: Assessing the competence of prospective physical education teachers, The Physical Educator **29**:93, 1972.

Gallup, G. H.: Fourth annual Gallup poll of public attitudes toward education, Phi Delta Kappan, September, 1972, p. 33.

Longo, P.: Opening the door to the open classroom, Kappa Delta Pi Record **11**:98, 1975.

University of the State of New York, The State Education Department, Newsletter of the Division of Teacher Education and Certification, No. 1, June, 1972, Competence Based Certification, Albany, N.Y.

Unruh, G. G., and Alexander, W. M.: Innovations in secondary education, New York, 1970, Holt, Rinehart and Winston, Inc.

Van Til, W.: Education: a beginning, New York, 1971, Houghton Mifflin Company.

14

THE PHYSICAL EDUCATOR AND TEACHING STYLE

INSTRUCTIONAL OBJECTIVES AND COMPETENCIES TO BE ACHIEVED

After reading this chapter the student should be able to—
1. Demonstrate those aspects of teacher-student relations necessary to effective teaching.
2. Define the term teaching style and describe the various styles that teachers use in actual practice.
3. Evaluate the worth of teaching-centered and student-centered styles.
4. Relate various general philosophies to teaching style.
5. Demonstrate that he or she has developed a viable teaching style.

Research studies have shown that the behavior and personality of one person when closely interacting with another person can have an effect on that person's behavior and personality. This is true of many human relationships whether in a family setting or some form of business or other relationship. It is especially true of the relationship between teacher and student. The teacher's personality and behavior can affect the pupils classroom behavior. Furthermore, since the personalities of teachers differ, it also follows that there are different teaching styles, with the result that the impact upon students is different.

Although in some occupations personality is secondary to accomplishing professional goals (carpentry, for example), teaching success in great measure depends upon the style that the teacher uses with his or her pupils. Indeed, the teacher's personality and the way he or she behaves in the classroom, gymnasium, or playfield may be one of the most important factors in determining the outcomes accomplished from the physical education experience. The excellent teacher is not only one who has command of the skills, subject matter, and other requirements for his or her field of specialization, it is also the teacher who successfully transmits these skills and subject matter to the students.

Alexander M. Mood* points out that some authorities feel that about 10 percent of the teachers may be classified as being excellent, 10 percent as hopeless, and the other 80 percent as having varying degrees of competence and effectiveness. Mood goes on to point out that a characteristic of most excellent teachers is that they are sympathetic to students and deeply concerned about their welfare and interests. He further points out that research indicates there are some points that teachers should be aware of if they wish

---

*Mood, A. M.: How teachers make a difference, Washington, D.C., 1971, U.S. Office of Education, Department of Health, Education, and Welfare.

to do an effective professional job of teaching. These are presented here in adapted form:

• *The teacher should listen to what the students have to say and put it to use.* The teacher should pay attention to each question or comment no matter how trivial it may be. Each student should be given a feeling that he or she is participating in the learning process and has something worthy to contribute.

• *Each student should be provided with a sense of personal worth.* Teachers should go out of the way to instill in each student the feeling that he or she has some knowledge, skill, or attitude that is important and therefore deserves to be complimented.

• *Each student should be imbued with a feeling of confidence, particularly in respect to ability to learn.* The teacher must be very careful not to erode the student's self-confidence. This means that the teacher must understand that some students will learn faster than others and that students are also different in other ways that are affected by the learning process.

• *The teacher should not appear to be superior morally or intellectually.* If this does happen it builds up antagonism between student and teacher. Furthermore, students become overprotective of their egos.

• *Conflicts of interest with students should be minimized.* Students must be convinced that the teacher reflects goodwill toward them and therefore conflicts of interest should be reduced to a minimum. Although some conflicts will naturally exist—for example, attendance may be considered unnecessary by pupils but important by the teacher, and disruptive behavior cannot be tolerated—the teacher should aim at enlarging the community of interests with students rather than decreasing them.

• *Lecturing should be kept to a minimum.* Students learn more readily if they can grapple with questions and problems. Although this process is slower than having teacher expound the truth, it is generally agreed that it is more effective when the students do some thinking and themselves arrive at the answer.

• *The gymnasium, swimming pool, playground, or classroom should be characterized by a relaxed atmosphere.* Greater student participation and learning will take place in an open, relaxed atmosphere than in one that is rigid and formal.

• *Students should be kept active.* Physical movement is needed by all students throughout the school day—it will enhance the learning that takes place.

• *Genuine concern should be shown by the teacher for each student in the class.* Each student should be given the feeling and be convinced that the teacher cares about him or her as a person.

• *Individual students should not be permitted to fall behind.* Everything possible should be done to make sure each student makes progress and learns. The whole class should be aware of this feeling so that when a student starts to falter, not only the teacher but the whole class plays a part in seeing that the student learns and moves ahead.

• *Apathy and boredom should be combated.* These are deterrents to learning. Students should be kept interested and make the learning an exciting experience.

• *Teaching should be diversified.* A variety of methods such as films, slides, curriculum packages, programmed devices, and records should be used in teaching. The teacher must keep abreast of new teaching ideas.

• *Student participation should be encouraged in making learning attractive.* Students should be consulted about teaching and how to make it more interesting. Many of their experiments and ideas should be utilized.

• *The teacher should do the best type of teaching job possible.* Each teacher must do the very best job each day. Effective teaching is an important responsibility, and pupils should not be cheated.

• *Colleague interaction will help.* An exchange of ideas, discussion of problems, and joint ventures with other teachers are excellent ways to improve one's own teaching.

• *Grading systems should be questioned.* Grades create problems between teacher and student. If possible, they should not be used or at least the importance of grades should be minimized.

• *The teacher should be a model.* Setting a

good example of what is right, honest, and scholarly is important to the learning process.

TEACHING STYLE AND METHODS AND MATERIALS

Courses in methods and materials in professional preparation curricula are typically concerned with instructing the future physical educator in how to teach a particular skill, how to correct student errors in skill performance, and how to direct the practice of a skill. Such courses may be said to be skill-centered. For example, the methods of teaching soccer are taught as a unit, and then the methods unique to other team, individual, and dual sports are taught as independent units. Methods and materials courses are also concerned with patterns of class organization for the teaching of a skill. The future physical educator learns how to teach the left-handed student, how to line the students up for instruction so that they do not face into the sun, and the most efficient methods of organizing a class for various drills and lead-up games.

Rarely do methods and materials courses consider the individuality and creativity of the teacher, and even more rarely do they take into account the individuality of the students to whom the methods will be applied. These courses do, however, serve an essential purpose as part of the professional preparation curriculum. They do introduce the future physical educator to effective methodology in teaching and class management, and they do help to prepare for the student teaching experience. What methods and materials courses frequently do not do is to provide the future teacher with experiences in developing a system and style of teaching that is unique to himself or herself.

DEFINITION OF THE TERM "TEACHING STYLE"

Teaching style and teaching methodology are two separate yet complementary phenomena. Teaching methodology is based on a standard philosophy of physical education and on the objectives of the physical education program. A physical educator's style of teaching is an expression of himself or herself as an individual and is related to personal philosophy and objectives. A physical educator adapts methodology to teaching style rather than the reverse.

We may thus define teaching style as an observable phenomenon that is an expression of the physical educator's individuality in relation to stated philosophy and program objectives. Additionally, a physical educator's teaching style is reflected in methodology of teaching and in class organization and management.

Historically the term "style" was related to a pen or stylus. Later, it referred to handwriting and eventually to the quality and nature of a literary work. In the psychological sense, as it is used in this chapter, it refers to personality and to individual behavior. Specifically, it refers to the behavior of the teacher in the classroom, gymnasium, swimming pool, playground, or other setting where learning takes place. It encompasses the basic characteristics of teachers as reflected in their personalities, which have implications for their relations with students and their outlook toward learning and teaching.

Some persons have confused teaching style with teaching method. In respect to teaching method, we are referring more to the techniques and procedures used by the teacher in presenting certain subject matter or skills, such as textbooks and audiovisual aids, which are outside the range of personality structure. However, the choice of teaching method is of course influenced by a teacher's personality and behavior.

PERSONALITY AND TEACHING STYLES

There are several types of teaching styles that have been identified by researchers in the field. Some of the more prominent of these styles are discussed for the reader. Hamachek* discusses four personality styles that are reflected in teacher behavior, which he points out were developed clinically by

---

*Hamachek, D. E.: Personality styles and teacher behavior, The Educational Forum **36:**313, 1972.

Shapiro.* These styles are the compulsive style, the suspicious style, the hysterical style, and the impulsive style.

Compulsive style

Hamachek refers to the teachers who possess this style as "living machines." They are rigid in their schedules and ways of behaving and thinking. A compulsive teacher might be one who is "dogmatic," "opinionated," or "bull-headed." He or she frequently does not listen to what a student is saying but instead spends time thinking about what he or she is going to say in response. This type of teacher is obsessed by detail, whether it be erasing the blackboards every night before going home, insisting that students perform a particular skill in exactly the way demonstrated, or giving back in an examination the same information initially passed on to them. He or she directs and tells students rather than interacting with them. This type of teacher is not sensitive to the individual differences that exist among students and has limited interests. The classroom is devoid of a social tone; education is serious business, interpersonal dynamics are not a part of the learning process. It is very difficult for this teacher to have fun with students. The teacher with the compulsive style prescribes for students in light of personal feelings and needs instead of in terms of the students' feelings and needs.

Suspicious style

The suspicious style is, according to Hamachek, a style that is characterized by some paranoidlike features. The teacher who has this type of style is often the one who feels the students are plotting against him or her. This teacher has a guilty and tense feeling about many things that happen and imagines colleagues or other persons are trying to find out about his or her personal life and so keeps a wary eye on them. Because of these suspicions it is difficult to enjoy teaching students. This teacher sees very little fun in teaching and rarely laughs. Since he or she

*Shapiro, D.: Neurotic styles, New York, 1965, Basic Books, Inc.

cannot accept or place trust in himself or herself it is difficult to do the same with others. Therefore this person is reluctant to place faith in other people, whether students or colleagues. Teachers who possess the suspicious style also are very conscious of those who possess power or position and may have an antagonistic relationship with these authority figures. Such teachers are particularly wary of administrators who evaluate them. They feel that the principal or superintendent may evaluate their teaching, for example, in terms of their character or personal habits rather than in terms of their teaching performance.

Hysterical style

The teacher characterized by the hysterical style is different from the other styles discussed, particularly in respect to awareness of the more colorful events that occur. In fact, the colorful events may be so highlighted by this person that the substance and fact of teaching may be overlooked. In other words, the reactions of such a teacher may be more in terms of impressions than facts. Such teachers are easily influenced by other persons' feelings, prejudices, fads, and objects or circumstances that excite them. Their attention is captured not so much by the details and facts but by the headlines and sensational happenings that occur. They are the teachers who accentuate rumors about students and colleagues using drugs, engaging in sex, getting traffic tickets, or squandering money at the races. They are apt to think of students in terms of these emotional characterizations and judgments, and in turn these characterizations may affect the manner in which they treat their students. It should be recognized that although the hysterical style may cause many teaching problems, it may also result in teaching behavior that is enthusiastic, colorful, and lively.

Impulsive style

The teacher who possesses this style is characterized by quick action that is unplanned and not carefully thought through. In such cases, judgment may be poor and reckless and result in poor decisions. In turn, these decisions may provide many disappointments. Such persons are unpredictable since behavior is often the result of whim or impulse. They usually are characterized by the immediate concerns of their own lives rather than permanent goals or values. As contrasted with the compulsive teacher, who critically evaluates a problem, the impulsive teacher acts on the spur of the moment, with initial impressions frequently becoming the basis for action.

Reflective style

Murphy and Brown* discuss a teaching style that is referred to as the "reflective" style. This is a style aimed at getting the students to think, analyze, reflect, and conceptualize. It encourages questioning and hypothesizing. The questioning and discussing take place in a climate of freedom and permissiveness, with the teacher serving as a guide rather than occupying a role of dispenser of the truth. There is a very warm, respected relationship between instructor and student that results in a high degree of motivation on the part of the student. The student experiences a feeling of freedom to discuss the subject in terms of his or her own attitude, experience, and opinion. This teacher is not inhibited. The subject becomes interesting and exciting to students in the democratic atmosphere that is provided.

BASIC TEACHING STYLES

There are two basic kinds of teaching style: teacher-centered and student-centered. Although other styles have been discussed briefly, these two basic styles are discussed much more completely. Of course, there is some overlapping with previously discussed styles.

Teacher-centered style

The teacher-centered physical educator is often described as autocratic. He or she

states the philosophy of physical education in terms of personal relationships to the profession and a personal conception of the goals of the profession in relation to his or her own teaching. Program objectives are stated in terms of what the teacher wishes to accomplish. Evaluation is made in relation to what was accomplished through his or her program. For example, the teacher-centered physical educator might list some of the daily objectives of a unit in basketball in the following manner:

1. To teach the dribble
2. To teach the hook shot
3. To teach foul shooting

The autocratic physical educator will evaluate the basketball unit as a successful learning experience if he or she has indeed taught the dribble, the hook shot, and foul shooting *and* has taught the class to perform these skills to a common standard. The satisfaction for the autocratic physical educator, then, is based not on student success but on teacher accomplishments in terms of teacher-centered objectives. The program evaluation is not derived from observing student success but rather from an analysis of the teaching and its effectiveness in terms of student learning.

The teacher-centered physical educator is somewhat of a perfectionist and expects that all students will be able to perform a certain skill in the same way. This teacher does not realize that all students do not have the ability to meet a single standard of performance, and teaching is frequently geared to those students who can measure up to the physical educator's criteria for success. This teacher tends to feel a sense of failure as a teacher when a student falls short of the expected goal. The teacher-centered physical educator strives to guide students toward the response or action he or she views as being the correct one in any given situation. In a rules quiz, for example, all the students may correctly answer that there are nine players on a baseball team. They may not know why there are nine players or what the players' duties are, but they have given the correct response, and that accomplishes the goal.

---

*Murphy, P. D., and Brown, M. M.: Conceptual systems and teaching styles, American Educational Research Journal 7:529, 1970.

The teacher-centered physical educator is generally a rather rigid individual, and this rigidity is transferred to the teaching situation. Classes tend to be dull rather than exciting, and students are more often externally motivated by fear of failure than by an inner-directed desire to succeed. This physical education stylist is often the delight of supervisors and administrators because he or she demands excellent discipline and maintains tight control over classes. It is difficult to be able to state accurately, however, whether or not the students in such classes derive any enjoyment from their physical education experience.

In a teacher-dominated physical education class, the instructor is most likely to follow tried and tested methodology rather strictly. This teaching stylist feels that only proved methods and techniques will work, and resists innovation because it threatens effectiveness as a teacher. He or she sometimes refers to educational innovations as fads that will not be fully accepted because their lasting value has not been demonstrated. A capsule analysis of this stylist would show one year of teaching experience that has been repeated "x" number of times.

The teacher-centered physical educator is less interested in the individual student than in the student group. The class is viewed as simply a group of bodies that need to be physically educated. For this reason, the teacher-centered physical educator is less apt to know students by name than to know them by their physical abilities. This teacher frequently can describe accurately the tumbling, softball, or other skills of the fourth student in the second squad, but may not know the student's name. Students often feel that they are less important to the teacher than the condition of the gymnasium floor, the cleanliness of the locker room, or the height of the grass on the playing field.

The teacher-centered physical educator is chiefly concerned with the cognitive areas of teaching and less often with the affective areas. As such, this teacher chooses the body of knowledge to be imparted to students and is interested only in their grasp of it as knowledge. In turn this teacher depends on observable motor skills and the scores on written and skill tests to tell whether the knowledge is being absorbed. He or she is not particularly interested in whether students appreciate, enjoy, or want to participate in certain physical education activities. The right of choosing the activities to be engaged in is reserved for the teacher, and the activity is taught for the sake of the activity.

The teacher-centered stylist feels the need to conform to the philosophy of the school administration, and this is frequently a traditionalist philosophy. Thus, the physical educator believes that it is also a duty to have students conform and feels that this can be accomplished only through a traditional teaching style. In the gymnasium or on the playing field it is the physical educator who demonstrates new skills, and the students are expected to mimic the instructor's technique. Student evaluations are thus subjectively arrived at in relation to their ability to conform, not only in regard to techniques of performing skills but in the areas of behavior and attitude as well. The results of written tests are sometimes discounted if they diverge either way from the physical educator's subjective evaluation of the student.

This style of teaching physical education often helps to stereotype the field as one that stands apart from the rest of the school program. The teacher-centered physical educator is primarily concerned with the relationship to his or her own field only and tends not to keep abreast of changes in general education. This person does not consider changes in general education any more seriously than he or she considers changes in physical education as important to teaching and professional growth.

Intramural and interscholastic sports programs and physical education clubs are also influenced by the teacher-centered physical educator in much the same way as the class program is influenced. Often, the intramural and club activities offered are not decided on the basis of student need and interest but rather on the basis of what the physical educator thinks the students ought to have.

Under the teacher-centered approach, a student may be barred from joining clubs and intramural teams if he or she also has an interest in other school clubs and activities. In some instances, a student whose band rehearsal makes him or her a few minutes late for a club meeting or game may be locked out of the gymnasium or locker room. The teacher-centered physical educator tends to theorize that the student cannot be seriously interested in the after-school program in physical education if he or she does not make the effort to arrive at the activity on time. This labels the student as a nonconformist in the eyes of the teacher and effectively drives the student away from after-school physical education activities. In some secondary schools, this lack of a cooperative relationship on the part of the physical educator with other school activities results in a marked failure of the intramural and club programs in physical education. Students will seek out and participate in those school activities that answer their needs and interest and that welcome them as individuals who have something to contribute.

With the teacher-centered physical educator, intramural teams in a rigid setting are frequently highly coached. Contests are instructional extensions of the class period rather than games played purely for enjoyment. The physical educator will supervise very closely, and at times will remove a student from a game if the student is not "giving his or her all." A contest may also be stopped to correct the skill errors of several players. Frequently, the physical educator will have formed the teams and appointed a captain for each without any student participation and will exercise the right to shift players from one team to another.

In varsity sports the teacher-centered physical educator will dominate the game completely. The physical educator in the coaching role will decide all lineups and lineup changes and direct all game strategy from the bench. In a sport such as football, for example, the coach will send the plays in to the quarterback rather than letting the quarterback direct the offense. A game in which this kind of team goes on to victory is another example of guiding students to the response desired by the teacher. The victory serves as a proof, for the physical educator, of the worth of the teacher-centered style of teaching, but such a victory makes a questionable contribution to the physical, mental, emotional, and social growth of the players involved.

Student-centered style

The student-centered physical educator is sometimes thought of as a democratic teacher. The student-centered physical educator's philosophy is stated in terms of the relationship of physical education to the total educational field and its goals. Goals of physical education are conceived as parallel to those of general education. The student-centered physical educator's program objectives are stated in terms of student needs and interests, and evaluation is based upon how well the program has succeeded in meeting those needs and interests. Some of the daily objectives of a unit in tennis might be listed in the following manner:

1. To be able to execute the forehand
2. To be able to serve
3. To be able to play a game of doubles

The student-centered physical educator will be pleased with this unit if, among the other basic tennis skills, students can return the forehand shot into the playing court, serve well enough to keep the ball in play, and cooperate with a partner in playing a game of doubles. This physical educator is not satisfied with teaching minimal skills. Rather, students learn skills as well as they can so that they will find success and pleasure in physical activity. He or she does not attempt to develop champion players in a sport such as tennis but is instead concerned with the ability of students to be able to play a recreational game of tennis, even if it is played on a beginning level. The student-centered physical educator does not expect or demand that all students attain a common level of skill; rather, each student attempts to reach his or her own potential. The satisfaction for this stylist is based on student success in terms of student-centered objectives.

Fig. 14-1. In the student-centered style the attention is focused on the student. Student in physical education class in Brockport Central Schools, Brockport, N.Y.

The program evaluation is derived from an observation of student success and from an objective analysis of the teaching in relation to its ability to meet student needs and interests. This physical educator uses evaluation as a guide to adaptations and modifications that might help to meet student needs even more effectively.

The student-centered physical educator is especially cognizant of differences in student ability and avoids setting common criteria for skill performances. Instead, the teacher prefers to devise charts or other devices that show the beginning, intermediate, and advanced level of performance for each skill or combination of skills. Each student can use these criteria to judge personal progress and

performance and to attempt to move from the beginning to the more advanced levels according to individual potential. Thus each student progresses at his or her own most comfortable rate and can find success that is meaningful. Because there are no artificial or induced standards toward which each student must strive, there is less chance for failure. The student-centered physical educator attempts to gear teaching to each individual in the class rather than to any one similarly skilled group of individuals. The teaching is then on a more personalized basis, and there is a decided emphasis on remedial help for those who need it, as well as on coaching tips for those who are more advanced. The student-centered physical educator strives to help students reach their own goals in regard to motor skill ability.

The student-centered physical educator is usually very flexible. In the teaching situation he or she will alter or adapt a lesson if it is not accomplishing its purpose. Other on-the-spot changes will be made if the class seems unusually tired or if a dreary day leads to student lethargy. The teacher will devise unique games or activities that will help to rekindle student interest and enthusiasm or will place a unique lesson in the program merely to provide a break in routine. Classes are exciting to watch, and students are enthusiastic about the class because they find it stimulating and challenging. These students have an inner motivation to succeed because they are encouraged to operate as individuals and to succeed as individuals. This helps them to discipline their own behavior. At times, this physical educator is criticized by supervisors and administrators because the noise emanating from the gymnasium or playing field is interpreted as a lack of control on the part of the physical educator, rather than being recognized as the sounds of boys and girls responding enthusiastically to their physical education experience. Discipline is an undertone, not a fear-inducing characteristic of the class period.

The student-centered physical educator welcomes innovations because he or she is contributing to students, to the profession, and to his or her own professional growth through the use of the latest techniques and methodology. The teacher will, for example, adopt the principles of movement education, giving them an objective and sufficiently lengthy trial before accepting them as a permanent part of the program or rejecting them because they make a questionable contribution to students. This type of person judges innovations on student relevance rather than on how they relate to the teacher. This stylist also appreciates traditional methodology but does not view it as unchanging or unchangeable. Each new school year represents new techniques and methodologies to be tested, new activities to introduce, new individuals to guide through the physical education ex-

perience, new challenges to be met, and new personal experiences to be gained.

The student-centered physical educator is interested in each student as an individual and realizes that physical education makes a unique contribution to the individual that is made by no other phase of the school program. This physical educator knows each student by name and can accurately describe each student's physical education needs, interests, and abilities. The teacher is interested in students as human beings and willingly gives time for individual guidance and counseling. Students prize this person as a teacher because they know that he or she views them as the most important part of the physical education program.

This physical educator attempts to teach students to think for themselves, to be creative, to express themselves, and to ask questions. He or she is concerned with the cognitive objectives of physical education but is also especially concerned with the affective objectives. This teacher is vitally interested in having students become aware of the values of physical activity and the varieties of physical activity. He or she wants them to enjoy and appreciate physical activity, to seek out new activities, and to participate in them on their own. This teacher employs a conceptual approach to physical education so that students will be able to base their knowledge of physical activity on scientific understanding. When new activities are introduced or new units initiated, the students understand the value of that activity and the need for it, aside from the fact that the activity is required by a syllabus.

The student-centered physical educator believes in a balance of activities presented in a logical progression but also very strongly feels that students should be able to select the activities that appeal to them. Rather than dictating the activity for each unit, the physical educator will present students with a list of several activities that will fulfill the same student needs as indicated by their motor ability and physical fitness test scores. If there is more than one teacher, the class may be divided into two interest groups. If there is only one teacher, the class may decide to select one activity, or the classes may be so arranged that two activities can be covered. Some student-centered physical educators will extend the number of class periods allocated to a unit to assure meeting the needs and interests of the students.

The student-centered physical educator is also interested in conforming to administrative dicta but does not view this as a hindrance to the program or to the desire to utilize the latest thinking in physical education. Before adopting any new method or technique that might be viewed as radically different, this teacher will present a plan to superiors for approval, showing how the innovation will make the physical education experience more meaningful for students. This physical educator further realizes that there are many alternatives in teaching and is willing to test any alternative that seems pertinent and logical. The teacher also knows that his or her performance of a skill is not necessarily the best way for students to perform it. Variations in body build, flexibility, strength, endurance, and experience are taken into account and students are asked to demonstrate a variety of techniques for their fellow classmates. This helps students to understand that there is more than one acceptable technique in performing a skill.

Student evaluations, for the student-centered physical educator, are based on many objective measures. He or she does not believe that a single grade should be given to a student, especially when the grade is expected to include skill, attitude, and behavioral outcomes. This physical educator prefers to evaluate students in a written, comprehensive statement that is more meaningful than a letter or number grade. Some secondary schools have permitted their physical education staffs to devise a separate physical education evaluation form based on just such a statement and including places for noting test scores and other factors. Such evaluation forms give a total picture of student progress.

The student-centered physical educator is interested in other areas of the curriculum as well as in physical education. He or she reads professional journals and attempts to understand the changes being made in general education. He or she views education and physical education as dynamic, and is aware of their many interrelationships and interdependencies. Through reading and meetings with other professionals, he or she strives to grow as a teacher in conjunction with the growth of education and physical education as professional fields of endeavor.

Intramural and interscholastic sports, as well as physical education clubs, are student-centered when the physical educator is student-centered. The intramural and club activities offered are directly related to student needs and interests. There are frequently different programs for students in different grades. For example, in the fall season ninth-grade students may be offered soccer and speedball, while senior students may be offered field hockey and lacrosse.

The student-centered physical educator wants students to be interested in all phases of the school program. He or she will work cooperatively with the art, drama, or music teacher to plan a schedule of after-school events that will not conflict or may set aside a special day for students whose diversity of interest makes cooperative scheduling difficult.

Intramural teams are organized by the students under the supervision of the physical educator, and captains are elected by the vote of team members. The games are played for their recreational value, regardless of the skill levels of the various players. While the intramural program is considered to be an extension of the class program, it is regarded not as a teaching-learning situation but as an opportunity for each student to practice skills and to enjoy the use of them in a chosen activity. Team lineups, substitutions, and the conduct of the intramural games will be student-directed. The teacher will supervise but will never control or dominate the games.

Varsity sports will also be student-directed. Although the physical educator will be directly responsible, as coach, for the overall administration of the team, the players themselves will take the most important role. Lineups, lineup changes, and game strategy will evolve from a dialogue between the players and the physical educator. Additionally, the quarterback in football or the catcher in baseball will have the responsibility for calling the game plays, with the physical educator suggesting plays only when the situation demands it. In victory, the glory belongs wholly to the players, and in defeat they will have learned invaluable lessons that will lead to future victories. The student-centered approach makes a definite contribution to the physical, mental, emotional, and social growth and development of the students and athletes in such a program because student initiative is the keynote.

Teacher-centered style versus student-centered style

The teacher-centered physical educator and the student-centered physical educator are equally knowledgeable about their subject matter. It is only their *approach* to teaching this subject matter that really differs. Although the subject matter is the prime focus of the former, the latter focuses on the student in the teaching-learning situation.

Neither style of teaching is perfect, nor is either free of disadvantages. Both styles have their merits, and both have been used successfully by many different teachers of many different subjects. Each style has been described from a puristic, theoretical point of view so that differences would be more easily recognized and understood, but it must be remembered that teachers tend to borrow elements of both styles and incorporate them into their own unique teaching systems.

In practice, physical educators may shift from style to style, depending on the particular lesson. In teaching team and dual sports, the physical educator may use an approach that is closer to the teacher-centered style and may do this for a variety of reasons. For example, he or she may have a class, or several classes, that have not developed the maturity required for a student-centered approach, or the physical educator may want to

teach a skill and have only a limited amount of time. This same physical educator may find that these same classes benefit most from the student-centered approach when its use is limited to such creative, expressive activities as dance, tumbling, gymnastics, swimming, and other individual sports. It is also possible to use the teacher-centered style during one part of a class period and the student-centered style during another part of the same class period.

A physical educator may use the teacher-centered style in the class program and in a varsity coaching situation but prefer the student-centered style for the intramural and club program, or the reverse may be true. Any number of combinations of teaching style may be observed in the individual physical educator, depending upon the activity, the needs of the students, and the physical educator's assessment of the most appropriate style for the situation.

The two teaching styles are not exclusive, and they do overlap. A physical educator may, in fact, state objectives and goals in student-centered terms, yet instruct through the teacher-centered style. However, the predominating style in use at the time will be readily identifiable to the observer.

PHILOSOPHY AND TEACHING STYLE

There are five major philosophies that influence education, educational thought, and teaching style. These philosophies are idealism, realism, pragmatism, naturalism, and existentialism. The ability to understand the key concepts of these philosophies and to relate these concepts to education helps a physical educator to articulate a philosophy of his profession and guides him in developing a teaching style that reflects his personal philosophy.

Idealism and teaching style

Idealism is a heritage from the ancient Greek thinkers and philosophers. The idealist places universal ideas at the center of the universe and says that these ideas represent absolute and universal reality. Further, the idealist believes very strongly in human powers of reasoning and intuition.

In regard to education, the idealist feels that the quest for knowledge is inner-directed and that the creativity and thought processes of the student are personal. The role of the teacher is to supply a learning atmosphere and mold the mind of the learner.

The idealist regards physical education as more than a purely physical experience. The physical education program is expected to provide opportunities for mental, social, and emotional growth as well. The idealist would strongly support a physical education program that encouraged student initiative and creativity and furthered intellectual attainment. Having the student understand the *why* of the activity would be approved. The teacher would be looked upon as the possessor of all culture and worthy of emulation by the student. The emphasis would be centered upon seeing how nearly the pupil could achieve the ideal.

Realism and teaching style

Realism as a philosophy took hold during the late nineteenth and early twentieth centuries, although its roots are as old as those of idealism. The realist places the laws of nature at the center of the universe and supports the scientific method as the best way of seeking and gaining knowledge.

Mathematics and science are, to the realist, the core of the educative process. The educative process as a whole is thought of as a system of learning how to acquire knowledge, acquiring knowledge, and putting knowledge to use. The role of the teacher is to be objective in methodology, testing, and student evaluation. The development of standardized tests was influenced by the philosophy of realism.

The realist values physical education because the physical education experience helps the student learn to adjust to the world. The outcome of the activity in terms of student adjustment is of prime importance to the realist. The realist would prefer a scientifically formulated program that follows a logical sequence. However, any activities offered in the program would have to be justified as valuable on the basis of scholarly research. This person would require that student evaluations be derived from the results of objective tests. The realist would approve of a physical education program that had a teacher strong in scientific procedures.

Pragmatism and teaching style

Pragmatism is considered to be an American philosophy in its modern concept. The word "pragmatism" was first used in the 1800s, the approximate time this philosophy began to evolve out of its earlier form, which was known as experimentalism. Pragmatism is the philosophy associated with John Dewey.

The pragmatist is a flexible person who believes in change, in the integration of human beings with their world, and in the scientific method. The pragmatist places experience at the center of the universe because man cannot know, or prove, anything that has not personally been experienced.

Dewey said that experience is the key to learning and that the problem-solving method gives the student the experience he or she needs in order to learn. The pragmatist stresses individual differences between students and demands a student-centered school. The role of the teacher is to inspire, guide, and lead the student through a variety of problem-solving activities.

The pragmatist demands a physical education program that meets the needs of the individual student. A wide variety of activities, with emphasis on creativity, is of prime importance. Rigidity and formality, which are inherent in drills and exercises, would not receive the approval of the pragmatist. The pragmatist believes in providing activities that arise from the interests and experiences of the student and in adapting the activity to the student. He or she also prefers that students sample innovative activities, that they be involved in deciding curriculum content, and that they participate as equals in program planning.

Naturalism and teaching style

Naturalism is the oldest philosophy known to the western world. It shares many of the concepts of realism and pragmatism because it has had a strong influence on the development of these philosophies.

The naturalist places at the center of the universe only those things that exist in actuality. In other words, only material or physical things have significance. The naturalist values society as a whole but is more concerned with each human being as an individual.

Naturalist thought has influenced the development of the educational philosophies of realism and pragmatism. The naturalist desires a student-centered school in which the educational process is geared to the growth, needs, and interests of each individual student. The problem-solving method is important to the naturalist, who feels that the role of the teacher is to guide the student through the process of investigation by the use of example and scientific demonstration.

The naturalist believes in a wide variety of physical activity and in vigorous exercise. All activities in the program must be geared to the student as an individual rather than as part of a larger group. The program should follow the natural pattern of the student's growth and development.

Existentialism and teaching style

Existentialism emerged as a philosophy in the late nineteenth century but did not receive significant recognition until after World War II. Existentialism is a thoroughly modern philosophy.

The concept of the individuality of human beings forms the core of existentialism. The existentialist believes that each person guides his or her own destiny, determines his or her own system of values, and occupies a place that is superior to that of the society at large.

The existentialist says that education is an adventure in the discovery of self and that the schools must be totally student-centered so that the individual student will not be hindered in attempts at discovery. The existentialist advocates that the student be given full freedom to learn what he or she is interested in learning at the time he or she is interested in learning it. The student selects not only the subject matter but the method through which learning will take place. Norms, standardized tests, and group tests would be entirely eliminated in favor of an individual evaluative process. The role of the teacher is to monitor the learning environment and to supply the needed tools and opportunity for learning, as well as to serve as a stimulus for the student.

In regard to physical education, the existentialist would prefer a balanced and varied program that has something for everyone. Additionally, the existentialist would prefer that each student have freedom in the choice of activities and that he or she be responsible for self-discipline, guiding learning, and evaluating progress. The teaching approach most preferred by the existentialist is that of the physical educator who is completely student-centered.

DEVELOPMENT OF A TEACHING STYLE

A teaching style develops gradually and is unique to each physical educator because of the myriad individual variations and shadings that may be applied to a style. There are various influences, however, that affect the development of an individual's teaching style. Two of the most important influences are the undergraduate professional preparation program and the student-teaching experience. A third influence is the philosophy of the school system in which the beginning teacher matures.

Influence of the undergraduate professional preparation program

It is in the undergraduate years that the future physical educator first explores the nonactivity aspects of physical education. Courses in the history and philosophy of education, psychology and other of the behavioral sciences, and physical education, in principles and practice of physical education, and in organization and administration of physical education form a foundation of understanding and comprehension of the breadth and depth of the field. Through such courses the future physical educator begins to form a personal philosophy of physical education. He or she is often required, as an adjunct to these courses or in methods and materials courses, to formulate a series of objectives for physical education, to plan course outlines and curriculum content, and to write lesson plans.

The philosophy and teaching style of the undergraduate instructors have a profound influence on the development of the student's teaching style. In general, a department will decide upon how the students in that department are to write their objectives and construct the lesson plans that will carry out these objectives. The decision may dictate student-centered terminology or teacher-centered terminology or some kind of compromise terminology. However, the point is too infrequently made that there is more than one way of writing objectives and that there is more than one style of teaching that will carry out the objectives satisfactorily. Experience in teaching gained in methods courses further influences and reinforces the dictated teaching style. It is this method of phrasing objectives and this style of teaching that is brought to the student-teaching experience.

Influence of the student-teaching experience

The student-teaching experience is often described as the culminating experience of the future physical educator's undergraduate preparation. This culminating experience is at times a traumatic one for the student teacher, but it is an invaluable experience because it provides an opportunity for further development of teaching style or drastic modification in it.

Not all the master teachers associated with a particular undergraduate school will state their objectives or design their lesson plans in exactly the same way. There may be many variations, and the student teacher who has begun to develop a student-centered style may find that his or her master teacher ad-

vocates a rigidly teacher-centered style. These stylistic differences can be a source of friction between the student teacher and the master teacher. It is typically the student teacher who adapts teaching style to gain the approval of the master teacher and to ensure a favorable evaluation at the end of the student-teaching experience.

The master teacher has an obligation to the student teacher but an even stronger obligation to the students being taught. Secondary school students are adaptable, and a change in teaching style at the beginning of a new unit will not have a detrimental effect on the students. A change in the middle of a unit could be less than beneficial. It is of no value to the student teacher to follow the example of the master teacher without question. Conferences between the two individuals can open doors to understanding, however, and may result in an enjoyable and worthwhile experience for the master teacher and the student teacher.

Influence of the philosophy of the school system

The beginning teacher may or may not have a well-defined teaching style, depending upon the strength of his undergraduate experience and willingness to express himself or herself as an individual in the teaching situation. The initial weeks of full-fledged teaching give the beginning teacher an opportunity to evaluate further undergraduate and student-teaching experiences.

In a one-teacher department, the beginning teacher will be free to test both teaching styles and to make adaptations, modifications, and compromises. Where there are several teachers in a department, the probationary teacher may be required to adhere to a preferred departmental style. In either case the philosophy of the school system as a whole will give the beginning teacher clues as to how much innovation he or she can attempt.

The beginning teacher may find that he or she is free to innovate and to teach by any style or that it is better to shift teaching style frequently until comfortable with the style and until students react favorably. An experienced teacher, too, will modify and change teaching style from time to time as student needs and interests change.

IDEAL TEACHING STYLE

There is no ideal teaching style. Each physical educator may find that the suitability of a particular teaching style depends on the circumstances and the teaching situation.

Teaching style must be the physical educator's unique expression of his or her role in relation to the role of students. The value system of the students balanced against the value system of the physical educator will help to influence the choice of a teaching style.

Teaching style should be viewed as dynamic rather than static. As student needs change and as the profession of physical education grows, the teaching style should be adapted to keep abreast of this growth and change. Fear of attempting the new and untried impedes the professional growth of the physical educator, but a willingness to be flexible enhances the physical educator as a professional member of a professional field of endeavor.

The kind of teacher a person becomes will depend upon the kind of person he or she is. These two factors cannot be separated because they are so closely interwoven and related. The student-teaching experience, as well as the actual teaching experience that comes later on, should reflect this important concept. The methods and materials used are important. However, it should never be forgotten that the process of teaching is never more important than the person who is doing the teaching. It is not only necessary for the prospective teacher to know about personality theories, it is even more important to know about his or her personality.

Self-assessment tests

The following are to assist students in determining if materials and competencies presented in this chapter have been mastered:

1. Identify and list examples to prove the validity of each of the principles identified by Alexander M. Mood as being important in developing an effective teacher-student relationship conducive to optimum learning.

2. Demonstrate to the class the behavior of a teacher who reflects each of the styles discussed in this chapter.
3. Compare the advantages and disadvantages of a teaching-centered and a student-centered style. Which do you recommend and why?
4. Describe the relationship of general philosophies to teaching style. Provide illustrations to show how each of the several philosophies are reflected in a teacher's style.
5. Assume the role of the teacher of one of your classes to demonstrate what you consider to be a viable teaching style. Have the class evaluate your performance.

Points to remember

1. The teacher should be able to exercise his or her individuality and creativity.
2. The student should be able to exercise his or her individuality and creativity.
3. A physical educator's style of teaching is an expression of himself or herself as an individual.
4. Teaching style is an observable phenomenon.
5. The teacher-centered physical educator is often autocratic.
6. The student-centered physical educator tends to be democratic.
7. The physical educator's philosophy of education influences teaching style.
8. There is no ideal teaching style.

Problems to think through

1. How can methods and materials courses be changed so that they take more cognizance of individual teaching styles?
2. How closely aligned are teaching style and teaching methodology?
3. How can the area of affective learning take place more effectively under the teacher-centered style?
4. How can we objectively evaluate teaching style in terms of student need?
5. How can we justify the teacher- or coach-dominated activity or sport in terms of contributions to student creativity and initiative?
6. How can a physical educator determine whether his or her teaching style is unique?

Case study for analysis

A student teacher finds that his teaching style and that of his master teacher are directly opposite. The student teacher feels that he is obligated to follow the example set by the master teacher, but he wishes to test his own theories, methods, and style of teaching. He hesitates to assert himself because he fears that he may be given a poor evaluation as a result. What steps should he take to resolve his dilemma?

Exercises for review

1. What are the characteristics of the teacher-centered style?
2. What are the characteristics of the student-centered style?

3. Under what circumstances should a physical educator change his teaching style?
4. How do the individual philosophies of education influence teaching style?
5. What factors help to determine the development of a teaching style?
6. Show why it is true that teaching style is dynamic rather than static.

Selected readings

Bruner, J. S.: Toward a theory of instruction, Cambridge, Mass., 1966, Harvard University Press.

Conant, J. B.: The education of American teachers, New York, 1963, McGraw-Hill Book Company.

Gage, N. L.: Can science contribute to the art of teaching? Phi Delta Kappan 49:339, 1968.

Hamachek, D. E.: The self in growth, teaching and learning: selected readings, Englewood Cliffs, N.J., 1965, Prentice-Hall, Inc.

Hamachek, D. E.: Personality styles and teacher behavior, The Educational Forum 36:313, 1972.

Hyman, R. T.: Teaching: triadic and dynamic, The Educational Forum 32:65, 1967.

Joyce, B., et al.: Conceptual development and information processing: a study of teachers, Journal of Educational Research 59:219, 1966.

Kagan, J.: Understanding children; behavior, motives and thought, New York, 1971, Harcourt Brace Jovanovich.

Katz, J. M.: Seniors view their student teaching, Kappa Delta Pi Record 4:75, 1968.

Lemen, M.: Implications of the problem-solving method for physical educators, Journal of Health, Physical Education, and Recreation 37:28, 1966.

Mood, A. M.: How teachers make a difference, Washington, D.C., 1971, U.S. Department of Health, Education and Welfare.

Murphy, P. D., and Brown, M. M.: Conceptual systems and teaching styles, American Educational Research Journal 7:529, 1970.

Shapiro, D.: Neurotic styles, New York, 1965, Basic Books, Inc.

Siedentop, D.: Behavior analysis and teacher training, Quest 18:26, 1972.

Solomon, D.: Teaching styles and learning, Chicago, 1963, The Center for the Study of Liberal Education.

Washburne, C., and Heil, L. M.: What characteristics of teachers affect children's growth? Scholastic Review 68:420, 1960.

Webb, D.: Teacher sensitivity—affective impact on students, Journal of Teacher Education 22:4, 1971.

PART FOUR

Teaching physical education

15

THE TEACHING PROCESS AND LEARNED BEHAVIORS

INSTRUCTIONAL OBJECTIVES AND COMPETENCIES TO BE ACHIEVED

After reading this chapter the student should be able to—

1. Describe two learning theories that provide the underlying foundation of teaching methodology.
2. Identify internal and external conditions found in any instructional setting that may influence the effectiveness of learning activities.
3. Explain the law of readiness and the law of transfer as applied to the teaching of a physical education skill.
4. Compare a variety of teaching methods in terms of student and teacher roles in each.
5. Evaluate a variety of teaching methods in terms of their advantages and disadvantages in an instructional setting.
6. Interpret the nature of the activity, the group, and its goals in relation to selection of appropriate teaching methodology.

In an earlier chapter an extensive analysis of the teacher-centered and student-centered styles of teaching was offered. These teaching styles are sometimes labeled by other authors as the direct versus indirect or the structured versus unstructured approaches to teaching.

The present chapter will be devoted to descriptions of teaching methods, with a detailed analysis of advantages and disadvantages of each. The conditions that influence the teaching process—conditions within the learning environment as well as within the learner—will also be discussed. It is important for the teacher of physical education to recognize the variety of conditions that affect instruction in order to select appropriate teaching methods from the many types presented here. Selection of teaching methodology should also be based on a sound knowledge and understanding of *how* students learn. Inasmuch as theories of learning mark the initial point from which a teacher should start this selection process, these theories will be presented first.

THEORIES OF LEARNING

Psychologists have attempted to explain the phenomenon of learning and to answer such questions as how it best takes place and what the laws are under which it operates. The basic theories of learning, for purposes of discussion, may be said to be divided into two broad categories. The first category may be called the connectionist theories. These theories state that learning consists of a bond or connection between a stimulus and a response or responses. The second category may be called cognitive theories. Those psychologists that support these theories feel that the various perceptions, beliefs, or attitudes (cognitions or mental images) that a human being has concerning his environment determine what type of behavior the human being will have. The manner in which these "cognitions" are modified by the experience that the human being has indicates the learning that takes place. The basic principles underlying the cognitive theories were developed by the Gestalt psychologists.

Thorndike's laws of learning

E. L. Thorndike, a psychologist whose theories of learning have had a great impact on educators and education, believed in a stimulus-response theory, or S-R bond theory. His laws of readiness, exercise, and effect have influenced educational programs.

Thorndike developed these laws that set forth the conditions under which learning best takes place. Because psychology is a relatively new science and because there are many contradictory views as to various psychological principles, laws of learning should not be regarded as the final word. However, they are working principles and, as such, deserve the attention of all physical educators who desire to seek the most efficient and effective ways of teaching.

Law of readiness. The law of readiness means that an individual will learn much more effectively and rapidly if he or she is "ready" and has matured and if there is a felt need. Learning will be satisfying if materials are presented when an individual meets these standards. This law also works in reverse. It will be annoying and dissatisfying to do something when the individual is not ready. The closer an individual is to reaching the point of readiness, the more satisfying the act.

In physical education activities the teacher should determine whether the child is ready in respect to various sensory and kinesthetic mechanisms and in respect to strength in some cases. The teacher should ask such questions as: Does the student have the capacity, at this time, for certain skills? Does he have the proper background of experience? Is the material being presented timely?

Should it be postponed until some future time, or is now the time to present it? Most physical educators agree, for example, that athletic competition on an interscholastic basis should not be part of the program for elementary school children. The child is not mentally, emotionally, and physically ready for such an experience. There is also considerable agreement that fine-muscle activity should not play too pronounced a part in the program for young children. Instead, their program should largely consist of activities that involve the large muscles.

The law of readiness also has implications for the learning of skills. An adult has difficulty hitting a baseball, riding a bicycle, throwing a football, and performing other physical activities if he or she has not developed some skill in these activities during youth. During youth, on the other hand, individuals can perform reasonably well in these skills without too much difficulty. They are at the proper maturation level for the learning of such skills, and their neuromuscular equipment has developed to a point where skills are learned more economically and effectively. They do not mind passing through an awkward trial-and-error period. Physical educators should bear this in mind and set as their goal the development in youth of many interesting and varied skills. In this way students will have the foundational equipment when they reach adulthood to engage in a variety of physical education activities that will provide many enjoyable hours of wholesome recreation.

Law of exercise. The law of exercise, in respect to the development of skills in physical education, means that practice makes for better coordination, more rhythmical movement, less expenditure of energy, more skill, and better performance. As a result of practice, the pathway between stimulus and response becomes more pronounced and permanent.

In many ways this law of learning is similar to the law of use and disuse. As a result of continual practice, strength is gained, but as a result of disuse, weakness ensues.

Learning in physical education is acquired

by doing. To master the skill of bowling, swimming, or handball a person must practice. However, it should be restated that practice does not necessarily ensure perfection of the skill. Mere repetition does not mean greater skill. Practice must be meaningful, with proper attention to all phases of the learning process. The learner, through repetition and a clear conception of what is to be done, steadily makes progress toward the goal he or she is attempting to attain. Repetition, however, should not be blind. It is during the process of "repetition" that learning takes place.

Law of effect. The law of effect maintains that an individual will be more likely to repeat experiences that are satisfying to him than those experiences that are annoying. If experiences are annoying, the learner will shift to other, satisfying responses.

This law of learning, as applied to physical education, means that every attempt should be made to provide situations in which individuals experience success and have a satisfying and enjoyable experience. Leadership is an important factor. Under certain types of leadership undesirable experiences would be satisfying. One coach might approve of hitting an opponent and make this an enjoyable experience. Under other coaches such an act would be an annoying experience because it would be condemned and would not be tolerated. Leadership is the key to good teaching.

Guthrie's contiguity theory

Edwin R. Guthrie* developed the contiguity theory of learning, which emphasizes the stimulus-response association. Contiguity means that a response that is evoked by a stimulus will be repeated whenever that same stimulus recurs. The strengthening of the connection between the stimulus and the response takes place in a single trial. Guthrie believed that since associations can occur with one trial and last forever, there is no need for anything like rewards or motivation to explain learning. However, although Guthrie holds that the full connection is established in one trial, it usually appears to take place gradually. This means that all stimuli cues are not always presented in the same manner, and for this reason many stimulus-response associations must be

*Guthrie, E. R.: The psychology of learning (revised edition), New York, 1952, Harper and Row, Publishers.

Fig. 15-1. Teacher from Hampton Institute, Hampton, Va., conducting physical education class for secondary school students.

made. In every learning situation, for example, there are various combinations of stimuli that are presented and the correct responses need to be established for each situation. Guthrie holds that repetition and practice are essential in learning in order for the individual to become aware of the stimuli that will evoke the correct response.

In physical education we can apply Guthrie's theory to the learning of a skill such as the high jump. If a youngster desires to be proficient in this skill, he or she must make sure that bodily movements are always the same each time he or she approaches the bar. The individual must be aware of all the surrounding stimuli such as the runway and position of the bar. The proficient high jumper will be one who has established a successful movement pattern and one who does not deviate from it. Even the slightest change in stimuli can evoke an incorrect response. The youngster who becomes distracted by the noise of the spectators finds it difficult to clear the bar if accustomed to practicing in complete silence. According to Guthrie's theory, this youngster should practice under conditions faced during actual competition, for to achieve optimal performance the competitor must be aware of all the stimuli that are present at the time of competition.

Hull's reinforcement theory

Clark L. Hull* sees learning as a direct influence of reinforcement. He has established his theory on the influence of need and its reduction as the prime elements in learning. In his theory Hull emphasizes that learning occurs when the individual adapts to the environment and that such adaptation is necessary for survival. When needs arise the individual's survival is threatened, and the individual must act in a certain manner to reduce the need. The responses that the individual makes that lead to the reduction of the need are reinforced, resulting in habits or learning. According to Hull's theory, a stimulus causes a response that results in a

---

*Hull, C. L.: Principles of behavior, New York, 1943, Appleton-Century-Crofts.

need. The need evokes a response on the part of the individual, which reduces the need. The response that resulted in the reduction of the need is then reinforced, which develops habits or learning. Hull employed drive and primary reinforcement in his early work. Later he used ideas such as drive stimulus reduction and secondary reinforcement.

Hull's theory emphasizes that habits or learning result from reactions set into motion by needs. In physical education the teacher plays an important part in satisfying the needs of the student. Teachers who explain the psychological and sociological bases for participating in an activity may stimulate students to a larger degree than those who present the activity without any rationale. To elicit correct responses from students, the teacher presents material that is meaningful, and therefore lesson plans consist of material important to the learner.

In Hull's theory the child learns by doing —drive reduction is a doing phenomenon. In physical education the child arrives at the solution to many problems through his or her own efforts. For example, the student practices the "kip" on the low bar and after many attempts becomes aware of not achieving success because of the position of the arms or other weakness. Upon discovering the correct position, the student repeats it over and over to reinforce it. The result is the correct movement on the low bar. The habit is learned. Further repetition of the activity with the correct response leads to a feeling of satisfaction on the part of the student, for the need is no longer a problem.

One of the major implications of Hull's theory to physical education is his finding that practice periods that are extremely long or lacking in reinforcement inhibit learning. An example of this is the pole vaulter who practices hour after hour. After a long period of practice without any reinforcement, he finds it difficult to clear his usual height. However, Hull states that the inhibitions decrease after rest periods, and the next day the vaulter can again clear his accustomed height. Thus practice periods play an important role in determining the performance of an individual.

Skinner's operate conditioning theory

The main feature of B. F. Skinner's* operant conditioning theory is the fact that the stimulus that reinforces the responses does not precede it but follows it. In operant conditioning, behavior is elicited by the individual rather than the stimuli. In this theory of learning the individual organism first makes the desired response and then is rewarded. Reinforcement is contingent on the desired response. Skinner's main emphasis is that the individual repeats at a future time the behavior that has been previously reinforced. Behaviors that are not reinforced are not usually repeated. When the individual is rewarded, he elicits that behavior again. Extinction occurs when the behavior is no longer reinforced.

Skinner makes the point that since teachers cannot always wait for behavior to manifest itself, they must sometimes shape the behavior of the individual. In teaching any physical skill it is recognized that reinforcement is extremely valuable. For example, the teacher who desires that a student learn how to make the jump shot encourages the student to learn the proper form. When the student is shooting at the peak of the jump, in the correct manner, the teacher indicates approval to the student. The student becomes aware of the proper form and continues to use it, knowing that the skill is being properly performed according to the teacher's standard.

Skinner has placed great emphasis on the use of audiovisual aids and teaching machines because of their reinforcement value. Since the teacher cannot reinforce the behavior of all children in a class, such machines may be useful, although some psychologists believe that they may interfere with the organization of materials into structural wholes. Through the use of such new innovations as the videotape replay, students see themselves in action and discover their deficiencies. Such de-

vices prove beneficial in reinforcing learning in large classes where the teacher cannot cope with all the individual problems that arise.

Gestalt theory

The Gestalt psychologists such as Max Wertheimer, Kurt Koffka, Wolfgang Kohler, and Kurt Lewin are greatly concerned with form and shapes. Gestalt theory is more concerned with perception than learning. One of the most important Gestalt principles having implications for physical education is the whole method theory. This theory is based on the premise that a person reacts as a whole to any situation. The whole individual attempts to achieve a goal. Furthermore, the greater the insight or understanding an individual has concerning the goal to be attained, such as paddling a canoe or guiding a bowling ball to a strike, the greater will be the degree of skill in that activity. An individual reacts differently each time he or she performs a physical act. Therefore it is not just a question of practice, as it would be if performed the same way each time. Instead, the more insight a student has of the complete act, the greater his or her skill. The individual performs the whole act and does it until gaining an insight into the situation or until getting the "feel" or the "hang" of it. Since insight is so important, dependent conditions such as a person's capacity, previous experience, and experimental setup are very important considerations.

Psychoanalytic theory of learning

Psychoanalysis is genetic as well as dynamic theory. Learning is related to the psychosocial stages of development and must take into account that it is affected by unconscious forces and in certain cases leads to repression, fixation, and regression. All these unconscious forces are involved in a psychoanalytic theory of learning. Freud's theory stressed the importance of cognitive control in the development of a rational ego.

Information processing theories

More recently educational psychologists have been investigating the relationship of

---

*Skinner, B. F.: The behavior of organisms, New York, 1938, Appleton-Century-Crofts.

central nervous system processes to learning itself. Two groups of information processing theorists have been looking at neurophysiologic and neurochemical functioning in the brain, giving particular attention to the feedback mechanisms involved from that center.

Of particular interest to physical educators is the work of another group of these investigators, the cyberneticists, whose theory on feedback mechanisms relates specifically to motor learning. According to the cybernetic theory, a motor response is the result of a three-phase process: (1) sensory input, (2) information processing through the central nervous system wherein selective attention to appropriate stimuli is rendered and then followed by (3) motor responses. Included in this process is kinesthetic feedback from the proprioceptors, (sensitive nerve endings in muscle fibers), which together with a knowledge of results from previous experiences combine to produce improved motor performances.

There is a critical need in our profession for further research in this area of motor learning and the conditions and factors that influence it. Because acquisition of motor skills is a primary objective throughout physical education activities, it is essential that teachers continue to further their understanding of motor learning concepts. Although many gaps in knowledge still exist, the following material and answers to critical questions may be helpful for development of motor skills in the classroom.

MOTOR LEARNING

The term "motor learning" is generally used in reference to the improvement of a motor performance or the development of a skill. For example, when, through practice, a golfer improves putting skill, an archer improves aim, or a pitcher improves delivery, motor learning has taken place.

Movement is a fundamental aspect of human behavior, and skills may be categorized in several different ways. Two frequently used categories of skills are types of action and function.

Motor skills, as they relate to types of ac-

tion, may be divided into fine versus gross motor skills or into sensory versus perceptual motor skills.

Fine motor skills are those requiring manual dexterity, such as typing, whereas *gross motor skills* involve large muscle activity, as in running.

Sensory motor skills are those that develop as a result of the sensory cues (feeling, tasting, hearing, seeing, and smelling). Serving a volleyball would involve a sensory cue, for example. *Perceptual motor skills* are developed whenever the perceptual process is involved (judgments concerning speed, depth, and background information). In archery, both types of skill are involved, because cues of feeling and seeing are used, as well as judgments concerning distance and point of aim.

Motor skills may also be categorized according to their function in human existence. Although some motor skills are essential for normal existence (walking, self-care), others may be classified in terms of their self-improvement or educational values (reading, writing), and others are recreational in nature. Physical education skills would be classified generally in this latter division.

How does a student learn a motor skill? Is motor skill ability inherited or acquired? Is it transferable from one type of activity to another? Researchers are beginning to find answers to some of these questions.

Process of motor learning

Motor learning involves the establishment of pathways within the complex neuromuscular system of the human body. The very simplest human movement, such as clapping the hands, involves a pathway that may be divided into three distinct parts: the sensory, the connecting, and the motor neurons. These neurons form a neural pathway to bring about muscular innervation, making the hands come together. Neuromuscular skills are merely different sets of pathways that have been established through practice. The following questions immediately come to mind concerning the development of skill.

- *Are all skills acquired, or are some move-*

ments inherited? Some movements may be categorized as inherited. For example, under normal circumstances, individuals walk, and they perform "swimming" movements in the water. Refinements of these motions can be acquired. Examples include hopping, skipping, and stroking in the water. Other inherited movements include those reflexes that are automatic and involuntary by nature, such as the knee jerk, eye wink, and breathing.

• *Once learned, are motor skills always remembered?* Retention of motor skills is dependent on many factors. Those skills that are easily acquired, are natural, are used frequently, or are "overlearned" usually remain with an individual for a long period of time. For example, riding a bicycle, swimming, skating, and throwing are rarely forgotten. The degree of perfection in performance may vary, but usually a well-refined skill may be reacquired in a relatively short period of time.

• *How much should a skill be practiced?* The amount of practice necessary to learn a skill depends on the individual's quickness in acquiring the skill, and the degree of perfection desired. It has been found helpful to practice a motor skill in a series of a few attempts, followed by rest, and then to return to a series again. By distributing practice and rest intervals, neural pathways may be developed and stabilized.

• *What about injuries?* In injuries where muscle tissue has been damaged, usually rest will allow a return to normal functioning. In instances where nerve endings are damaged, new neural pathways may need to be established, and relearning may take a little longer.

Principles and conditions that assist in the learning of motor skills*

Some of the major factors and conditions that promote the learning of motor skills are as follows:

• *Perception is important in motor learn-*

*Adapted in part from material in Bucher, C. A.: Foundations of physical education, ed. 7, St. Louis, 1975, The C. V. Mosby Co.

ing. Perception refers to the process of receiving and distinguishing among the available stimuli presented in any situation. It is essential in motor skill learning for an individual to perceive speed, distance, and shapes of objects. Deficiencies in any of these areas make the learning of motor skills more difficult. Various communication devices and techniques assist the learner in acquiring motor skills. Motion pictures, live demonstrations, knowledge of mechanical principles, and a realization and clear understanding of what is expected of the learner in performing a skill will be of particular value to beginners.

• *Effective motor learning is based on prerequisite factors.* Such factors are strength, dynamic energy, ability to change direction, flexibility, agility, peripheral vision, visual acuity, concentration, an understanding of the mechanics of the activity, and an absence of inhibitory factors are essential to motor learning.

• *Skills should not be taught unless students have reached a level of development commensurate with the degree of difficulty of the skill.* Maturation is growth that takes place without any special training, stimulus, or practice—it just happens. It is closely associated with the physiologic development of all individuals. Therefore the material must be adapted to individual maturation levels.

• *Each individual is different.* Teachers must be aware of the fact that individuals are different from one another and that these differences must be recognized if learning is to occur.

• *The learning curve is a consideration in motor learning.* Learning curves are not always constant, and they are different for each individual. The learning curve depends on the person, the material being learned, and the conditions surrounding the learning. Learning may start out with an initial spurt and then be followed by a period in which progress is not so rapid, or there may be no progress at all.

• *Learning takes place most effectively when the student has a motive for wanting to learn.* Motivation is an inducement to action.

Fig. 15-2. Physical education class in lacrosse at Wheaton High School in Wheaton, Md.

Usually the greater the motivation, the more rapid the learning. Motives should be of the intrinsic rather than the extraneous type. Rewards, awards, and marks should not be a means of motivating activity. The worth of the activity in itself should be the motive.

• *Learning takes place much more effectively when the student intends to learn.* If a boy makes up his mind that he intends to learn a certain skill, if he arrives at the point where he sees a need for the skill, he is much more open to learning.

• *The student should know the goals toward which he or she is working.* Learning progresses much faster when goals are clear. The student should have a clear picture of what constitutes a successful performance. For example, if high jumping is being taught, the proper form and technique should be clearly demonstrated and discussed.

• *The student should receive feedback that indicates the progress being made.* There are basically two kinds of feedback available to the student during the performance of a motor skill. Internal feedback is related to the concept of *kinesthesis*, whereas external feedback is related to the concept known as *knowledge of results*. Kinesthesis is associated with the feeling of the movement and has been recognized as being a conscious

muscle sense. External feedback or knowledge of results is also extremely valuable to the student during and after the completion of a motor skill. Knowledge that one is progressing toward a set goal is encouraging and promotes a better learning situation.

• *Progress will be much more rapid when the learner gains satisfaction from the learning situation.* Satisfaction is associated with success. As the learner is successful in mastering a particular physical skill, the desire to learn increases.

• *The length and distribution of practice periods are important considerations for effective learning. Massed practice* refers to long and continuous practice periods, whereas *distributed practice* refers to practice periods interrupted by rest intervals. There is some agreement that practice periods are most profitable when they are short and spaced over a period of time. The number of repetitions, such as shots at the basket or serves in tennis, should be considered as the unit of practice rather than the total number of minutes spent in the practice session.

According to some psychologists, when subject matter is very interesting and meaningful to the learner, practice periods may be made longer. Therefore it seems the length and spacing of periods should be adjusted to the class and material being learned.

• *As a general rule, learning is more effective when skills are taught as whole skills and not in parts.* In physical education it seems that the whole method should be followed when the material to be taught is a functional and integrated whole. This means that in swimming, which is a functional whole, the total act of swimming is taught. You learn to swim by using your arms and legs, and this can be taught as a whole. However, research indicates that complex skills should be broken down into their basic parts. In a complex sport such as football the game consists of blocking, broken-field running, tackling, passing, punting, and the like. In such a complex sport each of these skills represents a part of the whole that is football. However, they represent a functional and integrated whole by themselves and, as such, should be taught separately.

• *Overlearning has value in the acquisition of motor skills.* The initial practice in the learning of a motor skill is important in determining how long the skill remains in the possession of the learner. A partially learned skill does not remain in possession of the learner as long as one that is overlearned, that is, practiced until it establishes a pattern in the nervous system. If a skill is mastered and there is continual practice of the accomplishment, considerable time elapses before such a skill is lost to the learner.

• *Speed rather than accuracy should be emphasized in the initial stages of motor skill learning.* Physical educators are often required to make a judgment as to whether speed or accuracy should be emphasized in the initial stages of skill learning. Although some psychologists maintain that speed may lead in some cases to blindness in thinking, other researchers emphasize the speed factor. It would be desirable to be able to emphasize both speed and accuracy; however, this is not always possible. In physical education many skills are carried on primarily by momentum, and according to some research, speed should be emphasized in the initial stages of such learning. At this stage an em-

phasis on accuracy interferes with the development of momentum needed to carry on the movement. In teaching golf and tennis skills that require momentum to be performed successfully, it is important to emphasize speed in the early stages of learning.

• *Transfer of training can facilitate the learning of motor skills.* Transfer of training is based on the premise that a skill learned in one situation can be used in another situation. For example, the student who knows how to play tennis takes readily to badminton because both skills require similar strokes and the use of a racquet. Most psychologists agree that positive transfer most likely occurs when two tasks have similar part-whole relations involved.

Physical educators must be aware of the concept known as *negative transfer*. Negative transfer occurs when one task interferes with the learning of a second task. For example, a young man being introduced to the game of golf for the first time experiences difficulty in swinging the club, because of his previous experience in another skill such as baseball. Perhaps you have heard the expression: "You're swinging the golf club like a baseball bat."

• *Mental practice can enhance the learning of motor skills.* Mental practice is the symbolic rehearsal of a skill with the absence of gross muscular movements. The physical educator should be concerned with the role of mental practice in skill learning. Research seems to indicate that although physical practice is superior to mental practice, mental practice is better than no practice at all. A combination of physical and mental practice is best.

• *A knowledge of mechanical principles increases the student's total understanding of the activity in which he or she is participating.* A knowledge of mechanical principles that involve levers, laws of motion, gravity, and other factors are closely related to skill performance. Physical educators should be able to give their students sound rationale for the skills they are performing based upon a knowledge of basic mechanical principles.

• *Implementation of the principle of rein-*

forcement will enhance learning. One of the most fundamental laws of learning is reinforcement. In essence it means that the behavior most likely to emerge in any one given situation is one that is reinforced or found successful in a previous, similar situation. Therefore the best-planned learning situation will provide for an accumulation of successes. The reinforcement (reward) should follow the desired behavior almost immediately and should be associated with the behavior in order to be most effective.

• *Errors should be eliminated early in the learning period.* When instructing in such skills as field hockey and softball, the physical education teacher should attempt to eliminate incorrect performance as early as possible so that errors do not become a fixed part of the participant's performance. Inefficient methods, once learned, are difficult to correct.

• *The learning situation should be such that optimum conditions are present for efficient learning.* This means that distracting elements have been eliminated from the setting, the proper mental set has been established in the mind of the student, the proper equipment and facilities are available, the learner has the proper background to understand and appreciate the material that is to be presented, and the conditions are such that a challenging teaching situation is present.

• *A learning situation is greatly improved if the student diagnoses his or her own movements and arrives at definite conclusions as to what errors he or she is committing.* Self-criticism is much more conducive to good learning than teacher criticism. If the student discovers mistakes, they are corrected much more readily than if they are discovered by someone else. A masterful teacher will develop teaching situations in which the student is led to self-criticism. This is a sign of good teaching.

Implications of research for teaching motor skills

The application of scientific research findings to program planning and the teaching of physical education activities is important.

There is a gap between what is known and what is applied to teaching motor skills. Bell* has listed the results of some research and applied it to the teaching of selected physical education activities. A sampling of Bell's work is presented here in adapted form to show the implications of some research for the teaching of motor skills:

• *Archery:* Four days per week of massed practice was shown to be better than two days of distributed practice.
• *Badminton:* During the early stages of learning thirty minutes a day of distributed practice was found to be better than sixty minutes of massed practice per day, twice a week.
• *Basketball:* Learning the foul shot improved as a result of mental practice in basketball.
• *Baseball:* Knowledge of results helped to improve speed and accuracy in the baseball throw.
• *Bowling:* Demonstration via the motion picture was of help if the learners had already had some practice.
• *Football:* Mental practice in the football pass by reading an instruction sheet improved performance.
• *Golf:* The whole method of practice (total swing) was superior to the part method.
• *Gymnastics:* Videotape replay resulted in better performance.
• *Softball:* Instruction in mechanical principles utilized in softball enhanced performance.
• *Swimming:* The whole method of teaching was found to be superior to the part method.
• *Tennis:* The best results were achieved where emphasis on speed and accuracy was the same.
• *Tumbling:* No difference was found in the performance of two groups, one of which utilized motion pictures while the other did not.
• *Volleyball:* A knowledge of mechanical principles assisted in the performance of volleyball skills.

*Bell, V. L.: Sensorimotor learning, Pacific Palisades, Calif., 1970, Goodyear Publishing Company, Inc.

CONDITIONS FOR LEARNING

Knowledge of how students learn, and how they acquire motor skills provides the background for all methods of teaching. But an understanding of those conditions favorable to the learning process is also needed to ensure success with selected methodology. Conditions that influence learning experiences are internal and external to the instructional setting. Internally the student contributes hereditary influences and an individualistic learning style, whereas the home and school community provide influences of an external nature.

Heredity

Nature versus nurture as a contributing factor in personality development has long fascinated educators and psychologists. They are especially interested in the extent to which the genetic makeup of an individual affects the outcome of his or her developmental nature. Present-day knowledge has reached the point where science feels that genetic makeup will someday be able to be altered so that individuals can be produced who have desired, predetermined characteristics. In their studies of the makeup of intelligence, psychologists are finding that it may be possible to control portions of the intellect through the administration of such agents as ribonucleic acid. The significance of these discoveries holds many implications for education and physical education. Teachers need to remain up to date on discoveries and advances in these vital areas. Teachers need to know how these changes will affect the classrooms of the future and the physical abilities of the students of the future.

Home environment

Community and governmental agencies have long been striving to improve the environmental factors that serve as strong educational forces. Better homes, better jobs, better wages, and improved working conditions have been denied large segments of the population. In the typical middle-class home, books and conversation are a part of life and a way of life. In the homes of the disadvantaged, books are a rarity, and the home can be of little aid in preparing the child for school and an education. A few significant advances have been made in respect to the disadvantaged. Project Head Start, for example, was believed to be a help in preparing preschoolers for their first formal educational experience by offering the childhood experiences that are lacking in the home. Improved living conditions for the lower socioeconomic groups may someday make these homes vital contributors to the educational process. Teachers need to realize that not all students come from homes in which education is a potent force and that not all students are prepared for the challenge of school.

School environment

As time goes on, computerized education may bring about many changes in the structure of the school. Through computers, a student may be able to obtain references from sources across the country or retrieve information in a short period of time rather than spend hours of research in a variety of books and reference materials. The teacher may become more of a guide through the machine-controlled process, giving the praise, encouragement, and personal help that the machine cannot give. Some of these changes have already come about in school systems, but until computers are utilized on a national scale, the school will still depend on the teacher's training and abilities. In spite of the move toward computers, the teacher will still be the center of the educational process, for it is the teacher who must decide what the machine can do for each student, and it is the teacher who must evaluate what the machine is doing for the student. It is also the teacher who provides the human factor upon which good teaching and learning will always depend.

The school must ask itself what vital conditions and characteristics of a learning situation most influence a student during the developmental years. By knowing these determinants the school can adjust and adapt to future educational developments in every curricular area. By knowing the determinants of learning, the school will better be able to meet its responsibilities to its students.

If the teaching process is to be enhanced, several environmental factors need careful consideration. Each factor stems from basic individual needs and may be categorized according to four major areas of concern:

1. Physical needs
   a. Heat. Temperatures should be maintained within a comfortable range so that students do not become drowsy from too much heat or overstimulated from too much cold.
   b. Light. Proper lighting in all classroom areas protects and aids students' vision.
   c. Ventilation. Proper circulation of fresh air is important to the health and comfort of everyone in the classroom.
   d. Equipment. Equipment should be in safe condition, adequate to the number of students in the class, and of the proper size and weight for the particular age level.
   e. Facilities. Adequate and safe facilities are a necessity for proper conduct of classes.
2. Emotional needs. A positive approach should be maintained in the handling of students and their problems. The National Association for Mental Health lists several factors essential to good mental health that have significance in the school situation:
   a. Acceptance. Students should feel accepted as persons of worth by teachers and peers.
   b. Security. Students should know what is expected of them as persons and students.
   c. Protection. Students should not be made to feel that peers or teachers have marked them as failures or potential failures.
   d. Control. Students should understand and abide by proper standards of good conduct and courteous behavior.
   e. Independence. Students should feel freedom to express themselves as individuals as long as they do not impinge on the rights of others.
   f. Guidance. The student's efforts and successes need to be constructively criticized, praised, and recognized.
3. Social needs. Democratic group processes recognize both the larger group and the individual within the group.
   a. Cooperation. Through cooperative efforts with peers the students should feel they are making individual contributions to the larger group.
   b. Competition. Through controlled competition with peers the student should feel gratification in success, experience the adventure of competing, gain pride in accomplishment, and know the satisfaction that comes from wholehearted effort.
   c. Grouping. Through grouping techniques students should be placed in groups where they will feel most comfortable and where they will be encouraged to work to their capacity.
   d. Rapport. Good teacher-student relationships help the students to feel that they are respected as individuals.
4. Intellectual needs. Not all students' intellectual needs can be met in the same way, and not all students function best in a single kind of learning situation. Some students learn best in a democratic environment where they are encouraged to be creative through a problem-solving approach. These students have the maturity to be able to conceptualize knowledge and come to their own conclusions through personal discovery. Other students function best in a rather rigidly teacher-dominated situation because they are not as yet ready to help guide their own learning. A single classroom may contain either type of student, or students who alternate between the two systems, depending on the material to be learned. Only through a comprehensive knowledge of each student can the teacher determine how each individual learns best and adapt the teaching methods as the need dictates.

Creation of a favorable environment

The preceding discussion outlines the basic factors necessary for the creation of an environment in which learning may take place. Yet each of these components must be combined so that an effective teaching-learning atmosphere is created. If, for example, each factor is present save one, the atmosphere will not be as conducive to the educational process as it might be. An overheated gymnasium, a poorly ventilated locker room, or a teacher who concentrates only on the students with high motor skill ability will each have a negative effect on the teaching-learning atmosphere. The physical needs, such as heating, lighting, and ventilation, are often only minor problems that can be corrected at once if difficulties arise. However, the social, emotional, and intellectual needs of the students need much more care and attention. The complexity of these needs and their interdependencies demand far greater consideration from the teacher and far more time and effort. Meeting these needs usually is possible only through the establishment of effective teacher-pupil relationships. Unless the teacher is willing to become sincerely involved with students, effective learning cannot take place, no matter how ideal the physical environment may be. This genuine involvement with the student sets the teacher apart from the teaching machine and gains for him or her professional respect. Good teacher-student relationships provide one of the most vital keys to successful teaching and learning. This particular relationship is probably most noticeable in the physical education classroom or on the athletic field, where the physical educator is not only a teacher of skills but a counselor of students as well.

Learning styles

Learning does not take place simply because the proper atmosphere exists or because the physical tools for learning, such as books, pencils, or athletic equipment, are available. In order for learning to take place, there must first of all be an individual who is motivated to learn, incentives that will increase the motivation, challenges that make reaching the learning goal an adventure, and continued effort on the part of the individual to overcome the challenges and arrive at the goal.

Although all individuals are capable of learning, not all individuals learn at the same rate or in the same manner. Not all learners can be reached by a common methodology or teaching style. Many different kinds of learning styles have been identified, and learners tend to use each of these styles in varying degrees, depending on the material or concepts to be learned. Some learners are completely verbally oriented, for example, while other learners succeed best when the problem-solving technique is used. Memorization, concept formation, and trial-and-error learning are other examples of learning styles.

The incentives offered for learning are vital to the educational process because they enhance motivation. Grades for achievement, placement in a higher ability group, and teacher praise and recognition are forms of incentives that are commonly used in education.

The challenges presented to the learner also help to increase the individual's motivation to solve a learning problem. If a learning task is too easy and the goal is reached without much effort on the part of the learner,

very little real learning can take place. As the individual overcomes a variety of challenges that are set in his or her path and draws closer to a goal, he or she learns—that is, each individual's success in overcoming a challenge is a true learning experience. However, no challenge should be so difficult that eventual goal attainment is made an impossibility.

To learn and retain what has been learned, the individual must put forth a continued effort in order to overcome the challenges in his or her path and in order to arrive at a goal. A learner may experience failure in the first attempts at learning, but continued efforts will bring a successful response in a given situation. As the learner continues to put forth effort, he or she will continue to make more and more successful responses that lead to goal attainment.

METHODS OF TEACHING
Factors affecting method selection

The proper selection of an appropriate teaching method involves consideration of several factors. Although class size, equipment, and facilities merit some thought, these factors are more often considered in connection with organization of the class. Methods of teaching are determined by the nature of the activity itself, the particular purposes or goals to be achieved, and the age level and ability of the group.

Nature of the activity. The wide variety of activities included in a well-rounded physical education program necessitates utilization of different teaching methods, depending upon the nature or type of activity. Teaching an individual stunt such as a handspring requires a personal approach to improve an individual's performance, whereas teaching offensive team tactics requires total group knowledge. Therefore the selection of a method must take into account the nature of the activity.

Nature of the group goals. The nature of the group goals is an extremely important element to be considered in teaching methods. What do the students themselves expect to learn and achieve in a particular unit of work? In basketball, for example, they all want to play the game and to improve their skills only through playing. The creative teacher needs to develop exciting drills for skill practice, thus improving abilities of the individuals and upgrading game play while maintaining class enthusiasm.

Frequently the teacher needs to determine student objectives and goals for classwork. Providing an opportunity to hear students express their interests and desires will often bring out special individual hopes. Some girls may want to lose weight, and boys may want to improve game skill. Meeting these individual goals, revealed through democratic group processes, makes physical education a more meaningful experience for all.

Nature of the group. It is important to keep in mind the characteristics and interests of the students in the class. The differences between boys and girls, their physical abilities, their interests, and their attitudes all need consideration if teaching methods are to be appropriate. For example, on the junior high level, a variety of methods should be utilized to appeal to the students' widespread interests. Whereas a lengthy lecture would serve only to bore these younger students, it might be appreciated as a time-saver by older adolescents. The ability level of the students also needs clarification when methods are selected. Advanced students move rapidly through introductory and review sessions in a unit and should move on quickly into the advanced skills presentations.

Ways of presenting material

The theories of learning discussed previously provide the basis for all instructional methods. Recognizable within the several methods of teaching to be discussed in this chapter will be laws of readiness, laws of transfer, motor learning principles, and so on. No single method of teaching will be declared the best method of teaching physical education. Instead, the teacher will need to bring to each individual teaching situation a knowledge of growth and development, hereditary and environment, and theories of learning, and combine it with the best methods available under the given circumstances. Judgment and experience bring quality instruction to the teaching process.

The following descriptions of teaching methods include several factors that may be

Fig. 15-3. There are several different methods of teaching and presenting material in physical education. Class of students being taught by a teacher at Hampton Institute, Hampton, Va.

helpful to students and teachers in planning daily classes of physical education. The role of the teacher and the role of the student are pinpointed, and teaching style is identified as teacher-centered or student-centered. Important advantages and disadvantages are also listed with each method, followed by a question that is worthy of consideration.

First, however, two essential principles of teaching should be stressed as an introduction to methodology. The teacher of physical education should remember that instruction should progress from the known to the unknown with every class meeting. Whichever method of teaching is finally selected for presentation of material, the introductory activities should include a review of previous learnings to ensure progress.

A second principle involves the whole-part-whole organization of teaching materials. It has been found that learning may be more effective if students know or at least have an acquaintance with the total activity being studied. For example, when learning an individual or team sport for the first time, an introduction of the entire game on the opening day of the unit would provide an intellectual framework or background of concepts from which the student may be led towards learning of the component parts. In the same way, viewing a folk or square dance in its entirety gives students a mental image of how the various steps and patterns combine to create the whole dance. Thereafter, working on the steps or parts of the dance puts sense or orderliness into the practice. This whole-part-whole concept in teaching and the idea of going from what is known towards the unknown are basic principles underlying the teaching process. Once the appropriate material has been selected, providing for sequential, progressive programming by these principles, a method of teaching can be selected from those described below.

Lecture

• *Purpose.* To present information, usually cognitive in nature, such as facts (rules, history, etiquette) or concepts (physical laws, physiologic effects of exercise). It is also used to discuss the application, analysis, synthesis or evaluation of ideas and concepts.

• *Role of the teacher.* Speaker.

• *Role of the student.* Listener.

• *Style.* Teacher-centered.

• *Description.* A lecture is a verbal presentation of a body of knowledge. The material should be well-organized, and the mode of delivery clear and interesting. The speaker should be in clear view of all students, and the students should be comfortably seated within range of the speaker's voice or audio system.

• *Advantages*

1. A great deal of information may be presented to a very large audience in a single presentation, making very efficient use of time available.

2. The cognitive content of lecture later provides materials for evaluation purposes.

• *Disadvantages*

1. No interaction is allowed between students and teacher during lecture.

2. Students may not all be able to receive the information or assimilate the materials presented to the same degree.

• *Question for consideration.* Could the same amount of information be presented to the students as effectively through some other method of teaching? If so, which one(s)?

Verbal explanation

• *Purpose.* To explain the nature of a single concept or to analyze a single skill having immediate relevancy to activity of the class period.

• *Role of the teacher.* Explainer.

• *Role of the student.* Listener.

• *Style.* Teacher-oriented.

• *Description.* Verbal explanation provides information on a single problem or topic. It is similar to a lecture, but briefer, and addresses a particular point related to the day's activity. As with a lecture, the teacher should speak clearly and concisely to the point from a position in view of all students. Students may be gathered informally around the teacher.

• *Advantages*

1. May be used in the middle of a game or drill to make additions or corrections during skill learning, to promote more acceptable social behaviors, or to provide additional essential cognitive information.

2. May be initiated by the teacher or stem from questions or problems developing during the course of activity.

• *Disadvantages*

1. All students may not need the verbal explanation, yet may have their activity interrupted.

2. Time may be lost from activity.

• *Question for consideration.* Could the students acquire the same knowledge, information or ideas, or find solutions to their problems through some other method that does not cut down on activity?

Demonstration

• *Purpose.* To present information through the visual channel by presenting psychomotor examples of activity. Auditory stimuli may also be involved.

• *Role of the teacher.* Demonstrator, planner, or commentator.

• *Role of the student.* Receiver or listener.

• *Style.* Teacher-centered.

• *Description.* A demonstration is one of several types of audiovisual methods of presentation frequently used in physical education. The psychomotor skills and activities are performed by a single individual, by a group, or by a team while the remaining class members view the presentation. A verbal analysis may accompany the demonstration or be given immediately afterwards, as in the case of diving or gymnastics, where quiet is necessary for the performer.

When presenting a demonstration certain important factors should be kept in mind: (1) The demonstration should be well planned so that all important points are firmly fixed in the teacher's mind; (2) the demonstration should be organized so that all students are able to see and hear well. If student assistants are used, they should know the purposes and procedures necessary to show effectively the particular skill or activity

under study; (3) all necessary material and equipment should be on hand so that no time is wasted once the demonstration is begun. Safety concepts should be highlighted, and relevant information stressed; (4) helpful pointers for proper performance of the skill should be given. The skill should be analyzed or game broken down into its component parts and then shown in its entirety. Emphasis should be on correct methodology, not incorrect performance. Viewers should be involved in the demonstration through mimicry, whenever possible.

• *Advantages*

1. Demonstrations provide input from visual as well as audio stimuli. Inasmuch as 80 percent of all learning is said to be achieved through the visual sense, this is a most effective means of presenting information.

2. A demonstration provides a model of performance or activity that the student may then imitate.

Fig. 15-4. A demonstration in scuba diving is given to a physical education class in Homewood High School, Homewood, Ala.

3. When a student or group of students is selected to provide a demonstration, the self-concepts of the performers may be enhanced. Modeling by the teacher enhances his or her image in the eyes of the class.

4. A demonstration may provide strong motivation to some students.

• *Disadvantages*

1. Organization of a large group within view of a single performer may sometimes be difficult because of the physical arrangements of the learning area.

2. When a student or group of students is selected to perform there is always a chance of error in the presentation or of unsuitable or inappropriate behaviors occurring.

3. Those students who feel themselves incapable of imitating the model may be discouraged rather than encouraged.

• *Question for consideration.* Does the demonstration stifle the creation of original psychomotor responses? If so, when would demonstrations be inappropriate as a method of teaching?

Practice-drill (combined with reinforcement feedback)

• *Purpose.* To provide for the acquisition and improvement of skills that are essential components of games and activities.

• *Role of the teacher.* Drill designer.

• *Role of the student.* Executioner, practitioner.

• *Style.* Teacher-centered.

• *Description.* Practice-drill is a method of developing skills for physical education games and activities. Earlier in this chapter principles and conditions for motor learning were discussed. Drills are one method of teaching that promotes skill acquisition, provided that the drills themselves are properly constructed and effectively organized. Drills in physical education can be as dull as memorizing a multiplication table, or they can be nearly as much fun as the game from which they are derived. For real learning to take place they should be as interesting as possible, and this of course requires planning on the part of the teacher. The following principles

are important when planning drill formations:

1. Drills should be an outgrowth of the game situation. This gives meaning to the drill. The students are not asked merely to kick a ball, for example, but are instructed to kick the soccer ball through the goal posts for a score.

2. Drills should allow maximum participation for all class members. A student has the opportunity to practice more frequently if the class is divided into many units, each of which is composed of a small number of students. For a teacher to make as many practice units as possible, all available equipment must be put to use. These two factors (the size of the class and the available equipment) must be considered when planning drills.

3. Drills should be interesting and fun. Adding the competitive element to a drill formation or scoring points for adapted techniques makes the drill much more fun while the student is trying to learn a skill.

4. Drills should allow for individual instruction and total supervision. In setting up drill formations the teacher must remember his or her responsibility for the entire group and must therefore be able to supervise all working areas. At the same time, individual instruction should be given to students needing special help. Thus, in both instances proximity to the groups is essential.

5. Drills should be varied frequently to prevent boredom or loss of interest. Changing drill formations—for example, from the shuttle type to the circle—can be stimulating, which is necessary, particularly with junior high school students. However, every change must be planned so that time is not wasted unnecessarily in going from one line-up to another. For example, if groups are in four equal lines, it would be very difficult to set up three circles and wasteful to follow this change by going back to four units again. Groups should remain fairly constant, and formations should change smoothly from one to another.

6. Drills should not take the whole class period. Classes will lose interest in the per-

fection of skills if no opportunity to test them in the appropriate game situation is allowed.

7. Drills should progress from the simple to the more difficult. Drills should start with simple formations—either review old skills or practice new ones in simple form. When formations and patterns are changed, the skills should be made increasingly difficult or combined with other skills to maintain interest and utmost effort in participation.

The necessity of drills in teaching physical education is great, but for them to be most effectively used, they must be carefully and thoughtfully planned with all these factors in mind. Some teachers find it more satisfactory to teach one skill at a time, but others—feeling that good student leaders can direct skill practices—set up groups to provide for drilling on different skills at the same time. Under the direction of leaders, groups can rotate to different skill stations until all students have had practice within each assigned area. Such a procedure would depend, of course, upon the equipment and practice areas available, as well as upon effective leadership, but it would promote leadership and develop group responsibility and cooperation. This same division of groups may even be used on an elective basis, with students selecting the drill they need to practice most, and then rotating.

To ensure most effective learning from practice drill opportunities, the teacher must be concerned with another highly important factor: reinforcement-feedback. Considerable interest has been generated in this area because of recent emphasis on humanism in the classroom. The creation of a positive learning environment and the development of a positive self-concept in every student has been recognized as vital to the teaching process. Several types of positive feedback have been identified:

1. Simple verbal feedback ("Good job!" "Fine.")

2. Simple nonverbal feedback (applause, or slap on the back)

3. Informative verbal feedback (explains what was good about appropriate behavior, as in "Good use of team strategy!")

4. Judgmental verbal feedback (explains why appropriate behavior was good, as in "Keep on using that good strategy and we'll score more points!")

In instances when feedback includes informative and judgmental points, the reinforcement has greater value to the learner. However, it should be appropriately and discriminantly used for utmost effectiveness. The teacher who slaps everyone on the back, saying "good," "great," "terrific," loses credibility.

• *Advantages*

1. Practice-drill combined with reinforcement-feedback may be a challenging and interesting method of improving skill.

2. The controlled drill situation provides equal practice opportunities for all students.

• *Disadvantages*

1. Practice should be monitored to ensure correct performance of skills. It is sometimes difficult to monitor performances of many students in one class period.

2. Younger or less mature students may lose interest quickly when drilling over and over in the same pattern. Variations may need to be provided.

• *Question for consideration.* On what factors does an instructor base a decision when balancing time allocations for game-play and drill practice in a single class session?

Task (individualized approach)

• *Purpose.* To provide the student with an independent learning opportunity for acquisition of skill, for discovery of concepts, or developing solutions to problems.

• *Role of the teacher.* Task designer.

• *Role of the student.* Task performer.

• *Style.* Student-centered.

• *Description.* The task method of teaching allows the individual student to work singly or in small groups toward the accomplishment of specific tasks designed for achievement of particular learning objectives. The tasks themselves are generally of two types: (1) performance tasks or (2) information plus performance tasks. They may be simple in nature, with structured tasks described on reading cards or posters, or they may be more elaborate packets or a series of study units in task form. Such study units would be information-plus-performance tasks, sometimes described as an individualized instructional packet, including activities for skill development plus outside reading requirements, audiovisual aids, and self-evaluation instruments. This packet method of teaching, according to recent research, has proven to be very effective.

Task teaching may be organized at learning centers and designed specifically for independent study by one or more students. Necessary materials should be available at the center, along with instructions for proceeding through the learning activities. Specific objectives to be achieved should be carefully outlined in sequential form, with evaluation measures incorporated therein. (See behavioral objectives.) The student at the learning center is responsible for his or her own rate of achievement and is free to progress to different learning centers or other activities after completing the prescribed tasks.

• *Advantages*

1. Tasks provide an independent, self-directed learning situation.

2. Students are free to progress at their own rate and according to their own ability levels.

• *Disadvantages*

1. The teacher needs to design tasks and learning packets appropriate for the wide-spread variation in ability levels and interests found in adolescents.

2. Other measures of evaluation beside the self-evaluation tests may be necessary to check on progress of students.

• *Question for consideration.* To what extent should individualized learning experiences be balanced with team and large group activities in the total physical education curriculum?

Reciprocal teaching (partner-small group)

• *Purpose.* To provide independent learning experiences in all three domains of learning.

• *Role of the teacher.* Facilitator.

• *Role of the student.* Performer-helper.

• *Style.* Student-centered.

• *Description.* In the reciprocal method of teaching the student has a greater responsibility for achievement of many learning objectives than is found in some of the previous methods. The word reciprocal, as it is used here, indicates that at least two partners work together to accomplish established goals. While one partner is performing, practicing, or doing the desired activity, the second partner watches and assists the learner by evaluating performance and offering suggestions. The teacher, as facilitator, encourages the second partner by assisting in the correction phase of the experience. In the case where a third person is involved in the group,

Fig. 15-5. A ball-throwing machine is used to develop skill in softball at Wheaton High School, Wheaton, Md.

this third member may help with equipment or scoring procedures and later change places (roles) with all the other partners.

It may be seen from this description that objectives within all three domains of learning are involved in this method of teaching. The partner who analyzes and evaluates is forced to involve high level cognition. At the same time, sharing and working closely with a partner brings affective objectives into play. The psychomotor domain is utilized in the actual performance of tasks or activities.

• *Advantages*

1. Self-directed learning experiences are provided for all three learning domains.

2. The teacher is freed to guide the learnings of all the small groups.

• *Disadvantages*

1. At first some students may feel strange in the role of evaluator and be hesitant about correcting a partner's performance.

2. It may be difficult for the teacher to hear all partners when they are acting in the role of evaluator.

• *Question for consideration.* In what ways might the problem-solving and guided discovery methods be combined with reciprocal types of teaching?

Guided discovery

• *Purpose.* To allow students opportunities to discover for themselves appropriate solutions to a given series of sequential problems.

• *Role of the teacher.* Designer-sequencer.

• *Role of the student.* Explorer-discoverer.

• *Style.* Student-centered.

• *Description.* The guided discovery method of teaching requires a student to seek solutions to sequentially designed problems that will lead him or her to discover for himself or herself an appropriate result. In this method the teacher never provides an answer. Instead, the instructor designs a series of tasks on a given subject, such as facts, concepts, relationships, or movements, and through experimentation the student progresses step-by-step, finally arriving at a desirable result. This method of teaching has

been receiving widespread acceptance since the time when movement education programs were introduced into this country during the 1960s.

• *Advantages*

1. The student is allowed to discover the answers to given problems, thus achieving more permanent learning.

2. The teacher is freed to assist all students in the class.

• *Disadvantages*

1. Proper design of sequential problems is essential if students are to be guided to discover correct solutions. This is a difficult and time-consuming task for the teacher.

2. The process of discovery itself is time-consuming.

3. Some students may have difficulty in being motivated by this teaching method.

• *Question for consideration.* What about those students whose learning style is one that requires motivation by teacher-centered methods?

Problem solving

• *Purpose.* To provide students with independent opportunities to find for themselves one or more solutions to problems provided them in various learning experiences.

• *Role of the teacher.* Designer.

• *Role of the student.* Inventor.

• *Style.* Student-centered.

• *Description.* The problem-solving method of teaching promotes student inquiry and exploration to find new solutions to problems that have no predetermined answers. It is the responsibility of the teacher to design tasks that will require these cognitive processes and force the student to discover from several possible solutions that which is most appropriate. Many types of problems can be designed in physical education activities: skill problems, concepts, limitations of movement, and variations of movement, for example. Through the process of experimentation, the student (either singly or in a small group) arrives at possible solutions, all of which may be correct providing they meet the limitations of the given problem. This method, like guided discovery, has met with great success in movement education activities.

• *Advantages*

1. There are many opportunities for success provided in problem solving, thus contributing to a positive learning experience.

2. Students are responsible for directing their own learning experiences.

3. The teacher is freed to assist all students in the class.

• *Disadvantages*

1. Designing appropriate tasks without preconceived solutions is difficult and time consuming.

2. The process of problem solving is a time-consuming one for students.

• *Question for consideration.* How may the problem-solving method of teaching be adapted to suit those students who are less imaginative and creative than others?

Contract

• *Purpose.* To provide a self-directed learning experience in an area of personal interest to the student wherein the element of success is generally assured.

• *Role of the teacher.* Evaluator.

• *Role of the student.* Contractor.

• *Style.* Student-centered.

• *Description.* A contract is a form of individualized study in which the student embarks on a self-directed learning experience. After previous agreement with the instructor, the student identifies specific objectives to be achieved in the contract. These objectives may be in one, two, or all three learning domains. Included in the contract are specific tasks associated with accomplishment of each objective, and a time format indicating dates for completion. The standards for evaluation are usually identified with each task so that a final grade is automatically derived.

Contracts may be one of three types, depending on the role played by the student: (1) the student is required to fulfill all tasks; (2) the student is allowed to select from the total number of tasks a specific number of assignments to meet contract requirements; and (3) the student is allowed to design the total contract, including all tasks, assignments, and evaluation techniques. Content of the tasks may be derived from the cognitive, affective, and psychomotor domains.

• *Advantages*

1. The contract method allows the individual student to be responsible for his or her own learning experiences.

2. Measures of evaluation are previously detailed. Students generally know in advance exactly what is expected and what grades they will receive for their accomplishments. Therefore success is generally assured if qualitative and quantitative criteria are met.

3. Interaction between the teacher and student is usually an important ingredient, particularly in the planning stages of contracts.

4. The student is meeting personal needs and interest through individualization of contracts.

• *Disadvantages*

1. Derivation and implementation of this method are difficult.

• *Question for consideration.* Are there enough resources and materials available to meet the variety of needs and interest of students in the class?

Independent study

• *Purpose.* To provide an elective, self-directed learning opportunity (usually in upper secondary levels).

• *Role of the teacher.* Supervisor-evaluator.

• *Role of the student.* Initiator-performer.

• *Style.* Student-centered.

• *Description.* Independent study offers alternative program opportunities to students who are eligible according to prerequisites of the curriculum. These alternatives frequently are offered in the eleventh and twelfth years of school after required academic and performance standards have been met.

There are many types of independent study programs offered within elective phases of physical education. Contracts, as discussed in the previous section, represent one type of independent offering. Another type of elective being experimented with in some states is called an out-of-school program, in which students are allowed to attend activities sponsored by local Ys, JCCs, private classes, or similar programs. Courses taken as part of this alternative educational program are generally limited to once or twice a year and only to cases where certain established criteria are met. Activities might include figure skating, judo, horseback riding, or special swimming classes. Participation in such a course of study might be used

---

Checklist for quality and control of out-of-school physical education programs*

Completed (✔)

1. Proposed program meets standards and qualifications set by the New York State Commissioner's regulations in respect to alternatives allowed. ☐
2. Description of program contains:
    a. Nature of program ☐
    b. Who is eligible ☐
    c. Credit plan ☐
    d. Cost facts for pupils ☐
    e. Liability aspects ☐
    f. Transportation responsibilities ☐
    g. Time demands ☐
    h. Procedure for student to make arrangements with community agents ☐
    i. Clarification of evaluation procedures ☐
    j. Need for goal setting by pupil ☐
    k. Nature of supervision of program ☐
    l. Expectations for attendance ☐
    m. Nature of final report at end of experience ☐
    n. Range of activities and experiences accepted ☐
3. Pupils receive description of program before planning experience. ☐
4. Parents receive description of program before planning experience. ☐
5. Community participants receive description of program and final agreement between school and pupil. ☐
6. Form designed for agreement or contract between pupil and school contains time, credit, objectives and goals, starting and ending dates, evaluative procedures, signatures of pupil, community, instructor, authorized school personnel, and due date for final report. ☐
7. Authorized physical education personnel confers with community personnel and clarifies institutional expectations, pupil attendance, supervision, evaluation procedures. ☐
8. Authorized physical education personnel checks qualifications of community instructors. ☐
9. Authorized physical education personnel make recommended visit to most frequently used instructional sites and make periodical phone calls. ☐
10. Form designed for pupil evaluation of out-of-school experience and situation. ☐
11. Form designed for record keeping of out-of-school experience. ☐
12. Time allotted for physical education personnel for supervision and evaluation of program. ☐
13. Clerical services provided for record keeping. ☐
14. Plans for periodical evaluation of program and procedure and subsequent revision if necessary. ☐
15. Approval of administration of school and school board of program. ☐
16. Periodic report on progress of program to the faculty administration and school board. ☐
17. Occasional publicity releases describing program given to local media. ☐

---

*Developed by Evelyn L. Schurr, SUC Brockport November, 1975. Reprinted with permission.

to meet *some* of the total physical education requirements in a secondary school curriculum but only with prior administrative approval and for very limited periods of time.

Establishment of appropriate criteria is essential prior to the implementation of such a program to ensure quality instruction. The checklist below outlines some important factors that must be considered for proper administration of out-of-class programs.

Important, too, are decisions regarding the percentage of time that may be fulfilled by out-of-class programs. Some schools have found 10 percent or at most 20 percent to be reasonable allocations. In the same way, procedures for evaluation and marking must be predetermined before contracts with out-of-school personnel can be established. The problem of insurance coverage for accidents occurring on property other than school property is the most serious one needing consideration and must be carefully investigated prior to the introduction of these programs.

* *Advantages*
1. The student is allowed to pursue an area of study of particular interest to him or her.
2. The student is responsible for his or her own learning experience.
3. Program offerings of the secondary curriculum may be greatly expanded.

* *Disadvantages*
1. The responsibility for the instructional program is shifted to outside personnel. The teacher's responsibility becomes one of supervision and evaluation.
2. Record keeping needs to be carefully administered to cover both in-school and out-of-school requirements.

* *Question for consideration.* Should a school sanction programs taught by persons other than those on the regular teaching staff?

Question-answer

* *Purpose.* To promote cognitive processes within the students as well as to provide information on physical education activities.
* *Role of the teacher.* Questioner.

* *Role of the student.* Respondent.
* *Style.* Teacher-centered.
* *Description.* Questioning may be a very effective method of teaching, particularly when the instructor is knowledgeable in the teachniques of conducting a worthwhile question-and-answer session. This method may be utilized at the beginning of a class period as a means of imparting information or at the close of activities as an analyzing and synthesizing technique.

When conducting a question-and-answer session there are several factors the teacher needs to keep in mind:
1. Questions should be clearly stated.
2. Questions should be stated so that all students can hear, and they should *all* feel that their responses are welcome.
3. Questions should be addressed to all students, and a specific respondent named after the question has been asked.
4. Questions should be asked only once, and sufficient time should be allowed for answering.
5. Questions should be interesting, pertinent, and challenging and should incorporate different levels of cognitive responses. For example, questions asking for simple *facts* would be categorized at the first level of cognitive development, requiring only a recall of knowledge. Higher levels of questions would require an *analysis* of skill, perhaps, or a discussion of differences in performance. Top level questions would demand the highest cognitive processes, such as synthesis and evaluation. To answer such a question the student must use imagination and creativity. Then new ideas will result (see Bloom's taxonomy).
6. Question-and-answer periods should be carried on in a dignified atmosphere, with only relevant answers being tolerated. Off-subject responses should be discouraged as often as necessary, and all appropriate answers should be treated with respect.

* *Advantages*
1. High-level thought processes become involved in well-designed question-answer sessions.
2. High-level affective responses may be

fostered also as students learn to value and respect one another's responses.

• *Disadvantages*

1. Questions need to be carefully planned and outlined, which may be a time-consuming task for teachers.

2. Questioning may take an extended period of time, thus limiting activity sessions.

• *Question for consideration.* Which method provides a more effective learning experience: a brief verbal explanation followed by a long practice, or a long question period followed by a brief practice session?

Evaluation

• *Purpose.* To provide self-evaluation opportunities for students through various in-class and out-of-class experiences.

• *Role of the teacher.* Administrator, evaluator.

• *Role of the student.* Respondent.

• *Style.* Teacher-centered.

• *Description.* Evaluation may be classified as a method of teaching, inasmuch as the instructor, through careful selection of appropriate testing instruments, may afford students the opportunity to evaluate their own personal progress. In so doing, students come to know themselves and to view realistically their achievement of personal and course goals. Selected instruments may measure accomplishment of objectives in all three learning domains.

In the cognitive domain, evaluation instruments may be in the form of standardized or teacher-made tests, or written reports on reading assignments. In the affective domain, the student may be brought to deeper self-awareness through values clarification techniques and sociometry. Psychomotor testing in the form of skills and fitness testing provide a clear indication of progress to the student in the third learning domain.

• *Advantages*

1. Tests may serve diagnostic, prescriptive, and final evaluation purposes. (See Chapter 22).

2. The teacher is able to become better acquainted with student development in all three learning domains.

3. The student becomes better acquainted with his or her own development.

• *Disadvantages*

1. Testing takes time away from instructional periods.

2. In an individualized program the teacher will need to construct a variety of evaluation instruments, all of which will require correction and recording of results. With large classes this may be difficult.

• *Question for consideration.* What percentage of class time should be devoted to evaluation procedures during the course of a school year?

Audiovisual teaching

• *Purpose.* To supplement the learning process through interesting methods of presenting materials. This method relies on auditory and visual channels for sensory input.

• *Role of the teacher.* Arranger.

• *Role of the student.* Listener/viewer.

• *Style.* Teacher-centered.

• *Description.* The use of teaching aids and materials is a method of teaching that supplements the learning process. Students who are not stimulated by other teaching methods may be motivated by films, charts, or other resource materials, and highly skilled students may broaden the scope of their knowledge by studying enrichment materials. Well-chosen teaching aids are of special value in teaching the culturally disadvantaged or other students whose formal experience with physical education has been limited. Acquaintance with the wealth of outside resources and information from which all members of a class may benefit is an invaluable aid in teaching, and the physical educator should make good use of such information.

In recent years considerable progress has been made in regard to teaching aids. The equipment and tools have been vastly improved and the resources and services greatly extended so that all schools may take advantage of these instructional materials.

• *Advantages*

1. They enable the student to better un-

derstand concepts and the performance of a skill, events, and other experiences. The old cliché, "one picture is worth a thousand words," has much truth. The use of a film, pictures, or other materials gives a clearer idea of the subject being taught, whether it concerns how a heart functions or how to perfect a golf swing.

2. They help to provide variety to teaching. There is increased motivation, the attention span of children is increased, and the subject matter of a course is much more exciting when audiovisual aids are used in addition to other teaching techniques.

3. They increase motivation on the part of the student. To see a game played, a skill performed, or an experiment conducted before his eyes in clear understandable form helps to motivate the student to engage in a game, perform a skill more effectively, or want to know more about the relation of exercise to health. This is particularly true in video replay, for example, where a student can actually see how he or she performs a skill and then compare this performance to what should be done.

4. They provide for an extension of what can normally be taught in a classroom, gymnasium, swimming pool, or playground. Audiovisual aids enable the student to be taken to other countries, to experience sport events that occur in other parts of the United States, and to witness other events. All of these are important to physical education programs and the instructional program for students.

5. They provide a historical reference for the field of physical education. Outstanding events in sports and physical education that have occurred in past years can be brought to life before the student's eyes. In this way the student obtains a better understanding of how the field of physical education plays an important role in American society and in other cultures of the world.

• *Disadvantages*

1. Necessary equipment is expensive and bothersome to assemble or repair.

2. Films may become outdated.

3. There is little interaction between student and teacher.

4. The teacher may become overly dependent on these aids.

• *Questions for consideration.* Is a performance by an expert on film of greater value than a live demonstration by peers or teacher?

TEACHING AIDS AND MATERIALS

When selecting audiovisual aids or other resources and materials, the teacher of physical education should consider certain principles that make utilization of these aids effective and valuable. The similarity between these principles and those suggested in other methods of teaching should be noted, for the aim in each case is to create a worthwhile learning situation.

• *Materials should be carefully selected and screened.* The teacher should preview the materials to make sure they are appropriate for the unit and age level of the students and that they present information in an interesting and stimulating manner.

• *Proper preparation of materials should be made.* The teacher should check all equipment that may be necessary for the presentation of materials to make sure that it is in operating condition. Record players and movie projectors, in particular, need to be carefully checked before they are used.

• *The presentation of materials should be planned and integrated into the lesson.* Students should be properly introduced to the materials so that they know what to expect and so that they understand their relationship to the unit of study.

• *Materials should be presented to the students in a proper learning situation.* Students should be located so that all may hear, see, and learn from the material being presented to them. They should realize that they will be held responsible for the information being presented.

• *Materials should be varied.* Different types of materials should be chosen for presentation to stimulate the varying interests of the students. A teacher using films or slide films exclusively does not take full advantage of supplementary materials available for widespread appeal.

• *Use of supplementary materials should be limited.* The teacher should place a reasonable limit on the use of extra teaching materials to maintain a balance between supplementary learnings and those gained from regular instructional materials.

• *Care should be taken to avoid excessive expenses.* A reasonable part of the instructional budget should be set aside for supplementary materials. This amount should be in accordance with the emphasis placed on this phase of the teaching program.

• *Records and evaluations of materials should be maintained.* All supplementary materials should be carefully evaluated and records kept on file for future reference. This should save the unnecessary expense involved in reordering or duplicating materials and in maintaining outdated materials.

By following these principles the teacher is able to supplement learnings with materials that are valuable and interesting to the students.

A recent study by one of Bucher's students was concerned with current practices and trends in the use of audiovisual media for the teaching of motor skills in professional physical education programs. This study has implications for secondary school physical education programs in that it reveals the number of responding schools that offer or require a course in audiovisual media and techniques in their professional preparing programs.

The researcher developed and mailed a questionnaire that was returned by sixty-three physical education directors in a variety of colleges and universities. Of these respondents, five required a course in audiovisual media and techniques, and thirty-five offered such a course on an elective basis. A total of fifty-four of the individuals answering the questionnaire indicated that they felt that audiovisual media serve as a valuable supplement to instruction in the learning of motor skills.

The study also found that videotaping is increasing in use as an instructional tool. The audiovisual media used with the most frequency by the respondents in this study were, in order of frequency, 16 mm and 8 mm films, loop films, cartridge films, chalkboards, wall charts, slide films, filmstrips, and instructional television.

On the pages that follow, six categories of materials and resources are discussed in terms of their purposes, problems, and specific sources. Suggestions are listed under *reading materials, audiovisual aids, special aids, professional personnel, community activities,* and *clinics.* Although these are recent and fairly inclusive listings, new types of materials are always being placed on the market. Teachers should be on the lookout for the very latest items available as listed in journals, catalogs, and advertisements.

Reading materials

• *Purposes.* To provide up-to-date information and enrichment materials on all aspects of the program.

• *Problems.* To keep track of materials and assignments. A check-out system should be developed so that the teacher may know where materials may be located. In addition, some method of annotating particularly beneficial articles or resources should be devised, thus simplifying assignments.

• *Types*

1. Textbook.

Bucher, C. A.: *Physical Education for Life,* New York, 1969, McGraw-Hill Book Company.

This text for high school boys and girls provides information about physique, posture, physical skills, physical fitness, safety and first aid, and the body in motion. The book also includes basic instruction about twenty different sports and activities. Additional information is provided on the purchase and care of equipment. The textbook is informative and motivating and is an excellent means of giving high school students a rich physical education experience.

2. Magazines (research, historical, educational, informational, or supplementary):

All-American Athlete, Dept. J., 801 Palisade Ave., Union City, N.J. 07087

Athletic Journal, Athletic Journal Publishing Co., 1719 Howard St., Evanston, Ill. 60202

The Coach, Lowe and Campbell Athletic Goods, 1511 Baltimore Ave., Kansas City, Mo. 64108

Coach and Athlete, 1421 Mayon St., N.E., Atlanta, Ga. 31324

Dance Magazine, 268 West 47th St., New York, N.Y. 10036

Journal of Physical Education and Recreation, 1201 Sixteenth St., N.W., Washington, D.C. 20036

Research Quarterly, 1201 Sixteenth St., N.W., Washington, D.C. 20036

Scholastic Coach, Scholastic Magazine, Inc., 50 West 44th St., New York, N.Y. 10036

U.S. Gymnast Magazine, P.O. Box 53, Iowa City, Iowa 52240

3. Booklets, pamphlets, and catalogs (educational and supplemental information about health, safety, and related areas):

American Alliance for Health, Physical Education, and Recreation, 1201 Sixteenth St., N.W., Washington, D.C. 20036

American School and University, Product Catalog File, American School Publishing Co., 470 Fourth Ave., New York, N.Y. 10016

The Athletic Institute, 200 Castlewood Drive, North Palm Beach, Fla. 33408

American Medical Association, 535 N. Dearborn St., Chicago, Ill. 60610

Metropolitan Life Insurance Co., 1 Madison Ave., New York, N.Y. 10010

National Dairy Council, 111 N. Canal St., Chicago, Ill. 60606

Science Research Associates, 259 E. Erie, Chicago, Ill. 60611

Audiovisual aids

• *Purposes.* To give information to a large group at one time in such areas as skill breakdowns, game play, techniques and rules of sports, and enrichment materials; to provide musical or other rhythmical accompaniment.

• *Problems.* To keep an accurate and up-to-date file on current materials, with evaluative suggestions. Individual file cards are helpful for this purpose. Large school sys-

tems and new schools generally maintain departments for audiovisual instruction, with personnel specifically hired for the maintenance, distribution, selection, and follow-up of all equipment and materials in this area.

• *Types*

1. Motion pictures. Motion pictures for use in physical education classes are available in every area. They may be purchased in color or black and white or rented for nominal fees. Catalogs issued by film companies contain listings of films available for rental or purchase and generally include brief descriptions of the films themselves to help the teacher in making selections.

Guides are also available for filmstrips and for tapes, scripts, and transcriptions.

2. Slide films. Slide films have been developed for rental and purchase on both a sound and silent basis.

A source of full-color slide films is The Athletic Institute, 200 Castlewood Drive, North Palm Beach, Fla. 33408. To rent their slide films, contact must be made with Ideal Pictures, Inc., at one of their regional offices:

102 West 25th Street, Baltimore, Md. 21218

58 E. South Water St., Chicago, Ill. 60601

1840 Alcatraz Ave., Berkeley, Calif. 94703

Slide films are available in sports, including beginning archery, beginning badminton, beginning baseball, beginning bowling, campcraft, beginning fencing, beginning golf, beginning table tennis, gymnastics, beginning soccer, beginning softball, swimming, beginning tennis, track and field, beginning volleyball, and beginning wrestling, plus individual recreational sports such as fishing, ice skating, skiing, and judo. Excellent booklets accompany each of these slide films.

3. Learning loops. Several 8 mm learning loops may be purchased from the Athletic Institute. An 8 mm loop film projector is also available directly from the Institute. These loops are an excellent device for specific instruction in skill performance. They are available in each individual event in track and field for men, track and field for women, gymnastics, and tennis.

4. Loop movies. Loop movies consist of several 16 mm loops spliced together, end to end, for continuous projection. They are available for purchase from Champions on Film, 3666 South State St., Ann Arbor, Mich. 48104, with prices ranging between $20.00 and $50.00. These films cover such subjects as basketball, wrestling, swimming, baseball, golf, tennis, trampoline, and track.

5. Television. Although educational television (ETV) has widespread appeal at various age levels in all phases of the curriculum, its usage as a teaching technique in physical education is still rather limited.

Physical educators agree that the full potential of television has not been reached and recognize that recent developments in physical education, such as movement efficiency and sensory-perceptual experiences, contain concepts adaptable to television production.

6. Videotape. Videotapes are finding increased usage in many educational endeavors and are being recognized as an invaluable teaching aid in physical education activites. Several purposes illustrate the adaptability of this special type of recording device. It may be used in the following ways:

a. To videotape sports performances for later study of still frames, for closer analysis of action
b. To supervise several outdoor play areas from one location through a closed-circuit television monitoring device
c. To provide objective evaluation of an individual performance, such as diving or trampolining, through instant replay
d. To build up a school library of tapes for specific instructional purposes at later dates

These are only a few of the instructional possibilities of this versatile teaching tool. Its popularity will continue to increase because of its adaptability, the ease with which it may be operated, and its effectiveness. Current problems caused by tapes that fit improperly in some machines are being solved.

7. Phonographs and audiotape recorders. For extensive use in physical education classes, phonographs and audiotape recorders must be durable, portable, and provided with discrete volume controls. Transportation and storage of this valuable equipment may be a problem if safe closet space is not available relatively near the gymnasium.

8. Records (available in all speeds, some in unbreakable nylon materials, for teaching all rhythmic activities).

9. Drum (dance drum, bongo drum, and similar percussive devices). Drums are used extensively to provide rhythmical measures for creative activities. They should be kept in a dry place, for extreme dampness causes loss of tone. In such instances, placing the drum on a radiator for a few minutes restores tensity.

Special aids

• *Purposes.* To provide graphic, illustrative material to students in an interesting and educational manner.

• *Problems.* To find time to utilize displays effectively, to change displays for added interest, and to keep up to date with current events. Student assistants should be utilized to prepare and maintain the displays.

• *Types*

1. Charts, diagrams, and photographic materials (for materials in several different sports):

National Association for Girls' and Women's Sports, American Alliance for Health, Physical Education, and Recreation, 1201 Sixteenth St., N.W., Washington, D.C. 20036

Nissen Corp., 930 27th Avenue, S.W., Cedar Rapids, Iowa 52416

2. Bulletin boards and chalkboards (cork or beaver board, stationary or movable). These are excellent teaching devices for educational and motivational purposes. They should be colorful, interesting, neat, clear, uncluttered, and changed often. School administrators generally provide these materials.

3. Magnetic boards (blank-surfaced boards suitable for specific sports, such as soccer, football, or basketball, or all-purpose types of boards, suitable for all sports). These boards are excellent teaching devices for

team sports. Although the initial expense ($19.00 to $50.00) seems rather steep at first, the lasting value of this item over several years makes it a worthwhile investment.

Professional personnel

• *Purposes.* To provide an interesting incentive to students by having a visiting professional demonstrate, teach, or discuss a sport or related experience.

• *Problems.* To plan and organize for thorough effectiveness and safety. Preplanning with the guest is essential, and preparation with students allows them to gain more fully from the experience.

• *Types.* The directors and personnel of professional organizations such as the National Golf Foundation, United States Lawn Tennis Association, and Amateur Athletic Association.

Community activities

• *Purposes.* To promote good public relations with the community and to provide additional activities for student participation.

• *Problems.* To find time to plan and organize carefully the various details of the activities with community leaders.

• *Types.* Recreational activities (tennis meets); PTA sponsored special events and programs; benefit athletic demonstrations.

Clinics

• *Purposes.* To provide additional and valuable learning experiences to students attending these clinics as participants or observers. Taking an honor team, a leaders club, or an entire class to a special program of this type offers information and an opportunity for appreciation that they never forget because of the specialized nature of the experience.

• *Problems.* Planning, organizing transportation, obtaining parental permission, and providing supervision of the students. In many schools definite procedures for taking students on field trips are outlined, and they should be carefully followed.

• *Types.* Special games and programs put on by visiting professional clubs (basketball or football teams); special clinics sponsored by local or state teaching organizations; traveling college groups and community organizations.

Self-assessment tests

These tests are to assist students in determining if material and competencies presented in this chapter has been mastered:

1. Draw a diagram depicting the action of the components of the information-processing theory of learning. Compare this with a diagram of the stimulus-response theory.
2. Given two columns headed "internal conditions" and "external conditions," list those factors and subfactors that affect the learning environment.
3. Select a psychomotor skill (underhand pitching) and explain how the principle of transfer effects learning of this skill.
4. Describe a minimum of five different teacher roles as related to teaching methodology, including a description of the responsibilities of the teacher and student in each example.
5. Cite one advantage and one disadvantage to the following teaching methods:
   a. Contract
   b. Lecture
   c. Demonstration
   d. Audiovisual
   e. Reciprocal
   f. Evaluation
   g. Task
   h. Problem solving
6. You are assigned a group of beginning swimmers who have expressed a desire to learn water polo. Would you incorporate this activity into planning their learning experiences? In what ways?

Points to remember

1. Selection of teaching methods depends on many factors internal and external to the teaching environment and the learner.
2. Two important principles of teaching involve progressing from known to unknown material and introducing material first in its entirety and then part-by-part.
3. There are many effective methods of presenting information to learners, each one having its own unique set of advantages and disadvantages.
4. Acquisition of motor skills is dependent on a variety of factors requiring consideration for instruction.
5. Individualized methods of instruction allocate responsibility for learning to the student and allow the teacher freedom to facilitate the teaching process.
6. An understanding of learning theories should lay the foundations for planning effective instructional activities.

Problems to think about

1. Why is there no single best method for the teaching of physical education.
2. Which teaching methods would probably be more

effective with students who have poorly developed motor coordinations?

3. Which methods would probably be more effective with highly skilled boys and girls?
4. To what extent should students be allowed choices in the selection of activities?
5. To what extent should students be allowed to elect independent study in physical education?

Case study for analysis

You have accepted a teaching position in a small high school where there is only one other physical education teacher for all four high school grade levels. This teacher has been on the faculty for many years and may best be described as the "commander" or "drill sergeant" type of teacher. How would you effectively go about incorporating newer teaching methodology in this situation without causing friction between the two of you?

Exercises for review

1. What is teaching?
2. What environmental factors enhance the teaching process?
3. What are the values of individualized learning experiences?
4. Why should a teacher be familiar with a variety of teaching methods?

Selected readings

American Association for Health, Physical Education and Recreation: Guidelines for secondary school physical education, Washington, D.C., 1970, AAHPER.

American Association for Health, Physical Education, and Recreation: Physical education for high school students, ed. 2, Washington, D.C., 1970, AAHPER.

American Association for Health, Physical Education and Recreation: The new physical education, Journal of Health, Physical Education and Recreation, 1971, **42:**24-39, Sept., 1971.

American Association for Health, Physical Education and Recreation: Personalized learning in physical education, Washington, D.C., 1976, AAHPER.

Heitmann, H. M., and Kneer, M. E.: Physical education instructional techniques: an individualized humanistic approach, Englewood Cliffs, N.J. 1976, Prentice-Hall, Inc.

Kalakian, L., and Goldman, M.: Introduction to physical education; a humanistic perception, Boston, 1976, Allyn and Bacon, Inc.

Locke, L. F., and Jensen, M.: "Pre-packaged sports skills instruction: a review of selected research," Journal of Health, Physical Education and Recreation, **42:**7, 57-59, Sept., 1971.

Mosston, M.: Teaching physical education, Columbus, Ohio, 1966, Charles E. Merrill Publishing Company.

Siedentop, D.: Developing teaching skills in physical education, Boston, 1976, Houghton Mifflin Company.

Shulman, L. S., and Keisler, E. R., editors: Learning by discovery: a critical appraisal, Chicago, 1966, Rand McNally & Company.

Willgoose, C. E.: The curriculum in physical education, ed. 2, Englewood Cliffs, N.J., 1974, Prentice-Hall, Inc.

16

LEARNING OUTCOMES—END RESULTS OF THE TEACHING PROCESS

INSTRUCTIONAL OBJECTIVES AND COMPETENCIES TO BE ACHIEVED

After reading this chapter the student should be able to—

1. Define the terms learning, instructional objective, and behavioral objective.
2. List the taxonomies of instructional objectives in the three domains of learning.
3. Apply the taxonomies of instructional objectives to physical education.
4. Describe three values of instructional objectives.
5. Demonstrate an ability to write behavioral objectives, including all four basic components.
6. Discuss four specific values to the learner of behavioral objectives.

LEARNING OUTCOMES

Learning is generally defined as an observable change in behavior and as an outcome of the teaching process. In the previous chapter learning theories were presented, and several methods of teaching were described. In this chapter the results of this teaching process, or the *outcomes* of learning, will be analyzed. The recent trend to hold teachers accountable for what takes place within the classroom makes it imperative that actual learning be identified. How does a teacher know that learning has oc-

curred in the gymnasium or on the playing field? How does a teacher know for certain that a student has achieved specified educational goals?

It is the purpose of this chapter to help the teacher evaluate the teaching process by means of the identification of learning outcomes. These learning outcomes are in the form of observable, measurable behaviors that the teacher has brought about through the establishment of two types of objectives: instructional and behavioral. The first section of this chapter deals with *instructional* objectives—those goals or aims that the *teacher defines* for the program of activities or unit under study. The second part of this chapter concerns the writing of specific *behavioral* objectives—those outcomes of the learning process that the *student* should *achieve* during a particular class session.

DEVELOPMENT OF INSTRUCTIONAL OBJECTIVES

To meet the current demands for accountability several significant changes in teaching methodology have taken place. For example, the introduction of programmed learning materials, flexible schedules, and individualized instructional programs represents an attempt on the part of educators to improve educational methodology. These improved teaching approaches provided answers to the demands for measurement of teacher effectiveness by offering evidence that educational changes had taken place.

Of the many innovations that have been developed, perhaps one of the most significant is the classification of educational objectives within three identified domains of learning. These educational or instructional objectives may be defined as those goals of the instructional process that the teacher has identified as essential to learning.

Educational objectives in the learning domains

The first publication of educational objectives by Bloom and his associates in 1956 was the outcome of intense work by many educators to bring modern psychological thinking into the educational sphere. Although objectives have long been a part of the educational process, the classification of educational objectives into a taxonomy, or hierarchical form, using developmental theories as a basis for structuring objectives, was a totally new approach.

The first taxonomy to be developed dealt with learning in the cognitive or thinking domain of learning. From the research of developmental psychologists such as Piaget and others theories about stages of development emerged, indicating when or at what point in the developmental process a child would begin to assimilate facts and then proceed upward toward higher levels of cognitive activity. Development of specific cognitive skills could then be fostered at appropriate stages of intellectual development recognizable within the learning.

These same educators, Bloom, Krathwohl, and others further recognized that an individual does not learn facts or develop cognitive abilities without other factors influencing the learning process. Realizing that how a person feels about himself and his surroundings has a definite relationship to learning, they next developed a taxonomy of educational objectives in the affective or feeling domain. Here again the developmental nature of the organism was taken into account when classifying objectives in hierarchical form.

The third learning domain, the psychomotor domain, has recently been classified by educators in the fields of physical education and home economics, as well as by developmental psychologists. One of the first to publish a psychomotor taxonomy was Elizabeth Simpson, a home economist from Illinois, in 1966-1967. This was followed by publications from several physical educators, such as Cratty, Jewett, and Fleischman, who presented their ideas on the structures of psychomotor functioning. Because of the complex nature of development in this third domain the process of identification of a single taxonomy of educational objectives has been slow. However, the taxonomy published by Anita Harrow in 1972 seems to be receiving acceptance among physical educators at the present time. Therefore, her classification of instructional objectives will be utilized in this discussion of learning in the pyschomotor domain.

A fourth domain of learning, the emotional domain, has been suggested by some educators, but has not received widespread application as yet. Inasmuch as many of the objectives within this fourth domain are subsumed within the sociological aspects of the affective domain, the discussions that follow will be limited to the taxonomies of instructional objectives within just three domains: the cognitive, the affective, and the psychomotor domains of learning.

Physical educators, historically, have been dedicated to the teaching of the *whole* person. Therefore, it might seem that a discussion of objectives within three learning domains would be in no way innovative to teachers in the field. Yet, to meet the demands for accountability that are so widespread at the present time, physical educators, like all teachers, have to be able to prove that learning has indeed taken place in their gymnasiums and classrooms. Therefore the development of a taxonomy of instructional objectives, leading towards *measurable* behaviors, helped to answer these demands. With the utilization of the following series of instructional objectives in the three learning domains, the teacher of physical education is able to take the first step towards promoting changes in behavior. The second step, measurement of the specific outcomes of the learning process through behavioral objectives, will then be presented.

Cognitive domain

Developers of the taxonomy of educational objectives* within this learning domain recognized that cognition increases in complexity at each developmental stage of the individual. Initial stages of development allow learning of basic facts, while the mature individual is later able to understand and apply total concepts. Six basic levels or stages of cognitive learning were identified so that teachers could incorporate educational objectives on a hierarchical basis. The taxonomy of objectives in the cognitive domain is organized under the following six headings: (1) knowledge, (2) comprehension, (3) application, (4) analysis, (5) synthesis, and (6) evaluation.

Application to physical education. To apply this taxonomy of cognition to the instructional physical education program,

*From Bloom, B. S., editor: Taxonomy of educational objectives. Handbook I. Cognitive domain, New York, 1956, David McKay Co., Inc.

teachers must first keep in mind its hierarchical nature and develop objectives appropriate to the intellectual development of their students. For example, the cognitive development of first graders would allow simple objectives at the first level, that is, knowledge objectives. In other words, six-year-olds are capable of learning *facts* about games, about their bodies, or about equipment. Therefore the teacher would write instructional objectives suitable to this level of intellectual development. In secondary schools, where students' intellectual skills and abilities are more fully developed, the teacher should expect achievement of higher levels of cognition—application of strategy to game play, for example, or creation of new movements or games at the synthesis level. Thereafter instructional objectives demanding higher intellectual skills would be written.

To further clarify the utilization of this cognitive taxonomy in physical education it may be helpful to identify possible instructional objectives in a sample unit on tennis. To accomplish this, the teacher must first

Fig. 16-1. Volleyball class being conducted for students at Hampton Institute, Hampton, Va.

think through the body of knowledge in the game of tennis, identifying specific information to be included in the unit. Then the specific intellectual skills that are essential to the game should be determined. The teacher must ask, "What should the students *know* at the beginning tennis level?" The answer might include a knowledge of the rules of the game, knowledge of scoring, the history of the game, and knowledge of tennis etiquette. These four areas of knowledge would fall in level 1 of the cognitive taxonomy, requiring merely a recall of facts on the part of the student.

The next question the physical educator must ask is, "What do the students need to comprehend?" Here, at level 2 of the taxonomy, the teacher might identify basic concepts in tennis that the student should understand, such as concepts of spin, concepts regarding levers, and concepts of force applied to a moving object.

At the third level the student would need to apply the foregoing knowledge and understanding to playing the game. For example, the student might have to keep score during a game, explain rules to a partner, or move to anticipate spin of the ball appropriately.

The three remaining higher levels of intellectual skills may also be used to formulate instructional objectives in a beginning tennis unit. At the analysis level the teacher might seek to develop the students' abilities to analyze certain aspects of their own or their opponent's playing strategies, finding their weaknesses or their strengths in game play. Then, when providing opportunities for students to utilize this information by synthesizing and evaluating what they have learned, the teacher can expect the highest intellectual levels to become operative.

This is a very brief, and by no means complete, application of the cognitive taxonomy of educational objectives to a unit on beginning tennis. From this brief presentation, however, it should be understood that the levels of intellectual development form a foundation for writing specific instructional objectives for any unit of study or activity.

Affective learning domain

The affective learning domain encompasses the development of attitudes and appreciations for a particular subject or activity. The writing of educational objectives in this domain by Krathwohl, Bloom, and Masia in 1964 followed previous work on the cognitive domain. With acceptance of affect into the educational scene came recognition of the role of a student's feelings and interests in relation to achievement and a heightened awareness among educators of the importance of this learning domain.

Formulation of the taxonomy of instructional objectives* in the affective domain combined recent work of developmental psychologists, such as Abraham Maslow, who developed a hierarchy of needs, with the work of sociologists studying the changing patterns of society. It will be noticed that within this taxonomy the developing individual is aware first of his or her self, and his or her own responses to surroundings and gradually develops a value structure to his ever increasing social sphere. The taxonomy of objectives in the affective domain is organized under the following headings: (1) receiving, (2) responding, (3) valuing, (4) organization of values, and (5) characterization by value.

Application to physical education. The affective domain of learning formulates a significant part of physical education objectives. Traditionally teachers in this field have claimed that physical education activities contribute greatly to character development through the social skills of cooperation, leadership, and sportsmanship. However, there was little evidence to support these claims. Now, with the application of instructional objectives through an affective taxonomy and measurement of learning outcomes, proof will be available that students develop attitudes and values in physical activity.

To understand the application of the affec-

*From Krathwohl, D. R., Bloom, B. S., and Masia, B. B.: Taxonomy of educational objectives. Handbook II. The affective domain, New York, 1964, David McKay Co.

tive taxonomy to a particular instructional activity, the following hierarchy of objectives in an introductory unit on team handball is presented. Keep in mind that the teacher's general objective is to develop positive feelings and attitudes on the part of the students toward this new activity.

The first instructional procedure might be to establish a setting where the student would be exposed to a game of handball, perhaps in the form of a film or demonstration game. This class activity would meet the teacher's instructional objectives at the first level on the taxonomy in that the students would be *receiving* information on team handball. The next set of instructional objectives would necessitate a response from the students regarding the game of team handball, such as following directions or becoming involved in certain aspects of the game. As each student's interest in the game increases, the third level of objectives, valuing, would be achieved. The student might voluntarily practice the skills of the game or participate in a demonstration of the game, thus indicating his or her own valuing of the activity. At the fourth level of the taxonomy the student might show increasing valuing of the game by indicating a preference for the game over and above other elective activities. In so doing, the student points out inner feelings for the game by placing it in an *organizational structure* of those activities he or she most highly prizes. Finally, when this same student dedicates himself or herself to the furtherance of this activity by proclaiming a devotion to the game over a long period of time, and incorporating it into his or her total life style, he or she has reached the highest level in the taxonomy, *characterization by value.* The teacher must recognize that these higher levels in the affective domain may not be reached within a single unit of activity and, that evidence of their achievement might be presented at some future time. The teacher also needs to realize that all students will not highly prize all activities but will develop these attitudes and appreciations for only certain programs in the curriculum. Therefore, the teacher might set these top-level instructional objectives for a few of the students, with the hope that all students would achieve them in at least one or two activities during a secondary school career.

Psychomotor domain

The taxonomy of objectives in this third domain of learning, the psychomotor or doing domain, provides the foundation of programs of physical activities. Again, the taxonomy presented here is developmental in nature, relying on theories of physical development for its hierarchical structure.

Application to physical education. Although traditionally physical educators have used objectives in their instructional programs, the application of this hierarchy of objectives can provide an appropriate individualization of programming. By allowing students opportunities to develop motor tasks organized from simple to complex, a distinct progression in psychomotor abilities can be achieved.

The following taxonomy has been suggested by Harrow.* Its relevance to physical activity and to development of physical skills is easily recognized, and its application to physical education is obvious. The taxonomy of educational objectives in the psychomotor domain is organized under the following headings: (1) involuntary reflex movements, (2) voluntary purposeful movements such as locomotor movements, (3) perceptual abilities where sensory stimuli are communicated to the brain for interpretation, (4) physical abilities, which are the foundation of skilled physical movements, (5) skilled movements characterized by proficiency in performing a physical skill, and (6) nondiscursive communication as in dance.

Values of instructional objectives

For the teacher of physical education or of any subject matter area, these taxonomies of educational objectives provide concrete guidelines to develop *levels* of behavior or improvement in the learner. Moreover, the

---

*From Harrow, A.: A taxonomy of the psychomotor domain, New York, 1972, David McKay Co., Inc.

Fig. 16-2. Relay race being conducted for students at Hampton Institute, Hampton, Va.

organization and systematic ordering of behaviors found within each taxonomy also provides a framework for other important teaching functions. For example, the taxonomic framework of a unit of study may serve as a basis of comparison of that program with a similar program, allowing for judgment and evaluation of curricular offerings. Also taxonomic instructional materials provide necessary information for test development, which may be similarly organized to measure levels of development in the three learning domains and at the same time pinpoint needs of individual students.

Classifications of instructional objectives have been successfully used for the development of physical education programs already, and for the organization of activity units within those programs. In Ohio, a guide for the teaching of secondary school girls physical education was developed, based on key concepts that the teachers thought should be included from physiology, sociology, and psychology. On a national level, the American Alliance for Physical Education developed a booklet, *Knowledge and Understand-*

ing in Physical Education, in which were outlined cognitive concepts for elementary, junior high, and senior high school levels. This was followed by the development and publication of their standardized testing instrument, testing knowledge of physical education activities, and performance, again written for all three achievement levels.

Development of instructional objectives in taxonomic form for the many activities incorporated in a program of physical education is a very demanding task. Yet the outcomes, as evidence by concrete measurement of learning by students, are of extreme importance to the students and to the parents. Evidence that learning has indeed taken place because instructional objectives have been met thus answers their demands for accountability.

But how does the teacher determine that instructional objectives have been met? The second step, that of writing specific objectives for students based on outlined instructional objectives, is essential for completion of the teaching process. The students in the classroom must show evidence of learning by *doing* something specific and measurable. Therefore, after developing instructional objectives for a unit of study, the teacher must next formulate specific behavioral objectives for students to accomplish in each daily lesson.

BEHAVIORAL OBJECTIVES
Writing behavioral objectives

A behavioral objective, sometimes referred to as a performance objective, may be defined as an intended learning outcome achieved through the performance (an observable, measurable behavior) of a specified task. When a student accomplishes the established task, this behavior represents an outcome of the educational process; in other words, the student shows that learning has taken place.

In the tennis unit described previously, the instructional objective in the cognitive domain was written from the viewpoint of the teacher, who hoped that the students would know the rules of tennis. However, for the teacher to determine that this learning has taken place, the students have to demonstrate this knowledge by doing something, such as taking a written test, answering questions orally in class, or some similar measurable behavior. These test results or these student performances in the cognitive domain would then indicate not only what each student had learned but also would indicate to the teacher how well instructional objectives had been met. Proof of higher levels of cognitive skills should also be evaluated while students actually play their tennis matches, while analyzing each other's play and so forth. Student activities or performances should be based on written behavioral objectives, established to ensure that learning was taking place.

Translation of instructional objectives (the teacher's goals) into behavioral objectives (the students' goals) requires careful and thoughtful planning, for these behavioral objectives become the formula for planning a daily lesson. The fact that behavioral objectives then become the organizers of the instructional process must not be overlooked,

for herein lies the implementation of the several methods of teaching described previously. If a student's behavioral objective in the psychomotor domain involves learning to stroke a tennis ball, then within the daily lesson plan some activities must be organized that will develop that stroking. If an affective objective for the day seeks to develop sharing of equipment with a partner, then the activities during class must require sharing opportunities. Student achievement of established behavioral objectives, therefore, is synonymous with the learning process. They *are* the outcomes of learning.

Components of behavioral objectives

The writing of a behavioral objective based on instructional objectives requires careful delineation of four specific components or elements. It must first be stated *who* will be performing the behavior, the student, the tenth-grade girl or boy, or whoever it might be. In the second place, *what* the student will be doing must be identified, and thirdly the *conditions* under which the activity will be performed must be described. The fourth element is perhaps the most significant from the instructional standpoint. Here the quality of performance is measured by including a description of *how well* the performance has to be demonstrated.

Following are three behavioral objectives taken from a beginning tennis unit, and drawn from each learning domain. All four elements are incorporated in each objective.

- *Cognitive.* After studying instructional materials, the student will correctly explain (according to a partner's judgment) the concept "sweet part of the racket."
- *Affective.* The ninth-grade boy or girl will practice the forehand stroke against the tennis backboard throughout the class period.
- *Psychomotor.* The beginning tennis student will execute a controlled stroke against the tennis backboard by not losing the ball for five minutes.

Each of the above objectives contains the four necessary components. To clarify the factors, these objectives have been rewritten

Fig. 16-3. Golf instruction in physical education at Wheaton High School, Wheaton, Md.

Table 16-1. Components of behavioral objectives

Component	Objective		
	Cognitive	Affective	Psychomotor
Who will do it?	Student	Ninth-grade boy or girl	Beginning tennis student
What will be done?	Will explain verbally the concept of "sweet part of racket"	Will practice the forehand	Will execute a controlled forehand stroke
Under what *conditions?*	After studying the instructional materials	Against the tennis backboard	Against the tennis backboard
How well will it be done? By what *criteria?* To *what extent?*	Correctly, according to judgment of a partner	Throughout the class period	By not losing the ball for five minutes

with each element defined (Table 16-1).

When writing a behavioral objective the teacher must be careful to include the following:

1. A behavior that can be *performed*. The student must *do* something. Knowing how to do it is not enough, because it is hard to be sure what a student knows.

2. A behavior that is *measurable*. The student must do something that is observable. If the student *develops* a stroke, it is difficult to measure, so a different word should be selected.

Selection of verbs is the important factor here. General verbs, such as know, learn, appreciate, and comprehend, would be appropriate for instructional objectives. However, more specific verbs that involve *action* must be included in behavioral objectives. In the cognitive domain, such verbs as explains, describes, lists, identifies, diagrams, analyzes, and evaluates would be acceptable. In the affective domain a student might follow, respond, answer, obey, practice, select, volunteer, share, or prefer an activity, Psychomotor verbs are more easily included, in that they involve actions already, as in run, walk, swing, hit, catch, pass, jump, and so on.

3. A behavior that is *described*, with limiting specifications. How did the student explain? Verbally? In writing? Where did the student *run?* On the track? Out of the stadium?

4. A behavior that can *meet* certain established *criteria* or standards for evaluation purposes. Judgment of the quality of performance is required here, as in a score of 80 percent or better, to pass a written test, or successfully hitting a target in three out of five attempts.

The evaluation element is a critical component of a behavioral objective. If the major underlying purpose for establishing these behavioral objectives is to identify results of the teaching process—the learning outcomes—then measurement of performance must be obtained.

Relationship to teaching methods

Taking a closer look at the three behavioral objectives from a beginning tennis unit, it is easy to recognize teaching methodology incorporated within each one. In the cognitive domain, the student has been given instructional materials and is working with a partner. Therefore, this behavioral objective might be found with a reciprocal teaching arrangement, with small groups working at the centers. By having students work on stroking at the tennis backboard, the teacher has allowed students opportunities to practice, an affective response that shows valuing of the activity, throughout the entire class period. In expecting students to stroke without losing the ball it is the teacher's intent that the students work for control, again at a learning station established for individualization of instruction.

In most cases more than three objectives would be incorporated into a single lesson plan for physical education. Often these objectives would overlap by contributing to learning in more than one domain. (In the lesson above, the objective to practice might also be classified in the psychomotor domain, or working with a partner might be categorized as an affective objective.) Moreover, there may be a need for several objectives, stated at different achievement levels for an individualized learning experience described previously.

Of the utmost importance, however, is the *need* for writing objectives in all three learning domains, for learning takes place in all three of these domains constantly within any classroom. If the outcomes of the teaching process are to be educational in nature, then the *planning* of each learning experience is essential to the achievement of appropriate educational goals.

Values of behavioral objectives

The utilization of behavioral objectives offers the teacher of physical education concrete evidence of learning outcomes. At the same time, many other values are also afforded the student participant.

1. Guidelines for sequential learning and performance, from simple to complex, are generally developed in this behavioral format, thus allowing the student to select the task level appropriate for him or her and promoting individualized, self-directed learning.

2. Knowledge of the results of effort are almost immediate. This is provided by the evaluation or measurement process included in each objective.

3. A model of appropriate behaviors is often provided, in the form of written or audiovisual materials. The "condition" element expressed within each behavioral objective ensures this.

4. Meeting of a behavioral objective requires *action*. Therefore, the student is learning by doing something specific, with actions specified in the instructional verbs.

Critics of behavioral objectives point out that this standardization of performances is very mechanical and nonhumanistic and leaves little room for individualization and student interaction. Proponents of objectives answer these criticisms by emphasizing that one of their key values is individualization. When relevant behavioral objectives are established in terms of individual needs and interests and students are provided options regarding what learnings to pursue, these behavioral objectives become their guides and resources for further learning. With care and careful planning, the teacher can write behavioral objectives for all students at whatever stage of development they may be in and may plan execution of these objectives through appropriate individualized teaching methodology. Certainly not *all* learning that takes place within the classroom is measurable or even anticipated. But the utilization of instructional and behavioral objectives provides guidelines for teachers and students that in turn give evidence of results of that teaching process—the learning outcomes.

Self-assessment tests

These tests are to assist students in determining if material and competencies presented in this chapter have been mastered:

1. Without consulting your text state in your own words a definition of the terms *learning, instructional objective,* and *behavioral objective.* Give a sample of each.
2. Prepare a chart showing the levels of instructional objectives in taxonomic form for each of the three domains of learning. Cite an action verb appropriate for each level.
3. Select a physical education activity, such as basketball, and prepare a unit for instruction incorporating the taxonomy of instructional objectives in each learning domain.
4. An experienced teacher on your school faculty claims that traditional objectives are as effective as the newer behavioral objectives. Prepare a justification for behavioral objectives to convince this teacher of their value.
5. Write two behavioral objectives for measurement of learning outcomes in each of the three domains of learning. Select verbs from different levels in the hierarchy so that the developmental aspect of behaviors will be incorporated into your objectives.
6. You have just finished explaining testing procedures to a class of seventh-grade boys and girls who then begin to question you about the need for so many tests. Cite four reasons you might use to convince these learners of the value of assessment to them.

Points to remember

1. Through the writing of instructional objectives a teacher is better able to promote measurable changes in behavior.
2. Through the achievement of goals outlined in behavioral objectives the student is better able to assess his or her own learning.
3. Utilization of a taxonomy of instructional objectives

will ensure sequential and progressive learning activities.
4. Achievement of behavioral objectives lays the foundation for planning subsequent individualized learning experiences.
5. Achievement of behavioral objectives in one domain often may be dependent upon simultaneous achievement of objectives within the other learning domains.

Problems to think through

1. How are the needs and interests of each learner in the classroom met by behavioral objectives?
2. How much daily class time should be allocated to assessment procedures?
3. To what extent may students be relied upon to carry out self-assessment procedures? At what level may these procedures be introduced?
4. How do behavioral objectives become the "organizers" for teaching methodology within a daily lesson plan?

Case study for analysis

Parents in the high school community were concerned that students were not learning anything in physical education class. Explain how unit and lesson objectives might be utilized to answer these criticisms.

Selected readings

American Association for Health, Physical Education and Recreation: Knowledge and understanding in physical education, Washington, D.C., 1969, AAHPER.

American Association for Health, Physical Education and Recreation: Organizational patterns for instruction in physical education, Washington, D.C., 1971, AAHPER.

American Association for Health, Physical Education and Recreation: Curriculum improvement in secondary school physical education, Washington, D.C., 1973, AAHPER.

Bloom, B., editor: Taxonomy of educational objectives. Handbook I. Cognitive domain, New York, 1956, David McKay Co., Inc.

CSC Media Book: The cognitive domain, Washington, D.C., 1972, Gryphon House.

CSC Media Book: The psychomotor domain, Washington, D.C., 1972, Gryphon House.

Davis, R.: Writing behavioral objectives, Journal of Health, Physical Education and Recreation 44:47-49, 1973.

Gronlund, N. E.: Stating behavioral objectives for classroom instruction, New York, 1970, Macmillan Publishing Co., Inc.

Gruben, J. J., and Kirkendall, D. R.: "Effectiveness of motor, intellectual and personality domains in predicting group status in disadvantaged high school pupils," Research Quarterly 44:423-433, 1973.

Harrow, A. J.: A taxonomy of the psychomotor domain, New York, 1972, David McKay Co., Inc.

Hartman, B., and Clement, A.: Adventures in key concepts, The Ohio Guide for Girls Secondary Physical Education, Journal of Health, Physical Education and Recreation **44**:20-22, 1973.

Krathwohl, D. R., Bloom, B. S., and Masia, B. B.: Taxonomy of educational objectives. Handbook II. Affective domain, New York, 1964, David McKay Co., Inc.

Kryspin, W. J., and Feldhusen, J. F.: Writing behavioral objectives, Minneapolis, 1974, Burgess Publishing Company.

Simpson, E.: The classification of educational objectives, psychomotor domain, Illinois Teacher **10**:110-144, Winter 1966-1967.

Singer, R. N., and Dick, W.: Teaching physical education: a systems approach, Boston, 1974, Houghton-Mifflin Company.

Snider, R. C.: Should teachers say no to MBO?" Today's Education **65**:44-46, March-April 1976.

Tanner, D.: Using behavioral objectives in the classroom, New York, 1972, Macmillan Publishing Co., Inc.

17

METHODS AND MATERIALS FOR TEACHING TEAM SPORTS

INSTRUCTIONAL OBJECTIVES AND COMPETENCIES TO BE ACHIEVED

After reading this chapter the student should be able to—

1. Identify the values of team sports in a secondary school program of physical education.
2. Apply methods of teaching to team sports normally found in a physical education program.
3. Write instructional objectives in the three domains of learning for each of the team sports normally included in a program of physical education.
4. Select methods of teaching appropriate for the accomplishment of instructional objectives in each of the three domains of learning.
5. Incorporate considerations for the nature of the game and the nature of the group into selection of teaching methodology.
6. Derive behavioral objectives from instructional objectives in each of the three domains of learning.

It is the purpose of this chapter to discuss the implementation of teaching methods in activities classified as team sports. A team sport is one that generally involves the combined efforts of three or more players competing in a game situation against an equal number of opponents.

Team sports normally found in secondary school physical education include baseball, basketball, field hockey, football (touch football and flag football), ice hockey, lacrosse, recreational games (dodgeball, etc.), soccer, softball, speedball, team handball, volleyball, and water polo. They are often the favorite activity of adolescent students and are taught extensively throughout the upper levels of a progressive program. To meet standards now required by Title IX regulations, boys and girls will be participating together for the first time in many of these team games. Therefore, selected teaching methods must now take into consideration the extreme variations in needs, abilities, and interests found in coeducational classes.

The values of football, softball, soccer, and the many other team sports are numerous. The physical skill and fitness benefits, the opportunities for intellectual growth and development, and the multitude of social interactions combine to make team sports an excellent educational experience. Because of these inherent values and their widespread appeal, physical educators should strive to present team sports to students in a manner that will provide meaningful experiences throughout their secondary curriculum. Thoughtful selection of teaching methods will accomplish this end. Following is a brief discussion of each of the teaching methods presented in an earlier chapter, with a description of its application to the teaching of team games.

TEAM SPORTS
Methods for teaching team sports

Lecture may be effectively used to introduce a new game or unit to a large number of students in one class period. The content may include a history of the game, the nature of the game or activity, and objectives for the unit.

Verbal explanation may be used at the beginning of a class period to present new material briefly to a large or small number of students. Content of verbal explanation may include skill development hints, strategy concepts, team formations, promotion of social interactions, and cooperation.

Verbal explanation may also be used effectively in the middle of a class period to redi-

Fig. 17-1. Basketball game as part of physical education program at Regina High School in Cincinnati, Ohio.

rect group interactions or to stress or highlight important concepts to be learned. At the close of a period verbal explanations may be used to review specific daily objectives and to announce plans for future lessons.

Demonstration may be used to introduce the activity as a whole, as in a demonstration of a total game, or to introduce specific skills and concepts involved in the game. Offensive and defensive strategies may also be explained by means of a demonstration or teamwork and position play. Demonstrations may be given for large or small groups of players, and although they may be presented at any point during a class period, they are usually more effective at the beginning of a session, thus avoiding interruptions of activity.

Practice-drill and reinforcement-feedback are often used following demonstration of a specific skill being developed in a team game. Small groups may be organized for the practice of a single skill, or several skills may be practiced simultaneously and groups rotated to various drill stations. Feedback from practice sessions may be provided by group leaders, partners, or teachers, as well as by knowledge of results from the performance itself.

Tasks may also be used to develop skills found in team games. Individuals, singly or in small groups, may independently seek to improve their skills by striving to accomplish specific tasks (behavioral objectives) established from the game or activity. Because this method consists of independent modules, students may develop skills that are particularly weak. Also, because of the design of task experiences, students may have *more* developmental *opportunities* than in practice-drill situations. However, because of the larger number of students who usually elect or are assigned to team activities, the task method may be more difficult to organize than the practice-drill setup for skill development.

Reciprocal teaching requires the use of partners or small groups for skill development, as in the task method. Again, because of large numbers involved in team activities, this may be difficult to organize for all class members.

This method may be incorporated into game play by giving players the responsibility of analyzing a partner's playing skills and then alternating into an active role while the partner becomes the passive observer. Small groups may work effectively together to develop game strategies—offensive plays or defensive maneuvers during team scrimmages organized in class.

Guided discovery may be used to allow individuals or small groups to accomplish specific skill development objectives, or, more creatively, to discover teamwork patterns that use each member's skills most effectively.

Problem solving may be used to allow individuals or small groups opportunities to devise new strategies or game play regulations that may provide new challenges for competition as well as change the game. For example, changing field dimensions, the numbers of objects being used in a game, or the limitations on players may change a game structure in such a way that it becomes more demanding as far as skill objectives or teamwork operations. This method may also be used to develop totally new game situations based on given sets of equipment, facilities, and conditions.

Contract teaching may be adapted for individuals within a team setting. For example, cognitive objectives may be met through establishment of contracts so that students may study history, rules, etiquette, current events, or personalities involved in the game under study. Contracts may also be written that incorporate specific tournament regulations or position variations among team members that should be met by the end of the unit.

Independent study may not be as adaptable a method of teaching team games as other types of activities are. However, there may be opportunities for a student to play on an approved community team (ice hockey, for example, or a Babe Ruth League team) or to conduct an independent research project on a team activity, thereby meeting specified program requirements.

Question-answer may be used to further

cognitive development through implementation at the close of a class period. On the lower levels of the cognitive taxonomy, knowledge of facts, principles, and concepts underlying team sports can be elicited. Higher level questioning can promote application, analysis, synthesis, and evaluation processes concerning conceptualization of the sport under study.

Evaluation may be used at the close of each class period and at the end of a unit of study. Testing may be written or oral or may be performance-based examinations that have been standardized against national norms or are teacher-made instruments. Both self-evaluation and class-evaluation procedures may be used to measure achievement of objectives for the unit.

Audiovisual materials may be used in several different ways for the teaching of team games. Films, loop films, and videotapes may be used in combination with lectures at the beginning of a unit or with demonstrations, tasks, and contract teaching. Reading materials may be assigned for cognitive objectives in association with independent study assignments. Charts, posters, chalk boards, and magnetic boards are also particularly effective for developing skills and team strategies.

From the previous discussion it may be seen that all of the several methods of teaching may be in some way implemented in the teaching of team games. Selection of the most effective method should be based specifically on the instructional objectives established for the unit with daily behavioral objectives evaluating the results. The schematic representation on the next page shows how teaching methods based on theory and knowledge form the bridge between student and teacher and how evaluation through objectives provides feedback to complete the learning cycle.

Suggested instructional objectives for team sports

On the following pages some suggested instructional objectives are outlined for each of the team sports frequently found in pro-

Fig. 17-2. Cycle of learning.

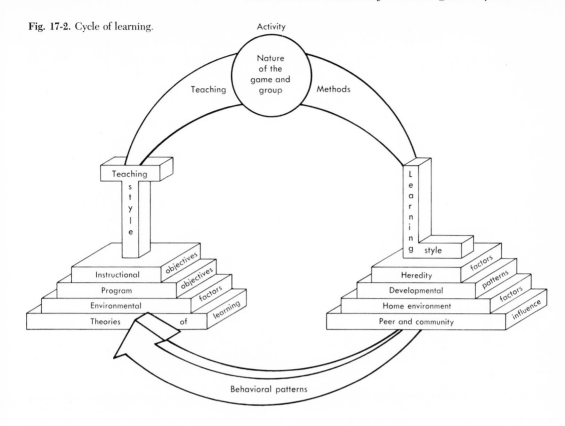

grams on an introductory level when students are first becoming exposed to an indepth study of a team sport. Only a few instructional objectives have been included from each of the three learning domains. They are not intended to represent the *totality* of instructional objectives that the instructor should incorporate in his or her unit of teaching. Rather, they are intended to point the direction and provide a basis for determining possible areas to be covered. It should be noted that many similarities exist among the objectives within the three learning domains for team sports. Differences in objectives generally stem from the nature of the game itself.

Methods of teaching have also been cited to indicate suggested ways in which material might be incorporated in the unit of study. Again these are only suggestions, and by no means are they intended to be required methods of teaching, or the *only* means available. Similarities in teaching methodology will be recognized with differences and selec-

tion depending again on the nature of the game and the group involved. For this reason a section covering special considerations for each team sport and its problems and possible solutions has also been included.

SOCCER/SPEEDBALL
Instructional objectives
Cognitive

• The student will acquire knowledge of rules and regulations of the game, history and development of the sport, international competition and tournaments, national leagues and players, and care and selection of safety equipment.

• The student will understand concepts of spin as it relates to the pathway of the ball in flight and to its rebounding.

Affective

• The student will strive to develop an awareness of position play by being responsible for covering his or her own area and marking his or her opponent.

• The student will practice all styles of kicking with the nonpreferred foot in order to improve his or her contribution to the team.

Psychomotor

• The student will develop the following basic skills: passing (inside and outside of foot), place kicking, dribbling (inside and outside of foot), heading, throwing, instep driving, chipping, volleying, and half-volleying. (For speedball, the additional skills of punting, drop-kicking, and catching will be developed.)

• The student will develop physical skills of endurance, eye-foot coordination, quickness, speed, agility, and leg power.

Methods
Cognitive

• The student will acquire knowledges through reading of textbook and rule books, through audiovisual demonstrations, and through reading of the local newspaper.

• The student will study concepts of spin in a reciprocal or small group teaching situation wherein types of spin are experimentally introduced.

Affective

• The student will watch films and demonstration games, then discuss position play within his small groups.

• The student will practice with his nonpreferred foot at learning stations doing tasks established for that purpose.

Psychomotor

• The student will practice-drill on his or her own to develop soccer skills after viewing films and demonstrations. Tasks, reciprocal teaching, and individualized learning packages may also be utilized (see sample modules).

• The student will develop physical abilities at the beginning of each class through individualized exercise programming.

Special considerations	Problems	Solutions
Nature of game		
Movement pace	Very rapid game	Use substitutes.
Safety	Contact injuries	Instruct to play the ball; wear equipment.
Equipment	Enough shin pads	Allow persons who are practicing skills to share pads with those who are playing.
Nature of group		
Size of group	Too large	Substitute in; play with more than eleven, if field large enough.
Skill level	Diversified	Individualize for practice; make homogeneous teams; put less skilled in backfield at beginning.
Coeducational	Boys may be more skilled; faster.	Use all girls in lines at forward, put all boys in backfield, and alternate.

Fig. 17-3. Soccer at Paul J. Gelinas Junior High School in Setauket, N.Y.

SOCCER SKILL MODULE*

DRIBBLING

Terminal skill objective: Given a slalom course consisting of five cones placed 5 feet apart in a straight line, you will start to the right of the first cone and be able to dribble a soccer ball down and back through the course and cross the finish line within a time limit you have set.

Inputs. Decide which ones you need or want. (Enter the numbers of these inputs in the progress section of your program record.)

1. Watch the loop film on dribbling (projector 1).
2. Read pages 10 to 12 in the *Soccer Skill Handbook*.
3. Watch and listen to the demonstration-explanation on the dribble by the teacher (Friday's class).
4. Watch a varsity or junior varsity soccer game at the high school (see the schedule in the main hallway).
5. Watch a professional soccer game on television.
6. Watch a classmate practicing the dribble.

Practices. Decide which ones you need or want. (Enter the numbers of these practices in the progress section of your program record.)

1. Get a soccer ball and practice dribbling with your right foot at a walk, then a fast walk, then a skip, then a run.
2. Do the same as in 1, but use your left foot.
3. Do the same as in 1, but you use your right and left feet.
4. Do the same as in 3, but ask a classmate to tell you if you are doing anything wrong.
5. Get a soccer ball and practice on the practice slalom course.
6. Attend open gym after school on Wednesdays to do any of the above.

Terminal test. Any time you feel you are ready:

1. Find one of the three class timers and go to the test slalom course.
2. Put the ball on the start mark and, at the timer's "go" signal, go through the course just as you did for the preassessment.
3. If you meet your goal, the timer should put his or her initials and your score in the proper "terminal objective complete" box in the progress section of your program record.
4. If you do not meet your goal, the timer should put his or her initials and your score in the proper "terminal objective attempt" box in the progress section of your program record. Then decide on the inputs or practices you should repeat or do for the first time.

TRAP AND KICK

Terminal skill objective: Given a line placed 15 feet from a 10-foot-wide goal marked on the wall and a soccer ball bounced to you from the left of the goal, you will stand behind the line and be able to trap the ball and score a goal within three seconds, at a success rate of at least 2 out of 5.

Inputs. Decide which ones you need or want. (Enter the numbers of these inputs in the progress section of your program record.)

1. Watch the loop film on trapping (projector 2).
2. Watch the loop film on passing (projector 3).
3. Read pages 14 to 16 in the *Soccer Skill Handbook*.
4. Read pages 21 to 24 in the *Soccer Skill Handbook*.
5. Watch and listen to the demonstration-explanation on trapping by the teacher (Friday's class).
6. Watch a varsity or junior varsity soccer game at the high school (see the schedule in the main hallway).
7. Watch a professional soccer game on television.
8. Watch a classmate practice trapping and kicking.

*Reprinted with permission of R. Hurwitz, State University of New York College at Brockport.

Continued.

SOCCER SKILL MODULE—cont'd

Practices. Decide which ones you need or want. (Enter the numbers of these practices in the progress section of your program record.)

1. Get a soccer ball and find a classmate who would like to practice trapping and kicking. Have the classmate roll the ball to you from about 10 feet away; trap the ball and pass it back. Then take your turn passing to the classmate. Tell each other if you are doing anything wrong.
2. Do the same as in 1, but stand about 15 feet away from your classmate and bounce the ball (low bounce) to each other.
3. If no one is taking the terminal test at the test area, practice the actual test with a classmate.
4. Attend open gym after school on Wednesdays to do any of the above.

Terminal test. Any time you feel you are ready:

1. Ask the teacher to give you the terminal test.
2. If you meet your goal, the teacher will put his or her initials and your score in the proper terminal objective complete box in the progress section of your program record.
3. If you do not meet your goal, the teacher will put his or her initials and your score in the proper terminal objective attempt box in the progress section of your program record. Then decide on the inputs or practices you should repeat or do for the first time.

REBOUND PASSING

Terminal skill objective: Given a line placed 8 feet from the wall, a soccer ball placed on the floor behind the line, and a time limit of thirty seconds, you will be able to rebound pass the ball off the wall from behind the line a number of times you have decided.

Inputs. Decide which ones you need or want. (Enter the numbers of these inputs in the progress section of your program record.)

1. Watch the loop film on passing (projector 3).
2. Read pages 21 to 24 in the *Soccer Skill Handbook*.
3. Watch and listen to the demonstration-explanation on passing by the teacher (Monday's class).
4. Watch a varsity or junior varsity soccer game at the high school (see the schedule in the main hallway).
5. Watch a professional soccer game on television.
6. Watch a classmate practicing rebound passing.

Practices. Decide which ones you need or want. (Enter the numbers of these practices in the progress section of your program record.)

1. Get a soccer ball and find a classmate who would like to practice passing. Stand about 5 feet from each other and pass the ball back and forth with your right feet. Do not stop the ball; try to keep it going. Tell each other what you are doing wrong.
2. Do the same as in 1, but use your left feet.
3. Do the same as in 1, but use both your right and left feet.
4. Do number 1, 2 or 3, but stand about 10 feet apart and pass a little harder.
5. Do any of the above, but try passing a foot or two to the right or the left of the other person each time.
6. Get a soccer ball, stand about 8 feet from an empty space on the wall, and practice rebound passing.
7. Attend open gym after school on Wednesdays to do any of the above.

Terminal test. Anytime you feel you are ready:

1. Find one of the three class timers, find a classmate who will count for you, and go to the rebound passing test area.
2. Put the ball on the floor behind the line and, at the timer's "go" signal, pass the ball against the wall as many times as you can before the timer says "stop" (thirty seconds). Do not go over the line except to get the ball if it stops. If this happens, put the ball on the floor behind the line before you start passing again.

SOCCER SKILL MODULE—cont'd

3. The counter should count the number of times the ball hits the wall before the timer says "stop." The counter should tell this number to the timer.
4. If you meet your goal, the timer should put his or her initials and your score in the proper terminal objective complete box in the progress section of your program record.
5. If you do not meet your goal, the timer should put his or her initials and your score in the proper terminal objective attempt box in the progress section of your program record. Then decide on the inputs or practices you should repeat or do for the first time.

PARTNER PASSING

Terminal skill objective: You and a partner will be able to pass a soccer ball back and forth at least four times while moving from the black line at one end of the gym to the black line at the other end of the gym within a time limit set by you and your partner, and with a maximum of three errors.

Inputs. Decide which ones you need or want. (Enter the numbers of these inputs in the progress section of your program record.)

1. Watch the loop film on passing (projector 3).
2. Read pages 21 to 24 in the *Soccer Skill Handbook.*
3. Watch and listen to the demonstration-explanation on passing by the teacher (Monday's class).
4. Watch a varsity or junior varsity soccer game at the high school (see the schedule in the main hallway).
5. Watch a professional soccer game on television.
6. Watch your classmates practicing partner passing.

Practices. Decide which ones you need or want. (Enter the numbers of these practices in the progress section of your program record.)

1. Get a soccer ball and find your assigned partner. Stand about five feet from each other and pass the ball back and forth with your right feet. Do not stop the ball; try to keep it going. Tell each other what you are doing wrong.
2. Do the same as in 1, but use your left feet.
3. Do the same as in 1, but use your right and left feet.
4. Do the same as in 3, but walk with your partner in a certain direction, passing the ball back and forth. Ask a classmate to watch you and your partner and tell you if you are doing anything wrong.
5. Do the same as in 4, but walk faster.
6. Do the same as in 4, but run.
7. Attend open gym after school on Wednesdays to do any of the above.

Terminal test. Any time you and your partner feel you are ready:

1. Find one of the three class timers and go to the partner passing test area with your partner.
2. Put the ball on the starting line in front of you or your partner, and at the timer's "go" signal, move to the finish line while passing the ball back and forth with your partner. Remember, you must pass the ball at least four times.
3. The timer will count the errors (each time one of you loses control of the ball or has to stop or back up to receive a pass).
4. If you meet your goal, the timer should put his or her initials and your scores in the proper terminal objective complete box in the progress section of your program record.
5. If you do not meet your goal, the timer should put his or her initials and your scores in the proper terminal objective attempt box in the progress section of your program record. Then decide on the inputs or practices you should repeat or do for the first time.

FOOTBALL (FLAG/TOUCH)
Instructional objectives
Cognitive

• The student will acquire knowledge of the basic rules of the game's history, development of the sport, care and selection of equipment, current national league teams, and leading personalities.

• The student will understand and apply basic concepts regarding receipt and propulsion of a football, in comparison with other balls.

• The student will develop basic offensive and defensive team strategies.

Affective

• The student will respond carefully and appropriately to game situations, avoiding unnecessary or overzealous body contact.

• The student will be aware of player positioning and responsibilities and try to react to game situations in a manner most helpful to the conduct of the game, rather than for self-gratification.

Psychomotor

• The student will develop skills of passing, punting, receiving, dodging, running, blocking, kicking, and tagging.

• The student will develop those physical abilities essential to the game, including speed, strength, endurance, eye-hand coordination, eye-foot coordination, agility, quickness, and power.

Methods
Cognitive

• The student will acquire knowledge of the game by reading assignments from a textbook and rule book, by watching other participants, by reading the local newspapers, and listening to lectures and verbal explanations on equipment, history, and development of the game.

• The student will study special tasks at learning centers wherein concepts regarding receipt and propulsion of a football are described. Through guided discovery the student will find his or her own answers to determine the best way to move the ball.

• Together with others in a small group the student will design offensive and defensive team strategies for use in tag and touch football situations.

Affective

• The student will study player positioning and responsibility in various game situations, analyzing effective maneuvers for each situation with others in a small group, to determine the best resultant play.

• When playing, the student will constantly be aware of the safety of others, and will strive to adapt his or her moves to the needs of the play, discussing these problems daily with small groups.

Psychomotor

• The student will develop physical skills necessary for the game through practice-drill with reinforcement feedback, through tasks at learning stations, and through films.

• The student will develop physical abilities necessary to improved playing of the game through performance of a series of tasks and exercises at the beginning of each daily period.

Special considerations	Problems	Solutions
Nature of game		
Movement pace	Very fast	Use substitutes.
Safety	Contact	Teach proper blocking and tagging procedures.
Equipment	Expensive	Improvise with hand-made flags; use plastic or less expensive footballs.
Nature of group		
Size of group	Too large	Use platoons or substitutes
Skill level	Extremely varied	Place less skilled players in drills; in homogeneous groups for playing.
Coeducational	Boys monopolize	Adapt rules; boys must tag with both hands; put girls only in front lines, then alternate.

SOFTBALL/BASEBALL
Instructional objectives
Cognitive

• The student will acquire knowledge of the rules and regulations of the game, the history and development of the game in this country and abroad, the structure of current national leagues, and leading personalities, and care and selection of equipment.

• The student will understand and apply basic concepts regarding the application of force to an object and the receipt and propulsion of an object.

• The student will develop strategies for offensive and defensive team play.

Affective

• The student will become aware of strengths and weaknesses in his or her own abilities and will select the position that maximizes his or her assets yet will practice on his own to improve.

• The student will remain alert during game play and will respond correctly to game situations by making appropriate play.

Psychomotor

• The student will develop skills essential to the playing of the game, including throwing, catching, hitting, bunting, base running, and pitching.

• The student will develop physical skills of quickness, speed, eye-hand coordination, and throwing power.

Methods
Cognitive

• The student will acquire knowledge through reading textbook and rule book, and newspaper articles, and through listening to lectures and verbal explanations related to the game.

• The student will study concepts of force in learning stations with tasks established for that purpose, paying particular attention to distinctions in throwing and bunting the ball.

Affective

• The student will discuss responsibilities of various positions on the team in small groups and the skills necessary to fulfill each position and will then determine a position most suitable to his or her own abilities.

• During game play the student will encourage all players to remain alert through chatter and with every play will be thinking what play would be necessary if the ball should come to him.

Psychomotor

• The student will study films and work in small groups to improve skills necessary to the game. Through task completion, guided discovery, and practice-drill with feedback the student will develop movements that are most effective for game play.

• The student will develop physical abilities necessary to the game through performance of exercises at the beginning of class.

Special considerations	Problems	Solutions
Nature of game		
Movement pace	Slow	Do running exercises prior to game play; adapt rules to change infield-outfield more often.
	All players may not get to bat or touch ball.	Play adapted games in small groups so that everyone is involved.
Safety	Injuries from bat, ball, sliding	Wear protective equipment; adapt rules until skill developed.
Equipment	Not enough for everyone	Let students bring own gloves.
Nature of group		
Size of group	Too large	Rotate groups through skill stations into game play.
Skill level	Varied; no one able to pitch	Use highly skilled as assistants; do not call strikes, balls.
Coeducational	Girls afraid of catching ball thrown by boys	Practice to develop skill; wear gloves.

ICE HOCKEY
Instructional objectives
Cognitive

• The student will acquire knowledge of the rules of ice hockey, proper care and selection of skates and equipment, history and development of the sport, current status of hockey league teams on a national level, and names of leading professionals.

• The student will understand and apply concepts of balance, speed, and force as they relate to puck handling and shooting.

• The student will design offensive and defensive team strategies for play at full strength and when killing penalties with one or two persons down.

Affective

• The student will become aware of personal skill strengths and weaknesses and put forth effort to improve bilaterally.

• The student will be concerned with and assume responsibility for the safety of others by trying to skate with control and by trying to body check correctly.

• The student will appreciate the need for positioning and teamwork in the development of offensive play patterns and power plays, as well as in defensive strategies.

Psychomotor

• The student will develop skating skills with equipment *on* (forward, backward, stopping, stance, and carriage) plus puck-handling skills, shooting (slap shots on both sides, snap shots, back hand, and wrist shots), checking, and goal tending.

• The student will improve physical abilities necessary for the game, such as endurance, speed, power, strength, agility, quickness, and eye-hand coordination.

Methods
Cognitive

• The student will acquire knowledge for ice hockey through loop films, game films, reading textbook and official rule book, special explanation on equipment and skates, and reading local newspaper articles of ice hockey league play.

• The student will study concepts of balance, speed, and force in tasks designed for that purpose at learning centers.

• The student will design strategies at chalkboard sessions with small groups where offensive and defensive tactics will be developed for teams at full strength and when playing short.

Affective

• Working independently to discover his or her own weaknesses, the student will examine his or her own skill development and then practice-drill to improve left-handed and right-handed shooting and stick handling.

• The student will study and apply positioning tactics for improved teamwork as an offensive and defensive player.

• The student will constantly be alert to the safety of others and will develop methods of control and body checking that will be appropriate in game situations.

Psychomotor

• During practice-drill with reinforcement feedback and during task assignments at learning centers, the student will develop skating and stick-handling skills necessary for game play.

• Prior to drills and game play each day the student will work out through power skating to improve physical abilities necessary for the game. Speed and power will be emphasized for a specified time limit at the beginning of class.

Special considerations	Problems	Solutions
Nature of game		
Movement pace	Very rapid	Change lines often
Safety	Checking injuries; stick injuries	Teach proper checking techniques and stick-handling; wear equipment at all times.
Equipment	Expensive	Budget over a long period; acquire slowly; teach proper care.

Special considerations	Problems	Solutions
Nature of group		
Size of group	Too large	Use platoon system.
Skill level	Varied	Group by ability; develop skills daily in drills.
Coeducational	Contact	Not required to be integrated by Title IX.

WATER POLO
Instructional objectives
Cognitive

• The student will acquire knowledge of rules and regulations for the game, history and development of the game, special safety procedures and etiquette in water polo, and game adaptations for different skill levels.

• The student will understand and apply principles of offensive and defensive strategies for teams of equal as well as unequal strength.

Affective

• Students will show a concern for the safety of participants at all times, with particular attention to fatigue and injury.

• The student will be aware of positions of teammates, encouraging utilization of entire swimming area.

Psychomotor

• The student will develop strong leg kicks, plus the following basic skills: ball carrying, passing, shooting, guarding, blocking, and goal tending.

• The student will develop stamina, endurance, leg strength, and eye-hand coordination for playing water polo. It will also be important to develop breath control and breath-holding techniques for underwater work.

Methods
Cognitive

• The student will learn the rules of the game from the bulletin board materials and verbal explanations. Safety procedures, etiquette, and adaptations will be discussed *each* day of the unit. History of the game will be learned through brief lecture.

• The student will develop offensive and defensive strategies in small groups for immediate utilization in team play. Adaptations or limitations will be designed to equalize teams whenever the need occurs on the basis of swimming levels of players each day.

Affective

• Nonparticipating students will be responsible for observation and life guarding of all students and will encourage game play using total swimming area available and keeping swimmers spread out.

Psychomotor

• The student will seek to develop leg strength in kicking drills designed specifically for that purpose. Ball-handling skills will be developed in small group work prior to game play.

• Physical abilities will be improved through daily workouts at the beginning of each class, with all swimming lanes utilized for individual practice of specific tasks.

Special considerations	Problems	Solutions
Nature of game		
Movement pace	Very rapid	Substitute frequently, or change lines.
Safety	Vitally important	Teach rescue skills, lifeguarding; enforce all rules.
Equipment	Goals are expensive	Improvise with cones, etc.
Water depth	Uneven, due to diving area	Change sides in game, so both teams have shallow.
Nature of group		
Size of group	Too large	Do not crowd pool or swimming area; use extras as guards.
Skill level	Variable	Must pass beginners test to play.
Coeducational	Boys monopolize ball	Play with all girls in forward positions, and boys in back; then alternate.

LACROSSE
Instructional objectives
Cognitive

• The student will acquire knowledge of the history and development of sport, the care and selection of equipment, and the rules and regulations of the game.

• The student will understand and apply concepts of levers as related to giving impetus to ball.

• The student will analyze offensive and defensive strategies during game play.

Affective

• The student will become aware of the importance of developing stick-handling skills and will practice for *control* of the ball.

• The student will encourage teammates to play proper positions for improvement of team play, as well as for safety purposes.

Psychomotor

• The student will develop basic fundamental skills of the game, including stick handling, cradling, scooping, throwing, catching, dodging, checking, shooting, and facing.

• The students will develop physical abilities essential to the game, including running speed, endurance, strength, and eye-hand coordination

Methods
Cognitive

• The student will acquire knowledge about the game through reading textbook and official rule book, watching films and a demonstration game, and will learn about the care and selection of equipment through lecture and application of information.

• The student will study lever concepts in independent study sessions organized with experiences designed for that purpose.

• The student will study offensive and defensive strategies through chalkboard discussions in small groups.

Affective

• Through practice-drill and task study at learning centers the student will develop *control* of the ball.

• In tournament games at the end of the unit the student will *vocally* encourage teammates to play in proper positions for safety and scoring purposes.

Psychomotor

• The student will practice-drill, complete tasks at learning centers, and work in small groups to develop skills necessary to the game.

• The student will accomplish a series of fitness exercises designed to improve necessary physical abilities for the individual.

Special considerations	Problems	Solutions
Nature of game		
Movement pace	Very intense	Use platoon system.
Safety	Contact injuries	Stress skills, position-play, proper equipment.
Equipment	Expensive; large quantities	Budget over a long period, add additional pieces each year; players should use equipment while drillers do without it.
Nature of group		
Size of group	Too many; too few	Use platoon system, use smaller field, adapt rules.
Skill level	Varied	Develop an established level of game skill before playing of game, use skilled players as assistants part of the time, homogeneously group players for games.
Coeducational	Contact injuries	Group players in lines according to sex if necessary.

VOLLEYBALL
Instructional objectives
Cognitive

• The student will acquire knowledge of the rules and regulations of the game, the history and development of the game, current international (Olympic) tournaments, leading teams, care of volleyball, and protective equipment.

• The student will comprehend and apply concepts of spin in relation to the striking of a volleyball in serving and receiving situations.

Affective

• The student will encourage teammates in the execution of setups and passes for improvement of teamwork.

• The student will combine alertness with teamwork in order to be ready to react appropriately at all times during game situations.

Psychomotor

• The student will develop volleyball skills including the volley, setup, spike, smash, and serve (underhand and overhead).

• The student will develop physical abilities of leg strength, arm strength, agility, and eye-hand coordination.

Methods
Cognitive

• The student will acquire knowledge through watching loop films and tapes, through reading textbook, official rule book, and current volleyball articles.

• The student will study concepts of spin in reciprocal or small group study situations, wherein types of spin are experimentally produced for practice.

Affective

• The student will participate in a series of volleyball games wherein he or she will be expected to encourage teammates from the sidelines in the execution of team play and, when it is his or her turn to play, will be ready to back up teammates on every play.

Psychomotor

• The student will improve volleyball skills through tasks set up at learning centers, through demonstration followed by practice-drill of skills, through loop films, and through reciprocal teaching with a partner or small group.

• The student will develop physical skills

essential to the game of volleyball through a series of exercises designed for those purposes to be carried out at the beginning of each class during the unit.

Special considerations	Problems	Solutions
Nature of game		
Movement pace	Slow for the unskilled	Adapt rules: lower net; combine unskilled with skilled players.
	Minimal cardiovascular development	Incorporate running activities into each daily lesson.
Safety	Injuries to fingers, knees, and from ball contact	Stress proper ball-handling technique; use of knee pads; courtesy.
Equipment	Setting up of standards and nets	Appoint student helpers, but supervise.
Nature of group		
Size of group	Too large	Rotate players in with each change of service, or play shortened games.
Size of individual	Too short	Alternate taller and shorter players in line-up; lower net for younger individuals.
Skill level	Extremely varied	Use skilled players to help develop skill in beginners, then group homogeneously for tournament play.
Coeducational	Boys dominate play	Stress courtesy; adapt rules—alternate turns and positions on court.

RECREATIONAL GAMES (WAR BALL, BOMBARDMENT, DOCTOR, PRISONER BALL, STICK BALL)
Instructional objectives
Cognitive

• The student will acquire a knowledge of rules and regulations for each of the games.

• The student will be able to apply concepts of game structure seen in existing games in developing new games for recreational activity.

Affective

- The student will appreciate the recreational value of games, feeling relaxation and satisfaction from participation.
- The student will follow all the rules of the recreational games and be able to serve fairly as his or her own referee.

Psychomotor

- The student will develop game skills necessary for each of the recreational activities, including throwing, catching, dodging.
- The student will improve physical abilities, particularly eye-hand coordination, in playing the games.

Methods
Cognitive

- The student will acquire knowledge of the rules of each game prior to participation through brief verbal explanation of the activity.
- The student will work with other small groups to develop new games based on given limitations of space, equipment, and numbers of players.

Affective

- The student will discuss in small groups the personal values and benefits received from participation.
- The students will be expected to call their own outs, violations, and fouls during recreational games and will be judged by peers.

Psychomotor

- The student will develop game skills and physical abilities through playing recreational games.

Special considerations	Problems	Solutions
Nature of game		
Movement pace	Variable	Provide many balls.
Safety	Ball thrown too hard at opponents	Partially deflate balls; instruct players to use control.
Equipment	Having enough balls	Use various types.

Special considerations	Problems	Solutions
Nature of group		
Size of group	Too large	Less aggressive players do not become involved.
Skill level	Less skilled never touch the ball or are eliminated	Allow players to return to activity after time limit or after a fly ball is caught.
Coeducational	Boys tend to monopolize balls and throw too hard	Adapt rules: boy must give ball to girl at certain times, or girls must play in certain zones in front.

FIELD HOCKEY
Instructional objectives
Cognitive

- The student will acquire knowledge of rules and regulations of the game, care and selection of equipment as related to size, history and development of the game, and safety procedures.
- The student will acquire an understanding of concepts of levers, in application of force to a stationary and moving target.
- The student will comprehend and apply techniques of teamwork and position play for offensive and defensive strategy.

Affective

- The student will be aware of positioning of teammates during scrimmage games and will cover, back up, and attack opponent as necessary.
- The student will control his or her stick to protect self and others during practice-drills and scrimmages.

Psychomotor

- The student will develop basic fundamental skills for hockey including dribbling, passing, shooting, dodging, tackling, lunging, the bully, scoop, and flick.
- The student will improve physical abilities of quickness, speed, endurance, agility, and eye-hand coordination.

Methods
Cognitive

• The student will acquire knowledge through lecture, audiovisual demonstrations, reading textbook and rule book assignments, and verbal explanations on equipment.

• The student will study concepts of levers in a problem solving center set up for that purpose.

• The student will work in small groups to develop offensive and defensive strategies, practicing against one another in different game situations.

Affective

• The student will participate in small discussion groups and in scrimmage practice sessions to develop signals with partners and nearby teammates to develop awareness of positions while playing together.

• The student will work with a partner on passing, keeping the stick low, and will be evaluated after each practice session.

Psychomotor

• The student will develop stickwork at learning centers, working in small groups on specified tasks at different levels of difficulty.

• The student will improve physical skills through assignment of individualized exercises to be completed at the beginning of each class. Developmental levels will be incorporated in items to be practiced.

Special considerations	Problems	Solutions
Nature of game		
Movement pace	Highly intense in game situations; speed essential	Substitute often; practice stick work at normal speed, not slow motion.
Safety	Hit shins; dangerous hitting	Wear shin pads; stress careful skill development in stick handling.
Equipment	Expensive; varied lengths of sticks needed; many shin pads	Buy a little each year; take good care of it; take turns; have only active players wear pads while others drill.

Special considerations	Problems	Solutions
Nature of group		
Size of groups	Too large	Use platoon system.
Skill level	Broad range	Play lead-up games with less skilled; develop skills in centers, use leaders to assist.
Coeducational	Boys less familiar with game	Allow girls to help teach; place boys in backfield positions at first, with girls as forwards playing against opposing girls.

BASKETBALL
Instructional objectives
Cognitive

• The student will acquire knowledge of rules and regulations of the game, history and development of the game, and of current leagues and leading players.

• The student will develop an understanding of physical laws governing giving and receiving of impetus.

• The student will comprehend and apply offensive and defensive team strategy.

Affective

• The student will experience playing offensive and defensive positions and will select that position most suited to his or her own abilities.

• The student will develop an appreciation for the complexities of the game of basketball and will support interscholastic programs and/or enter intramural tournaments.

Psychomotor

• The student will develop ball-handling skills of passing, catching, dribbling, and shooting.

• The student will improve physical abilities of quickness, speed, agility, and endurance. Leg strength and arm strength will be developed.

Fig. 17-4. Basketball in the Brockport Central Schools, Brockport, N.Y.

Methods
Cognitive

• The student will acquire knowledge through lecture, audiovisual films, and reading textbook and rule book assignments, plus local sports pages.

• The student will study physical laws in tasks at learning centers wherein guided discovery promotes understanding of concepts.

• The student will participate in chalkboard sessions in which offensive and defensive patterns and strategies are explained and developed.

Affective

• The student will play offensive and defensive positions during class sessions and be asked to select his or her preferred position for the tournament at the end of the unit.

• The student will be encouraged to attend interscholastic events and/or to enter intramural tournaments by being given a point toward his or her grade.

Psychomotor

• The student will develop ball-handling skills through practice-drill with reinforcement feedback at learning stations set up around the gymnasium. (See lesson plan in earlier chapter.) Tasks for individualized improvement and for reciprocal teaching will also be utilized.

• Physical skills will be improved through individualized warm-up tasks at the beginning of class.

Special considerations	Problems	Solutions
Nature of game		
Movement pace	Highly intense in game situations	Substitute often.
	Slow waiting for turn during practice	Provide as many balls and stations as possible.
Safety	Contact in games	Develop stops and starts and control.

Special considerations	Problems	Solutions
	Ball-handling injuries	Develop passing, catching skills, and stress ball control.
Equipment	Balls expensive	Stress proper care.
Nature of group		
Size of group	Too large	Play cross court; substitute often.
Skill level	Diversified	Group by skill level for games; use skilled players as assistants in a reciprocal arrangement.
Coeducational	Contact sport	Not required to be integrated.

TEAM HANDBALL
Instructional objectives
Cognitive

• The student will acquire knowledge of rules and regulations of the game, the history and development of the game, and of Olympic competition.

• The student will understand and apply offensive and defensive tactics for improved team play.

Affective

• The student will develop an appreciation for this new sport and will encourage others to participate in it.

Psychomotor

• The student will develop basic fundamental skills necessary to the game, including controlled ball-handling skills combined with running, dodging, and scoring.

• The student will improve physical abilities necessary to the game, especially working on arm power, endurance, speed, accuracy, eye-hand coordination, and agility.

Methods
Cognitive

• The student will acquire knowledge of team handball through reading assignments and demonstrations of games and will learn about the development of the sport through lecture presentations.

• The student will be given an opportunity to develop offensive and defensive team tactics in small group session during which strategies are discussed.

Affective

• The student will be given an opportunity to participate in the organization of this sport on an intramural level and will be given an opportunity to encourage others to join in this new activity.

Psychomotor

• The student will work on skill development through tasks at specified learning centers, through drilling with immediate feedback from partners or small groups, and through game play.

• The student will develop physical abilities essential to the game through exercises and drills performed prior to participation in game play.

Special considerations	Problems	Solutions
Nature of game		
Movement pace	Very fast	Use substitutes or platoon system.
	Unfamiliar	Motivate by using leaders to build enthusiasm; add to intramural program; invite others to watch a demonstration.
Nature of group		
Size of group	Very large	Use additional players in game by adapting rules or use platoon system.
Skill level	Varied	Use less skilled in backfield until ball-handling skills are developed.
Coeducational	Boys monopolize ball	Adapt rules—must use girls; put all girls in forward lines and boys in backfield; alternate.

Table 17-1. Suggested behavioral objectives for team sports*

Cognitive	Affective	Psychomotor
Basketball		
After studying an analysis of offensive and defensive strategies, student will design a successful offensive out-of-bounds play.	Student will assist partner for 5 minutes during shooting practice and offer suggestions and evaluative criticisms.	Student will score ten out of fifteen foul shots; student will successfully complete four types of passes during a scrimmage game.
After reading the rules for officiating, student will referee regular class game for 5 minutes, making correct calls 75% of time, according to judgment of partner.	Student will attempt to improve shooting accuracy by practicing on his or her own two or three times per week during unit.	Student will dribble in and out a zig-zag relay course with nonpreferred hand in less than 20 seconds.
Football		
Following chalkboard session, student will verbally distinguish between (1) roll-out, (2) spring-out, (3) drop-back passes to teammate.	Student will demonstrate effective teamwork by using the three following passes appropriately during scrimmage: (1) roll-out, (2) sprint-out, (3) drop-back.	Student will be able to initiate a fake and correctly run a flag pattern, post pattern sideline pattern, and button-hook pattern, according to task card instructions.
During loop film demonstration student will describe correctly to a partner the differences between flag pattern, post pattern sideline pattern, and button-hook pattern.	Students will remain after class to practice on his own the four passes on the loop film.	
Recreational games		
Student will add challenge to game by suggesting rule change that increases difficulty of competition as determined by teammates.	Student willingly abides by rules of the game, calling self out each time ball hits him/her, during game.	Student demonstrates improved catching ability by not dropping ball more than once during 5-minute game.
Given two balls, a pin, and a small group (10-12) of players, student will devise game using passing, throwing, and dodging skills.	Student exhibits appreciation for others by controlling his/her throws during game rather than bombarding opponent.	Student throws ball with accuracy, hitting opponent below waist 50% of time during 5-minute game.
Volleyball		
Student will formulate five test questions on rules of volleyball to be used in written test at end of class period.	Student will cover his/her position throughout the 15-point game, missing a return no more than three times.	Student will successfully execute three out of five overhand serves into opponent's court during drill.
Given two volleyballs and group of 6 players, the student will design drill for practice serves.	Student will offer verbal positive feedback to teammates throughout 15-point game each time serve comes to his/her side.	Student will set up ball effectively, getting 10-12 feet height 80% of time during a 15-point game.

*Sample objectives in all three domains of learning are provided to demonstrate how various methods of teaching may be applied to the teaching of team sports in a daily lesson.

Fig. 17-5. Volleyball game in progress at Homewood High School in Homewood, Ala.

SUGGESTED BEHAVIORAL OBJECTIVES FOR TEAM SPORTS

Following are suggested behavioral objectives that might be drawn from unit instructional objectives. Implicit within each is a teaching method that will elicit a measurable response from the student. This behavior, a result of the teaching methodology, serves as the indicator of learning—the learning outcome—as discussed in an earlier chapter. Based on the results of this evaluative process, the teacher and the student are able to plan future appropriate learning activities.

Because behavioral objectives are dependent upon previous learning, only a few samples are included here. The instructor will need to develop many individualized behavioral objectives if he or she hopes to promote individualized learning in team sports.

MATERIALS FOR TEACHING TEAM SPORTS
Special reading materials

National Association for Girls' and Women's Sports (NAGWS), AAHPER Publication Sales, 1201 16th St. N.W., Washington, D.C. 20036
Guides
Basketball guide
Field hockey–lacrosse guide
Soccer–speedball–flag football guide
Softball guide
Volleyball guide

Selected articles
Basketball
Field hockey–lacrosse
Softball
Wm. C. Brown Co., Publishers, 2460 Kerper Blvd., Dubuque, Iowa 52001
Activity booklets
Soccer
Softball: slow and fast pitch
Field hockey
Basketball
Ice hockey
Lacrosse for girls and women
The Athletic Institute, 200 Castlewood Drive, North Palm Beach, Fla. 33408
Sports technique books (paperback or hard cover)
Baseball
Basketball
Women's basketball
Ice hockey
Power volleyball
Soccer
Women's softball

Other publishers of sports series
Allyn & Bacon, Inc., 470 Atlantic Ave., Boston, Mass. 12210
Goodyear Publishing Co., Pacific Palisades, Calif. 90272
Prentice-Hall, Inc., Englewood Cliffs, N.J. 07636
Amateur Athletic Union, 233 Broadway, New York, N.Y. 10007

Slide films (sound and silent for purchase or rental)

The Athletic Institute, 200 Castlewood Drive, North Palm Beach, Fla. 33408
Baseball (7 units)

Basketball (7 units)
Basketball (girls; 8 units)
Field Hockey (5 units)
Soccer (3 units)
Softball (8 units)
Volleyball (4 units)
Student manual for each sport
Instructor's guide

Special charts (techniques)

National Association for Girls' and Women's Sports, AAHPER, 1201 16th St. N.W., Washington, D.C. 20036.
Basketball (twelve charts)
Softball (eleven charts)
Volleyball (eleven charts)

Self-assessment tests

These tests are to assist students in determining if material and competencies presented in this chapter have been mastered:

1. Cite values for boys and girls that are gained from participating in team sports during secondary school.
2. Select five methods of teaching that are particularly effective in meeting instructional objectives for team sports.
3. List several items the instructor wants students to know, to value, and to be able to do while learning a team sport.
4. Identify teaching methods that are particularly effective for meeting objectives in the cognitive domain. The affective domain. The psychomotor domain.
5. Discuss factors incorporated within a team game that require special consideration in selection of teaching methodology.
6. Evaluate learning a team sport through development of two behavioral objectives in each of the three domains of learning.

Points to remember

1. Methods used in teaching team sports in physical education classes should be selected to meet specific instructional objectives.
2. Many different methods may be utilized within a teaching unit, thus providing variety and an opportunity for meeting varying learning styles.
3. Factors found within the nature of the game and the group require consideration when planning a lesson on a team sport.
4. Evaluation through behavioral objectives provides an essential background for sequential planning.
5. Special consideration must be given to teaching coeducational team activities because of Title IX regulations.

Problems to think through

1. To what extent should psychomotor skill be developed prior to playing in a team game situation?
2. To what extent should game rules be modified during the introductory phases of a unit to promote activity in a game situation?
3. On what basis should lack of proper equipment be a determinant of participation in an activity?
4. To what extent should student officials be utilized in class activities?
5. To what extent should game play be incorporated in class-time or should students be encouraged to participate in intramural games instead?

Case study for analysis

To meet Title IX regulations the physical education instructor finds it necessary to combine unskilled boys with skilled girls in the field hockey unit, and unskilled girls with skillful boys in the football class. Plan a series of learning activities that will motivate these students to participate in the new activity.

Exercises for review

1. Design a contract in which the student may select from a series of tasks those that are most interesting to him or her for learning a team sport.
2. Plan an informative verbal explanation covering major points for position play in a team sport, and write three or four questions on the material presented.
3. Develop a practice-drill designed to incorporate *three* psychomotor skills utilized in one team sport.
4. Select a *concept*, such as application of force to an object, and design a series of tasks that will lead to an understanding of this concept as it relates to a team sport.
5. Develop a series of sequential problems that will lead to *discovery* about performance of a motor skill selected from a team sport.

Selected readings

American Association for Health, Physical Education and Recreation: Organizational patterns for instruction in physical education, Washington, D.C., 1971, AAHPER.
Bucher, C. A.: Physical education for life, New York 1969, McGraw-Hill Book Company.
Knapp, C., and Leonhard, P. H.: Teaching physical education in secondary schools, New York, 1968, McGraw-Hill Book Company.
Nixon, J. E., and Jewett, A. E.: Physical education curriculum, New York, 1964, The Ronald Press Company.
Smith, C. D., and Prather, S.: Group problem solving, Journal of Health, Physical Education and Recreation **46:**20-21, Sept. 1975.
Vannier, M., and Fait, H. F.: Teaching physical education in secondary schools, ed. 4, Philadelphia, 1975, W. B. Saunders Company.
Walker, J.: Cowell and Schwehn's Modern methods in secondary school physical education, Boston, 1973, Allyn & Bacon, Inc.
Willgoose, C.: The curriculum in physical education, ed. 2, Englewood Cliffs, N.J., 1974, Prentice-Hall, Inc.

18

METHOD AND MATERIALS FOR TEACHING INDIVIDUAL AND DUAL SPORTS

INSTRUCTIONAL OBJECTIVES AND COMPETENCIES TO BE ACHIEVED

After reading this chapter the student should be able to—

1. Adapt teaching methods to the meeting of instructional objectives for individual and dual sports.
2. Identify special problems relating to teaching individual and dual sports stemming from the nature of the game as well as from the nature of the group.
3. Discuss special solutions related to problems in teaching individual and dual sports.
4. Identify sources of materials for teaching individual and dual sports, including records for the inclusion of rhythmic activities.

A wide variety of activities is included in the area of individual and dual sports. Their values are numerous in terms of challenges to the individual student to develop and improve physical skills, many of which will be used in leisure activities in later years.

Individual and dual sports have long been a part of the American way of life. Recent years have seen the mushrooming of business interests in some of these sports, which matches the increase in leisure time enjoyed by people in every walk of life. The inclusion of these activities in secondary school physical education has been recognized as vital to the preparation of adolescents in recreational pursuits. Development of knowledge and understanding of these activities (cognitive), of wholesome attitudes and appreciation toward these activities (affective), and of proper skills and techniques for participation (psychomotor) will provide lasting enjoyment to each individual in the program.

DUAL SPORTS

For the purposes of this text, dual sports are identified as those games and activities in which one or two players compete against an equal number of opponents. Included in this classification are badminton, combatives (wrestling, judo, karate, fencing), handball, racquet ball, shuffleboard, squash, table tennis, and tennis.

Methods for teaching dual sports

All of the methods for teaching described in an earlier chapter may be adapted for teaching dual sports in secondary school. However, because the nature of these activities requires a small number of participants, certain methods may be more appropriate in a school setting. Motivation to achieve affective objectives—valuing these sports for life—is of particular importance in teaching methodology and must constantly be kept in mind during the planning stages of units of study.

Lecture may be used to introduce a unit, giving information to large or small numbers of students as needed. Because of the carryover value of these sports, motivation is extremely important, and an introductory lecture given by an outstanding player or professional from the community might greatly stimulate interest in the activity under study.

Verbal explanation may be used effectively to meet skill objectives, particularly in small groups, and to explain cognitive materials. Because fewer players are involved in these activities than in team sports, the explanation of roles of each player is simpler and may be accomplished in less time than in the more complex team games. For example, in the game of tennis, the player needs to learn his or her role as a singles player and as a doubles partner, whereas in the larger team games there are many different positions with which each player should become familiar.

Demonstrations of the game itself or of game elements may be handled with ease on the playing courts or in areas smaller than those required for dual games. Because of the popularity of many of these sports it is generally quite easy to arrange for skilled players to present a demonstration lesson that will have great motivational value early in a unit.

Practice drill and reinforcement-feedback may be used to develop physical skills for dual sports. However, because drills should be drawn from gamelike situations and inasmuch as only a few players are involved in games of this type, this method of teaching is not quite as functional for dual games as for team games. This would be especially true with very large classes, as students would need to take turns and would therefore spend quite a bit of class time being inactive.

Task teaching, guided discovery, problem solving, and reciprocal teaching may be more easily adapted to dual sport situations than some of the previous methods. With the small number of participants, objectives in all three learning domains may be met. For example, in the cognitive domain, concepts regarding levers (combatives) may be stressed; in the affective domain, working with a partner and developing an appreciation for the values of the activities; and in the psychomotor domain, developing strength and agility and developing striking skills. All these objectives may be introduced through small group arrangements

Fig. 18-1. Tennis at Paul J. Gelinas Junior High School in Setauket, N.Y.

and individualized instructional techniques.

Contracts and independent study projects may also be incorporated into dual sport activities very easily. Out-of-class programs in many of these activities may easily be arranged with community agencies or other private associations. Meeting administrative and curricular requirements to substitute these sports for school offerings is an important factor that will need to be handled, and extensive records will need to be kept on individual participation and progress.

Question-answer and evaluation methods may be useful in dual sports in the same way as in the team activities discussed earlier. Also audiovisual aids and materials may be used to provide supplementary information in dual sports just as in team sports. Excellent materials are becoming available, as may be seen from the listings at the close of this chapter.

Suggested instructional objectives for dual sports

On the following pages some suggested instructional objectives for each of the dual sports frequently found in programs of physical education are outlined. As was the case in the previous chapter, these objectives might be utilized in beginning or introductory classes and represent only some of the myriad of objectives that the teacher might identify in a particular situation.

BADMINTON
Instructional objectives
Cognitive

• The student will acquire knowledge of the rules and regulations of the game, terminology, care and selection of equipment, and history and development of the game.

• The student will understand and apply concepts of flight.

Fig. 18-2. Trampoline workout as part of the physical education program at Regina High School in Cincinnati, Ohio.

• The student will design tactics for working effectively with a partner in doubles.

Affective

• The student will analyze his or her own playing ability in terms of his or her strengths and weaknesses and practice those skills that most need development.

• The student will analyze his or her opponent's playing ability and adapt playing style accordingly in order to increase his or her score.

Psychomotor

• The student will develop basic physical skills necessary to the game, including the serve, clear, smash, lob, drop shot, and net shot.

• The student will develop physical abilities essential to the game, including eye-hand coordination, agility, and quickness.

Methods
Cognitive

• Through out-of-class assignments the student will read a sports technique book and a rule book on badminton. A handout with explanations of badminton terminology will also be provided.

• A brief verbal explanation at the opening of the unit will give necessary information on equipment, its care and selection.

• Material on the history and development of the game will be provided at the audio-visual center where pictures and loop films will be available to help the student acquire knowledge of the game.

• While working in small groups the student will experiment on the application of light, medium and strong force applied to the shuttlecock, in order to understand concepts of flight.

• The student will work with a partner to design playing strategies which will effectively be used against opponents in a doubles game.

Affective

• Working in individualized modules and following pretesting on basic skills, the student will analyze his or her own test results in comparison with others and will determine those strokes that need most improvement.

• During game situations the student will analyze opponents' weaker shots and will use this information to best advantage in order to win.

Psychomotor

• The student will work at learning centers to improve physical skills. Through reciprocal teaching by partners or small groups, loop films, and individualized modules, the student will set his or her own goals and strive to improve by posttesting at the end of the unit.

• Physical abilities of eye-hand coordination, agility, and quickness will be improved by practice at the various stations or centers.

Special considerations	Problems	Solutions
Nature of game		
Movement pace	Slow for beginners	Alternate playing and running by groups.
Equipment	Fragile	Teach proper care and control.
Safety/ space	Space needed *between* and *above* courts	Consider outdoors; caution partners to watch out for each other and side courts.
Nature of group		
Size of group	Too large	Rotate small groups to centers and/or exercise and running.
Skill level	Varied	Individualize in modules; set up tournaments by levels.
Coeducational	Younger boys may not want to team up with girls.	Have several different kinds of tournaments; allow options for mixed and unmixed groups.

COMBATIVES (fencing and wrestling)
Instructional objectives (fencing)
Cognitive

• The student will acquire knowledge of the history and development of fencing, care and selection of equipment, types of weapons, especially light-weight practice foil, tournament rules, regulations, and etiquette.

• The student will understand concepts of balance as applied to fencing in attacking and parrying strategies.

Affective

• The student will honor the formality of fencing bouts by following saluting procedures.

• The student will develop an awareness of body movements of his opponents, and will try to react quickly with appropriate countermoves.

Psychomotor

• The student will develop the skills necessary for fencing, including footwork (advance, retreat, lunge, combinations), attacks (thrusts, coupes), defenses (parry, counter).

• The student will develop necessary physical abilities, including leg strength, flexibility, and eye-hand coordination with balance.

Methods
Cognitive

• The student will acquire knowledge of fencing through watching a demonstration, researching the history and development of the sport, studying about weapons and their care and selection in a special handout.

• The student will study in a learning center about the relationship of a broad base of support to balance and stability as it relates to fencing.

Affective

• After observing fencing etiquette the student will follow saluting procedures and will encourage others to do so in order to participate in tournaments.

• The student will practice moves and counter moves with partner without weapons and with light-weight practice foils.

Psychomotor

• The student will develop the physical skills essential to fencing by practice sessions alone, with partners, trying to achieve out-lined objectives, both without and with lightweight practice foil. Partners will help to instruct one another. A tournament will provide appropriate learning challenges.

• The student will develop necessary physical abilities of leg strength, flexibility, eye-hand coordination and improved balance through a series of drills and warm-up activities prior to participation in bouts.

Special considerations	Problems	Solutions
Nature of game		
Movement pace	Variable; tiring	Alternate with other types of activity.
Equipment	Essential	Share; students in drills need not use.
Safety	Seldom a problem	Use lightweight practice foils; full-size jackets (not half-jackets).
Nature of group		
Size of group	Too large	Alternate drill groups and bouts.
Skill level	Varied	Group by level of skill.
Coeducational	Seldom a problem; mixed competition acceptable	Group by skill level.

Instructional objectives (wrestling)
Cognitive

• The student will acquire knowledge of rules for competition, weight classifications, proper dieting and weight control, and history and universality of sport.

• The student will understand concepts of mechanical principles as they apply to wrestling holds.

Affective

• The student will develop an awareness of his own strength and weaknesses and will practice to improve skills.

• The student will anticipate opponents' moves and respond appropriately.

Fig. 18-3. Wrestling as part of physical education program at Paul J. Gelinas Junior High School in Setauket, N.Y.

Psychomotor

• The student will develop balance, endurance, flexibility, agility, and strength, particularly neck strength.

• The student will learn to perform basic wrestling holds and moves, both as man on bottom, man on top, the take down, and the pins.

Methods
Cognitive

• The student will acquire knowledge of wrestling facts through reading assignments, will study and apply dieting and weight control suggestions, attend demonstrations and matches, compare Olympic and popular forms of wrestling.

• At learning centers where particular tasks are described the student will study and apply principles of levers in various wrestling holds and positions.

Affective

• The student will study pretest strength scores and set individual goals to improve special areas of weakness.

• The student will be alert to opponents options from both the mat and the top positions and will apply appropriate counter movements as instructed.

Psychomotor

• Before competing the student will concentrate on developmental tasks which will

improve strength in various muscle groups, paying particular attention to the neck muscles, through bridging exercises.

• In bouts with opponents of equal size and weight and ability the student will practice-drill, according to instructions, suggested moves; then he will participate in practice bouts.

Special considerations	*Problems*	*Solutions*
Nature of game		
Movement pace	Great effort sustained	Alternate periods of activity with rest and watching others.
Equipment	Mats needed to cover all surfaces and obstructions (pillars)	Save used mats for meeting additional needs.
Safety	Lack of mats; mats not properly taped or enough coverage; partner errors	Restrict participation on matted area until sufficient supply obtained; teach proper passive resistance in drills.
Nature of group		
Size of group	Too large	Offer other alternatives; rotate groups from mats to other learning centers.
Skill level	Varied	Group by ability, size, and weight classifications; motivate

Special considerations	Problems	Solutions
		the smaller boy to build strength so that he can succeed in this sport.
Coeducational	Not required by Title IX	

HANDBALL
Instructional objectives
Cognitive

• The student will acquire knowledge of the rules of the game, terminology, etiquette, and care and selection of equipment.
• The student will understand and distinguish different strategies utilized in singles and doubles play.

Affective

• The student will appreciate the value of developing skill in his or her nonpreferred hand and will practice additionally to achieve this goal.
• The student will anticipate opponent's moves and will react appropriately and swiftly to try to win the point or serve.

Psychomotor

• The student will develop physical skills essential to handball, including the serve (drive, lob, z-serve), back-wall shots, kill shots, volley shots, ceiling shots, and fist shots.
• The student will develop physical abilities necessary to the game including quickness, eye-hand coordination, agility, and endurance.

Methods
Cognitive

• The student will acquire knowledge of the game of handball through reading assignments in texts and rulebooks, observation of a demonstration game, and printed material on equipment.
• The student will meet in groups of two and three to design cutthroat and partner strategies to be applied in tournament games.

Affective

• Following pretesting with the nonpreferred and preferred hands, the student will spend additional time in meeting established individual goals for the nonpreferred hand.
• In tournament and practice games the student will strive to keep his or her opponent moving and off-balance so that he or she is unable to return the shot.

Psychomotor

• The student will develop physical skills through practice-drill and reinforcement feedback, sequential practice of a variety of shots and reciprocal teaching situations.
• The student will improve physical abilities through participation in practice games and tournaments.

Special considerations	Problems	Solutions
Nature of game		
Movement pace	Rapid	Take turns; adapt scoring system for game.
Equipment	No problem	
Safety-space	Availability of courts	Adapt to corners of gym
Nature of group		
Size of group	Too large	Rotate; offer alternatives.
Skill level	Varried	Pretest for homogeneous grouping.
Coeducational	Girls lack strength	Develop arm strength; adapt game in beginning.

RACQUETBALL/SQUASH
Instructional objectives
Cognitive

• The student will acquire knowledge of the history and development of the game, rules of the game, etiquette, and care and selection of equipment.
• The student will understand different strategies involved in singles, cutthroat and doubles play, with particular attention to angling and rebounding of the ball.

Affective

• The student will be aware of personal strengths and weaknesses, as well as those of his or her opponent during practice games and tournaments and strive to outplay his or her opponent to gain points or the serve.

• The student will appreciate the physical fitness values of these games and try to incorporate them into free time outside of class.

Psychomotor

• The student will develop necessary basic skills for these games, including forehands, backhands, back-wall shots, kills, volleys, and serves.

• The student will try to improve physical abilities necessary for these games, including eye-hand coordination, agility, flexibility, and quickness.

Methods
Cognitive

• The student will acquire knowledge of the game through watching demonstration games, reading textbooks and rule books, and printed materials, and verbal explanations.

• The student will work in small groups of twos, threes, and fours in order to design tactics that are successfully utilized in game situations.

• The student will experiment with angle shots, as described on task cards at assigned learning stations.

Affective

• The student will enter a class tournament and will compete to the best of his or her ability.

• The student will seek out opportunities to play these games in out-of-class time and on weekends and will improve physical fitness, as measured by endurance jogging and in games.

Psychomotor

• The student will practice with a partner on assigned skills, strive to meet individualized goal objectives for various strokes in learning stations, and participate in practice games and class tournaments.

• The student will improve physical abilities by participating in these activities, both in and out of class, and by doing additional jogging for improved endurance.

Special considerations	Problems	Solutions
Nature of game		
Movement pace	Rapid	Rotate groups in game situations.
Equipment	Not enough	Students may have own racquets and balls.
Safety-space	Courts not available, accessible	Use corners of gyms or three walls; adapt game.
Nature of group		
Size of group	Too large	Allow observers to substitute often; play short games.
Skill level	Varied	Pretest; group by abilities for games; use advanced players to assist beginners.
Coeducational	Girls feel less skilled	Allow options for mixed and unmixed games.

SHUFFLEBOARD/TABLE TENNIS
Instructional objectives
Cognitive

• The student will acquire knowledge of the rules and regulations of the games, terminology of the games, and the care and selection of equipment.

• The student will comprehend and apply effective strategies for singles and doubles matches.

Affective

• The student will appreciate the recreational values of these games and will encourage others to enjoy them by organizing tournaments.

• The student will practice on his or her own to develop skills.

Psychomotor

• The student will develop essential skills for playing of these games including a controlled application of force in shuffleboard and of serves, volleys, chops, and slices in table tennis.

• The student will try to improve eye-hand coordination.

Methods
Cognitive

• The student will acquire knowledge of these games through observation of demonstration games and reading articles and booklets on rules and terminology and will listen to verbal explanations regarding care of various types of equipment.

• Through the playing of games with partners the student will discover various effective offensive and defensive strategies that will improve his or her doubles and singles games.

Affective

• The student will join with other members of the class in organizing tournaments for class members and other interested students.

• The student will seek opportunities to

Fig. 18-4. Table tennis in the Brockport Central Schools, Brockport, N.Y.

practice on his or her own to improve his or her game skills.

Psychomotor

• The student will practice in small groups to meet objectives on task cards designed to incorporate various levels of force in shuffleboard and table tennis; he or she will experiment with various types of spins and placement of table tennis serves and other shots; he or she will practice singly against the backboard in tennis table or shoot at the shuffleboard goal to improve physical skills.

• The student will attempt to improve eye-hand coordination through repeated striking of objects with the hand or small paddle. This may be done at learning centers specifically designed with tasks for this purpose.

Special considerations	Problems	Solutions
Nature of game		
Movement pace	Light activity	Alternate with more strenuous games.
Equipment	Sufficient quantities	Students may bring table tennis items from home.
Safety	No problem	
Nature of group		
Size of group	Too large	Partners can rotate in; other options can be offered.
Skill level	Varied	Combine weaker and stronger players as teams for practice; play tournaments by skill level.
Coeducational	No problem	

TENNIS
Instructional objectives
Cognitive

• The students will acquire knowledge of the history and development of the game of tennis, the care and selection of equipment, tennis etiquette, on and off the court rules, scoring, match regulations, and current leading personalities and international tournaments.

• The student will understand strategies involved in singles and doubles play.

Affective

• The student will honor accepted tennis etiquette and encourage classmates to do so also.

• The student will seek out players of similar skill level, and engage in tournament play at his or her own level.

Psychomotor

• The student will develop basic footwork and fundamental skills of tennis, including forehand, backhand, serve, lob, volley, half-volley, and overhead smash.

• The student will develop physical abilities necessary to the game of tennis, including quickness, endurance, eye-hand coordination, strength, agility, and balance.

Table 18-1. Suggested behavioral objectives for dual sports*

Cognitive	Affective	Psychomotor
Tennis		
After reading an assignment on etiquette student will hand in a list of ten important rules to follow.	After making a list, student will follow ten rules of etiquette during class.	Student will collect balls and give to opponent with each change of service during class match (etiquette).
Student will analyze partner's form on a serve and suggest changes according to descriptive handout.	Student will allow weaker opponent three serves while playing in a tennis game during class.	Student will serve to opponent's backhand each time during class match.
Handball		
Student will explain to a partner three types of serves: lob, drive, and z-serve, according to previous instructions.	Student practices shots with nonpreferred hand as defensive weapon.	Student will correctly execute the lob, drive, and z-serve in competitive setting, according to loop film instructions.
Student will diagram effective use of kill shot, back-wall kill shot, and ceiling shot on written test.	Student will volunteer to demonstrate a kill shot, a back-wall kill shot, and a ceiling shot in front of class.	Student will earn at least 5 points with kill shot, back wall, and ceiling kill shot in game situation against partner.
Badminton		
Student will assemble badminton equipment and tighten net at correct height.	Student will report to class early and help set up badminton equipment.	Student will serve into opponent's service court with 80% accuracy during warmup.
Student will explain to younger students the method of scoring in badminton.	Students will volunteer to assist in teaching badminton to younger class for the next three weeks.	Student will demonstrate for younger students the correct ready position for receiving badminton serve.
Wrestling (beginner)		
Following a verbal explanation, student will, when doing a switch, apply concept of working against a joint, successfully, two out of three times against an opponent.	When working with partner, student will provide appropriate resistance for techniques simulating competitive situations during class.	From referee's position student will successfully execute three of following four: sit-out, stand-up, wrist-roll and switch, by end of class.
After viewing loop film on the four take-downs, student will verbally analyze situation necessary for successful applications of takedowns.	Student will work overtime on four takedowns with less-skilled opponent.	Student will successfully takedown opponent, using each one of four: double-leg, single-leg, duck-under, and arm-drag.

*Sample objectives in all three domains of learning are provided to demonstrate how various methods of teaching may be applied to the teaching of dual sports in a daily lesson.

Methods
Cognitive

• The student will acquire knowledge of the game through televised programming, audiovisual loop films, reading textbooks, rule books, and articles appearing in magazines and newspapers.

• The student will obtain information from class discussions and verbal explanations.

• While working in small groups students will discuss and develop effective strategies for singles and doubles play.

Affective

• During class the student will exhibit knowledge of tennis etiquette by following given suggestions and teaching other students.

• Following pretesting the student will group himself or herself with students of similar skill level and will set up a tournament for these players to enjoy during and after class.

Psychomotor

• The student will develop basic physical skills for tennis through audiovisual aids, individualized learning programs for skill development, pretesting and posttesting evaluations, and practice-drill combined with reinforcement feedback. The student may also select his own best methods for performing tennis skills through the problem solving and guided discovery approach.

• Before class the student will warm up with a series of exercises that promote development of physical abilities necessary to the game of tennis. These exercises should be individually prescribed, according to the personal development of the student.

Special considerations	Problems	Solutions
Nature of game		
Movement pace	Slow for beginners; rapid for skilled	Work in homogeneous groups at progressive tasks.
Equipment	Insufficient quantity	Students may supply own; alternate with other activities.

Special considerations	Problems	Solutions
Safety	No problem	
Nature of group		
Size of group	Too large	Drills in large groups; alternate officiating and playing of a short game.
Skill level	Varied	Stronger players occasionally can assist weaker ones.
Coeducational	Boys too strong	Separate for practices; occasionally allow options for mixed practices and tournament play.

INDIVIDUAL SPORTS AND ACTIVITIES

One definition of an individual sport or activity stems from the type of competition or competitive element that exists. For the purpose of this text, an individual sport or activity is one that is *not* played against an opponent. Instead the participant is competing against himself or herself, trying to produce the best performance of which he or she is capable. This may be accomplished by beating his or her own earlier records or scores, as in swimming times, by beating bowling, golf, and archery scores, or by presentation of perfected routines, as in dance or synchronized swimming. Personal efforts may be combined with those of other team members for scoring purposes, as at a gymnastics or swimming meet or may be combined with a partner or group, as in figure skating, folk dancing, and so on. Nevertheless, the activity or sport is actually engaged in by the individual alone, facing a challenge inherent in the activity itself, rather than a challenge provided by external opponents.

Included in this category are aquatics, archery, bicycling, bowling, conditioning, environmental education (hiking, camping, orienteering, pioneering), figure skating, golf, gymnastics, rhythms (folk dance, square dance, ethnic dance, nonpartner dance and modern, jazz, and social dancing), track and field (including cross country), skiing, and weight training.

Methods for teaching individual sports and activities

Teaching methods for these individualized activities are similar to those used in the teaching of dual sports. Lectures, demonstrations, audiovisual materials, and evaluation instruments may all be used with large classes, but essentially, the nature of these games necessitates using more of the student-centered methods of presenting materials. Cognitive concepts, affective values, and psychomotor skills may be more readily learned through individualized approaches and through teacher-student interaction within small groups.

One distinctive feature of individual sports lies in the realm of feedback mechanisms, for in these activities there is an immediate relay of knowledge of results to the performer. For example, scores from archery, golf, and bowling are known after each motor act, providing the student with instant feedback on accuracy. Feedback may also be transmitted readily to a performer through videotape, as with gymnastic stunts, diving, or figure-skating routines. This teaching method, although applicable to team games, is particularly useful for filming single performances. Analysis of form by the individual, peers, older students, and the teacher will assist the learner in meeting educational objectives.

Like dual sports, individual activities have tremendous carry-over value and are becoming increasingly popular in school programs. In instances where schools may not be able to provide all of the necessary facilities and equipment to organize individual sports, as in bowling and golf, arrangements may be made to utilize nearby community facilities. Independent study programs of this type greatly increase the curricular offerings in secondary schools and thus provide students with enough skills and satisfying experiences that they will want to continue participation in these activities in later life. When these affective goals are achieved, whether by in-school or out-of-school programs, physical education has made a lasting contribution to the growth and development of adolescents.

Special mention should be made of the increased interest in environmental education in schools throughout the country. Taking their cues from the Outward Bound programs in Great Britain, where individuals developed inner security through survival training, today's high schools are now providing similar challenging experiences in the wilderness and the out-of-doors. These programs include survival techniques on land, mountains, desert, and water, orienteering, ecological studies, and recreational skills in the out-of-doors. Students acquire greater insights into their own personalities as they develop self-control and self-discipline, plus a sense of cooperation through group processes. The problem-solving method of teaching is incorporated into these programs, with small groups being forced to seek answers to group survival situations.

Suggested instructional objectives for individual sports and activities

On the pages that follow are suggested instructional objectives for the twelve sports and activities listed in the introduction to this section. Because of duplication in teaching methodology and similarities in objectives, specific methods will not be discussed for each topic. It should be clear at this point that cognitive objectives are generally achieved through reading assignments, films, lectures, verbal explanations, and question-answer, whereas psychomotor objectives are generally met through individualized tasks or modules, through audiovisual materials, problem solving, guided discovery, reciprocal teaching, and of course practice-drill with reinforcement feedback and evaluation. In each case subject matter needs careful preparation, according to the types and availability of materials. Inasmuch as these are individual areas of study, independent methods, and contract methods can easily be utilized. For the accomplishment of affective objectives, grouping arrangements and out-of-class opportunities need to be organized. For all teaching, the instructor should strive to use a variety of teaching methods in order to appeal to the wide range of learning styles found in every class room.

Although specific methodology has been omitted for the activities, special considerations have been outlined as in the previous chapter, with selected problems and solutions highlighted. Factors drawn from the nature of the sport or activity and the nature of the group again provide categories for the problems themselves.

AQUATICS (instructional, competitive, synchronized)
Instructional objectives
Cognitive

• The student will acquire knowledge of safety regulations in a swimming area, cardio-respiratory functioning, component parts of basic strokes and adaptations for competition and rhythmic presentation, and American Red Cross standards for performance.
• The student will understand and apply basic concepts of force, propulsion, buoyancy, and resistance as related to moving through water.

Affective

• The student will observe all safety regulations and be alert to the safety of others.
• The student will recognize the value of developing swimming abilities for greater life-long enjoyment of swimming and other related recreational activities (boating, canoeing, sailing, water-skiing).

Psychomotor

• The student will develop skills in basic swimming strokes, basic entry and exit skills in water, basic reach and rescue techniques, and artificial-resuscitation procedures.
• The student will develop specific swimming physical abilities for aquatics, including strength, endurance, flexibility, and breath control.

Special considerations	Problems	Solutions
Nature of activities		
Safety (the first consideration)	Hazardous	Teach proper reach and resuscitation techniques; assign
		many life guards; enforce safety rules.
Equipment	Pool maintenance	Get outside help.
Movement pace	Exhaustion (with fright in beginners)	Allow rest periods; use buddy system.
Nature of group		
Size of group	Too large	Use buddies; take turns in water.
Skill level	Extremely varied	Group according to abilities, as in American Red Cross; arrange low pupil-teacher ratio.
Coeducational	Not necessarily a problem	Use grouping procedures to overcome any difficulties.

ARCHERY
Instructional objectives
Cognitive

• The student will acquire knowledge of selection of equipment, care and storage of equipment, rules of tournaments, etiquette and terminology; history of the sport, and names of Olympic leaders and other record holders in the field.
• The student will understand concepts of flight (as related to point of aim-distance) and will apply to his or her own shooting stance.

Affective

• The student will become aware of personal body structure and postures in determining his or her own most appropriate shooting stance.
• The student will appreciate the value of archery as a life-time recreational activity.

Psychomotor

• The student will develop appropriate stance for archery, together with proper shooting technique at increasing distances.
• The student will try to increase strength in arms and shoulders, as well as eye-hand coordination.

Special considerations	Problems	Solutions
Nature of sport		
Safety (first consideration)	Injury from equipment	Teach *group* shooting and recovery in wave formations.
Equipment	Varied for size, skill	Purchase some bows and arrows of each size; share.
Movement pace	Slow	Combine with more active sports or preliminary running.
Nature of group		
Size of group	Too large; left-handedness	Work in pairs, trios; put at far end of shooting line.
Skill level	Varied	Group homogeneously; shoot at increasing distances.
Coeducational	No problem	

BICYCLING
Instructional objectives
Cognitive

• The student will acquire knowledge of the structure and function of bicycle parts, traffic rules and safety regulations for cycling, and repair of equipment.

• The student will understand and apply concepts of cardiovascular development as related to cycling activity.

Affective

• The student will choose to cycle to and from school, weather permitting.

• The student will be aware of safety to himself or herself and others during all cycling experiences.

Psychomotor

• The student will develop cycling skills.

• The student will improve physical abilities, especially endurance and leg strength through cycling experiences.

Special considerations	Problems	Solutions
Nature of activity		
Safety	Traffic hazards	Teach rules of the road.
Equipment	Many types and styles	Teach functioning of all types; let students supply own.
Movement pace	Tiring	Allow rest stops.
Nature of group		
Size of group	Too large	Plan alternative learning stations for noncyclers.
Skill level	No problem	
Coeducational	No problem	

BOWLING
Instructional objectives
Cognitive

• The student will acquire a knowledge of the history and development of the sport, the rules and scoring of the game, etiquette and terminology, care and selection of equipment, and the conduct of tournaments.

• The student will understand concepts of force as applied to straight-line and hooking techniques in bowling.

Affective

• The student will assist other students in the development of skill, keeping score, and setting of pins.

• The student will appreciate the recreational value of this activity for later leisure time.

Psychomotor

• The student will develop physical skills necessary for bowling, including four-step approach, smooth back-swing, and release.

• The student will develop eye-hand coordination plus strength to improve his or her bowling technique.

Special considerations	Problems	Solutions
Nature of sport		
Safety	No problem	Teach caution, control; bowlers release simultaneously.

Special considerations	Problems	Solutions
Equipment	Plastic type, unlike real equipment	Use local facilities whenever possible.
Movement pace	Slow	Use more active activities to meet other physical objectives.
Nature of group		
Size of group	Too large	Work in groups; alternate roles of scorer, setter, bowler.
Skill level	Varied	Pretest; use skilled to assist except in tournament play.
Coeducational	No problem	

CONDITIONING/WEIGHT TRAINING
Instructional objectives
Cognitive

• The student will acquire knowledge of the physiologic structure and function of the human body and its systems (particularly muscular development), diet and exercise and their relationships to one another, and exercise equipment.

• The student will understand and apply principles of weight control, conditioning exercises, and weight training.

Affective

• The student will become aware of his or her personal deficiencies and design a program for improvement.

• The student will incorporate his or her personal conditioning or weight training program into daily routine.

Psychomotor

• The student will perform daily conditioning-weight training exercises at increasing degrees of difficulty.

• The student will develop physical abilities through weight training and conditioning programs, according to his or her own needs, especially muscular strength, endurance, and control.

Fig. 18-5. Physical conditioning as part of program in the Brockport Central Schools, Brockport, N.Y.

Special considerations	Problems	Solutions
Nature of activity		
Safety	Muscle strains	Teach proper care; exercise increments.
Equipment	Expensive (universals, etc.)	Convince administration of its long-lasting values; have fund-raising projects involving all students.
Movement pace	Steady	Allow self-pacing.
Nature of group		
Size of group	Too large	Restrict numbers; rotate groups, number of meetings; provide independent work.
Skill level	Varied	Individualize.
Coeducational	No problem	Individualize.

ENVIRONMENTAL EDUCATION
(camping, orienteering, hiking)
Instructional objectives
Cognitive

• The student will acquire knowledge associated with local environment, particularly regarding ecology and pollutants.
• The student will understand and apply techniques for safety, survival, and conservation, particularly related to local environments.

Affective

• The student will experience (singly and in small groups) challenging situations that involve an understanding of factors within given environments and a realization of his or her own capacities.
• The student will contribute to the safety of others in small group situations while cooperating with them for the solutions to problems and challenges presented by environments.

Psychomotor

• The student will perform camping, orienteering, and hiking tasks (dependent upon available environments).

• The student will develop physical skills necessary for accomplishing tasks in the given environments, including strength, endurance, and speed.

Special considerations	Problems	Solutions
Nature of activities		
Safety	Hazardous	Teach safety and first aid pertinent to given environments.
Equipment	Complex (bridges, ropes, etc.)	Dependent upon environment; adapt.
Movement pace	Challenging; tasks too strenuous	Adapt to abilities and capacities of individuals.
Nature of group		
Size of group	Too large	Restrict; work in small groups at many given problems.
Skill level	Varied	Vary degree of challenge in tasks.
Coeducational	No problem	Boys assist girls.

GYMNASTICS
Instructional objectives
Cognitive

• The student will acquire knowledge of the care, structure, and function of various types of apparatus and of the scoring systems at various types of apparatus in competition.
• The student will understand and apply concepts of balance, force, and flow in combining moves on various apparatus and mats.

Affective

• The student will become aware of weaknesses in own techniques and strive to correct in practice sessions.
• The student will appreciate the aesthetic qualities of gymnastics.

Psychomotor

• The student will develop specific physical skills for apparatus and mats: *unevens*, mount (back-pullover), back hip circle, dismount; *balance beam*, chasse, stag leap, scales, support mount, hitchkick, dismounts; *vaulting*, bent-hip squat, straddle; *parallel bars*, mounts, traveling, swings, dismounts; *trampoline*, bounces, knee-drop, seat drop, hand-and-knee drop, front drop, back drop, twists; *floor exercise*, basic tumbling (rolls, cartwheels, headstands); *movements*, walk, run, leap, hop, jump, slide, chase, turns, falls.

• The student will develop necessary physical abilities for gymnastics, including strength, balance, agility, flexibility, endurance, and power.

Special considerations	Problems	Solutions
Nature of activities		
Safety	Injury	Teach spotting.
Equipment	Varied; expensive	Acquire singly; teach proper care.
Movement pace	Steady	Individualize.
Nature of group		
Size of group	Too large	Work in small groups; use films at centers.
Skill level	Varied	Individualize tasks.
Coeducational	No problem	Boys assist.

FIGURE SKATING (beginning)
Instructional objectives
Cognitive

• The student will acquire knowledge of proper selection, lacing and tightening of boots, structure and function of edges, school figures, terminology, types of competition and leading personalities.

• The student will understand and apply the concepts of balance (on inner and outer edges) related to body positioning for control.

Affective

• The student will develop confidence in his or her ability to skate with control through practicing to music.

• The student will appreciate the aesthetic qualities inherent in rhythmic skating patterns.

Psychomotor

• The student will develop physical skills necessary to figure skating, including stops and starts, falls, stroking (forward and backward), turning (cross-overs, clockwise, and counterclockwise), and combinations.

• The student will develop physical abilities necessary to figure skating, including strength, endurance, balance, speed, power, flexibility, and agility.

Special considerations	Problems	Solutions
Nature of sport		
Safety	Injury (falling on ice) Momentum	Teach proper way to fall; teach stops and starts.
Equipment	Figure and ice hockey skates	Let students provide own; teach about differences.
Movement pace	Rapid, after learning basics	Allow rests.
Nature of group		
Size of group	Not usually a problem (depends on size of arena)	Work in homogeneous groups at tasks; share areas.
Skill level	Varied	Group by pretesting in homogeneous groups.
Coeducational	Not a problem	

GOLF
Instructional objectives
Cognitive

• The student will acquire a knowledge of the history and development of golf, golf terminology, etiquette, and tournament regulations, care and selection of equipment, and current champions of leading tournaments.

• The student will understand and apply to his or her playing the correct stance in addressing the ball and the correct club selection in relation to lie of the ball and remaining distance.

Affective

• The student will become aware of personal strengths and weaknesses in golf stroking and will practice on his or her own for improvement.

• The student will develop an appreciation for the recreational values of golf as a future life-time activity.

Psychomotor

• The student will develop proper technique and skills for golf including stance, grip, swing, chipping, and putting.
• The student will try to improve flexibility and strength, as well as eye-hand coordination.

Special considerations	Problems	Solutions
Nature of sport		
Safety	Injury, from others practice swinging	Watch overcrowding; organize students to face in same directions.
Equipment	Expensive; varied	Ask students to bring some in; use practice golf balls.
Movement pace	Slow	Provide running or other more active activities during part of class.
Nature of group		
Size of group	Too large	Alternate active and passive groups.
Skill level	Varied	Use skilled players to assist nonskilled; provide competition by skill level.
Coeducational	No problem	

RHYTHMS (including folk, square, social, dances-without-partners, creative)
Instructional objectives
Cognitive

• The student will acquire knowledge of basic creative movement, folk dance (American as well as other countries), square dance (traditional and modern), dances-without-partners, social dances, and rhythmic gymnastics (balls, ropes, hoops, wands, ribbons).
• The student will comprehend, apply, and interpret basic movements to given rhythmic patterns.

Affective

• The student will become aware of body parts, body shapes, and relationships to others (in space, with and without apparatus).
• The student will develop an appreciation for the aesthetics of rhythmic movements.

Psychomotor

• The student will perform and create axial and locomotor movements appropriate to given types of rhythms (folk, square, etc.)
• The student will develop physical abilities necessary to the performance of dance movements, including balance, strength, agility, flexibility, endurance, and eye-hand coordinations.

Special considerations	Problems	Solutions
Nature of activities		
Movement pace	Tiring	Allow rest periods.
Equipment	Records; apparatus limited	Allow students to provide; develop partner routines.
Safety	No problem	Keep apparatus under control.

Fig. 18-6. Dance is an important part of the physical education program at the Bel Air Middle School in Bel Air, Md. Videotape equipment is being used here to analyze student performance.

Special considerations	Problems	Solutions
Nature of group		
Size of group	No problem	Work in alternating groups.
Skill level	Varied	Group by interest, ability
Coeducational	No problem	

SKIING
Instructional objectives
Cognitive

• The student will acquire knowledge of equipment and its care and selection, clothing and other gear, types of ski tows, and types of environmental conditions.

• The student will understand types of skiing conditions and will apply appropriate safety measures and techniques.

Affective

• The student will appreciate the many values inherent in skiing activities.

• The student will voluntarily ski outside of class, conditions permitting.

Psychomotor

• The student will develop basic skiing skills, including walking, straight running, gliding, snowplowing, wedge turns, and basic christie.

• The student will develop necessary physical abilities necessary for skiing, including endurance, leg strength, and balance.

Special considerations	Problems	Solutions
Nature of activity		
Movement pace	Rapid	Allow rests.
Equipment-area	Varied conditions	Plan alternate learning activities.
Safety	Falls	Teach caution with equipment and conditions
Nature of group		
Size of group	Too large	Alternate active-passive groups.
Skill level	Varied	Pretest; group by skill.
Coeducational	No problem	

TRACK AND FIELD
Instructional objectives
Cognitive

• The student will acquire knowledge of at least four events (including both field and running events), plus knowledge of effects of performance on cardiovascular efficiency.

• The student will comprehend and apply concepts of force to throwing and jumping events.

Affective

• The student will become aware of own capacities in selecting types of events (both track and field) at which he or she is best able to perform.

• The student will practice for improvement in times and distances in the running and fielding events.

Psychomotor

• The student will develop physical skills related to running, hurdling, passing a baton, throwing, and jumping.

• The student will develop physical abili-

Fig. 18-7. Track and field at the Paul J. Gelinas Junior High School in Setauket, N.Y.

Table 18-2. Suggested behavioral objectives for individual sports and activities*

Cognitive	Affective	Psychomotor
Aquatics		
Student will explain concept of buoyancy to the satisfaction of teacher.	Student will join a synchronized swimming group that meets after school.	Student will bob twenty times in a row without supporting self on side of pool for 20-25 seconds.
In a written paragraph, student will analyze correct form for performing flutter kick.	Student will practice on own until time on 100-yard freestyle improves by 2 sec.	Student will perform jackknife dive in good form, according to rating of three judges.
Archery		
After studying diagram of bow and arrow, student will correctly name all parts of bow and arrow.	After receiving instructions student will respond by assuming correct body position in preparation for shooting with each arrow.	Student will hit target with three out of six arrows from 25 feet away.
After studying materials on relationship of point of aim to increased distances, student will apply this concept by adjusting point of aim at three distances and hitting target with 60% accuracy.	After reading information provided, student will select bow and arrows appropriate to own size, weight, strength, and abilities.	Student will shoot five out of six balloons on target face from distance of 30 yards.
Gymnastics (beam)		
After reading materials on scales, student will describe four scales to partner while performing on beam.	Student will voluntarily demonstrate one-minute routine on beam for class.	Student will walk length of beam without falling.
Student will evaluate performance of classmates according to official standards and will be in agreement with an expert panel 85% of time.	The student will organize and join a gymnastic club meeting twice a week during lunch hour.	Student will perform a one-minute routine judged satisfactory by panel of classmates.
Skating		
Following review of material student will describe to class four methods of stopping forward motion on ice.	Student will feel difference between inside and outside edges and assist partner in discovering same.	Student will skate backward, without falling, from one end of rink to another.
Cycling		
Student will correctly reassemble gears according to diagram and get bicycle in proper working order.	Student will cycle to school and home whenever weather permits.	Student will control bicycle by staying in line while bicycling through traffic during class trip.
Folk dance		
Given test of five musical themes student will recognize and correctly distinguish between 3/4 and 4/4 tempo by doing appropriate foot patterns.	Student will stay in step with partner while performing polka once around the gymnasium.	Student will correctly perform three out of five basic folk dance steps according to previous instruction.
Student will interpret five-minute musical selection by combining axial and locomotor movements that, in judgment of teacher, match rhythm of selection.	Student will, in combination with three other classmates, create an original ending to given dance routine.	Student will be able to control a balance on one-half toe for 15 seconds.

*Sample objectives for some of the individualized sports and activities are included, showing various teaching methods applied to a daily classroom session.

ties essential to the activities, including strength, endurance, speed, agility, flexibility, balance, and eye-hand coordination and power.

Special considerations	*Problems*	*Solutions*
Nature of activities		
Movement pace	Fast and slow	Alternate stations.
Equipment	Varied	Teach care, handling.
Safety	Injuries from others or from strains	Organize practice sessions carefully; space activities generously; condition carefully; progress by degrees.
Nature of group		
Size of group	Too large	Group at several activities; alternate passive-active roles.
Skill level	Varied	Individualize.
Coeducational	No problem	Establish separate standards.

MATERIALS FOR TEACHING INDIVIDUAL AND DUAL SPORTS
Special reading materials

National Association for Girls' and Women's Sports (NAGWS) 1201 16th Street N.W., Washington, D.C. 20036
  Guides
    Aquatic guide
    Archery-golf guide
    Bowling-fencing guide
    Gymnastics guide
    Tennis-badminton-squash guide
    Track and field guide
  Selected articles
    Archery
    Gymnastics
    Riding
    Track and field
Wm. C. Brown Co., Pub., 2460 Kerper Blvd., Dubuque, Iowa 52001
    Advanced badminton
    Advanced tennis
    Archery
    Badminton
    Bowling
    Circuit training
    Conditioning and basic movements
    Dance: from magic to art
    Fencing
    Figure skating

Folk dancing for students and teachers
    Gymnastics for men
    Gymnastics for women
    Handball
    Judo
    Karate
    Modern dance
    Raquetball
    Skiing
    Skin and scuba diving
    Swimming
    Tumbling and apparatus stunts
    Weight training
Mayfield Publishing Co., 285 Hamilton Avenue, Palo Alto, Calif. 94301
    Ballet Basics
    Beginning Diving
    Bowling
    Fitness and Figure Control
    Golf
    Introduction to Women's Gymnastics
    Practical Personal Defense
    Tennis, Anyone?
    The Dancer Prepares (modern)
    This is Ballroom Dance
National Federation of State and High School Athletic Associations, 7 South Dearborn St., Chicago, Ill. 60603
    Track and Field Rules
    Wrestling Official's Manual
The Athletic Institute, 200 Castlewood Drive, North Palm Beach, Fla. 33408
    Sports technique books (paperback and hard cover)
    Archery
    Badminton
    Bowling
    Golf
    Gymnastics—floor exercise
    Gymnastics—horizontal bars
    Gymnastics—parallel bars
    Gymnastics—rings
    Gymnastics—side horse and long horse vaulting
    Women's gymnastic—balance beam
    Women's gymnastics—floor exercise-vaulting
    Women's gymnastics—uneven parallel bars
    Skiing
    Tennis
    Track and field
    Women's track and field

Other sources of reading materials

Amateur Athletic Union, 233 Broadway, New York, N.Y. 10007
Allyn & Bacon, Inc., 470 Atlantic Avenue, Boston, Mass. 02210
Goodyear Publishing Co., Pacific Palisades, Calif. 90272
Prentice-Hall, Inc., Englewood Cliffs, N.Y. 07636
United State Figure Skating Association, 178 Tremont Street, Boston, Mass. 02158 (figure-skating kit by Mary Maroney)

Slide films (sound and silent—for purchase or rental)

The Athletic Institute, 200 Castlewood Drive, North
Palm Beach, Fla. 33408
  Archery (4 units)
  Badminton (6 units)
  Bowling (4 units)
  Camp craft (4 units)
  Competitive swimming (3 units)
  Cycling (8 units)
  Diving (3 units)
  Fencing (4 units)
  Golf (6 units)
  Gymnastics (girls and women, 4 units)
  Ice skating (4 units)
  Judo (6 units)
  Life-saving (3 units)
  Skiing (6 units)
  Skin and scubadiving (6 units)
  Swimming (4 units)
  Table tennis (2 units)
  Tennis (6 units)
  Track and field (9 units)
  Track and field (girls, 2 units)
  Trampolining (3 units)
  Tumbling (3 units)
  Tumbling—advanced (3 units)
  Wrestling (5 units)
  Student manual with each sport
  Instructor's guide

Special aids

American Alliance for Health, Physical Education, and
  Recreation, 1201 16th St., N.W., Washington, D.C.
  20036 (fitness emblems, awards)
American Red Cross, local chapters. (Charts, skill
  sheets, and other free instructional materials)
Castello's, 30 East 10th St., New York, N.Y. 10003
  (Fencing, judo, and karate equipment)
Educational Activities, Inc., Box 392, Freeport, N.Y.
  11520 (Records, instructional kits)
Harvard Table Tennis Co., 265 Third Street, Cam-
  bridge, Mass. 02142 (Table tennis tournament charts
  and booklet)
Hoctor Products for Education, Waldwick, N.J. 07463
  (Records)
Kimbo Educational, P.O. Box 246, Deal, N.J. 07723
  (Records)
Life-Time Sports, AAHPER 1201 16th St., N.W., Wash-
  ington, D.C. 20036 (Posters)
National Association for Girls' and Women's Sports,
  AAHPER, 1201 16th St., N.W., Washington, D.C.
  20036 (Swimming and diving charts)
Nissen Corporation, 930 27th Avenue, S.W., Cedar
  Rapids, Iowa 52406 (Gymnastic technique charts)
Youngjohn Enterprises, Inc., P.O. Box 4522, Cleveland,
  Ohio 44124 (Instructional swimming charts)

Self-assessment

These tests are to assist students in determining if
material and competencies presented in this chapter
have been mastered:

1. List instructional objectives from each domain of
   learning for a selected individual or dual sport and
   list methods that might be utilized for their achievement.
2. Plan a demonstration for the introduction of an individual sport to a large class of ninth-grade boys and
   girls.
3. Design a bulletin board that would include motivational materials for students participating in an individual sport or activity.
4. Make a list of reading materials appropriate for assignments to meet cognitive objectives in individual or
   dual sports.

Case study for analysis

You are a new teacher in a "traditional" physical
education program that includes only team sports plus
limited gymnastics and rhythms. Identify objectives and
activities that you would select to expand the program,
giving the rationale you would use to convince the administration and the local community of the need for
them.

Exercises for review

1. Identify basic types of instructional objectives that
   should be achieved in the cognitive learning domain.
   The affective domain. The psychomotor domain.
2. Write a behavioral objective that tests learning of an
   individual sport in the cognitive domain. The affective domain. The psychomotor domain.
3. Select a specific manipulative skill and write a series
   of tasks designed to improve an individual's skill
   level.
4. Write a short answer test on rules and regulations of
   a selected individual or dual sport that consists of at
   least ten questions.
5. Develop an answer that would explain your denial of
   seventh graders' requests to participate in teams of
   their own selection in a tournament ending a unit on
   a dual sport.

Points to remember

1. Individual and dual sports should be an integral part
   of a well-rounded program of physical education.
2. Instructional objectives from all three learning domains may be achieved through individual and dual
   sports.
3. Through adaptations of teaching methodology the
   special problems inherent in individual and dual
   sports may be eliminated.
4. Many materials are now available to help in the individualization of instruction in these activities.

Problems to think through

1. How may large classes be organized to afford adequate instruction and skill development in individual
   and dual activities?
2. How may environmental activities be incorporated
   into the physical education curriculum?
3. Should beginning levels of swimming be required for
   graduation from high school?

4. Should class organization be homogeneous or heterogeneous for skill practices? For games?
5. In how many individual and dual sports should a high school student become proficient?

Selected readings

American Alliance for Health, Physical Education and Recreation: Ideas for secondary school physical education, Washington, D.C., 1976, AAHPER.

American Alliance for Health, Physical Education and Recreation: Personalized learning in physical education, Washington, D.C., 1976, AAHPER.

American Association for Health, Physical Education and Recreation: Physical Education and Recreation: Physical Education for High School Students, Washington, D.C., 1970, The Alliance

American Association for Health, Physical Education and Recreation: Organizational patterns for instruction in physical education, Washington, D.C., 1971, AAHPER.

Heitmann, H. M., and Kneer, M. E.: Physical education instructional techniques: an individualized humanistic approach, Englewood Cliffs, N.J., 1976, Prentice-Hall, Inc.

Knapp, C. and Leonhard, P. H.: Teaching physical education in secondary schools, New York, 1968, McGraw-Hill Book Company.

Vannier, M., and Fait, H. F.: Teaching physical education in secondary schools, ed. 4, Philadelphia, 1975, W. B. Saunders Company.

Walker, J.: Cowell and Schwehn's modern methods in secondary school physical education, Boston, 1973, Allyn & Bacon, Inc.

19

METHODS AND MATERIALS FOR MAINSTREAMING AND TEACHING THE HANDICAPPED STUDENT

INSTRUCTIONAL OBJECTIVES AND COMPETENCIES TO BE ACHIEVED

After reading this chapter the student should be able to—

1. Define the terms "adapted," "handicapped," and "mainstreaming."
2. Explain the advantages and disadvantages of mainstreaming and the principles that should apply when this concept is utilized.
3. Identify the various kinds of handicapped students, their characteristics and needs, and the type of physical education activities and programs that are most adaptable to each.
4. Demonstrate how each type of handicapped student should be provided for in a mainstreamed physical education class.
5. Define and outline a program for the physically gifted and creative student.

In a recent annual report to Congress, the United States Commissioner of Education indicated that change is prevalent throughout the field of education and that federal monies are being provided to see that education for all students becomes a reality. The Commissioner particularly stressed the fact that increased educational opportunities should be provided the gifted and the handicapped.

During recent years much legislation has been enacted by Congress to meet the educational needs of the handicapped student. This legislation has encouraged such things as stronger cooperative ties between school and community guidance services, interdisciplinary cooperation in educational programs, and pilot studies designed to improve the lot of the approximately seven million preschool and school-age handicapped children in the nation. Much of this legislation has implications for the adapted program in physical education.

The public attitude, as reflected in government action designed to provide equal education for all persons, has been changing. Today there is a strong feeling and a conviction on the part of the public that the handicapped child not only has a moral but a legal right to a sound education. This changing public opinion also affects the definition of the handicapped child. For example, in New York State the handicapped child is defined as one who can benefit from special services and programs because of mental, physical or emotional reasons. The American Alliance for Health, Physical Education, and Recreation interprets adapted physical education in terms of a physical activity program that is diversified and adapted to students with disabilities who have individual limitations and capacities.

MAINSTREAMING

Mainstreaming is a term that is applied to programs concerned with handicapped persons, such as those who are health impaired, mentally retarded, blind and visually deficient, deaf or hard of hearing, brain damaged, emotionally disturbed, or having learning disabilities arising from such conditions. In substance the term means developing programs to include handicapped students in regular educational programs and activities. In other words, it is taking handicapped students from special or segregated status and integrating them with so-called normal children in regular school programs. It also implies that although handicapped students will be scheduled in regular classes whenever and to what extent possible, special education will be provided them, and that selected experiences for which they are capable will constitute their program.

The legal aspects of mainstreaming have been set forth in various court cases that have maintained that handicapped children have the same right to public education as other children and that special provisions must be made for them. As a result of such court decisions, laws and guidelines have been passed and established in most states mandating such services and providing appropriate education for this segment of the population. Some examples of state laws: in Kansas the law says in part "the board of education of every school district shall provide special education services for all exceptional children in the school district . . . not later than July 1, 1979." The State of Wisconsin school code requires that "preference is to be given whenever appropriate to education of the child in classes along with children who do not have exceptional educational needs. . . ." In Maine the law states that "if after the compliance date (July 1, 1975) all eligible children have not been provided with the necessary education by the appropriate administrative unit, the state

commissioner of education may withhold all in such portion of the state aid as, in his judgment, is warranted."

The federal government has passed legislation promoting mainstreaming. For example, Public Law 93-380, Education Amendments of 1974, was signed into law by President Ford on August 21, 1974. Part VI, B of the law, Education of the Handicapped, states that "to the maximum extent appropriate handicapped children should be educated with children who are not handicapped and that special classes, separate schooling or other means of removal of handicapped children from the regular educational environment occurs only when the nature or severity of the handicap is such that education in regular class with the use of supplementary aids and services cannot be achieved satisfactorily." In November, 1975, the Education of all Handicapped Children Act became Public Law 94-142, appropriating $100 million for the handicapped; this will expand to $3.1 billion by year 1982. In regard to physical education, a survey by AAHPER showed that twenty-seven states in 1973 provided physical activities to children with various handicapping conditions, but only twelve states required physical educators working with handicapped children to have special preparation. The number of states providing for mainstreaming in physical education has increased since 1973 as has the emphasis upon special preparation for physical educators who work with such students.

Some historical facts concerning education for the handicapped

It is estimated by the United States Office of Education that there are 7.8 million handicapped children in this nation between the ages of 3 and 21. Of this number, it is estimated that one million are not receiving any education and only about one-half of them are in satisfactory educational programs. The nation has been slow to recognize the importance of providing for handicapped persons.

In 1817 Thomas Gallaudet opened a special school for deaf children in Hartford, Connecticut. At this time in our history it was generally thought that such students could be best served in institutions where they were segregated from the rest of society. By the early twentieth century, however, boards of education began to accept some responsibility for the education of the handicapped. As a result, by 1911, more than 100 cities had established special schools within public schools for the handicapped, and colleges began to prepare teachers for this segment of the education population. World War II provided an impetus for education of the handicapped when large numbers of disabled soldiers returned to civilian life.

Mainstreaming, although practiced to a very limited degree in the 1920s, developed into a major emphasis in the 1950s when Lloyd Dunn and others questioned the practice of special classes for the handicapped. When the civil rights movement became prominent, parents of handicapped children along with special education personnel went to court to insure fairer treatment for this group of students. In 1971 the legal case involving the Pennsylvania Association for Retarded Children versus the Commonwealth reached a momentous decision when a United States district court ordered the state to provide education at public expense for all retarded children. As a result of this court decision, there was action throughout the country with approximately forty-eight states now having laws mandating special education.

Advantages of mainstreaming

Reasons for the trend toward mainstreaming, in addition to those already mentioned, include the fact that studies have been done on the effectiveness of special class versus regular class placement. These studies have failed to come up with any conclusive results. In addition, many educators feel there are many benefits to having handicapped children in educational contact with nonhandicapped children. Studies have shown there is improvement among handicapped students in coping with interpersonal relationships. Finally, educators also feel that nonhandicapped children benefit from their association with handicapped children.

Other advantages that have been set forth for mainstreaming are that it helps handicapped students to better meet life situations, gives them a better feeling of belonging, makes them feel more self-sufficient, eliminates labeling, which has a detrimental effect on all students, enhances the learning situation, provides a more diversified program for all children, and enriches the lives of all children.

Disadvantages of mainstreaming

Some of the disadvantages of mainstreaming as pointed out by educators include the arguments that it will restrict the educational growth of the average normal child, that it places more pressure on teachers, and that the handicapped student requires more time and attention by teachers than does the so-called "normal" child. Some of the rationale for this last argument is that the scholastic pace and projects must be tailored to meet the needs of the handicapped. These educators also point out that scheduling is a major problem, that many teachers do not feel adequately prepared to teach handicapped children in their classes, and that class size becomes a problem.

Principles that should apply to mainstreaming

Some principles that should apply and guide the mainstreaming concept include:

1. All students should be provided satisfactory learning experiences whether or not they are handicapped or are so-called normal students.

2. Class size should be such that an adequate educational offering and effective teaching can be provided all students.

3. Facilities should be adapted to meet the needs of all students, including the handicapped (ramps, if necessary, etc.).

4. Mainstreaming should be used only for those students who can benefit from such a practice. In other words, severely handicapped students may benefit more from special classes.

5. Periodic evaluation should take place in order to objectively determine the effective-

ness of mainstreaming in terms of students' progress.

6. Adequate supportive services should be provided for handicapped students. Example: if a speech therapist or a person trained in physical education for the handicapped is needed, these persons should be provided.

7. The administration should support the program and make it possible for those teachers involved in such a program to have the necessary instructional supplies, space, time, and other resources necessary to adequately do the job that is required.

8. Adequate preservice and in-service teacher preparation should be provided for all teachers who will be or who are involved in working with handicapped students.

9. In order that full public support can be assured, an adequate public information program should be carried on by the school to ensure that parents, the community, and the public in general are aware of the program, its needs, and what it is doing for children.

Physical education program for handicapped with mainstreaming

Physical education must be aware of the various mainstreaming concepts that have been discussed thus far. Physical education is a subject through which much can be done for handicapped students if they are mainstreamed and if the physical educators in charge understand handicapped individuals and the type of program that will best meet their needs. Whether the program is successful will depend upon the teacher and his or her ability to individualize the offering to meet the needs of each student in the class. The program of activities must be carefully selected, the starting point must be where the student is at present, and progress should be made within the capabilities of the individual.

The physical educator should utilize several approaches in teaching various types of handicapped students. A thorough medical examination should be a first step. Personal assistance will be needed from time to time. Modification of the activities will be necessary in many cases. Rapid progress in skill

development should not be expected. Handicapped students should feel they have achieved and are successful in their efforts. Complete records on each student should be kept with notations concerning the nature of the handicap, recommendations of the physician, and activities that are appropriate or inappropriate.

Each handicapped student must be made to feel a part of the physical education program. For example, mentally retarded children should gain self-confidence, and physically handicapped students should have fun meeting the challenges that certain activities and exercises provide. In addition, the activities should be challenging and rewarding for the development of a positive self-concept. Some types of handicapped students should be taught leisure-time activities and ways to play. The need for physical fitness must be stressed. Finally, some points that physical educators should remember are that it is important not to underestimate a student's abilities and that many handicapped children have a short attention span, tire easily, and are easily distracted. Safety must be stressed at all times.

THE ADAPTED PHYSICAL EDUCATION PROGRAM

The emphasis upon adapted physical education has resulted in many innovations in school systems in the United States and provisions for students will all types of handicapping conditions. A select few are listed here, particularly for the blind and visually handicapped, to indicate the nature and scope of such changes throughout the nation. It should be recognized, however, that adapted physical education programs are needed and exist for all kinds of handicapped students, including the mentally retarded, emotionally disturbed, culturally disadvantaged, and physically handicapped.

Washington Irving Junior High School, Los Angeles, California. Blind children are provided a physical education program that enables them to participate in such activities as track and field, tug-of-war, weight lifting, combatives, rope skipping, basketball, and wrestling.

Robert E. Lee School, Long Beach, California. Blind children are enrolled and participate in the same activities as those offered normal children. The normal classmates assist the blind children in such activities as the 50-yard dash and playing softball.

Buena Vista School, Walnut Creek, California. At this school when the blind student is at bat in softball, a batting tee is used. Other activities in which the student engages are whoopla ball, folk dancing, tether ball, and flag football.

Fargo Public Schools, Fargo, North Dakota. Visually handicapped students in the schools of this community meet with the regular physical education classes and engage in such activities as tumbling, self-testing activities, balance beam exercises, ice skating, relays, physical fitness tests, rope jumping, and conditioning exercises.

Physical education in the State of Michigan. The program is designed to help students to become aware of personal potential. They do not participate in those activities for which they are not physically fit. This goal applies to handicapped and normal children.

Wheeling High School, Wheeling, Illinois. In the physical education program at this school, blind students play softball with sighted classmates. Such modifications are made as roping off the diamond to guide the blind student when running bases, sighted classmates giving signals to blind students to bat and to throw to a particular base, using a 23-inch soft playground ball, and rolling rather than throwing the ball to the batter.

Other activities, events, and associations that have been organized and developed for the handicapped person on national and international levels include International Special Olympics for the Mentally Retarded, National Wheelchair Basketball Association, International Paralympics, Pan American Wheelchair Games, and National Mail-A-Graphic Bowling Tournament.

These innovative programs have many implications for physical education at the secondary school level. Educators are now in an era in which adapted physical education has come into its own and in which federal sub-sidy is extensive. Of course, the key to success of the adapted program, as is the case of all physical education programs, is the teacher. Particularly, in this special type of physical education, the teacher must be well prepared, dedicated, and sensitive to the needs of handicapped students.

THE CHALLENGE OF THE HANDICAPPED STUDENT

A beginning physical educator soon discovers that the students in a single physical education class cannot accurately be said to form a homogeneous group. While all the boys or all the girls in a single physical education class may be in the same secondary grade and while all of them may fall within a certain narrow age range, they will not possess the same physical and mental abilities. Not all of them will have developed to the same levels of emotional and social maturity. Most of these students will fall into the classification "average" or "normal" for their age and grade. Other students will deviate considerably from their peers on a physical, mental, emotional, or social measure or on a combination of these measures. This latter group may be said to be handicapped.

Handicapped students in physical education present a challenge to the teacher, for they may fall into any of several different categories. The culturally disadvantaged child is atypical, as are the physically gifted student, the creative student, and the awkward student with low motor ability. Atypical groupings also include emotionally disturbed as well as mentally retarded students. Each of these groups needs a strong and well-planned physical education experience. In schools where facilities and teaching personnel are available, adapted programs are developed especially to meet the needs of the handicapped student. With mainstreaming the physical educator must be prepared to make both program and instructional adaptations to meet special physical education needs.

It is a rare secondary school that does not have at least a few handicapped students on its class rolls. It is a definite possibility that someday each physical educator may have to teach at least some students who fall outside the norm. Each physical educator should know how to best provide for the handicapped student.

THE CULTURALLY DISADVANTAGED STUDENT

Culturally disadvantaged students have always made up a segment of the school population, but it is only recently that they have become a real concern to various communities and to the schools serving these communities. It is a common error for the public to associate only the black child with cultural deprivation. Professional educators, especially, must realize that cultural deprivation crosses all color lines and ignores none of them.

The culture of poverty is especially apparent in the large urban centers. Ten years ago one in three city children was classified as culturally disadvantaged in estimates made by the Ford Foundation. At the present time an estimated 50 percent of the children living in cities are culturally disadvantaged. Many of the inhabitants of Appalachia, suburban communities, and isolated small towns and rural villages all across the United States are culturally disadvantaged.

Characteristics of the culturally disadvantaged student

The culturally disadvantaged student feels isolated from the mainstream of life. Home and neighborhood environment are negative influences that destroy confidence, rob the student of a chance for success, and defeat aspirations. The goals of middle-class culture, as represented by the school, seem to be unreachable goals to someone who lives in the culture of poverty.

A culturally disadvantaged student may not achieve success in school because the cultural standards of the school and the home environment are usually inconsistent. Even schools in inner city areas are staffed by teachers who represent the middle-class segment of society.

In a classroom situation the culturally dis-

advantaged student is unable to compete successfully scholastically, emotionally, or socially. Because reading and conversation have not been encouraged at home, the student is severely restricted in ability to communicate and finds it extremely difficult to use logic or form concepts or to think in abstract terms. The culturally disadvantaged student is, for these reaons, often behind proper grade level in achievement. This boy or girl frequently attains low scores on intelligence and standardized tests because these tests are not designed to measure him or her accurately. As the culturally disadvantaged student continues to meet failure, there is loss of any motivation to achieve, and levels of ambition and aspiration continue to decline.

Continual failure in the classroom negatively affects the school behavior of the culturally disadvantaged student. Short attention span, emotional instability, excitability, and restlessness often contribute to disruptive behavior patterns.

Educational needs of the culturally disadvantaged student

Many culturally disadvantaged students come from itinerant families. The children of migratory workers, in particular, will attend several different schools throughout the course of a single school year. Other culturally disadvantaged families are mobile because they constantly search for higher-paying jobs or better living conditions. This mobility further increases the educational deprivation of the culturally disadvantaged student.

Educational curricula for the culturally disadvantaged cannot be conventional middle-class curricula with conventional middle-class objectives and goals. The teacher cannot employ traditional middle-class methodology and impose middle-class standards of discipline. The traditional and conventional approaches to education do not help the culturally disadvantaged student to rise out of poverty; they only succeed in driving him or her deeper into a narrow existence.

Many authorities have criticized the unrealistic educational atmosphere to which the culturally disadvantaged student is systematically exposed. On the elementary school level especially, it is pointed out, reading books and textbooks illustrate and espouse a way of life that is totally alien to the culturally disadvantaged. It is further noted that if the student does indeed continue education in a secondary school, the curriculum choices offered are really only weak attempts to resolve long-standing educational inequities. On the secondary school level the culturally disadvantaged student is sometimes arbitrarily channeled into a terminal vocational program, without regard to hidden potential for seeking a higher education and a professional career.

Educators are constantly seeking to adjust curricula or to introduce innovative curricula that will better serve the culturally disadvantaged. As yet, definite answers as to how a curriculum can realistically meet the needs of culturally disadvantaged students have not been found. However, educators have been able to identify three broad curriculum designs in secondary education for the disadvantaged. These three educational patterns may be termed remedial education, curriculum adjustment, and methodological modification. These patterns are not mutually exclusive.

Remedial education is a genuine need of the disadvantaged, but an entire secondary school curriculum cannot be based on such a program. However, many communities are engaged in out-of-school remedial education through such a program as Upward Bound.

Curriculum adjustment involves a slowing down of the educational pace. Curriculum content is identical for all segments of the school population, but classes made up of disadvantaged students spend proportionately greater amounts of time in each subject area. A regularly paced class will cover a unit of work in mathematics, for example, in many fewer class periods than will a slower-paced class of disadvantaged students. In these latter classes, discipline is very rigid—a concession to the teacher but not necessarily the most conducive atmosphere for the students. This slower method of teaching makes a questionable contribution to the disadvantaged student. It does not guarantee that educational or vocational needs are being met. However, it does allow the student to move into regularly paced classes when ability permits and to move more slowly in those courses where there is a need to increase confidence and knowledge.

Methodological modifications are nothing more than the extreme adaptation of existing standard courses or specially designed standard courses. This educational technique is sometimes known as "tracking." When this method of educating disadvantaged students is adopted, the curriculum is made up almost entirely of vocationally oriented subject matter designed to prepare the student for the job market. Very few courses with a purely academic orientation are included in the programs, which may close the door on higher education. For example, courses in mathematics will be geared toward learning to make change, while courses in English will concentrate on writing a business letter or going to an interview. In the former there will be no attempt to teach the concepts of secondary school mathematics, such as algebra and geometry, and in the latter there will be no attempt to teach literature or theme writing. In some secondary schools, placement of a student in a program of this sort is undertaken in spite of the student's personal aspirations or untapped academic ability that might be revealed through exposure to a more academic curriculum.

These three systems may have more disadvantages than advantages, but they will be continued to be used until better methods are found to reach the needs of these youth in secondary schools. Culturally disadvantaged students do need vocational training, but they also need to be free to select courses that meet their individual needs and interests. The culturally disadvantaged student will not succeed educationally if all courses are dictated or if he or she is confined by a tracking system or otherwise educationally isolated. The secondary schools must be as dedicated to educating culturally disadvantaged students as they are to educating the more advantaged segments of the school population.

The physical educator and the culturally disadvantaged student

In the physical education classroom the culturally disadvantaged student can be given an opportunity to meet success. Physical activity has a strong appeal for these youngsters, whether they are students in a school in their neighborhood or community or part of the student body in a school in an advantaged area.

The physical educator is the most important single factor in a secondary school physical education program for the disadvantaged. The physical educator must have a sincere interest in these students and must be willing to assume the responsibility for physically educating them. He or she should have an adequate background and special training in general education and physical education courses concerned with teaching the disadvantaged. These courses will help in gaining a fuller understanding of the culturally disadvantaged student and the educational problems this student faces. The physical educator must have the ability to develop rapport with culturally disadvantaged students in order to better respect, understand, and help these students. The physical educator must be able to provide an enriched program that will help motivate the culturally disadvantaged student to make the best use of his or her physical, intellectual, and creative abilities.

The physical education program and the culturally disadvantaged student

The school physical education program frequently is the only supervised physical activity program for the culturally disadvantaged student. These students usually do not have a neighborhood recreational facility available and must conduct their sports and games on unsupervised streets or in dangerously littered lots. The school physical education experience must be designed to afford this student the physical education and recreational activities that are denied him or her elsewhere.

• *The physical education program must be carefully tailored to meet the needs and interests of the students.* Culturally disadvantaged students enjoy vigorous activity as well as creative and self-testing activities. There must be a wide choice of activities offered so that these students can select not only those experiences they find pleasurable but also those in which they can find success. As fundamental challenges are met successfully, new challenges must be presented in a logical progression.

• *The physical education program must be designed to increase the physical fitness and motor skill abilities of the students.* The program should include activities that will help the students to increase their physical fitness levels. Lack of structured programs outside the school denies culturally disadvantaged students the opportunity to participate in a regular program of physical activity, which often prevents them from maintaining even minimal fitness levels. Motor skill abilities are also often minimal simply because some students may never have had the benefit of a good physical education program in school.

• *There must be provision for suitable competition.* Culturally disadvantaged students need and enjoy competition. Competitive sports and games must be a part of the class program, but time must also be alloted for the individual to compete with himself or herself in order to raise a physical fitness test score or to improve in a skill performance. Intramural programs are an invaluable extension of the class program, and the culturally disadvantaged student should be encouraged to participate. Likewise, culturally disadvantaged students should be encouraged to seek membership on interscholastic teams.

• *The program must provide for carryover interests.* The culturally disadvantaged students need to develop a background in the lifetime sports. Swimming, dancing, and tennis, as well as other recreational activities such as bowling, should be included among the lifetime sport activities offered.

• *Equipment must be carefully purchased to suit the program.* There should be records, a phonograph, and a variety of rhythm instruments. Culturally disadvantaged students enjoy rhythmical activities and find that they are successful in such areas as dance, gymnastics, and tumbling, where they can demonstrate their creativity and express their individuality. Many warm-up activities, as well as many games, can be done to a musical accompaniment.

• *The program must allow for each student to be treated as an individual.* Culturally disadvantaged students are especially conscious of their individuality, and the program should allow ample opportunity for self-expression and creativity. Teacher recognition and praise for the most minor accomplishment are of utmost importance to the continued success of these students.

• *The program should help to instill good health habits and attitudes.* Where possible, showers should be available to the students. Each student should be provided with an individual locker, and cleanliness and proper maintenance of uniforms should be required.

• *The size of classes should be so arranged that discipline is easy to maintain.* Secondary school physical education classes are frequently overcrowded, and discipline is a major problem. If possible, culturally disadvantaged students should not be in a large class because little teaching takes place and because the individual student becomes lost in the mass. These students need and want to follow firm, consistent, and appropriate disciplinary standards. As much as any student, they must know what is expected of them and should be made to conform to the standards. However, any disciplinary standards imposed must relate directly to the students. Artificial standards will result in a total lack of discipline.

• *The physical education program should attempt to instill values that will extend into the classroom situation.* Through the activities of physical education, culturally disadvantaged students can obtain a release of tension in an acceptable way. They can also learn, from the give and take of sports, how to get along with others and will become more aware of the needs, abilities, and talents of their classmates. If these experiences are provided in the physical education class, at least some of the lessons will be transferred to the academic classroom.

• *The program should be correlated with the general education program of the school.* Through physical education activities much general educational knowledge and many such skills and abilities can be enhanced. Through folk dances, for example, it is possible to acquaint the student with the dress and customs of various cultures. This knowledge will help a class in history to become more interesting to the student and will help to develop pride in his or her own culture. Through a sport such as baseball, mathematics can be brought to life. The students will be able to see the relationship between mathematics and its uses for such practical purposes as determining baseball batting averages, computing team won-lost percentages, and understanding angles so that this knowledge can be applied to laying out a baseball diamond.

THE PHYSICALLY HANDICAPPED STUDENT

The physically handicapped student may have a temporary disability, such as a broken arm, or he may be in a postoperative stage of recovery. Other physically handicapped students suffer from more permanent disabilities, such as blindness, deafness, or irremediable orthopedic conditions. The range of physical handicaps extends from minor to major in severity and directly affects the kinds and amounts of participation in physical activity.

Whatever the disability, a physical education program should be provided. Some handicapped students will be able to participate in a regular program of physical education with certain minor modifications. A separate, adapted program should be provided for those students who cannot participate in the basic instructional program of the school. The physically handicapped student cannot be allowed to sit on the sidelines and become only a spectator. He or she needs to have the opportunity to develop and maintain adequate skill abilities and fitness levels.

There are about three million children and youth between the ages of 4 and 19 years in the United States who are physically handicapped in varying degrees. About 500,000 of these handicapped individuals are of secondary school age. These figures are based on estimates made by the Bureau of the Census through its ongoing United States National Health Survey. Many authorities feel, however, that accurate statistics have not as yet been made available and that the number of physically handicapped youth may be somewhat higher than these estimates. Further, these surveys sometimes classify mental retardation under the broad category of physical handicaps.

Many of the more severely handicapped secondary school children attend special schools where their unique needs can be met by highly trained staff members. The remainder are enrolled in the public secondary schools. It is this latter group with which the physical educator must be especially concerned.

Characteristics of the physically handicapped student

The presence of a physical handicap does not mean that the student also has a mental handicap, although this is sometimes true. Physical handicaps may stem from congenital or hereditary causes or may develop later in life through environmental factors, such as malnutrition, or from disease or accident. Sometimes negative psychological and social traits develop because of the limitations imposed on the individual by a severe physical handicap.

A physically handicapped student is occasionally ignored or rebuffed by classmates who do not understand the nature of the disability or who ostracize the student because a disability prevents full participation in the activities of the school. These attitudes toward handicapped persons force them to withdraw to avoid being hurt, which results in their becoming further isolated from the remainder of the student body. Some experts have noted that the limitations of the handicap often seem more severe to the observer than they in fact are to the handicapped individual. When this misconception occurs, the handicapped student must prove his or her abilities to gain acceptance and a chance to participate and compete on an equal basis with nonhandicapped classmates.

The blind or deaf student or the student with a severe speech impairment has different problems from those of the orthopedically handicapped student. The student who is partially sighted, blind, deaf, or impaired in speech cannot communicate with great facility. The orthopedically handicapped student is limited in the physical education class but not necessarily in the academic classroom. The student with vision, hearing, or speech problems may be limited in the physical education classroom and the academic classroom.

Educational needs of the physically handicapped student

Physically handicapped students in general have the same academic needs, interests, and abilities as do their nonhandicapped peers. While special arrangements must be made for students who have speech, hearing, or visual disabilities, these students are capable of competing successfully in the classroom atmosphere.

Physically handicapped students need preparation for vocations, technical schools, or college. They can contribute to the school through participation in social and service activities. They are far less limited in the general education program and activities of the school than in the physical education program.

The physical educator and the physically handicapped student

There is a lack of physical educators who are specifically trained to teach the physically handicapped. School systems find that the cost of providing special classes taught by specially trained physical educators is prohibitive. Where there are no special classes, the physical educator must provide, within the regular instructional program, those activities that will meet the needs of the handicapped student. Further, placing the physically handicapped student in a regular physical education class will help in providing a feeling of belonging. This advantage is not always possible where separate, adapted classes are provided.

To be able to provide an adequate program for physically handicapped students, the physical educator needs special training. Advanced courses in anatomy, physiology, physiology of activity, and kinesiology are essential, along with special work in psychology and adapted physical education. The professional preparation curriculum should also include courses in movement education and body mechanics.

The physical educator must have an understanding of the physical disability of each handicapped student and must be aware of any psychological, social, or behavioral problems that may accompany the disability. The physical educator must know the capacities of each handicapped student so that he or she can provide an individualized program.

The physical education program and the physically handicapped student

No two physically handicapped students will have the same limitations in regard to the activities of the physical education program. Under no circumstances can the physical educator diagnose the disability and prescribe a physical activity program. This must be accomplished by the student's physician. The physician's recommendations for students whose conditions have been previously diagnosed should be followed. If in the course of the year the physical educator observes that a student seems to have some kind of physical handicap that is not noted on the record cards of the school, the physical educator must refer the student to the family physician or the proper agency through the normal administrative process of the school. After the disability has been medically diagnosed and activity recommendations made, it becomes the responsibility of the physical educator to provide the proper program.

Some handicappped students will be able to participate in almost all the activities that nonhandicapped students enjoy. Blind students, for example, have successfully engaged in team sports where they can receive aural cues from their sighted teammates. Some athletic equipment manufacturers have placed bells inside game balls, and the blind student is then able to rely on this sound as well as on the supplementary aural cues. Ropes or covered wires acting as hand guides also enable the blind student to participate in track-and-field events. Still other activities, such as swimming, dance, calisthenics, and tumbling, require little adaptation or none at all, except in regard to heightened safety precautions.

In general, deaf students will not be restricted in any way from participating in a full physical education program. Some deaf students experience difficulty in activities requiring precise balance, such as balance-beam walking, and may require some remedial work in this area. The physical educator should be prepared to offer any extra help that is needed.

Other physically handicapped students will have a variety of limitations and a variety of skill abilities. Appropriate program adaptations and modifications must be made in order to meet this range of individual needs. The following general guidelines are helpful in physically educating the physically handicapped on the secondary school level.

• *Cooperate with the physician in planning each student's program.* The physician is the individual most knowledgeable about the history and limitations of a student's handicap. He or she is therefore in the best position to recommend a physical activity program for the student.

• *Test the motor skill ability and physical fitness levels of each student.* The student's abilities and levels of fitness should be tested in areas where medical permission for participation has been granted. This will not only ensure a proper program for the individual but will help in placing the student in the proper class or section of a class.

• *Keep the program under constant evaluation.* Careful records should be kept showing the student's test scores, activity recommendations, activities engaged in, and progress through the program. In this way, the physical educator will know whether the program is reaching its objectives, the student will be able to discuss progress with the physical educator, and the school health team and the student's physician will be able to be kept up to date on the student's progress and needs.

• *Keep the adapted and regular programs as similar as possible.* Where the two programs are totally divergent, the physically handicapped student is isolated from classmates. When the programs are as similar as possible, the handicapped student can be made to feel a part of the larger group and will gain self-confidence and self-respect. Similarity in the programs will also effectively serve to motivate the physically handicapped student.

• *Provide challenges for the student.* Physically handicapped students need the challenge of a progressive program. They welcome the opportunity to test their abilities and should experience the fun of a challenge and the success of meeting it.

• *Provide time for extra help.* Handicapped students should be given an opportunity to seek extra help and extra practice after school hours. During this time they can benefit from more individualized instruction than is possible during the class period.

• *Select activities on an individual basis.* Although several handicapped students in a single class may be able to participate in several activities in common, they may not have a common interest in these activities. The fitness level and ability, recreational needs, sex, age, and interests of each student will help to determine the activities the student will engage in pleasurably.

• *Adapt the activity to the student rather than the student to the activity.* The student's disability determines the activities in which he or she can participate. Therefore, any modifications or adaptations that are made must be made in the activity.

• *Provide safe facilities and safe equipment.* Safe facilities and safe equipment are essential in any physical education program.

Extra safeguards must be taken when a physical education class includes physically handicapped students.

• *Provide suitable extraclass activities.* Experts feel that physically handicapped students are placed in an unduly hazardous situation when they engage in highly competitive activities. Intramural and club programs should be provided, but they must be of such a nature that physically handicapped students can enjoy them in a safe, controlled atmosphere that precludes the danger of injury.

THE MENTALLY RETARDED STUDENT

There are special schools in many states that serve mentally retarded students either on a residential or a day-care basis. Public secondary schools also offer specially designed curricula and employ teachers who have the comprehensive background and training needed to teach in programs for the retarded. In some public schools, special physical education classes are offered for these students, while in still other schools, mentally retarded students participate in the regularly scheduled physical education classes.

Mental retardation can be a result of hereditary abnormalities, a birth injury, or an accident or illness that leads to impairment of brain function. There are degrees of mental retardation ranging from the severely mentally retarded, who require custodial care, to the educable mentally retarded, who function with only a moderate degree of impairment.

Each year in the United States more than 126,000 babies are born who have some degree of mental retardation. At present, there are more than seven million mentally retarded children and adults in the United States.

Many agencies are conducting research in the field of mental retardation in an attempt to discover the causes of mental retardation, the nature of mental retardation, and the methods through which it may be prevented. Some agencies are operating innovative training schools for mentally retarded students. The Joseph P. Kennedy, Jr., Foundation is spearheading much of the research concerned with mental retardation and is also a leader in providing camping and recreational programs for the mentally retarded. The Kennedy Foundation has also sponsored training programs for teachers of the mentally retarded. The United States government has sponsored an experimental physical education program for the mentally retarded at the Austin State School in Austin, Texas. This program is cooperatively conducted by a staff of special education teachers, specially trained physical educators, vocational rehabilitation technicians, and architectural engineers. A special program and special equipment have been designed especially for use with the mentally retarded. Climbing devices, obstacle courses, and unique running areas, as well as a swimming pool, are part of the special facilities. The objectives of this program include social and personal adjustment, as well as the development of physical fitness, sports skills, and general motor ability.

Characteristics of the mentally retarded student

Mentally retarded students show a wide range of intellectual and physical ability. The experts seem to agree that a mentally retarded child is usually closer to the norm of chronological age in physical development than in mental development. Some mentally retarded students are capable of participating in a regular physical education class, while others have been able to develop only minimal amounts of motor ability. In general the majority of mentally retarded students are two to four years behind their normal peers in motor development alone.

Despite a slower development of motor ability, mentally retarded students seem to reach physical maturity faster than do normal boys and girls of the same chronological age. Mentally retarded children tend to be overweight and to lack physical strength and endurance. Their posture is generally poor, and they lack adequate levels of physical fitness and motor coordination. Some of these physical problems develop because mentally retarded children have had little of the play and physical activity experiences of normal children. The problems of some mentally retarded youngsters are further multiplied by attendant physical handicaps and personality disturbances.

A mentally retarded student does not have the ability to think in the abstract or to remember isolated facts well. A short attention span, a tendency to overreact emotionally, and a low threshold of irritability also contribute to the classroom problems of the mentally retarded student. While not all mentally retarded students have the same personal characteristics, some of them also tend to be very restless, destructive, and impulsive.

Educational needs of the mentally retarded student

Mentally retarded students need a sound foundation in educational skills. Many of them will seek and be able to hold jobs at the conclusion of their secondary education, and there must be vocational training courses for them. Girls in particular need and enjoy courses in home economics, while both boys and girls benefit from instruction in money management and the techniques of using the telephone and writing acceptable letters.

While special classes are usually conducted in many subject areas of the school curriculum, it has been found that the mentally retarded student can join with peers in some subjects. Vocational and shop courses, art, music, home economics, and physical education are a few of the subjects in which mentally retarded students can find success outside of the special class. Likewise, the mentally retarded student can enjoy intramural activities and school clubs and can contribute to special events, school committees, and service organizations.

The physical educator and the mentally retarded student

The mentally retarded student requires a physical educator with special training, special skills, and a special brand of patience.

Such a student lacks confidence and pride and therefore needs a physical educator who will help to change his or her negative self-image. The physical educator must be able to provide a program designed to give each student a chance for success. The goals of the program cannot be so high that they are unreachable.

The physical educator must be ready to praise and reinforce each minor success. He or she should be capable of demonstrating each skill and giving simple and concise directions and willing to participate in the physical education activities with the students. Discipline must be enforced and standards adhered to, but the disciplinary approach must be a kind and gentle one.

The physical educator must be especially mindful of the individual characteristics of each mentally retarded student. Students who need remedial work should be afforded this opportunity, while students who can succeed in a regular physical education program should be placed in such a class or section. Above all, the physical educator must remember that he or she cannot proceed with a class of mentally retarded students in the same manner as he or she would proceed with a class of students with average intelligence and physical ability.

The physical education program and the mentally retarded student

Most mentally retarded students need to be taught how to play. They are frequently unfamiliar with even the simplest of childhood games and lack facility in the natural movements of childhood, such as skipping, hopping, and leaping. They are often seriously deficient in physical fitness and need work in postural improvement. Further, mentally retarded students find it difficult to understand and remember game strategy, such as the importance of staying in the right position, and cannot relate well to the rules of sports and games.

Many mentally retarded students need a specially tailored physical education experience. For those who can participate in a regular physical education class, care must be taken that these students are not placed in a situation where they will meet failure. In a special physical education class, the mentally retarded student can be exposed to a variety of physical education experiences. Physical fitness and posture improvement, along with self-testing activities and games organized and designed according to the ability and interests of the group, will make up a vital part of the special program. In such a class, activities can be easily modified and new experiences introduced before interest wanes. Research has indicated that specially tailored physical education classes can help mentally retarded students to progress very rapidly in their physical skill development.

Physical education can make a very positive contribution to the mentally retarded. Not only must the program be a suitable one, but the physical educator must also be adequately prepared and emotionally and intellectually dedicated to teaching these students.

• *The program should provide opportunities for increasing physical fitness.* Mentally retarded students do not usually initiate play experiences or seek out physical activity. Lack of a regular program of physical exercise, as well as lack of understanding of the need for such a program, means that the mentally retarded student may be lacking in physical fitness. A sound program that includes physical fitness activities can help these students to become more physically fit.

• *Provide a background of basic motor activities.* Movement education is especially suited to mentally retarded students. These students have often not engaged in the natural play activities of childhood and need to develop their gross motor skill abilities in order to be able to find success in some of the more sophisticated motor skills.

• *Provide a wide variety of self-testing activities.* Mentally retarded students enjoy even the smallest success in physical activity. Giving such a student an opportunity to compete against himself or herself will help him or her to gain confidence and pride in accomplishment.

• *Provide a carefully structured, progres-*

AAHPER-KENNEDY FOUNDATION

SPECIAL FITNESS TEST
for the
mentally retarded

A manual explaining the purpose of this test, administrative procedures, and how to record and use the results is available from:

**AAHPER
NEA PUBLICATIONS—SALES
1201 SIXTEENTH STREET, N.W.
WASHINGTON, D. C. 20036**

It presents graphs showing changes in the performance of retarded children with age, national norms for educable retarded boys and girls 8 to 18 years of age, and suggestions for improving their physical fitness.

It is highly recommended that anyone using this test obtain a copy of the manual.

Special Fitness Record Forms (score cards) are also available

1. FLEXED ARM HAND

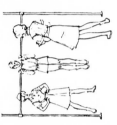

—horizontal or doorway gym (about 3½" dia.) bar adjusted to aproximately the student's height.
—overhand grasp, pull chin above bar and hold as long as possible
—may use stool or tester may lift to position
—score is time *in seconds* from when he hangs unaided until his chin touches or falls below bar.

2. SIT-UP

—student lies on back, fingers interlaced behind head, legs extended. Partner holds ankles down
—sit up, touch elbow to knee and return keeping fingers behind head.
—"curl up," no pushing off with elbows, back flat on mat each time.
—score is *number of complete sit ups in one minute*

3. SHUTTLE RUN

—2 lines, 30 feet apart, 2 blocks of wood (2" x 2" x 4") behind far line.
—on "GO!" student runs down, picks up one block, runs back and *places* it behind starting line, runs down and picks up second block, runs back and *carries* it across starting line
—score is time in *seconds to the nearest tenth* from "GO!" until he crosses finish line.

4. STANDING BROAD JUMP

—toes behind take-off line with feet several inches apart
—bend knees and swing arms backward
—jump by extending legs and swinging arms forward
—score is distance *in feet and inches* from take-off line to back of heel *nearest* take-off line

5. 50-YARD DASH

—starter raises hand, says "READY?—GO!" and sweeps hand down to signal timer who stands at finish line
—any starting position may be used
—score is time *in seconds to the nearest tenth*

6. SOFTBALL THROW FOR DISTANCE

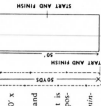

—12" softball thrown from between two parallel lines, six feet apart (see figure)
—must be thrown overhand
—score is distance *in feet from point of throwing to point of landing*

7. 300-YARD RUN-WALK

—if indoors, six times around 50' x 25' course
—if outdoors, three times up and back a 50-yard shuttle course
—walking permitted but object is to cover distance in shortest possible time.
—score is the elapsed time *in minutes and seconds*

Special Note

Some retarded children must be restricted in their physical activity for medical reasons. It is strongly recommended that each child be examined by a medical doctor before beginning any physical testing or training program.

STANDARDS FOR AAHPER SILVER AWARD
(Qualified by achieving the standard on any five test items)

GIRLS

Age	Flexed Arm Hang (sec.)	Sit Ups (no.)	Shuttle Run (sec.)	Standing Broad Jump (ft.—ins.)	50-yd. Dash (sec.)	Softball Throw (ft.)	300-yard Run-Walk (min.—sec.)
8	5	13	15.0	3' 1"	11.3	27	1:34
9	6	15	14.2	3' 4"	10.5	34	1:33
10	8	18	13.3	3' 10"	9.3	41	1:23
11	7	18	12.9	4' 0"	9.1	46	1:23
12	5	19	12.2	4' 3"	8.8	56	1:18
13	5	18	12.3	4' 3"	8.9	57	1:16
14	6	20	12.1	4' 6"	8.7	63	1:15
15	5	20	12.0	4' 6"	8.6	65	1:20
16	5	21	12.1	4' 8"	9.0	67	1:18
17	4	20	12.5	4' 9"	9.0	62	1:22
18	7	20	12.2	4' 9"	9.0	61	1:20

BOYS

Age	Flexed Arm Hang (sec.)	Sit Ups (no.)	Shuttle Run (sec.)	Standing Broad Jump (ft.—ins.)	50-yd. Dash (sec.)	Softball Throw (ft.)	300-yard Run-Walk (min.—sec.)
8	7	16	14.0	3' 4"	10.5	43	1:33
9	8	17	13.1	3' 10"	9.9	58	1:24
10	8	20	12.6	3' 11"	9.2	66	1:20
11	11	22	11.9	4' 6"	8.9	80	1:15
12	12	24	11.6	4' 10"	8.3	95	1:12
13	10	25	11.3	5' 0"	8.2	104	1:10
14	13	26	11.0	5' 3"	8.0	112	1:07
15	17	31	11.2	5' 9"	7.5	137	1:01
16	17	29	11.1	6' 1"	7.3	154	0:59
17	17	30	10.6	6' 2"	6.9	159	0:56
18	25	31	10.6	6' 6"	7.1	159	0:57

STANDARDS FOR AAHPER GOLD AWARD
(Qualified by achieving the standard on any five test items)

GIRLS

Age	Flexed Arm Hang (sec.)	Sit Ups (no.)	Shuttle Run (sec.)	Standing Broad Jump (ft.—ins.)	50-yd. Dash (sec.)	Softball Throw (ft.)	300-yard Run-Walk (min.—sec.)
8	10	18	13.8	3' 8"	10.1	33	1:28
9	11	21	12.9	3' 9"	9.1	46	1:24
10	13	25	12.1	4' 5"	8.8	52	1:16
11	12	24	11.9	4' 8"	8.4	65	1:15
12	10	24	11.5	4' 11"	8.1	71	1:09
13	11	22	11.6	4' 10"	8.3	72	1:10
14	12	25	11.3	5' 1"	8.2	86	1:08
15	11	25	11.0	5' 1"	8.0	84	1:12
16	11	24	11.2	5' 3"	8.1	82	1:11
17	10	24	11.7	5' 3"	8.2	81	1:13
18	10	24	11.5	5' 3"	8.5	84	1:11

BOYS

Age	Flexed Arm Hang (sec.)	Sit Ups (no.)	Shuttle Run (sec.)	Standing Broad Jump (ft.—ins.)	50-yd. Dash (sec.)	Softball Throw (ft.)	300-yard Run-Walk (min.—sec.)
8	11	20	12.6	3' 9"	9.4	57	1:23
9	13	23	12.1	4' 5"	8.9	73	1:17
10	16	26	11.8	4' 8"	8.5	81	1:13
11	19	27	11.1	5' 1"	8.2	99	1:08
12	19	30	11.0	5' 4"	7.9	114	1:05
13	19	30	10.8	5' 6"	7.7	125	1:04
14	22	30	10.4	5' 11"	7.4	142	1:00
15	26	34	10.7	6' 4"	7.1	159	0:58
16	29	34	10.2	6' 9"	6.9	181	0:55
17	29	35	9.8	7' 2"	6.3	176	0:51
18	39	36	9.9	7' 1"	6.5	187	0:52

STANDARDS FOR KENNEDY FOUNDATION CHAMP AWARD
(Qualified by achieving the standard on all seven test items)

GIRLS

Age	Flexed Arm Hang (sec.)	Sit Ups (no.)	Shuttle Run (sec.)	Standing Broad Jump (ft.—ins.)	50-yd. Dash (sec.)	Softball Throw (ft.)	300-yard Run-Walk (min.—sec.)
8	14	22	13.0	3' 10"	9.6	36	1:26
9	16	25	12.4	4' 1"	8.8	58	1:19
10	16	29	11.9	4' 8"	8.5	59	1:12
11	17	27	11.5	5' 0"	8.2	75	1:13
12	14	28	11.1	5' 4"	7.8	82	1:06
13	14	25	11.2	5' 1"	7.9	81	1:07
14	16	27	11.0	5' 6"	7.8	95	1:04
15	15	27	10.6	5' 6"	7.8	94	1:06
16	14	26	11.0	5' 7"	7.9	97	1:05
17	13	27	11.1	5' 6"	7.9	98	1:10
18	13	28	11.2	5' 8"	8.1	93	1:09

BOYS

Age	Flexed Arm Hang (sec.)	Sit Ups (no.)	Shuttle Run (sec.)	Standing Broad Jump (ft.—ins.)	50-yd. Dash (sec.)	Softball Throw (ft.)	300-yard Run-Walk (min.—sec.)
8	15	22	12.4	4' 1"	9.1	61	1:22
9	19	27	11.9	4' 9"	8.6	85	1:14
10	21	29	11.4	4' 11"	8.2	89	1:08
11	24	29	10.9	5' 4"	8.0	108	1:05
12	25	32	10.7	5' 6"	7.5	123	1:03
13	25	33	10.5	5' 10"	7.5	140	1:00
14	32	34	10.1	6' 4"	7.1	151	0:56
15	33	36	10.3	6' 9"	6.9	181	0:56
16	37	38	9.9	7' 0"	6.5	188	0:52
17	34	38	9.6	7' 5"	6.1	187	0:49
18	49	38	9.7	7' 4"	6.3	204	0:49

For boys and girls who achieve the CHAMP standards on all seven test items and engage in at least 30 hours of sports and recreational activity.

Fig. 19-1. Kennedy Foundation Special Fitness Test for mentally retarded.

sive program. Mentally retarded students have the same physical activity needs as do normal students. A progressive program will help to interest and motivate them in a variety of physical activities.

• *Provide opportunities for competition in games of low organization.* Mentally retarded students enjoy the give-and-take of competition, but any competition must be geared specifically to their needs and abilities. The experience of competing will aid in the development of desirable social traits.

• *Introduce new activities at the beginning of a class period.* Mentally retarded children tire easily and have a short attention span. New activities will be learned more easily and will be enjoyed more before fatigue sets in and while interest is still high.

• *Provide for a choice of activities.* This will help the mentally retarded student to feel important. Further, if a choice of activities is offered, motivation, morale, and discipline will remain higher.

• *Provide for lifetime recreational skills.* These skills are essential for any student, but mentally retarded students, especially, need to learn the value of recreation. Through specially designed intramural and club programs, additional recreational experiences can be introduced.

• *Stress positive health and safety habits.* Provide each student with a locker and require that proper care be taken of the physical education uniform. Where possible, provide time in the program for showers. Stress should be placed on the relationship between health and physical activity. Safety must be constantly stressed in all activities and must be related to other phases of the school program.

• *Keep accurate, up-to-date records.* Records will help in guiding the student and in assessing his abilities and limitations. The students' parents are also interested in their progress, and keeping them informed of gains will help to establish good public relations. Accurate and complete records will be invaluable to the student's guidance counselor, the school health team, and the student's personal physician. Complete records will also help the physical educator in making an objective evaluation of the program.

THE DISRUPTIVE STUDENT

The disruptive student may suffer from deep-seated emotional disturbances or may simply be in need of guidance and counseling to help resolve less serious problems that lead to disruptive behavior. Some students who dislike school will be disruptive in classes even though there is no serious emotional problem involved. In any case, the disruptive student presents special problems for the physical educator, who must be concerned not only with teaching but also with the safety of the students in the class.

A single disruptive student can have a disastrous effect on the conduct of a class as well as on the behavior of the rest of the students in that class. Effective teaching cannot take place when discipline deteriorates.

Characteristics of the disruptive student

Emotionally unstable students have difficulty in maintaining good relationships with their classmates and teachers. Some of their abnormal behavior patterns stem from a need and craving for attention. Sometimes the disruptive student exhibits gross patterns of aggressiveness and destructiveness. Other emotionally unstable students may be so withdrawn from the group that they refuse to participate in the activities of the class, even to the extent of refusing to report for class. In the case of physical education, the disruptive student may refuse to dress for the activity. These measures draw both student and teacher reaction, focusing the desired attention on the nonconforming student.

Emotionally unstable students are often restless and unable to pay attention. In a physical education class they may poke and prod other students, refuse to line up with the rest of the class, or insist on bouncing a game ball while a lesson is in progress. These are also ploys to gain attention, and the student behaves similarly in the academic classroom for the same reason.

Some disruptive students may have physical or mental handicaps that contribute to their behavior. Others may be concerned about what they consider to be poor personal appearance, such as extremes of height or weight, or physical maturity not in keeping with their chronological age. Still other disruptive students may simply be in the process of growing up and are finding it difficult to handle their adolescence.

Educational needs of the disruptive student

The disruptive student is in need of guidance and counseling. The school should not impose discipline on the disruptive student before the causes for his or her behavior have been ascertained. The school has many services available to it through which it can help the disruptive student. School psychologists can test the student, and social welfare agencies can assist by working with both the student and his family. Case studies of the student and conferences with all the student's teachers can be invaluable in determining his or her needs. The school health team will also have pertinent information to contribute, as will the student's guidance counselors. Conferences with the student also help to open the doors to understanding.

The school cannot take the responsibility for arbitrarily expelling or suspending the disruptive student without first carefully and comprehensively examining the causes for such behavior. Expulsion or suspension often serve to heighten the negative feelings of the student and make it more difficult to draw the student back into the life of the school.

The physical educator and the disruptive student

If the physical educator is faced with many disruptive students in a single class, he or she must first examine his or her relationship to that class. The physical educator's rapport with the entire class, relationships with individual students, disciplinary standards, and program will all affect student behavior to some degree.

If negative student behavior stems from some aspect of a student's personality, then the physical educator must take positive steps to resolve the problem so that teaching can take place. The physical educator must deal with each behavioral problem on an individual basis and seek help from the school personnel best equipped to give aid. The student's guidance counselor will have information that will be of help to the physical educator. A conference with this individual may reveal methods that have proved effective with the student in the past. Further, the observations made by the physical educator will be of value to the guidance counselor's continuing study of the student.

The physical educator will find that not all disruptive students are continual and serious behavior problems, since students as well as teachers have their good and bad days. The physical educator should have a private conference with the student whose behavior suddenly becomes negative and try to understand why the student has reacted in such a way. Such a conference will lead to mutual understanding and often help to allay future problems with the same student.

Much of the physical educator's task is student guidance. In individual cases of disruptive behavior, the physical educator should exhaust personal resources in order to alleviate the problem before enlisting aid from other sources. Any case of disruptive behavior demands immediate action on the part of the physical educator to prevent minor problems from becoming major ones.

The physical education program and the disruptive student

A majority of secondary school pupils enjoy physical activity and physical education. They look forward to the physical education class as one part of the school day in which they can express themselves and gain a release of tension in an atmosphere that encourages it. For this reason, the student who is disruptive in the classroom is often one of the best citizens in the physical education class.

Physical education is in a unique position to help the disruptive student. Most students profit from the activities of physical education, and through their actions in this phase of the school curriculum it is possible for teaching personnel to gain many insights into student behavior.

• *Know each student by name and as an individual.* Individual knowledge of each student is of utmost importance in physical education and in understanding individual behavior patterns. Recognizing a student's needs and problems early in the school year will help to prevent future behavior problems.

• *Be certain that students understand the behavior required of them.* While physical education classes are conducted in a less formal manner than are classroom subjects, this does not mean that lower standards of behavior are acceptable. Students should know what the standards are on the first day of class and should be expected to adhere to these standards in all future classes.

• *Discipline must be firm and consistent.* When rules are rigid one day and relaxed the next, students will not know how to react. Discipline must be enforced in a firm and consistent manner for all students during all classes.

• *Discuss behavioral problems with the individual student.* Respect for the individual student is a necessity. No student likes to be criticized or embarrassed in front of peers. When a student is singled out from a group and used as a disciplinary example, the atmosphere in the class will deteriorate. Respect for the student means maintenance of respect for the teacher. If disciplinary matters are handled on a one-to-one basis, rapport is enhanced.

• *Expect good behavior from all students.* If the disruptive student knows that the physical educator expects bizarre behavior, the student will react in just this way. Good behavior should be expected until the student acts otherwise.

• *Try to ensure that the disruptive student will be successful in the physical education class.* Constant failure only abets disruptive behavior. If a student is known to be hostile and disruptive, an attempt should be made to avoid placing him or her in situations where he or she feels inadequate. If, for ex-

ample, a disruptive student does not run well, he or she may still make a superior goalie in soccer, a position that would not require running.

• *Give praise as often as possible.* If the disruptive student has a special skill talent, ask him or her to demonstrate for the class. This will provide the recognition and attention needed. Give praise for a skill that is well performed and notice the minor accomplishments of the student.

• *Allow the student to help with equipment.* Make the position of equipment leader a reward rather than a punishment. See that each deserving student, including the disruptive ones, receive this honor when they merit it.

• *Welcome the disruptive student to intramural and club activities.* No student is going to participate in extraclass activities unless so motivated. Set behavioral standards for these activities and open them to all students in the school who meet the standards. Acceptance into a club or participation on an intramural team may help the disruptive student gain self-respect and peer recognition and approval.

• *Keep the student's guidance counselor informed of his or her progress.* The guidance counselor should know of any progress made by the pupil. Too often these individuals are informed only of failures or increasing behavior problems. Progress in one area of the school curriculum may have a positive effect on progress in other areas of the curriculum.

THE POORLY COORDINATED STUDENT

Well-coordinated students are the bright lights of the physical education class. Often held up as examples by the physical educator, they find success easily and receive much individual attention because they respond well to instruction and coaching. There is another segment of the school population, however, that needs individual instruction even more—the awkward, uncoordinated students who are frequently left to learn skills as best they can.

The student with low motor ability is often

ignored by the physical educator. This student is often unpopular with classmates because he or she is considered a detriment in team sports. This student is undesirable as a partner in dual sports and therefore is often paired with equally uncoordinated and awkward partners. The student with low motor ability needs special attention so that physical skill performances can be improved and success can be gained in the activity.

Physical education makes special arrangements for the physically handicapped, the mentally retarded, and the athlete. Very little is done for the poorly coordinated student.

Characteristics of the poorly coordinated student

The poorly coordinated student exhibits a measurable lack of physical ability. Less often considered is the psychological effect of the student's physical inabilities. The poorly coordinated student who is not given special help in the secondary school often becomes the adult who abhors any physical activity and is reticent about participating in adult recreational activities.

Poorly coordinated students are usually placed in regular physical education classes when they have no mental or physical handicaps. The only concession made to their problem is through ability grouping in schools where facilities and personnel are adequate. Even then, ability grouping sometimes is used only to separate the "duds" from the "stars," thus increasing the poorly coordinated student's feelings of inadequacy. The poorly coordinated student may be held up to ridicule by fellow students as well as by physical education teachers, who tend to use him or her as an example of how not to perform a physical skill.

The poorly coordinated student will resist learning new activities because the challenge this presents offers little chance for success. The challenge of a new skill or activity to be learned may create such tension within the student that he or she becomes physically ill. In other instances this tension may result in negative behavior.

Poor coordination may be the result of several factors. The student may not be physically fit, may have poor reflexes, or may not have the ability to use mental imagery. For some reason such as a lengthy childhood illness, the poorly coordinated student may not have been normally physically active. Other poorly coordinated students will enter the secondary school physical education program from an elementary school that lacked a trained physical educator, had no facilities for physical education, or had a poor program of physical education. A single factor or a combination of any of them will help to retard motor skill development.

Educational needs of the poorly coordinated student

The physical education program frequently motivates students with specific problems to perform better in the academic classroom by offering an opportunity for success in physical activity. This process may work in reverse with the poorly coordinated student. A student's dread of physical education class will have a detrimental effect on ability to perform well in the classroom. Both behavior and academic achievement may be adversely affected.

When classroom performance declines, it is the classroom teacher who will become aware of the problem first. As with any other student problem, the first step in resolving that problem is a conference with the student and then with the student's guidance counselor. It may be only through such conferences that the cause of the problem is revealed and the physical educator made aware of his or her contribution to the problem. Unless the physical educator is made aware of the problem, steps cannot be taken to remedy it. Many problems of this nature in a single school cast shadows of doubt on the value of the physical education program, its philosophy, and objectives. If measures are not taken to adequately resolve the problems, poor relations will develop between the physical educator, the student body, the remainder of the school faculty, the administration, and the community.

The physical educator and the poorly coordinated student

The physical educator must understand child growth and development and formulate a physical education program that is based on sound principles of growth and development. A knowledge of adolescent growth and development and of adolescent psychology is also an essential prerequisite to teaching on the secondary school level. Additionally, the physical educator must be able to use personal knowledge to select activities and devise progressions that are appropriate to the age and grade level of the students in the program.

In working with poorly coordinated students the physical educator must exercise the utmost patience. He or she must know why the student is poorly coordinated and be able to devise an individual program that will help the student to move and perform more effectively. The physical educator must be sure that the student understands the need for special help and should try to motivate him or her to succeed. When a skill is performed with even a modicum of improvement, the effort must be praised and the achievement reinforced.

With a large class and only one instructor, there can be relatively little time spent with each individual. The buddy system, in which a poorly coordinated student is paired with a well-coordinated partner, often enables both students to progress faster. Immediate successes will not be forthcoming for the poorly coordinated student, and the physical educator must be careful not to push the student beyond desirable limits. An overly difficult challenge, coupled with the fatigue that results from trying too hard, may result in retarding, rather than accelerating, improvement. Any goal set for the poorly coordinated student must be an attainable goal.

The physical educator has a very definite responsibility to the poorly coordinated student. Poor attitudes concerning physical activity can too easily be carried over into adult life. If these negative attitudes can be reversed by the physical educator early in the student's secondary school career, the student may be motivated to develop abilities in several of the lifetime sports.

The physical education program and the poorly coordinated student

The objectives of the program for poorly coordinated students will not differ from the objectives of any physical education program, but the emphases will lie in different areas, and many activities will be modified or adapted as the need arises.

Before a program is devised, the status of the students will need to be known so that their individual abilities and needs can be identified. Physical fitness and motor ability testing must be ongoing phases of the program. Through the physical education program the students must come to realize that their special needs are being met because they are as important as the well-skilled students in the eyes of the physical educator.

• *Carefully weigh the advantages and disadvantages of ability grouping.* Separating students into ability groups may cause poorly coordinated students to feel that they are being pushed out of the way. If ability grouping is used, they must receive adequate instruction and a meaningful program and have equal access to good equipment and facilities.

• *Select the proper activities.* If a student has poor eye-hand or eye-foot coordination, it will be difficult to succeed in such activities as tennis or soccer. Activities must be chosen that suit the abilities of the students and at the same time help them to develop the needed coordination.

• *Offer a varied, interesting, and progressive program.* Work on improving fitness and self-testing activities should form only a part of the program. Games of appropriate level, rhythmics and dance, and such activities as swimming and archery will help to stimulate and maintain interest.

• *Offer a club program for all students.* Physical fitness clubs, swimming clubs, and other clubs open to all students will benefit poorly coordinated students. If ability grouping is used in class, a common club program will help to remove the stigma of separateness.

• *Include competition in the program.* With carefully arranged teams and schedules in an intramural program, poorly coordinated students can be given a chance to compete on their own level. Preparation for intramural competition should be a part of the class program.

• *Include some activities of a coeducational nature.* Dancing in particular lends itself to coeducational instruction. When classes can be combined and coeducational instruction offered, poorly coordinated students have an opportunity to develop social skills.

• *Group students on a flexible pattern.* Different groupings for different activities will stimulate interest and provide students with a variety of partners.

• *Provide for upward progression.* Reassess the students periodically to see how they are progressing. When an adequate level of success has been attained in a particular activity, move the student into a faster-moving and more highly skilled group.

• *Involve the students in program planning.* Offer a selection of activities that will appeal to poorly coordinated students and guide their selections in relation to their abilities.

• *Provide for lifetime sports skills.* Swimming and dance are ideal for future recreational use. Poorly coordinated students need a background of lifetime sports skills to help them offset the tensions that will arise in their lives and receive the fullest enjoyment from life. Rather than attempting to develop championship-level skill, these students need to develop enough skill to be able to appreciate and engage voluntarily in physical activity.

THE PHYSICALLY GIFTED OR CREATIVE STUDENT

By what criteria do we judge the gifted or creative student in physical education? Is it the boy who captains the basketball team, the girl who scores the most goals for the field hockey team, the boy who wins a state gymnastics title, or the girl who aspires to a career as a professional dancer? Is it the student who decides to be a professional physical educator? The gifted or creative student in physical education has a combination of many qualities, the depth of each quality varying with the individual. Gifted and creative students in physical education are handicapped when they do not receive a specially tailored physical education experience.

In this section we are not concerned with the secondary school student who is gifted intellectually. These students may also be gifted physically, but some intellectually gifted students have only low or average motor ability. We are concerned here with the student who is exceptional because of his or her motor skill abilities and who perhaps is also gifted intellectually.

Characteristics of the physically gifted or creative student

The physically gifted student is not the student who is a star athlete in one sport or activity. The physically gifted student has superior motor skill abilities in many activities and maintains a high level of physical fitness. He or she may be a star athlete but in general is simply a good all-around performer.

The physically gifted student learns quickly and requires a minimum of individual instruction. This student is usually enthusiastic about physical activity and practices skills of his or her own volition. Any individual instruction required is in the form of coaching rather than remedial correction. The physically gifted student has a strong sense of kinesthetic awareness and understands the principles of human movement. The student may not be able to articulate these latter two qualities, but observation by the physical educator will reveal that the student has discovered how to exploit the body as a tool for movement.

The physically creative student also has a well-developed sense of kinesthetic awareness. This student is the girl who dances with ease and grace or who is highly skilled in free exercise. It is the boy who is the lithe tumbler or gymnast. These students develop their own sophisticated routines in dance, tumbling, gymnastics, apparatus, and synchronized swimming. They may or may not be extraordinarily adept in other physical education activities but are as highly teachable as are the physically gifted.

Educational needs of the physically gifted or creative student

The physically gifted student or the physically creative student may or may not exhibit similar extraordinary abilities in the academic classroom. A student who is doing very poorly academically may be the superior student in physical education, or may be superior in all phases of the secondary school program.

For the academically gifted student, most secondary schools offer honors courses, opportunities to conduct independent research, or courses that lead to college credits. Where a student shows exceptional talent in physical education but none in the classroom, appropriate measures must be taken to discover, and perhaps remedy, the cause of this disparity. Exceptional students in physical education should be identified to the guidance personnel by the physical educator in a con-ference, since grade reports will reveal a superior mark only and reveal little of the student as an individual. Guidance personnel should be informed of these exceptional students as early in the school year as a reliable and valid judgment can be made.

The physical educator and the physically gifted or creative student

The beginning physical educator, especially, may find it difficult to teach a student who seems to possess many more physical abilities than the teacher. However, there is no student in a secondary school who knows all there is to know about an activity. Students' knowledge is limited by what they have been taught or have learned on their own. Many experiences will still be new to them.

The physically gifted student or the physically creative student may not have attempted participation in a wide range of activities—he or she may have experienced only those activities offered in the school physical education program. Both the physically gifted and the physically creative student, as well as the average student, will be stimulated and challenged by the introduction of new activities. The creative student in dance may be introduced to a new kind of

Fig. 19-2. The physical educator must meet the needs of physically gifted and creative students. **A,** Student at Walt Whitman High School, South Huntington Schools, New York. **B,** Student at Mount Pleasant Senior High School in Wilmington, Dela.

music, or the boy who is skilled on apparatus may enjoy adding new moves to his routines. The athlete may be a good performer, but he may need to become a better team player. He may rely on his superior skills rather than on a complete knowledge of the rules and strategies of sports and games.

The physical educator has a contribution to make to each student in the physical education program. The challenges presented by students of exceptional ability will help to keep the physical educator alert, stimulated, and enthusiastic about teaching.

The physical education program and the physically gifted or creative student

A well-planned physical education program will be adaptable to the needs of all the students it serves. Before the program can be definitely developed, however, the specific needs, limitations, and abilities of the students in the program must be defined. The activities offered must be adapted to the needs of the students, since the students cannot be adapted to the program. Objectives are not achieved in the latter manner.

The exceptional student needs a structured program of physical activity, since this is a vital part of his mental, social, emotional, and physical development. Some schools have made it a policy to excuse athletes from the activity program when their varsity sport is in season. This is a disservice to the student, especially when the varsity sport and the unit being taught in class are different. A student benefits from physical activity in a regular program. The physical educator can keep the interest of the exceptional student high by adopting some tested methods.

• *Develop a leaders' program.* This type of activity has proved valuable in many secondary schools. Leaders can assist the physical educator in innumerable ways and develop a sense of responsibility for the program because they are directly involved. Members of leaders' clubs have served as gymnastics and tumbling spotters in classes other than their own and can assist as officials in the class program and during intramural contests. Members of leaders' clubs still partici-

pate in the activities of their own class but at the same time receive the benefit of extra exposure to activities.

• *Utilize audiovisual materials.* Movies, filmstrips, loop films, and slides interest and benefit all students, but by watching these materials the exceptional student can compare performance with those of experts, gain new insights into skills, and discover new techniques of performing skills.

• *Provide special challenges.* Textbooks in physical education are not in wide use in secondary school physical education programs. While all students could benefit from the use of a textbook, special outside readings, assignments, and research problems would provide an additional challenge for the exceptional student. Bucher has written a physical education textbook for high school boys and girls, *Physical Education for Life*, which should be especially helpful. (See Selected Readings at end of chapter.)

• *Encourage the exceptional student to assist in class.* Many of the highly skilled or creative students will be able to assist students who have low motor skill abilities. By working on a one-to-one basis, the amount of individualized instruction will be increased. The student with low motor ability will receive the special assistance needed, and the gifted student will be helped to realize that not all students possess high levels of ability.

• *Assign the student to coaching responsibilities.* The exceptional student can assist in the intramural program by acting as a coach on a day when the team is not playing. Coaching a team will help the student to become more cognizant of the importance of team play, sportsmanship, and the need for rules. Such coaching, however, should be done under the close supervision of the physical educator.

• *Provide challenges within the program.* A skilled gymnast would not benefit from a beginning unit in tumbling. If the class is on this unit, the exceptional student might be assigned to work on advanced skills or on an advanced routine. A girl who shows great creativity in dance could be assigned to design a new dance or to devise some new steps.

Self-assessment tests

These tests are to assist students in determining if material and competencies presented in this chapter have been mastered:

1. Write out a definition in your own words of the terms "adapted," "handicapped," and "mainstreaming."
2. Your classmates maintain that handicapped students should be segregated from so-called normal students. Present a report to your class outlining the advantages and disadvantages of mainstreaming. Furthermore, assume it is required by law in your state and therefore must be implemented. Provide in your report the guidelines you feel are necessary in implementing this concept in physical education classes.
3. Prepare a chart. For each of the following classifications of handicapped students, list their characteristics, needs, the physical education activities that meet their needs, and the methods and materials that will assure a viable physical education program for each:
   Culturally disadvantaged
   Mentally retarded
   Physically handicapped
   Disruptive
   Poorly coordinated
4. Given a physical education class where mentally retarded and physically handicapped students are enrolled, outline a program of physical education, and the methods and materials you would use.
5. Justify why physically gifted and creative students should also be provided for in the physical education program.

Points to remember

1. Every physical educator will at some time have handicapped students in class.
2. There are many different categories of handicapped students.
3. Physical education has a strong appeal for the culturally disadvantaged.
4. Physically handicapped students may exhibit a wide range of disabilities.
5. Some mentally retarded students can participate in regular physical education classes.
6. A disruptive student may affect the safety of a physical education class.
7. A poorly coordinated student may become a behavior problem if he or she does not receive special assistance.
8. The physically gifted or physically creative student can benefit from participation in regular physical education classes.
9. The meaning of mainstreaming.

Problems to think through

1. Should the objectives of physical education be the same for all secondary school students?
2. What is the advantage of having specially trained physical educators for special students?
3. What are the advantages and disadvantages of having special physical education classes for handicapped students?
4. What special concern should physical education have for the student with average physical ability?
5. How can physical educators best plan a program for the resistive student?
6. What implications does ability grouping have for the handicapped student? implications for mainstreaming?

Case study for analysis

You are a beginning physical educator in a medium-size secondary school and are the only member of your department. On the first day of activity in the fall, you notice that one of your students is refusing to put on the physical education uniform. The remainder of your class is dressed for activity and ready to report to the playing area. What steps will you take to resolve this problem?

Exercises for review

1. What special responsibilities does the physical educator have for the handicapped student?
2. How can the physical educator best adapt the program to the needs of the mentally retarded student?
3. What special physical education needs does the creative student have?
4. To what other resources can the physical educator turn when needing assistance in understanding and working with the handicapped student?
5. Through what means outside of the class program can physical education contribute to the handicapped student?
6. What special challenges does the physically gifted student present?

Selected references

American Alliance for Health, Physical Education, and Recreation: a guide for programs in recreation and physical education for the mentally retarded, Washington, D.C., 1968, AAHPER.

American Alliance for Health, Physical Education, and Recreation: Guidelines for professional preparation programs for personnel involved in physical education and recreation for the handicapped, Washington, D.C., 1973, AAHPER.

Adams, R., et al.: Games, sports and exercises for the physically handicapped, Philadelphia, 1975, Lea & Febiger.

Arnheim, D. D., Auxter, D., and Crowe, W. C.: Principles and methods of adapted physical education, St. Louis, 1977, The C. V. Mosby Company.

Arnheim, D., and Sinclair, W.: The clumsy child: a program of motor therapy, St. Louis, 1975, The C. V. Mosby Co.

Barach, R.: Achieving perceptual motor efficiency, Seattle, 1968, Special Child Publications.

Bucher, C.: Physical education for life, New York, 1969, McGraw-Hill Book Company.

Buell, C.: Physical education and recreation for the

visually handicapped, Washington, D.C., 1973, AAHPER.

Cratty, B.: Active learning, Englewood Cliffs, N.J., 1971, Prentice-Hall, Inc.

Cratty, B.: Motor activity and the education of retardates, Philadelphia, 1969, Lea & Febiger.

Cratty, B.: Remedial motor activity for children, Philadelphia, 1975, Lea & Febiger.

Fait, H.: Special physical education, Philadelphia, 1972, W. B. Saunders Company.

National Advisory Council on Education Professions Development: Mainstreaming: helping teachers meet the challenge, Washington, D.C., 1976, The Council.

Vodola, T.: Individualized physical education program for the handicapped child, Englewood Cliffs, N.J., 1973, Prentice-Hall, Inc.

Wheeler, R., and Hoally, A.: Physical education for the handicapped, Philadelphia, 1969, Lea & Febiger.

20

METHODS AND MATERIALS FOR DEVELOPING PHYSICAL FITNESS

INSTRUCTIONAL OBJECTIVES AND COMPETENCIES TO BE ACHIEVED

After reading this chapter the student should be able to—

1. Define the term physical fitness and discuss its relationship to total fitness.
2. Demonstrate effective methods and techniques for teaching adolescents in the area of physical fitness.
3. Discuss with students the value of being physically fit.
4. Identify the ways in which the various class and out-of-class parts of the physical education program can contribute to the physical fitness of secondary school students.

How fit are young people today? Recent information indicates that although there was a real improvement in the general physical fitness of American youth from 1958 to 1965, there was no gain in the ten-year period following. More girls than boys showed improvement, especially in endurance tests. However, girls' performances on all but one test were not as good as that of boys. This was based on a national sample of 7,800 boys and girls between the ages of 10 and 17, among 12 million who took the six-part youth fitness test.

The President's Council on Physical Fitness and Sports reports that there are nine million students in school physical education programs. Four out of every five of these students are able to pass standard physical fitness tests. only two out of three could pass in 1961.

There is still much progress to be made in improving the physical fitness of young people. There are many students who do not take part in school physical education programs or in other fitness programs. Many such students are unable to pass certain parts of physical fitness achievement tests.

The terms "physical fitness" and "fitness" have been defined and interpreted in many different ways during the past few years. There are some persons who believe that these terms refer only to body building and motor performance. Others, including most physical educators, prefer to think in terms of *total fitness* of the individual—physical, social, emotional, and intellectual fitness—and recognize this as the more valuable educational goal.

Physical educators have a very real responsibility to their students and the community in the area of physical fitness and its role in total individual fitness. Increased public awareness and curiosity about what is being done in the schools have forced teachers in this field to come up with concrete programs and answers. However, the public does not yet realize that physical fitness is but a part of the total fitness picture, and thus teachers have a dual educational role: explaining to students and to parents alike the overall story of total fitness and one of its components, physical fitness.

The current high level of interest in fitness is the result of a massive campaign sponsored by the President's Council on Youth Fitness, established first during President Eisenhower's administration and later changed by President Kennedy in 1961 to the President's Council on Physical Fitness. It is now known as the President's Council on Physical Fitness and Sports. Under the leadership of such men as Shane McCarthy, Bud Wilkinson, Stan Musial, and James A. Lovell, Jr., the Council has attempted to raise the standards and level of physical fitness of people across the entire country. Their nationwide campaign reached out in many different educational areas, striving to accomplish the following:

1. To improve programs of physical education, with increased emphasis on physical fitness
2. To increase state leadership and supervision of physical fitness and sports programs
3. To increase the number of school personnel doing physical education work
4. To conduct regional clinics in physical fitness
5. To establish demonstration centers in schools where high-level fitness programs were organized
6. To develop adult fitness programs
7. To improve standards in Armed Forces testing and training programs
8. To publish pamphlets, booklets, and other resource materials
9. To inform the public and develop their interest in physical education through advertising in public media

Statistics indicate the remarkable effectiveness of the Council's work. Not only have physical education programs been improving, but the number of teaching specialists has increased, state supervision and leadership has been extended, and the physical fitness levels of students has substantially improved. Many states now have a gover-

nor's physical fitness council or commission. Fitness programs for cycling, swimming, jogging, and running specified distances have been developed, with badges and awards issued across the country to those who qualify.

Yet physical educators and Council members realize that only a beginning has been made. Other statistics indicate that much more has to be done—in the many states that do not yet have full-time people employed in the department of education to supervise the program and in the nearly 40 percent of schools where no daily physical education classes are held for all students.

In March of 1968, President Johnson changed the Council's name to President's Council on Physical Fitness and Sports and located the Council in the Department of Health, Education and Welfare. This was done for the purpose of extending the scope of the Council and promoting sports and fitness in America.

TEACHING FOR PHYSICAL FITNESS

The task of teaching for physical fitness is a difficult one, particularly in regard to teaching adolescent students. The following reasons account for this:

1. Lack of interest. Adolescent girls are sometimes more interested in interests other than physical pursuits, and boys often want to become star athletes without extensive effort.

2. Lack of understanding. Adolescents do not fully understand the term "physical fitness" as it relates to their growth and development and their all-round health and total performance.

3. Lack of uniformity. Physical fitness is an individual attainment and cannot be achieved by a total group through an identical process.

Furthermore, the very nature of physical fitness requires maintenance. It is not a fact, like the multiplication tables, that once learned may be set aside. Physical fitness is a condition that must be maintained. Healthful attitudes toward fitness must be developed in students, along with an appreciation for its significance.

Fig. 20-1. Students using Universal Gym. Courtesy Bill Henderson, Toms River, N.J.

Achievement of physical fitness is another difficulty, for fitness itself varies in relation to the individual's personal requirements. The scholar needs physical skills different from those of the football player and therefore requires a different level of fitness. However, the basic components of fitness—such as good posture, desirable health habits, and social, emotional, and mental well-being—are necessary for all. It is the responsibility of the physical education teacher to promote the development of these components to their fullest degree. Students must be made aware of their need for physical fitness and led toward achievement of this goal. This should be done through both the instructional and the noninstructional phases of the total physical education program.

TEACHING METHODS AND TECHNIQUES*

There are many methods and techniques useful for teaching adolescents in the area of physical fitness. The instructional program

*See also Chapter 22 on evaluation.

itself should contain definite steps for appraisal, guidance, and testing throughout the school year, and related discussions, assignments, and studies should be included for special emphasis.

Appraisal

The appraisal of physical fitness in secondary school is an important teaching method that serves many purposes. Appraisal of fitness provides the teacher with a picture of the fitness level of each student and the overall school population. These data may then be helpful in determining individual student needs and the needs of the total program. Statistics on speed, accuracy, and other components of fitness should be used throughout the year to aid in program planning and to promote fitness.

The process of appraisal should be very beneficial for the student. It should provide an understanding of the true nature of fitness. Having endurance, efficiency, and coordination enough to complete satisfactorily the everyday tasks required in secondary school should be recognized as one of the fitness objectives. Students also need to recognize that physical fitness is not the same for each individual, and this attitude may be promoted through the appraisal process. Furthermore, appraisal helps to motivate students toward improvement of their own physical abilities. Instead of mistaking physical fitness for mere muscular strength, they see that exercise is necessary for proper growth and development and healthy resistance to disease.

Many materials have been developed for appraisal of physical fitness. They will be discussed in greater detail later in the chapter. However, it should be noted here that some of the physical fitness tests include norms, or scoring scales, for evaluation of physical performance. These are helpful in student appraisal, because they offer a more precise technique for comparing scores of students of the same age, height, and/or weight. Students, too, prefer to picture their own test results in terms of the achievements of hundreds of their peers, instead of just their classmates.

Norms do not provide the total picture in the assessment of physical fitness, however. A physical education teacher should be cautious in applying norms since these scores vary according to the basis used for their development (age, height, and so on). One study indicates that both physique (height and weight) *and* developmental level (accelerated, normal, or retarded growth pattern) are important determinants in physical performance levels. Norms that do not consider the overweight factor, for example, may be scaled too high for accomplishment by such persons.*

A study of 7,600 boys and girls, 10 to 18 years of age, analyzed the relationship of age, height, and weight to performances in the California Physical Fitness Test. Results brought about recommendations that *age* be used as a basis for test norms, for steady prog-

ress was shown by students each year in nearly all test items.*

Obviously, more research is needed in this area of testing physical fitness and establishing norms for guidance. The physical educator should recognize the limitations while taking advantage of the values.

Guidance

The teaching program should provide an opportunity for individual guidance of students in the area of physical fitness. This may be done in connection with the appraisal program, with individual conferences scheduled for each student to discuss personal problems and weaknesses. When a teacher is able to offer this personal attention to each student and can suggest exercises and methods of improvement, the boy or girl consciously puts forth effort to improve.

Group guidance in the general aspects of physical fitness should also be included in the instructional program through a unit of study. For girls, stress should be placed on proper posture and good body mechanics in daily activities—that is, in standing, sitting, walking, lifting, carrying books, studying, and so on. By appealing to the girls' desire to be attractive and to develop balance, grace, and poise in movement, the teacher may motivate these students toward improved fitness. Physical fitness for boys should stress increasing their achievement levels in strength, endurance, flexibility, accuracy, balance, and other physical traits. In this way they, too, are motivated toward improving physical fitness. A successfully taught unit should have carryover value not only into daily life but also into college and later years, by developing a wholesome attitude toward fitness and its importance in effective living.

Guidance in physical fitness should not only be included as a unit of study for students but should also be emphasized in each class in the *daily* instructional program. The

---

*Wear, C. L., and Miller, K.: Relationships between physique and developmental level to physical performance, Research Quarterly 33:4, 1962.

*Espenschade, A. S.: Restudy of relationships between physical performance of school children and age, height and weight, Research Quarterly 34:2, 1963.

value of daily calisthenics and warm-up exercises should be stressed in terms of their role in developing physical fitness. A study comparing the physical fitness of Japanese children to boys and girls in Iowa showed that Tokyo children scored higher in nearly all motor performance tests. Furthermore, it was shown that Japanese students had longer and more frequent physical education classes in which to develop these skills. Students in the United States must recognize the importance of daily workouts for developing and maintaining a high level of performance in physical fitness activities. Guidance of this kind is of utmost importance to students while in school, for then in later years, as they organize themselves for adulthood, exercise will form an integral part of daily living.

Testing

Testing should be a regular part of the total physical education program, and testing for physical fitness should be included as one phase of evaluation. The materials for testing different components of physical fitness are extensive. One of the best tests for boys and girls is the Physical Fitness Test Battery developed by the American Alliance for Health, Physical Education, and Recreation. The motivational and educational value of these tests should be recognized.

Discussion

Students in secondary school should have an opportunity to discuss various aspects of physical fitness as part of their instructional program. Related problems such as dieting, relaxation, and menstruation are topics that arouse much interest in girls. Narcotics and alcohol studies provide excellent learning possibilities for both boys and girls. Special studies in these and similar subjects related to physical fitness in everyday life should be a regular part of the instructional program.

Assignments

Homework assignments on fitness that are coordinated with the regular instructional program should be given. These assignments may be in the form of improving performance of particular physical fitness exercises such as push-ups or sit-ups, or they may be in the form of readings related to this particular subject. Studying about young girls and boys who have accomplished unusual feats in athletics is both interesting and inspiring to adolescents. In schools using teaching teams, wherein students have an opportunity to do independent research, the topic of physical fitness may well be a fitting assignment.

Bucher has written a physical education textbook for high school students entitled *Physical Education for Life*. It devotes considerable space to the subject of physical fitness and how it can be developed and maintained. (See Selected Readings at the end of the chapter.)

Other techniques

In order to emphasize physical fitness in the instructional program, there are a few supplementary techniques that are particularly helpful. The use of audiovisual aids is an excellent way to stimulate student interest. Bulletin boards, performance charts, records, and similar devices serve as reminders when displayed prominently. In addition, having the students conduct drills and take turns in leading the class permits personal experience in promoting physical fitness. Of most importance is making physical fitness enjoyable, for when students see that activities are fun, they will profit more fully from the instructional program.

MATERIALS FOR TEACHING, DEVELOPING, AND TESTING PHYSICAL FITNESS

At the present time the quantity of materials for teaching physical fitness continues to increase as a result of nationwide interest, fostered by the President's Council on Physical Fitness and Sports, and increased emphasis on health status, drugs, and medical care. Physical educators have found greater interest in and reception for their programs among parents and lay people and have found it an ideal time to expand and extend their programs and facilities.

There is a wealth of material presently available to teachers for use in physical education classes. The President's Council on Physical Fitness and Sports, Washington, D.C., 20201, and the American Alliance for Health, Physical Education and Recreation, Washington, D.C., 1201 16th St., N.W., 20036, are excellent sources for such materials.

There are many other materials available in the area of physical fitness. Many state departments of education have developed their own testing instruments (California,

Oregon, Washington, Iowa, Virginia, New York), as have some cities (Tucson, Denver, Omaha, Louisville, Kansas City). Teachers should also investigate their own state departments of education, for not only have testing programs been initiated from their offices but also publications on courses of study, programs, and clinic suggestions.

The physical fitness checklist included here is another helpful education tool for teachers interested in this type of material for their students.

Chapter 18 contains other films and rec-

A physical fitness checklist

Medical aspects

Yes | No

1. Thorough dental and health examination each year
   a. Fit heart and circulatory system, digestive system, nervous system, and so on
   b. Proper body development, according to age and sex (height and weight)
2. Correction of remediable health defects—vision, hearing, overweight

Physical activity

1. At least one and one-half to two hours a day spent in vigorous physical activity, preferably outdoors
2. Adequate muscular strength and endurance*
3. After running 50 yards, heart and breathing return to normal rates within ten minutes
4. Average skill in running, jumping, climbing, and throwing
5. Control of body in activities involving balance, agility, speed, rhythm, accuracy
6. Skill in recreational activities—arts and crafts, bowling, dancing

Posture

1. When student is standing upright, string dropped from tip of ear passes through shoulder and hip joints and middle of ankle.
2. When student is sitting in a chair, trunk and head are erect, weight balanced over pelvis, or trunk slightly bent forward.
3. When student is walking, slumping is avoided, body is in proper balance, and excessively wasteful motions of arms and legs are eliminated.

Health habits

1. Rest: at least eight hours of sleep each night
2. Diet: four servings daily from each of the four basic food groups
   a. Meat, poultry, fish, and eggs
   b. Dairy products
   c. Vegetables and fruits
   d. Bread and cereals
3. Cleanliness
   a. Daily bath
   b. Teeth brushed after every meal
   c. Clean hair, nails, and clothing
4. Abstain from use of tobacco and alcohol

---

*The school health or physical education teacher can help to determine proper standards.

Record form for identification of physically underdeveloped pupils

Teacher _____   School year _____

Period or section _____   Date of 1st test _____

School _____

Girls

Name of pupil	Modified pull ups ages 10-17; 8			Sit ups ages 10-17; 10			Squat thrust ages 10-17; 3			Remarks*
	1st test		Retest	1st test		Retest	1st test		Retest	
	Pass	Fail	Date passed	Pass	Fail	Date passed	Pass	Fail	Date passed	

*Enter here any conditions, e.g., obesity, posture, etc., that may affect physical performance.

Fig. 20-2. Record form for identification of physically underdeveloped pupils used at Guymon Junior High School, Guymon, Okla.

ords, listed according to manufacturers, that may be useful in the area of physical fitness.

Isometrics

Widespread attention has been focused on isometrics, an exercise system developing one particular facet of physical fitness—strength. Physical education teachers should understand the principle behind isometrics and recognize its values and limitations in order to place isometrics in its proper perspective within the physical education program.

Definition. Isometrics is a series of exercises designed to develop strength in particular muscle groups. In isometrics muscle groups are contracted against an immovable force, or resistance, and "held tight" before relaxing after a count of six to ten. The tension produced in the muscles increases their strength through this isometric contraction. Isometric contractions should not be confused with isotonic, or dynamic, contractions, in which the muscle groups work against a resistant force that is overcome, as in weight lifting.

Values. An important value of isometric exercise is conditioning. Through daily application of isometrics, muscles learn to work efficiently and effectively in performance of activity. It is believed that increased muscular strength improves speed, power, and flexibility, all of which are important components of body conditioning and fitness. For this reason, isometrics has gained in popularity not only in school programs but also in amateur and professional athletics as well.* It is important, however, to evaluate carefully the equipment and literature that are on the market on isometrics.

Isometric exercises are also valuable in corrective, or remedial, programs of physical education. Whenever a student has identifiable weakness in specific muscle groups,

such as arm and shoulder muscles, isometric routines are particularly helpful.

Limitations. Certain limitations exist in the isometric program of exercise when it is applied to a school program of physical education. As has been previously stated, the value of isometrics lies in meeting *individual* needs for strengthening and conditioning. In large physical education classes it would be very difficult to individualize this program sufficiently for instructional purposes.

Furthermore, while students may become motivated at first with this approach to exercising, enthusiasm may soon be lost if no tangible results are seen. Dynamometers, machines that measure strength, are not standard equipment in most schools, and students may not recognize the progress they are making without them.

Also, emphasis should not be placed merely on isometrics. Isometrics, like weight lifting, has specific values that should be utilized whenever possible, within the limits of proper programming for physical fitness.

Out-of-class program

The noninstructional program, which includes all activities held outside the regularly scheduled physical education class, is equally important to the promotion of physical fitness. The intramural and extramural activities, clubs, demonstrations, contests, and other activities all serve to focus student attention on physical pursuits.

Intramural activities. The intramural program should be available to as many students as possible. By providing an interesting and exciting program of intraclass games in a wide variety of sports and in an atmosphere in which all students believe their participation is welcome, the teacher is able to increase the overall interest in physical fitness and skills.

Extramural activities. A program of interscholastic competition serves to heighten the interest of boys and girls, and their efforts to make the honor squads or varsity teams also induce improvement in physical fitness.

Clubs. There are several clubs that may be sponsored by the physical education depart-

---

*Some manufacturers have developed special exercise kits, charts, and handbooks of isometrics. Bucher's book, *Physical Education for Life*, lists many excellent isometric and isotonic exercises for high school boys and girls. (See Selected Readings at the end of the chapter.)

Fig. 20-3. Students participating in physical fitness program at Wheaton High School, Wheaton, Md.

ment to provide benefits for physical fitness. Cheerleaders, baton twirlers, drill team, gymnastics, tumbling, cycling, and physical fitness clubs all promote physical fitness. The avid interest that many students have in these types of activities should be developed. Leaders' clubs and modern dance groups also play a role in the physical education program, and membership should be open to all interested students.

Demonstrations. Public demonstrations and performances by club participants, such as those of the modern dance group, not only improve the physical fitness of participants but also serve to increase the interest in and appreciation of these activities.

Contests and campaigns. Sometimes a special contest or campaign to promote good posture or a similar component of physical fitness is an excellent technique for arousing and enhancing interest in physical fitness. Student planning as well as participation in such events should be fostered to gain the most value from them.

Organizations. Organizations such as an athletic association, Hi-Y, or scouting and

explorer troops may serve to promote fitness both among its members and on a schoolwide basis.

Outings. Field trips, clinics, and outdoor camping expeditions are very popular with students, and they provide fitness experiences not otherwise available. The physical education teacher should try to sponsor such events whenever feasible.

Awards. For students who have shown much improvement or have performed exceptionally well in specific areas of physical fitness, a ribbon or small award may be presented. The American Alliance for Health, Physical Education, and Recreation has special awards and certificates that may be given in connection with the administration of their physical fitness test. The President's Council on Physical Fitness and Sports also has presidential sports awards.

Cosponsored activities. Much interest can be stimulated with coeducational activities sponsored by both the boys' and the girls' departments or with special events sponsored cooperatively with community organizations. The local Dads' Club or Chamber of

Fig. 20-4. Students playing flag football to develop physical fitness in the Lexington Public Schools, Lexington, Mass.

Commerce is usually interested in physical fitness activities and willingly conducts field days, contests, and sports days. The physical education teachers should work with the leaders of these organizations to ensure proper management and supervision for the benefit of the students.

Self-assessment tests

These tests are to assist students in determining if material and competencies presented in this chapter have been mastered:

1. Give a description to your class of the characteristics you consider to be a part of a physically fit person.
2. Assume your methods class is a group of eleventh-grade students. Demonstrate what you consider to be some effective methods and techniques for stimulating their interest in being physically fit.
3. Arrange a meeting with a group of high school students during which you discuss the values of physical fitness.
4. Prepare a chart that includes a heading for each of the following: (a) the basic instructional class program, (b) adapted program, (c) intramural and extramural program, and (d) interscholastic program. List under each heading the various ways in which that component of the overall program can contribute to the development of physical fitness in secondary school students.

Points to remember

1. The physical fitness goal of physical education requires special emphasis because of increased national concern in this area.

2. The instructional program of physical education should be geared to physical fitness through methods of teaching that include appraisal and guidance.
3. The additional teaching techniques of testing and assignments should stress physical fitness in the instructional program.
4. The noninstructional program should emphasize fitness through its many components.
5. Students in secondary school need to be guided in physical fitness to become aware of its importance to everyday living.
6. Students need to realize the individuality of physical fitness and should understand their own personal requirements in this area.

Problems to think through

1. How can the results of the appraisal of physical fitness be most effectively used for the benefit of the students?
2. In a community that sponsors few recreational programs, how may the physical education department of the secondary school promote community-wide interest in physical fitness activities?
3. The administration of a secondary school is disturbed about students smoking on school property, contrary to regulations. Students and some members of the community are in favor of a student smoking lounge. In what ways may the physical education department help in solving this problem?
4. In a small secondary school there is only one woman and one man teaching physical education. Activities after school are therefore limited to the supervision and facilities available to these two instructors. How may an adequate intramural program be set up that would promote physical fitness for the greatest number of students?
5. What methods may be used to improve physical fitness in students scoring low on appraisal?
6. In what ways may individual personal guidance be offered to students needing special attention in physical fitness work?

Case study for analysis

The physical education department in a large secondary school plans to promote a year-long campaign for physical fitness, not only for students in the school but also for the community-at-large. The administration has approved the idea and offered some financial assistance to back their campaign. What steps would the staff take in carrying out their campaign within the instructional program? In the noninstructional program? In the community? What special activities and events may be sponsored? In what ways may students become involved in the program?

Exercises for review

1. What are the advantages and disadvantages in running a physical fitness appraisal program more than once during a year?
2. What particular objectives should be established for

a unit on physical fitness with eighth-grade boys and girls?

3. What aspects of physical fitness should be stressed in team sports? Individual sports? Formal activities? Rhythms? Aquatics?

4. What exercises are particularly valuable for developing strength? Endurance? Flexibility? Balance? Other components of physical fitness?

5. What types of charts and diagrams would serve effectively to motivate students in physical fitness?

6. What current outside reading materials may be valuable homework for high school students?

7. In what ways may a leaders' club assist the physical education teacher in testing and promoting physical fitness?

8. What types of awards would be appropriate for performances in physical fitness?

9. What topics for discussions in physical fitness would be of particular interest to high school girls? Boys? Both?

10. What are the advantages and disadvantages to choosing a "most physically fit" boy and girl?

Selected readings

Allsen, P. E., et al.: Fitness for life, Dubuque, Ia., 1976, Wm. C. Brown Co.

Bucher, C. A.: Physical education for life, New York, 1969, McGraw-Hill Book Company.

Bucher, C. A.: Foundations of physical education, St. Louis, 1975, The C. V. Mosby Co.

Bucher, C. A.: Exercise, it's plain good business, Reader's Digest, March, 1976.

Bucher, C. A., et al.: The foundations of health, Englewood Cliffs, N.J., 1976, Prentice-Hall Inc.

Cooper, K. H.: How to feel fit at any age, Reader's Digest, March, 1968.

Jones, K. L., et al.: Total fitness, New York, 1972, Harper & Row.

President's Council on Physical Fitness and Sports: Basic understanding of physical fitness, Physical Fitness Research Digest, Washington, D.C., 1971, The Council.

President's Council on Physical Fitness and Sports: Physical activity and coronary heart disease, Physical Fitness Research Digest, Washington, D.C., 1972, The Council.

President's Council on Physical Fitness and Sports: Circulatory-respiratory endurance, Physical Fitness Research Digest, Washington, D.C., 1973, The Council.

President's Council on Physical Fitness and Sports: Introduction to physical fitness, Washington, D.C., The Council.

President's Council on Physical Fitness and Sports: Youth physical fitness, Washington, D.C., The Council.

PART FIVE

Class management

21

CLASS MANAGEMENT—
ORGANIZATION FOR INSTRUCTION

INSTRUCTIONAL OBJECTIVES AND COMPETENCIES TO BE ACHIEVED

After reading this chapter the student should be able to—

1. Encourage development of self-management techniques in students through activities designed for that purpose.
2. Explain several important purposes for good class management.
3. Identify important details that should be prepared prior to the beginning of the school year.
4. List the characteristics of a well-managed classroom.
5. Identify several methods of grouping students.
6. Describe verbal and nonverbal communications, both positive and negative, which promote discipline and control in the classroom.
7. Explain four aspects of an individual's "learning state," indicating readiness to be motivated.
8. Differentiate between intrinsic and extrinsic motivations.

The well-managed physical education classroom may best be described as one that allows desired educational goals to be achieved. From the point of view of the teacher this means making effective and ef-

ficient use of each minute of class time. For the student it means developing good self-management skills and assuming responsibility for his or her own learning. The teacher's role in class management has therefore changed, according to current educational practices. Instead of maintaining tight control over student performances throughout a single class period, the teacher has now become an effective planner and organizer of each daily session, and the responsibility for learning has shifted to the student. Management of the class is the result of individual self-management by each student, whose active involvement and productivity promotes accomplishment of educational goals.

Although effective class management is a primary concern of all educators, it is perhaps an even greater concern of the physical educator because of the special equipment, facilities, and programs that must be coordinated for a large school population. Moreover, the partial loss of class time needed for dressing and showering procedures necessitates particular effectiveness in the remaining minutes of class. This can only be done through efficient class management.

CLASS MANAGEMENT

Class management includes attention to all the necessary procedures and routines that are a part of the daily instructional program. Roll call, excuses, and showers all require certain procedures to make the most efficient use of the time available.

Class management should not be confused with teaching method. The preparation of the setting and the organization of the class so that instruction takes place most effectively is the major concern.

The main purposes of good class management are as follows:

1. To make the most effective and efficient use of class time
2. To ensure the safety of the group through class routines and procedures
3. To provide a controlled classroom atmosphere in which instruction may take place
4. To promote self-discipline and self-motivation on the part of each individual in the class
5. To develop within the students a sense of responsibility toward themselves and toward each other
6. To enhance rapport between teacher and student that will promote learning
7. To create a group spirit in which each individual feels good within himself and feels comfortable with his group
8. To recognize and provide for the needs and interests of each individual within the group
9. To make the most effective use of the teacher's time and energy
10. To provide the most effective organization and arrangement of the class in order that instruction may be given and learning will take place

Effective class management is brought about through careful and thoughtful planning on the part of the teacher with the students. This mutual and cooperative planning should be the backbone of class organization so that students willingly maintain the standards they have established. Boys and girls understand and respect the mutual benefits derived and in a sense they manage themselves. When this happens it is class management at its best.

The teacher's role in developing this ideal type of class management is one of guidance and leadership during the planning periods and orientation of students at the beginning of the school year. Advance preparation, class orientation, and class procedures are the main areas with which the teacher must be concerned. These three topics will receive detailed attention in the first part of this chapter.

ADVANCE PREPARATION

Early preparation includes attention to the many details to which the physical education teacher should attend before school opens in the fall. The opening program, the equipment, the lockers, the records, and the schedule all need to be prepared. This readiness is a basic step to good class management, for it prepares the teacher in advance, and he or she is then able to devote full attention to the requirements of the students when they arrive.

Program planning

An outline of the program for the year should be formulated in view of departmental objectives. Plans for the opening unit and the first week of school should be drawn up in detail so that the teacher knows exactly what needs to be accomplished in the first meeting of all classes. In schools in which team teaching exists, the entire team should be involved in the planning. Of course, the program should remain flexible so as to provide for student involvement in the final plans.

Equipment and facilities

All equipment and facilities should be checked with the inventory that was made the year before. The teacher should make sure that all necessary repairs have been completed and that everything is ready and safe for use. This includes playing fields, gymnasiums, swimming pools, and other facilities. The special equipment needed for the first teaching unit, whether it concerns hockey, soccer, or football, should be taken from storage and placed in an appropriate place where it is easily accessible. The teacher will thus be prepared to make use of it as soon as the class is organized.

Locker room

Necessary preparations should be made in the locker room. A check to ensure that the lockers are clean and in working order will save much confusion. It is very frustrating to assign a locker to a student only to find that it does not work.

If there are bulletin boards in the locker rooms, they should be attractively prepared with appropriate pictures and materials. When the students come into the locker room and see these careful preparations, it will help to establish an atmosphere that is conducive to effective learning in physical education.

Class lists and records

The physical education teacher will find class lists very helpful. Preparing record files and grade books ahead of time saves confusion later on. It is usually quite difficult to find time to take care of these clerical duties once school has begun. There are always other urgent matters that require immediate attention, which means that sometimes paper work remains undone. The mental attitude of the teacher is greatly improved, too, when these details have been cared for beforehand, because he or she is not burdened with thoughts of additional work that needs to be accomplished.

Schedules

Another detail that should be given attention before school opens is the teaching schedule. Any changes or errors that occur regarding teaching stations and assigned instructors should be provided for in advance of the initial class meeting. The scheduling of facilities should be cooperatively worked out by the men's and women's departments so that the instructional classes as well as the after-school program can be organized without delay. This includes games scheduled with other schools.

CLASS ORIENTATION

Proper orientation of each physical education class is important because it affects the outcome of the classwork throughout the year. It is during the first week of school that the students are introduced to physical education and are made aware of their personal responsibilities. This period of orientation also includes student registration, locker assignments, and group planning sessions and discussions.

Registration of students

Usually at the first class session some form of class registration is necessary. The information required and the form of registration vary, depending on the uses for which the registration is held. Customarily it is thought valuable to have on file the following items about each student:

Name
Address
Home telephone number
Age and birthday
Locker number and combination
Health status
Record of fee payments
Family physician
Activities (electives, intramural activities, honor teams)
Test scores and achievement records from previous grades
Awards, varsity letters

Only a part of this information is recorded during the registration period. Other factors regarding such matters as electives and awards would be reported later on. By maintaining a personal record of each student from year to year, an overall picture of his or her accomplishments is readily available.

The form on which information is recorded should be a printed card where appropriate details may be filled in. The cards may be used to call the roll until squad cards are made out (if this is the procedure), and then they may be filed in the physical education office.

Locker assignment

Another item of business that can be taken care of during the orientation period, when students do not yet have uniforms and sneakers available for participation, is the assignment of lockers. This routine procedure becomes difficult when combinations to built-in locks must be explained, but even in such instances no more than one class period should be necessary to accomplish this task.

Locker rooms are generally organized according to a regular pattern, with rows of lockers and benches arranged alternately. The room itself should be well lighted and ventilated and kept as clean as possible. There are different types of lockers used in school locker rooms: baskets, full-length lockers, half-size lockers, and combinations of baskets or small lockers. In each of these cases locks may be built in, with the teacher having a master list of combinations and a master key, or individual locks may be provided by the students. If students provide the locks, the teacher must keep an accurate record of students' locker combinations, for occasions arise when it is essential that the teacher have access to all lockers.

A major point to be kept in mind when assigning lockers is the spacing of class members. Aisles and sections must not be overcrowded, in order to guard against accidents and to facilitate dressing as rapidly as possible.

Lockers may be selected by the individuals in the class or specifically assigned by the teacher, but whichever method is used, it probably should be consistently followed by the teacher with all class groups. The choice of method depends on class size, locker room conditions, and departmental procedures that may have been established.

Group planning

The teacher may wish to devote part of one of the orientation periods to a discussion of the physical education program so that the students will understand the objectives and purposes of the program and have an oppor-

Fig. 21-1. Basketball game in progress at Regina High School, Cincinnati, Ohio.

tunity to ask questions. The teacher should prepare in advance a general outline of points to be used in the discussion to ensure that all phases of the program are covered.

The extent of the discussion depends largely upon the course of action the teacher intends to follow. During the orientation a discussion of the year's program by the students may bring out suggested elective units or special requests in regard to the intramural and interscholastic programs. On the other hand, the teacher may use the time to introduce the program the particular class will be following, as determined by departmental requirements. The nature of the discussion will therefore depend on the degree of flexibility in program arrangement, as determined by the philosophy of the department in respect to student planning.

During the discussion period, time should be taken to determine, through class suggestion and selection, the rules and regulations that will be a necessary part of class organization. The students themselves should establish a code of conduct for the locker room, the showers, roll call, and other class situations in order to give them an opportunity to realize the need for such codes and hopefully to accept their own regulations more willingly.

The teacher must carefully moderate the discussion so that all individuals have an opportunity to express opinions and to ensure a constructive approach to the problems under consideration.

The orientation period may also be an appropriate time for the election or appointment of class leaders or captains. Valuable pointers on the qualifications of leaders may be brought out at this time.

CLASS PROCEDURE

Proper management of a class is brought about by giving considerable attention to many small details covering teacher and student behavior. The suggestions that follow govern various phases of a single class period except the actual instruction of the class. It is this class organization that is the key to promoting a valuable instructional period. Important factors in class procedure include locker room regulations, roll call, shower procedures, costume regulations, excuses, and preclass preparations.

Before class

When students come to a class in physical education the teacher should be completely prepared for them. The teacher should be properly dressed for class and stationed where students may easily locate him or her for advice or questioning. Plans for the class organization should be fixed in the teacher's mind, and all equipment should be in readiness.

The students should come to class in an orderly fashion, just as they proceed to all school classes. This businesslike atmosphere should continue throughout the dressing time.

Locker room regulations

Locker room regulations, determined and enforced by the class, should include the following:

Benches. Benches between lockers should remain clear of books and clothing to prevent these items from being crushed, pushed around, or lost. Benches are to be used to sit on while changing clothes.

Books. A special place should be set aside where students may place their books. Usually they may be placed on top of the lockers, provided the lockers are not too high. Such a location helps to prevent damage or loss to this important property.

Clothing. All clothing should be hung up neatly in long lockers, and shoes should be placed on the floor of the locker. This protects the clothing and prevents it from becoming dirty or damaged. Even where half-size lockers are used this regulation should be enforced as far as possible. Lockers should be closed and locked during class to ensure the protection of all belongings.

Valuables. Valuable jewelry and wallets should, of course, be locked inside a locker during the physical education class. Some teachers require all jewelry to be put away in this manner, thus preventing damage to or loss of the jewelry.

Lights. Locker room lights should be turned out when all students proceed to the gymnasium. A member of the class may be given this particular responsibility, or the job may be shared by many students during the course of the school year.

Routine. The routine followed by students within the locker room should be a matter of changing clothes in the quickest and easiest manner. Students should attend to the business at hand without any undue nonsense or fooling around. Loud and raucous behavior should not be permitted.

Time. The time allotted for changing clothes before class should be established by the students in the orientation week discussions. Customarily, five minutes is sufficient time for all students to change and proceed to their places.

Costume

The costume or gymnasium uniform may vary in style, shape, and color. The requirements governing its use, preferably established by the groups concerned, may also vary, from rigid to loose restrictions. The following considerations are pertinent.

Types of uniforms. Girls' uniforms range from one-piece gym suits with a skirt or short type of bottom to a two-piece outfit of blouse and shorts. Boys' uniforms are generally shorts and a T-shirt, perhaps marked by the school insignia.

Requirements. Besides determination of the basic outfit, there should be requirements concerning sneakers, socks, and sweatshirts for participants. Students are usually required to dress in these items for every class. Furthermore, all clothing should be clearly labeled with the owner's name, with indelible ink, chain stitching, or name tags.

Improper preparation. Regulations may need to be established regarding students who do not fulfill all requirements concerning the prescribed uniform. Students should realize their responsibilities in this matter.

Laundering. It is usually important to set definite time periods at which clean uniforms are required. For girls in classes meeting twice a week, a clean uniform is probably necessary every two or three weeks. For boys, the time period may have to be shorter. Effective means of checking on clean uniforms, probably during roll call, should be established to ensure enforcement of this requirement. Of course, if students can be impressed with the need for clean wearing apparel and thereby dress in this manner voluntarily, it is much better.

Roll call

A teacher is responsible for the group in his or her charge and should therefore keep an accurate record of attendance for each class session. Symbols are usually needed to denote excuses, absences, tardiness, and similar situations. Roll call can become a very complicated and time-consuming process and therefore needs careful consideration.

Methods. Teachers of physical education have devised various means of calling roll for the purpose of saving time and promoting efficiency. Some of the better methods are worthy of attention.

1. Number check. The students are assigned a certain number painted on the floor and must be standing on it when roll is taken. The numbers are painted, in order, along the sidelines of the gymnasium floor, and the teacher merely notes vacant numbers.

2. Number call. The students are given a certain number that they must call out at the appropriate time. Numbers not mentioned are then noted by the teacher as absent.

3. Roll call. The teacher calls out the names of all students and listens for their responses.

4. Squad call. Names of the students are checked according to organized squads, with leaders assisting the teacher by checking attendance.

Each of these methods has its own merits. However, the first suggestions are rather impersonal, and a more friendly atmosphere can be promoted through the use of the last method. Furthermore, the use of student leadership—while requiring more time on the part of the teacher for instruction and training—has the advantage of fostering leadership qualities.

Systems. There is no established rule about when class roll should be taken or what symbols should be used. It is customary for attendance to be taken at the beginning of a class period so that a report of students absent from class but not listed on the daily absence list may be sent to the office. This is an important function of every teacher. Offenders should be discovered as soon as they are found absent from any part of the school day. Besides fulfilling the responsibility for taking roll at the beginning of the class, the teacher will find proceeding from roll call formations to the next activity a convenient way of organizing the group for instruction. Taking roll in the middle of the period may interrupt drill practice, and sometimes there is not enough time at the end of the period, no matter how well the lesson is planned.

In regard to the use of symbols, most teachers develop their own systems. The main criteria that should be kept in mind are speed, clarity, uniformity, and exactness. If leaders are used, they must be able to understand the procedure and in the case of a teacher's absence the substitute should be able to interpret the system. Symbols most often required cover the following items:

Absence	Uniform cut
Tardiness	Suit
Excuse	Sneakers
Office	Not clean
Illness	
Observing	

Safety. Roll call is a very convenient time for checking on safety regulations. This important factor needs special emphasis in physical education, and it is at this point in the daily lesson that equipment rules and safety regulations can be reviewed. Each class member should know and accept its personal responsibilities for the safety of others.

Excuses from class

The problems concerning temporary and permanent excuses from class are always prevalent in physical education. Methods of handling these problems depend upon the size of the department, the department's philosophy, the facilities available, and the teacher.

Basic philosophy. A physical education program should include some kind of modified or adapted activities program for individuals who are injured, disabled, or recently recovered from illness. Limited activities under these circumstances should be prescribed by a physician and administered by the teacher. Because most physical education teachers understand the need for an adapted program, it is possible for them to carry out such instructions. When this type of program is in operation, there is no need for temporary or permanent excuses.

Methods of handling excuses. Temporary or permanent excuses from physical education class may be accepted by the teacher but should have the authorization of nurse or physician. This procedure channels health problems through health services, who are aware of health deficiencies. Some teachers send excused students directly to a study hall if they have no alternate program established within their classes and no adapted program is available. However, this is a questionable practice. Theoretically, students should participate in as much of the regular class activity as possible or in a program specially adapted to their needs. Whenever a particular activity is more than the student should undertake, he or she should have an assignment related to physical education. Students should be engaged in a purposeful activity. If it is possible to assign a remedial type of exercise, with permission of the physician, this should be done. Whatever course of action is taken, the teacher needs time and patience to motivate excused students to spend class time wisely and to help them achieve educational objectives.

Showers

The amount of time allotted for dressing at the close of the physical education class depends upon the shower requirement. Because of the health-teaching opportunity provided by a showering program, students should be encouraged to meet this regulation. Certain rules must be established in this regard, however, and procedures for enforcement set up. A well-run showering program requires certain restrictions for efficiency, safety, and consistency in their application. Towels, too, may become a problem unless properly handled.

In respect to the time necessary for efficient showering, twelve to fifteen minutes is the usual amount of time allocated. However, this can only be relative to the number of students in the class and the number of shower stalls available. Girls generally require a longer period of time to shower than boys, so this should also be considered.

Because of the danger of slipping on a wet locker room floor, students should dry completely in the drying area, which is usually constructed adjacent to the showers. If none exists, the teacher should designate a particular portion of the locker room, near the shower exit, "for drying only." In connection with safety, it is also essential that soap, deodorants, and other personal items be kept in unbreakable plastic containers.

The problem of towels can best be solved when the school provides them. Each student is then given a clean, dry towel that is returned at the end of the period. When students bring their own towels from home, they frequently allow them to mildew in the lockers, for lack of proper drying and cleaning. Squad captains should assist the teacher in the collecting and counting of towels, especially when towels are rented and the teacher is responsible for the exact number of towels supplied by the rental company. If showers are required of all students, the teacher may find it of value to send students into the showers by squads. In schools where no individual shower stalls and dressing areas are provided, girls who are menstruating should be permitted to sponge off carefully at the sinks while partially dressed. In addition, a doctor's excuse from showering should be honored. All other students well enough to be in school and to participate in physical activity should be encouraged to take a shower.

Grading

Grading in physical education, as in any academic subject, is a very difficult matter. It should be kept in mind that the purpose of grading is to report an individual's progress to the individual and his or her parents. Each party should understand exactly what the grade represents if it is to have any real meaning and subsequent effect. It must be pointed out that a grade in physical education represents many different factors—not skill alone. For an extensive discussion of this topic, see Chapter 22.

Cumulative records

Record keeping in physical education, as in every field of endeavor, is a time-consuming process. However, time devoted to this aspect of the program is well spent if the material collected is pertinent, useful, and up-to-date. Some of the main considerations regarding the records that should be kept are discussed in the following paragraphs.

The registration card referred to in connection with class orientation is the basic item to be included in the individual record file. Each year a new registration card is added to the file with up-to-date information. Other data that should be on file—either on the same card if there is room, or separately—should include such information as items concerning medical excuses, grades, skill accomplishment, attendance, awards, and honors.

Records, efficiently kept from year to year, provide an accurate picture of an individual's growth and development and a meaningful basis for determining particular needs.

Problems and interruptions

Flexibility in the management of classes should be a byword for all teachers but particularly for physical educators. Many unforeseen occurrences create interruptions in the established school routine, and the teacher who can remain flexible and adapt suddenly yet wisely is a real master. There are several types of interruptions that merit attention: assemblies, class outings, fire drills, and injuries. (Weather may sometimes cause an interruption if the teacher has not considered this factor when planning.)

Assemblies. In schools where a combination auditorium-gymnasium is used, assemblies become a major source of interruptions. Book week, the science fair, and special examinations are all held in the auditorium, in addition to the regular assembly programs. Even when assemblies do not interfere with the scheduled physical education classes, the chairs may have to be put up or taken down. In this event the physical education teacher must have alternate plans to follow: written work, textbook assignments, the use of audiovisual materials, or discussion. Fortunately, in good weather classes can be held outdoors.

Class outings or trips. When class groups are taken on special field trips or outings, the physical education teacher is often left with half a group. In this instance the regular classwork should be adapted to the smaller group.

Fire drills and shelter drills. Safety drills are essential in all schools, and regular, prescribed procedures should be followed when such drills occur during physical education class. Instructions are usually issued by the administration as to where the groups should exit. The teacher is responsible for his or her particular group and must see that orders are carried out. These drills can be a source of confusion, particularly when students are showering. The teacher should try to point out this difficulty to the principal so that the situation may be avoided.

Injuries. Injuries occur even where safety precautions exist. The teacher must be calm in following regular accident procedures. All instructions—to send for the nurse, carry out activity, or dismiss the class—should be given with unruffled authority, to prevent students from becoming unduly alarmed or excited and perhaps from creating further danger because of thoughtless actions.

CHARACTERISTICS OF GOOD CLASS MANAGEMENT

Careful observation of a single physical education class should reveal to a large extent the degree of management the teacher has promoted. Thoughtful analysis of the conduct of the *students* and their application to the day's work should point out certain characteristics of good class management. The following questions provide a guideline for such an analysis:

1. How much time is used in locker room procedures before class? After class?

2. How much time is required to check attendance?

3. How much time is required for students to become organized into working groups?

4. Are the students properly prepared for participation?

5. Are the students motivated to improve and engaged in purposeful activity?

6. Do the students display eagerness? Enthusiasm? Cheerfulness? Attentiveness? Respect?

7. Are *all* students thoughtfully engaged in some form of activity related to the unit or classwork for that day?

8. Do the students display an understanding of the purpose(s) of the day's lesson?

9. Are the students aware of their responsibilities for the safety and welfare of the group?

Observation of teacher behaviors would also serve as an indicator of the extent to which the teacher has promoted the development of self-management skill in the students. The following questions on *teacher* behaviors relates to these class management skills.

1. To what extent does the teacher feel the need to impose controls on student behaviors?

2. To what extent does the teacher feel the need to control the conduct of all activities?

3. How much time does the teacher spend introducing activities? In presenting information? In organizing groups? In repeating instructions or directions?

4. How much time does the teacher spend controlling disturbances rather than assisting students with activities?

The degree to which a teacher is able to reduce time spent in managerial activities and management of behaviors represents the degree to which self-management skills have been developed in students—skills essential to effective teaching.

It has been suggested by some physical educators that self-management skills, which are themselves learned behaviors, should specifically be taught early in the school year to secondary students. For example, management *games* may be used, in which members of a group or team must appropriately react to signals for quiet in order to earn points, praise, or a reward of some kind. Participation in *elective activities* is another reward offered for appropriate team conduct due to self-management of its members.

The important point that perhaps should be underscored here is that good class management allows for an effective teaching environment in which *students assume responsibility for learning.*

Development of self-management skills is one of several factors that contribute to a learning environment. The teacher must also give careful consideration to techniques of *grouping, discipline,* and *motivation* in the conduct of the class. These additional three components of the classroom setting, because of their contributions to the instructional scene, need particular attention here.

GROUPING

The problems of grouping within an educational setting are not new. Researchers have been arguing the values of heterogeneous and homogeneous grouping for many years and are still seeking conclusive answers to these problems. In a recent two-year study of 150 Philadelphia schools involving some 1,896 student researchers, Summers and Wolfe found that low achievers performed better in classes when combined with high achievers. Moreover, they concluded that classes of thirty-four or more were detrimental to all types of students, whereas small classes were particularly helpful to those students classified as disadvantaged.

Traditionally students have been grouped by grade level, and physical educators, like other classroom teachers, have designed programs progressively on a grade level basis. More recently, however, emphasis has been placed on individualized, humanistic instruction, as was once found in the early one-room school house. In physical education there are many techniques for grouping available to the instructor. Selection of an appropriate scheme would depend on several factors, such as class objectives and the number of students and equipment. Recently AAHPER has identified many organizational patterns for instruction, citing several purposes of grouping, including health, competition, safety, effective learning, and interaction for students. Although grade level distribution of students continues to be a normal condition in school, the teacher may be able to reallocate students according to some of these other purposes. Or class groupings may be based on some of the following criteria: social structures, anthropometric data (height, weight, and age), ability preferences, interest groups, achievement levels, physical capacity scores, or some other learning characteristics. In general, administrative procedures determine the type of grouping that the instructor is assigned in the fall of the year, although in some school systems, teachers may request special groupings. However, even if the teacher is unable to request certain types of class groupings, he or she may still organize smaller subgroups within each class unit, according to the above purposes or criteria.

The major goal of any grouping procedure is to establish an instructional setting wherein increased learning opportunities may take place. It is the responsibility of the physical education teacher to choose the method of grouping that is most appropriate to his or her teaching situation. In the discussion that follows the various *types of groups* and *factors* affecting procedures for grouping will be analyzed in greater depth in order to help the teacher in making enlightened decisions on this important problem.

Types of groups

Methods of grouping may be classified according to the type of *control* that determines the selection of the group. Control may be in the hands of the teacher or the student, or it may be left to chance. Each type of grouping has its own particular advantages and problems, and each should be considered carefully by the teacher when he or she is grouping a class for instruction.

Teacher-controlled methods of grouping. In the teacher-controlled type of grouping the teacher determines the groups. Teams or squads are selected according to scores on fitness tests, according to a particular skill or ability such as basket-shooting or speed, or on the basis of some other single underlying factor, such as height or weight. The teacher then distributes students on different squads into homogeneous or heterogeneous groups.

Homogeneous groups

Samples
1. Low, average, or highly skilled gymnasts
2. Slow, average, or fast runners
3. Tall, medium, or short students

Advantages
1. The teacher knows individual needs in the area under study.
2. The teacher can select teaching methods appropriate to the levels and abilities of a particular group.
3. Individual students feel at home in their group when the abilities of all are similar.
4. Opportunities for leadership are provided students in the low and medium groups that otherwise may not be available.
5. The teacher may control cliques of students through their distribution on teams.
6. Students formulate realistic assessments of their own abilities and may be motivated to improve.

Problems
1. It is an unrealistic classroom setup: groups are not generally composed of people of like ability.
2. There may be a lack of motivation and incentive among some students in the lower groups.
3. There may not be adequate leadership in low ability groups.
4. Teachers may have a difficult time finding opportunities to retest and change groups of students showing improvement.
5. Record keeping and evaluation of students may become complicated if groups change frequently within a unit.

Heterogeneous groups

Samples
1. Highly skilled students evenly distributed
2. Tallest players evenly distributed
3. Leaders evenly distributed

Advantages
1. The teacher controls the distribution of students of high, average, and low skills to make even teams.

2. The teacher may control cliquishness in the same manner.
3. Leadership in all groups may be assured.
4. Students of high ability are motivated to assist others on their own team, and those of low ability are motivated to improve.
5. Opportunities are provided for students to learn how to work together effectively with others.

Problems
1. Students dissatisfied with the group may be resentful and blame the teacher.
2. It is a very time-consuming method of grouping for the teacher because it requires much thought and preparation; well-balanced teams may not be the result.
3. A team or squad that does not perform well together immediately loses its spirit instead of trying harder to work together.
4. It is difficult to teach groups composed of different levels of skills.

Note: Schools presently engaged in the team-teaching approach have found teacher-controlled methods of grouping most helpful in dividing large classes into smaller study groups.

Student-controlled methods of grouping. In the student-controlled method of grouping, students select the teams. Captains previously elected by the class or appointed in some other manner select the members of their own teams. This may be done in front of the group or separately at a different time or place. Another method of grouping in this manner is to have captains select only part of their teams and allow the remaining students an opportunity to divide themselves evenly on teams of their choice.

Advantages
1. Captains are generally well-respected individuals and good leaders, for they have been elected by the group or otherwise selected for their abilities.
2. Initial selections by the captains generally provide an even distribution of highly skilled players to effect balanced teams.
3. Team spirit is promoted because players are generally pleased about being chosen or having an opportunity to select their own team.

Problems
1. Students waiting to be chosen by captains often feel left out and uncomfortable while hoping to be selected.
2. This is a time-consuming method if the entire class waits for teams to be selected.
3. The teams that result from this method are not necessarily balanced.
4. Cliques are not necessarily broken up by this method.

5. Some animosity may develop between students and captains.

Note: This method may be used most effecitvely to select teams for tournament games that end a special unit of study, such as basketball or volleyball, especially if captains select entire teams without the class in attendance.

Methods controlled by chance. In this type of grouping, chance is the determining factor. Teams or squads are formed on the basis of homeroom groups or from numbers drawn from a hat. The system of lining students up and having them number off by "threes" or "fours" is frequently used. The line itself then offers a new factor of control, in that students may be lined up by alphabet, by height, or just haphazardly. The resulting teams are all heterogeneous in nature.

Advantages
1. Groups are realistic and competitive.
2. Skilled players assist others in their group.
3. Intraclass games and tournaments are usually interesting.
4. Students learn to play and get along well with all other students in their class.
5. Groups may be created and changed quickly and easily.
6. Many leadership opportunities are allowed if terms are changed often and if individuals are not allowed to serve as leaders a second time.
7. The teacher maintains standards of fairness and quality, because chance is the controlling factor.
Problems
1. It is difficult to meet the needs and interests of the individuals in these groups.
2. Teaching methods may not be appropriate for all students.
3. Teams may come out unbalanced, thereby hampering class tournaments and games.
Note: A teacher must vary methods used for selecting groups, for students are quick to catch on to repetitive methods. For example, if a teacher always divides groups by having students number off by fours, the students will soon begin to station themselves at intervals of fours as they line up.

These various methods of grouping have their advantages and problems. Before selecting the type of grouping most suitable to his or her teaching situation, the teacher needs to give careful consideration as to what is best for the students.

Other factors involved in grouping

• *How many squads or teams should be established?* The teacher should keep in mind the ultimate goal of providing the most practical opportunities possible by creating the most groups according to equipment. The activity itself, the number of students, the number of teachers, and the facilities and teaching stations available are all determinants in answering this initial question. The samples given in Table 21-1 indicate the different numbers of teams that may result because of the difference in the situation, not the activity.

• *With which type of working groups may the objectives for physical development best be met in this unit?* Some units of study may require special groupings for drills, for example, forwards and guards in basketball, defensive and offensive players in football, and heavyweight and lightweight students in wrestling. Therefore, the teacher must determine whether heterogeneous or homogeneous groupings would be more suitable for the activity.

• *With which type of working groups may the objectives for social development in this unit best be met?* Teams providing opportunities for leadership and for establishing harmonious relationships may result from selections made by either teachers or students. Perhaps there are special cliques that need to be separated for a more smoothly functioning class, and the teacher may therefore prefer to control the groupings for a particular unit.

• *With which type of working groups may the objectives for intellectual development best be met?* Homogeneous groups may un-

Table 21-1. Factors involved in grouping

Activity	Number of students	Number of teachers	Teaching stations and equipment	Squads/ members
Volley-ball	48	1	2 courts 8 balls	4/12
	120	2	2 courts 8 balls	8/15
Basket-ball	60	1	6 goals 10 balls	6/10
	120	2	6 goals 10 balls	10/12

derstand certain types of instruction more quickly when it is geared to each group's particular level. For example, rules and historical development of games may be learned more quickly by groups of lower abilities when audiovisual aids (charts, magnetic boards, and the like) are utilized in teaching. However, lectures would probably be suitable in giving this information to other groups.

• *With which type of grouping may the objectives for emotional development in this unit best be met?* With a class of highly stimulated junior high school girls, for example, who are just being introduced to the game of speedball, squads may best be selected by the teacher in order to maintain calm and control. Then, at the end of the unit, the students may select teams for a tournament to climax the unit.

The teacher must weigh the answers to these questions before deciding which method to follow in grouping the class. The problem of heterogeneous versus homogeneous grouping in education has been and still is being argued from many different viewpoints. However, each teacher must determine the most suitable method in the existing circumstances.

DISCIPLINE

Any discussion of discipline or control in a classroom generally involves two aspects of this problem—encouragement of those behaviors that are consistent with educational goals and discouragement of disorderly conduct that would interfere with the instructional process. Student behaviors that would be classified as appropriate to an educational setting include concentrating on a task, listening and responding to signals and directions, and engaging in productive activity. Inasmuch as these are learned behaviors, it is the goal and responsibility of the teacher to promote learning of these self-management skills in students.

Techniques to be used in learning these management skills are similar to those used for motivational purposes in the learning of other educated behaviors. For example, verbal and nonverbal communications (praise or a pat on the back) are common techniques used by classroom instructors. Grades, too, are frequently used as a stimulus to promote appropriate behaviors. All of these techniques will be discussed further in the motivation section of this chapter. However, it is important for the teacher to realize that self-management skills are learned behaviors and may be encouraged in much the same way as other learning. It should also be realized that the maintenance of a warm, humanistic climate where self-control and self-discipline predominate is an ideal setting for the accomplishment of educational goals.

Alternately, the discouragement of disruptive behaviors is the other side of the problem of discipline in the classroom. Again, verbal and nonverbal communication techniques may be used, as well as punishment and grades. Whereas techniques utilized to promote appropriate behaviors are generally classified as positive in nature, those required to discourage disturbances are usually very negative. Because of the negative quality to these interactions between student and teacher, current educators suggest the following guidelines for their use:

1. Negative interactions or "chides" should be used sparingly, for they accomplish very little. It is generally more effective to ignore disruptive behaviors and offer positive communication when appropriate.

2. If negative comments seem necessary, they should be directed carefully at the offender, timed immediately following the misdemeanor, and be severe enough to be effective.

Teachers need to develop real skills for handling discipline problems so that, rather than reacting ineffectively out of anger and perhaps mistakenly calling down the wrong individual or the wrong behavior, the teacher will respond properly to the appropriate person or persons. It should be kept in mind that negative interactions of any kind—verbal disdain, sarcasm, lowering of grades, corporal punishment, removal of rewards, removal from the classroom, or additional assignments—are generally ineffective, and only contribute further to hostility.

Courtesy Gwen R. Waters.

Fig. 21-2. Archery class at Paul J. Gelinas Junior High School in Setauket, N.Y.

One problem of discipline that needs further discussion here concerns the administration of corporal punishment. Most educational theorists agree that corporal punishment is not a useful way to maintain discipline because of its negative effect on the classroom setting as well as on the student involved. Although some school boards have established definite rules forbidding its use in their school systems, others have established policies permitting paddling or similar punishment under certain restrictive conditions. It is the responsibility of the teacher to find out school policy in regard to this important issue and to govern his or her disciplinary responses accordingly.

Ultimately teachers should seek to develop self-management skills in students, thereby creating a controlled setting. It is generally advisable to establish only a few rules for conduct—with *seven* regulations being a suggested limit—and to be consistent in enforcing them. Manner of enforcement should be as humanistic and individualized as possible, using personal conferences whenever possible, as well as other management techniques. Just as the best defense is often described as a strong offense, so might effective discipline begin with *prevention* of problems. The development of self-management skills is therefore a key to a disciplined classroom.

MOTIVATION

The place of motivation in the learning process is indeed distinctive. It has been defined as the desire within an organism (the student) to act and continue to be involved in the learning process. Another description of motivation calls it "that which gives both direction and intensity to human behavior."* Recent studies of all types of students, from dropouts to overachievers, have led investigators to certain conclusions about the motivated student.

1. Girls tend to be more positively motivated than boys.

2. Students from more favorable socioeconomic situations are better motivated.

3. Motivation to learn appears to be a fairly stable and constant phenomenon.

4. There can be too much motivation. We need optimal rather than maximal motivation.*

Recognizing these factors about motivation, the teacher must provide external motivation for those students who need it. Because styles of learning vary—some are visual, some aural, and others physical—the teacher must attempt to reach each individual student in class.

Sources of motivation vary and are generally found to be one of two types: intrinsic or extrinsic. Both play an important part in the teaching-learning process and need to be understood by the teacher.

Intrinsic motivators

Intrinsic motivators are factors found within the individual that prompt practice, review, and improvement in any phase of learning. A sincere desire to learn, because of a genuine need to use the material or skill, is probably one of the greatest forces promoting learning. When students strive to improve performance for their own sake—when they believe it is important to know how to swim or to play golf, for example—then they will be more likely to master the subject and retain skills.

Intrinsic motivation brings about the more desirable type of learning, learning that will not be disturbed by the emotional tensions of competition or external stress. This type of motivation produces learning that in and of itself is its own greatest reward. The student recognizes improvement and is satisfied

with the results of the effort. The transfer of knowledge is more likely to take place when learning is self-motivated. The student who drives himself or herself to a better performance in one skill area, such as ball handling, will probably do better in other ball games as a result. Transfer and retention of knowledge and skill are a vital aspect of any educational endeavor, and the teacher should strive to promote this type of learning.

How does the teacher foster intrinsic motivation to promote learning? Educators generally believe that students who share in the planning of their programs of study are more likely to have a greater interest in it. The goals and objectives students set for themselves are usually those that they will sincerely strive to attain. Teachers who establish goals and objectives that take into account the needs and interests of their students and who allow students to share in their specific program planning, can surely expect greater and more effective learning to result.

Extrinsic motivators

While some students are perhaps more highly motivated from within, teachers realize that extrinsic motivational factors are not without value. Grades, awards, trophies, and point systems fall into the category of extrinsic motivators—factors that originate outside the individual. There are some students who will work hard just to earn the coveted "A" or the trophy that the school awards. When the student does this, learning takes place.

Pressure from the peer group may also be classified as an extrinsic motivator. The desire of adolescents to be a part of the team or a star on the athletic field promotes much learning in physical education.

A third extrinsic motivator is especially important for a teacher to understand and use. In simplest terms, genuine praise may do more to promote individual learning than all the ribbons and medals the school can provide. When students know they are performing correctly, several things happen: they continue to perform in the same manner,

---

*From Frymier, J. R.: Motivating students to learn, NEA Journal **57**:37, 1968.

thereby creating a pattern of automatized movement in performing a skill, they feel pleased with themselves, and they develop a positive self-image that further promotes the learning process. Educators generally agree that punishment (fear or threat) in some way actually shatters the entire learning situation and disturbs the total teaching-learning process. This seems to hold true for every age level, in all subject matter areas. Particularly, though, it is applicable to physical education, in which a confident self-image and a skilled performance (achieved through practice that has been guided by constructive criticism and praise) combine to help produce better physically educated individuals.

In connection with this discussion of intrinsic and extrinsic motivational factors, it is interesting to speculate about the aptness of Fig. 21-3. Assuming that individuals are motivated both from within and without in an inverse relationship, consider as ideal those students whose intrinsic motivation is so high that overall goals of education are nearly achieved. Students fall somewhere on this line as they approach this general purpose of education. It is for teachers in their role as planners, organizers, and motivators to move students upward on this ladder, or scale, toward effective behavior.

Other researchers have attempted to distinguish differences in the types of motives of students at different age levels. In studies of secondary school students they found several different motives influencing behaviors: a desire to understand the growth and development process within their own bodies, a desire to impress members of the opposite sex, and a desire for affection, adventure, and self-discovery.

A knowledge and understanding of the motives, interests, and needs of students will assist the teacher in motivating them toward learning appropriate behaviors in the classroom. Because students' motives, needs, and interests vary, the teacher must attempt to reach each individual class member through a variety of motivational techniques.

Planning motivational techniques

Success in using *intrinsic* or *extrinsic* motivational techniques is dependent upon selection of a technique appropriate to the "learning state" of the individual students. This learning state may be identified by answering the following four questions:

1. Are they *capable* of learning the behavior?
2. Are they *motivated* to learn the behavior?
3. Do they have the *incentive?*
4. Can they expect *success?*

These four aspects describe the learning state or readiness of the individual student to be motivated. The final element, that of success, is of particular importance because of its relationship to the self-concept that the student is developing. To ensure successful experiences that will further contribute to the developing self-concept, it may be helpful for the teacher to assess the needs, interests, and attitudes of students towards physical education.

Student assessment techniques

Student assessment is a broad area in educational process—too broad to be completely covered within a single chapter of a specialized text. However, physical educators should be knowledgeable of the many assessment techniques available that will enable

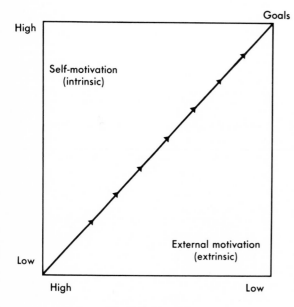

Fig. 21-3. Motivation.

them to understand the attitudes, interests, and needs of students. Teacher-devised instruments such as rating systems, reports, records, and simple question-and-answer tests have been found to be very effective in this area. The information thus acquired can be most useful in program planning and motivating students toward desirable educational goals.

A FINAL NOTE

Good class management is the result of many interrelated factors. The overall goal of self-management by students may best be accomplished by development of these skills, and by careful attention to grouping, discipline, and motivational techniques. If a student is motivated by reachable, interesting goals and by positive interactions from the teacher, the classroom will become self-managed, and the teacher will then be free to make effective and efficient use of all instructional time.

Self-assessment tests

These tests are to assist students in determining if material and competencies presented in this chapter have been mastered:

1. Develop a procedure for utilization at the beginning of class that will promote quiet and orderly behavior while students are dressing for class.
2. Prepare a two-minute lecture for students explaining why self-control and self-management are essential to the learning environment.
3. Design a bulletin board for the opening day of school on which is displayed important information about the program and procedures for class.
4. Write a brief paragraph describing the behaviors of the student and the teacher in a well-managed classroom.
5. Draw up two plans for grouping thirty students in basketball, giving reasons for procedures used.
6. You have a new student in class who is hard of hearing. List five ways in which you would communicate praise for improvement in skill performance.
7. A descriptive student continually interferes with the conduct of your class. Cite three possible actions you might take to correct the situation.
8. Given a choice, several students in your class would prefer to sit on the bleachers than participate in any active game or contest. Explain what your first step would be in trying to change their attitudes.

Points to remember

1. Good class management means effective and efficient utilization of class time.

2. Self-management skills are learned behaviors and may be developed in the classroom.
3. Grouping patterns may have helpful or detrimental effects on the conduct of activity.
4. Discipline is an individual problem.
5. Motivational techniques should be geared to the needs and interests of the students.

Problems to think through

1. Why should self-management techniques be encouraged in the classroom?
2. Why should negative verbal communication be avoided in controlling descriptive behavior?
3. Why should students be responsible for their own learning?
4. Of what value is the element of "success"?

Case study for analysis

In a large high school there are two men and two women physical education instructors assigned to each class of 120 students. To fulfill Title IX regulations for providing equal programs to boys and girls the administration has scheduled coeducational classes in all subject matter areas, including physical education. Design a grouping arrangement that would satisfy coeducational activity requirements for a fall semester in which three lifetime sports (archery, bowling, and tennis) are offered along with field hockey and soccer.

Exercises for review

1. Identify all appropriate information that should be recorded on a registration card for each student enrolling in physical education at the beginning of a school year.
2. Develop a recording system that would efficiently record absences and excuses from class and any other information that you feel might be pertinent for evaluation and other purposes.
3. Determine a set of standards for desirable behaviors to be followed in the locker rooms before and after class, and draw up a list of possible consequences that would be carried out in instances where undesirable behaviors became evident.
4. Devise one or more motivational schemes other than grading that would promote minimal levels of participation by less skilled and disinterested students scheduled in a daily, required program of physical education.
5. In the case where chance groupings result in squads of vastly unequal abilities, what action should the instructor take?

Selected readings

Classroom teachers and Rowan, C.: Motivating students, Today's Education, 64:21-30, Sept.-Oct. 1975.

Gallup, G.: The public looks at the public schools, Today's Education **64**:16-20, Sept.-Oct. 1975.

Kagan, J.: Love for learning, Today's Education **64**: 47-48, March-April, 1975.

Heitmann, H. M., and Kneer, M. E.: Physical education instructional techniques: an individualized humanistic approach, Englewood Cliffs, N.J., 1976, Prentice-Hall, Inc.

Martens, R., Burwitz, L., and Newell, K. M.: Money and praise: do they improve motor learning and performance? Research Quarterly **43**:429-442, Dec. 1972.

McKenna, B. H., and Olson, M. N.: Class size revisited, Today's Education **64**:29-31, March-April, 1975.

Pratt, T. M.: A positive approach to descriptive behavior, Today's Education **64**:60-62, March-April, 1975.

Shepardson, R. D.: Don't just say great! Today's Education **64**:32-33, Nov.-Dec., 1975.

Seidentop, D.: Developing teaching skills in physical education, Boston, 1976, Houghton Mifflin Company.

Summers, A. A., and Wolfe, B. L.: Schools do make a difference: the Federal Reserve Bank of Philadelphia study, Today's Education **64**:24-27, Nov.-Dec., 1975.

Van DerBur, M.: Motivating students. Today's Education **63**:68-70, Sept.-Oct., 1974.

22

PUPIL EVALUATION AND GRADING

INSTRUCTIONAL OBJECTIVES AND COMPETENCIES TO BE ACHIEVED

After reading this chapter the student should be able to—

1. Discuss various innovative methods that are being utilized in today's physical education programs to evaluate students.
2. Indicate what constitutes a minimal program for evaluating the degree to which students are accomplishing professional physical education objectives.
3. List selective methods and materials for evaluating pupil achievement.
4. Evaluate physical education tests utilized in the secondary school and select those that best meet established criteria.
5. Apply sound principles of evaluation to grading pupils in the secondary school.

John is in the twelfth grade at Ft. Pierce, Florida, and is scheduled to take golf as part of his physical education requirement. In advance of taking the course he has signed a contract with his teacher that spells out in detail the work in golf that he must complete to earn a grade of his choice. For example, John knows he can earn 10 points as part of the contract if he learns to swing a club properly, demonstrates proper technique to the instructor, and writes a short report that analyzes the sequence of movements to be followed in using the club effectively. Another part of the golf contract that is valued at 20 points requires John to read a book on golf

and then write a summary and critique of the publication. There are other contract options that permit John to earn additional points. To get a grade of A in golf John must earn a minimum of 125 points. If he wants a B, he needs 100 points; a C, 90 points; and a D, 80 points. No completed contract receives a failing grade. If the quality is not acceptable, the contract time is extended.

Contract learning is an innovation that some school teachers are utilizing in various subjects in order to individualize learning and provide for students who have different interests and motivations. These teachers have described the "contract-for-grade" system as a way in which they can interact with students and where both have the opportunity to indicate their expectations for the course.

What students accomplish in the contract system depends entirely upon their own efforts and how they apply themselves. In physical education at Ft. Pierce, Florida, the sports contracts are designed to be utilized by students on an individual basis and working at their own pace. The goal is not necessarily to create superskilled players but, instead, to have each boy and girl learn the basic fundamentals, rules, and etiquette of the sport and be able to participate in the activity with some degree of understanding and enjoyment.

To fulfill contract requirements, students frequently use as resources the school library, programmed texts, and other supplemental materials, teacher-student discussions, visual aids, the community, and consultants who are familiar with the subject. The teacher is on call to advise students during and after school hours. The sources of information for the students are as great as their imagination and ingenuity. Attendance is not always required. In some schools the students check in to class daily but thereafter are free to go where their resources are located.

Student reaction to contract learning has been favorable. For example, at Madison Consolidated High School in Indiana, students were asked to express their opinions. About 80 percent said they enjoyed contract better than traditional learning and wanted to use it again. Three out of every four students felt they learned more under the contract system than under methods that had been in use in past years. Nearly nine out of every ten students liked the independent method of work, the opportunity to earn the grade they wanted, and the statement of exactly what must be done to be awarded a specific grade. Some representative student comments include: "You get the grade you want." "It gives the student a chance." "The system helped me more than the teacher." "I knew exactly what was required in order to get a certain grade." "It permitted me an opportunity to work at my own pace." "It places the responsibility upon the student and this is as it should be."

Contract learning is an innovation that school systems will want to consider as a possible method to personalize and motivate student learning.

Student contracting for grades in physical education is an innovative procedure where teachers of physical education are trying to make pupil evaluation more meaningful for the student. Other innovative procedures are also being used.

INNOVATIONS REGARDING EVALUATION

A physical growth report card has been used by the Abraham Lincoln High School in Philadelphia. The report card consists of ten different growth items broken down into physical components and personal character-

Fig. 22-1. Measuring physical fitness at Wheaton High School, Wheaton, Md.

istics. The physical components include muscle strength, muscle endurance, flexibility, cardiovascular endurance, and neuromuscular coordination. The personal characteristics include height, weight, age, posture, muscle tone, health habits, and work habits. Although all of these components are not graded for each marking period, throughout the entire school year all do receive attention. By the end of the year a physical profile can be seen that shows the strong and the weak points of the pupil. A student receives a grade of A (exceptional), B (above average), C (good), D (poor), or E (very poor) for each component.

At Jessie M. Clark Junior High School in Lexington, Kentucky, each member of the physical education class participates in the evaluation of other students and also rates himself or herself. In addition, the teacher rates each student. Thus far, in practice there is much agreement among all three ratings. A conclusion reached by those who utilize this method is that the student feels more a part of the learning process and as a result is more concerned and plays a more active role in class.

At Framingham North High School in Framingham, Massachusetts, the members of the physical education class formulate goals they wish to achieve. Then they plan the steps by which they will achieve these goals, and, finally, they are rated on the degree to which the goals are achieved.

At Herrick Public School in Herrick, Long Island, New York, students also think through and write out the goals that they wish to achieve. They are told they should take a look at themselves, decide what they wish to achieve in physical education, define goals for themselves in light of their wishes, plan how to achieve these goals, and, finally, evaluate what they have accomplished. Student and teacher grades are averaged together in order to arrive at the final grade.

It would appear that evaluation and grades will continue to be used in our schools since the American society seems to demand them. At the same time, methods must be devised that will judge more accurately the work accomplished by students and, in addition, help the student to better understand himself or herself and the degree to which progress is being made toward desirable educational and personal goals.

EVALUATION IN PHYSICAL EDUCATION

Physical education teachers have the responsibility for evaluating the degree to which they are accomplishing professional objectives. This process of evaluation should cover two general areas: pupil achievement, which includes the progress report or grade, and program administration. In Chapter 23 details of the evaluation of program administration and teaching are discussed, whereas in this chapter the main topic is pupil evaluation and grading.

Evaluation of pupil achievement should

YOU EARN YOUR MARK IN PHYSICAL EDUCATION

(You earn **6** points a day for full participation)

Participation and Health	240 points
Skills (ability)	60 points
Knowledge of the Rules	20 points
Maximum Total	320 points

		Bonus Points—	
A	320 - 306		
B	305 - 286	Class Intramural Champ	10
C	285 - 261	Leader in Decathlon	5
D	260 - 241	Satisfactory Captain	10
F	240 - Below	Oiler Leader	15

Make-Up — 6 points a week on scheduled day.

Fig. 22-2. How a student earns mark in physical education at Richmond Union High School, Richmond, Calif.

PHYSICAL EDUCATION REPORT CARD
NASHVILLE CITY SCHOOLS

Pupil_____School_____

Homeroom_____Classroom _____Year 19_____ 19_____

GRADE LEVEL	FALL					SPRING					YEAR'S AVERAGE
	1	2	3	Ex	Av	4	5	6	Ex	Av	

Items checked (✔) below need improvement

	1	2	3	4	5	6
Develops co-ordination						
Shows knowledge of rules						
Develops physically						
Strength						
Endurance						
Weight						
Participates						
Dress						
Playing						
Shower						
Attendance (Days absent from class)						
Conduct						

CODE
(Teacher may add plus or minus if she wishes)

A=90 - 100—Consistently does ex-cellent work
B =82 - 89—Does good work
C=75 - 81—Does fair work
D=70 - 74—Low, but, passing
F =Below 70—Failing

Comments enclosed   Date_____ Date_____ Date_____
                     Date_____ Date_____ Date_____

Teacher_____

(Front)

Fig. 22-3. Physical education report card in Nashville City Schools, Nashville, Tenn.

determine to what extent program objectives are being met. Evaluation should reveal levels of student development toward each of the four major goals: physical fitness, physical skills, knowledge and appreciation, and social development. The results of this evaluation process should serve many purposes. Besides providing a basis for grading pupil progress, evaluation techniques should also provide essential information for the motivation, guidance, and grouping of students and for program planning and curriculum building.

Current emphasis on meeting individual needs has increased the importance of evaluation, particularly for the purpose of identify-ing exceptional children. In order for orthopedically handicapped, gifted, and retarded children to receive equal opportunities in education, special adapted programs, both in physical education and in general education, are being developed to meet their particular needs.

There are many techniques of evaluation that are useful in measuring pupil achievement. Selection of a particular instrument depends on several factors, including time, facilities, and type and purposes of information sought. Physical education teachers must devise a program of evaluation suitable to the philosophy and objectives of their par-

ATTITUDES AND PRACTICES	Items checked (✔) below need improvement					
	1	2	3	4	5	6
SOCIAL						
Uses self-control						
Is courteous in speech and action ...						
Co-operates						
Cares for property (incl. textbooks).						
Is considerate toward others						
Respects and obeys school rules						
WORK						
Makes good use of abilities						
Follows directions promptly						
Completes each task						
Works independently						
Uses initiative						
HEALTH						
Maintains personal cleanliness						
Maintains correct posture						
Obeys safety precautions						

PARENT'S SIGNATURE

1. _____

2. _____

3. _____

4. _____

5. _____

6. _____

(Back)

Fig. 22-3, cont'd. For legend see opposite page.

ticular school situation and physical education program. However, at least a minimum program of evaluation should be instituted to fulfill the teachers' responsibilities in this area. A minimum program of measurement and evaluation in physical education should include at least a medical examination and some objective means of determining a student's progress toward each goal established for the physical education program.

A more comprehensive program of measurement and evaluation would include several other testing techniques, such as sports skill tests, attitude and interest inventories, checklists, and questionnaires. The develop-ment of a program of evaluation for a particular school requires a great deal of thought and study on the part of the staff.

Methods and materials for evaluation of pupil achievement and various systems of reporting pupil progress are presented and discussed.

METHODS AND MATERIALS FOR EVALUATING PUPIL ACHIEVEMENT

An evaluation program of pupil achievement should be designed to determine level of achievement in relation to the four principal objectives of the physical education program. The following testing techniques,

identical progress scores, such as three more baskets on the second testing round. The teacher must then consider which student making a score of three evidenced greater improvement: the low scorer who managed to make three more baskets or the expert who scored high originally, yet still increased his score by three. Only by evaluating each student's performance can a teacher make proper use of charts in grading.

Knowledge and appreciation

In the area of knowledge and appreciation, tests differ from those of physical fitness and skills in that an intellectual process is involved, rather than a motor performance. Standardized written tests are available in some of the sports and may be found in rule books and source books of the various sports. Unfortunately, many standardized tests are limited to the college level. Teachers may therefore have to devise their own tests, using either the oral, essay, or objective form. In so doing, the teacher can make sure that the test covers assigned materials and that it is suitable for the age level being tested.

Principles of test construction. There are certain principles of test construction that should be followed when developing a knowledge test.

1. The items selected should cover the entire subject matter, with emphasis placed on the most important facets of the game.

2. The length of the test should be related to the time available for testing.

3. The test should be appropriately worded and geared for the age level to be tested.

4. Directions should be simple and clear.

Techniques of testing. There are different techniques that may be utilized in test construction. True-and-false items, matching questions, sentence completion, multiple-choice, and diagrams, as well as short essays, may be combined to make an interesting and comprehensive examination of knowledge.

The following are a few suggestions regarding the wording of objective tests.

1. Questions or test items should be worded so as to avoid ambiguity and triviality.

2. Statements should be simple and direct, not tricky, involved, or based solely on opinion.

3. Words such as *never, always, none,* or *all* should be omitted in sentences requiring true or false answers.

Knowledge tests are generally developed in objective form, but evaluation of appreciation requires other techniques. To determine attitudes and opinions in physical education, the teacher will find that short-answer questionnaires, opinion polls, and surveys are useful. These testing techniques are not designed to determine factual comprehension, as knowledge tests are, but to discover student preferences in the area of program content or their attitudes toward class conduct. Results of these tests, therefore, are not computed on an individual basis but are used to determine overall class opinions or estimations. Because of the personal nature of these testing techniques, the forms are, of necessity, teacher-made. Construction of these questionnaires or surveys depends on the information sought and the purposes to be served.

Administration of tests. When a written test is administered, directions should be read aloud as well as written on the test paper. A few questions as to the timing or scoring of the test may be answered, but they should be limited. Following the signal "go," no further questions or talking should be allowed. Nothing is more disconcerting to the teacher or the students than unnecessary questioning. If directions are clear and the test well constructed, a satisfactory examination should result.

Social development

Social development is a goal of the physical education program that also requires evaluation, but unfortunately, it is one aspect that is often neglected by teachers. The social development of the adolescent is a complex process. However, various techniques of testing have been devised to measure some of its aspects: social adjustment, attitudes and interests, social efficiency, and social status.

Testing social adjustment. Measurements

of social adjustment may be made through the administration of standardized inventories (such as the Bell Adjustment Inventory) that have been developed specifically for this purpose. Such inventories should be used cautiously, however, and the results regarded only as clues to or indications of adjustment problems. The guidance department of a large school system is probably better equipped to administer and interpret these tests, but the physical education teacher should be familiar with them. A list of some of the other tests for social adjustment includes the following: Science Research Associates Inventory, Minnesota Multiphasic Personality Inventory, Washburne's Social Adjustment Inventory, and the Bernreuter Personality Inventory. These tests are usually concerned with common adolescent problems or worries about the home, health, friends, and so on. Such tests or inventories are for general educational use, not for physical education personnel alone; therefore, the school psychologist or guidance counselor should be consulted in regard to this phase of testing.

Testing attitudes and interests. The guidance department should also be able to assist the physical educator in testing the attitudes or interests of adolescents. Attitudes may be measured in different ways. As an example, three techniques are mentioned: (1) teacher evaluation (observation of students, with an anecdotal record being kept by the teacher), (2) opinion polls, and (3) rating scales. The physical education teacher should ask for the assistance of other teachers, and particularly of the guidance personnel, in this type of testing. Teachers work together because of a mutual interest in student problems, and sharing the test results promotes greater understanding among all concerned. This type of faculty cooperation would apply also to interest inventories such as the Strong Vocational Interest Blank or the Kuder Preference Record. The development of social interests, attitudes, and adjustment, while being a goal of physical education, is also a general educational goal, and testing them is the concern of the entire teaching staff.

Testing social efficiency. In regard to testing social efficiency, rating scales have been developed by leaders in the field of physical education specifically for use within the program. In these tests, ratings of the frequency of behavior are measured by observer judgment. By referring to the original sources indicated, the teacher may learn the techniques of administering these tests for social efficiency.

Testing social status. Sociometrics is the measurement of social relationships as determined by use of a sociogram. The sociogram is useful in physical education as a method of teaching and of testing the social status of individuals in a class, team, or squad. The results of the sociogram point out the natural leaders in the groups and the outsiders trying to become members. When the device is used more than once with the same group, a comparison of the results indicates social growth or change. A sociogram may be taken, for example, by asking all members of a team to list two people whom they would most like to have as their friends, with their choices limited to a given group or team. Results may be pictured with arrows pointing to the names listed, as shown in Fig. 22-4.

It may be interpreted from the particular sociogram shown here that John is the strongest leader, with Bill following closely behind. John, Larry, and Ed seem to form a rather small social clique, while Bill, who would like to join them, returns friendship with Fred only. It may be said also that Allen may be trying to break up this friendship and that Charlie, who was chosen by no one, would be happy with either Bill or Allen for a friend.

An indication of social development in such a group would be the movement of Charlie and Allen into an acceptable position in the group and the enlargement of the clique so that friendships are more spread out. A second sociogram would then show partial proof of social development and accomplishment through teamwork in whatever the group activity may have been. This is a simple technique of testing social development. It is useful as a tool in teaching be-

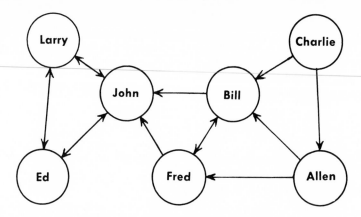

Fig. 22-4. A sociogram indicates social status.

cause it indicates social interactions and points out possibly dangerous cliques, as well as those individuals who need assimilation into the group. The teacher, knowing this, can gear teaching to avoid social upsets and to improve social relationships.

Problems in evaluating student achievement

The testing of student achievement and the analysis of results necessary for their future application are essentials of the teaching program. For the new teacher, five main problems stem from this responsibility: (1) alloting time for testing, (2) selecting tests, (3) administering tests, (4) keeping records, and (5) using the results.

Allotting time. The time necessary for adequate evaluation of students' achievements must be set aside as a regular part of the teaching program. In situations where classes meet every day, one class period every other week may be devoted to testing. When classes meet only two or three times a week, the teacher should plan for evaluation procedures at least at the beginning and end of each unit of study in order to obtain accurate records of growth and progress.

Selecting tests. In selecting tests the new teacher should survey the available instruments to determine whether they are pertinent to his or her school situation. Proper selection of tests helps to overcome the problems of large classes, short periods, and individual rating needs. Because good organization and wise use of leaders also help to eliminate loss of valuable time, the beginning teacher should plan testing periods very carefully in order to make the most of them. Testing itself is a teaching method, with its promotion of good performances and its motivational purposes, and time taken for evaluation is therefore not wasted.

In selecting a test for administration to a class, the teacher should be concerned with five elements of the particular test: validity, objectivity, reliability, norms, and administrative feasibility. If the test is satisfactory in all these respects, the teacher may be assured that the results will be accurate.

Validity. The test should measure what it is supposed to measure. If the teacher is measuring balance, for example, the test should measure balance and not some other physical characteristic, such as speed or endurance.

Objectivity. The scoring of the test should be exact and well defined and as free as possible from personal opinion or subjective judgment. If two or more judges evaluate the performances of a class group, their answers or scores should be similar. This is an important factor in testing, and it affects the students to a great extent. They recognize the value of exact scoring methods for particular performances and generally prefer them to scaled value judgments.

Reliability. The testing device should consistently produce the same results. If a test were repeated under very similar conditions with the same group, the results should be equivalent—with the better performers again scoring high and so on. Extraneous factors such as practice, distance, or time should not influence the results.

Norms. The test should have an accepted scale of performance scores normal for particular age levels and groups. Norms are useful for comparison of the achievements of one group with those of a similar group. Norms are valuable, however, only if they are based on a large population, which ensures a wide range of performance levels.

Administrative feasibility. It should be possible to administer a test to a class group without too much expense, loss of time, or other complication. It is logical to expect that testing student achievement consumes a reasonable amount of time, expense, and consideration. Evaluation should not, however, result in excessive loss of teaching time, to the detriment of the program. This factor often determines the feasibility of administration of a particular type of test. Taking into account class size, available equipment, and length of class periods may eliminate an otherwise sound testing device.

Making the selection of a testing instrument according to these five factors is necessary if accurate and worthwhile results are to be obtained. The teacher of physical education should take great care in surveying available tests before making a final choice.

Administering tests. The feasibility of administering a particular instrument of testing is not the only consideration involved prior to selection. Other factors unrelated to the test itself may become problems during test administration and therefore need to be anticipated by the teacher.

• *What provisions can be made in regard to changing climactic conditions?* For example, in a test for accuracy in archery or punting in football, wind direction and velocity may be disturbing factors. Can retests be administered?

• *What provisions can be made for make-up testing of pupils who may be absent on the day the test is given?* Will time be set aside after school or during the regular class program to accommodate these pupils? Will the identical test be given, or will a substitute be used to prevent preparation on the basis of rumors or gossip?

• *What provisions can be made to correct errors made by student assistants in timing, for example, or in scoring test results?* Will retesting solve this problem, or will the advantage of previous practice produce a higher score by the testee?

• *What provisions can be made for the maintenance of testing targets, line makers, and the like during the test administration?* Chalk lines frequently become blurred or erased during test administration. Can masking tape be used, or is it possible to assign a student leader the task of keeping lines or circles visible?

• *What provisions can be made for students who err throughout the entire test, either through a misunderstanding of the directions or through a lack of sufficient time?* Should such students automatically fail because of their unacceptable performances, or should they be allowed the opportunity to take the test again in the makeup period?

These are questions that the teacher must answer when administering tests, whether they be written or performance tests of student achievement.

Keeping records. The clerical duties attached to the testing program pose other difficulties. Records should be kept up to date and new test results constantly analyzed in terms of student progress and program planning for most effective use. The teacher must take time to do this if the true values of evaluation are to be realized.

To ease this difficulty somewhat, schools have been making use of community volunteers or teacher aids to free regular teachers from these clerical duties, which consume so much time. The physical education teacher should investigate this possibility in regard to record keeping. The form of the record itself may help to make the task less burdensome. Some schools have been finding the use of IBM cards to be a real help in solving the problem of recording test results. The

Evergreen Park Community High School uses this system to record physical fitness test results and to send reports home as well. A sample card is seen in Fig. 22-5.

It may also be helpful for the teacher to maintain a record file of evaluative tests used, adding comments concerning possible success or problems involved in their administration. This procedure would prevent repetition of testing with unsuitable instruments.

Using test results. The results of all types of tests of student achievement should be put to use if the process of evaluation is to have any direct value for the students. There are several ways in which this may be done, and the choice depends on the purpose of the particular test.

Tests administered at the beginning of a unit—whether skill, knowledge, or fitness tests—serve as prognostic devices to determine the needs of the group in relation to that specific activity. The teacher should interpret test results immediately and use them in planning the unit of study. Special groups may need to be formed on the basis of skills, or a special area of the activity may need emphasis because of a general weakness of the group. The motivational aspect of prognostic tests is also a valuable teaching tool.

Tests administered in the middle of a unit serve a diagnostic purpose, since results can indicate to the teacher those areas wherein teaching has not been sufficiently clear to make learning complete. The teacher then knows that the remaining class sessions need to include review and clarification of ideas to cement learning.

Tests at the close of a unit of study indicate pupil progress and achievement. When they are compared with preliminary tests, a vital measure of improvement and effort is obtained.

Evaluation of student achievement should do more than produce figures of present status. It should promote improvement of this status. This can be accomplished only through appropriate use of accurate test results.

Scores on all tests administered within a given unit, course of study, or semester should be averaged and combined with other determinants to equal a student's grade for that particular report period. The problems of using test results and developing a grading system are extremely important ones, and the physical education teacher must consider them very carefully and thoughtfully.

METHODS AND MATERIALS FOR GRADING

Grading in physical education is a complex process, for a single grade represents many different facets of pupil achievement, all of them important. In simplest terms, a grade is a teacher's (or teachers') estimation of pupil status. It may take several different forms, it

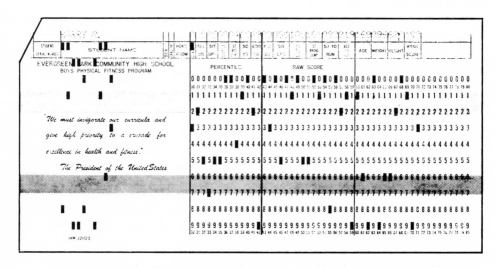

Fig. 22-5. IBM card used in Evergreen Park Community High School, Evergreen Park, Ill.

may be arrived at by many different techniques, and it may serve many purposes.

Purposes of grading

In general, a grade serves two primary purposes: it informs the student of present status, and it also notifies the parents. Grades may also serve several subsidiary functions: (1) a motivational device for some students, (2) a guide to program planning and regrouping of students, because grades identify areas of strength and weakness in the curriculum and in the youngsters, and (3) a basis for counseling students, for abrupt changes in a student's grades would probably be indicative of problems. Unfortunately, grades are sometimes used as a threatening device to push or force students into activity, which is not a desirable purpose of grading.

Principles of grading

To be of real value, a grade in physical education should be developed according to certain well-defined principles:

1. It should be representative of an individual pupil's achievement in relation to the established objectives of physical education. Comparision of achievement with other students should be avoided.

2. It should be developed on the basis of all four objectives of physical education. Emphasis should be placed on physical skills and physical development to the same degree that these factors are stressed in the program of instruction.

3. It should be understood by the student. He or she should know its components, the method of derivation of the grade, and how the various items in the test were weighted.

4. It should be understandable to parents. It should be explicit enough so that the objectives of the program are clearly understood.

5. It should be expressed in the same manner as grades in other subject matter areas throughout the school. This not only facilitates record keeping and transfer of credits but also places physical education on the same level as other subjects.

6. It should be determined on the basis of several different evaluative techniques.

Both subjective and objective measurements should be used.

7. It should be fair—a just estimation of the student's achievement and proper consideration should be given to other factors, such as improvement, effort, sportsmanship, and citizenship.

Methods of grading

There are several methods utilized in grading, not only in the field of physical education but also throughout the general educational complex in this country. Some examples include the following:

1. Letter grades: A, B, C, D, and E or F
   H, S, and U
   P and F
2. Numerical grades: 1, 2, 3, and so forth
3. Explanatory paragraphs
4. Checklists: often used to check weaknesses in such areas as effort, improvement, or citizenship

Problems in grading

In physical education the main problem is trying to arrive at a single grade that truly represents the pupil's achievement toward the various objectives. To what degree should performance and ability be weighted in relation to achievement in knowledge and social development? Some teachers believe that the former should have twice the value of the latter, because physical skills and development are the primary raison d'être of a program of physical education. Others believe that all four objectives should be considered equally. Another problem in grading centers around improvement. To what degree should improvement in skills affect the final grade? Should the student who has low motor ability but who shows real improvement in a sports unit be rated in the same manner as the highly skilled individual who merely loafs along throughout the unit?

A third question arises out of the procedures necessary in physical education class. Should credit for grading be given for having a clean gym suit, for being dressed for participation in every class, for showering, and for attendance? In addition, there is the problem of effort in physical education class.

How does a teacher determine maximum effort, and is such effort accorded an automatic A? These are some of the questions the physical educator must answer before developing a grading system suitable for use in his or her school situation.

Dr. Lynn McCraw of the University of Texas proposes a plan for grading that offers some solutions to these problems (Table 22-1).

Ideally, the report card should be clear, concise, accurate, and explicit. It should show achievement in physical skills, general ability, social development, and all the objectives that were stressed throughout the program. Perhaps more than one grade is necessary to clarify the many facets of the program for the parents.

It is always revealing to discuss the problem of grading with the students themselves, to determine what elements they feel a physical education grade should encompass and to allow them to estimate a grade for themselves. In a survey of high school girls, it was interesting to note that those whom the teacher rated A− or A ranked themselves

only B or B+, while students whom the teacher ranked C+ or lower often rated themselves above the teacher's estimate. This typifies the attitudes of many students toward themselves: those who do little often think they deserve more, while those who put forth real effort rarely feel that they are deserving.

In a survey of eighth graders who were asked about the components of a physical education grade, the element cited with greatest frequency was effort. One astute remark made by an eighth-grade girl included the following observations:

> I think that physical education should be graded, but not on a scale, just by the level that one person can reach by himself. It is up to the physical education teacher to get to know her students and learn just how far their abilities go, and then grade each person on the basis of how much he or she is improving. This could probably best be done by having a place on the report card where the physical education teacher can make a statement about the child's improvement.

The chart shown in Fig. 22-6 depicts another method by which various factors might be weighted in determining an individual's

Table 22.1. Proposed plan for grading*

Components	Weightings	Instruments
Attitude in terms of Attendance Punctuality Suiting out Participation	5% to 25%	Attendance and other records Teacher observation
Skills in terms of Form in execution of skill Standard of performance Application in game situation	20% to 35%	Objective tests Teacher observation Student evaluation
Physical fitness with emphasis on Muscular strength and endurance Cardiovascular-respiratory endurance Agility Flexibility	20% to 35%	Objective tests Teacher observation
Knowledge and appreciation of Skills Strategy Rules History and terms	5% to 25%	Written tests Teacher observation
Behavior in terms of Social conduct Health and safety practices	5% to 25%	Teacher observation Student evaluation

*From McCraw, Lynn W.: Principles and practices for assigning grades in physical education, Journal of Health, Physical Education, and Recreation 35:2, 1964.

grade. Ability factors such as physical fitness, game skills, and knowledge scores are included in percentages along vertical lines, while attitudes, adjustment, and improvement are diagrammed along the horizontal percentage line. If a student ranks in the fiftieth percentile in ability and in the eightieth percentile for his attitudes and effort, his final grade would be C+. On the other hand, a student with excellent physical skills and high ability who loafs during class period, putting forth little or no effort, would fall into the C range.

Grading in team teaching

Grading in schools using teaching teams for instruction has been a difficult problem to solve. It has been found that members of the teaching teams must formulate criteria for grades together in order to provide consistency throughout the school. The master teacher in charge of a particular unit, such as volleyball, is responsible for all grades during that grading period, and the helping teachers turn their grades in to him for compilation. In this way a student accumulates several grades in many areas during one grading period. Teachers who have taught under this system seem to believe that it works out satisfactorily for everyone concerned.

Self-assessment tests

These tests are to assist students in determining if material and competencies presented in this chapter have been mastered:

1. Close your text and identify at least three innovative methods that are being utilized in today's secondary school physical education program to evaluate student progress and achievement.
2. Identify each major objective of physical education. For each objective indicate the method or test you would use to determine a student's achievement in regard to this objective.
3. Utilizing one or more of the selective methods discussed in this chapter, evaluate the physical fitness status of one of your classmates.
4. Select five tests utilized in physical education and rate each according to each of the following criteria: validity, objectivity, reliability, norms, and administrative feasibility.
5. Prepare a report card that you would recommend for use in a high school physical education class that would indicate a student's status in regard to each of the major objectives of physical education that the class is designed to achieve.

Points to remember

1. There are many important factors to be considered when selecting tests for evaluation, such as validity and reliability.

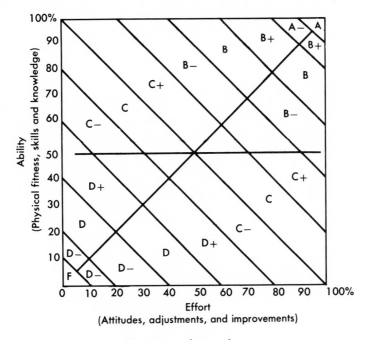

Fig. 22-6. Evaluation chart.

2. There are many types of tests useful in evaluating pupil achievement in the four goals of physical education.
3. Teacher-made tests of knowledge and skills must be constructed according to certain principles.
4. A system of grading should be developed on the basis of certain well-defined principles.
5. A grade should be a true measure of pupil status and and should be expressed in a form similar to that used in other academic areas in the school.

Problems to think through

1. Should skill tests be administered both at the beginning of a sports unit and at the end? What factors should be considered in planning them?
2. Should a written knowledge test be given at the close of every sports unit?
3. When should physical fintess testing be done—at the beginning, middle, and/or end of the year?
4. Should tests of social development be given within a single sports unit? What type? At what other times of the year may they be given?
5. Under what circumstances may teacher-made tests be more valuable than standardized tests?
6. Of what value are tests of social interests and attitudes?
7. To what uses may the results of physical fitness tests be put?
8. A student of low motor ability would probably never be graded higher than a C in physical education class.

Case study for analysis

A high school physical education program consists of classes that meet twice a week. The department wishes to gather factual evidence that would point up to the administration the need for expanding the program and convince them of the value of a daily class in physical education. What evaluation techniques would be useful to promote this argument?

Exercises for review

1. Define validity of a test, and explain.
2. Define reliability of a test, and explain.
3. Devise a sample knowledge test of volleyball rules for seventh-grade girls or boys.
4. Administer one physical fitness test item to a group and compare the scores with national norms.
5. Prepare a set of directions to be given orally before administering a written knowledge test to a class.
6. Select a specific skill essential to the game of basketball and devise a simple test for measuring its performance.
7. Look up a standardized skill test in one of the source books and evaluate its suitability for use in a nearby high school.
8. Make a sociometric study of a group or team presently established and evaluate the individual status of participants.

Selected readings

American Alliance for Health, Physical Education, and Recreation: Sports skills test manuals, Washington, D.C. 1966-1967, AAHPER.

Barrow, H. M., and McGeen, R.: A practical approach to measurement in physical education, Philadelphia, 1972, Lea & Febiger.

Bucher, C. A.: Administration of health and physical education programs, including athletics, St. Louis, 1975, The C. V. Mosby Co.

Franks, B. D., and Deutsch, H.: Evaluating performance in physical education, New York, 1973, Academic Press, Inc.

Kirschenbaum, H., et al.: Wad-ja-get? the grading game in American education, New York, 1971, Hart Publishing Co.

Safrit, M. J.: Evaluation in physical education, Englewood Cliffs, N.J., 1973, Prentice-Hall, Inc.

Wilhelms, F., editor: Evaluation as feedback and guide, Washington, D.C., 1967, Association for Supervision and Curriculum Development.

23

TEACHER AND PROGRAM EVALUATION

INSTRUCTIONAL OBJECTIVES AND COMPETENCIES TO BE ACHIEVED

After reading this chapter the student should be able to—

1. Identify the reasons why teachers should be evaluated.
2. Explain the items on which teachers should be evaluated.
3. List and discuss the various methods utilized for evaluating teachers.
4. Utilize effective techniques and methods for evaluating the physical education program.

Educators today are taking a very close look not only at programs but also at teachers themselves. Recent advances in education have necessitated the development of more accurate methods of rating teachers and their abilities. In this chapter the two important factors, teacher evaluation and program administration evaluation, are discussed.

TEACHER EVALUATION

Today's educational programs require a system of teacher evaluation that is in tune with the times. Appraisal should be carried out as a mutually desirable procedure for the purpose of helping both the student and the teacher. Emphasis should be placed upon such items as how effective the materials utilized are, to what extent the teacher un-

derstands the personalities of the students with whom he or she is working, and how well the teacher understands the subject matter of his or her field. Appraisals should be conducted by persons who are competent in this area. In a day of specialization it has been suggested that persons who are specialists in this area of evaluation should be the ones to evaluate teachers.

Reasons for teacher evaluation

Castetter* has outlined several reasons why evaluation of personnel is important and necessary. These reasons are presented here in adapted form.

1. To determine whether a teacher should be retained. Administrators evaluate teachers to determine whether they make a desirable contribution to the school system where they are employed and whether they should become a permanent part of the faculty.

2. To determine the potential of a teacher. Evaluation can help in indicating the nature and scope of a teacher's potential to the school system.

3. To assign the teacher to responsibilities where the best performance will result. Through periodic evaluation it will be known

---

*Castetter, W. B.: The personnel function in public administration, New York, 1971, The Macmillan Publishing Co., Inc.

where the teacher's abilities can best be utilized in the school system.

4. To improve the performance of the teacher. Evaluation can help the teacher to understand his or her weaknesses and strengths and how these weaknesses can be eliminated and strengths utilized best.

5. To uncover abilities. Evaluation offers an avenue for determining teacher abilities that otherwise may go undetected.

6. To serve as a guide for salary raises. Where salary raises are determined on the basis of merit and productivity, evaluation provides important information for these raises.

7. To identify important factors concerning program and students. Evaluation not only determines the teacher's effectiveness but also the desirability and effectiveness of the program and the reaction of students to the program.

8. To test the procedure by which the school recruits teachers. Teacher evaluation can assist in determining whether the recruitment procedure for new teachers is effective.

9. To provide motivation for teachers. A sound evaluation procedure can motivate teachers to do better work.

10. To improve the understanding between teachers and administration. Through an effective evaluation system teachers will be better able to understand the role and responsibilities of the administration, and in turn the administration will better understand the role of the teacher.

11. To provide some basis for the transfer, promotion, or dismissal of teachers. Many objective facts must be mobilized if teachers are to be promoted, dismissed, or transferred in a just manner. Evaluation offers a means of obtaining some of these facts.

12. To motivate self-development. A very important reason for evaluation is to encourage the teacher to develop and become a better teacher.

TEACHER EVALUATION TODAY

Methods and techniques measuring teacher effectiveness and ability have been greatly expanded, and information concerning a teacher's personal history and growth has acquired greater importance, as evidenced by the bulging record folders filed in principals' offices.

Increased stress on the teacher and teaching has resulted from many factors. Educators today have recognized more and more the importance of the teacher-pupil relationship and therefore have been more concerned with the personality patterns of individual teachers. Then, too, with increasing emphasis upon teacher accountability, the effectiveness of teaching has assumed greater importance. Other factors, such as merit pay schedules and teaching team programs, have forced principals and supervisors to differentiate teachers in accordance with their productivity. Increased community pressures and criticisms of educational policies and procedures have brought about the need for greater professionalism among educators and, in turn, more effective appraisal of teachers and teaching has been encouraged.

The emphasis today is upon teachers possessing competencies in the form of knowledge, skill, and attitudes. Teacher education programs are becoming competency based. In other words, the teacher is evaluated on the basis of competencies developed rather than, as traditionally done, on courses taken. Similarly, there is an emphasis upon teachers changing the behavior of their students in an observable manner. In other words, teachers are evaluated in more and more school systems on whether their students develop specific competencies in the subject matter and classes they teach. (For a more complete discussion on competency-based learning, see Chapter 12).

Evaluation of teachers and their effectiveness involves several steps. As in other phases of evaluation, school systems vary in the extent and degree to which they fulfill this need. In general, however, a teacher's personal record file would include information regarding the following:

1. Personal status
   a. Health and physical status
   b. Intellectual abilities
   c. Social and emotional stability

2. Professional status
   a. History
   b. Experiences
   c. Teaching effectiveness
   d. Relationship with pupils
   e. Relationship with colleagues
   f. Relationship with the profession
   g. Relationship with the community

The process of evaluation—that is, the actual collection of information—should encompass opinions from several sources. The teacher should be responsible for some self-evaluation; other sources are the administrator and colleagues.

Personal status

Health. A teacher should be in good health and physical condition. Some schools require periodic health examinations and chest x-ray films. The rigors of teaching demand a healthy, vigorous person, particularly in the field of physical education. However, physical perfection is not necessarily a requisite of any teaching position. There are countless handicapped persons who have been effective teachers in spite of their handicap. (A decade ago the New York City schools had a regulation stating that vision of all swimming teachers had to be nearly 20/20 and that no person wearing corrective lenses could be hired for this activity. However, this restriction has been lifted.)

Intellectual abilities. A teacher should be well educated, well read, and able to apply knowledge to everyday pursuits. Many schools require evidence of this ability, expecting prospective teachers to take the National Teachers Examination or the Teacher Education Examination Program. Other statistics are also used, such as college entrance examination scores and transcripts of college records.

Social and emotional stability. A teacher should be a well-adjusted person, finding contentment in his or her surroundings while making contributions to it. Administrators have several instruments and methods available to them for comprehensive appraisal of teachers' personalities. The Minnesota Teacher Attitude Inventory, the Minnesota Multiphasic Personality Inventory, and the

Rorschach Test are some of the well-known tests that have been used. Other methods are observations, interviews, anecdotal records, and student opinion.

Professional status

Preparation. A teacher should have a broad knowledge of educational psychology and history and be particularly well schooled in his or her subject matter. Administrators are particularly interested in the teacher's professional preparation and expect teacher-training institutions to make recommendations on the basis of fair and honest appraisal techniques. Grades in the major field and in student-teaching work may be of special importance.

Experience. A teacher should seek outside experiences that are both broadening and educational to expand the background brought to a teaching position. Administrators generally take a close look at all summer experiences, such as counseling and recreation work, as well as travels, in assessing a teacher's experiences. Past experiences in the teaching field are naturally important aspects that would also be studied.

Teacher effectiveness. A teacher should be able to apply knowledge and teaching techniques to the classroom situation and be able to communicate effectively with the students.

Methods of appraisal

Administrators have several methods of appraisal available for use in teacher evaluation.

New methods

A survey conducted recently regarding administrator and teacher evaluation procedures in school systems enrolling 25,000 or more pupils and conducted by the Educational Research Service, sponsored jointly by the National Education Association and the American Association of School Administrators, indicates the following new approaches that are being utilized in the evaluation of teachers.

Multiple evaluators. Instead of a teacher being evaluated by one or two persons, in some school systems the evaluation is taking on a multifaceted basis. Teachers are evaluated by a committee, students, subordinates, parents, and/or outside groups. The aim is for consensus evaluations, for example, among a committee or between the teacher and the evaluators.

Performance objectives. Objectives of desirable accomplishments are set by the teacher, administration, or both. Then the teacher is evaluated on the degree to which the objectives are achieved. For example, short- and/or long-range goals are set and stated in terms of measurable objectives. An example of a performance objective might be: "I will provide a special program for my students who are subpar physically." The teacher is then evaluated in terms of whether or not or to what degree this objective is achieved.

Multiple bases for evaluation. Some school systems feel that a combination of evaluation on the basis of performance objectives and also a procedure that lists predetermined characteristics of the effective teacher is best. In other words the teacher is evaluated not only on the basis of whether he achieved certain objectives but also in regard to the degree to which he acquired the characteristics of a model teacher.

In-basket data. In this procedure a file is kept on various incidents that occur and details of teacher performance during the evaluation period. Such a file might contain notations on class observations, reports from students, complaints from parents, graduate courses taken, conferences held, and the like. Then, on the basis of all these items, the evaluation of the teacher takes place.

Traditional evaluation techniques

Observation. Administrators may make personal assessments of a teacher's abilities through periodic visitations to class. Criteria such as those listed in the chapter on class management would be helpful (control of the class, type of discipline used, attitude of the youngsters).

Student opinion. A periodic checkup of student opinions may be used to determine specific qualities of teaching. Students may be asked to rate teachers (one to four, or poor to excellent) on such factors as cheerfulness, preparation, discipline, and so on. The Morris Trait Index* is another survey that may be used by students.

Anecdotal record. An administrator may keep a file on problems that come to his or her attention as a result of a particular teacher's classroom activities. Complaints from students or teachers would fall into this category. (For example: Where was the teacher when those boys started that fight in the locker room? Or why are students always late to classes following gym class?)

Standardized instruments. An administrator may use one of several standardized evaluation charts to appraise teacher effectiveness.

Relationship with pupils. Administrators may take into consideration teacher-pupil relations. Requests for a particular teacher to serve as a chaperone or as a sponsor for a club activity might be indicative of that teacher's concern for students. Also, complaints from students and parents may be given due consideration by administrators.

Relationship with colleagues. An administrator may record a teacher's contributions at teachers' meetings, at workshops, or on voluntary committees. Holding an elective office in a faculty association, credit union, or committee would certainly be an indicator of status among one's associates, and administrators would take note of this.

Relationship with profession. Administrators may become acquainted with a teacher's professionalism through his or her activities in local, state, and national organizations (committee work and office-holding). Within the school an administrator may look for innovations and changes in teaching techniques and programming. He or she may also check a teacher's familiarity with the current literature in education.

Relationship with the community. Administrators recognize that good public relations are a vital force between a school and its community. Each teacher should foster

---

*Morris, E. H.: Morris Trait Index L, Bloomington, Ill., Public School Publishing Co.

good school-community relations. The teacher should show evidence of loyalty to the school and its administrative policies and practices—such as at PTA functions and board meetings—and should be a loyal contributor to the community, working for its betterment through cooperation with and promotion of its interests, such as the Memorial Day Parade and the summer recreation program.

The appraisal practices set forth here are not intended to be an absolute formula. They are merely suggestions of possible practices that individual school systems may employ. Three other points should be emphasized in this regard:

1. Administrators generally evaluate all teachers in a similar manner. Physical education teachers should not expect special consideration because they have winning teams or bring in valuable gate receipts.

2. Consideration would naturally be given to length of experience in a particular school situation. The beginning teacher would not be expected to evidence the same degree of effectiveness or competency as the teacher with five or ten years of experience in that school.

3. Standards of evaluation are themselves indicative of the school's expectations. For example, submitting weekly lesson plans or not smoking on the job are regulations with which a prospective teacher may not wish to comply. A teacher who does not agree with the standards expected of him or her in a school situation would probably be more effective in another school system.

PROGRAM ADMINISTRATION EVALUATION

Evaluation of program administration may be a yearly procedure, handled by members of the department for the purpose of curriculum organization, or it may be an examination of the whole school by a visiting team of specialists from the state department of education or professional association for the purpose of accreditation. The process of evaluation itself involves rating or judgment of the program according to selected criteria and standards. Some standardized forms have been developed to evaluate various phases of the physical education curriculum.

Where standardized tests are not available to judge program administration, criteria based on authoritative textbook sources or the judgment of experts in the field must be established.

The following are sample questions that may be formulated for teacher rating of program administration. They may be answered poor, fair, good, or excellent, or be scored on a scale of one to ten. Areas of the program are listed, and questions are raised concerning the various factors.

Class program

1. Does the teaching program devote equitable time to team sports, individual sports, rhythms and dance, and gymnastic activities?

2. Are the available equipment and facilities adequate to allow maximum student participation?

3. Are reasonable budgetary allotments made for the class teaching program?

4. Are accurate evaluation procedures carried out and are worthwhile records kept?

5. Are minimal participation requirements met by all students?

Fig. 23-1. Cross-country at Paul J. Gelinas Junior High School, Setauket, N.Y.

6. Are students meeting proper physical education requirements in regard to dressing and showering?

7. Are proper safety measures taken in all activities?

8. Are opportunities for developing student leadership being provided in the class program?

Adapted program

1. Do adequate screening procedures determine all possible participants in this program?

2. Are adequate facilities, equipment, time, and space made available to the program?

3. Are proper supervision and instruction afforded each individual participant?

4. Is medical approval obtained for each individual's regimen of activity?

5. Do participants engage in some of the regular class work, as well as remedial classes, when advisable?

6. Are careful records and progress notes kept on each student?

7. Is the financial allotment to the program reasonable?

8. Does student achievement indicate the value of the program?

Intramural and extramural programs

1. Are intramural and extramural sports offered to all students in as many activities as possible?

2. Has participation in these programs increased during the past year?

3. Is maximum coaching supervision available to players?

4. Is adequate financial assistance given to this phase of the program?

5. Are accurate records maintained concerning the participants, their honors, award, and electives?

6. Does the reward or point system emphasize the joys of participation rather than stress the value of the reward?

7. Is equipment well cared for and properly stored to gain the most use from it?

8. Are competitive experiences wholesome and worthwhile for all participants?

Interscholastic program

1. Is financial support for this program provided by the physical education budget?

2. Is there equitable financial support for all sports in the interscholastic program?

3. Are interscholastic sports available to all students, boys and girls alike?

4. Are adequate health standards being met in respect to number of practices and games, fitness of participants, and type of competition?

5. Is competition provided by schools of a similar size?

6. Is the program justifiable as an important educational tool?

7. Are academic standards for participants maintained?

8. Are good public relations with the community furthered through this program?

Aquatics

1. Are maximum instruction and participation opportunities made available to all students?

2. Is superior care taken in cleaning and maintaining the pool area—with proper checks on water chlorination, temperature, and filter system?

3. Is adequate supervision by qualified personnel available at all times?

4. Are health standards of cleanliness and rules requiring freedom from infection enforced at all times?

5. Are proper safety regulations enforced at all times?

6. Does student achievement indicate the value of the program?

7. Are competitive swimming and diving events properly officiated and controlled?

8. Is swimming on the intermediate level a requirement for graduation?

Administration

1. Is the teaching staff well qualified and capable of carrying out the program?

2. Is the program run efficiently, with little loss of teaching time or space, and is maximum use made of facilities?

3. Are professional standards maintained as to class size and teacher assignment?

Fig. 23-2. Basketball at Paul J. Gelinas Junior High School, Setauket, N.Y.

4. Is the departmental organization on a democratic basis, with all members sharing in the decisions?

5. Do members of the staff have a professional outlook, attend professional meetings, and keep up with the latest developments in the field?

6. In what areas have scientific tests and research been made for contribution to the profession?

These are just a few sample questions that may be used in evaluating program administration. The key to successful evaluation of this type lies in the follow-up steps for improvement.

Whatever method of program evaluation is selected, it should be realistic, functional, and continuous, in order to fulfill its major purpose of benefiting the students.

Self-assessment tests

These tests are to assist students in determining if material and competencies presented in this chapter have been mastered:

1. As a prospective teacher, list the ways by which a meaningful evaluation of your performance will assist you in becoming a better teacher.
2. Prepare a list of items on which a teacher should be evaluated. List each of these items in order of priority, giving your reason as to its importance and place on your list.
3. Utilizing a class situation demonstrate the various methods by which a teacher may be evaluated.
4. Prepare what you consider to be an effective checklist for evaluating each component part of a physical education program.

Points to remember

1. Teacher evaluation is a growing responsibility of administrators.
2. Evaluation is a continuing process.
3. Steps involved in teacher evaluation encompass every aspect of a teacher's personal and professional status.
4. Program evaluation may be accomplished within a school system or by a visiting team of specialists.
5. All evaluation procedures must take into account special factors related to the particular community involved.

Problems to think through

1. To what extent should self-rating procedures be included in a teacher's personal record file?
2. What is the primary purpose of program evaluation?
3. Should the teaching staff be informed of the methods of teacher evaluation in use within their school system?
4. For what reasons would test scores be evidence of effective teaching? For what reasons would they not?
5. Should a teacher be well liked by students in order to be an effective teacher?

Case study for analysis

A large new suburban high school is preparing for a visitation from the state accreditation committee. The physical education department is expected to collect concrete evidence of student achievement in all phases of the program. What materials would provide concise information for this purpose?

Exercises for review

1. Take a survey of at least ten people by asking them to list in order of importance the five most important qualities of a good teacher. Make a composite listing of these qualities.
2. Compare the complete evaluation instruments presented partially in this chapter and note differences.
3. Evaluate as completely as possible a high school in the college community.
4. Interview a teacher, and on the basis of that discussion, write a description of the teacher's personal and professional status. What key questions may be used?

Selected readings

Bucher, C. A.: Administration of health and physical education programs, including athletics, St. Louis, 1975, The C. V. Mosby Co.

Safrit, M. J.: Evaluation in physical education, Englewood Cliffs, N.J., 1973, Prentice-Hall, Inc.

Wilhelms, F., editor: Evaluation as feedback and guide, Washington, D.C., 1967, Association for Supervision and Curriculum Development.

INDEX